THE WORKS

OF

LORD BOLINGBROKE

THE WORKS

OF

LORD BOLINGBROKE

IN FOUR VOLUMES

VOLUME II

REPRINTS OF ECONOMIC CLASSICS

Augustus M. Kelley, Bookseller
New York, 1967

Published by
FRANK CASS AND COMPANY LIMITED
67 Great Russell Street, London W.C.1

Published in the U.S.A. by A. M. Kelley,
24 East 22nd Street, New York, U.S.A.

First edition of this collection   1844
Reprinted   1967

Library of Congress Catalog Card No. 67–16351

Printed in Great Britain

THE

WORKS

OF

LORD BOLINGBROKE.

WITH

A LIFE,

PREPARED EXPRESSLY FOR THIS EDITION,

CONTAINING ADDITIONAL INFORMATION RELATIVE
TO HIS PERSONAL AND PUBLIC CHARACTER,

SELECTED FROM THE BEST AUTHORITIES.

IN FOUR VOLUMES.

VOL. II.

LONDON:

HENRY G. BOHN, YORK STREET, COVENT GARDEN.

MDCCCXLIV.

CONTENTS.

VOL. II.

A

DISSERTATION UPON PARTIES.

TO THE RIGHT HONORABLE

SIR ROBERT WALPOLE,

KNIGHT OF THE MOST NOBLE ORDER OF THE GARTER, CHANCELLOR AND UNDER-
TREASURER OF THE EXCHEQUER, FIRST COMMISSIONER OF THE
TREASURY, AND ONE OF HIS MAJESTY'S MOST
HONORABLE PRIVY COUNCIL, &c.

SIR:—As soon as the demand of the public made it necessary to collect the following papers together, and to prepare a second edition of them, I took the resolution of addressing them to you. The style of my dedication will be different from that which is commonly employed to persons in your station. But if you find nothing agreeable in the style, you may find perhaps something useful, something that will deserve your serious reflection, in the matter of it. I shall compare you neither to Burleigh nor Godolphin. Let me not profane the tombs of the dead, to raise altars to the living. I shall make you no compliments on the wisdom of your administration, nor on the wonders you have performed, to the honor and advantage of this kingdom, in the course of fourteen or fifteen years, either at home or abroad. I shall leave these copious themes to others, and shall confine myself to reasons of another kind, that induced me to this dedication. If these reasons prove sufficient to convince the public of the extreme propriety of it, I have all that I propose to myself. Give me leave to present to you, in one short view, the general design of these little essays.

They are designed, then, to expose the artifice, and to point out the series of misfortunes, by which we were divided formerly into parties, whose contests brought even the fundamental prin-

ciples of our constitution into question, and whose excesses
brought liberty to the very brink of ruin.

They are designed to give true ideas of this constitution, and
to revive in the minds of men the true spirit of it.

They are designed to assert and vindicate the justice and honor
of the revolution; of the principles established, of the means employed, and of the ends obtained by it.

They are designed to explode our former distinctions, and to
unite men of all denominations in the support of these principles, in the defence of these means, and in the pursuit of these
ends.

They are designed to show how far these ends were answered
at the revolution, or have been answered since; and by consequence how much, or how little is wanting, to render that
glorious work complete, according to the original plan, and agreeably to the engagements taken, at that time, with the nation.

Let me now appeal to you, sir.—Are these designs which
any man, who is born a Briton, in any circumstances, in any
situation, ought to be ashamed, or afraid to avow? You cannot
think it. You will not say it. That can never be the case, until
we cease to think like freemen, as well as to be free. Are these
designs in favor of the Pretender? I appeal to the whole world;
and I scorn, with a just indignation, to give any other answer
to so shameless and so senseless an objection. No; they are
designs in favor of the constitution; designs to secure, to fortify,
to perpetuate that excellent system of government. I court no
other cause; I claim no other merit.

Stet fortuna domûs, et avi numerentur avorum.

Let the illustrious and royal house, that hath been called to
the government of these kingdoms, govern them till time shall
be no more. But let the spirit, as well as the letter of the constitution, they are intrusted to preserve, be, as it ought to be,
and as we promise ourselves it will be, the sole rule of their
government, and the sole support of their power: and whatever
happens in the various course of human contingencies, whatever
be the fate of particular persons, of houses, or families, let the
liberties of Great Britain be immortal.

They will be so, if that constitution, whose genuine effects
they are, be maintained in purity and vigor. A perpetual attention to this great point is therefore the interest and duty of
every man in Britain; and there is scarce any man, who may
not contribute to the advancement of it, in some degree. The
old may inform the young, and the young may animate the old.
Even they, who are most retired from the scene of business,
may be useful in this cause, to those, who are in it; to those,

who are heated by the action, distracted by the cares, or dissipated by the pleasures of the world. I say, they may be useful: and I add, that they ought to be so to the utmost that their situation allows. Government is the business of those, who are appointed to govern, and of those, who are appointed to control them. But the British constitution is the business of every Briton. It is so more particularly, indeed, of persons raised, like you, to the highest posts in the government. You lie under particular obligations of this kind, besides the general engagements of interest and duty, that are common to all: and a neglect in others would be a breach of trust in you. We say that our kings can do no wrong. The maxim is wisely established, and ought to be followed, no doubt, as far as the conduct of princes renders the observance of it practicable. But from the establishment of this maxim results the necessity of another, without which the exercise of the executive power would remain under no control. Though our kings can do no wrong, and though they cannot be called to account by any form our constitution prescribes; their ministers may. They are answerable for the administration of the government; each for his particular part, and the prime, or sole minister, when there happens to be one, for the whole. He is so the more, and the more justly, if he hath affected to render himself so, by usurping on his fellows; by wriggling, intriguing, whispering, and bargaining himself into this dangerous post, to which he was not called by the general suffrage, nor perhaps by the deliberate choice of his master himself. It follows, then, that ministers are answerable for every thing done to the prejudice of the constitution, in the same proportion as the preservation of the constitution in its purity and vigor, or the perverting and weakening it, are of greater consequence to the nation than any other instances of good, or bad government.

Believe me, sir, a reverence for the constitution, and a conscientious regard to the preservation of it, are in the political, like charity in the religious system, a cloak to hide a multitude of sins: and as the performance of all other religious duties will not avail in the sight of God, without charity, so neither will the discharge of all other ministerial duties avail in the sight of men, without a faithful discharge of this principal duty. Should a minister govern in various instances of domestic and foreign management, ignorantly, weakly, or even wickedly; and yet pay this reverence, and bear this regard to the constitution, he would deserve certainly much better quarter, and would meet with it too from every man of sense and honor, than a minister, who should conduct the administration with great ability and success, and should at the same time procure and abet, or even

connive at such indirect violations of the rules of the constitution
as tend to the destruction of it, or even at such evasions as tend
to render it useless.   A minister, who had the ill qualities of
both these, and the good ones of neither; who made his administration hateful in some respects, and despicable in others;
who sought that security by ruining the constitution, which he
had forfeited by dishonoring the government; who encouraged
the profligate, and seduced the unwary, to concur with him in
this design, by affecting to explode all public spirit, and to ridicule every form of our constitution; such a minister would be
looked upon most justly as the shame and scourge of his country; sooner or later he would fall without pity; and it is hard to
say what punishment would be proportionable to his crimes.—
To conclude this head therefore; since the obligations of interest
and duty on every man, especially on every minister, and more
especially still on a prime, or sole minister, to reverence the constitution, to conform his conduct to it, and neither to invade, nor
suffer it to be invaded by others, are so undeniable, and so
strong; and since the means, which the minister's power gives
him to preserve it in purity and vigor, or to corrupt and weaken
it, are so many; nothing could be more proper than a dedication
to one, in your exalted station, of papers, that are written to explain this interest, and to enforce this duty, and to press them on
the understanding and conscience of every man in Britain, but
of him most, who is most concerned.

After the general reasons, that have been given, and suggested,
for addressing this dedication to you, give me leave to descend
into some, that are a little more particular, and that regard the
man, as well as the minister.

If the principles of the revolution, and the means employed in
it, have not been vindicated by me, with as great force of reason
and eloquence, as they were by you, in a famous oration you
made at Sacheverel's trial, they have been vindicated however
to the best of my power.   The cause is the same, though the
performances are not equal: and since the cause is the same, the
cause will recommend my writings to your good opinion, how
little soever you may like the advocate.   But I have something
more to urge in my own favor.   You had a sermon to condemn,
and a parson to roast; for that, I think, was the decent language
of the time: and, to carry on the allegory, you roasted him at so
fierce a fire, that you burnt yourselves.   Your arguments being
confined to the propositions this preacher had advanced, you
may seem rather to have justified resistance, or the means employed to bring about the revolution, than the revolution: for
though the principles of the revolution were, and must for ever
remain true, and though the means were just, and will for ever

be so, in cases of the like nature; yet true principles, and just means, require to be farther sanctified by their ends. The man, who should affect the greatest zeal for the principles then established, and the means then used, would deserve, I think, to be ranked among the false brethren, and would prove himself a treacherous, and a mercenary friend to the revolution, if he showed any indifference about the ends obtained, or endeavored in any manner to defeat those, that were intended to be obtained by it. The people, who run so great a risk, and bring about so great an event, in order to restore their constitution, and to secure their liberties against dangers of every kind, and especially against those which recent experience hath taught them to apprehend, have surely a good right to the whole benefit of such a revolution; and they cannot be deprived of any part of this benefit, or left exposed to any shadow of the same dangers, by any rule of justice, or good policy.

Such considerations as these made me think that, to assert and vindicate fully the honor and justice of the revolution, it was necessary that the ends of the revolution should be insisted upon in my arguments, whether they were so or not in yours; and that the importance of the subject, as well as the difference of the occasions, for the whole lay open before me, would be a sufficient reason for supplying in the copy what was wanting in the original. I have endeavored, therefore, to show how much our constitution hath been improved, how far our liberties have been better secured by the revolution, and how little is wanting to complete that glorious design, and to render the British constitution the most perfect system of a free government that was ever established in the world. If all the ends of the revolution are already obtained, it is not only impertinent to argue for obtaining any of them, but factious designs might be imputed, and the name of incendiary be applied with some color, perhaps, to any one, who should persist in pressing this point. On the other hand, if any of these ends have not been fully obtained, the reproach of faction and the title of incendiary will belong to every person who raises a contest by his opposition to these instances, and who endeavors to make the friends of the constitution pass for enemies to the government. Thus it is easy to join issue: and when issue is once joined, it cannot be difficult to decide. If a principal end of the revolution was to secure the nation for the future against all the dangers, to which liberty, as well as religion, had been exposed before the revolution; if one of these dangers arose from the corruption, that had been employed to create a dependency of the two houses of parliament on the crown; if this corruption might have succeeded very probably then, had the means been sufficient to support it; if no pro-

vision was made, at the revolution, to secure the independency
of the two houses, and the freedom of elections, against corruption; if no provision hath been made against this danger, since
the revolution, proportionable to that increase of the possible
means of corruption, which hath happened since the revolution,
by the increase of the revenue of the crown, of debts, of taxes,
of officers, and powers to raise these taxes; if all this be so, and
the whole merits of the cause may be safely rested there, how
can it be pretended that all the ends of the revolution have been
already obtained? They have not most certainly. When, and in
what manner, they shall be obtained, it would be presumption
in any private persons so much as to insinuate. They may represent such things as they judge to be of use to the public, and
may support their representations by all the reasons, that have
determined their opinions. Thus far their province extends.
All beyond this belongs to their superiors; and, in the case before
us, to the wisdom of the nation assembled in parliament. This
however I would add; that as a consistency of character seems
to exact from you a zeal for obtaining all the ends of the revolution, suitable to that which you have expressed for the principles
it established, and the means it employed; so the particular obligations you lie under to promote the honor and interest of his
present Majesty, and of his royal family, seem to exact the
same: for, after all, the revolution is the foundation of the present settlement; whatever strengthens the foundation strengthens
the superstructure; and there can be no need of going about
to prove, that to obtain all the ends of the revolution is to
strengthen that foundation. The arguments, that prevailed
formerly with many against the principles and means of the
revolution, are quite exploded; the prejudices against them
are quite worn out. We may therefore persuade, without flattering ourselves, that the foundation of our present settlement,
and of all our future national happiness, is laid immovably in
these two respects. Shall it not be so, and does it not become
you, in a particular manner, to endeavor that it should be so, in
every respect? Could you forgive yourself, if you neglected the
first opportunity of concurring to remove the least pretence from
the disaffected, nay from the well affected, to say that the ends
of particular men, of parties, and of families, have been answered
by the revolution, even beyond their several expectations; but
that the national expectations have not been so fully answered,
nor the ends of the revolution entirely obtained? No man knows
better than you the truth and force of what hath been here advanced. No man, therefore, is able to make a juster application
of it to the most important interests of your country, to the true
interests of your royal master, and to your private interest too;

if that will add, as I presume it will, some weight to the scale; and if that requires, as I presume it does, a regard to futurity, as well as to the present moment. Upon the whole matter therefore, I cannot but expect that you should receive favorably an address, made so properly, and in which, if I have pressed you a little warmly, yet I have done it with the decency that every gentleman owes to another, at least to himself. You will allow me, and every friend of the revolution and of liberty, leave to hope that the time is coming, when you will not oppose, or shall not have it in your power to oppose, the endeavors of those, who promote the entire completion of all the ends proposed by the first, and the full security of the last. Whenever this happens; whenever the independency of the two houses of parliament, and the uninfluenced and uninfluenceable freedom of elections are once effectually secured against the dangers that may possibly arise hereafter from the growth of corruption; then will all our future kings be reduced to the agreeable necessity of establishing their thrones, as we are obliged to acknowledge that the throne is now established, not on the narrow and sandy foundations of courtcraft, and unconstitutional expedients, but on the popularity of the prince, and the universal affection of the subjects: foundations of the kingly authority so evidently supposed by our constitution, that a king, who will add weight to his sceptre, must govern by them, or govern against this constitution, against the very rule of his government.

I am now come to the last reason, drawn from the subject of these writings, that I shall trouble you with, for dedicating them to you. The attempt to extinguish the animosities, and even the names of those parties that distracted the nation so long, so fatally at first, and so foolishly at last, entitles this volume to your kind reception of it, at least, as properly as the attempt to expose the dangers that may possibly arise hereafter, from corruption, to the independency of parliament, and to the freedom of elections. Whilst a real difference of principles and designs supported the distinction, we were divided into national parties: and this was misfortune enough. It was lamented as a great one, at the time, by every good man of every party. But if the distinction should remain, when the difference subsists no longer, the misfortune would be still greater, because they, who maintained the distinction, in this case, would cease to be a party, and would become a faction. National interests would be no longer concerned; at least, on one side. They would be sometimes sacrificed, and always made subordinate to personal interests; and that, I think, is the true characteristic of faction. This attempt, therefore, ought to have your approbation. To dedicate it to you may be construed to suppose that it will have your

approbation: and he, who supposes that it will, makes you no
indifferent compliment.

When the court fomented our national divisions, the very
worst designs were carried on: for to divide can never be an
expedient for good purposes, any more than to corrupt; since
the peace and prosperity of a nation will always depend on
uniting, as far as possible, the heads, hearts and hands of the
whole people, and on improving, not debauching their morals.
" Divide et impera," is a maxim often quoted. How are we to
apply it?   There is no place for it in arbitrary governments; for
in them, the interest of the governors requires that a servile
union, if it may be called an union, should be maintained by
the weight of power, like that of slaves in a galley, who are
united by their chains, and who tug the oar together, at the
sound of a whistle.   In free governments, it can have place as
little, whilst they, who are at the head, intend the maintenance
of liberty.   To what case then can it be applied?   There is but
one, and that is the case of those, who aspire at more power
than a free constitution of government gives them.   Such governors must divide and incense parties one against another, that
they may be always able to bribe the passions of one side, and
so usurp on both.   But the prince who pursues this method,
risks the power he hath for a power he does not want.   He
would be the more inexcusable, under such a constitution as
ours; because, if he could not gain esteem by his great, he might
gain affection by his good qualities: and this principle would
carry him, even better, perhaps, than the other, to the power he
would obtain.   What can a prince desire more than to be placed
at the head of a united people; among whom he may have as
many friends as he pleases, and can have no enemies, unless he
creates them, by supposing them to be such, and by treating
them accordingly?   If the designs of a prince, in fomenting the
divisions, are to invade the liberties of his people, his designs
are laid in the utmost iniquity: and if these are not his designs,
they must be laid in the utmost folly.   When a people submits
quietly to government, and is willing to obey on the terms on
which alone their prince hath a right to command, how extravagant must his demands be, and how unaccountable his conduct, to divide such a people?   Shall he expect, for instance,
that all his people should think like him and his council, about
every occurrence, about every measure he takes, and every man
he employs? and since this is too much to ask of freemen, nay
of slaves, if his expectation be not answered, shall he form a
lasting division upon such transient motives?   Shall he proscribe
every man, as an enemy to his government, who dislikes the
administration of it?   Proscriptions are abominable, and in-

human, when they are backed by a fulness of arbitrary power. But to hang up the tables of proscription, without the power of sending centurions to cut off every head that wears a face disliked at court, would be madness in a prince. Such a conduct cannot suit his interest, however it may his passions, in any circumstance whatever. There are indeed circumstances, wherein it may suit the interest of a minister. Till the sword of civil war be drawn, a prince can scarce become irreconcilable with his people, and be reduced, for want of national strength, to support his power and dignity by the force of faction. But a minister may fall easily, and soon, into this desperate state: and after fomenting, as long as he could, the divisions of parties, he may have no refuge but in faction. There may be such a conduct, as no national party will bear, or at least will justify. But faction hath no regard to national interests. Faction, therefore, will bear anything, share in anything, justify anything. If the minister, who takes this method to support himself, hath any art, he will endeavor to disguise his faction under the name and appearance of a national party. But even this disguise will soon fall off. The best of those, who were engaged in the party, will quit the faction, and then the latter must stand confessed to public view. But it is not only the criminal conduct of a minister, and the fear of resting his administration on the national judgment, that may oblige him to govern by division, and by faction. As the most opposite notions are often united in the head, so are the most contrary sentiments in the heart of man. Incapacity often begets sufficiency; and yet a consciousness of incapacity often begets a jealousy of power, grounded on a sense of the superior merit of other men. The minister, who grows less by his elevation, like a little statue placed on a mighty pedestal, will always have this jealousy strong about him. He must of course select a faction to himself; and this faction must be composed, to answer his purposes, of men servilely obsequious, or extremely inferior to him by their talents. Whenever this happens, the reign of venality, of prostitution, of ignorance, of futility, and of dulness commences. The minister will dread to see the persons employed whom he secretly esteems, for this very reason, because he esteems them. Abilities to serve the commonwealth will be an objection sufficient to outweigh the strongest proofs of attachment to the person of the prince, and of zeal for his government; nay, even the merit of a whole life spent in giving these proofs. In short, the very reasons that should determine the prince to employ men, will determine the minister to proscribe them. Dislike, or contempt of him, will pass with his master for disaffection to the government; and, under this pompous name of government, will nothing but the paltry in-

terest, or humor, of the minister be couched.   The minister
will reap, perhaps, for even that may be doubtful, the immediate benefit of dividing, or maintaining the divisions of the
nation, and of nursing up faction, by continuing longer in power,
his sole security, and, by deferring, if not escaping, the evil day,
the day of account and retribution.   But the prince will reap, in
this case, the permanent mischief of establishing division and
faction; and may possibly make the lamentable exchange of his
own popularity, for his minister's impunity.   I need not finish
up this picture of imagination, since I write to you, who know
so much better than I pretend to do the characters of men, and
the arts of government.   It is sufficient that I have hinted at the
general causes and effects of the endeavors, that are sometimes
used, and to which Great Britain hath not been a stranger, to
foment national divisions, and to govern by the faction of a
minister, armed with the power of the prince, against the sense
and spirit of a nation, and the interest of the prince himself.
This may serve, and it is all I shall say, to bespeak your appro
bation of the papers that follow, on account of the matter they
contain.

But, sir, the reasons I have given, how pertinent soever they
may be, are not the only reasons I had for addressing myself in
this manner, and upon this occasion, to you.   There are reasons
of another kind; reasons, that come still more home to yourself;
reasons, that appear very important to me, and that will appear
so to you, perhaps, when you have reflected duly on them, and
have weighed impartially the consequences of them.   I shall
press these reasons with all the plainness and force that decency
permits, in so public and personal an application; because, though
truth may sometimes offend, I am very indifferent to offences
taken with truth on my side.   If you hearken to truth, which
men in your station seldom hear, you may be the better for it.
If you do not, the author of this dedication cannot be the worse;
for I will add, upon this occasion, that whoever he is, he is one
you cannot impose upon, in your private capacity, neither as a
man, nor as a gentleman; and that you can as little do it, in
your public capacity.   You cannot disappoint him; because the
temper of his mind gives you no hold on him.   He hath neither
avarice to make him desire riches, nor ambition to make him
desire power, nor vanity to make him desire honors.   You cannot oppress him, because he is free from guilt, and from every
probable, for no man is free from every possible, imputation of
guilt.   The laws of his country are his protection; and they are
sufficient to protect every Briton who reverences and obeys them,
in how peculiar a situation soever he may be found.   They who
act against these laws, and they alone, may have reason to fear,

let their situation be never so high, or their present power never so great.

Having said this, I proceed to observe to you, that you are in the right most certainly to retort by yourself, or others, in the best and smartest manner that you, or they can, whatever the writings published in the Craftsman* may contain, which you judge to be injurious to yourself, or reflecting on your administration. The public will judge uprightly upon the whole matter. The laughers will be for those who have most wit, and the serious part of mankind for those who have most reason on their side. Again: As to affairs of peace or war, public occurrences, domestic management, foreign negotiations, in short, the news of the day, and the current business of the time, weekly and daily papers, or more elaborate, anniversary treatises, are properly employed by you to explain, in your own favor, the series of your conduct; to refute Caleb; or, which is still more easy, and by some thought as useful, to keep up the cavil on one point till a new one is started, that draws off the attention of the world. All this may be called fair war; and whoever prevails in the judgment of the public, the public will reap information from the contest, and will have reason to be pleased with these appeals, which present an image of the custom that obtained in the ancient commonwealths of Greece and Rome, where the greatest interests of the state were debated, and the greatest men in those governments were accused and defended, in public harangues, and before the whole people.

But the writings of the Craftsman have not been confined to these subjects, that are personal or temporary. The cause of the British constitution hath been pleaded through the whole course of these papers; every danger to it hath been pointed out; every security, or improvement of it, hath been explained and pressed. Now here, sir, begins my complaint. I said that the cause of our constitution hath been pleaded in the Craftsman; and I am sorry that the expression is so precisely just, that no other would come up to the case. The cause of the constitution hath been pleaded, for the constitution hath been attacked—openly, insolently attacked, and is so every day by those against whom the Craftsman so often employs his pen. Who could have expected, for I will give an instance or two, who could have expected, at this time, and under the present establishment, to hear the necessity of maintaining standing armies, in times of peace, even against the people of Britain who maintain them, contended for and asserted. Who could have expected to hear a dependency, a corrupt dependency

---

* A political paper published weekly at that time, under the assumed name of Caleb D'Anvers.

of the parliament on the crown, contended for, and asserted to be a necessary expedient to supply a want of power, which is falsely supposed in the crown; as if our fathers had opposed, and at length destroyed that chimera, called prerogative, formerly so dangerous to our liberties, for no other reason but to furnish arguments for letting loose upon us another monster, more dangerous to our liberties by far? Who could have expected that attempts to revive the doctrines of old whiggism, and the principles and spirit of the revolution, in opposition to such manifest contradictions of them all, would give any umbrage, or cause any alarm, among men, who still affect to call themselves whigs, and pretend zeal for a government, that is founded on the revolution, and could not have been established without it? This could not have been expected, I think; and so it is. There are persons who take to themselves the title of ministerial writers, and have sometimes the front to assume that of writers for the government. These persons are not content to ring, in daily panegyric, encomiums on the wisdom and virtue, the justice and clemency, the success and triumphs of your administration, and to answer, or to attempt to answer, the almost innumerable objections that have been made, it matters not here whether justly or unjustly, to your conduct at home, and your own, and that of your brother abroad: but they take fire, they show an alarm, and they grow angry, whenever any thing is written, nay, when a word is dropped, in favor of the fundamental articles of British liberty. Sometimes they argue directly, and in plain terms against them. Sometimes they perplex and puzzle the cause, evade what they cannot deny, and, when they cannot impose a fallacy, endeavor at least to hinder men from discerning a truth. Thus, sir, they mingle your justification with the condemnation of our constitution; and labor, as much as in them lies, to make your preservation and the destruction of this constitution a common cause. If you could possibly doubt the truth of what is here advanced, I might refer you to the particular pamphlets and papers, which are known at least by the answers that have been given to them, till such time as an extract of all the passages hinted at here be made public, as I hope it will; and whenever it is, I dare appeal beforehand to your private thoughts, whether the principles they contain, and the consequences deducible from them, would not destroy, if they were to take place, the whole scheme of the British constitution. It hath been asked, why do the writers on one side eternally harp on liberty and the constitution? Do they mean to instil jealousy and distrust, and to alienate the minds of the people? In what instances have the laws been broken, or hath the constitution been invaded by those who govern? These questions deserve an answer; and I shall answer the first, by asking another question.

Why do the writers on one side eternally labor to explain away liberty, and to distinguish us out of our constitution? If nothing had been said of this kind, I am persuaded that much less would have been said of the other; and I can assure you, with great truth, that the public had not been troubled, particularly, with this dissertation upon parties. As to the other two questions, they may be taken together. There is a plain and real difference between jealousy and distrust, that may be observed in the present case. Men may be jealous on account of their liberties, and I think they ought to be so, even when they have no immediate distrust that the persons who govern design to invade them. An opportunity of invading them opened, is reason sufficient for awakening the jealousy; and if the persons who have this jealousy, apply to those who govern to help to cure it, by removing the opportunity, the latter may take this, if they please, as a mark of confidence, not distrust: at least, it will be in their power, and surely it will be for their interest, to show that they deserved confidence in this case, not distrust. But it will be always trifling, and foolish, to ask what laws have been broken, what invasions on the constitution have been made; because, as nothing of this sort will be done, when there are no designs dangerous to the constitution carried on; so that when there are such designs, whatever is done of this sort will be private, indirect, and so covered, that the greatest moral certainty may be destitute of proof. Whenever any of these things are done publicly, directly, and in a manner to be easily proved, the danger will be over, the constitution will be destroyed, and all fear for it and concern about it will be impertinent, because they will come too late. If ever that old trite maxim, " principiis obsta," was well applied, it is so in the case we speak of here.

The reasons I have given for mentioning these writers ought to excuse me for it, at least to you, and even to you I shall say very little more about them. The flowers they gather at Billingsgate, to adorn and enliven their productions, shall be passed over by me, without any reflection. They assume the privilege of watermen and oyster-women. Let them enjoy it in that good company, and exclusively of all other persons. They cause no scandal; they give no offence; they raise no sentiment but contempt in the breasts of those they attack; and it is to be hoped, for the honor of those whom they would be thought to defend, that they raise, by this low and dirty practice, no other sentiment in them. But there is another part of their proceeding, which may be attributed by malicious people to you, and which deserves for that reason alone some place in this dedication, as it might be some motive to the writing of it. When such authors grow scurrilous, it would be highly unjust to impute their

scurrility to any prompter; because they have in themselves all
that is necessary to constitute a scold; ill manners, impudence, a
foul mouth, and a fouler heart. But when they menace, they
rise a note higher. They cannot do this in their own names.
Men may be apt to conclude, therefore, that they do it in the
name, as they affect to do it on the behalf of the person, in whose
cause they desire to be thought retained. Many examples of these
menaces might be quoted, and most of them would be found
directed against one particular person. After employing the
whole impotence of their rhetoric against him, and venting for
many years together, almost without notice on his part, as much
calumny as their imaginations could furnish, a pamphlet hath
been lately published; the professed design of which is to call
for a vigorous proceeding in parliament against this man. To
introduce this proposal, it is preceded by a long series of facts;
some notoriously false; some, which it is impossible should be
true; others, which it is impossible this writer should know to
be true, if they were so; and others again, not only destitute of
proof, but even of probability. Such accusations must be brought
by some creature,* of so notoriously prostituted a conscience,
that his evidence would be rejected in any common cause, and
should not be refuted therefore by me, if I was concerned to
refute him. But, sir, if I take notice of this live libel, or refer
to others of the same kind, it is not done out of regard to these
authors, whom I despise, as I am persuaded the person does,
against whom all the virulence of their malice is directed. My
concern, upon this occasion, is for you alone; and you will allow
me to represent what that concern dictates. It is possible that
you may have very strong resentments against this person, and
he against you. It is possible that you may have shown yours,
and he may have shown his, according to the different circumstances you have been in, and the different opportunities you
have had. But this will not become a matter of state, though
you are a minister of state. The public will espouse your passions no more than his; nor concern itself to inquire who gave
the first occasion to these resentments; who hath acted the part
of a fair, and who of a treacherous enemy. It is, I doubt, too
certain that the public hath been employed sometimes to revenge
private quarrels, and to serve the low turns of envy or jealousy.
But, in all these cases, the public hath been imposed upon; these
motives have been concealed; others have been pretended; and
the others have been of a public nature alone; because the bare
suspicion of any private interest, or passion, in a public prosecution is sufficient, and most justly so, to create invincible preju-

* See the Grand Accuser, &c. p. 77.

dices to it. The scribblers I speak of have laid you therefore under great disadvantages, notwithstanding your elevation, and your power, whether you design any thing against the person so obnoxious to you or not. They should have concealed industriously what they have affected to proclaim; since it is certain that, how great soever your popularity in the nation may be, they will never bring up mankind to think that any person should be prosecuted by methods extraordinary, or even ordinary, purely for your ease, your pleasure, or your safety. If they could prove, what they frequently throw out, that every man is a friend to the Pretender who is not a friend to you; and that he who objects to your conduct in the administration, endeavors to pull down the present government, and set up another; then, indeed, they might raise a spirit against this particular person, for aught I know; but most certainly against many others, of much greater consequence, who appear every day, in the face of the world, not to be your friends, and who make no scruple of objecting, with the utmost freedom, to your conduct. But such assertions as these will only serve to make men angry, or laugh. They, who have the best opinion of your abilities, will no more agree that the present establishment is supported, than that it was made by you. They will never be wanting in their respect to the crown so much as to confound the cause of the king with the cause of his minister, or to suppose that the reins of government would grow weaker in his majesty's hand, if you was out of power, or out of the world. In short, sir, you may pass, and I believe you do pass justly, for a man of extreme good parts, and for a minister of much experience; but you would not desire, I think, to be represented as the Atlas who supports this state; and your brother will not certainly pass for the Hercules who relieves you, and who sustains, in his turn, the important burthen.

I know very well that something is added to supply, if that were possible, this defect, and to make the cause more plausible. It is pretended that the writings imputed to this particular person, and several others published in the Craftsman, contain reflections of a very extravagant, indecent, and even seditious nature; such as they alone, who are capable of supposing them, are capable of making. But then these reflections are to be proved by the constructions which the accusers make of the expressions employed by those whom they accuse; constructions as arbitrary and as forced as many of those by which some of the best men at Rome were brought within the interpretation of the law of majesty, by some of the worst. Examples of much the same sort have been set even in Britain, whilst the practice prevailed of supposing innuendoes, and parallels, and oblique meanings, and prosecuting and condemning men on suppositions and interpretations. But there is no room to fear that any such examples should be renewed, whilst a British spirit prevails in a British parliament.* Whilst that spirit prevails, no parliament will condemn any man upon principles which parliaments have always condemned as unjust and tyrannical. Less than any will they condemn those who write in defence of this constitution, at the request and on the instance of those who attack it. A British spirit and the spirit of the British constitution are one and the same;† and therefore if ever there arises a British spirit in a British parliament, of which I presume no doubt ought to be made at this time, vengeance will not overtake the former; it may be the latter.

What hath been said might suffice to show how foolish and vain it is to throw out menaces against those who have nothing to fear, at a time, when zeal to preserve the constitution in every part inviolate seems daily to increase. But since I have entered on the subject, and the matter seems of some concernment to you, give me leave to add one consideration more, that may serve to show how foolish and vain such a proceeding would be, even at any other time. Let us suppose that the very person pointed at was, and could be proved to be, the author of this Dissertation upon Parties, for instance, which I now dedicate to you. Let us suppose that the resolution was taken to follow the generous and equitable advice of the pamphlet-writer, who thinks he ought to be proceeded against in a peculiar manner. Let us even suppose that we lived in an age, when parliaments were brought, in some degree, under that very dependency, against which so much is said in this dissertation. In short, let us suppose that the most innocent man, who was obnoxious to those in power, might have reasonable grounds to fear an exorbitant exercise of this power against him. But then let us make one single supposition on the other side. Let us suppose that this obnoxious man was really in earnest; that he wrote from his heart; and that he felt there the same warmth for the British constitution, which he expressed in his writings, and labored to infuse into the breast of every other man. I would ask you, sir, do you think such a man would be ashamed to avow, in the face of his country, the contents of the following sheets, or be afraid to suffer for them? Could any eloquence, even yours, if you would employ it so unworthily, expect, by the help of false surmises and invidious comments, the base inventions of little railers, to make him pass for an enemy to the present establish-

---

* See Some Considerations concerning the Public Funds, &c., p. 98.
† Ibid.

ment, who had proved himself a friend to that constitution, in consequence of which, and for the sake of which alone, this establishment was made? Would his endeavors to reconcile parties, and to abolish odious distinctions, would pleading for the attainment of all the ends proposed by, and promised at the revolution, for securing the independency of the two houses of parliament, and the freedom of elections, as effectually against corruption, as they are already secured against prerogative; would this, I say, make him pass for the greatest of criminals? No, sir, not in the breasts even of those who gave sentence against him, if men capable of giving such a sentence could be found. Among the rest of mankind his innocency would be acknowledged; his constancy would be applauded; his accusers, and his grand accuser in the first place, would pass alone for criminal. He might fall a victim to power; but truth, and reason, and the cause of liberty would fall with him; and he who is buried in their ruins, is happier than he who survives them. Thus I am persuaded the person here intended would be found, upon trial, to think. The event therefore of such a prosecution, whatever it might be, could not turn to his disadvantage; and consequently to threaten him with it would be ridiculous, even at such a time as we have supposed, much more at the present. Void of all ambition, except the ambition of honest fame, he might stand the efforts of violence in such a cause, not only with little concern, but with much inward complacency. Weary of the world, determined and preparing to retire totally from it, he would surely suspend his retreat to face the persecution; and whatever his persecutors might imagine, they would erect a sort of triumphal arch to the man they hated. He would leave the world with more honor than they would remain in it. By suffering in defence of the constitution of his country, they who had thought favorably of him, would think that he crowned the good, and they who had entertained prejudices against him, that he atoned for the ill which had been imputed to him. Such different judgments, you know, sir, will attend every man's character who acts on our divided stage; and he is happy who can reconcile them so nearly. It never happens that there is a man of whom all speak well, as it rarely, very rarely, happens that there is a man of whom all speak ill, except those who are hired to speak well.

I find it hard to leave off, when I have the honor of writing to you, sir; but having now explained the principal reasons that induced me to address this dedication to you, it is time that I should force myself to a conclusion, and conclude by recommending the following sheets to your serious perusal. I recommend them to nothing else. I do not apprehend that they will want your patronage any more than the person who wrote them. Let them stand or fall in the public opinion, according to their merit. But if you should find any thing in them that deserves your notice, you will have an obligation to one, from whom you least expected any; to,

Sir, your most humble servant,

The AUTHOR OF THE DISSERTATION UPON PARTIES.

LETTER I.

SIR:—To corrupt and to divide are the trite and wicked expedients, by which some ministers in all ages have affected to govern; but especially such as have been least capable of exerting the true arts of government. There is, however, a difference to be made between these two expedients, to the advantage of the latter, and by consequence between the characters of those who put them in practice.

Every busy, ambitious child of fortune, who hath himself a corrupt heart, and becomes master of a large purse, hath all that is necessary to employ the expedient of corruption with success. A bribe, in the hand of the most blundering coxcomb that ever disgraced honor and wealth and power, will prevail as much as in the hand of a man of sense, and go farther too, if it weigh more. An intriguing chamber-maid may slip a bank note into a griping paw, as well as the most subtle demon of hell. H**e may govern as triumphantly by this expedient as the great knight his brother, and the great knight as Burleigh himself.

But every character cannot attempt the other expedient of dividing, or keeping up divisions, with equal success. There is, indeed, no occasion for any extraordinary genius to divide; and true wisdom despises the infamous task. But there is need of that left-handed wisdom, called cunning, and of those habits in business, called experience. He that is corrupted, co-operates with him that corrupts. He runs into his arms at the first beckon; or, in order sometimes to raise the price, he meets him but half way. On the other hand, to divide, or to maintain and renew the divisions of parties in a state, a system of seduction and fraud is necessary to be carried on. The divided are so far from being accessory to the guilt, that they would not be divided, if they were not first deceived.

From these differences, which I have observed between the two expedients, and the characters and means proper to put them in practice with success, it may be discovered perhaps why, upon former occasions, as I shall hereafter show, the expedient of dividing prospered so much better than that of corrupting; and why, upon some later occasions, the expedient of corrupting succeeds so well in those hands, which are not, and, I trust, will not be so lucky in maintaining or renewing our party divisions.

Much hath been written by you, Mr. D'Anvers, by your correspondents and others, who have drawn their pens in the cause of truth, virtue, and liberty, against the right reverend, as well as undignified, the noble, as well as ignoble assertors of corruption; enough surely to shame those who have not lost all sense of shame, out of so ignominious a crime; and to make those who have not lost every other sense, tremble at the consequences of it. We may flatter ourselves that these honest endeavors have had some effect; and have reason to hope that far greater will follow from those illustrious examples of repulses, which have been lately given to the grand corrupter, notwithstanding his frequent and insolent declarations that he could seduce whomsoever he had a mind to gain. These hopes are farther confirmed to us by repeated declarations of the sense of parliament, and will be turned, we doubt not, into certainty, whenever the wisdom of the two houses shall again think it proper to raise new barriers of law against this encroaching vice.

In the mean time, I think nothing can better answer the designs of your papers, nor promote the public good more effectually in the present conjuncture, than to put our countrymen frequently on their guard against the artifice, which is clumsily, but industriously employed to maintain, and, if it be possible, to create new divisions amongst them. That day, which our fathers wished to see, and did not see, is now breaking upon us. Shall we suffer this light to be tured again into party-darkness by the incantations of those who would not have passed for conjurers, even in the days of superstition and ignorance? The nation is not only brought into an uniformity of opinion concerning the present administration, by the length and the righteous conduct of it; but we are grown into an unanimity about principles of government, which the most sanguine could scarce have expected, without extravagance. Certain associations of ideas were made so familiar to us, about half a century ago, and became in the course of time so habitual, that we should not have been able, even a few years ago, to break them, nor have been easily induced to believe, on the faith of any prediction, that experience and the evidence of facts would, in a few years more, break them for us, destroy all our notions of party, and substitute new ones in their room.

The power and majesty of the people, an original contract, the authority and independency of parliament, liberty, resistance, exclusion, abdication, deposition; these were ideas associated, at that time, to the idea of a whig, and supposed by every whig to be incommunicable, and inconsistent with the idea of a tory.

Divine, hereditary, indefeasible right, lineal succession, passive obedience, prerogative, non-resistance, slavery, nay, and sometimes popery too, were associated in many minds to the idea of a tory, and deemed incommunicable and inconsistent in the same manner, with the idea of a whig.

But now that which neither side would have believed on the faith of any prediction, is come to pass;

> ————quod divûm promittere nemo
> Auderet, volvenda dies en! attulit ultro.

These associations are broken; these distinct sets of ideas are shuffled out of their order; new combinations force themselves upon us; and it would actually be as absurd to impute to the tories the principles, which were laid to their charge formerly, as it would be to ascribe to the projector and his faction the name of whigs, whilst they daily forfeit that character by their actions. The bulk of both parties are really united; united on principles of liberty, in opposition to an obscure remnant of one party, who disown those principles, and a mercenary detachment from the other, who betray them.

How this change for the better comes to have been wrought in an age, when most things have changed for the worse; and since it hath been wrought, why the old distinctions are kept up in some measure, will I think be accounted for in treating this subject farther. At present, what shall we say to those who publicly speak of this national union as impracticable and chimerical; yet privately act against it, with all their might, as a practicable thing, and a real evil to them? If it be as complete and as well cemented, as I imagine it is, and as every honest Briton wishes it may be; nay, if there be nothing more than a strong tendency on all sides towards it, which no man of the least observation and candor will deny; it is surely the duty of every one, who desires the prosperity of his country, to seize the opportunity, to cultivate and improve it. If men are to be known by their works, the works of those, who oppose this union, denote them sufficiently. Wicked and unhappy men! who seek their private safety, in opposing public good. Weak and silly men! who vainly imagine that they shall pass for the nation, and the nation for a faction; that they shall be judged in the right, and the whole body of the people in the wrong. On whom would they impose? How long do they imagine that so unequal a contest can last?

There is no complaint which hath been more constantly in the mouths, no grief hath lain more heavily at the hearts of all good men, than those about our national divisions; about the spirit of party, which inspires animosity and breeds rancor; which hath so often destroyed our inward peace; weakened our national strength, and sullied our glory abroad. It is time, therefore, that all, who desire to be esteemed good men, and to procure the peace, the strength and the glory of their country by the only means, by which they can be procured effectually, should join their efforts to heal our national divisions, and to change the narrow spirit of party into a diffusive spirit of public benevolence.

That we may be more encouraged to do so, it will be of use perhaps to consider, in some particulars, what advances are already made towards that national union, without which no national good can be expected in such circumstances as ours.

Let us begin with the present temper of the members of the church of England towards the dissenters. Those laws, by which the latter were debarred from serving God after their own way, have not been these many years a terror to them. Those which were designed to hinder the propagation of their principles, and those which shut the door of all public preferment, even to such amongst them as conformed occasionally, are repealed. Far from desiring to impose any new hardships upon them, even those who have been reputed their enemies, and who have acted as such on several occasions, acknowledge their error. Experience hath removed prejudice. They see that indulgence hath done what severity never could; and from the frankness of these, if I was a dissenter, I should sooner entertain hopes of future favor, than from the double dealing of those who lean on the dissenters when they are out of power, and who esteem them a load upon them when they are in it. We are now in the true and only road, which can possibly lead to a perfect reconciliation among protestants; to the abolition of all their differences; or to terms of difference so little essential, as to deserve none of distinction. These happy ends must be obtained by mutual goodwill. They never can be obtained by force. It is true, indeed, that force, which is the effect of a majority and superior power, may support a rivalship and erect even counter-establishments. But then, by the same means, our ancient disputes will be revived; the church will be thought really in danger; and religious feuds, which have been so long and so beneficially kept down, will once more disturb the peace of the state. It is a certain truth, that our religious and civil contests have mutually, and almost alternately, raised and fomented each other. Churchmen and dissenters have sometimes differed, and sometimes thought,

or been made to think, that they differed, at least, as much about
civil as religious matters.   There can be, therefore, no way so
effectual to compose their differences on the latter, as to improve
the growing union between them on the former.   "Idem sentire
republicâ," to think alike about political affairs, hath been esteemed necessary to constitute and maintain private friendships.   It
is obviously more essential in public friendships.   Bodies of men
in the same society can never unite, unless they unite on this
principle; and if they once unite on this principle, they will unite
on all others, or they will readily and cheerfully make one another
easy about them.   Let me speak plainly.   It becomes a man to
do so, who means honestly.   In our political divisions of whig
and tory, the dissenters have adhered to the former; and they
want no apology for doing so.   They joined themselves to those
with whom they agreed, and stood in opposition to those with
whom they differed in principles of government.   There could
be no objection brought against them on this account.   They
certainly did not follow power.   They did not act like a sect, or a
faction, who had, and pursued an interest distinct from the interest
of the whole.   Their non-comformity hath nothing to do here.
They concurred with conformists; and if they had been conformists
themselves, as they were dissenters, they would have acted in
the same manner.   But if this division of parties, on the same
principles, subsists no longer; if there be in truth neither a tory,
nor a whig, as I have said above, but a court and a country
party in being, if the political principles, which the dissenters
have formerly avowed, are manifestly pursued on one side; and
those which they have opposed, or others equivalent to them in
their effects, are pursued on the other; can the dissenters hesitate
about the option they are to make?   I am persuaded they cannot.   I know that several amongst them do not.   What might
be, and certainly would be said, if they made their option to
stand by the m * *, I will not so much as suggest.   What must
be the consequence of their standing by the nation, in opposition
to him, for between these two powers the present contest lies, it
is easy to tell, and impossible to deny.   They will prove, in this
case, to the whole world, that the spirit of liberty animates, and
conscience alone determines their conduct.   They, who could
never brook a regal, will have the merit of saving their country
from a ministerial tyranny; and their country will owe them all
the acknowledgments, which are due from good and grateful
citizens of the same commonwealth.

As to the other great and national division of whig and tory,
he who recollects what hath passed in parliament, and observes
what passes out of it, can differ very little in his opinion from
what hath been said concerning it.   The principal articles of your

civil faith, published some time ago, or, to speak more properly, the civil faith of the old whigs, are assented and consented to by the country party; and I say, upon good authority, that if this creed was made a test of political orthodoxy, there would appear at this time but very few heretics amongst us. How different the case is on the other side, will appear not only from the actions, but from the principles of the court-party, as we find them avowed in their writings; principles more dangerous to liberty, though not so directly, nor so openly levelled against it, than even any of those, bad as they were, which some of these men value themselves for having formerly opposed.

In short, the revolution is looked upon by all sides as a new era; but the settlement then made is looked upon by the whole country party as a new Magna Charta, from whence new interests, new principles of government, new measures of submission, and new obligations arise. From thence we must date both king and people. His majesty derives his title from acts, made in consequence of it. We likewise derive, not our privileges, for they were always ours, but a more full and explicit declaration, and a more solemn establishment of them from the same period. On this foundation all the reasonable, independent whigs and tories unite. They could unite on this alone; for the whigs have always professed the principles which paved the way for the revolution; and whatever the tories may have professed, they acted upon the same principles, or they acted upon none, which would be too absurd to assert, when they brought about that great event, in concert with the rest of the nation, as I shall some time or other prove.

To this Magna Charta, and these principles, let us adhere inviolably, in opposition to the two extremes mentioned by me at the beginning of this letter, viz: to those who disown them, and to those who betray them. Let neither the polemical skill of Lesly, nor the antique erudition of Bedford, persuade us to put on again those old shackles of false law, false reason, and false gospel, which were forged before the revolution, and broken to pieces by it. As little let us suffer the arch slyness of G**, the dogmatical dryness of H**, or the soucing prostitution of S** to slip new shackles on us, which are inconsistent with the constituent principles of our establishment. Let us maintain and improve the national union, so happily begun, and bless God for disposing the temper of the nation almost universally to it. Such a coalition hath been long wanted in this kingdom, and never more than at this important crisis; for on this it will depend, whether they, who not only oppose the progress of that growing corruption, which had well nigh overspread the land, but endeavor to extirpate it by the roots, shall prevail; or they who nourish and propagate it, who eat themselves, and tempt others to eat the baneful fruit it bears.   On this it will depend whether they shall prevail, who constantly insist against the continuance of a standing army in time of peace, agreeably to the principles of our constitution; or they who plead for it, and endeavor to make it a necessary part of that constitution, though incompatible with public liberty.   On this it will depend whether they shall prevail, who endeavor to conceal the frauds which are practised, and to screen the fraudulent, at the risk of ruining credit, and destroying trade, as well as to monopolise in the hands of a few the whole wealth of the nation; or they who do their utmost to bring the former to light, and the latter to punishment, at a time when glaring fraud, or very strong symptoms of fraud, appear in so many parts of public management, from some of the greatest companies down to the turnpike at Hyde-park corner.   On this it will depend whether they shall prevail, who desire that Great Britain should maintain such a dignity and prudent reserve in the broils of Europe, as become her situation, suit her interest, and alone can enable her to cast the balance; or they who are eager, on every occasion, to prostitute her dignity, to pawn her purse, and to sacrifice her commerce, by entangling her not only too much with the other great powers of Europe, from whom she may sometimes want reciprocal engagements, but even with those diminutive powers, from whom it would be ridiculous to expect any.

I am, sir, yours, &c.

LETTER II.

Sir:—Whilst I was writing my last letter to you, it came into my thoughts that nothing would illustrate the subject better, nor enforce more strongly the exhortation to an union of parties, in support of that constitution, on the terms of which alone all right to govern us, and all our obligation to obey is now founded, than an inquiry into the rise and progress of our late parties; or a short history of toryism and whigism from their cradle to their grave; with an introductory account of their genealogy and descent.

Your papers have been from the first consecrated to the information of the people of Britain; and I think they may boast very justly a merit singular enough, that of never speaking to the passions, without appealing to the reason of mankind.   It is fit they should keep up this character, in the strictest manner, whilst they are employed on the most important subject, and published at the most important crisis. I shall therefore execute my design with sincerity and impartiality. I shall certainly not flatter, and I do not mean to offend. Reasonable men and lovers of truth, in whatever party they have been engaged, will not be offended at writings, which claim no regard but on this account, that they are founded in reason and truth, and speak with boldness what reason and truth conspire to dictate. As for the drummers and trumpeters of faction, who are hired to drown the voice of both in one perpetual din of clamor, and would endeavor to drown, in the same manner, even the dying groans of their country, if she was already brought into that extreme condition; they shall not provoke me to break a most contemptuous silence. The subject is too solemn. They may profane it, by writing on it. Far be it from me to become guilty of the same crime, by answering them.

If the inquiry I am going to make into the rise and progress of our late parties should produce in any degree the good which I intend, it will help to confirm and improve the national union, so happily begun, by taking off some remains of shyness, distrust and prejudice, which may still hang about men, who think alike, and who press on from different quarters to the same common point of view. It will help to unmask more effectually the wicked conduct of those, who labor with all the skill, and, which is much more considerable, with all the authority they possess, to keep up the division of parties; that each of these may continue to be, in its turn, what all of them have been too often and too long, the instruments and the victims of private ambition. It will do something more. A few reflections on the rise and progress of our distemper, and the rise and progress of our cure, will help us of course to make a true judgment on our present state, and will point out to us, better perhaps than any other method, the specific remedies still necessary to preserve our constitution in health and vigor.—Having premised this, I come to the point.

Queen Elizabeth designed, and the nation called, king James to the throne, though the whole Scotish line had been excluded by the will of Henry the Eighth, made indeed under the authority of an act of parliament, and yet little regarded either by the parliament, or the people. As soon as he was on the throne, a flattering act of recognition passed; for though all princes are flattered on their first accession, yet those princes are sure to be flattered most, who deserve panegyric least. In this act the parliament acknowledged, on the knees of their hearts, such was the cant of the age, the indubitable right, by which they declared

that the crown descended to him immediately, on the decease of
queen Elizabeth. Of this act, and of the use which some men,
very weakly I think, endeavored to make of it, I shall have occasion to speak hereafter. I would only observe here, that this
is the era of hereditary right, and of all those exalted notions,
concerning the power and prerogative of kings, and the sacredness of their persons. All together they composed such a system of absurdity as had never been heard of in this country, till
that anointed pedant broached them. They have been spoken
of pretty much at large in your papers; particularly in some of
those published under the name of Oldcastle. To them I refer.

To assert that the extravagant principles of ecclesiastical and
civil government, which began to be propagated in this reign,
and were carried still higher in the next, gave occasion to those
of another kind, or of another extreme, which were taught with
success, and gained by degrees great vogue in the nation, would
be too much. Opinions very different from those which received
the sanction of a legal establishment in church and state, had
crept about obscurely, if not silently, even whilst the government of Elizabeth lasted. But this I say, that the principles by
which king James and king Charles the First governed, and the
excesses of hierarchical and monarchical power, exercised in
consequence of them, gave great advantage to the opposite
opinions, and entirely occasioned the miseries which followed.
Phrenzy, provoked phrenzy, and two species of madness infected the whole mass of the people. It hath cost us a century
to lose our wits, and to recover them again.

If our grievances under king Charles the First had been redressed by a sober, regular, parliamentary reformation of the
state; or, if the civil war happening, a new government had
been established on principles of the constitution, not of faction,
of liberty, not of licentiousness, as there was on the abdication
of king James the Second; we may conclude, both from reason
and experience, that the absurd and slavish doctrines I have
mentioned would have been exploded early. They would
have been buried in the recent grave of him who first devised
them; and the memory of him and of them would have stunk
together in the nostrils of mankind. But the contrary fell out.
The state was subverted, instead of being reformed; and all the
fury of faction and enthusiasm was employed to destroy the
constitution to the very foundations. A natural consequence
followed. If the principles of king James's and king Charles's
reigns had been disgraced by better, they would not have risen
again: but they were only kept down for a time by worse; and,
therefore, they rose again at the restoration, and revived with
the monarchy. Thus that epidemical taint, with which king

James infected the minds of men, continued upon us: and it is scarce hyperbolical to say, that this prince hath been the original cause of a series of misfortunes to this nation, as deplorable as a lasting infection of our air, of our water, or our earth, would have been. The spirit of his reign was maintained in that of his son, (for how could it well be otherwise, when the same ministers were continued in power?) and the events of both produced the civil war. The civil war ended in the death of the king, and the exile of his family. The exile of these princes reconciled them to the religion of Rome, and to the politics of foreign nations, in such degrees as their different characters admitted. Charles sipped a little of the poisonous draught, but enough, however, to infect his whole conduct. As for James,

> —— Ille impiger hausit
> Spumantem pateram.

he drank the chalice off to the lowest and foulest dregs.

That principles as absurd as these in their nature, and as terrible in their consequences, such as would shock the common sense of a Samojede, or a Hottentot, and had just before deluged the nation in blood, should come into vogue again at the restoration, will not appear strange to those who carry themselves back as it were to that point of time. The wounds of the civil war were bleeding, and the resentments of the cavaliers, who came into power at court and in parliament, were at their height. No wonder then if few men had, in such a ferment as this, penetration enough to discern, or candor enough to acknowledge, or courage enough to maintain, that the principles we speak of were truly and primarily the cause of all their misfortunes. The events, which proved them so, were recent; but for that very reason, because they were recent, it was natural for men in such a circumstance as this, to make wrong judgments about them. It was natural for the royal party to ascribe all their and their country's misfortunes, without any due distinction, to the principles on which king Charles and even king James had been opposed; and to grow more zealous for those on which the governments of these two princes had been defended, and for which they had suffered. Add to this the national transport, on so great a revolution; the excess of joy which many felt, and many feigned; the adulation employed by many to acquire new merit; and by many to atone for past demerit; and you will find reason to be surprised, not that the same principles of government, as had threatened our liberties once, and must by necessary consequence do so again, were established; but that our liberties were not immediately, and at once given up. That they were saved, we owe not to parliament, no not to the convention parliament, who brought the king home; but to those great and good men, Clarendon and Southampton. Far from taking advantage of the heat and fervor of the times, to manage parliaments into scandalous jobs, and fatal compliances with the crown, to their immortal honor, with gratitude and reverence to their memories be it spoken, they broke the army, stinted the revenue, and threw their master on the affections of his people.—But I return.

Besides these reasons, drawn from the passions of men, others of a more sober kind may be given, to account for the making a settlement at the restoration upon principles too near a-kin to those, which had prevailed before the war, and which had in truth caused it. Certain it is, that although the non-conformists were stunned by the blow they had just received, and though their violence was restrained by the force of the present conjuncture; yet they still existed. Symptoms of this appeared, even whilst the government was settling, and continued to appear long after it was settled. Now, every symptom of this kind renewed the dread of relapsing into those miseries, from which the nation had so lately recovered itself; and this dread had the natural effect of all extreme fears. It hurried men into every principle, as well as measure, which seemed the most opposite to those of the persons feared, and the most likely, though at any other risk, to defeat their designs, and to obviate the present danger, real or imaginary. May we not fairly conjecture, for it is but conjecture, something more? In such a temper of mind, and such a situation of circumstances, might not even those, who saw how groundless and dangerous such extravagant notions about the right, power and prerogative of kings were, imagine however that it was a part of prudence to give way to them, and to countenance them in the present conjuncture; to suffer the opinions of the nation to be bent too far on one side, as they had been bent too far on the other; not that they might remain crooked, but that they might become straight?

The same spirit and much the same reasons that determined our settlement, at the restoration, upon such high principles of monarchy, prevailed relatively to our religious differences, and the settlement of the church. I shall speak of it with that freedom which a man may take, who is conscious that he means nothing but the public good, hath no bye-ends, nor is under the influence of serving any particular cause.

I say then very frankly, that the church and the king having been joined in all the late contests, both by those who attacked them, and those who defended them, ecclesiastical interests, resentments and animosities came into the aid of secular, in making the new settlement. Great lenity was shown at the restoration, in looking backwards; unexampled and unimitated mercy to particular men, which deserved no doubt much applause. This conduct would have gone far towards restoring the nation to its primitive temper and integrity, to its old good manners, its old good humor, and its old good nature, (expressions of my Lord Chancellor Clarendon, which I could never read without being moved and softened,) if great severity had not been exercised immediately after, in looking forwards, and great rigor used to large bodies of men, which certainly deserves censure, as neither just nor politic.—I say, not just, because there is, after all, a real and a wide difference between moral and party justice. The one is founded in reason; the other takes its color from the passions of men, and is but another name for injustice. Moral justice carries punishment as far as reparation and necessary terror require, no farther. Party justice carries it to the full extent of our power, and even to the gorging and sating of our revenge; from whence it follows that injustice and violence once begun, must become perpetual in the successive revolutions of parties, as long as these parties exist.—I say, not politic; because it contradicted the other measures taken for quieting the minds of men. It alarmed all the sects anew, confirmed the implacability, and whetted the rancor of some, disappointed and damped a spirit of reconciliation in others, united them in a common hatred to the church, and roused in the church a spirit of intolerance and persecution. This measure was the more imprudent because the opportunity seemed fair to take advantage of the resentments of the presbyterians against the other sectaries, and to draw them, without persecuting the others, by the cords of love into the pale of the church, instead of driving them back by severe usage into their ancient confederacies. But when resentments of the sort we now mention were let loose, to aggravate those of the other sort, there was no room to be surprised at the violences which followed; and they, who acted greater, could not complain of these, great as they were, with any very good grace.

If we may believe one,* who certainly was not partial against these sects, both presbyterians and independents had carried the principles of rigor in the point of conscience, much higher, and acted more implacably upon it than ever the church of England hath done in its angriest fits. The securing themselves therefore against those who had ruined them and the constitution once already, was a plausible reason for the church party to give, and I doubt not the true and sole motive of many for exercising and persisting in the exercise of great severity. General, prudential arguments might, and there is reason to believe

* Dr. Burnet, afterwards Bishop of Salisbury, in one of his tracts.

they did weigh with particular men; but they could have little force, at such a time, on numbers. As little could some other considerations have then, whatever they have now. The promises at Breda, for instance, and the terms of the declaration sent from thence could not be urged with force to a parliament who had no mind, and was strictly under no obligation, to make good such promises as the king had made, beyond his power of promising, if taken absolutely, or from which, if taken conditionally, he was discharged, on the refusal of parliament to confirm them. Thus again, the merit pleaded by the presbyterians, on account of the share they had in the restoration, which was very real and very considerable, could avail however but little. That they went along with the national torrent, in restoring the constitution of church and state, could not be denied. But then it was remembered too that these fruits of repentance came late; not till they had been oppressed by another sect, who turned upon them, wrested the power out of their hands, and made them feel, what they had made others feel, the tyranny of a party.

Such reasons and motives, as I have mentioned prevailed; and worse than these would have been sufficient, when the passions of men ran so high, to lay the dissenters, without any distinction, under extreme hardships. They seemed to be the principal object of the fears and jealousies of parliament. Addresses were continually made, and the edge of the law continually whetted against them, from 1660 to 1669, when the law for suppressing conventicles, and the last of these penal statutes passed, as I remember. Experience will justify me for saying that this long and extreme rigor was unwise, as well as unjust. It appears, indeed, from the memorials of those times, that they who suffered had given abundant provocation, though not sufficient excuse, to the rigor under which they suffered. Some former hardships which the dissenters had endured from the church, made them more violent against it, when they got possession of an usurped power. Just so the violence which they exercised at that time, stimulated the severity they felt in their turn, when the legal constitution of the church was restored. Notwithstanding all which, I incline, upon very good reasons, to think that this severity was not in the first design of the ministers, nor would have been shown, if another fatal influence had not prevailed. The influence I mean is that of popery. It prevailed from the first moments to the last of the reign of king Charles the Second. The best ministers were frequently driven off their bias by it. The worst had a sure hold on their master, by complying with it. On the occasion now mentioned, this influence and the artifice of the popish faction worked very fatally on the passions of parties, and the private interests of individuals; and the ministers, and the church, and the dissenters, were bubbles alike of their common enemy. Barefaced popery could ask no favor, because popery could expect none. Protestant dissenters were therefore to serve as stalking horses, that papists might creep behind them, and have hopes of being some time or other admitted with them. The church party was hallooed on the dissenters; whilst the dissenters were encouraged to unite and hold out; whilst they were flattered with an high opinion of their own strength, and the king's favor; and whilst some leading men amongst them, who thought it better to be at the head of a sect than at the tail of an establishment, were perhaps encouraged and confirmed in that thought, by the private applications of the court.

These arts, these wicked arts (for such they were) prevailed; and though the two thousand ministers, who went out of their churches on one day, were far from being all of the same mind, or having one positive consistent scheme; though many of them must have lost their benefices, even if they had complied with the act of uniformity, because they were intruders, and in actual possession of benefices legally belonging to others; yet, by uniting in the point of non-conformity, they appeared as one body, and in some sense they were so. Several of them were popular for certain modes of devotion, suited to the humor of the time; and several were men eminent for true learning and unaffected piety. They increased the zeal of their flocks, and created compassion in others. Here the court began to reap the fruits of of their management, in the struggle for a toleration. I use the word, though I know it may be simply cavilled at. The first step made was an application to the king, who declared himself ready and willing to dispense, in their favor, with several things in the act of uniformity: and thus the dissenters were made, by the severity of the parliament and the intrigues of the court, the instruments of introducing a dispensing power. Such attempts were made more than once; but happily failed as often as made, through the vigorous opposition of parliament; till at last the scene began to open more, and the dissenters to see that they were made the tools of promoting what they never intended, the advancement of the prerogative above law, and the toleration of popery against it.

To conclude. By such means as I have described, the constitution of parties after the restoration preserved unhappily too near a resemblance to the constitution of parties before the war. The prerogative was not, indeed, carried so high in some instances, as James and Charles the First had attempted to carry it. Nay, some supports of it were bought off, and taken away; and others more dangerous, as we have observed, were prevented by the virtue of the men at that time in power. But still the government was established on principles, sufficient to invite a king to exercise arbitrary power, and support him by their consequences in the exercise of it afterwards; so that, in this respect, the seeds of future divisions were sowed abundantly. The dissenters had, indeed, lost much of their credit and all their power. But still they had numbers, and property, and industry, and compassion for them; so that here was another crop of dissensions planted to nurse up, and to strengthen the other. They did not inflame the contest which followed, into a civil war, as they had helped to do formerly; but I think that without them, and the disunion and hatred among protestants, consequent upon them, the zeal against popery could not have run into a kind of factious fury, as we shall be obliged to confess it did. I think that fears of falling once more under presbyterian, or republican power, could not have been wrought up in the manner they were, towards the end of this reign, so as to drown even the fear of popery itself; so as to form a party, in favor of a popish successor; so as to transport both clergy and laity into an avowal of principles, which must have reduced us to be at this time slaves, not freemen, papists, not protestants; if the very men, who had avowed such principles, had not saved themselves and us, in direct opposition to them. But I am running into the subject of another letter, when this is grown too prolix already.

I am, sir, yours, &c.

LETTER III.

Sir:—The sum of what hath been said, concerning the settlement of church and state, and the division of parties at the restoration, amounts to this; that as the attempts of king James and Charles the First, against the spirit of the constitution, threw the nation into a civil war, and all the miserable consequences, both necessary and contingent, of that calamity; so the fury, enthusiasm and madness of those factions which arose during that unnatural ferment, frightened the nation back, if not into all, yet more generally, perhaps, than before, into most of the notions that were established to justify the excesses of former reigns. Hereditary, indefeasible right, passive obedience and non-resistance, those corner-stones, which are an improper foundation for any superstructure, but that of tyranny, were made, even by parliament, the foundation of the monarchy; and all those, who declined an exact and strict conformity to the whole establishment of the church, even to the most minute parts of it, were deprived of the protection, nay, exposed to the prosecution of the state. Thus one part of the nation stood proscribed by the other; the least, indeed, by the greatest; whereas a little before the greatest stood proscribed by the least. Roundhead and cavalier were, in effect, no more. Whig and tory were not yet in being. The only two apparent parties were those of churchmen and dissenters; and religious differences alone at this time maintained the distinction.

Such was the state of party, upon the meeting of the first parliament called by king Charles the Second, and for some years afterwards, as nearly as I have been able to observe by what I have read in history, and received from tradition. How the notions then in vogue began to change; and this spirit to decline, some time after the restoration; how the zeal of churchmen and dissenters against one another began to soften, and a court and country party to form themselves; how faction mingled itself again in the contest, and renewed the former resentments and jealousies; how whig and tory arose, the furious offspring of those inauspicious parents, roundhead and cavalier; how the proceedings of one party might have thrown us back into a civil war, confusion and anarchy; how the success of the other had like to have entailed tyranny on the state, and popery in church; how the revolution did, and could alone, deliver us from the grievances we felt, and from the dangers we feared; how this great event was brought about by a formal departure of each side from the principles objected to them by the other; how this renewal of our constitution, on the principles of liberty, by the most solemn, deliberate, national act, that ever was made, did not only bind at least every one of those, who concurred in any degree to bring it about; (and that description includes almost the whole nation,) but how absurd it is for any man, who was born since that era, or who, being born before it, hath been bound by no particular, legal tie to any other settlement, to be willing to give up the advantages of the present constitution, any more than he would give up the privileges of the great charter, which was made and ratified so many ages ago; all these points are to be now touched in that summary manner which I have prescribed to myself, and which will be sufficient, in so plain a case, where men are to be reminded of what they know already, rather than to be informed; and to be confirmed, not to be convinced.

I proceed therefore to observe, that the nation began to be indisposed to the court, soon after the restoration. The sale of Dunkirk helped to ruin a great and good minister, though it be still doubtful at least, notwithstanding the clamor raised, and the

negotiations with D'Estrades, so much insisted upon, whether he
was strictly answerable for this measure. Who knows how soon
the re-establishment of the same port and harbor may be laid in
form to the charge of those two men, who are strictly and undeniably answerable for it, and who stagger already under the
weight of so many other just imputations?

The first Dutch war, which was lightly and rashly undertaken,
and which ended ignominiously for the nation, augmented the
public indisposition.   Nay, misfortunes, such as the plague, and
the burning of London, as well as mismanagement, had this effect.
But we must place at the head of all, a jealousy of popery, which
was well founded, and therefore gathered strength daily.   This
soon heated the minds of men to such a degree, that it seems
almost wonderful the plague was not imputed to the papists, as
peremptorily as the fire.

The death of my Lord Southampton, and the disgrace and
banishment of my Lord Clarendon, made room for new causes
of jealousy and dissatisfaction; and the effects increased in proportion.   These two noble lords had stood in the breach against
popery and foreign politics; and what one of them said of the
other, that is, Southampton of Clarendon, may be applied with
justice to both.   They were true protestants, and honest Englishmen.   Whilst they were in place, our laws, our religion, and our
liberties were in safety.   When they were removed, England
felt the ill effects of the change; for when they were removed, all
these were in danger.   How glorious a panegyric is this, in which
the unanimous voice of posterity does and must agree?   It is preferable surely to all the titles, honors, and estates, which those
illustrious patriots left behind them: and so I persuade myself it is
esteemed by the young noblemen, who are heirs to their virtues
as well as their fortunes.

King Charles, and more than him, the duke and the popish
faction, were now at liberty to form new schemes, or rather to
pursue old ones, with less reserve, against the religion and liberty
of England.   As soon as the famous cabal had the whole administration of affairs, these designs were pushed almost without
any reserve at all.   I am not writing the history of this reign; nor
have I undertaken any thing more than to make a few observations on the several turns of parties in it.   I need not, therefore,
descend into particular proofs of the designs which I attribute to
the court, nor into a deduction of the measures taken to promote
them, and the efforts made to defeat them.   That these designs
were real, can be doubted of by no man; since, without quoting
many printed accounts, which are in the hands of every one, or
insisting on other proofs, which have not seen the light, and such
there are, the Abbot Primi's relation of the secret negotiations

between the king and his sister, the Duchess of Orleans, published in 1682, as I think, and immediately suppressed, as well as the history of the jesuit D'Orleans, written on memorials furnished to him by king James the Second, put the whole matter out of dispute, and even beyond the reach of cavil. It is sufficient for my purpose to observe, that the tide of party, which had run so strongly for the court, and had been seldom so much as slackened hitherto, began now to turn, and to run year after year more strongly the other way.

When this parliament sat down, for it deserves our particular observation, that both houses were full of zeal for the present government, and of resentment against the late usurpations, there was but one party in parliament; and no other party could raise its head in the nation. This might have been the case much longer, probably as long as king Charles had sat on the throne, if the court had been a little honester, or a little wiser. No parliament ever did more to gain their prince than this. They seemed for several years to have nothing so much at heart as securing his government, advancing his prerogative, and filling his coffers. The grants they made him were such as passed for instances of profusion in those days; when one million two hundred thousand pounds a year for the civil list, the fleet, the guards and garrisons, and all the ordinary expenses of the government, was thought an exorbitant sum; how little a figure soever it would make in our times, when two-thirds of that sum at least are appropriated to the use of the civil list singly. But all this was to no purpose: a foreign interest prevailed; a cabal governed; and sometimes the cabal, and sometimes a prime minister had more credit with the king than the whole body of his people. When the parliament saw that they could not gain him over to his own, and to their common interest; nor prevail on him by connivance, compliance, and other gentle methods, they turned themselves to such as were rough, but agreeable to law and the custom of parliament, as well as proportionable to the greatness of the exigency. That they lost their temper, on some particular occasions, must not be denied. They were men, and therefore frail: but their frailties of this kind proceeded from their love of their country. They were transported, when they found that their religion and liberty were constantly in danger from the intrigues of a popish faction; and they would have been so transported, no doubt, if liberty alone had been attacked by a protestant faction. Then it was that this high-church parliament grew favorable to protestant dissenters, and ready to make that just distinction, so long delayed between them and popish recusants, that the whole protestant interest might unite in the common cause. Then it was, that this prerogative parlia-

ment defied prerogative, in defence of their own privileges, and
of the liberties of their country.   Then it was that this passive
obedience and non-resistance parliament went the utmost lengths
of resistance, in a parliamentary way; and the necessary consequence of the steps they made in this way, must have been resistance in another, if the king had not dropped his ministers,
retracted his pretensions, redressed some and given expectation
of redressing other grievances.   In fine, this pensioner parliament, as it hath been styled, with some corruption in the house,
and an army sometimes at the door of it, disbanded the army in
England, and protested against the militia settled in Scotland by
act of parliament, and appointed to march for any service wherein the king's honor, authority, and greatness were concerned, in
obedience to the orders of the privy council.   That I may not
multiply particular instances, they not only did their utmost to
secure their country against immediate danger, but projected to
secure it against remote danger, by an exclusion of the Duke of
York from the crown, after they had endeavored strenuously,
but in vain, to prevent his entailing popery more easily upon us,
by his marriage with a popish princess; for he had declared himself a papist with as much affectation as if he expected to grow
popular by it; had already begun to approve his zeal, and exercise his talent in conversions, by that of his first wife; and was
notoriously the agent of Rome and France, in order to seduce
his brother into stronger measures than king Charles was willing
to take.   King Charles, to use an expression of the Lord Halifax
of that age, would trot; but his brother would gallop.

When I reflect on the particulars here mentioned, and a great
many others, which might be mentioned to the honor of this
parliament, I cannot hear it called the pensioner parliament, as
it were by way of eminence, without a degree of honest indignation, especially in the age in which we live, and by some of
those who affect the most to bestow upon it this ignominious
appellation.   Pensions, indeed, to the amount of seven or eight
thousand pounds, as I remember, were discovered to have been
given to some members of the house of commons.   But, then,
let it be remembered, likewise, that this expedient of corrupting
parliaments began under the administration of that boisterous,
overbearing, dangerous minister, Clifford.   As long as there remained any pretence to say that the court was in the interest of
the people, the expedient of bribery was neither wanted, nor
practised.   When the court was evidently in another interest, the
necessity and the practice of bribing the representatives of the
people commenced.   Should a parliament of Britain act in compliance with a court, against the sense and interest of the nation,
mankind would be ready to pronounce very justly that such a

parliament was under the corrupt influence of the court. But, in the case now before us, we have a very comfortable example of a court wicked enough to stand in need of corruption, and to employ it; and of a parliament virtuous enough to resist the force of this expedient, which Philip of Macedon boasted that he employed to invade the liberties of other countries, and which had been so often employed by men of less genius, as well as rank, to invade the liberties of their own. All that corruption could do in this parliament, was to maintain the appearance of a court party, whilst the measures of the court united a country party, in opposition to them. Neither places nor pensions could hinder courtiers in this parliament from voting, on many signal occasions, against the court; nor protect either those who drew the king into ill measures, nor those who complied with him in them. Nay, this pensioner parliament, if it must be still called so, gave one proof of independency, besides that of contriving a test in 1675, to purge their members on oath from all suspicion of corrupt influence, which ought to wipe off this stain from the most corrupt. They drove one of their paymasters out of court, and impeached the other, in the fulness of his power, even at a time when the king was so weak as to make, or so unhappy as to be forced to make, on account of pensions privately negotiated from France, the cause of the crown and the cause of the minister one, and to blend their interests together.

What I have said to the honor of the long parliament is just; because, in fact, the proceedings of that parliament were agreeable to the representation I have given of them. But now, if some severe censor should appear, and insist that the dame was chaste, only because she was not enough tempted; that more pensions would have made more pensioners; that much money and little prerogative is more dangerous to liberty than much prerogative and little money; and that the worst and weakest minister king Charles ever had, might have been absolute in this very parliament, whose character I defend, if such a minister had been able to enlist, with places, pensions and occasional bribes, not a slender majority, which the defection of a few might at any time defeat, but such a bulky majority, as might impose on itself: if any one, I say, should refine in this manner, and continue to insist that such a minister, with such a purse, would have stood his ground in the parliament I speak of, with how much contempt and indignation soever he might have been every where treated by the people; I shall not presume to assert the contrary. It might have been so. Our safety was owing as much, perhaps, to the poverty of the court, as to the virtue of the parliament. We might have lost our liberties. But then I would observe before I conclude, that if this be true, the preservation of our religion and liberty, at that time, was owing to these two circumstances; first, that king Charles was not parsimonious, but squandered on his pleasures, what he might have employed to corrupt this parliament; secondly, that the ministers in that reign, fingering no money but the revenue, ordinary and extraordinary, had no opportunity to filch in the pockets of every private man, and to bribe the bubbles very often with their own money; as might be done now, when funding hath been so long in fashion, and the greatest minister hath the means of being the greatest stockjobber, did not the eminent integrity of the minister, and the approved virtue of the age, secure us from any such danger.

We have now brought the deduction of parties very near to the era of whig and tory; into which the court found means to divide the nation, and by this division to acquire in the nation a superiority, which had been attempted ineffectually, even by corruption in parliament.—But this I reserve for another letter, and am,

Sir, yours, &c.

LETTER IV.

Sir:—There is a passage in Tully so extremely applicable to the mischievous, but transitory, prevalence of those principles of government, which king James the First imported into this country, that since it occurs to my memory, I cannot begin this letter better than by quoting it to you, and making a short commentary on it. " Opinionum commenta delet dies, naturæ judicia confirmat."* Groundless opinions are destroyed, but rational judgments, or the judgments of nature, are confirmed by time. It is Balbus, who makes this observation very properly, when he is about to prove the existence of a Supreme Being. The same observation might have been employed as properly, on other occasions, against Balbus himself; and the truth of it might have been exemplified, by comparing the parodoxes and superstitious opinions of his own sect, as well as the tales of an hippocentaur, or a chimera, with the eternal truths of genuine theism, and sound philosophy. In short, the application of it might have been justly made then, and may be so now in numberless instances, taken from the most important subjects, on which the

* L. 2, De Nat. Deor.

thoughts of men are exercised, or in which their interest, as men and members of society, are concerned.

The authority of a sect, and much more of a state, is able to inspire, and habit to confirm, the most absurd opinions. Passion, or interest, can create zeal. But nothing can give stability and durable uniformity to error. Indolence, or ignorance, may keep it floating, as it were, on the surface of the mind, and sometimes hinder truth from penetrating; or force may maintain it in profession, when the mind assents to it no longer. But such opinions, like human bodies, tend to their dissolution from their birth.— They will be soon rejected in theory, where men can think, and in practice, where men can act with freedom. They maintain themselves no longer, than the same means of seduction, which first introduced them, or the same circumstances, which first imposed them, attend and continue to support them. Men are dragged into them, and held down in them, by chains of circumstances. Break but these chains, and the mind returns with a kind of intellectual elasticity to its proper object, truth. This natural motion is so strong, that examples might be cited of men embracing truth in practice, before they were convinced of it in theory. There are cases, where reason, freed from constraint, or roused by necessity, acts in some sort the part of instinct.— We are impelled by one, before we have time to form an opinion. We are often determined by the other, against our opinion; that is, before we can be said properly to have changed it. But observe here the perverseness of that rational creature, man.— When this happens; when the judgment of nature, for so we may speak after Tully, hath prevailed against the habitual prejudice of opinion; instead of acknowledging the victorious truth, which determined him to act, instead of condemning the erroneous opinion, against which he acted, he is too often apt to endeavor, peevishly and pedantically, to reconcile his actions to his error; nay, to persist in renouncing true, and asserting false maxims, whilst he reaps the benefit, and maintains the consequences of the former.

You see whither we are brought by these general reflections. The absurd opinions, ("fictæ et vanæ" our Roman orator would have called them) about the right, power and prerogative of kings, were so little able to take a deep root, and to stand the blasts of opposition, that few of those who drew their swords on the side of king Charles the First were determined to it by them. I assert this fact on cotemporary authority, on the authority even of some who were themselves engaged in that cause, from the beginning to the end of our civil wars. A more recent tradition assures us, that when the same opinions revived at the restoration, they did not sink deep even then into the minds of

men, but floated so superficially there, that the parliament (the
very parliament who had authorised them, and imposed them,
as I observed in the last letter) proceeded a great way, and was
ready to have proceeded farther, in direct opposition to them.
A tradition still more recent will inform us, and that is to be the
subject of this letter; that when these opinions revived again,
at the latter end of the same reign, with an appearance of
greater strength, and of a more national concurrence than ever,
they revived but to be exploded more effectually than ever.
King Charles made use of them to check the ferment raised
against his government; but did not seem to expect that they
would subsist long in force.   His wiser brother depended much
on them: but his dependence was vain.   They were, at that
time, wearing out apace; and they wore out the faster by the
extravagant use which was made of them.   They were in the
mouths of many, but in the hearts of few; for almost all those
who had them in their mouths, acted against them.   Thus were
these wicked and ridiculous principles of government twice revived, and twice destroyed again, in less than thirty years from
the restoration.

> Ter si resurgat murus aheneus,
> ————Ter pereat!

The second revival of these principles, for enough hath been
said of the first, happened soon after the dissolution of the long
parliament; and there, I think, we must place the birth of whig
and tory, though these parties did not grow up into full maturity,
nor receive their names till about two years afterwards.   The
dissolution of this parliament was desired by men of very different complexions; by some, with factious views; by others, on
this honest and true maxim, that a standing parliament, or the
same parliament long continued, changes the very nature of the
constitution, in the fundamental article on which the preservation
of our whole liberty depends.   But whatever motives others
might have to desire this dissolution, the motives which prevailed on the king, were probably these.   This parliament not
only grew more reserved in their grants of money, and stiff and
inflexible in other matters, but seemed to have lost that personal
regard which they had hitherto preserved for him.   They
brought their attacks home to his family; nay, to himself, in the
heats which the discovery and prosecution of the popish plot
occasioned.   That on the queen provoked him.   That on his
brother embarrassed him.   But that which provoked and em-
barrasted him both, was the prosecution of the Earl of Danby,
in the manner in which it was carried on.   I will not descend
into the particulars of an affair, at this time so well understood.

This minister was turned out, and might have been punished in another manner, and much more severely than I presume any one, who knows the anecdotes of that age, thinks that he deserved to be. But the intention of this attack, according to Rapin, was to show that the king, as well as his brother, was at the head of a conspiracy to destroy the government, and the protestant religion. This is a very bold assertion, and such a one as I do not pretend to warrant. But thus much is certain; that if the Earl of Danby's impeachment had been tried, he must have justified himself, by showing what every one knew to be true, that the secret negotiations with France, and particularly that for money, were the king's negotiations, not his.

Now, whether the king hoped, by dissolving the parliament, to stop this prosecution; or to soften that of the popish plot; or to defeat the project of excluding the Duke of York; his hopes were all disappointed. The following parliaments trod in the steps of this. How, indeed, could they do otherwise in those days, when the temper of the people determined the character of the parliament; when an influence on elections by prerogative, was long since over, and private, indirect means of gaining another more illegal influence were not yet found, or the necessary supports of such means were not yet acquired; when any man, who had desired people, who knew neither his fortune, his character, nor even his person, to choose him their representative in parliament, that is, to appoint him their trustee, would have been looked upon and treated as a madman; in short, when a parliament, acting against the declared sense of the nation, would have appeared as surprising a phenomenon in the moral world, as a retrograde motion of the sun, or any other signal deviation of things from their ordinary course in the natural world.

There was, indeed, one point, which this parliament had taken extremely to heart, and which was no longer open to the parliaments that followed; I mean the conduct of the king in foreign affairs, during the war between France, and Holland and her allies, which ended by the treaty of Nimeguen. This war was not made in remote countries. It was made at our door. The motives to it, on the part of the aggressor, were neither injuries received, nor rights invaded; but a spirit of conquest, and barefaced usurpation. The interest we had in it was not such as depended on a long chain of contingencies, and required much subtlety to find out, but plain and immediate. The security, and at one time, the very existence of the Dutch commonwealth depended on the event of it. No wonder then, if the conduct of the king, who joined openly with France at first, and served her privately to better purpose at last, furnished ample matter to the public discontent, and helped to increase the ill humors of succeeding parliaments on two other points, which were still open, and continued to draw their whole attention, as long as king Charles suffered any to sit, during the rest of his reign.

These two points were the prosecution of persons involved in the popish plot, and the exclusion of the Duke of York. The first of these had prepared mankind for the second. The truth is, that if nothing which affected the duke had been produced, besides Coleman's letters, these proofs of his endeavors to subvert the religion and liberty of the people he pretended to govern, joined to so many others of public notoriety, which showed the whole bent of his soul, and the whole scheme of his policy, would have afforded reason more than sufficient for sacrificing the interest, or even the right (if you will call it so) of one man to the preservation of three kingdoms. I know how partial we are in the judgments we make, concerning ourselves, and our own interest. I know that this partiality is the immediate effect of self-love, the strongest spring in the human, nay in the whole animal system; and yet I cannot help being surprised that a man should expect to be trusted with a crown, because he is born a prince, in a country where he could not be trusted by law, and ought not to be trusted in reason, with a constable's staff, if he was born a private person. Let me add, that such an expectation must be deemed more unreasonable in a descendant of Henry the Fourth of France, if possible, than in any other man. The hereditary title of the house of Bourbon, on the extinction of that of Valois, was certainly as clear, and much better established by the laws and usages of France, than the hereditary right of any prince of the house of Stuart to the crown of England; and yet Henry the Fourth, with all the personal qualifications which could recommend a prince to the esteem and love of his subjects, would never have been received into the throne by the French nation, if he had not been of the religion of that nation. On what foundation then could it be expected that a protestant and a free people should be less animated by religion and liberty both, than their neighbors had been by religion alone; for liberty had nothing to do in that contest? Our fathers were thus animated, at the time I am speaking of. The long parliament projected the exclusion; and if the design had been carried on, in the spirit of a country party, it would probably have been carried on with a national concurrence, and would consequently have succeeded in effect, though not perhaps at once, nor in the very form at first proposed.

The violent and sanguinary prosecution of the popish plot was intended, no doubt, to make the success of the exclusion more secure, by raising the passions of men so high, that no expedient but an absolute and immediate exclusion, in the terms of the bill, should be thought sufficient. I cannot help saying on this occasion, that I wish this laudable and just design had not been pursued, by wading through the blood of so many men: enemies to our religion and liberty, indeed; but convicted, for the most part, on evidence which could hardly have passed at any other time. I wish we had done nothing which might be interpreted to the disrepute of our own religion, whilst we attempted to proscribe theirs. In fine, I wish, for the honor of my country, that the prosecutions on account of this plot, and much more on account of another, which was set up as a kind of retaliation for this, and which caused some of the noblest, as well as some of the meanest blood in the nation to be spilt, could be erased out of the records of history. But there is still a farther reason to wish that greater temper had been joined, at this time, to the same zeal for religion and liberty. Men were made to believe that the king, who had yielded on so many other occasions, would yield on this; that he, who had given up so many ministers, would give up his brother at last; and that if the parliament would accept nothing less than the exclusion in their own way, it would be extorted from him. Now in this they were fatally deceived: and I must continue to suspect, till I meet with better reasons than I have yet found to the contrary, that they were so deceived by the intrigues of two very opposite cabals; by the Duke of York's, who were averse to all exclusions, whether absolute, or limited, but most to the last; and by the Duke of Monmouth's, who could not find their account in any but an absolute exclusion; nor in this neither, unless the bill passed without any mention of the duke's daughters, as next in succession: to which, as bishop Burnet tells us, the prince of Orange was willing to comply, on the faith of assurances he had received from hence; a fact, which the bishop might know, and we may therefore take on his word, as extraordinary as it seems. I would only observe that king William, then prince of Orange, could have no reason for consenting that his wife's pretensions to the crown should not be confirmed by an act which excluded her father, except one; and that was the necessity, real or apparent, of uniting different private interests in the public measure of excluding the Duke of York. Now, if this was his reason, the same reason proves, what shall be farther confirmed in the next letter, that a spirit of faction ran through the proceedings of those who promoted the bill of exclusion: and when faction was opposed to faction, there is no room to wonder, if that of the court prevailed. The king, who had not used to show firmness on other occasions, was firm on this: and the consequence of pushing the exclusion in this manner, was giving him an opportunity of breaking the country party; of dividing the nation into whig and tory: of governing himself without parliaments; and of leaving the throne open to his brother, not only without our limitations or conditions, but with a more absolute power established, than any prince of his family had enjoyed.

As soon as the court had got, by management, a plausible pretence of objecting a spirit of faction to those in the opposition, the strength of the opposition was broken, because the national union was dissolved. A country party must be authorised by the voice of the country. It must be formed on principles of common interest. It cannot be united and maintained on the particular prejudices, any more than it can, or ought to be, directed to the particular interests of any set of men whatsoever. A party, thus constituted, is improperly called party. It is the nation, speaking and acting in the discourse and conduct of particular men. It will prevail in all struggles sooner or later, as long as our constitution subsists; and nothing is more easy to demonstrate than this, that whenever such a party finds it difficult to prevail, our constitution is in danger; and when they find it impossible, our constitution must in fact be altered. On the other hand, whenever the prejudices and interests of particular sets of men prevail, the essence of a country party is annihilated, and the very appearance of it will soon be lost. Every man will resort in this case to that standard, under which he hath been marshalled in former divisions; to which his inclinations lead him; or which, though he does not entirely approve, yet disapproves the least.

Such a dissolution of a country party was brought about at the period to which we are now come in our deduction of parties, by the passions, the public pique, and private interest of particular men, and by the wily intrigues of the court. The dissolution of this party, and the new division of the nation into whig and tory, brought us into extreme danger. This extreme danger reunited the nation again, and a coalition of parties saved the whole. Such an experience might have shown them that how opposite soever their professions were, yet they really differed more on negative thad on positive principles; that they saw one another in a false light, for the most part, and fought with phantoms, conjured up to maintain their division, rather than with real beings. Experience had not this happy effect soon. The swell of the sea continued long after the storm was over; and we have seen these parties kick and cuff like drunken men, when they were both of the same side. Let us hope that this scene of tragical folly is over, to the disappointment of those who are conscious of past iniquity, or who meditate future mischief. There are no others who wish and endeavor to prolong it.

I am, sir, &c.

LETTER V.

Sir:—Nothing is more useful, nothing more necessary, in the conduct of public affairs, than a just discernment of spirits. I mean here not only that natural private sagacity which is conversant about individuals, and enables some men to pry, as it were, into the heads and hearts of others, and to discover with them those latent principles which constitute their true characters, and are often disguised in outward action; but I mean principally that acquired, public, political sagacity, which is of the same kind, though I think not altogether the same thing as the former; which flows from nature, too, but requires more to be assisted by experience, and formed by art. This is tnat superior talent of ministers of state, which is so rarely found in those of other countries, and which abounds so happily at present in those of Great Britain. It is by this that they discover the most secret dispositions of other courts; and, discovering those dispositions, prevent their designs, or never suffer themselves to be surprised by them. It is by this that they watch over the public tranquillity at home; foresee what effect every event that happens, and much more every step they make themselves, will have on the sentiments and passions of mankind. This part of human wisdom is therefore every where of use; but is of indispensable necessity in free countries, where a greater regard is to be constantly had to the various fluctuations of parties; to the temper, humor, opinion, and prejudices of the people. Without such a regard as this, those combinations of peculiar circumstances, which we commonly call conjunctures, can never be improved to the best advantage, by acting in conformity, and in proportion to them; and without improving such conjunctures to the best advantage, it is impossible to achieve any great undertaking, or even to conduct affairs successfully in their ordinary course.

A want of this just discernment of spirits, if I am not extremely mistaken, defeated the designs of those who prosecuted with so much vigor the popish plot, and the exclusion of the Duke of York. Several of them were men of very great abilities; and yet we shall have no reason to be surprised that they fa led in this point, if we reflect how unfit even the greatest genius is to discern the spirit of others, when he hath once overheated his own. All men are fallible: but here lies the difference. Some men. such as I have just mentioned, crossed by difficulties, pressed by exigencies, transported by their own passions, or by the passions of those who fight under their banner, may now and then deviate into error, and into error of long and fatal consequence.

But there are some men, such as I shall not mention upon this occasion, (because I reserve them for another and a better) who never deviate into the road of good sense; who, crossed by no difficulties, pressed by no exigencies, meeting scarce opposition enough to excite their industry, and guiding a tame well-tutored flock, that follow their bell-wether obstinately, but never tread on his heels: there are men, I say, whose special privilege it is to proceed with all these advantages, deliberately and superciliously, from blunder to blunder, from year to year, in one perpetual maze of confused, incoherent, inconsistent, unmeaning schemes of business.

But having nothing to do with the men of this character at present, I return to those of the former class; to the men who led the whig party, at its first appearance in the time of king Charles the Second. The foundation upon which they built all their hopes of success, was this; that they should frighten and force the king into a compliance with them: but they did not enough consider that the methods they took were equally proper to frighten and force a great part of the nation from them, by reason of the particular circumstances of that time. They did not enough consider, that when they began to put their designs in execution, scarce twenty years had passed from the restoration; and that the highest principles, in favor of the church and the monarchy, had prevailed almost universally during one half of that time, and very generally during the other half; that they had the accidental passions of the people for them, but the settled habits of thinking against them; that they were going off from a broad to a narrow bottom; from the nation to a part of the nation; and this at a time, when they wanted a more than ordinary concurrence of the whole body. They did not enough consider that they were changing the very nature of their party, and giving an opportunity to the court, which was then become, in the strict sense of the word, a faction, to grow up into a party again, and such a party as would divide, at least, the people with them, upon principles, plausible in those days, and sufficient to raise a spirit capable to disappoint all their endeavors.

The same resentments and prejudices, the same jealousies and fears, which burst out with violence, upon many occasions a few years before, lay still in the hearts of men; latent and quiet, indeed, and wearing out by degrees, but yet easy to be revived, and to be blown up anew. If we compare the conduct of the long parliament in 1674 and 1675, with the attempts which had been lately made, during the administration of the cabal; with the secret of the second Dutch war, and many other designs and practices of the court, which were then come lately and very authentically to light; with the state of Scotland, which was then subdued under a real tyranny, and with that of Ireland, where, to say no more, the act of settlement was but ill observed; if we make this comparison, it will not yet appear that the proceedings of the house of commons were immoderate, though they were warm; nor factious, though they were vigorous; nor that any danger could be then reasonably apprehended from them, except to the enemies of the constitution in church and state; and yet even then the old resentments, prejudices, jealousies and fears began to revive; and an apprehension of falling back under the influence of presbyterians and republican principles began to show itself in the house of lords, and in the nation. It is true, that this had no immediate consequence; because the popish plot broke out soon afterwards like a mighty flame, in which these little fires, that began to burn anew, were lost. This great event made the church and the dissenters continue to run into one, as they had begun to do before; and the sole division of parties was that of the court and the country, as long as this parliament lasted. But still it was evident with how delicate a hand every thing that related to our former disputes, required to be touched. It was evident that the least alarm given to the church, or to those who value themselves on the principles of loyalty then in fashion, would be sufficient to open those wounds which were just skinned over, and to raise two new parties out of the ashes of the old.

These parties were not raised, whilst the long parliament sat; because a general opinion prevailed, and well enough founded on their precedent conduct, that however angry the king might be with the parliament, or the parliament with the king, a few popular steps made on one side, and a little money granted on the other, would soften matters between them, and dispose them to forget all former quarrels. As hot, therefore, as the parliament grew, and as much as some people might think that they exceeded their bounds; yet still it was difficult to persuade even these people that a parliament, like this, would push things to the last extremity; destroy the constitution they had settled and supported with so much zeal; or draw the sword against a prince, to whom they had borne so much affection. But in the parliaments which followed, the case was not the same; and I will state as shortly as I can, upon authorities, which no man likely to contradict me must refuse, what made the difference. These authorities, shall be that of Burnet, and that of Rapin; whom I quote, on this occasion, for the same reason that I would quote my Lord Clarendon against king Charles the First, or Ludlow for him.

In the year 1676, before we have grounds sufficient to affirm that the design of excluding the Duke of York, was formed, but not before we have reason to suspect that it might be in the thoughts of several,* those who stood foremost in the opposition to the court, were very industrious to procure a dissolution of the long parliament, so industrious, that they negotiated † the affair with the duke, who had concurred in a vote for an address to dissolve it; and they undertook ‡ that a new parliament should be more inclinable to grant the papists a toleration, than they would ever find this would prove. The papists were in earnest for this measure; since Coleman drew a declaration for justifying it, and since their design in it was to divide the king and his people.§ It is fair to conclude that the protestants, who had been in it at the time I mention, upon party views, were at least as much so, when their views rose higher. This parliament had pushed a strict and thorough examination into the popish plot, with great sincerity and zeal. Nay, the project of the exclusion had been started, though not prosecuted, in the last session. May we not take it for granted, however, that they, who were now resolved to carry the exclusion, in a manner in which they soon attempted to carry it, and who foresaw by cousequence the dfficulties that would be opposed to them, and the strong measures they should be obliged to pursue, in order to overcome these difficulties; I say, might not they think this parliament much less proper than any other to engage and persist in such measures? They thought thus, without doubt; and so far they judged better than the king, who came into the dissolution upon very different motives. But as to the consequence of engaging a new parliament in such strong measures, the event showed that the king judged better than they, in the progress of this affair.

The dissenters, who had been long persecuted by the parliament, and bantered and abused by the court, were encouraged by the conjuncture to lift up their heads. They took advantage of the horror and indignation which the discovery of the popishplot, and the use made of this discovery, had raised all over the kingdom. They could not be more zealous in this cause than the members of the established church had shown themselves to be; but they cried, perhaps, louder for it. In short, whatever their management was, or however they were abetted, certain it is that they were very active, and very successful too, in the elections of the parliament which followed the long parliament, according to Rapin, who asserts that many of the members, chosen into this house of commons, were presbyterians. He might have said as much, upon just as good grounds, of the two parliaments which followed this; and I shall speak of them indiscriminately.

---

* Burnet's history of his own times, vol. i, p. 393.
† Ibid.   ‡ Ibid.   § Ibid.

The leaders, who mustered all their forces, in order to push the bill of exclusion, looked on this turn in the elections as an advantage to them; and it might not have been a disadvantage, if they and the dissenters had improved it with more moderation. But they were far from doing so, as Rapin himself seems to own a little unwillingly, when he says, that complaisance for the presbyterians was carried, perhaps, too far in the bill for the comprehension of protestant dissenters. Bishop Burnet speaks more plainly. He owns that many began to declare openly in favor of the non-conformists; that upon this the non-conformists behaved themselves very indecently; that they fell severely on the body of the clergy; and that they made the bishops and clergy apprehend that a rebellion, and with it the pulling the church to pieces, was designed. Several other passages of the same strength, and to the same purpose, might be collected from this historian; and he who reads them, will not be surprised, I think, to find that such proceedings as these, both in parliament and out of it, gave an alarm to the clergy, and set them to make parallels between the late and the present times; and to infuse the fears and the passions, which agitated them, into the nation. The bishop accuses them, indeed, of doing this with much indecency. But they, who are frightened out of their wits will be apt to be indecent; and indecency begets indecency.

At the same time that the jealousies of a design to destroy the church prevailed, others prevailed likewise of a design to alter the government of the state; of a design not only against the successor, but against the possessor of the crown. Many well-meaning men, says Bishop Burnet upon one occasion, began to dislike these practices, and to apprehend that a change of government was designed.—The king came to think himself, says the same author upon another occasion, levelled at chiefly, though for decency's sake his brother only was named. Rapin goes farther; for, speaking of the same time, he uses this remarkable expression; that "Things seemed to be taking the same course as in the year 1640; and there was reason to think that the opposing party had no better intentions towards the king now than the enemies of king Charles the First had towards him." But whatever some particular men, who knew themselves irreconcilable with the king, as well as the duke, or some others, who had still about them a tang of religious enthusiasm and republican whimsies, might intend; I am far from thinking that the party, who promoted the exclusion, meant to destroy, on the contrary, it is plain that they meant to preserve, by that very measure, the constitution in church and state. The reason why I quote these passages, and refer to others of the same kind, is not to show what was really designed, but what was appre-

hended; for as the distinction of whig and tory subsisted long
after the real differences were extinguished, so were these parties
at first divided, not so much by overt acts committed, as by the
apprehensions which each of them entertained of the intentions
of the other. When the resolution was once taken of rejecting
all limitations, on the belief artfully, and, I think, knavishly propagated, that the king would yield, if the parliament persisted;
the necessary consequences of the king's adhering inflexibly to
his brother, were those which followed, those "fulmina parlia-
mentaria," harsh votes, angry proceedings, addresses that were
in truth remonstrances, projects of associations, pretensions to a
power of dispensing with the execution of laws, (that very prerogative they had so justly refused to the crown) and many
others, which I omit. All these would have been blasts of wind,
"bruta fulmina," no more, if the king had yielded: and that they
were pushed in this confidence by the bulk of the party who
pushed them cannot be doubted; since it cannot be doubted that
the bulk of the party depended on the king's yielding almost,
perhaps, even to the last. Some few might be willing, nay desirous, that he should not yield, and hope to bring things into a
state of confusion; which none but madmen, or those, whom
their crimes, or their fortunes render desperate, can ever wish to
see. But it would be hard, indeed, if parties were to be charac-
terised, not by their common view, or the general tenor of their
conduct, but by the private views imputed to some amongst
them, or by the particular follies, into which mistake, surprise or
passion, hath sometimes betrayed the best-intentioned, and even
the best-conducted bodies of men. Whig and tory were now
formed into parties; but I think they were not now, nor at any
other time, what they believed one another, nor what they have
been represented by their enemies, nay by their friends. The
whigs were not roundheads, though the measures they pursued,
being stronger than the temper of the nation would then bear,
gave occasion to the suspicions I have mentioned. The tories
were not cavaliers, though they took the alarm so sudden and
so warm for the church and the king; and though they carried
the principles in favor of the king, at least, whilst the heat of
their contests with the opposite party lasted, higher than they
had been ever carried before. The whigs were not dissenters
nor republicans, though they favored the former, and though
some inconsiderable remains of the latter, might find shelter in
their party. The tories had no disposition to become slaves, or
papists, though they abetted the exercise of an exorbitant power
by the crown, and though they supported the pretensions of a
popish successor to it.--Thus I think about the parties which
arose in the reign of king Charles the Second; and as I deliver

my thoughts with frankness, I hope they will be received with candor. Some farther and stronger reasons for receiving them so, may perhaps appear in a subsequent letter.

I am, sir, yours, &c.

LETTER VI.

SIR:—If king Charles the Second could have been prevailed upon to sacrifice the chimerical divine right of his brother to the real interest, and right too, of his people, that happy event would have made him ample amends, in future ease and quiet, and the nation in future security, for all precedent disorders, dangers, and fears of danger. But instead of this, he was every day confirmed in the resolution of not giving up, directly and in terms, that right to his brother, which he thought reflected strength on his own. The very measures taken to force him to submit, enabled him to resist. The opposite spirit spent itself in blood and violence. The spirit of him rose visibly in the nation, and he saw very soon the time approach when he might venture to appeal to his people against his parliament. This time was come, when men were once convinced that a country party prevailed no longer, but that faction had taken its place. Many appearances, which I have not room to enumerate, served to propagate this opinion; particularly the behavior and almost avowed pretensions of the Duke of Monmouth, which were carried on even in defiance of the solemn declaration made by the king, that he had never married the duke's mother.

Some of the worthiest and warmest men, who were engaged for the exclusion, complained themselves, even from the first, of the private interests and factious intrigues which prevailed amongst them. "I must confess," says a very considerable man,* who laid down his life for this cause afterwards, and whose original letter is still extant; "I must confess, that I do not know three men of a mind; and that a spirit of giddiness reigns amongst us, far beyond any I have ever observed in my life." And yet he had lived and acted in as factious a time as this nation ever saw. He proceeds: "Some look who is fittest to succeed. They are for the most part divided between the Prince of Orange and the Duke of Monmouth. The first hath plainly the most plausible title. I need not tell you the reasons against Monmouth.

* Algernon Sidney.

The strongest for him are, that whoever is opposed to York will have a good party; and all Scotland, which is every day like to be in arms, doth certainly favor him, and may probably be of as much importance in the troubles that are now likely to fall upon us, as they were in the beginning of the last. Others are only upon negatives," &c.

I could easily multiply proofs of this kind; but I think I need not take any pains to show that there was such a faction formed at this time; nor to refute Welwood, who asserts that the Duke of Monmouth was not ambitious to the degree of aspiring to the crown, till after his landing in the west. I will only remark, that the efforts of this faction amongst those who drove on the bill of exclusion, furnished another motive to the division and animosity of parties. The tories, who had divided from the others, on jealousies of designs to change the constitution in church and state, began now to apprehend that the opposite party might succeed in another view, and set up a king of their own nomination. A notion then entertained by many, that the worse title a man had, the better king he was likely to make, did not persuade them. They had suffered under the tyranny of a party; many of them had been themselves the abettors of a party administration; and they feared, with reason, a party king. Thus personal interests were mingled on both sides with public considerations; and the Duke of York gained a great number of adherents, not by affection to him, but by an aversion to Monmouth, which increased among the tories in proportion as the duke's popularity increased among the whigs; not by any favorable disposition in the tories to popery and arbitrary power, but by a dread, as I have observed already, of returning in the least degree under the influence of those principles, and the power of those men, whose yoke had galled the necks of many that were still alive and active on the stage of public affairs. " Men grew jealous of the design," (says Bishop Burnet, speaking of Monmouth's popularity) " and fancied here was a new civil war to be raised. Upon this, they joined with the duke's party;" meaning the Duke of York's.

I say nothing of the apprehensions entertained on one side, and the expectations entertained on the other from Scotland; because though there was, even in the beginning of these struggles, a concert between those who were oppressed by the court there, and those who opposed it here, which grew afterwards into a closer correspondence, and became riper for action; yet the seditious spirit, that gave occasion to these apprehensions and expectations, was roused and exasperated by the inhumanity of the Duke of Lauderdale, who, though a presbyterian himself, was the butcher of that party, pushed the warmest of them into unjustifiable excesses, revived their silly zeal for the covenant,

and wrought up their enthusiasm even to assassination and rebellion.   Let me only observe, that this was plainly the fault of
the court, and could not, therefore, be imputed to the whigs,
whatever use some of that party might propose to make of such
a disposition.   The violence of the conventiclers was sounded
high, in order to palliate the severities exercised in the government of that kingdom.   But the reasonable men of all parties
thought then, as they think now, and always will think, that it
is the duty of those who govern, to discern the spirit of the
people, to consider even their passions, to have a regard to their
weaknesses, and to show indulgence to their prejudices, and that
ministers, who punish what they might prevent, are more cul-
pable than those who offend.

As the two parties were formed, so was their division maintained by mutual jealousies and fears, which are often sufficient
to nourish themselves, when they have once taken root in the
mind, and which were, at this time, watered and cultivated with
all the factious industry possible.   The most improbable reports,
the most idle surmises, carried about in whispers, were sufficient, as I might easily show in various instances, to raise a
panic terror in one party, or the other.   In both, there were but
too many persons on the watch, to improve and to propagate these
terrors, and by a frequent repetition of such impressions to raise
the alarm and hatred of parties to the highest pitch.   He, who
went about to allay this extravagant ferment, was called a trim-
mer; and he, who was in truth a common friend, was sure of
being treated like a common enemy.   Some, who voted for the
bill of exclusion, were very far from being heartily for it; but I
have seen good reasons to believe, and such there are even in
our public relations, that some of those who voted against it,
and declared for limitations, concurred in the end, though they
differed in the means, with those who promoted the bill.   And
yet such men were constantly marked out as favorers of popery
and enemies to their country.   Thus, in the other party, men,
who had no other view but that of securing their religion and
liberty, and who meant nothing more than to force the court
into such compliances as they judged necessary to establish this
security, were stigmatised with the opprobrious names of fanatic
and republican.   Thus it happened in those days, and thus it
happens in ours, when any man who declares against a certain
person, against whom the voice of the nation hath already declared, or complains of things which are so notorious, that no
man in the nation can deny them, is sure to be followed by the
cry of jacobitism, or republicanism.   But there is a great difference, God be praised, between the two cases.   The present cry

being void of pretence, is therefore without effect. It is heard in few places, and believed only in one.—But to return.

When the nation was divided in this manner, the heat of the parties increased as their contest lasted, according to the usual course of things. New engagements were daily taken; new provocations and offences were daily given. Public disputes begot private pique; and private pique supported public disputes with greater rancor and obstinacy. The opposite principles advanced by the two parties, were carried higher and higher, as they grew more inflamed; and the measures they pursued, in order to get the better each of his adversary, without overmuch regard to any other consequence, became stronger and stronger, and, perhaps, equally dangerous. The meeting of the parliament at Oxford had a kind of hostile appearance; and as soon as parliaments were laid aside, which happened on the sudden and indecent dissolution of this, the appearance grew worse. No security having been obtained by parliamentary methods, against the dangers of a popish succession, it is probable that they, who looked on these dangers as nearest and greatest, began to cast about how they might secure themselves and their country against them, by methods of another kind; such as extreme necessity, and nothing but extreme necessity can authorise. Such methods were happily pursued and attended with glorious success, a few years afterwards, when this succession had taken place; and, by taking place, had justified all that had been said against it, or foreboded of it; when the nation was ripe for resistance; and the Prince of Orange ready and able, from a multitude of fortunate, concurring circumstances, to support so great an enterprise. But the attempts, which were wise at one time, would have been desperate at the other; and the measures which produced a revolution in the reign of king James, would have produced in the reign of king Charles, a civil war of uncertain event at best: I say of uncertain event at best; because it seems to me, that whoever revolves in his thoughts the state of England and Scotland, as well as the situation of our neighbors on the continent, at that time, must be of opinion, that if the quarrel about the exclusion had broke out into a war, the best cause would have been the worst supported. The king, more united than ever with his brother, would have prevailed. What was projected in 1670, and, perhaps, more than was then intended, would have been effected; and the religion and liberty of Great Britain would have been destroyed by consequence. We cannot say, and it would be presumption to pretend to guess, how far the heads of party had gone, in Scotland, or in England, into measures for employing force. Perhaps, little more had passed, in which they who became the principal sacrifices, were any way concerned, than rash discourse about dangerous, but rude, indigested schemes, started by men of wild imaginations, or desperate fortunes, and rather hearkened to than assented to; nay, possibly despised and neglected by them. But the court, who wanted a plot to confirm and increase their party, and to turn the popular tide in their favor, took the first opportunity of having one; which was soon furnished to them by the imprudent, but honest zeal of some, and by the villany, as well as madness of others: and they prosecuted it so severely, with the help of forward sheriffs, willing juries, bold witnesses and mercenary judges, that it answered all their ends.* The design of assassinating the king and the duke, was certainly confined to a few desperate villains; but too many had heard it from them, who were both so foolish and so wicked, as not to discover them;† and this reflected great prejudice, though I doubt not in many cases very unjustly, against all those who had acted upon better principles, but yet were involved in these prosecutions.

As this event disarmed, dispirited, and broke one party, so it strengthened, animated, and united the other. The tories, who looked on the dangers they apprehended from the whigs to be greater and nearer than those which they had apprehended, as well as the whigs, before this new division of parties, from a popish succession, were now confirmed in their prejudices. Under this persuasion, they ran headlong into all the measures which were taken for enlarging the king's authority, and securing the crown to the Duke of York. The principles of divine hereditary right, of passive obedience, and non-resistance, were revived and propagated with greater zeal than ever. Not only the wild whimsies of enthusiasts, of schoolmen and philosophers, but the plainest dictates of reason were solemnly condemned in favor of them, by learned and reverend bodies of men, who little thought that in five years time, that is in 1688, they should act conformably to some of the very propositions, which at this time they declared false, seditious, and impious.

In short, the Guelphs and Gibellines were not more animated against each other at any time, than the tories and whigs at this; and in such a national temper, considerable steps were made, as they well might be, towards the destruction of our constitution. One of those which Rapin enumerates, and insists upon very gravely, can scarcely be mentioned without smiling. "The king," says he, "in order to make his people feel the slavery he had newly imposed on them, affected to review his troops; and these troops amounted, by the return of the garrison of Tangier, to four thousand men, effective, and well-armed." The whigs,

---

* Burnet.   † Burnet.

indeed, in those days, were so averse to standing armies, that they thought even those troops, commonly called guards, unlawful; and Bishop Burnet argues, in his reflections on my Lord Russel's trial, that a design to seize on them amounted to no more than a design to seize on a part of the king's army. But it is possible that the tories, who had showed their dislike of standing armies sufficiently in the long parliament, might think it however no unreasonable thing, when designs of insurrections, and even of assassinations had come so lately to light, that a number of regular troops, sufficient to defend the person of the king, but not sufficient to oppress the liberties of the people, and five times less than we have since seen kept up in the midst of the most secure tranquillity, should be winked at till these distempers were entirely over.

Another step, which the same author mentions, was indeed of the greatest consequence, and laid the axe to the root of all our liberties at once, by giving the crown such an influence over the elections of members to serve in parliament, as could not fail to destroy that independency, by which alone the freedom of our government hath been, and can be supported. I mean the proceedings by quo warranto, and the other methods taken to force or persuade the corporations to surrender their old charters, and accept new ones, under such limitations and conditions as the king thought fit to innovate. These proceedings were violent, the judgments upon them arbitrary, and the other methods employed scandalous. But still it was the end, it was the consequence, that alarmed and terrified all those who had not sold themselves to the court, or who had not lost, in their zeal for party, all regard to their country, much more than the means that were employed upon this occasion. If, instead of garbling corporations by prerogative, the court could have purchased their elections by money, we may reasonably believe that the surer and more silent way would have been taken. But would the alarm have been less among all the friends of liberty? Certainly not. They would have seen that the end was the same, and have disliked these means the more, for being less liable to observation and clamor. A prince, asserting an illegal and dangerous prerogative, and applauded for doing so, and seconded in the attempt by a numerous party in the nation, carried no doubt a very terrible aspect. But still there was room to hope, the violent character of the Duke of York considered, (and that hope was actually entertained by many) that the party, who abetted these usurpations of the prerogative, might be soon frightened back again from a court to a country interest; in which case there was room to hope likewise, the milder character and better understanding of the king considered, that the evil might be in some degree redressed, and the consequences of it prevented. It was reasonable for the friends of liberty to expect that men, who were injured, would complain and seek relief on the first favorable opportunity. But if they had been corrupted, and the practice of selling elections had been once established, I imagine that the friends of liberty would have thought the case more desperate. It is certainly an easier task, and there is somewhat less provoking, as well as less dangerous in it, to struggle even with a great prince who stands on prerogative, than with a weak, but profligate minister, if he hath the means of corruption in his power, and if the luxury and prostitution of the age have enabled him to bring it into fashion. Nothing surely could provoke men, who had the spirit of liberty in their souls, more than to figure to themselves one of these saucy creatures of fortune, whom she raises in the extravagance of her caprice, despatching his emissaries, ecclesiastical and secular, like so many evil demons, to the north and to the south, to buy the votes of the people with the money of the people, and to choose a representative body, not of the people, but of the enemy of the people, of himself.

This was not the case at the time we are speaking of. It was prerogative, not money, which had like to have destroyed our liberties then. Government was not then carried on by undertakers, to whom so much power was farmed out for returns of so much money, and so much money entrusted for returns of so much power. But though the case was not so desperate, yet it was bad enough in all conscience; and among all the excesses into which the tories ran, in favor of the crown, and in hopes of fixing dominion in their own party, their zeal to support the methods of garbling corporations was, in my opinion, that which threatened public liberty the most. It hath been reproached to them by many; but if among those who reproached them, there should be some who have shared since that time in the more dangerous practice of corrupting corporations, such men must have fronts of brass, and deserve all the indignation which is due to iniquity, aggravated by impudence. The others abetted, in favor of a prerogative, supposed real by many in those days, and under the pretence at least of law, a power which gave the crown too much influence in the elections of members of the house of commons; but these men, if there are any such, have been concerned in a practice, for the sake of their own vile interest, which spreads like a gangrene over the whole body of a nation, and to every branch of government, and which hath never failed, in any one instance, where it hath been suffered, to become the bane of liberty.

We have now carried the two parties through that period of

time when the conduct of both was most liable to the objections made to them by their adversaries. The tories acted on the most abject principles of submission to the king; and, on those of hereditary right, were zealous for the succession of a prince, whose bigotry rendered him unfit to rule a protestant and a free people. The whigs maintained the power of parliament to limit the succession to the crown, and avowed the principle of resistance; in which they had law, example, and reason for them. But then the fury of faction was for doing that without parliament, which could only be legally done by it: and, in order to do this, the principles of resistance were extended too far; and the hottest men of the party taking the lead, they acted in an extravagant spirit of licence, rather than a sober spirit of liberty; and the madness of a few, little inferior to that of Cromwell's enthusiasts, dishonored the whole cause for a time. My intention was not to have left them here, but to have carried these observations on so far as to justify, notwithstanding these appearances, what is said at the conclusion of my last letter, concerning the true characters of both parties. But either the abundance of matter hath deceived me, or I have wanted skill and time to abridge it; so that I must defer this part of my task, and crave your indulgence, as well as that of your readers, for my prolixity.

I am, sir, &c.

LETTER VII.

SIR:—I advanced, in the first of these essays, something to this effect; that every clumsy, busy, bungling child of fortune, on whom she bestows the means and the opportunity of corrupting, may govern by this infamous expedient; and, having gratified his ambition and avarice, may have a chance to secure himself from punishment, by destroying the liberties of his country. It was advanced, likewise, in the same paper, that every character is not equally fit to govern a people by dividing them; because some cunning, some experience, nay, some skill to form, and some address to conduct a system of fraud, are necessary in this case. I persuade myself that no man, who read that paper, was at a loss to find an instance to confirm the truth of the first of these propositions; and we have now before us another, which may serve to confirm the truth of the second.

Though I do not think the designs of king Charles the Second either deeply laid, or deeply fixed in his own mind, yet in general they were founded on bad principles, and directed to bad ends. He desired indeed to be easy, and to make his people so; but then he desired both these on such conditions as were inconsistent with good government, dur'ng the whole course of his reign, and with the security of religion and liberty, during the latter part of it. We have seen how the intemperate conduct of many, and the flagitious designs of some among the whigs, weakened their own party, and gave new strength and provocations to the other. But we have not yet considered some other advantages, without which these divisions could neither have been fomented nor supported as they were. Now these advantages arose chiefly from the character and conduct of the king himself. If king Charles had found the nation plunged in corruption; the people choosing their representatives for money, without any other regard; and these representatives of the people, as well as the nobility, reduced by luxury to beg the unhallowed alms of a court; or to receive, like miserable hirelings, the wages of iniquity from a minister: if he had found the nation, I say, in this condition, (which extravagant supposition one cannot make without horror) he might have dishonored her abroad, and impoverished and oppressed her at home, though he had been the weakest prince on earth, and his ministers the most odious and contemptible men that ever presumed to be ambitious. Our fathers might have fallen into circumstances which compose the very quintessence of political misery. They might have sold their birth-right for porridge, which was their own. They might have been bubbled by the foolish, bullied by the fearful, and insulted by those whom they despised. They would have deserved to be slaves, and they might have been treated as such. When a free people crouch, like camels, to be loaded, the next at hand, no matter who, mounts them, and they soon feel the whip and the spur of their tyrant; for a tyrant, whether prince or minister, resembles the devil in many respects, particularly in this. He is often both the tempter and tormentor. He makes the criminal, and he punishes the crime.

But this was not the state of the English nation, at the time we speak of. We were not yet corrupted, nor even quite ripe for corruption. Parties there were; and the contests of these parties gave occasion to the rise and growth of factions; some of which ran into the most seditious practices against the government, and others into the vilest submission to it. But still a spirit of liberty remained in many, uncorrupted and unextinguished, and such as worked our national deliverance in the days of distress, that soon followed. We were freemen then, in the proper sense and full extent of the words; because not ouly the laws, which asserted our common rights, were maintained and

improved, but private independency, which can alone support
public liberty under such a government as ours; was itself supported by some of that ancient economy and simplicity of manners, that were growing, but not grown, out of fashion.   Such a
people, as we then were, could neither be bought nor driven;
and I think king Charles could not have divided and led them,
if he had wanted any of the qualities he possessed, or had held
another conduct than he held.   Far from being proud, haughty,
or brutal, " he had not a grain of pride, or vanity, in his whole
composition;"* but was the most affable, best-bred man alive.
He treated his subjects like noblemen, like gentlemen, like freemen, not like vassals or boors.   Whatever notion he had of his
hereditary right, he owned his obligation for the crown he wore
to his people, as much as he would have been bound to do, in
reason, in justice, in honor, and in prudence, if he had stood at
the greatest distance from it, in the course of lineal succession,
and had been called to it from the low state in which he was
before, by the free gift and choice of the nation.   His professions
were plausible, and his whole behavior engaging; so that he won
upon the hearts, even whilst he lost the good opinion of his subjects and often balanced their judgment of things, by their personal
inclination.   These qualities and this part of his conduct went a
great way to give him credit with his people, and a hold on their
affections.   But this was not all.   He observed their temper, and
he complied with it.   He yielded to them in points, from which
he had determined, and declared too, that he would never depart.   To know when to yield in government, is at least as necessary, as to know when to lose in trade, and he who cannot do
the first, is so little likely to govern a kingdom well, that it is
more than probable he would govern a shop ill.   King Charles
gave up to the murmurs of his people, not one or two such ministers as may be found almost behind every desk; those awkward
pageants of courts, those wooden images, which princes gild and
then worship; but several great and able men, nay, whole cabals
of such, who had merit with him, though they had none with
the nation.   He started often out of the true interest of his people,
but the voice of his people almost as often reclaimed him.   He
made the first Dutch war, but he made the triple alliance too.
He engaged with France in the war of 1672, but he made a
separate peace with Holland.   True it is, indeed, that neither
the representations of his parliament, nor the desires of his people, could prevail on him to go farther, and to enter in earnest
into the war against France.   But the confidence between him
and his parliament was so broken at that time, that they would

* Sir William Temple.

not trust him, nor he them. At this I am not surprised, and for that very reason, I confess, I have always been so at the strong and repeated instances made to force him into that war; since it cannot surely be better policy to drive a prince into a war, which he has no inclination to make, than it would be to be drawn by him into a war, if he had no ability to conduct it. In home affairs, besides his frequent concessions, whenever the nation took umbrage at his proceedings, he passed the test and the habeas corpus bills, and many others for the public benefit; and I scarce remember any popular act, which stopped at the throne in his time, except that about the militia, which he apprehended to be a dangerous encroachment on his prerogative, and another in favor of the dissenters, which was contrived, meanly enough, to be stolen off the table in the house of lords.

What has been touched here, and in former papers will be sufficient to show, in some measure, how king Charles was enabled to divide a nation so united and so heated as this nation was, on the discovery of the popish plot; to oppose so avowedly and so resolutely the exclusion of his brother: the prospect of whose succeeding to the crown was become still more dreadful, even by that small part of Coleman's correspondence, which had come to light; and yet to attach so numerous a party to himself, nay to his brother; to lay aside parliaments for several years, and not only to stand his ground, but to gain ground in the nation, at the same time. But there is still something more to be added. He had not only prepared for the storm, but he acquired new strength in the midst of it; that is, in the proceedings on the popish plot, and the bill of exclusion. He would gladly have kept the former out of parliament; but when it was once there, he put on the appearances of great zeal for the prosecution of it. These appearances helped him to screen his brother; as the ill success of the exclusion-bill in the house of lords, where it was rejected by sixty-three against thirty, helped to screen himself from the violence of the house of commons. But that which gave him the principal advantage, in the present contests, was another management. As soon as the first preparatory steps were made to the bill of exclusion in 1678, he declared himself, in a speech to his parliament, ready to pass any bills to make his people safe in the reign of his successor, so they tended not to impeach the right of succession, nor the descent of the crown in the true line. He persisted in his declaration to the last; and if he had nothing else, I imagine that he would have gained no great popularity. When a free people lie under any grievance, or apprehend any danger, and try to obtain their prince's consent to deliver them from one, or prevent the other, a flat refusal, on his part, reduces them to the melancholy alter-

native of continuing to submit to one, and to stand exposed to
the other, or of freeing themselves from both, without his consent;
which can hardly be done by means very consistent with his and
their common interest. King Charles was too wise to push the
nation to such an extremity. He refused what his parliament
pressed on him, in the manner and on the principle they pressed
it; but then his refusal was followed by expedients, which varied
the manner, and yet might have been managed so as to produce
the effect; and which seemed to save, rather than actually saved,
the principle. Numbers concurred, at that time, in avowing the
principle; and the tests had made many persons think religion
safe; as the king's offers made them think it no fault of his, if it
was not made safer. The council had prepared some expedients; and the limitations, and other provisions against a popish
successor, proposed directly from the throne by the chancellor in
1679, went a great way towards binding the hands of such a
successor, and lodging the power, taken from him, in the parliament. But the scheme of expedients, debated in the Oxford
parliament, was a real exclusion from every thing, but the title
of a king. The first article banished the Duke of York, during
his life, to the distance of five hundred miles from England, Scotland and Ireland; and the tenth, to mention no more, excluded
him *ipso facto*, if he came into any of these kingdoms; directed
that he should suffer, in this case, as by the former bill, and that
the sovereignty should vest forthwith in the regent; that is, in
the Princess of Orange. Surely this was not to vote the lion in
the lobby into the house. It would have been to vote him out
of the house and lobby both, and only suffer him to be called
lion still. I am not ignorant of the refinements urged by Sir
William Jones and others against this scheme: but I know that
men run into errors from both extremes; from that of seeing too
much, as well as that of seeiag too little; and that the most
subtle refiners are apt to miss the true point of political wisdom,
which consists in distinguishing justly between what is absolutely best in speculation, and what is the best of things practicable in particular conjunctures. The scheme, no doubt, was
built on a manifest absurdity, and was liable to many inconveniences, difficulties and dangers; but still it was the utmost that
could be hoped for at that moment: and the single consideration
one would think, should have been this; whether, united under
such an act of parliament, they would not have opposed the
succession of the Duke of York, with less inconveniency, less
difficulty and danger, than disunited, and with the laws against
them. The truth is, that as there were men at this time desirous
that the king should be on desperate terms with his parliament,
because they were so themselves; in like manner there were

others, who desired, for a reason of the same nature, that the parliament should be on desperate terms with the king. These were factious interests, and they prevailed against the national interest; which required that the king should be separated at any rate from his brother, instead of being united to him by a fear made common to both. But the die was thrown; and the leaders of the whig party were resolved "to let all lie in confusion, rather than hearken to any thing besides the exclusion."* Obstinacy provoked obstinacy. The king grew obstinate, and severe too, against his natural easiness and former clemency of temper. The tory party grew as obstinate, and as furious on their side, according to a natural tendency in the disposition of all parties: and thus the nation was delivered over, on the death of king Charles, "à la sottise de son frere;† to the folly and madness of his brother."

It was this folly and madness, however, that cured the folly and madness of party. As the common danger approached, the impressions of terror, which it made, increased. Whig and tory then felt them alike, and were brought by them, as drunken men sometimes are, to their senses. The events of king James's reign, and the steps by which the revolution was brought about, are so recent, and so well known, that I shall not descend into any particular mention of them. A few general remarks on the behavior of this prince, and on the behavior of parties in his reign, and at the revolution, will be sufficient to wind up the history of whig and tory, and to prove what I have so often asserted, that both sides purged themselves on this great occasion, of the imputations laid to their charge by their adversaries; that the proper and real distinction of the two parties expired at this era, and that although their ghosts have continued to haunt and divide us so many years afterwards, yet there neither is, nor can be any division of parties at this time, reconcilable with common sense, and common honesty, among those who are come on the stage of the world under the present constitution, except those of churchmen and dissenters, those of court and country.

The behavior and conduct of king James the Second would be sufficient, if there was no other instance, and there are thousands, to show that as strong prejudices, however got, are the parents, so a weak understanding is the nurse of bigotry, and injustice and violence and cruelty its offspring. This prince was above fifty, when he came to the throne. He had great experience of all kinds, particularly of the temper of this nation,

---

* Burnet's History.
† An expression used by king Charles on many occasions.

and of the impossibility to attempt introducing popery, without hazarding his crown. But his experience profited him not. His bigotry drew false conclusions from it. He flattered himself that he should be able to play parties against one another, better than his brother had done, (which, by the way, was the least of his little talents,) and to complete his designs by an authority, which was but too well established. He passed, I think, for a sincere man. Perhaps he was so; and he spoke always with great emphasis of the word of a king: and yet never was the meanest word so scandalously broken as his. In the debate in 1678, about the test, when he got a proviso put in for excepting himself, it has been advanced in print, and not denied that I know of, that speaking with " great earnestness, and with tears in his eyes, he solemnly protested that whatever his religion might be, it should only be a private thing between God and his own soul, and that no effect of it should ever appear in the government."* At his accession to the throne, in council first, and after that in full parliament, in the face of the nation, he made the strongest declaration in favor of the constitution in church and state, and took the most solemn engagements to defend and support it. But bigotry burst through all these cobwebs; for such they are to men, transported by a religious delirium, who acquire a strength that those. who are well, have not, and conscientiously break all the obligations of morality. These admirable dispositions in the king were encouraged by the state in which his brother left and he found the nation, and by the complaisance of the parliament which he called soon after his accession. They were confirmed, and he was determined to pull off the mask entirely, by the ill success of the Duke of Monmouth and the Earl of Argyle. Bishop Burnet speaks of this parliament very indecently, and I think very untruly. They were neither men of parts, nor estates, according to him. The truth is, that the circumstances under which we were brought by the factious proceedings of both parties, in the late reign, for and against the court, were such as might perplex the best parts, and puzzle the heads even of the wisest men. A professed, zealous papist, in full and quiet possession of the throne, and, instead of any provision made, or any measures taken against him, the notion and the exercise of the prerogative established at an extravagant height, were such circumstances, as laid the nation almost at the mercy of the king. They, therefore, who were the most determined not to part with either their religion or their liberty, and yet had more to lose in the fray than Dr. Burnet, might be willing to look round them, to wait

* Burnet's History.

opportunities, and not undertake rashly what can seldom be undertaken twice.   It is impossible to believe that their confidence in the king's word was such as they affected.   But like drowning men, who saw nothing else to catch at, they caught at a straw.   The Duke of Monmouth's expedition into England, and the Earl of Argyle's into Scotland, were so far from affording the nation any opportunity of mending their condition, that the declaration of the former might draw some of the dissenters to his standard, as it did; but was calculated to drive the tory party, most of the whigs, and in short the bulk of the people from him.   The declaration of the latter was founded in the solemn league and covenant, and gave so much reason to apprehend that a revival of the same principles, and a renewal of the same tyranny was intended, that we cannot wonder it had no better an effect, though we lament the fate of a worthy and gallant man, whose crime was refusing a test, that should never have been imposed on protestants and freemen, and who had been driven into these extreme resolutions by a series of unjust and tyrannical usage.

Thus were these invasions, in the very beginning of his reign, favorable in some respects to the designs of king James.   They fortified, in the minds of men, the jealousies and fears which had a few years before formed the tory party, and disposed them, by consequence at least, to keep measures and not break with the king.   They gave him the pretence, which he seized very readily, of raising and keeping up a standing army.   But, in the event, they forwarded our deliverance from all the dangers to which we were exposed under his government, by precipitating his attempts against our religion and liberty.   The same day that the news of the invasion in Scotland was communicated to the parliament here, the commons voted that great revenue, which they gave him, and gave him for life.   After these invasions were over, they voted a supply, which was intended for the charge of maintaining the additional forces.   They offered to pass a law for indemnifying his popish officers from the penalty they had incurred, and to capacitate such others as he should name in a list to be given to the house.   In short, they suffered themselves to be drawn to the brink of the precipice: but there they stopped.   They would neither give him the whole supply of one million two hundred thousand pounds, which he asked, nor sanctify, by the authority of parliament, the practice of keeping up a standing army in time of peace; but rejected the words moved for that purpose.   They would neither repeal the test and penal laws, nor submit to his dispensing, or suspending, which was in effect a repealing power: that is, they would not cast themselves headlong down the precipice.   And because they would not, he quarrelled with them, lost the seven hundred thousand pounds they had voted, rather than suffer them to sit any longer; and never met them more.

Things hastened now to a decision. The king's designs were openly avowed, and desperately pushed. The church of England opposed them with the utmost vigor. The dissenters were cajoled by the court; and they who had been ready to take arms against king Charles, because he was unwilling to exclude his brother, and who had taken arms against this prince, since he was on the throne, became abettors of his usurpations. It were easy to prove this, even by bishop Burnet's account, as much as that is softened; and if the excuses which have been made for their silence against popery in this critical moment, or for their approving and encouraging the exercise of a dispensing power, are to be received, one may undertake to excuse, on the same principles of reasoning, all those instances of misconduct in the church party, which I have presumed to censure so freely. But the truth is, these excuses are frivolous. I could quote some that are even burlesque. Let us reverence truth, therefore, and condemn the dissenters as frankly, on this occasion, as we have condemned the members of the church of England on others.

The revolution soon followed. Many of the most distinguished tories, some of those who carried highest the doctrines of passive obedience and non-resistance, were engaged in it, and the whole nation was ripe for it. The whigs were zealous in the same cause; but their zeal was not such as, I think, it had been some years before, a zeal without knowledge: I mean, that it was better tempered, and more prudently conducted. Though the king was not the better for his experience, parties were. Both saw their errors. The tories stopped short in the pursuit of a bad principle. The whigs reformed the abuse of a good one.— Both had sacrificed their country to their party. Both sacrificed, on this occasion, their party to their country. When the tories and the whigs were thus coalited, the latter stood no longer in need of any adventitious help. If they did not refuse the assistance of those, who had weakened their cause more by the jealousies and fears to which they gave both occasion and pretence, than they had strengthened it by their number, yet they suffered them to have no influence in their councils, no direction of their conduct. The cause of liberty was no longer made the cause of a party, by being set on such a bottom, and pushed in such a manner, as one party alone approved. The revolution was plainly designed to restore and secure our government, ecclesiastical and civil, on true foundations; and whatever might happen to the king, there was no room to suspect any change in the constitution. There were some, indeed, concerned in this great and glorious undertaking, who had obstinately preserved, or lightly taken up the republican and other whimsies that reigned in the days of usurpation and confusion. If they could have prevailed, and it was no fault of theirs they did not, the coalition of parties had been broken; and, instead of a revolution, we might have had a civil war, perhaps not even that sad chance for our religion and liberty. But this leaven was so near worn out, that it could neither corrupt, nor seem any longer to corrupt the mass of the whig party. The party never had been presbyterians, nor republicans, any more than they had been quakers; any more than the tory party had been papists, when, notwithstanding their aversion to popery, they were undeniably under the accidental influence of popish councils. But even the appearances were now rectified. The revolution was a fire, which purged off the dross of both parties; and the dross being purged off, they appeared to be the same metal, and answered the same standard.

I shall deliver my thoughts, on some other occasion, concerning the disputes that arose about the settlement of the crown after the revolution; and show, if I do not very much deceive myself, that no argument can be drawn from thence against any thing I have advanced.

I am, sir, &c.

LETTER VIII.

Sir:—The slavish principles of passive obedience and non-resistance, which had skulked perhaps in some old homily before king James the First, but were talked, written and preached into vogue in that inglorious reign, and in those of his three successors, were renounced at the revolution by the last of the several parties who declared for them. Not only the laity, but the clergy embraced and co-operated in the deliverance which the prince of Orange brought them. Some of our prelates joined to invite him over. Their brethren refused to sign an abhorrence of this invitation. The university of Oxford offered him their plate, and associated for him against their king. In one word, the conduct of the tories, at this crisis, was such as might have inclined a man to think they had never held resistance unlawful, but had only differed with the whigs about the degree of oppression, or of danger, which it was necessary to wait, in order to sanctify resistance. Now, it may appear at first a little strange that these principles, which had always gone hand in hand with those of the divine, hereditary, indefeasible right of kings, that were just as well founded in reason, in support of which the example of the primitive Christians might be pompously cited, and to countenance which some texts of the Bible might be piously strained, should not keep their hold, and maintain their influence, as well as the others.

This attachment to hereditary right will appear the more strange, if we consider what regard was shown, at this time, to the difficulties they who had pawned themselves, as it were, for the principles, would be under, when they came to concur in establishing a settlement repugnant to it. That great and solemn resolution, about the abdication of king James, and the vacancy of the throne, might have been expressed in terms much stronger and plainer than it was. I have heard there were persons who had a mind it should be so, and who, more attached to the honor, that is, the humor of party, than to the national interest, in this great event, would have turned this resolution, as well as the declaration of the prince of Orange, to a more express approbation of the whig, and a more express condemnation of the tory tenets and conduct. But a wiser and honester consideration prevailed. Instead of erecting the new government on the narrow foundations of party systems, the foundations of it were laid as wide, and made as comprehensible as they could be. No man, I believe, at this time thinks that the vote asserted too little; and surely there was no color of reason, on the side of those who cavilled against it at that time, for asserting too much.

The disputes about the words abdicate, or desert, and about the vacancy of the throne, were indeed fitter for a school than a house of parliament, and might have been expected in some assembly of pedants, where young students exercised themselves in disputation, but not in such an august assembly as that of the lords and commons, met in solemn conference upon the most important occasion. The truth is, that they who formed the opposition, were reduced to maintain strange paradoxes; stranger, in my opinion, than most of those which cast so much ridicule on the stoics of old. Thus, for instance, they were forced to admit that an oppressed people might seek their remedy in resistance, for they had sought it there themselves; and yet they opposed making use of the only remedy, which could effectually secure them against returns of the same oppression, when resistance had put it in their power, as oppression had given them a right to use this remedy. Surely this must appear a paradox, and a very absurd one too, if we consider that resistance, in all such cases, is the mean, and future security the end; and that the former is impertinent, nay, wicked in the highest degree, if it be not employed to obtain the latter. Thus again, the same men declared themselves willing to secure the nation against the return of king James to that throne which he had abdicated, or, according to them, deserted; nay, some of them were ready, if we may credit the anecdotes of that time, to proceed to such extreme resolutions, as would have been more effectual than justifiable in the eyes of mankind; and yet they could not prevail on their scrupulous consciences to declare the throne vacant. They had concurred in the vote, that it was "inconsistent with the laws, liberties and religion of England to have a papist rule over the kingdom." King James had followed the pious example of Sigismond, who, not content to lose the crown of Sweden himself for his religion, had carried his son away, that he might be bred a papist, and lose it too; and yet they maintained, though they did not expressly name him, that if the throne was then, or should be at any time vacant of the father, it must be reputed instantaneously full of the son, upon the foundation of this silly axiom, that the king never dies. According to this law, and these politics, king James and his successors, to the twentieth generation, might have continued abroad, a race of royal exiles, preserving their indefeasible right to govern, but debarred from the exercise of it; whilst the nation continued, during all this time, from century to century, under the dominion of regents, with regal authority, but without any regal right; an excellent expedient sure to keep the monarchy in a hereditary succession! But there remained none better, on the principles of these men, since the Prince of Orange had committed the fatal oversight of neglecting to conquer the nation. His sword would have cut the gordian knot of hereditary right, and they could have submitted with safe consciences to a conqueror. But to give the crown to a prince, though they had put the whole administration into his hands; which, by the way, was high treason, unless the throne was, what they denied it to be, actually vacant: to give the crown, I say, to a prince who would not take it, when it was in his power to take it, without their consent; to settle a new government by agreement and compact, when the glorious opportunity of establishing it by force and conquest had been unhappily lost; these were propositions to which they could not consent. King James had violated the fundamental laws, which he had promised over and over, and sworn to maintain. He had shown by his first escape, when nothing more was imposed on him than to wait the resolution of a free parliament, that he would renounce his crown rather than submit to secure effectually the observation of these laws. He had made a second escape, which was voluntary as well as the first, and made on the same principle, against the entreaties of his friends, and the instigations of the same council that had directed his former conduct, and on a letter from the queen, claiming his promise to do so. Notwithstanding all these reasons, they who maintained the hereditary right of our kings, reduced themselves, and would have reduced their country, to the absurd necessity of altering their constitution, under pretence of preserving it. No king, except a Stuart, was to reign over us: but we might establish a doge, a lord archon, a regent, and thus these warm assertors of monarchy, refusing to be slaves, contended to be republicans. Many more paradoxes of equal extravagance might be cited, which were advanced directly, or which resulted plainly from the arguments employed on one side of the question in those disputes; but the instances I have cited may suffice for our present purpose, and may serve to show, that although difficulties hard to solve in speculation or to remove in practice, will arise in the pursuit of the most rational principles, yet such absurdities as these can never arise, except from the most irrational, and always must arise from such.

In the persons who maintained this divine, hereditary, indefeasible right of our kings, had thought fit to drop these principles, when they laid aside those of passive obedience and non-resistance, and no tolerable reason can be given why they did not, their conduct would have been consistent and uniform on this great occasion; and this consistency and uniformity would have been productive of great good, by taking away at once even the appearances of all political divisions in the bulk of the nation. But whilst they labored to reconcile their present conduct to their ancient system, they were true to neither. They had gone much farther than this would allow, and then they refused to go as far as the other required, in order to be safe, and therefore in order to be justified. They lost every kind of merit, the chimerical merit of adhering to a set of silly principles, the real merit of sacrificing their prejudices to the complete deliverance of their country from the recent danger of popery and arbitrary power. Nay, they did worse; for the mischievous consequences of their conduct were not hurtful to them alone, and at that time alone, but to the public, and even down to these times. They furnished pretence to factions, who kept up a division under the old names, when the differences were really extinguished by the conduct of both parties, because the conduct of both parties were no longer conformable to the principles imputed to them. The tories had no longer any pretence of fearing the designs of the whigs, since the whigs had sufficiently purged themselves from all suspicion of republican views, by their zeal to continue monarchical government, and of latetudinarian schemes in point of religion, by their ready concurrence in preserving our ecclesiastical establishment, and by their insisting on nothing farther, in favor of the dissenters, than that indulgence which the church was most willing to grant. The whigs had as little pretence of fearing the tories, since the tories had purged themselves, in the most signal manner, from all suspicion of favoring popery or arbitrary power, by the vigorous resistance they made to both. They had engaged, they had taken the lead in the revolution, and they were fully determined against the return of king James. The real essences of whig and tory were thus destroyed, but the nominal were preserved, and have done since that time a good part of the mischief which the real did before. The opposition made to the settlement of the crown brought this about. An over-curious inquiry into the motives of this opposition would be a task too invidious for me to undertake. Something, however, may be said upon it. We may say in general, without offence, that private ambition mingled itself early in the great and national concerns of the revolution, and that it did so more as the prospect of a new settlement, and of the elevation of the Prince of Orange, approached. Expectations were raised, disappointments were given or foreseen, and a variety of motives of the same kind began to influence very strongly the conduct of the principal actors. Some endeavored to lay the foundations of their future fortune by demonstrations of a personal attachment to the prince, which were carried on, I doubt, a little too independently of the regard due to their country in some cases; particularly, if I mistake not, in that of the declaration of rights, of which we may pronounce, and experience will justify us, that it was too loose, too imperfect, and nothing less than proportionable to the importance of the occasion, and the favorable circumstances of the conjuncture. Others there were who imagined that the shortest and surest way for them to take, in pursuit of the same view, was to make themselves considerable by opposition, to form a party, and maintain a struggle for personal power, under the pretence and umbrage of principle. This was, without doubt, the motive of some particular leading men, and could not be, at least at first, the motive of numbers. But there was another motive, which easily became that of numbers, because it arose out of a fund common to all men, the perversity of human nature, according to an observation made in one of these letters. Whilst the event of the Prince of Orange's expedition was undecided, men remained under the full influence of their fears, which had determined them to act against their prejudices. But when the revolution was secure, and these fears were calmed, these prejudices resumed in some degree their former power, and the more for being revived and encouraged by men of reputation and authority, who argued for some, and might as reasonably have argued for all the errors, in contradiction to which most of them had acted, nay, and were ready to

act. With such views, and by such means, were many brought,
at this time, to entangle themselves in a maze of inextricable
absurdities. Had they owned candidly and fairly that their principles, as well as those of the whigs, were carried too high in the
former disputes of parties, and that these principles could not be
true, since they found themselves actually in a situation wherein
it was not possible to act agreeably to them, without manifest
absurdity, the distinction, as well as the difference, of whig and
tory had been at an end. But contrary measures produced a
contrary effect. They kept up the appearances, and they could
keep up no more, of a whig and a tory party, and with these
appearances a great part of the old animosity. The two names
were sounded about the nation, and men who saw the same ensigns flying were not wise enough to perceive, or not honest
enough to own, that the same cause was no longer concerned,
but listed themselves on either side, as their prejudices at first,
and their inclinations, or other motives, which arose in the progress of their contests, directed them afterwards: whigs very often
under the tory standard, tories very often under the whig
standard.

This general representation which I have made of the state of
parties at the revolution is, I am verily persuaded, exactly just;
and it might be supported by many particular proofs, which I
choose rather to suggest than to mention. But if any doubt remains, let us analyse the several parties of that time a little more,
reduce them to their first and real principles, and then pronounce
whether we find the whig or the tory party subsisting among
them.

In the first place, there was a party that concurred in making
the new settlement; a party that prevailed in parliament, and was
by much the majority of the nation out of it. Were the whigs
this majority? was this party a whig party? No man will presume to affirm so notorious an untruth. The whigs were far from
being this majority, and king James must have died on the
throne, if the tories had not concurred to place the Prince of
Orange there in his stead. Was this party a tory party then? Certainly no. The whigs had been zealous in the same cause, and
had contributed to make it successful by their temper, as well as
their zeal, by waiting the time of the tories, or rather the maturity of the conjuncture, and by moderating their principles and
their conduct in favor of that coalition, without which the revolution could have succeeded no more than the exclusion did. We
find then here neither a whig nor a tory party; for in coalitions
of this kind, where two parties are melted as it were into one,
neither of them can be said, with truth and propriety, to exist.

There was another party directly opposite to this; a certain number of men, on whom the original taint transmitted down from king James the First, remained still in the full strength o its malignity. These men adhered to those principles, in the natural sense and full extent of them, which the tories had professed. But yet, the tories having renounced these principles, or distinguished themselves out of any obligation to observe them this inconsiderable faction could not be deemed the tory party, but received the name of jacobite with more propriety.

Two other parties there were at this time, formed on one common principle, but widely different, however, by the different consequences they drew from it. The principle I mean is that contained in the distinction of a king de jure and a king de facto. The famous statute of Henry the Seventh authorised this distinction. The statute was designed principally, no doubt, for the advantage of the subjects, that they might be safe, whichever side prevailed, in an age when the epidemical folly of fighting for different pretenders had spilt oceans of blood on the scaffold, as well as in the field; and yet the statute was designed for the service of kings de facto too, and particularly of Henry the Seventh. The author of "Hereditary Right Asserted," would have us believe otherwise; and yet surely nothing can be more evident than this, that if king Henry the Seventh's right had been as unquestionable as he supposes, and I presume to deny that it was, yet he would have been declared a king de facto only, if the intrigues of the Duchess of Burgundy and the faction of York had succeeded; and consequently this provision for the safety of his adherents, in that possible contingency, gave strength to him, as it would have given strength to any other prince, whilst it attached his adherents to him by the apparent security it provided; for this author contends that it did not establish a real security, and advises us to suspend our judgment on the validity of this statute, till we see what the "opinion of parliament or the judges may be, whenever a king de jure shall dispossess a king de facto." He refers us ad Calendas Græcas.

But there are two observations to be made to our present purpose on this statute, which seem to me natural and plain. First, it confounds in effect the very distinction it seems to make; since it secures alike, and, by securing alike, authorises alike those who adhere to the king de jure, and those who adhere to the king de facto, provided they adhere to the king in possession. Secondly, it was contrived to hinder people, according to my Lord Bacon's sense of it, "from busying themselves in prying into the king's title, and that subjects might not trouble themselves with inquiries into the justness of the king's title or quarrel." Now, upon the foundation of this distinction and this statute, thus understood, they who demurred on the settlement of the crown at the revolution, might plausibly, though I think very unreasonably, resolve neither to vote, nor act themselves, against those maxims and principles which they had entertained and professed, as maxims of law, and principles of the constitution, and yet resolve to submit sincerely, and adhere faithfully to a new establishment, when it was once made. But the other of the two parties I mentioned drew from the same principle, of distinguishing between a king de facto and a king de jure, a very different conclusion. They acknowledged one king, and held their allegiance still due to another. They bound them- selves by oath to preserve a settlement which they pretended themselves in conscience obliged to subvert. This was to justify perfidy, to sanctify perjury, to remove the sacred boundaries of right and wrong, and, as far as in them lay, to teach mankind to call good evil, and evil good.

Such were the three divisions into which men broke at the revolution, in opposing the settlement then made, whilst the great body of the nation concurred in it, and whig and tory formed in reality but one party. The first of these divisions continued, and became a faction in the state, but made no prose- lytes, and is worn out by time. The principle of the second was wrong, but it could not be reputed dangerous whilst it lasted, and it seems to have been built on so narrow and slippery a foundation, that it did not continue long in force. I may be more bold in asserting this, since if we look back to the era of the revolution, and to the times which followed, we shall find among those who voted for a regent, not a king, on the abdica- tion of king James, some illustrious persons who served king William faithfully, who adhered inviolably to our new establish- ment, and who have been distinguished friends of the succession that hath now taken place. That there have been persons, who deserved to be ranked under the third head, is too notorious to be denied; but I persuade myself that this division hath consisted always of a flux body. On one hand, it is scarce possible to be- lieve that any number of men should be so hardened, as to avow to themselves, and to one another, the acting and persisting to act on a principle so repugnant to every notion and sentiment that harbor in the breasts of social creatures. On the other, we know how the sallies and transports of party, on some occasions, can hurry even reasonable men to act on the most absurd, and honest men to act on the most unjustifiable principles, or both one and the other on no principle at all, according as the object which the prevailing passion presents to them directs. This hath been the case of many since the revolution, and there are some of all sides, I believe, still alive; sure I am that there were

some a few years ago, who know that no side is absolutely unexceptionable in this respect.

I am, sir, &c.

LETTER IX.

Sir:—But whatever the state of parties was at the revolution,
and for some time afterwards, the settlement made at that time
having continued, that state of parties hath changed gradually,
though slowly, and hath received at length, according to the
necessary course of things, a total alteration. This alteration
would have been sooner wrought, if the attempt I have mentioned, to defend principles no longer defensible, had not furnished the occasion and pretence to keep up the appearances of
a tory and a whig party. Some of those who had been called
tories furnished this pretence. They who had been called whigs
seized and improved it. The advantages to one side, the disadvantages to the other, the mischiefs to the whole, which have
ensued, I need not deduce. It shall suffice to observe, that these
appearances were the more easy to be kept up, because several
men, who had stood conspicuous in opposition to one another
before the revolution, continued an opposition, though not the
same, afterwards. Fresh provocations were daily given, and
fresh pretences for division daily taken. These contests were
present; they recalled those that had past in the time of king
Charles the Second, and both sides forgot that union which their
common danger and their common interest had formed at the
revolution. Old reproaches were renewed, new ones invented,
against the party called whigs, when they were as complaisant
to a court as ever the tories had been; against the party called
tories, when they were as jealous of public liberty and as frugal
of public money as ever the whigs had been. Danger to the
church, on one side, and danger to the state, on the other, were
apprehended from men who meant no harm to either; for though
dissenters mingled themselves on one side, and jacobites on the
other, and notwithstanding the leanings of parties in favor of
those, by whom they were abetted, yet is it a certain truth, that
the struggle was in the main for power, not principle; and that
there was no formal design laid on one side to destroy the
church, nor on the other the state. The cavils which may be
made, and the facts which may be cited, some of older and some
of fresher date, against what hath been here said, do not escape

me. Men of knowledge, and of cool and candid thought, will answer one, and account for the other, without my help; and I cannot resolve, for the sake of the passionate, nor even of the ignorant, to descend upon this subject into a greater detail.

I pass to that which is closer to my present purpose, and of more immediate use; and I say, that as the natural dispositions of men are altered and formed into different moral characters by education, so the spirit of a constitution of government, which is confirmed, improved and strengthened by the course of events, and especially by those of fruitless opposition, in a long tract of time, will have a proportionable influence on the reasoning, the sentiments, and the conduct of those who are subject to it. A different spirit and contrary prejudices may prevail for a time, but the spirit and principles of the constitution will prevail at last. If one be unnatural, and the other absurd, and that is the case in many governments, a vigorous exercise of power, signal rewards, signal punishments, and a variety of other secondary means, which in such constitutions are never wanting, will however maintain, as long as they are employed, both the spirit and the principles. But if the spirit and principles of a constitution be agreeable to nature and the true ends of government, which is the case of the present constitution of the British government, they want no such means to make them prevail. They not only flourish without them, but they would fade and die away with them. As liberty is nourished and supported by such a spirit and such principles, so they are propagated by liberty. Truth and reason are often able to get the better of authority in particular minds; but truth and reason, with authority on their side, will carry numbers, bear down prejudices, and become the very genius of a people. The progress they make is always sure, but sometimes not observable by every eye. Contrary prejudices may seem to maintain themselves in vigor, and these prejudices may be kept up long by passion and artifice. But when truth and reason continue to act without restraint, a little sooner or a little later, and often when this turn is least expected, the prejudices vanish at once, and truth and reason triumph without any rival.

The constitution of England had been seen in two very different lights for almost a century before the revolution; so that there is no room to be surprised at the great opposition that appeared, when the whig and tory parties arose a very few years before that era, between principles which, as opposite as they were, each side pretended to establish on the nature of one and the same constitution. How this happened hath been often hinted, and I have not here room to explain any farther. Let us be satisfied that it is no longer the case. Our constitution is no longer a mystery; the power of the crown is now exactly limited, the chimera of prerogative removed, and the rights of the subject are no longer probelematical, though some things necessary to the more effectual security of them may be still wanting. Under this constitution the greatest part of the men now alive were born. They lie under no pretence of obligation to any other, and to the support of this they are bound by all the ties of society, and all the motives of interest.

Let us prove what we advance; and that we may do so ad homines, let us borrow our argument from the great champion of hereditary right. Having mentioned in his introduction what he endeavors pompously, but vainly, to establish in his book in favor of hereditary right, " a prescription of nine centuries, a continual claim of five hundred and fifty years," he attempts to convince us by a " novel law, and a modern constitution." This modern constitution is the act of recognition, in the first of king James the First. The declarations there made in favor of hereditary right, are no doubt as strong as words can frame, and the words are such as would tempt one to think, by the fustain they compose, that his majesty himself had penned them. From hence it is concluded, that since " the vows and acts of fathers bind their posterity, this act, till the society hath revoked it lawfully, lays the same obligations on every member of the society, as if he had personally consented to it." If this act then was lawfully revoked, or repealed, another novel law, contrary to it, might be made equally binding; but neither this act, nor the act of the twelfth of Charles the Second, affirming the crown to appertain by just and undoubted right to the king, his heirs and lawful successors, having been expressly repealed, we still lie under the same obligations, and every settlement, contrary to them, and by consequence the settlement made at the revolution is unlawful. Now I ask, was not the will of Henry the Eighth, which excluded the whole Scotish line, made in pursuance, and by the authority, of an act passed in the twenty-fifth year of his reign? Hath not this author justified the validity of this will much to his own satisfaction, and, I believe, to that of his readers? Was this will lawfully revoked? Was this statute expressly repealed? I ask farther, whether hereditary right, and the obligations of subjects to it, could be made immutable and eternal, as this author asserts that they were by the act of recognition, without a manifest contradiction to the act of queen Elizabeth, which declares the power of parliament to limit and bind the succession to the crown? Was this act expressly repealed? That king James the First succeeded lawfully against law, our author is fond to maintain; and the proposition is not unlike that of some popish casuists, who assert that his holiness "jure potest contra jus decernere, can decree rightfully against right." But if these questions are fairly answered, it will result from such answers, and from the arguments I have quoted, that this novel law, this modern constitution, is a mere illusion; that it never bound any member of the society, and that the parliament had as much right to make the settlement in 1688, notwithstandiug the act of recognition, as the parliament had to make this act in 1603, notwithstanding the two acts I have mentioned, and the will of Henry the Eighth, made by virtue of the first of them. This wayward and forlorn hereditary right must, therefore, fall to the ground, or be supported by the supposed prescription of nine centuries, and claim of five and a half, which no intelligent man, who reads this book, will be persuaded that the author hath proved a jot better, than the uninterrupted succession of popes, from St. Peter down to his present holiness, is proved by the learned antiquaries of Italy. If this act of recognition be urged, as it sometimes is, to show the declared sense of the three estates of the kingdom, which declaration was obtained, it seems, in a hurry, since the act was read three times in one house the same day; the declared sense of the three estates, not pronounced in a hurry, but after the most solemn debates and conferences, may be urged with much greater weight, in favor of our present settlement. If this act of recognition, notwithstanding what hath been objected, be urged as a law which had the assent of the king, in opposition to the proceedings of the convention, by which king William and queen Mary were raised to the throne, the answer is obvious and conclusive. The circumstances of the two cases are very different, but when they come to be weighed in a fair balance, those which attended the settlement of the crown on the revolution, will be found at least as conformable to reason, to law, and to practice, as those which attended the establishment of the Stuart family. Queen Elizabeth designed king James the First to be her successor; the nation concurred to make him so; neither she nor they paid any regard to the law which stood in his way. Their reasons for acting in this manner are easy to be discovered in the history of that time, and on the same authority we may certainly conclude, that they would not have acted in this manner, if king James had been, like his mother, a professed papist. Thus he got into the throne, and when he was there, he got, like other kings, such a title as he chose to stand upon, agnised, or recognised by his parliament. The settlement at the revolution was made by a convention of the lords spiritual and temporal, and a full and free representative of the whole body of the people. When king William and queen Mary were once settled in the throne, this settlement was continued and confirmed by an assemblage of all the legislative powers. He who will dispute the validity of these proceedings, must show, therefore, first of all, what hath never yet been shown, no, not by the author I have so often quoted, the invalidity of the proceedings of those parliaments, which raised Edward the Third and Henry the Fourth to the throne, which were called as irregularly, though by writs in the names of Edward the Second and Richard the Second, as it can be pretended that the convention was. He must show the invalidity of the proceedings even of that assembly, by which Charles the Second was called home, till their proceedings became valid by a subsequent confirmation. He must show, farther, how any of the laws of the princes of the house of Lancaster came to be constantly received and executed, a little better than the author of "Hereditary Right Asserted" hath done, by assuring us on his word that it was by the "sufferance of Edward the Fourth and his successors, and the approbation of the people." He must account for the continuance in force of the laws of Richard the Third, and of Henry the Seventh, a little better than the same author does, by the deficiency of Henry the Seventh's title, which, upon another occasion, he magnifies, though upon this he affirms it to have been no better than that of Richard the Third, and by the great respect of Henry the Eighth for his father. When this hath been once shown, it will be time to think of a reply. In the meanwhile we will observe, that besides the passion and party-spirit which possess almost all those who write on this subject, there is a distinction which should be constantly made in cases of this nature, and which they never make, or never make exactly enough. They compare the proceedings without comparing the situation. Necessity and self-preservation are the great laws of nature, and may well dispense with the strict observation of the common forms of any particular constitution. Either the convention must have fallen into the absurdities I have already mentioned, or have called back king James, which would have been still a greater absurdity, or have left their country in absolute anarchy, or have done what they did. What they did, was done as near as possible to the spirit of our constitution, the forms of our laws, and the examples of former times. They had the merit, their posterity hath the benefit, nay, he who would say that they had the guilt, not the merit, must still allow that their posterity hath the benefit, without sharing the guilt; and, upon the whole matter, I will venture to assert, that he who scruples, or pretends to scruple, at this time, the validity of our present constitution, is no wiser, or else no honester, than he would be, who should scruple, or pretend to scruple, the validity of Magna Charta. I have often wished that some profound antiquary of much leisure, would write an elaborate treatise, to assert royal prerogative against the great charter, as well as hereditary right against the revolution. I am persuaded that he would succeed alike in both. Why, indeed, should a charter, extorted by force, and, therefore, vicious in its principle, stand on a better foot, or have more regard paid to it, than a settlement made in opposition to a divine, and, therefore, indefeasible right? I say, and, therefore, indefeasible; because if it be not proved to be something more than human, it will hardly be proved indefeasible. But I quit this subject; upon which, perhaps, you may think I have spent my time as ill, as I should have done if I had preached against the Koran at Paul's. It is time to speak of the motives of interest, by which we are bound, as well as by the ties of duty, to support the present constitution.

Upon this head a few words will be sufficient, since I presume that no prejudices can be strong enough to create much diversity of opinion in a case so very clear, and capable of being stated so shortly. Whether the revolution altered our old constitution for the better, or renewed it, and brought it back to the first principles, and nearer to the primitive institution, shall not be disputed here. I think the latter, and every man must think that one or the other was necessary, who considers, in the first place, how the majesty and authority of the prince began to swell above any pitch, proportionable to the rank of chief magistrate, or supreme head, in a free state; by how many arts the prerogative of the crown had been stretched, and how many precedents, little favorable to liberty, had been set, even before the accession of the Scottish line; and who considers, in the next place, the direct tendency, confirmed by experience, of those principles of government so frequently mentioned, which composed an avowed system of tyranny and established slavery as a political, a moral, and a religious obligation, which king James the First was too successful in establishing, but neither he nor his descendants were able to pursue. What these considerations made necessary, was done at the revolution, at least, so far as to put it into our power to do the rest. A spirit of liberty, transmitted down from our Saxon ancestors, and the unknown ages of our government, preserved itself through one almost continual struggle, against the usurpations of our princes, and the vices of our people; and they, whom neither the Plantagenets nor the Tudors could enslave, were incapable of suffering their rights and privileges to be ravished from them by the Stuarts. They bore with the last king of this unhappy race, till it was shameful, as it must have been fatal, to bear any longer; and whilst they asserted their liberties, they refuted and anticipated, by their temper and their patience, all the objections which foreign and domestic abettors of tyranny are apt to make against the conduct of our nation towards their kings. Let us justify this conduct by persisting in it, and continue to ourselves the peculiar honor of maintaining the freedom of our Gothic institution of government, when so many other nations, who enjoyed the same, have lost theirs.

If a divine, indefeasible, hereditary right to govern a community be once acknowledged; a right independent of the community, and which vests in every successive prince immediately on the death of his predecessor, and previously to any engagement taken on his part towards the people; if the people once acknowledge themselves bound to such princes by the ties of passive obedience and non-resistance, by an allegiance unconditional, and not reciprocal to protection; if a kind of oral law, or mysterious cabbala, which pharisees of the black gown and the long robe are always at hand to report and interpret as a prince desires, be once added, like a supplemental code, to the known laws of the land: then, I say, such princes have the power, if not the right, given them, of commencing tyrants; and princes who have the power, are prone to think that they have the right. Such was the state of king and people before the revolution. By the revolution, and the settlement since made, this state hath received considerable alterations. A king of Britain is now, strictly and properly, what kings should always be, a member, but the supreme member, or the head of a political body: part of one individual, specific whole, in every respect, distinct from it, or independent of it in none: he can move no longer in another orbit from his people, and, like some superior planet, attract, repel, influence, and direct their motions by his own. He and they are parts of the same system, intimately joined and co-operating together, acting and acted upon, limiting and limited, controlling and controlled by one another; and when he ceases to stand in this relation to them, he ceases to stand in any. The settlements, by virtue of which he governs, are plainly original contracts. His institution is plainly conditional, and he may forfeit his right to allegiance, as undeniably and effectually, as the subject may forfeit his right to protection. There are no longer any hidden reserves of authority, to be let out on occasion, and to overflow the rights and privileges of the people. The laws of the land are known, and they are the sole springs from whence the prince can derive his pretensions, and the people theirs. It would be to no purpose to illustrate any farther a matter which begins to be so well understood; or to descend into a more particular enumeration of the advantages that result, or may result from our present settlement. No man, who does not prefer slavery to liberty, or a more precarious security to a better, will declare for such a government, as our national divisions, and a long course, seldom interrupted, of improvident complaisance to the crown, had enabled king James the Second to establish against such a government as was intended by the subsequent settlement: and if there be any such man, I declare that I neither write to him nor for him.

I may assume, therefore, without fearing to be accused of begging the question, that the constitution under which we now live, is preferable to that which prevailed at any time before the revolution. We are arrived, after many struggles, after a deliverance almost miraculous, and such a one as no nation hath reason to expect twice, and after having made some honest improvements on the advantages of our new constitution, very near to that full security, under which men who are free and solicitous to continue so, may sit down, not without watchfulness, for that is never to be suffered to relax under such a government as ours, but without anxiety. The sum therefore of all these discourses, and of all our exhortations to one another, is, and ought to be, that we should not stop short in so important a work. It was begun at the revolution; but he who thinks it was perfected then, or hath been perfected since, will find himself very much mistaken. The foundations were laid then. We proceeded for some time after that, like the Jews in rebuilding their temple; we carried on the holy work with one hand, and held our swords in the other to defend it. That distraction, that danger is over, and we betray the cause of liberty without any color of excuse, if we do not complete the glorious building, which will last to ages yet remote, if it be once finished, and will moulder away and fall into ruins, if it remain longer in this imperfect state.

Now that we may see the better how to proceed in the cause of liberty, to complete the freedom, and to secure the duration of our present constitution, it will be of use, I think, to consider what obstacles lie, or may hereafter lie, in our way, and of what nature that opposition is, or may hereafter be, which we may expect to meet. In order to this, let us once more analyse our political divisions; those which may possibly exist now, or hereafter, as we did those which were formed at the revolution.

One possible division then, is that of men angry with the government, and yet resolved to maintain the constitution. This may be the case at any time; under the present wise, virtuous and triumphant administration, and therefore to be sure at any other.

A second possible division is that of men averse to the government, because they are so to the constitution, which I think can never be the case of many; or averse to the constitution, because they are so to the government, which I think may be the case of

more. Both of these tend to the same point. One would subvert the government, that they might change the constitution.—
The other would sacrifice the constitution, that they might subvert the government.

A third possible division, and I seek no more, is that of men
attached to the government; or, to speak more properly, to the
persons of those who govern; or, to speak more properly still,
to the power, profit, or protection they acquire by the favor of
these persons, but enemies to the constitution.

Now, as to the first and second of these possible divisions, if
there be any such among us, I do not apprehend that we are at
present, or can be hereafter in much danger, or that the cause of
liberty can meet with much opposition from them; though the
second have certainly views more likely to bring slavery upon
us, than to promote liberty; and though prudence requires that
we should be on our guard against both. The first, indeed,
might hope to unite even the bulk of the nation to them, in a
weak and oppressive reign. If grievances should grow intolerable under some prince as yet unborn; if redress should become
absolutely desperate; if liberty itself should be in imminent
peril; the nature of our constitution would justify the resistance,
that we ought to believe well enough of posterity to persuade
ourselves would be made in such an exigency. But without
such an exigency, particular men would flatter themselves extremely, if they hoped to make the nation angry because they
were so. Private motives can never influence numbers. When
a nation revolts, the injury is national. This case therefore is
remote, improbable, nay, impossible, under the lenity, justice,
and heroical spirit of the present government; and if I mentioned
such an imaginary party, it was only done that I might omit none
which can be supposed. The projects of the second division,
stated in the same hypothetical manner, are surely too extravagant, and their designs too wicked to be dangerous. Disputes
may arise hereafter, in some distant time, about ministers, perhaps about kings; but I persuade myself that this constitution
will be, as it ought to be always, distinguished from, and preferred to both, by the British nation. Reasons must arise in process of time, from the very nature of man, to oppose ministers
and kings too; but none can arise, in the nature of things, to oppose such a constitution as ours. Better ministers, better kings,
may be hereafter often wanted, and sometimes found, but a better constituted government never can. Should there be therefore
still any such men as we here suppose, among us, they cannot
expect, if they are in their senses, a national concurrence: and
surely a little reflection will serve to show them, that the same
reasons which make them weaker now than they were some

years ago, must make them weaker some years hence than they are now.

As to the third division, if any such there be, it is in that our greatest and almost our whole danger centres. The others cannot overthrow, but these may undermine our liberty. Capable of being admitted into power in all courts, and more likely than other men to be so in every court except the present, whose approved penetration and spotless innocence give a certain exclusion to them, they may prevent any farther securities from being procured to liberty, till those already established are dissolved or perverted. Since then our principal danger must in all times arise from those who belong to this division, it is necessary to show, before we conclude these discourses, by what means such men may carry on their pernicious designs with effect, and by what means they may be defeated. These considerations will lead us to fix that point, wherein men of all denominations ought to unite, and do unite, and to state the sole distinction of parties, which can be made with truth at this time amongst us.

I am, sir, &c.

LETTER X.

Sir:—It may be asken, perhaps, how men who are friends to a government, can be enemies at the same time to the constitution upon which that government is founded. But the answer will be easy, if we consider these two things: first, the true distinction, so often confounded in writing, and almost always in conversation, between constitution and government. By constitution we mean, whenever we speak with propriety and exactness, that assemblage of laws, institutions, and customs, derived from certain fixed principles of reason, directed to certain fixed objects of public good, that compose the general system, according to which the community hath agreed to be governed. By government we mean, whenever we speak in the same manner, that particular tenor of conduct which a chief magistrate, and inferior magistrates under his direction and influence, hold in the administration of public affairs. We call this a good government, when the execution of the laws, the observation of the institutions and customs, in short, the whole administration of public affairs, is wisely pursued, and with a strict conformity to the principles and objects of the constitution. We call it a bad government, when it is administered on other principles, and directed to

other objects, either wickedly or weakly, either by obtaining new
laws, which want this conformity, or by perverting old ones
which had it; and when this is done without law, or in open violation of the laws, we term it a tyrannical government.   In a
word, and to bring this home to our own case, constitution is the
rule by which our princes ought to govern at all times; government is that by which they actually do govern at any particular
time.   One may remain immutable; the other may, and, as human nature is constituted, must vary.   One is the criterion by
which we are to try the other; for surely we have a right to do
so, since if we are to live in subjection to the government of our
kings, our kings are to govern in subjection to the constitution;
and the conformity or non-conformity of their government to it,
prescribes the measure of our submission to them, according to
the principles of the revolution, and of our present settlement; in
both of which, though some remote regard was had to blood, yet
the preservation of the constitution manifestly determined the
community to the choice then made of the persons who should
govern.   Another thing to be considered is this: when persons
are spoken of as friends to the government, and enemies to the
constitution, the term friendship is a little prostituted, in compliance with common usage.   Such men are really incapable of
friendship; for real friendship can never exist among those who
have banished virtue and truth.   They have no affection to any
but themselves; no regard to any interest except their own.   Their
sole attachments are such as I mentioned in the last letter, attachments to power and profit, and when they have contracted a
load of infamy and guilt in the pursuit of these, an attachment to
that protection, which is sufficient to procure them appearances
of consideration, and real impunity.   They may bear the semblance of affection to their prince, and of zeal for his government;
but they who are false to the cause of their country, will not be
true to any other; and the very same minister who exalts his
master's throne on the ruins of the constitution, that he may govern without control, or retire without danger, would do the
reverse of this, if any turn of affairs enabled him to compound,
in that manner, the better for himself.

Under a prince, therefore, tolerably honest, or tolerably wise,
such men as these will have no great sway; at least, they will
not hold it long.   Such a prince will know, that to unite himself to them, is to disunite himself from his people; and that he
makes a stupid bargain, if he prefers trick to policy, expedient to
system, and a cabal to the nation.   Reason and experience will
teach him that a prince who does so, must govern weakly, ignominiously and precariously; whilst he, who engages all the hearts,
and employs all the heads and hands of his people, governs with

strength, with splendor, and with safety, and is sure of rising to
a degree of absolute power, by maintaining liberty, which the
most successful tyrant could never reach by imposing slavery.
But how few men (and princes, by their leaves, are men) have
been found in times past, or can be hoped for in times to come,
capable of governing by such arts as these?   Some cannot propose the ends, nor some employ the means; for some are wicked,
and some are weak.   This general division runs through the
whole race of mankind, of the multitudes designed to obey, and
of the few designed to govern.   It was this depravity of multitudes, as well as their mutual wants, which obliged men first to
enter into societies, to depart from their natural liberty, and to
subject themselves to government.   It was this depravity of the
few, (which is often the greater, because born no better than
other men, they are educated worse,) which obliged men first to
subject government to constitution, that they might preserve
social, when they gave up natural liberty, and not be oppressed
by arbitrary will.   Kings may have preceded lawgivers, for
aught I know, or have possibly been the first lawgivers, and
government by will have been established before government by
constitution.   Theseus might reign at Athens, and Eurytion at
Sparta, long before Solon gave laws to one, and Lycurgus to the
other of these cities.   Kings had governed Rome, we know, and
consuls had succeeded kings, long before the decemviri compiled
a body of law; and the Saxons had their monarchs before Edgar,
though the Saxon laws went under his name.   These, and a
thousand other instances of the same kind, will never serve to
prove what my Lord Bacon would prove by them, " that monarchies do not subsist, like other governments, by a precedent
law, or compact; that the original submission to them was natural, like the obedience of a child to his parents; and that allegiance to hereditary monarchs is the work of the law of nature."*
But that which these examples prove very plainly is, that however men might submit voluntarily in the primitive simplicity of
early ages, or be subjected by conquest to a government without a constitution, yet they were never long in discovering that
"to live by one man's will became the cause of all men's
misery:"† and therefore they soon rejected the yoke, or made it
sit easy on their necks.   They instituted commonwealths, or they
limited monarchies: and here began that struggle between the
spirit of liberty and the spirit of dominion, which always hath
subsisted, and that we may not flatter ourselves nor others, must
always subsist, except in those instances, of which the most

* Argum. in the case of Postnati.
† Hooker's Eccles. Pol. l. 1, sect. 10.

ancient histories furnish so few, the reigns of a Titus, or a Trajan; for it might look like flattery to quote the present most auspicious reign.

To govern a society of freemen by a constitution founded on the eternal rules of right reason, and directed to promote the happiness of the whole, and of every individual, is the noblest prerogative which can belong to humanity; and if man may be said, without profaneness, to imitate God in any case, this is the case: but sure I am he imitates the devil, who is so far from promoting the happiness of others, that he makes his own happiness to consist in the misery of others; who governs by no rule but that of his passions, whatever appearances he is forced sometimes to put on, who endeavors to corrupt the innocent and to enslave the free, whose business is to seduce or betray, whose pleasure is to damn, and whose triumph is to torment. Odious and execrable as this character is, it is the character of every prince who makes use of his power to subvert, or even to weaken that constitution, which ought to be the rule of his government. When such a prince fills a throne with superior parts, liberty is in the utmost peril; nor does the danger diminish in proportion, if he happens to want them. Such men as we are now to speak of, (friends to the government and enemies to the constitution) will be always at hand to supply his defects; for as they are the willing instruments of a wicked prince, they are the ready prompters of a weak one. They may sink into the mass of the people, and disappear in a good and a wise reign, or work themselves into power under false colors. "Sed genus immortale manet." Their race will continue as long as ambition and avarice prevail in the world, and there will be bad citizens as long as there are bad men. The good ought, therefore, to be always on their guard against them, and whatever disguise they assume, whatever veils they cast over their conduct, they will never be able to deceive those long, who observe constantly the difference between constitution and government, and who have virtue enough to preserve the cause of the former, how unprofitable soever it may be at all times, and how unpopular soever at some. But I ramble too long in generals. It is high time I should come to those particular measures, by which the men I have described are most likely to carry on their designs against our constitution; after which I shall say something of the methods, by which alone their designs may be prevented, or will be defeated, if a national union oppose itself by such methods as these, in time, to them.

Now that I may do this the better, and make what I have to say the more sensibly felt, give me leave to suppose, though I speak of a remote time, and such an one as we ought to hope will never come, that our national circumstances will be just the same as they are now, and our constitution as far distant as it now is from that point of perfection, to which the revolution ought to have brought it, might have brought it, and hath given the nation a right to expect that it should be brought. The completion of that glorious deliverance is still imperfect, after five and forty years, notwithstanding the hopes then given, the engagements then taken, and the opportunities that have since arisen. How this hath happened, by what arts this justice to the constitution hath been hitherto evaded, sometimes in favor of one government, and sometimes in favor of another, might easily be shown, and proved too, beyond contradiction. But I had rather exhort than reproach, and especially at a time when a strong tendency appears among men of all denominations to such a national union, as will effectually obtain the complete settlement of our constitution, which hath been so long delayed, if it be honestly, prudently, and vigorously improved.

It is certain then, that if ever such men as call themselves friends to the government, but are real enemies of the constitution, prevail, they will make it a capital point of their wicked policy to keep up a standing army. False appearances of reason for it will never be wanting, as long as there are pretenders to the crown; though nothing can be more absurd than to employ, in defence of liberty, an instrument so often employed to destroy it; though nothing can be more absurd than to maintain that any government ought to make use of the same expedient to support itself, as another government, on the ruins of which this government stands, was subverted for using; though nothing can be proved more manifestly by experience than these two propositions, that Britain is enabled, by her situation, to support her government, when the bulk of her people are for it, without employing any means inconsistent with her constitution; and that the bulk of the people are not only always for the government, when the government supports the constitution, but are even hard and slow to be detached from it, when the government attacks or undermines the constitution, and when they are by consequence both justified in resisting, and even obliged in conscience to resist the government.

I have heard it argued lately, that Pretenders abroad are a security at home, and that a government exposed to their attacks, will never venture to attack the constitution. I have been told too, that these notions were entertained by some who drew many political consequences from them at the revolution. But if any of those persons are still alive, I persuade myself that they have altered this opinion, since such a situation will furnish at all times pretences of danger; since pretences of danger to a government, whether real or imaginary, will be always urged with plausibility, and generally with success, for obtaining new powers, or for straining old ones; and since whilst those who mean well to the government, are imposed upon by those who mean ill to the constitution, all true concern for the latter is lost in a mistaken zeal for the former, and the most important is ventured to save the least important, when neither one nor the other would have been exposed, if false alarms had not been rashly and too implicitly taken, or if true alarms had not given unnecessary strength to the government, at the expense of weakening the constitution.

Notwithstanding what hath been said, I do not imagine that an army would be employed by these men, directly and at first, against the nation and national liberty. I am far from thinking that any men can arise in future times, capable of attempting, in this manner, what some men in our age, who call themselves friends to the government, have been so weak and so imprudent as to avow in print, and publish to the nation. To destroy British liberty with an army of Britons, is not a measure so sure of success as some people may believe. To corrupt the parliament is a slower, but might prove a more effectual method; and two or three hundred mercenaries in the two houses, if they could be listed there, would be more fatal to the constitution, than ten times as many thousands in red and in blue out of them. Parliaments are the true guardians of liberty. For this principally they were instituted; and this is the principal article of that great and noble trust which the collective body of the people of Britain reposes in the representative. But then no slavery can be so effectually brought and fixed upon us as parliamentary slavery. By the corruption of parliament, and the absolute influence of a king, or his minister, on the two houses, we return into that state, to deliver or secure us from which parliaments were instituted, and are really governed by the arbitrary will of one man. Our whole constitution is at once dissolved. Many securities to liberty are provided, but the integrity which depends on the freedom and the independency of parliament, is the key-stone that keeps the whole together. If this be shaken, our constitution totters. If it be quite removed, our constitution falls into ruin. That noble fabric, the pride of Britain, the envy of her neighbors, raised by the labor of so many centuries, repaired at the expense of so many millions, and cemented by such a profusion of blood; that noble fabric, I say, which was able to resist the united efforts of so many races of giants, may be demolished by a race of pigmies. The integrity of parliament is a kind of palladium, a tutelary goddess, who protects our state. When she is once removed, we may become the prey of any enemies. No Agamemnon, no Achilles will be wanting to take our city.

Thersites himself will be sufficient for such a conquest. But I need not dwell any longer on this subject. There is no man, who thinks at all, can fail to see the several fatal consequences which will necessarily flow from this one source, whenever it shall be opened. If the reason of the thing does not strike him enough, experience must. The single reign of Henry the Eighth will serve to show that no tyranny can be more severe than that which is exercised by a concert with parliament: that arbitrary will may be made the sole rule of government, even whilst the names and forms of a free constitution are preserved; that for a prince, or his minister, to become our tyrant, there is no need to abolish parliaments; there is no need that he who is master of one part of the legislature, should endeavor to abolish the other two, when he can use, upon every occasion, the united strength of the whole; there is no need he should be a tyrant in the gross, when he can be so in detail; nor in name, when he can be so in effect; that for parliaments to establish tyranny, there is no need, therefore, to repeal Magna Charta, or any other of the great supports of our liberty. It is enough, if they put themselves corruptly and servilely under the influence of such a prince or such a minister. On the whole, I conclude, that in the possible case here supposed, the first and principal object will be to destroy the constitution, under pretence of preserving the government, by corrupting our parliaments. I am the better founded in concluding that this may happen in some future age, by what we may observe in our own. There is surely but too much reason to suspect that the enemies of our constitution may attempt hereafter to govern by corruption, when we hear and see the friends and advocates of our present most incorrupt minister harangue and scribble in favor of corruption; when it is pleaded for and recommended, as a necessary expedient of government, by some men, of all ranks and orders; not only by professed hirelings, who write that they may eat, but by men who have talked and written themselves already out of their native obscurity and penury, by affecting zeal in the cause of liberty: not only by such as these, but by men whose birth, education, and fortune, aggravate their crime and their folly; by men whom honor at least should restrain from favoring so dishonorable a cause; and by men whose peculiar obligations to preach up morality should restrain them, at least, from being the preachers of an immorality, above all others, abominable in its nature, and pernicious in its effects.

These men are ready, I know, to tell us, that the influence they plead for is necessary to strengthen the hands of those who govern; that corruption serves to oil the wheels of government, and to render the administration more smooth and easy; and that it can never be of dangerous consequence under the present father of our country.—Absurd and wicked triflers! "According to them, our excellent constitution" (as one of your correspondents hath observed extremely well) "is no better than a jumble of incompatible powers, which would separate and fall to pieces of themselves, unless restrained and upheld by such honorable methods as those of bribery and corruption." They would prove, "that the form of our government is defective to a degree of ridiculousness." But the ridicule, as well as the iniquity, is their own. A good government can want no power, under the present constitution. A bad one may, and it is fit it should. Popularity is the expedient of one, and will effectually support it. Nothing but corruption can support the other. If there was a real deficiency of power in the crown, it ought to be supplied, no doubt. The old whimsies of prerogative should not be revived; but limitations ought to be taken off, or new powers to be given. The friends of liberty acknowledge that a balance of the powers, divided among the three parts of the legislature, is essential to our constitution, and necessary to support it. The friends of liberty therefore would concur, at least to a certain point, with the friends of the ministry; for the former are friends to order, and enemies to licence. For decency's sake, therefore, let the debate be put on this issue. Let it be such a debate as freemen may avow without blushing. To argue from this supposed deficiency of power in the crown, in favor of a scheme of government repugnant to all laws divine and human, is such an instance of abandoned villanous prostitution, as the most corrupt ages never saw, and as will place the present age, with infamous pre-eminence, at the head of them, unless the nation do itself justice, and fix the brand on those who ought alone to bear it.—Thus much for the iniquity of the practice pleaded for. As to the danger of it, let us agree that a prince of such magnanimity and justice as our present monarch, can never be tempted by any sordid motives to forget the recent obligation which he and his family have to the British nation, by whom they were made kings; nor to aim at greater power and wealth than are consistent with the safety of the constitution they are intrusted to preserve, and obliged to secure. Allowing this to be our present case, (and concerning our present case, there are not two opinions, I dare say, in the whole nation,) yet still the symptoms I have mentioned, show that the poison, with which these pretended friends of the government, and real enemies of the constitution, corrupt the morals of mankind, hath made some progress; and if this progress be not immediately checked by proper antidotes, and the power of poisoning taken from these empirics, the disease will grow incurable. The last dismal effect of it may not, or if you please, cannot happen in this reign; but it may, nay it must happen in some other, unless we prevent it effectually and soon: and what season more proper to prevent it in, and to complete the security of our liberties, than the reign of a prince, for whom the nation hath done so much, and from whom, by consequence, the nation hath a right to expect so much? King William delivered us from popery and slavery. There was wisdom in his councils, and fortitude in his conduct. He steered through many real difficulties at home, and he fought our battles abroad; and yet those points of security, which had been neglected, or not sufficiently provided for in the honeymoon of his accession, were continually pressed upon him, during the whole course of his reign. The men who pressed them were called jacobites, tories, republicans, and incendiaries too; not from the throne indeed, but by the clamor of those, who showed great indifference at least for the constitution, whilst they affected great zeal for the government. They succeeded however in part, and we enjoy the benefit of their success. If they did not succeed in the whole; if the settlement necessary to secure our liberty, and therefore intended at the revolution, be not yet complete, let us be persuaded, and let us act on that persuasion, that the honor of completing it was reserved to crown the glories of the present reign. To finish the great work, which king William began, of establishing the liberties of Britain on firm and durable foundations, must be reputed an honor surely; and to whom can this honor belong more justly than to a prince, who emulates, in so remarkable a manner, all the other heroic virtues of his renowned predecessor?

I am, sir, &c.

LETTER XI.

Sir:—If it was possible for any man, who hath the least knowledge of our constitution, to doubt, in good earnest, whether the preservation of public freedom depends on the preservation of parliamentary freedom, his doubts might be removed, and his opinion decided, one would imagine, by this single, obvious remark, that all the designs of our princes against liberty, since parliaments began to be established on the model still subsisting, have been directed constantly to one of these two points, either to obtain such parliaments as they could govern, or else to stand all the difficulties, and to run all the hazards of governing without parliaments. The means principally employed to the first of these purposes have been undue influences on the elections of members of the house of commons, and on these members when chosen. When such influences could be employed successfully, they have answered all the ends of arbitrary will; and when they could not be so employed, arbitrary will hath been forced to submit to the constitution. This hath been the case, not only since, but before that great change in the balance of property, which began in the reigns of Henry the Seventh and Henry the Eighth, and carried a great part of that weight into the scale of the commons, which had lain before in the scale of the peers and clergy.

If we look back as far as the close of the fourteenth century, an era pretty near to that when parliaments received their present form, we shall find both these means employed by one of the worst of our kings, Richard the Second. That he might obtain his will, which was rash, he directed mandates to his sheriffs, (officers of the crown, and appointed by the crown; for such they were then, and such they still are) to return certain persons nominated by himself: and thus he acquired an undue influence over the elections. In the next place, he obliged the persons thus returned, sometimes by threats and terror, and sometimes by gifts, to consent to those things which were prejudicial to the realm: and thus he acquired an undue influence over the house of commons. So that, upon the whole, the arbitrary will of a rash, headstrong prince, and the suggestions of his wicked ministers, guided the proceedings of parliament, and became the law of the land. I might pursue observations of the same kind through several succeeding reigns; but to avoid lengthening these letters, which are grown, perhaps, too long already, let us descend at once to the reign of king Charles the Second, for in that we shall find examples of all the means which a court that hath common sense, and a prince who will not set his crown on the cast of a die, can take to undermine the foundations of liberty, either by governing parliaments, or by governing without them.

Now the first attempt of this kind which king Charles made against the constitution, was this: he improved and managed the spirit of the first parliament he called, so as to render the two houses obsequious to his will in almost every case; and having got the triennial bill repealed, he kept the same parliament in being for many years by prorogations, which crept into custom long before his time, but were still a modern invention with respect to the primitive institution of parliaments, and wholly repugnant to the ancient practice. Thus he established a standing parliament, which is, in the nature of it, as dangerous as a standing army, and may become, in some conjunctures, much more fatal to liberty. When the measures of his administration grew too bad,

and the tendency of them too apparent to be defended and supported, even in that parliament, and even by a party spirit, he
had recourse to a second attempt—that is, to corruption; and Clifford first listed a mercenary band of friends to the government
against the constitution. Let us observe on this occasion, and as we
pass along, that a national party, such a party as the court adopts,
in contradistinction to such a party as it creates, will always retain some national principles, some regard to the constitution.
They may be transported, or surprised, during the heat of contest especially, into measures of long and fatal consequence.
They may be carried on, for a certain time and to a certain point,
by the lusts of vengeance and of power, in order to wreak one
upon their adversaries, and to secure the other to themselves.
But a national party will never be the instruments of completing
national ruin. They will become the adversaries of their friends,
and the friends of their adversaries, to prevent it; and the minister who persists in so vallanous a project, by what name soever
he may affect to distinguish himself and his followers, will be
found really at the head of a faction, not of a party. But the difference between one and the other is so visible, and the boundaries where party ceases and faction commences are so strongly
marked, that it is sufficient to point at them.

I return, therefore, and observe that when the spirit of party
failed king Charles, and the corruption he employed proved ineffectual, he resolved to govern for a time without parliaments,
and to employ that time, as soon as he had checked the spirit
of one party, by inflaming that of another, in garbling corporations. He had found by experience, that it was impossible to
corrupt the stream in any great degree, as long as the fountain
continued pure. He applied himself, therefore, to spread the
taint of the court in them, and to poison those springs, from
whence the health and vigor of the constitution flow. This was
the third, the last, and by much the most dangerous expedient
employed by the friends of the government, in the reign of king
Charles the Second, to undermine our liberties. The effect of it
he did not live to see, but we may easily conjecture what it
would have been.

The use I make of what hath been here said is this: the
design of the revolution being not only to save us from the immediate attempts on our religion and liberty, made by king
James, but to save us from all other attempts which had been
made, or might be made, of the same tendency; to renew and
strengthen our constitution; "to establish the peace, honor and
happiness of these nations upon lasting foundations, and to procure a settlement of the religion, and of the liberties and properties of the subjects, upon so sure a foundation, that there

might be no danger of the nation's relapsing into the like miseries at any time hereafter."* This being, I say, the avowed
design of the revolution, and the nation having engaged in it on
a confidence that all this would be effectually performed, the
design of the revolution was not accomplished, the benefit of it
was not secured to us, the just expectations of the nation could
not be answered, unless the freedom of elections, and the frequency, integrity and independency of parliaments were sufficiently provided for.   These are the essentials of British liberty.
Defects in other parts of the constitution can never be fatal, if
these are preserved entire.   But defects in these will soon destroy
the constitution, though every other part of it should be so preserved.   However, it happened, the truth and notoriety of the
fact oblige us to say, that these important conditions, without
which liberty can never be secure, were almost wholly neglected
at the revolution.   The claim of right declares, indeed, that
" elections ought to be free; that freedom of speech and debates
ought not to be impeached or questioned out of parliament; and
that parliaments ought to be held frequently."   But such declarations, however solemnly made, are nothing better than
pompous trifles, if they stand alone; productive of no good; and
thus far productive of ill, that they serve to amuse mankind in
points of the greatest importance, and wherein it concerns them
the most nearly neither to be deceived, nor so much as amused.
These were rights, no doubt, to which the nation had an indisputable claim.   But then they ought to have been more than
claimed, since they had been so often and so lately invaded.
That they were not more than claimed, that they were not
effectually asserted and secured, at this time, gave very great
and immediate dissatisfaction; and they who were called whigs
in those days, distinguished themselves by the loudness of their
complaints.   Thus, for instance, they insisted that there could
be no " real settlement; nay, that it was a jest to talk of a settlement, till the manner and time of calling parliaments, and their
sitting when called, were fully determined:"† and this in order
to prevent the practice of " keeping one and the same parliament so long on foot, " till the majority was corrupted by offices,
gifts and pensions."   They insisted that the assurances given at
the revolution had led them to think, that " the ancient, legal
course of annually chosen parliaments would have been immediately restored;"‡ and the particular circumstances of king Wil-

---

* See the Prince of Orange's declaration.
† See Considerations Concerning the State of the Nation, by Mr. Hamb-
den, published in 1692.
‡ An Inquiry, or a Discourse, &c., published in 1693.

liam, who had received the crown by gift of the people, and
who had renewed the original contract with the people, which
are precisely the circumstances of the present royal family,
were urged as particular reasons for the nation to expect his
compliance.

The frequent sitting of parliament was indeed provided for,
indirectly and in consequence, by the exigencies of the war,
which soon followed the revolution. This war made annual
supplies necessary; and, before it was over, the same necessity
of annual sessions of parliament came to be established, as it
continues to this hour, by the great alteration made with relation
to the public revenue. The whole public revenue had been the
king's formerly. Parliamentary aids were, in those days, extraordinary and occasional; and things came to that pass at last,
that parliaments were more frequently, or more rarely convened,
just as courts had more frequent or more rare occasions for such
supplies. But king William began to be, and all our princes
since him have continued to be, only proprietors for life of that
part of the public revenue, which is appropriated to their civil
list; although they are intrusted still with the management of
the whole, and are even the stewards of the public creditors for
that part which is the private property of these creditors. This
is the present state, sufficiently known, but necessary to be mentioned particularly on this occasion: and this must continue to
be the state, unless some prince should arise hereafter, who,
being advised by a desperate minister, abetted by a mercenary
faction, supported by a standing army, and instigated, like Richard
the Second, by the "rashness of his own temper,"* may lay
rapacious hands on all the funds that have been created, and by
applying illegally what he may raise legally, convert the whole
to his own use, and so establish arbitrary power, by depriving
at one stroke many of his subjects of their property, and all of
them of their liberty. Till this happens, (and heaven forbid that
it should be ever attempted!) sessions of parliament must be
annually held, or the government itself be distressed. But neither is this such a direct and full security as the importance of
the thing requires; nor does the security of our liberty consist
only in frequent sessions of parliaments, but it consists likewise
in frequent new parliaments. Nay, it consists so much more in
this than in the other, that the former may tend without the latter, even more than the discontinuance of parliaments, to the loss
of liberty. This was foreseen by the wisdom of our constitution. According to that, although it became in time, by the
course of events, and insensible alterations, no longer necessary

* Per immoderatam voluntatem.

to call parliaments once, or even twice in a year, which had been the more ancient practice, yet still our kings continued under an incapacity of proceeding long in government, with any tolerable ease and safety to themselves, without the concurrence and assistance of these assemblies. According to the same constitution, as parliaments were to be held, so they were to be chosen frequently; and the opinion, that the "holding and continuance of parliaments depended absolutely on the will of the prince," may be justly ranked amongst those attempts, that were made by some men to set the law, whilst others endeavored to set the gospel, on the side of the arbitrary power. This is the plain intent and scheme of our constitution, which provides that the representatives of the people should have frequent opportunities to communicate together about national grievances; to complain of them, and to obtain the redress of them, in an orderly, solemn, legal manner; and that the people should have frequent opportunities of calling their representatives to account, as it were, for the discharge of the trust committed to them, and of approving or disapproving their conduct, by electing or not electing them anew. Thus our constitution supposes that princes may abuse their power, and parliaments betray their trust; and provides, as far as human wisdom can provide, that neither one nor the other may be able to do so long, without a sufficient control. If the crown, indeed, persists in usurping on the liberty of the people, or in any other kind of mal-administration; and if the prince who wears it proves deaf, as our princes have sometimes been, to the voice of his parliament and his people, there remains no remedy in the system of the constitution. The constitution is broken by the obstinacy of the prince, and the "people must appeal to heaven in this, as in all other cases, where they have no judge on earth."* Thus if a parliament should persist in abetting mal-administration, or any way give up those liberties which they were intrusted to maintain, no doubt can be made but that the people would be in the same case; since their representatives have no more right to betray them, than their kings have to usurp upon them: and by consequence they would acquire the same right of appealing to heaven, if our constitution had not provided a remedy against this evil, which could not be provided against the other; but our constitution hath provided such a remedy in the frequent succession of new parliaments, by which there is not time sufficient given, to form a majority of the representatives of the people into a ministerial cabal; or by which, if this should happen, such a cabal must be soon broken. These reflections, and such others as they

* Locke's Essay upon Government, chap. 14.

naturally suggest, are sufficient to convince any thinking man, first, that nothing could make it safe, nor therefore reasonable, to repose in any set of men whatsoever, so great a trust as the collective body delegates to the representative in this kingdom, expect the shortness of the term for which this trust is delegated. Secondly, that every prolongation of this term is therefore, in its degree, unsafe for the people; that it weakens their security, and endangers liberty by the very powers given for its preservation. Thirdly, that such prolongations expose the nation, in the possible case of having a corrupt parliament, to lose the great advantage which our constitution hath provided, of curing the evil, before it grows confirmed and desperate, by the gentle method of choosing a new representative, and reduce the nation, by consequence, to have no other alternative than that of submitting or resisting; though submission will be as grievous, and resistance much more difficult, when the legislature betrays its trust, than when the king alone abuses his power. These reflections, I say, are sufficient to prove these propositions; and these propositions set before us, in a very strong light, the necessity of using our utmost efforts that the true design of our constitution may be pursued as closely as possible, by the re-establishment of annual, or at least of triennial parliaments. But the importance of the matter, and the particular seasonableness of the conjuncture, invite me to offer one consideration more upon this head, which I think will not strike the less for being obvious and plain. It is this. Should a king obtain, for many years at once, the supplies and powers which used to be granted annually to him, this would be deemed, I presume, even in the present age, an unjustifiable measure and an intolerable grievance, for this plain reason; because it would alter our constitution in the fundamental article, that requires frequent assemblies of the whole legislature, in order to assist, and control too, the executive power which is intrusted with one part of it. Now I ask, is not the article which requires frequent elections of the representative, by the collective body of the people, in order to secure the latter against the ill consequences of the possible weakness or corruption of the former, as fundamental an article, and as essential to the preservation of our liberties as the other? No man dares say that it is not; at least, no man who deserves our attention. The people of Britain have as good a right, and a right as necessary to be asserted, to keep their representatives true to the trust reposed in them, and to the preservation of the constitution, by the control of frequent elections, as they have to keep their kings true to the trust reposed in them, and to the preservation of the constitution, by the control of frequent sittings of parliament. How comes it then to pass, that we may observe so great a difference in the sentiments of mankind, about these two cases? Propose the first, there is no servile friend of government, who will not affect all that horror at the proposition, which every friend of the constitution will really feel. Propose the keeping up septennial, nay the making decennial parliaments, the same friends of government will contend strenuously for one, and by consequence for both; since there can be no reason alledged for the first, which is not stronger for the last, and would not be still stronger for a longer term. These reasons, drawn from two or three common-place topics of pretended conveniency and expediency, or of supposed tranquillity at home, and strength abroad, I need not mention. They have been mentioned by others, and sufficiently refuted. But that which may very justly appear marvellous, is this: that some men, I think not many, who are true friends of the constitution, have been staggered in their opinions, and almost, seduced by the false reasonings, of these friends of government; though nothing can be more easy than to show, from reason and experience, that convenience, expediency, and domestic tranquillity may be, and in fact have been as well, nay, better secured under triennial, nay, annual parliaments, than under parliaments of a longer continuance; and as for strength abroad, that is, national credit and influence, it will depend on the opinion foreign nations have of our national dispositions, and the unanimity of our sentiments. It must be chiefly determined, therefore, by their knowledge of the real sense of the nation. Now that can appear no way so much as in the natural state of our constitution, by frequent elections; and when it does appear so, it must have another kind of effect than the bare resolutions of a stale, ministerial parliament; especially if it happens, as it may happen in some future time, that the sense of the nation should appear to be different from the sense of such a parliament; and that the resolutions of such a parliament should be avowedly dictated by men, odious and hated, contemptible and contemned both at home and abroad.

But in the supposition that some inconveniences may arise by frequent elections, which is only allowed for argument's sake, are such inconveniences, and the trifling consequences of them, to be set in the balance against the danger of weakening any one barrier of our liberty? Every form of government hath advantages and disadvantages peculiar to it. Thus absolute monarchies seem most formed for sudden and vigorous efforts of power, either in attacking or in defending, whilst, in free constitutions, the forms of government must be necessarily more complicated and slow; so that in these, the same secrecy cannot be always kept, nor the same despatch always made, nor the same steadiness of measures always pursued. Must all these forms, instituted to preserve the checks and controls of the several parts of the constitution on one another, and necessary by consequence to preserve the liberty of the whole, be abandoned therefore, and a free constitution be destroyed, for the sake of some little conveniency, or expediency the more, in the administration of public affairs? No certainly. We must keep our free constitution, with the small defects belonging to it, or we must change it for an arbitary government, free perhaps from these defects, but liable to more and to worse. In short, we must make our option; and surely this option is not hard to be made, between the real and permanent blessings of liberty, diffused through a whole nation, and the fantastic and accidental advantages which they who govern, not the body of the people, enjoy under absolute monarchies. I will not multiply instances, though they crowd in upon me. Two consuls were chosen annually at Rome, and the proconsular power in the government of provinces was limited to a year. Several inconveniences arose, no doubt, from the strict observation of this institution. Some appear very plain in history: and we may assure ourselves, that many arguments of conveniency, of expediency, of preserving the tranquillity of the city, and of giving strength and weight to the arms and counsels of the commonwealth, were urged to prevail on the people to dispense with these institutions, in favor of Pompey and of Cæsar. What was the consequence? The pirates were extirpated, the price of corn was reduced, Spain was held in subjection, Gaul was conquered, the Germans were repulsed, Rome triumphed, her government flourished; but her constitution was destroyed, her liberty was lost. The law of habeas corpus, that noble badge of liberty, which every subject of Britain wears, and by which he is distinguished so eminently, not from the slaves alone, but even from the freemen of other countries; the law of habeas corpus, I say, may be attended perhaps with some little inconveniences, in times of sedition and rebellion. The slow methods of giving money, and the strict appropriations of it, when given, may be attended with some inconveniency likewise, in times of danger, and in great exigencies of the state. But who will plead for the repeal of the habeas corpus act; or who would not press for the revival of it, if it stood suspended for an indefinite, or even a long term? Who will say that the practice of giving money without account, or passing votes of credit, by which the purse of the people is taken out of the hands of those whom the people trusted, and put into the hands of those whom they neither did, nor would have trusted; who will say that such a deviation from those rules of parliament, which ought to be deemed sacred and preserved inviolate, may be established, or should not be opposed by all possible means, if it was established?

If all this be as clear as I imagine it is; if the objections to

frequent elections of parliaments do not lie; or, supposing them
to lie, if the danger on one side outweighs vastly the supposed
inconveniency on the other; nay, if laws and institutions, not
more essential to the preservation of liberty than this ancient
and fundamental rule of our constitution, be maintained; and if
all men are forced to agree, even they, who wish them perhaps
abolished; that they ought to be maintained, for the sake of preserving liberty; let me ask again, how comes it to pass, that we
observe so great a difference between the sentiments and reasonings of mankind about frequent sessions of parliament, and
frequent parliaments; about the case now before us, and all the
others that have been mentioned? The only manner in which I
can account for such an inconsistency, is this. The sight of the
mind differs very much from the sight of the body, and its operations are frequently the reverse of the other. Objects at a distance appear to the former in their true magnitude, and diminish
as they are brought nearer. The event that created much astonishment, indignation, or terror in prospect, creates less and less
as it approaches, and by the time it happens, men have familiar-
ised themselves with it. If the Romans had been told, in the
days of Augustus, that an emperor would succeed, in whose
reign a horse should be made consul, they would have been extremely surprised. I believe they were not so much surprised
when the thing happened, when the horse was consul and Caligula emperor. If it had been foretold to those patriots at the
revolution, who remembered long parliaments, who still felt the
smart of them, who struggled hard for annual, and obtained
with much difficulty, at the end of five or six years, triennial
parliaments, that a time would come when even the term of triennial parliaments would be deemed too short, and a parliament
chosen for three years would choose itself for four more, and
entail septennial parliaments on the nation; that this would
happen, and the fruits of their honest labors be lost, in little
more than twenty years; and that it would be brought about,
whilst our government continued on the foundations they had
then so newly laid: if all this had been foretold at the time I
mention, it would have appeared improbable and monstrous to
the friends of the revolution. Yet it hath happened; and in less
than twenty years, it is grown, or is growing, familiar to us. The
uniform zeal and complaisance of our parliaments for the crown,
leave little room to apprehend any attempt to govern without
them, or to make them do in one session the work of seven;
though this would be extremely convenient, no doubt, a great
ease to future ministers, and a great saving of expense and time
to country gentlemen. But suppose, for I desire it may be remembered that we reason hypothetically, suppose a parliament

should think fit to give, in the first session, all the money, all the credit, and all the powers necessary for carrying on the government, during seven years, and then let those persons, who will be shocked at this supposition, and yet declare themselves for septennial parliaments, lay their hands on their hearts, and consider whether such an alteration of the constitution might not grow familiar to them, and even gain their approbation. I think it would do so. I am sure it might as reasonably as the other. They would find the ease, in one case, of little attendance, as much as that of distant elections in the other. The arguments of conveniency, expediency, public tranquillity, and strength to the government, would be just as well applied; and if the ministers should, by miracle, make no very exorbitant ill use of such a situation, I doubt whether he who should plead for annual parliaments then, would be much better heard by the same persons, than he who pleads for frequent elections of parliaments is now. But let not the lovers of liberty, the friends of our constitution, reason in this manner. Let them remember that danger commences when the breach is made, not when the attack is begun; that he who neglects to stop the leak as soon as it is discovered, in hopes to save his ship by pumping, when the water gushes in with violence, deserves to be drowned; and, to lay aside figures of speech, that our constitution is not, like the schemes of some politicians, a jumble of disjointed, incoherent whimsies, but a noble and wise system, the essential parts of which are so proportioned, and so intimately connected, that a change in one begets a change in the whole; that the frequent elections of parliament are as much an essential part of this system, as the frequent sittings of parliament; that the work of the revolution is imperfect, therefore, and our future security precarious, unless our ancient constitution be restored, in this essential part; and that the restoration of it, in this part, is one of those methods, by which alone the pernicious designs of such men as we have mentioned in a former letter, if any such should be ever admitted into power, (enemies to the constitution, under the mask of zeal for the government) may be defeated.

I am, sir, &c.

LETTER XII.

SIR:—We have observed already, that the constitution of the British government supposes our kings may abuse their power, and our representatives betray their trust, and provides against both these contingencies, as well as human wisdom can provide. Here let us observe, that the same constitution is very far from supposing the people will ever betray themselves; and yet this case is possible, no doubt. We do not read, I think, of more than one nation,* who refused liberty when it was offered to them; but we read of many, and have almost seen some, who lost it through their own fault, by the plain and necessary consequences of their own conduct, when they were in full possession of it, and had the means of securing it effectually in their power. A wise and brave people will neither be cozened, nor bullied out of their liberty; but a wise and brave people may cease to be such: they may degenerate; they may sink into sloth and luxury; they may resign themselves to a treacherous conduct; or abet the enemies of the constitution, under a notion of supporting the friends of the government: they may want the sense to discern their danger in time, or the courage to resist, when it stares them in the face. The Tarquins were expelled, and Rome resumed her liberty. Cæsar was murdered, and all his race extinct, but Rome remained in bondage. From whence this difference? Machiavel† shall account for it. In the days of Tarquin the people of Rome were not yet corrupted. In the days of Cæsar they were most corrupt. A free people may be sometimes betrayed; but no people will betray themselves, and sacrifice their liberty, unless they fall into a state of universal corruption: and when they are once fallen into such a state, they will be sure to lose what they deserve no longer to enjoy. To what purpose therefore should our constitution have supposed a case, in which no remedy can avail; a case which can never happen, till the spirit which formed this constitution first, and hath preserved it ever since, shall be totally extinguished; and till it becomes an ideal entity, like the Utopia, existing in the imagination, or memory, no where else? As all government began, so all government must end by the people; tyrannical governments by their virtue and courage, and even free governments by their vice and baseness. Our constitution, indeed, makes it impossible to destroy liberty by any sudden blast of popular fury, or by the treachery of a few; for though the many cannot easily hurt, they may easily save themselves. But if the many will concur with the few; if they will advisedly and deliberately suffer their liberty to be taken away by those to whom they delegate power to preserve it; this no constitution can pre-

---

* The Cappadocians, vid. Strabo, lib. 12.—" Libertatem repudiaverunt, ut quam sibi dicerent intolerabilem."

† Discourses, lib. 1, c. 17.

vent. God would not support even his own theocracy against
the concurrent desire of the children of Israel, but gave them a
king in his anger. How then should our human constitution of
government support itself against so universal a change, as we
here suppose, in the temper and character of our people? It cannot be. We may give ourselves a tyrant in our folly, if we
please. But this can never happen till the whole nation falls
into a state of political reprobation. Then, and not till then,
political damnation will be our lot.

Let us descend into a greater detail, in order to develope these
reflections fully, and to push the consequences of them home to
ourselves, and to our present state. They deserve our utmost
attention, and are so far from being foreign to the subject of
these essays upon parties, that they will terminate in the very
point at which we began: and wind up the whole in one important lesson.

To proceed then: I say, that if the people of this island should
suffer their liberties to be at any time ravished, or stolen from
them, they would incur greater blame, and deserve by consequence less pity, than any enslaved and oppressed people ever
did. By how much true liberty; that is, liberty stated and
ascertained by law, in equal opposition to popular licence and
arbitrary will, hath been more boldly asserted, more wisely or
more successfully improved, and more firmly established in this
than in other countries, by so much the more heavy would our
just condemnation prove in the case that is here supposed. The
virtue of our ancestors, to whom all these advantages are owing,
would aggravate the guilt and the infamy of their degenerate
posterity. There have been ages of gold and of silver, of brass
and of iron, in our little world, as in the great world, though not
in the same order. In which of these ages we are at present,
let others determine. This, at least, is certain, that in all these
ages Britain hath been the temple, as it were, of liberty. Whilst
her sacred fires have been extinguished in so many countries,
here they have been religiously kept alive. Here she hath her
saints, her confessors, and a whole army of martyrs, and the
gates of hell have not hitherto prevailed against her: so that if a
fatal reverse is to happen; if servility and servitude are to overrun the whole world, like injustice, and liberty is to retire from
it, like Astræa, our portion of the abandoned globe will have, at
least, the mournful honor, whenever it happens, of showing her
last, her parting steps.

The ancient Britons are to us the Aborigines of our island.
We discover little of them through the gloom of antiquity, and
we see nothing beyond them. This, however, we know, they
were freemen. Cæsar, who visited them in an hostile manner,

but did not conquer them, perhaps was beaten by them;* Cæsar,
I say, bestows very liberally the title of kings upon their chief-
tains, and the compilers of fabulous traditions deduce a series of
their monarchs from Samothes, a cotemporary of Nimrod. But
Cæsar affected to swell the account of his expedition with pompous names; and these writers, like those whom Strabo mentions,
endeavored to recommend themselves by publishing romances to
an ignorant generation, instead of histories.† These supposed
monarchs were the heads of little clans;‡ " reguli, vel melioris
notæ nobiles;" and if our island knew any authority of the kingly
sort in those days, it was that of occasional and temporary monarchs, elected in great exigencies, " communi consilio, suffragiis
multitudinis,"§ like Cassivellaunus in Britain or Vercingetorix in
Gaul; for, in some cases, examples taken from either of these
people will conclude for both. The kings who ruled in Britain
after the Romans abandoned the island, in the beginning of the
fifth century, held their authority from the people, and governed
under the control of national assemblies, as we have great reason
to believe, and none to doubt. In short, as far as we can look
back, a lawless power, a government by will, never prevailed in
Britain.

The Saxons had kings, as well as the Britons. The manner
in which they established themselves, and the long wars they
waged for and against the Britons, led to and maintained monarchical rule amongst them. But these kings were in their first
institution, no doubt, such as Tacitus describes the German kings
and princes to have been: chiefs, who persuaded, rather than
commanded; and who were heard in the public assemblies of the
nation, according as their age, their nobility, their military fame,
or their eloquence gave them authority.‖ How many doughty
monarchs, in later and more polite ages, would have slept in
cottages, and have worked in stalls, instead of inhabiting palaces,
and being cushioned up in thrones, if this rule of government had
continued in force? But the Saxon kings grew into power in
time; and among them, as among other nations, birth, instead of
merit, became, for the sake of order and tranquillity, a title to the
throne. However, though these princes might command, and
were no longer under the necessity of governing by persuasion,
they were still under that of governing to the satisfaction of the
people. By what other expedient could they govern men, who
were wise enough to preserve and exercise the right of electing

* Territa quæsitis ostendit terga Britannis.
† Geog. lib. 11.
‡ Sel. Anal. Anglo Brit. lib. 2, cap. 3, Cam.
§ Cæs. de Bell. lib. 5 et 7.
‖ De situ mor. et pop. Germ. lib. 11.

their civil magistrates and military officers, and the system of whose government was upheld and carried on by a gradation of popular assemblies, from the inferior courts to the high court of parliament; for such, or very near such, was the Wittena Gemote, in nature and effect, whenever the word parliament came into use?

The first prince of the Norman race was an absolute conqueror, in the opinion of some men; and I can readily agree that he assumed, in some cases, the power of a tyrant.   But supposing all this to be true in the utmost extent, that the friends of absolute monarchy can desire it should be thought so, this, and this alone will result from it; unlimited or absolute monarchy could never be established in Britain; no, not even by conquest. The rights of the people were soon re-asserted; the laws of the Confessor were restored; and the third prince of this race, Henry the First, covenanted in a solemn speech to his people, for their assistance against his brother Robert and the Normans, by promising that sacred charter, which was in other reigns so often and so solemnly confirmed, by engaging to maintain his subjects in their ancient liberties, to follow their advice, and to rule them in peace with prudence and mildness.*

I need not descend into more particulars, to show the perpetuity of free government in Britain.   Few men, even in this age, are so shamefully unacquainted with the history of their country, as to be ignorant of the principal events and signal revolutions, which have happened since the Norman era.   One continued design against liberty hath been carried on by various methods, almost in every reign.   In many, the struggles have been violent and bloody.   But liberty still hath triumphed over force, over treachery, over corruption, and even under oppression.   The altars of tyranny have been demolished as soon as raised; nay, even whilst they were raising, and the priests of that idol have been hewed to pieces: so that I will affirm, without the least apprehension of being disproved, that our constitution is brought nearer than any other constitution ever was, to the most perfect idea of a free system of government.—One observation only I will make, before I leave this head, and it is this.   The titles of those kings which were precarious, from circumstances of times and notions that prevailed, notwithstanding the general acquiescence of the nation in them, afforded so many opportunities to our ancestors of better securing or improving liberty.   They were not such bubbles as to alter, without mending the government; much less to make revolutions, and suffer

* In antiquis vestris libertatibus.   Vestris inclinando consiliis.   Consultius et mitius, more mansueti principis.—Vid. Mat. Par.

by them. They were not such bubbles as to raise princes to the throne, who had no pretence to sit in it but their choice, purely to have the honor of bettering the condition of those princes, without bettering their own in proportion.—If what I have been saying appears a little too digressive from the main scope of this essay, I shall hope for indulgence from this consideration, that the natural effect of such reflections as I have made and suggested, must be to raise in our minds the honest ambition of emulating the virtue and courage of our forefathers, in the cause of liberty; and to inspire a reasonable fear, heightened by shame, of losing what they preserved and delivered down to us, through so many mixtures of different people, of Britons with Saxons, of both with Danes, of all three with Normans, through so many difficulties, so many dangers, so many revolutions, in the course of so many centuries.

There is another reason to be given why the people of this island would be more inexcusable than any other, if they lost their liberty; and the opening and enforcing of this reason will bring us fully into our subject.

I supposed just now that our liberty might be ravished or stolen from us, but I think that expression must be retracted, since it will appear, upon due consideration, that our liberty cannot be taken away by the force or fraud alone of those who govern; it cannot be taken away, unless the people are themselves accomplices; and they who are accomplices, cannot be said to suffer by one or the other. Some nations have received the yoke of servitude with little or no struggle; but if ever it is imposed upon us, we must not only hold out our necks to receive it, we must help to put it on. Now, to be passive in such a case is shameful; but to be active, is supreme and unexampled infamy. In order to become slaves, we of this nation must be beforehand what other people have been rendered by a long course of servitude; we must become the most corrupt, the most profligate, the most senseless, the most servile nation of wretches, that ever disgraced humanity: for a force sufficient to ravish liberty from us, such as a great standing army is in time of peace, cannot be continued, unless we continue it; nor can the means necessary to steal liberty from us, be long enough employed with effect, unless we give a sanction to their iniquity, and call good evil, and evil good.

It may be said, that even the friends of liberty have sometimes different notions about it, and about the means of maintaining or promoting it; and therefore that even the British nation may possibly, some time or other, approve and concur in measures destructive of their liberty, without any intention to give it up, and much more without changing from the character which they have hitherto borne among the societies of mankind, to that infamous character I have just now supposed. If this were true, it would only furnish more reasons to be always on our guard, to be jealous of every extraordinary demand, and to reject constantly every proposition, though never so specious, that had a tendency to weaken the barriers of liberty, or to raise a strength superior to theirs. But I confess I do not think we can be led blindfold so far as the brink of the precipice. I know that all words, which are signs of complex ideas, furnish matter of mistake and cavil. We dispute about justice, for instance, and fancy that we have different opinions about the same thing; whilst, by some little difference in the composition of our ideas, it happens that we have only different opinions about different things, and should be of the same opinion about the same thing. But this, I presume, cannot happen in the case before us. All disputes about liberty in this country, and at this time, must be disputes for and against the self-same fixed and invariable set of ideas, whatever the disputants on one side of the question may pretend, in order to conceal what it is not yet very safe to avow. No disputes can possibly arise from different conceptions of any thing so clearly stated, and so precisely determined, as the fundamental principles are, on which our whole liberty rests.

If liberty be that delicious and wholesome fruit, on which the British nation hath fed for so many ages, and to which we owe our riches, our strength, and all the advantages we boast of; the British constitution is the tree that bears this fruit, and will continue to bear it, as long as we are careful to fence it in, and trench it round, against the beasts of the field, and the insects of the earth. To speak without a figure, our constitution is a system of government suited to the genius of our nation, and even to our situation. The experience of many hundred years hath shown, that by preserving this constitution inviolate, or by drawing it back to the principles on which it was originally founded, whenever it shall be made to swerve from them, we may secure to ourselves, and to our latest posterity, the possession of that liberty which we have long enjoyed. What would we more? What other liberty than this do we seek? And if we seek no other, is not this marked out in such characters, as he that runs may read? As our constitution therefore ought to be, what it seldom is, the rule of government, so let us make the conformity, or repugnancy of things to this constitution, the rule by which we accept them as favorable, or reject them as dangerous to liberty. They who talk of liberty in Britain on any other principles than those of the British constitution, talk impertinently at best, and much charity is requisite to believe no worse of them. But they who distinguish between practicable and impracticable liberty, in order to insinuate what they mean, or they mean nothing, that the liberty established by the true scheme of our constitution is of the impracticable kind; and they who endeavor, both in speculation and practice, to elude and pervert the forms, and to ridicule and explode the spirit of this constitution: these men are enemies, open and avowed enemies to it, and by consequence to British liberty, which cannot be supported on any other bottom.   Some men there are, the pests of society I think them, who pretend a great regard to religion in general, but who take every opportunity of declaiming publicly against that system of religion, or at least against that church-establishment, which is received in Britain.   Just so the men of whom I have been speaking, affect a great regard to liberty in general, but they dislike so much the system of liberty established in Britain, that they are incessant in their endeavors to puzzle the plainest thing in the world, and to refine and distinguish away the life and strength of our constitution, in favor of the little, present, momentary turns, which they are retained to serve.   What now would be the consequence, if all these endeavors should succeed? I am persuaded that the great philosophers, divines, lawyers, and politicians, who exert them, have not yet prepared and agreed upon the plans of a new religion, and of new constitutions in church and state.   We should find ourselves therefore without any form of religion or civil government.   The first set of these missionaries would take off all the restraints of religion from the governed, and the latter set would remove, or render ineffectual, all the limitations and controls, which liberty hath prescribed to those that govern, and disjoint the whole frame of our constitution.   Entire dissolution of manners, confusion, anarchy, or perhaps absolute monarchy, would follow; for it is possible, nay probable, that in such a state as this, and amidst such a rout of lawless savages, men would choose this government, absurd as it is, rather than have no government at all.

But here again it may be said, that as liberty is a word of uncertain signification, so is constitution; that men have taught the most opposite doctrines, and pretended at least to build them on the principles of the constitution; that the rule, therefore, of determining our notions of liberty by the principles of our constitution is no rule, and we are by consequence just where we were before.   But the answer is ready.   It is true that there were formerly men who persisted long in the attempt to talk and write that chimera called prerogative into vogue; to contend that it was something real, a right inherent in the crown, founded in the constitution of our government, and equally necessary to support the just authority of the prince, and to protect the subject.   How we had like to have lost our liberty by the prevalence of such doctrines, by the consequences drawn from them, and the practices built upon them, hath been touched in the deduction of the state of parties. But happily this kind of progression, from a free to a slavish constitution of government, was stopped at the revolution, and the notions themselves are so exploded in the course of six-and-forty years, that they are entertained at this hour by no set of men, whose numbers or importance give them any pretence to be reckoned among our national parties. It is as true, that there are now men who pursue the very same design by different methods. The former attacked, these undermine our liberty. The former were the beasts of the field, hinted at above; these are the insects of the earth; and like other insects, though sprung from dirt, and the vilest of the animal kind, they can nibble, and gnaw, and poison; and, if they are suffered to multiply and work on, they can lay the most fruitful country waste. Corruption and dependency are their favorite topics. They plead for the first as a laudable expedient of government, and for the last, I mean corrupt, private dependency, as an essential part of our constitution. When they have perplexed, as much as they are able, our ideas of dependency and independency, they reason, if I may give their sophisms so good a name, as if the independency of each part of the legislature, of the king particularly, arose from the dependency of the other parts on that part. Now this is both false and absurd. It is false, because the constitutional independency of each part of the legislature arises from hence, that distinct rights, powers and privileges, are assigned to it by the constitution. But then this independency of one part can be so little said to arise from the dependency of another, that it consists properly and truly in the free, unbiassed, uninfluenced and independent exercise of these rights, powers and privileges, by each part, in as ample an extent as the constitution allows, or, in other words, as far as that point where the constitution stops this free exercise, and submits the proceedings of one part, not to the private influence, but to the public control of the other parts. Before this point, the independency of each part is meant by the constitution to be absolute. From this point, the constitutional dependency of each part on the others commences. To talk of natural independency belonging to the kingly office, to a house of peers, or a house of commons, the institutions of art, not of nature, is impertinent. It is absurd, because it absolutely destroys the very thing it is advanced to establish; for if A's independency arises from the dependency of B, and B's independency from the dependency of A, then are A and B both dependent, and there is no such thing as constitutional independency at all. The crown is the source of honors, and hath the disposal of public employments. This no man disputes; nor would any man, I believe, go about to alter. But will it follow that the constitutional independency of the king would be lost,[*] because the house of commons give the supplies, if he had not the power of giving part of this money, in places and pensions, back again to the members of that house? It would be easy for me to turn this whole profound reasoning into many, even ridiculous lights; but the subject creates other sentiments than those of mirth, though the logic employed about it deserves a ludicrous, not a serious treatment. I ask pardon for having said so much upon so slight an occasion, and I proceed.

Notwithstanding all these endeavors to puzzle our constitution, formerly in favor of that prerogative, by the weight of which it must have been crushed, and actually at this time in favor of that corruption and corrupt dependency by which it would be soon demolished; the main principles of the British constitution are simple and obvious, and fixed, as well as any truths can be fixed in the minds of men, by the most determinate ideas. The state of our constitution then affords an easy and unerring rule, by which to judge of the state of our liberty. The improvement or decay of one, denotes the improvement or decay of the other; and the strength or weakness of one, the safety or danger of the other. We cannot lose our liberty, unless we lose our constitution; nor lose our constitution, unless we are accomplices to the violations of it; for this constitution is better fitted than any, ancient or modern, ever was, not only to preserve liberty, but to provide for its own duratiou, and to become immortal, if any thing human could be so.

I am, sir, &c.

LETTER XIII.

Sir:—Much hath been said occasionally, in the course of these letters, concerning the beauty and excellency of the British constitution. I shall make, however, no excuse for returning to the same subject, upon an occasion which introduces it so naturally, and, indeed, so necessarily. Nothing can be more apposite to the professed design of these writings; nothing of more real, and more present use. Let me speak plainly. We have been all of us, those of every side, and of every denomination, accustomed too long to value ourselves, foolishly or knavishly, on our zeal for this or that party, or for this or that government; and to

[*] Vide London Jour. Sept. 28, 1734.

make a merit of straining the constitution different ways, in order to serve the different purposes of each.   It is high time we should all learn, if that be still possible, to value ourselves in the first place on our zeal for the constitution; to make all governments, and much more all parties bow to that, and to suffer that to bow to none.   But how shall this constitution be known, unless we make it the subject of careful inquiry, and of frequent and sober reflection?   Or unknown, how shall it become, what it ought to be, the object of our admiration, our love and our zeal?   Many of those who reap the greatest advantages from it, pass it by unregarded, with equal folly and ingratitude.   Many take a transient, inattentive view of it.   Many again consider it in part only, or behold it in a narrow, pedantic light.   Instead of this, we should view it often.   We should pierce through the form to the soul of it.   We should contemplate the noble object in all its parts, and in the whole, and render it as familiar to our intellectual sight, as the most common sensible objects are to our coporeal sight.*   " Quam illa ardentes amores exitaret sui, si videretur?"   Well may it be allowed me to apply to so glorious an effort of human wisdom, what Tully says after Plato, in the Phædrus, if I mistake not, of wisdom herself.

"All public regiment," says Mr. Hooker, "hath arisen from deliberate advice, consultation and composition between men." The proposition is undoubtedly and universally true.   It is as true in the kingdom of Morocco, as it is in the kingdom of Britain; and the undeniable consequences which flow from it are obvious.   We are not to wonder, however, if men do not look up to this original of government, nor trace these consequences from it in most countries.   In the institution of governments, too great powers have been usually given, and too great confidence reposed, either at first, or in process of time.   These powers have subsisted, have been confirmed by more time, and increased by the very nature of power, which is the properest instrument of its own propagation.   But the original composition, for want of being expressed, or sufficiently implied, or frequently recurred to by the forms of the government, hath been forgot, or hath grown so obsolete, that they whose interest required that no such thing should be believed, have thought themselves at liberty boldly to deny it; and not only so, but to suppose some other original of government.   Strange systems of policy, and stranger of religion, have been devised to support and sanctify these usurpations.   Education hath been set on the same side; and saucy authority hath prevailed against the clearest light of nature, and the plainest dictates of common sense.   No man who hath read and looked abroad into the world, and made

* Cic. de finib., l. 2.

a reasonable use of either, will think this too strange to be true; since there is no demonstrated truth (such truths I mean as are here spoken of) which may not be rendered, at least, very prob lematical, by long, uniform, positive contradiction; nor any demonstrated lie, which may not be rendered probable to many, and certain to some, by a long, uniform, positive affirmation; according to a just observation made by father Paul somewhere or other, on occasion of Constantine's supposed grant, and other cheats of the court of Rome.   But we of this country have been more happy.   Our original contract hath been recurred to often, and as many cavils as have been made, as many jests as have been broke about this expression, we might safely defy the assertors of absolute monarchy and arbitrary will, if there were any worth our regard, to produce any one point of time, since which we know any thing of our constitution, wherein the whole scheme of it would not have been one monstrous absurdity, unless an original contract had been supposed.   They must have been blinded therefore by ignorance, or passion, or prejudice, who did not always see that there is such a thing necessarily, and in the very nature of our constitution; and that they might as well doubt whether the foundations of an ancient, solid building were suited and proportioned to the elevation and form of it, as whether our constitution was established by composition and contract.   Sure I am that they must be worse than blind, if any such there are, who do not confess at this time, and under the present settlement, that our constitution is in the strictest sense a bargain, a conditional contract between the prince and the people, as it always hath been, and still is, between the representative and collective bodies of the nation.

That this bargain may not be broken, on the part of the prince with the people, (though the executive power be trusted to the prince, to be exercised according to such rules, and by the ministry of such officers as are prescribed by the laws and customs of this kingdom,) the legislative, or supreme power, is vested by our constitution in three estates, whereof the king is one.   Whilst the members of the other two preserve their private independency, and those estates are consequently under no dependency, except that which is in the scheme of our constitution, this control on the first will always be sufficient; and a bad king, let him be as bold as he may please to be thought, must stand in awe of an honest parliament.

That this bargain may not be broken, on the part of the representative body, with the collective body of the nation, it is not only a principal, declared right of the people of Britain, that the election of members to sit in parliament shall be free, but it hath been a principal part of the care and attention of parliaments, for more than three hundred years, to watch over this freedom, and to secure it, by removing all influence of the crown, and all other corrupt influence, from these elections. This care and this attention have gone still farther. They have provided, as far as they have been suffered to provide hitherto, by the constitutional dependency of one house on the other, and of both on the crown, that all such influence should be removed from the members after they are chosen. Even here the providence of our constitution hath not stopped. Lest all other provisions should be ineffectual to keep the members of the house of commons out of this unconstitutional dependency, which some men presume, with a silly dogmatical air of triumph, to suppose necessary to support the constitutional independency of the crown, the wisdom of our constitution hath thought fit that the representatives of the people should not have time to forget that they are such; that they are empowered to act for the people, not against them. In a word, our constitution means, that the members of this body should be kept, as it were, to their good behavior, by the frequent returns of new elections. It does all that a constitution can do, all that can be done by legal provisions, to secure the interests of the people, by maintaining the integrity of their trustees: and lest all this should fail, it gives frequent opportunities to the people to secure their interests themselves, by mending their choice of their trustees; so that as a bad king must stand in awe of an honest parliament, a corrupt house of commons must stand in awe of an honest people.

Between these two estates, or branches of the legislative power, there stands a third, the house of peers; which may seem in theory, perhaps, too much under the influence of the crown, to be a proper control upon it, because the sole right of creating peers resides in the crown; whereas the crown hath no right to intermeddle in the electing commoners. This would be the case, and an intolerable one indeed, if the crown should exercise this right often, as it had been exercised sometimes with universal and most just disapprobation. It is possible too, that this may come to be the case, in some future age, by the method of electing peers to sit in parliament, for one part of the same kingdom, by the frequent translations of bishops, and by other means, if the wisdom and virtue of the present age, and the favorable opportunity of the present auspicious and indulgent reign do not prevent it. But in all other respects, the persons who are once created peers, and their posterity, according to the scheme of the constitution, having a right to sit and debate, and vote in the house of peers, which cannot be taken from them, except by forfeiture; all influence of the kind I have mentioned seems to be again removed, and their share in the government depending neither on the king nor the people, they constitute a middle order, and are properly mediators between the other two, in the eye of our constitution.

It is by this mixture of monarchical, aristocratical and democratical power, blended together in one system, and by these three estates balancing one another, that our free constitution of government hath been preserved so long inviolate, or hath been brought back, after having suffered violations, to its original principles, and been renewed, and improved too, by frequent and salutary revolutions.   It is by this that weak and wicked princes have been opposed, restrained, reformed, and punished by parliaments; that the real, and perhaps the doubtful, exorbitances of parliaments have been reduced by the crown, and that the heat of one house hath been moderated, or the spirit raised, by the proceedings of the other.   Parliaments have had a good effect on the people, by keeping them quiet; and the people on parliaments, by keeping them within bounds, which they were tempted to transgress.   A just confidence in the safe, regular, parliamentary methods of redressing grievances hath often made the freest, and not the most patient people on earth, bear the greatest grievances much longer than people held under stronger restraints, and more used to oppression, who had not the same confidence, nor the same expectation, have borne even less.   The cries of the people, and the terror of approaching elections, have defeated the most dangerous projects for beggaring and enslaving the nation; and the majority without doors hath obliged the majority within doors, to truckle to the minority.   In a word, two things may be said with truth of our constitution, which I think neither can, nor ever could be said of any other.   It secures society against the miseries which are inseparable from simple forms of government, and is liable as little as possible to the inconveniences that arise in mixed forms.   It cannot become uneasy to the prince, or people, unless the former be egregiously weak or wicked; nor be destroyed, unless the latter be excessively and universally corrupt.   But these general assertions require to be a little better explained.

By simple forms of government, I mean such as lodge the whole supreme power, absolutely and without control, either in a single person, or in the principal persons of the community, or in the whole body of the people.   Such governments are governments of arbitrary will, and, therefore, of all imaginable absurdities the most absurd.   They stand in direct opposition to the sole motive of submission to any government whatsoever; for if men quit the state, and renounce the rights of nature, (one of which is, to be sure, that of being governed by their own will,) they do this, that they may not remain exposed to the arbitrary will of other men, the weakest to that of the strongest, the few to that of the many. Now, in submitting to any simple form of government whatever, they establish what they mean to avoid, and for fear of being exposed to arbitrary will sometimes, they choose to be governed by it always. These governments do not only degenerate into tyranny, they are tyranny in their very institution; and they who submit to them are slaves, not subjects, however the supreme power may be exercised: for tyranny and slavery do not so properly consist in the stripes that are given and received, as in the power of giving them at pleasure, and the necessity of receiving them, whenever and for whatever they are inflicted. Absolute democracy may appear to some, in abstracted speculations, a less deviation from nature than monarchy, and more agreeable to reason, because here it is the will of the whole community that governs the whole community, and because reason does certainly instruct every man, even from a consciousness of his own frailty, the impotentia animi of the Latin writers, to trust as little power as possible to any other man. But still it must be confessed, that if it be unsafe for a people to trust too much power to a prince, it is unsafe for them likewise to keep too much power to themselves. Absolute monarchy is tyranny; but absolute democracy is tyranny and anarchy both. If aristocracy be placed between these two extremes, it is placed on a slippery ridge, and must fall into one or the other, according to the natural course of human affairs; if the few who govern are united, into tyranny, perhaps, more severe than any other; if they are disunited, into factions and disorders as great as those of the most tumultuous democracy.

From such observations, and many of the same kind and tendency, it hath been concluded very reasonably, that the best form of government must be one compounded of these three, and in which they are all so tempered, that each may produce the good effects, and be restrained by the counter-workings of the other two, from producing the bad effects that are natural to it. Thus much is evident. But then how to fix that just proportion of each, how to hit that happy temperament of them all in one system, is a difficulty that hath perplexed the wisest politicians, and the most famous legislators. Let me quote one of the greatest writers of antiquity. Tacitus acknowledges, in the fourth book of his annals, what is here advanced; but he thinks such a constitution of government rather a subject of fine speculation than of practice.* He thinks it much more likely that

---

* Cunctas nationes et urbes populus, aut primores, aut singuli regunt. Delecta ex his et constituta reipublicæ forma, laudari facilius quam evenire; vel, si evênit, haud diuturna esse potest.

such a system should continue to be admired and praised in idea, than established in fact; and if it happens ever to be established, he does not imagine it can be supported long. Not only the real difficulties which his sagacity presented to his mind, but his reflections on the constitution and fate of the Roman commonwealth might lead Tactitus into this despondency. But what the refinements of Roman policy could not do, hath been done in this island, upon foundations laid by the rough simplicity of our northern ancestors.

It would be a curious and entertaining amusement, to reduce the constitutions of the Roman government, and of those which were formed on the ruins of that empire, particularly of our own, to their first principles; to observe in which they agree, and in which they differ, and the uniform or various tendencies of each; to mark the latent, as well as apparent causes of their rise and fall; how well or how ill they were contrived for triumphs abroad, or peace at home; for vain grandeur or real prosperity; for resisting corruption, or being ruined by it. Such an analysis and inquiry would be, I imagine, not only amusing, but useful. At least, it would be more so than any rhapsody of general reflections, huddled together with little order or design; for these leave no systematical impressions on the mind; nothing but a confusion of ideas, often bright and glittering, seldom instructive. But a work of this kind would be too voluminous and too aspiring for these little essays, and the humble author of them. He will therefore keep to his point, and content himself to make some of those observations alone, which seem proper to illustrate and prove what he hath advanced, that the British constitution is a plain and sufficient rule of judgment and conduct to us in every thing that regards our liberty; for preserving of which, as well as for securing its own duration, it is better fitted than any other.

There was so great a mixture of monarchical power in the Roman commonwealth, that Livy* dates the original of liberty from the expulsion of the Tarquins, rather because the consular dignity was made annual, than because the regal power had suffered any diminution in that change. The dictatorial power the most absolute that can be imagined, was introduced in eight, or at farthest in eleven years afterwards, and may therefore be reckoned coeval with the commonwealth; and whatever diminution either this or the consular power might suffer, the axes and the rods were terrible to the last, especially when they were

* Libertatis originem inde magis, quia annuum imperium consulare factum est quam quod diminutum quicquam sit ex regiâ potestate, numeres. Omnia jura, omnia insignia primi consules tenuere. Lib. cap. 1.

carried before a dictator, for whom the tribunes of the people were not a match, as they were for the consuls. But though there were three sorts of power exercised, there were but two orders, or estates established in this commonwealth, the patricians and the plebeians; and the supreme power was divided accordingly between the senate and the collective, not a representative body of the people. These two orders or estates had frequent contests, and well they might, since they had very opposite interests. Agrarian laws,* for instance, began to be promulgated within three-and-twenty years, and continued to the end of the commonwealth to produce the same disorders. How inconsistent, indeed, was that plan of government, which required so much hard service of the people; and which, leaving them so much power in the distribution of power, left them so little property in the distribution of property? Such an inequality of property, and of the means of acquiring it, cannot subsist in an equal commonwealth; and I much apprehend that any near approaches to a monopoly of property, would not be long endured even in a monarchy.—But I return to my first observation.

Though the Romans made frequent experience of the cruel mischiefs, and even extreme danger to liberty, which attended almost every variance of the two estates, yet did they never fall upon any safe or effectual method of preventing these disputes, or of reconciling them without violence. The old expedients alone subsisted; and surely they were not only violent, but extra constitutional. When the senate was inflexible, the people had immediate recourse to sedition. When the people was refractory, the senate had recourse to a dictator. The latter had an approbation which could not be given to the former, and was a legal institution; notwithstanding which I make no scruple of saying that it was at least as inconsistent with a free constitution of government as the former. Sedition was temporary anarchy. A dictator was a tyrant for six months, unless he thought fit to abdicate sooner. The constitution was suspended, and endangered by both. It might have been destroyed by the excesses of one. It was destroyed by the bare duration of the other. If the Romans had annually elected out of their tribes a certain number of men to represent the people, instead of depending on their tribunes; (a sort of bullying magistracy, and often a very corrupt one) and if this representative body had been one estate, and had acted as such, the consuls might very well have supplied the place of a third estate, and have been safely trusted, even more independently of the senate than they were, with the

* Tum primum lex agraria promulgata est; nunquam deinde usque ad hanc memoriam fine maximis motibus rerum agitata. Liv. l. 2, c. 41.

executive power.   But the want of a third estate in the Roman system of government, and of a representative body, to act for the collective body, maintained one perpetual ferment, which often increased into a storm, but never subsided into a calm. The state of Rome, and of the greatest men in that commonwealth, would have deserved pity rather than envy, even in the best times, if their defective constitution had not made such a state of trouble and tumult the price they paid for the maintenance of their liberty.*   But this was not the whole price.— Whilst Rome advanced triumphantly in conquering the world, as her orators, poets, and historians have expressed themselves; that is, a few nations round the Mediterranean sea, and little more; her citizens turned against one another those weapons, which were put into their hands against the enemies of Rome. Mutual proscriptions and bloody massacres followed: each party triumphed in its turn; they were more animated and better disciplined by their contests; both grew stronger; the commonwealth alone grew weaker; and Pompey and Cæsar finished the last tragical scene which Marius and Sylla began.   In fine, the Roman commonwealth would have been dissolved much sooner than it was, by the defects I have mentioned, which many circumstances concurred to aggravate, if such a spirit of wisdom, as well as courage, and such an enthusiasm for the grandeur, the majesty, and the duration of their empire had not possessed this people, as never possessed any other.   When this spirit decayed, when this enthusiasm cooled, the constitution could not help, nay, worked against itself.   That dictatorial power, on which the senate had always depended for preserving it, completed the ruin of it, in the hands of Cæsar; and that tribunitial power to which the people had always trusted the defence of their liberty, confirmed their slavery in the hands of Augustus.

I am, sir, &c.

LETTER XIV.

SIR:—The defects, which I have presumed to censure in the Roman constitution of government, were avoided in some of those that were established on the breaking of that empire, by

---

* Conciones magistratuum pæne pernoctantium in rostris.—Accusationes potentium reorum et assignatæ etiam domibus inimicitiæ.—Procerum factiones, et assidua senatûs adversum plebem certamina.—Dial. de Orat. Quinctil. Tacito inscrip.

the northern nations and the Goths; for I suspect that the Goths were not properly and strictly a northern nation, any more than the Huns and the Alans, though they have been often confounded, and I believe by myself.—Let us cast our eyes on Spain and France.

We cannot arrive, as far as my scanty knowledge informs me, at any particular and authentic account of the scheme of that government which the western Goths established, when, driven out of Gaul by the Franks, they drove the Vandals and the Alans out of Spain; nor distinguish very accurately between such institutions as were parts of the original Gothic plan, and such as were introduced into the several kingdoms that formed themselves on the re-conquest of the country by the Spaniards from the Arabs and Moors. The original of the Cortes particularly is quite in the dark, as we are assured by a very industrious inquirer and judicious writer.* Thus much, however, we may assert, that the Gothic kings were at first elective, and always limited, even after they became hereditary; and that the Cortes, whenever it was established, was an assembly, that may be more truly compared to a British parliament than the assembly of the states of France could ever pretend to be. Churchmen had wriggled themselves into a share of temporal power among the Goths, as they did in every country where they were admitted to preach the gospel, though without any authority from the gospel; so that the Cortes consisted of prelates, as well as dukes, masters of orders, earl and ricoshomes, who composed the whole body of the nobility; and of the procurators of the commons; that is, of the citizens and burgesses, chosen by the cities and boroughs to represent and act for the whole body of the commons. To preserve the independency of this assembly, these procurators were to be paid by the corporations for which they served; the king was to give no office or salary to any of them; nay, a " resumption of rewards, granted to members of the Cortes,"† was once at least debated, if not enacted. In short, he was not to name their president, nor even to send letters unopened to any of them. No money could be raised on the subjects, without the consent of this assembly; and it was a standing maxim, or order, that redress of grievances should precede the grants of supplies. Such a frame of government as this seems built for duration; and, in fact, if it had not been undermined, it could not have been demolished. The manner in which it was both undermined and demolished totally at last, deserves the attention of every man in Britain. It was undermined by the influence of the court, too much connived at and

---

* Dr. Geddes in his Miscell. Tracts.   † Ibid.

too long tolerated, on the members of the Cortes. Prostitute wretches were found in those days, I doubt not, as well as in ours, to maintain that the necessary independency of the prince could not be supported, without allowing a corrupt dependency of the Cortes on him; and they had in those days such success in Castile, as we ought to hope they will never obtain in Britain. When corrupt majorities were thus secured, pretences were not wanting, nor will they ever be so, for making concessions to the crown, repugnant to the spirit of the constitution, and even inconsistent with the forms of it. Such pretences, however plausible, would not have been admitted by men zealous to preserve their liberty; because any real danger, remote as well as immediate, to a free constitution, would in their balance outweigh all considerations of real expediency, and much more all the frivolous pretences of that kind. But the members of the Cortes* were no longer such men, when Castile lost her liberties under Charles the Fifth. The custom of bribing the representatives of the commons, by gifts and promises, and so securing a majority to the court, had long prevailed, as we have just now said; and after that, it is not to be wondered at if excises, given for eight years only, became perpetual; if money was granted before grievances were redressed; and if the precedent set in the time of Henry the Second, was followed in all succeeding reigns.——The Cortes gave this prince a supply, for making war on the Moors; but the sum being represented by the court to be insufficient for the service, it was carried that, in case of a deficiency, the king might raise, without calling a Cortes, the money necessary to make good that deficiency.† This vote of credit gave an incurable fatal wound to that constitution. I call it a vote of credit, though the powers it gave seem to be less than those which are given by some modern votes of credit; for surely there is a difference, and not a small one, between a power to raise money directly on the people, for a service known, and already approved, and provided for in part, by their representatives, and a power to borrow money, on the national credit, for services unknown, and to lay the nation under an obligation of paying for that which it is possible their representatives may disapprove.

This precedent having been made in favor of one king, and in one particular conjuncture, it became a prevailing argument in favor of every other king, and in every other conjuncture: for though it may be, nay must be, in the vast variety of characters, and of conjunctures, prudent and just to grant in favor of some princes, and upon some occasions, what it would be neither prudent nor just to grant in favor of other princes, and upon other

---

* Dr. Geddes in his Miscell. Tracts. † Ibid.

occasions, yet such is the merit of every prince who fills a throne, or rather such is the servile adulation paid to power, in what hands soever it be lodged, that general and almost universal experience shows this rule, which no man of sense would break in the management of his private interests, absolutely reversed in the management of the most important, national interests.— The inference to be drawn from hence is plainly this, that the inconveniency or danger of refusing to every prince, and in every conjuncture, such things as are inconsistent with the constitution of a free government, must be always less than the inconveniency or danger of granting them to any prince, and in any conjuncture.

Let me add this farther observation, which presents itself so naturally after the former. Though it be proper in all limited monarchies, to watch and guard against all concessions, or usurpations, that may destroy the balance of power, on which the preservation of liberty depends; yet is it certain, that concessions to the crown from the other constituent parts of the legislature are almost alone to be feared. There is no danger that the crown should make them to the others; and on this head the people may very safely trust to those who wear it, and those who serve it. The nobility will not make them to the commons, without great struggles, which give time for interpositions, nor the commons to the nobility. But both may be easily induced to make them to the crown. The reasons of this difference are obvious enough; for, first, a king is really nothing more than a supreme magistrate, instituted for the service of the community, which requires that the executive power should be vested in a single person. He hath, indeed, a crown on his head, a sceptre in his hand, and velvet robes on his back, and he sits elevated in a throne, whilst others stand on the ground about him; and all this to denote that he is a king, and to draw the attention and reverence of the vulgar. Just so another man wears a mitre on his head, a crosier in his hand, and lawn sleeves, and sits in a purple elbow chair, to denote that he is a bishop, and to excite the devotion of the multitude, who receive his benediction very thankfully on their knees. But still the king, as well as the bishop, holds an office, and owes a service. " Officium est imperare non regnum." The king, when he commands, discharges a trust, and performs a duty, as well as the subject, when he obeys. Notwithstanding which, kings are apt to see themselves in another light, and experience shows us, that even they who made them what they are, are apt to take them for what they are not. From hence it happened in Spain, and may happen possibly in other countries, that the kings, instead of being satisfied with, and thankful for the dignity, honor, power and wealth, which they possessed in so eminent a degree, above all other magistrates and members of the commonwealth, repined at their being possessed of no more. What they had was given them by the constitution; and what they had not was reserved by the same authority to the nobility and to the commons. But they proceeded, and their sycophants reasoned, as if the sole power of the government, and the whole wealth of the nation, belonged of right to them, and the limitations of the monarchy were so many usurpations on the monarch. In the second place, besides this constant desire of encroaching, there is another reason why concessions to the crown are more to be guarded against than others, in limited monarchies. The regal power resides in one person. The other shares of the supreme power are assigned to bodies of men. From hence it follows that the interest of the king, and the interest of the crown, cannot well be divided in the mind of a prince; whereas the interest of each individual may be distinguished from the interest of the nobility or of the commons, and still more from that of the nation, in the minds of those who compose a house of peers, or who are representatives of the people. A king cannot be tempted to give up the interest of the crown, because he cannot give up this public interest, without giving up his private interest; whereas the members of such assemblies may promote their private interest, by sacrificing to it that of the public. Several other reasons might be insisted upon, to establish the truth of the observation we have made, and to show how unfairly they argue, who all along suppose that the independency of the crown may as easily be lost, and the balance of power be destroyed on that side, by concessions from the prince, and usurpations on him, as the independency of the lords or commons may be lost, and the balance of power be destroyed on that side, by concessions to the prince, and by his usurpations. Such reasons, for instance, might be drawn from the difference of that influence which the crown hath on the other estates, and which the other estates have on the crown; as well as from the difference of the pretences, which may be urged on behalf of the crown, or of the nobility, or commons, to obtain such concessions; for supposing them all co-equal, as parts of the legislature, yet if it be considered that the executive power is solely in the crown; that the disposition of public money, as well as public employments, is a part of this power, that this power is in continual exercise, and may immediately affect, more or less, at one time or at another, every particular man, peer as well as commoner; whereas the other powers are exercised occasionally, are continued or suspended, in great measure, at the will of the prince, and are employed chiefly in matters of general, not particular concern; in fine, if it be considered farther, that the powers exercised by assemblies of peers

and commoners, whether these assemblies be regarded as parts
of the legislature, as the great councils of the nation, or as the
judges and prosecutors of enormous offenders, are few and simple, directed to notorious purposes, conducted by rules always
known, always the same, and always sufficient to these purposes:
whereas the branches of executive power are numerous and complicated, the rules various, and the purposes often unknown, often
contingent; so that it may become difficult to judge either of the
utility of the purposes, or of the sufficiency of the powers: if all
these things be considered, I say, we shall not be at a loss to determine on which side the danger to liberty, in a limited monarchy, lies; and whether concessions to the crown, in prejudice
of the constitution, are not more likely to be made, than concessions from it.

Happy had it been for the people of Castile, if they had seen
this danger in time, and had remedied, whilst the remedies were
in their power, those defects in their constitution, whatever they
were, which gave their kings by degrees such an influence over
the Cortes, as overturned at last the whole constitution, and gained
to the German race, that began to reign in Charles the Fifth, (for
his father Philip is scarce to be reckoned) such an absolute power
as the Gothic kings had never been able to obtain.   Though
Charles the Fifth was a very able prince, yet the honor, for such
it will be esteemed by some men, or more truly the infamy of
enslaving Castile must not be ascribed to his superior capacity,
nor to that of his ministers.   Had he been the merest tool, a
thing of straw, but something less than a scarecrow, and unable
to protect the property of his subjects, he might still have taken
their liberties from them in that conjuncture, as he did most
effectually.   Corruption was established; a majority of the Cortes
was bribed; the nobility was detached from the common interest
by titles, places, pensions and grants; and the clergy in general,
for exceptions there were, took no farther share in it than their
particular piques, or some indirect and fleeting considerations
inspired them to take.   The nation saw itself betrayed, and the
commons protested loudly against the proceedings of their representatives.   But this was the very point for which the enemies
of the Castilian constitution waited; and as soon as a pretence
for employing force was given, they muffled themselves up in
that threadbare cloak of zeal for the government, and stabbed
their country to the heart.   An ordinance of the Cortes had been
made about a hundred years before, against increasing the
standing forces of the kingdom to more than four thousand
soldiers in garrisons, and fifteen hundred ginets.   This ordinance
had not been very well observed.   The long wars with the
Moors made armies often necessary, when there was no actual

war. The danger of being invaded by the Moors, for every Moorish king was deemed a pretender to the throne, might serve to make them so represented; and when this reason failed entirely, as it did by the conquest of Granada, the last possession of these people in Spain, pretences for keeping armies on foot were still to be found. There were still Moorish factions; the new Christians were Moors in their hearts; amongst the old Christians there were several who favored them; the people were not to be trusted with their own preservation. Chievres, the rapacious minister of Charles the Fifth, and his journeymen, for so were those Spaniards called, according to Dr. Geddes, who did not care how much their country was plundered by foreigners, provided they shared the spoils; Chievres, I say, and his journeymen, a real faction, and perhaps not a great one, were the fast friends of the government. The rest of the nation were open or secret enemies. According to this excellent logic, the former were to be protected in blundering, for they were guilty of that too, as well as in plundering; and the latter were to be oppressed for complaining. The nation was sacrificed to a faction, and an excellent constitution destroyed, in favor of a profligate government. This destruction however would not have been so easily accomplished, nor would Castilians alone have enslaved Castile to a foreign race, after asserting their liberty so often, and so boldly, against princes of their own country, if two other circumstances had not concurred. Ferdinand had conquered Navarre, and a regular, disciplined army defended that conquest against the French. This army, which was at hand, marched into Castile, defeated the commons, and extinguished liberty in a country where it had been long declining. The nobility was detached from the commons by grants of land, amongst other considerations, as I said above; and the commons renewed their contest on this head, perhaps unjustly, to be sure very unseasonably. The commons however were justified for taking arms, in the opinion of the nobility, and even in that of Adrian, who governed during the absence of Charles, whose preceptor he had been; for this honest man, too honest to be long endured on the papal throne, where he was afterwards placed, affirmed that all the troubles of Castile were caused by the king, and by his covetous and tyrannical ministers. The conduct of the commons, upon this great occasion, was in many instances rash and violent, as well as ill advised and weak. But they were tumultuous assemblies driven into despair; and the nobility, who might have had great sway amongst them, and might have helped to regulate their fire, and to keep them sober, helped on the contrary to make them mad, either by neglecting them, or by taking part against them, till it was too late; and

then complained of their being mad, with as ill a grace as the
principal men of Rome, who helped to corrupt that people,
complained of their corruption, and assigned it as a reason for
depriving them of their liberty.

There cannot be a greater solecism in politics than that of a
nobility, under monarchical government, who suffer the liberty
of the commons to be taken away. In aristocracies, the nobility
get whatever the commons lose; but in monarchies, the crown
alone is the gainer, and the certain consequence of their helping
to enslave the commons, must be that of being enslaved themselves at last. How, indeed, should it be otherwise, since the
liberty of the commons cannot be taken away unless the constitution be first broken; and since neither the peers, nor any one
else, can hold their privileges or their properties, by a better
tenure than that of arbitrary will, when the constitution is once
broken? Was it possible to doubt of this truth, we might find
the proof of it, without going out of the country where we are—
I mean Spain. Among all the surprising phenomena which have
appeared in the world of late years, there are none that have
struck mankind with more astonishment than those instances of
persons raised to the highest posts of power, authority and command, nay to empire, who had not, either from their obscure
birth, or their low talents, or their still lower habits, the least
occasion even to dream of such elevation. Among other countries, Spain hath had her share of them; and the grandees, as they
are pompously styled, the successors of those men who thought
to rise on the ruin of the commons of Castile; they, who have
the vain honor of cocking their hats in the presence of their prince,
have been seen to stand at awful distance, or approach with re-
spectful cringe, in the presence of a parasite and buffoon.

I know full well that in such govern ments as we speak of here,
it is both the duty and interest of the nobility to oppose the excesses of the commons; but I know too that they have another
duty, which they are not to leave undone; another point of interest, which they are not to neglect: and, therefore, I have spoken
of this second estate in our government as of a middle order, that
are properly mediators between the other two, in the eye of our
constitution. Whilst the peers maintain this character, they will
be able to discharge this duty; but they would cease to be so, if
it was possible they should ever become the tools of faction, or
the vassals of a minister. In mediations of this kind, different
from those that are more commonly called such, mediators mingle
in the contest, are parties concerned, and can by that alone expect to mediate with effect, whether they be considered as bodies
of men or individuals. When the commons are assisted by the
peers in their reasonable endeavors to promote or restore fruga-

lity, to secure liberty, and to correct all sorts of mal-administration, the peers will have, both collectively and separately, a credit with the people, as well as with the representatives of the people; by which they may contribute to check the latter, whenever a house of commons shall grow unreasonable, factious, or seditious. But if the peers of the realm neglect, or oppose the commons in their just attempts, and forfeit by consequence the character of impartiality, and even the air of independency, the peers will then add little strength to the crown, whenever the evil day comes, and have as little power to prevent it from coming. There was a time, our fathers saw it, when a house of commons destroyed, instead of supporting, the constitution, and introduced tyranny, under pretence of excluding slavery. I think it might be shown, from the anecdotes of that age, that this could not have happened, if the court had not been so long and so partially abetted by the greatest part of the nobility and clergy, both in the house of lords and out of it. A universal and timely concurrence with the spirit of the commons, which was pious in the true sense of the word at first, would have had, I presume, the full effect that every honest man proposed in a parliamentary reformation of the state; and those fatal opportunities, that were afterwards given to the republican, presbyterian, and independent factions, would have been avoided. But they who could have trimmed (for there is a wise and honest, as well as a silly and corrupt trimming) or have mediated with success, lost the power of doing either; some by abetting the crown so long, for fear of the commons, and others by concurring with the commons so far, for fear of the crown, that the people in general had no confidence in the former, and the latter were afraid to trust their prince after all they had done against him. If any men had trusted to the plausible professions of the court at that time, and the court had subdued the opposite party, we may judge, without any breach of charity, that these men would have found themselves deceived. Just so, if any men who meant the reformation, not the destruction of the state, believed in the canting reformers of that age, such men were no doubt egregiously deceived. But I confess myself of opinion, and surely upon no improbable grounds, that there were few, or no such men. The good intentions of the court were distrusted even by those who took arms for the king; and the ill intentions of many of the leaders on the other side were suspected, no doubt, by many who took arms for the parliament. But two of the three estates being ripe for the rashest enterprises, and the third being in no condition to mediate, the extremes clashed, without any power sufficient to interpose; and when the sword was drawn, the sword could alone decide. I conclude, therefore, from these two examples, that as there cannot be a greater error in politics than that of a nobility, who assist a prince to take away the liberties and privileges of the commons, which was the case in Castile, so the surest way of preventing that terrible dilemma, wherein men are obliged to choose either submission to tyrannical government, or concurrence with an enraged and no longer governable people, which hath been the case in Castile and Britain both, is for the nobility, and the principal men amongst the commons, to engage so early in the cause of liberty, that the former may be always in condition to mediate with effect, and the latter have always power to allay the intemperate heat of their own body.

I am, sir, &c.

LETTER XV.

Sir:—But to resume the comparison of other constitutions of government with our own, I say, that if the Gothic constitution in Spain, either by original defects, or by deviating from, and not being reduced again in time to its first principles, was destroyed through the corruption of parliaments, and by the force of an army, one of which betrayed, and the other conquered the commons of Castile; the commons of France seem either not to have had, or to have lost, in the dark beginnings of that monarchy, all share in the supreme, legislative power. The great, original defect of having but two estates to share the supreme power, is an objection common to the Roman, and to the French constitutions, with this difference; of the three simple forms of government, the monarchical, the aristocratical, and the democratical, Rome wanted the first, and France hath always wanted the last. Rome had a nobility and a commonalty, but no magistracy fitted by its institution to answer the purposes of that supreme magistrate, who is called king even in limited monarchies. France hath always had a king and a nobility, and hath felt in their turns all the evils of monarchical and aristocratical tyranny. But the people have not had, I presume, since the government of the Franks was fully established on this side of the Rhine, and the form of their monarchy settled, any share in the supreme power, either collectively or representatively, how much soever a contrary notion may have been countenanced by some writers, and have been generally entertained, at least in other countries.

There is no nation in the world, says Mezerai, more illustrious, nor any whose original is more obscure than that of the French. They who would dispute the first, could hardly dispute the last; and it is no business of mine to controvert either. As dark as their original is, we may discover enough to establish what hath been said, and to carry on the comparison we are making.

The Franks were a nation of Germany, seated at one time between the Elbe, Rhine and Neckar, and at another, that is, in the reign of Theodosius the younger, extending themselves on the German side of the Rhine, from Cologne down to Nimighen, and still lower. What is known therefore of the government of the ancient Germans, either from Tacitus, or any other good authority, may be properly applied to their government, whilst they continued in Germany, and even after they settled in Gaul, till such times as we find, by relations more modern, that a different form of government prevailed amongst them. Now it seems to me extremely plain, that a different form of government did prevail amongst them even from the time of Clovis, the conqueror of Gaul. Thus, for instance, that passage in Tacitus, where he says, " that the ancient Germans took their kings on account of nobility, and their generals on account of valor; that the power of their kings was not absolute and unlimited; and that their generals commanded by the authority which their example, rather than their power gave them;"* that passage, I say, is properly enough applied to the Franks before, and perhaps during the conquest of Gaul; but very improperly afterwards, when Clovis, both king and general of that people, had founded the monarchy which he transmitted to his posterity.† That the nation of the Franks was divided into several tribes, or clans, and that these were governed by several little princes, cannot be doubted.— " Habebat quot pagos, tot pæne duces." That a general was chosen to command the whole with sovereign authority, but according to certain rules made by common consent, whenever any great enterprize was undertaken, and that Clovis himself, though he succeeded his father Childeric in commanding over a part of the Franks, was chosen in this manner, and for this purpose, is certain. In his first expedition, he led an army of freebooters, and was obliged by compact to divide the spoil by lots amongst them. The story, which so many authors have told, after Gregory of Tours, of a private soldier, who refused to leave to his disposition a vessel of gold, that had been taken out of a

---

* Reges ex nobilitate, duces ex virtute sumunt; nec regibus infinita, nec libera potestas; et duces exemplo potiùs quam imperio præsunt. De Mor. Germ.

† Boulainv. Mem. Hist.

church at Rheims, and broke it before his face, is a proof that he was nothing more at first than I have represented him, the head of a troop of adventurers, who chose him to lead them, but made their conditions with him. The Franks therefore might be at this time, in some sense, " all free, perfectly equal, and independent;"* but will it follow from hence that they continued to be so, in any sense, after Clovis had founded their monarchy; had destroyed all their little kings; united in one body, and under his own domination, all their little states, and changed the form of their government, by appointing dukes, earls, vicars, and other magistrates, to govern under him, according to the model of government in the latter Roman empire? Certainly not. However this change was brought about, and to whatever it was owing, the monarchy of the Franks in Gaul was built on the ruins of their former government. This Boulainvilliers himself confesses, when he says, (though not very accurately nor consistently, as I imagine, in calling their former government a kind of aristocracy,) that " the principle of union, which founded the monarchy on the ruins of a kind of aristocracy, was the mistaken ambition of particular men." In short, proofs enough may be collected out of this very author, to show that the government of the Franks, even under the first race of their kings, was not only different from the German governments, but in some respects founded on quite opposite principles. One of these respects, which is immediately to my purpose, I shall mention.

The general assemblies that were held at first in the month of March, and afterwards in the month of May, were national assemblies, indeed, but not such as the ancient Germans held; among whom the principal men consulted and decided about the least, and the whole body of the people about the greatest affairs.† In these assemblies of the French, the people had nothing to do, unless we reckon for something the function of hollowing,‡ which the author I have just now quoted assigns them, and which he says that custom had rendered necessary. In one word, the people had not any share in the supreme power, either collectively or representatively; in the original plan of the French government. Whether they acquired any share in this power afterwards, let us inquire next. Mezerai§ pretends, and

* Boulainv.   Mem. Hist.
† De minoribus principes, de majoribus omnes.—Tacit.
‡ Ills (that is the French) laisserent passer aux hauts magistrats, les ducs, les comtes, et les vicaires, le droit de la nation entiere; de sortque le commun n'eut plus d'autres fonctions dans assemblées réelles, que d'y paroitre pours les acclamations, que l'usage rendoit necessaires.—Boulainv. Mem. Hist.
§ L. 2.

indeed the whole history of France vouches for him, "that no nation ever honored their nobility so much as the French; amongst whom the nobility was not only exempt from all sorts of impositions and charges, but commanded absolutely all inferior ranks, who were almost in a state of servitude."* How could it be otherwise, when the nobility, and chief magistrates, and the clergy, composed alone the national councils, or parliaments, and even exercised distributive justice all over the kingdom? Their power increased, as that of the kings of the first race diminished. Charles Martel, indeed, who trusted to that battle-axe which gave him his name, and to foreign troops, laid aside the national assemblies, neglected the nobility, and misused even the clergy, who damned him for it. But Pepin found it necessary to regain both, and attach them to his interest, in order to mount the throne. By attaching them, he attached the whole nation to him. Childeric was deposed, and he chosen king in a general assembly held at Soissons, which Mezerai calls most improperly, since the expression communicates a false idea to his reader, the states, "les etats." These assemblies, in his time, in that of his son Charles the Great, and so on, consisted of the nobility and clergy alone; and once more it is beyond all dispute certain, that the people had no more share in these national councils, under the Second, than under the first race of the kings of France.

When the third race of these kings began in Hugues Capet, the lords were so powerful in their estates, and so independent in their governments, that he was forced to come to a kind of composition with them. They became sovereigns, each in his territory, but held of the crown, and acknowledged the king for the supreme lord. There was scarce a town which had not a little sovereign, scarce a castle without some little tyrant. The parliaments, in these ages, took several turns; "Ills prirent divers plis,"† as Pasquier expresses himself; but still they consisted of princes, great lords, bishops and abbots, who decided in them their disputes with one another, and with the king, and maintained by these means a sort of national confederacy, or federal union of many states, politically united under one head. Such assemblies as these, under the second and third race, were the original institutions, from whence the parliaments of France have proceeded,‡ as many alterations as they have received, and as much as they are now changed: so that we may safely affirm

---

* Jamais nation n'honora tant la noblesse que celle la; car non seulement elle etoit exempte de toute sorte d'impots, et corvées, mais commandoit à baguette à ses inferieurs, sur lesquels elle avoit presque droit de servitude.

† Recherches de la France.

‡ Primitive origine et institution des parlemens. Ibid.

the parliaments of France never gave the people any share in the government of that kingdom; and whoever entertains a notion that the assemblies of the states did, or that these assemblies are of great antiquity,* or that they are the foundation of the liberty of the people of that country, will find himself, on due examination, grossly deceived.

These assemblies of the three estates, the nobility, clergy and commons, were invented first by Philip de Bel.† They were entirely unknown before the year 1301. The people had no right to any such assemblies; and when they were instituted, they were plainly designed for nothing less than the good of the people. Long after the establishment of the Capetian race, when taxes grew heavy, and were laid on and levied very arbitrarily, seditions and rebellions of an oppressed people, who had no other recourse, followed.‡ To prevent these, not only writs, or orders, were sent to the nobility and clergy, in the several sheriffwicks and bailywicks, but to the commons, to assemble and take into consideration how to redress grievances, and support the public expenses; and after such consideration had amongst themselves, to depute some persons of each order, or estate, to confer together in the place appointed for holding such general assemblies. "The commons were added to these assemblies," says Pasquier, "against the ancient order or practice of France, for no other reason than this, that the principal burthen, or charge, was to fall upon them."§ This was the true reason. Redress of grievances had no part in the schemes of that rapacious and profuse prince, who was the author of this institution; and he that considers the manner in which these assemblies were convened, the powers they were suffered to exercise, the subordination in which the commons particularly were kept, and the habitual, unavoidable influence under which they lay, will be easily convinced that such assemblies were fitted to do the jobs and sanctify the iniquity of the court, and nothing more. If at any time they make any good ordinances for the reformation of the state, "these ordinances are," says honest Pasquier, "like fine pieces of tapestry, hung up to make a show to posterity."‖ They have no other effect. "But the

* Primitive origine et institution des parlemens.

† L'assemblée des etats—fut une idée toute nouvelle de Philippe le Bel, et jusqu' alors entierement inusitée.—Boulainv. let. sur les anciens parl. de France.

‡ Pasqu. Rech.

§ Le roturier fut expres ajouté, contre l'ancien ordre de la France, à cette assemblée, &c.

‖ —— Ces sont belles tapisseries, qui servent seulement de parade à une posterité. Cependant l'impost que l'on accorde au roy est fort bien mis à effet.

imposition granted to the king hath its full effect." I conclude therefore, and upon sufficient grounds, that even since the establishment of these assemblies of the estates, in the beginning of the fourteenth century, the people of France have had no real share in the supreme power of the government, either collectively or representatively.

I might illustrate and prove what is here advanced; by the example of every assembly of the states of France, of which we have any good accounts, from the first in 1301 to the last that was held, as I remember, in 1614. But such a deduction would carry us too far. I shall content myself, therefore, with making two observations.

First, that these farces, for such these assemblies were, and such they were designed to be, owe their institution not only to one of the worst kings, but to one of the worst ministers that France ever saw, Enguerand de Marigny, who was called the coadjutor and the governor of the kingdom; the most insolent, the most avaricious, and the most prodigal man of his age. The great ability of this minister, on which his whole merit with a greedy master was raised, consisted in making his administration a system of violence and fraud, in order to plunder and enslave the people. When he durst not employ one, he turned himself to the other; and how grossly and impudently he managed even fraud, it may not be improper to take notice, in one instance, because we shall see the better, by this instance, what the nature and effect of these assemblies were, of which we speak, and what use the court made of them from their first institution. Enguerand de Marigny then meeting with great opposition to some taxes he had devised,* proposed the calling an assembly of the states, and hoped probably that he might gain the commons to favor the intention he had of extending these taxes to the nobility and clergy. A great scaffold was erected. The king, the lords, and the clergy, took their places on it. The commons attended at the foot of it. The minister made a most vehement declamation, to stir the passions of the audience, and made no scruple of insinuating in it, what neither he nor his master intended to perform, a promise of reimbursing, after the expedition proposed, what the people should give to the king. The king rose from his throne, and advanced to the extremity of the scaffold, that he might second by his looks the harangue of his treasurer, and see who those were that refused, or consented to the aid he demanded. The deputies of Paris promised to give a sufficient supply, or to follow the king in their persons to the war. The other deputies concurred in this general engagement,

* Boulainv. let. sur les anciens parl. de France.

and the assembly broke up, without any farther deliberation, or
any ordinance of the estates. But an ordinance of the king soon
followed; a general excise* was imposed by his authority, as if
it had been the grant of the estates to him; and his minister had
a number of harpies ready, whom he let loose to desolate the
kingdom, by levying this infamous tax, for the consideration of
some little advance made to the king. If you ask what were
the consequences of these proceedings, it will be sufficient to
mention two. The tax of a fifth on the revenues of the subject,
which is the proportion of our land tax of four shillings in the
pound, was continued, though the general excise had been imposed; and Enguerand de Marigny was hanged† in the succeeding reign for this amongst other crimes, though not by an assembly of the estates; for the estates had neither the opportunity nor
the power of resenting the greatest insult that could be offered
them, and the greatest injury that could be done to the nation.

The next observation I have to make is very short, but I think
very pertinent, and very important. This example shows us
clearly how true it is, that no instruments of tyranny can be
found so sure and effectual as the assembly of the estates of a
realm, when such an assembly is so constituted as to want the
power, which was from the first the case of the three estates in
France, and the same must happen when they are so managed
as to want the will, which became at last the case of the Cortes
in Spain, to secure the liberty and defend the property of the
people, against such kings as Philip le Bel, and such coadjutors
as Marigny. This prince and his minister had strained prerogative to the utmost, and had governed by it very tyrannically.
Whilst this expedient would do, they tried no other; but when
they apprehended it might fail them, they added a deputation of
the commons to the assembly of the estates; that, seeming to
create a new control on the crown, they might in reality give
greater scope and freer exercise to arbitrary will. The friends
of liberty, therefore, who live under limited monarchies, cannot
be too careful to preserve their constitution in vigor, nor too fearful lest their representatives should be so influenced as to neglect
their privileges, misapply their powers, and depart from their
integrity; since these friends of liberty see that the greatest masters of tyranny have judged the form, without the spirit, of a
free government more favorable to their schemes of oppression,
than all the authority that absolute monarchy can give; and that

---

* ———— Six deniers par livre de toutes les merchandises, victuailles,
boissons, and denrées, ———— Vendues dans le royaume.—Boulainv. let.
sur les anciens parl. de France.

† Mezerai, Daniel, &c.   Sous Lovis Hutin.

they made an innovation in the form of their government on this very motive, and for this very purpose.

I am, sir, &c.

LETTER XVI.

Sir:—I have dwelt long, perhaps too long, on the last head. I was induced to it, not only because the account I have given, according to the truth of history, is contrary to the national prejudices of many people on this subject, as I hinted before; but principally because the great point of strength and security, on which the freedom of our constitution rests, will appear in a fuller light, by being thus contrasted with the constitution of the French government. Both their ancestors and ours came out of Germany, and had probably much the same manners, the same customs, and the same forms of government. But as they proceeded differently in the conquests they made, so did they in the establishments that followed. The conquest of Britain was a work of time, and the Saxon monarchy was long in forming. The conquest of Gaul was carried on with greater rapidity, and the French monarchy was sooner formed. From hence some reasons might be drawn to account, amongst others, for that great difference between the constitutions of the two monarchies, which these two German nations founded, at no great distance of time, in Britain and in Gaul. But I shall not indulge myself in guessing at the reasons, or accidents, that determined the Franks to the division they made of their people, and to the form of government they established. Whatever reasons or accidents determined them, this is certain, that the distinction of lord and vassal became the general distinction of the whole nation; that the commons* amongst them were little better than slaves, whatever they had been in Germany; and that they were so inured to servitude under their kings, prelates and lords, that they looked on themselves at last, not justly, but unjustly, as men who had no right, no, not even a right by nature, to any share in the government of that community whereof they made so vastly the principal part.

In Britain another constitution was formed, and another spirit

---

* Le peuple, d'un autre coté, se fait justice, reconnoissant combien la condition naturelle le droit eloigner du concours du government, et dans se sentiment ne se fait entendre que par requete. Boulainv. let. sur les an. parl.

prevailed. The Saxons had a nobility* too, arising from personal valor, or wisdom, continued by blood, and sometimes conferred by the prince, however legally at first it matters not to
inquire, on such as held great offices about his person. All these
were the adelings, or nobles, a handful in comparison of the
frilingi, or free-born, who made the body of the Saxon people.
The freedom of this people was erected on two columns, that
have proved more durable than brass. They were parties to the
making, and to the executing all the general laws of the kingdom.
They shared the legislative power; were joined to the lords in
the administration of justice; and no magistrate, or officer, could
exercise jurisdiction, nor authority over them, no not ecclesiastical, without their consent and election. The comites ex plebe,
who were chosen for this last function, the administration of
justice, made one rank amongst the Saxon commonalty. The
custodes pagani, such as had a helmet, a coat of mail, and a
gilt sword, for their ordinary arms, whether they fought on foot,
or on horseback, made another rank; and the plain pagani, or
ceorles, made the lowest. But even these were totally distinct
from, and far superior to the lazzi, or slaves, nay to the free lazzi,
such as had been slaves, and were become free. The ceorles
were freemen to all intents and purposes, and in all the essentials
of liberty, as much as the Saxons of any superior rank, and were
capable of rising to any superior rank by merit, or by favor.

These are the sources, from which all the distinction of rank
and degree, that exist at this day, amongst us, have flowed. These
are the general principles of all our liberties. That this Saxon constitution hath varied in many particulars, and at several periods
of time, I am far from denying. That it did so, for instance, on
the entry of the Normans, though certainly not near so much as
many have been willing to believe, and to make others believe,
is allowed. Nay, let it be allowed, for argument's sake, and not
otherwise, that during the first confusion, and the subsequent
disorders which necessarily accompany and follow so great and
so violent a revolution, the scheme of the Saxon constitution
was broken, and the liberties of the people invaded, as well as
the crown usurped. Let us even agree that laws were made,
without the consent of the people; that officers and magistrates,
civil, military and ecclesiastical, were imposed without their
election; in one word, that these Norman kings, and the lords,
had mounted each other too high to be lords over freemen, and
that the government was entirely monarchical and aristocratical,
without any exercise of democratical power. Let all this be
granted, and the utmost that can be made of it, will amount to

* Nat. Bacon. Hist. and Pol. Dis.

this, that confusion and violence at the entry, and for some time after, under the government of the foreign race, introduced many illegal practices, and some foreign principles of policy, contrary to the spirit, and letter too, of the ancient constitution; and that these kings and the lords "abused their power over the freemen by extortion and oppression, as lords over tenants." But it will remain true, that neither kings nor lords, nor both together, "could prevail over them, or gain their consent to give their right, or the law, up to the king's beck. But still the law remained arbiter both of king and people, and the parliament supreme expounder and judge both of it and them."* Though the branches were lopped, and the tree lost its beauty for a time, yet the root remained untouched, was set in a good soil, and had taken strong hold in it; so that care and culture, and time were indeed required, and our ancestors were forced to water it, if I may use such an expression, with their blood; but with this care, and culture, and time, and blood, it shot up again with greater strength than ever, that we might sit quiet and happy under the shade of it; for if the same form was not exactly restored in every part, a tree of the same kind, and as beautiful, and as luxuriant as the former, grew up from the same root.

To bring our discourse to that point which is here immediately concerned, parliaments were never interrupted, nor the right of any estate taken away, however the exercise of it might be disturbed. Nay, they soon took the forms they still preserve, were constituted almost as they now are, and were entirely built on the same general principles, as well as directed to the same purposes.

When I say that they were constituted almost as they now are, I do not mean to enter into any of those minute questions, about which a man may employ much time and study, and have as little true and useful knowledge of our constitution as the most ignorant man alive. But I propose to make a short reflection or two on the property and power of the three estates that compose our parliament as they stood formerly, and as they now stand; because although our parliaments were composed of king, lords and commons in those days, as well as these, yet the difference of the weight which each of these estates hath cast into the scale of government, at different periods, does in effect make some difference in the constitution of parliaments: and by considering this difference, our thoughts will be led the better to judge of the true poise of our constitution, on maintaining which our all depends; since the nearer we keep to it, the safer our liberty is, and since every variation from it is dangerous to our

---

* Nat. Bacon, Summary Conclusion of the first part of Hist. and Pol. Dis.

liberty, in a degree proportionable to such variations.   Property then, and power by consequence, have changed hands, or rather have shifted much in the same hands since the Norman era. Kings, lords, and the church were in those days, and long after-wards, the great proprietors; and by the nature of tenures, as well as by the bulk of their estates, they held the commons in no small subjection, and seem to have governed without much regard to them, or to their concurrence, in many cases.   But the regard that was not paid them at first, the kings, the lords, and the church found it necessary to pay them in a short time; and that authority, that weight in the balance of power, which pro-perty did not give them, they soon acquired, or rather resumed by their numbers, and by the circumstances that followed.   By the circumstances that followed, I mean the great disorders in the state, and the civil wars, which the ambition of princes, of the nobility, and of the church too, created.   In all these con-flicts, some of the commons "holding for the king, who pro-mised liberty from the lords, and others siding with the lords, who promised them liberty from the king,"* they came off bet-ter in the end than their principals, and an example rarely to be parallelled was set; for general liberty was nursed by these means under the wings of particular ambition.   In later days, when the nation, harassed and spent by the long wars of York and Lan-caster, seemed glad to settle under any stable government; and in this temper gave many advantages to the cunning of Henry the Seventh, which the violence of his son improved; it is cer-tain that the commons suffered extremely from the avarice of one, the profusion of the other, and the high-strained prerogative of both.   But then their sufferings were temporary, and may be said to have ended with these reigns; whereas the sufferings of the nobility and the church were permanent and irretrievable. "The king and his council," says the author I quoted last, "under color of liveries and retainders, brought the whole kingdom to be of their livery."   It was so.   But still the com-mons lost nothing, and gained much.   They were more under subjection to the crown; but they were less under subjection to the lords and the church.   Not only the dependences on these were broken, but the lords and the church were made more dependent on the crown than the commons had been on them. The lords were obliged to attend the court at their own expense, and might alienate their estates to defray this expense.   A great part of the lands of the church were confiscated and parcelled out to those who could buy, at very cheap rates; and the increase of trade, which begun about this time to be very considerable,

---

* Nat. Bacon, Hist. and Pol. Dis. conclusion of the second part.

put the commons into a condition of being the buyers. Thus were the old foundations of property and power sapped on one side, and new foundations laid on the other. Some of the weight of the church continued in the scale of the lords, and some of it hath gone since into that of the commons. The parliamentary control of the crown did not become less, but it became more equally and more usefully placed. Democracy was so well poised with aristocracy, after this great change, that if they divided, they could not invade one another; and if they united they could not be invaded by the monarchy. Far different was the case in other countries, where the crown got the better of the lords, and baffled, at least in some degree, the monstrous attempts of ecclesiastical usurpation. In France, for instance, when the encroachments of the papal power were checked, the church compounded with the crown, and an alliance succeeded, of the monarchy with the hierarchy. But if the church was able to compound, the nobility was forced to submit in that kingdom: so that the authority and wealth of the church being fixed on the side of the crown, the whole strength and influence of the nobility being taken from them, and incorporated with the power of the crown, and the commons having nothing to do in that government but to pay taxes and carry arms, the kings of France are become absolute monarchs; and whatever liberty, or appearance of liberty there was in that constitution, it is totally destroyed.

When I say that parliaments were entirely built on the same general principles, as well as directed to the same purposes, as they still are, I shall be justified by the whole tenor of our history, and of our law. Let us consider this in a case the plainest imaginable, though it suffers so much debate through the effrontery of some men. Let us consider it relatively to that great principle, that parliaments ought to be independent of the crown, in all respects, except such as are settled by the law and custom of parliament, and concerning which there is no dispute. Now, this general principle hath not only been always the same, but it hath been always so declared, in the most authentic and solemn manner; and parliaments have not been more intent on any national concern whatever, than on maintaining this principle, and securing the effects of it. I say, parliaments have been constantly thus intent, and especially in the best times, during more than three centuries at least; for I would not go back too far, nor grope unnecessarily in the dark. What else did those laws mean, that were made in the time of the Lancaster kings, to regulate the elections, and to prevent the influence which Richard the Second had illegally and arbitrarily employed, and which there was room to fear that other princes might employ? What else do all those resolutions, all those declarations, all those remonstrances, all those acts of parliament mean, that have been made so often, and enforced so strongly, from time to time, and from those days to these, against the influence of the crown, either on the elections, or on the members of parliament? I should be ashamed to ask any more questions of this kind, or to descend into any detail, in order to prove what every clerk of a justice of peace, nay, almost every day-laborer, knows. But there is another question, which I must ask. If this be so, what do these men mean, who are employed, or rather, what does he mean who employs them, to plead in all places, and on all occasions, even the most solemn, in favor of this very influence, nay, of the very worst sort of it, of that influence which is created immediately by corruption; for to that their arguments reach by undeniable consequences? Reason is against him and them; since it is a plain absurdity to suppose a control on the crown, (and they have not yet ventured to suppose the contrary, that I know of,) and to establish, at the same time, a power, and even a right, in the crown, to render this control useless. Experience is against them; since the examples of other countries, and at some times (former times I mean) of our own, have proved, that a prince may govern according to his arbitrary will, or that of his more arbitrary minister, as absolutely, and much more securely with, than without the concurrence of a parliament. Authority, even the uniform authority of our whole legislature, is against them. The voice of our law gives them the lie. How then shall we account for this proceeding; this open and desperate attack upon our constitution, and therefore upon our liberty? Have these great men made any nice discovery, that escaped the blunt sagacity of our ancestors formerly, and is above the narrow conceptions of all other men, except themselves, at this time? Is it less fit than the wisdom of this nation hath judged it to be, for so many ages, that kings should govern under the constitutional control of two other estates? Or is it less fit that they should govern so for the time to come than it was for the time past? We shall hear, for aught I know, even in this age, that kings are God's vicegerents; that they are, next to him and his son Christ Jesus, supreme moderators and governors. We shall hear again, perhaps, of their hereditary, their divine, their indefeasible right, and the rest of that silly cant, which was invented to make the usurpations of prerogative go down the better. But will even this alter the case? Will this make it unworthy of them to submit to the full control of such a constitution as God himself approved, in the institution of the Jewish senate? Moses was undoubtedly God's vicegerent. He was, if ever man was

so, next and immediately under God, a supreme moderator and
governor. He was inspired,* and assisted in a supernatural manner; and yet he took the advice of his father-in-law Jethro, the
priest of Midian. He associated to himself in the government of
the commonwealth, or he bade the people take, as he says in
another place, or choose, " wise men and understanding, and
known among the tribes,"† that they might be associated to him.
He found himself unequal to the task of governing alone, and he
expostulated with God upon it. " I am not able to bear all this
people alone. Have I conceived all this people? Have I begot-
ten them? If thou deal thus with me, kill me, I pray thee, out
of hand."‡ Whether they, who deduce from hence the institution of sanhedrins, are in the right, or they who assign them a
more modern date, against the opinion of the Jewish doctors
themselves, whose authority our doctors receive implicitly enough
in some cases, and reject as arbitrarily in others, it matters not to
inquire. Let us leave the dispute to the partisans of Joseph Scaliger, and Petavius, of father Simon and Le Clerc. Thus much
is certain. A great sanhedrin subsisted at Jerusalem, even at the
coming of the Messiah, as well as inferior sanhedrins in several
parts of Palestine; which form of government bore some resemblance to our old Saxon constitution; and he who takes the trouble of looking into Mr. Selden,§ will find that the great sanhedrin
had as much authority, and exercised as much power, as ever
parliaments did, or wittenagemots could claim. That God approved a kind of parliamentary establishment, and a division of
the supreme power between his vicegerent Moses and the seventy
elders, to whom he gave some of the spirit that was on Moses,
the quotations I refer to from Holy Writ do sufficiently prove.
After this, it cannot be said, I think, to derogate from the majesty
of any prince, let us entertain as high notions of this majesty as
we please, that he is relieved from the burthen of governing
alone; that he is obliged to share the supreme power with the
nobility and commonalty of the realm; and that he is hindered
from destroying, either directly or indirectly, that independency
of those other estates, which can alone preserve this division of
the supreme power, really as well as apparently. But perhaps
these great and honest men have discovered a necessity of putting the members, or a majority of the members of parliament,
under the influence of the crown, in order to preserve this very
constitution. Let us see, therefore, what dangers this expedient
is fitted to prevent. Are we afraid that a house of commons,
unless restrained by places and pensions, should give up the con-

---

* Exod. xviii.　　　　　† Deut. i.　　　　　‡ Numb. xi.
§ Seld. de Synod. et Præf. Invid. vet. Ebræorum.

stitution to the lords, and establish an aristocracy? This fear would be ridiculous, surely; and he who should argue against such a supposition, would make himself so. Are we afraid that a house of commons, unless restrained in this manner, should usurp more power than belongs to them, and establish a kind of democratical tyranny? But they would have, in opposition to them, a power sufficient to defeat their designs; the united power of the crown, and of the house of lords. Formerly, indeed, they succeeded in an attempt of this kind; and the king and the lords may, at any time, throw too much power into their scale, and set the sense and spirit of the people on their side, as was done at that time. But this neither hath been, nor can be done, unless both king and lords conduct themselves so ill, that the mischiefs to be apprehended from their prevalency appear as great, or greater, than those which are to be apprehended from the prevalency of the commons. Let it be remembered too, that as the king and lords may give too much power and popularity to the commons, so the lords and commons may give too much power to the crown. The difference will lie only here; that the king and lords will never do the first designedly; whereas there is a possibility that the lords and commons may be induced, in some age less virtuous than the present, by places, pensions, and other gratifications, bestowed on a majority of those assemblies, to do the last designedly. What now remains to be urged in favor of this expedient? From danger are we to be protected by it? Shall we be told that parliament will not pursue the national interest, unless their members are bought into it by the crown? Something like this hath been advanced, I have heard; and nothing more impudent, nor more silly, could be advanced. A court that is truly in the interest of the nation will have, nay, must have a concurrence of parliament, as it would be easy, if it was needful, to show. Time and trouble, indeed, may be sometimes required to lead independent men, who judge for themselves, and comply because they are convinced; whereas neither one nor the other are wanting to determine such as hold to a court by a corrupt dependency on it: for they are soon disciplined, and ready to perform the whole exercise of parliamentary mercenaries at the beat of a drum. Some inconveniences may likewise arise, for that which I have just mentioned does not deserve the name, from the independency of parliaments. Ministers, for instance, may be called to account by the passion, by the prejudice, if you will, of such assemblies, oftener, perhaps, than they deserve to be; or their errors may be censured, or their faults be punished, in a greater degree, and with more rigor, not only than true political justice requires, which should always be tempered with mercy, but even than strict justice exacts. But as one of these is a fault, if it be a fault, on the best side, and as the other will certainly happen very seldom, it does not seem reasonable that a door should be opened to corruption and dependency in order to prevent them. Nay, farther, this vigilance and this severity of parliaments, which we here suppose, will not fail to have some very good effects, that are more than sufficient to balance the supposed ill effects. Among the rest, they may render the rash, who are in power, more cautious, and the bold more modest. They may render fools less fond of power, and awe even knaves into honesty. It were better, surely, that able and good men should now and then suffer, nay, the good man who suffered would be himself of this opinion, than that the adulation and servility of parliaments, which are the necessary consequences of corruption and dependency, should ever contribute to make the court become, in any future age, a sanctuary for pickpockets, and an hospital for changelings.

I am, sir, &c.

LETTER XVII.

Sir:—The great alteration we have spoken of, in property and power, brought our constitution, by slow degrees, and through many struggles and dangers, so near the most perfect idea of a free system of government, that nothing would be now wanting to complete it, if effectual means were found of securing the independency of parliament against corruption, as well as it is secured against prerogative. Our kings have lost little of the gaudy plumage of the crown. Some of their superfluous power, indeed, hath been bought, and more hath been wrested from them. Notwithstanding which, it is a very demonstrable truth, that the crown must sit lighter and more secure on the head of a wise prince, (and no constitution provides for, though every constitution should provide against, a weak prince,) since the great change of property and power in favor of the commons, than ever it did before. Our kings are no longer exposed, as some of the greatest of them have been, to the insults of turbulent, ambitious lords, or haughty prelates. It is no longer in the power of a few factious noblemen to draw armies into the field, and oblige their prince to fight for his crown, to fight to gain it, and to fight to keep it; as Edward the Fourth did, I think, in nine pitched battles. To make the prince uneasy, or insecure, as we are now constituted, the whole body of the people must be uneasy under his government. A popular king of Great Britain will be always not only easy and secure, but in effect absolute. He will be, what the British constitution alone can make any prince, the absolute monarch of a free people; and this popularity is so easily acquired, a king gains the public confidence and affection at so cheap a rate, that he must be poor indeed in all the kingly virtues, who does not purchase them, and establish true popularity upon them.

If the condition of our kings is mended in many respects, and made worse in none, that of the nation is mended in every respect, by the great improvements of our constitution; which are due principally to the change I have mentioned, as the advances we have made in trade, and in national wealth and power, are due principally to these improvements. It is by these, that the subjects of Great Britain enjoy hitherto such a freedom of their persons, and such a security of their property, as no other people can boast. Hence that great encouragement of industry; hence that broad and solid foundation of credit, which must always continue, unless the weight of taxes, and the oppression of tax-gatherers make it worth no man's while to be industrious any longer, and unless national credit be reduced, by length of time, and private management, to rest no longer on its natural and original foundation, but on the feeble props of yearly expedients, and daily tricks; by which a system, that ought to be the plainest and fairest imaginable, will become of course a dark, intricate, and wicked mystery of stockjobbing.

But the great advantage we are to insist upon here, which hath arisen to the whole nation from the alteration in the state of property and power, is this: that we have been brought by it to the true poise of a mixed government, constituted like ours on the three simple forms. The democratical power is no longer kept under the same dependencies; and if a house of commons should now fail to assert that independent share in the supreme legislative power, which the constitution assigns to this assembly, it could not proceed, as it might and sometimes did formerly, from the nature of tenures, and many other unavoidable restraints; it could proceed alone from the corruption of particular men, who threw themselves into a voluntary dependency. The democratical power of our constitution is not sufficient to overtop the monarchical and aristocratical; but it is sufficient to counterwork and balance any other power by its own strength, and without the fatal necessity of favoring the ambition of the crown against the lords, or that of the lords against the crown. Nay more, as our government is now constituted, the three estates have not only one common interest, which they always had; but they have, considered as estates, no separate, contradictory interest. Our constitution gives so much grandeur, so much authority and power to the crown, and our parliaments give so immense a revenue, that no prince hath any real interest to desire more, who looks on himself as the supreme magistrate of a free people; for if we suppose inordinate ambition, or avarice, to make part of his character, these passions are insatiable: but then for this very reason, because they are so, there ought to be no account held of them; and though a prince may measure his demands, a people, who are in their senses, will never measure their concessions by them.

The property of the commons is not only become far superior to that of the lords upon the whole, but in the detail there are few, very few, instances to be produced of greater shares of private property amongst the latter, than amongst the former; and as the property of the commons is greater, so it is equally free. There are no badges of servitude on one side; no pretence of any superiority, except those of title and rank, on the other. The peers are, in some points, I speak it with all the respect due to them, commoners with coronets on their coats of arms; and affecting to act as such, it is plain they desire very wisely to be taken for such, on many occasions. The interests of these two estates then, with regard to property, are the same; and their particular rights and privileges are now so well ascertained, and so distinguished, that as the proximity of their interests of one sort should always unite them, so the distance of those of another sort cannot easily make them clash. In short, these two orders, according to the present constitution, (and how different is it from that of Rome, or, in the last respect, even from that of Spain, not to mention that of France?) have no temptation, and scarce the means, of invading each other: so that they may the better, and the more effectually, employ their vigilance, and unite their efforts, whenever it shall be necessary, against the encroachments of the crown, from whose shackles they have both emancipated themselves, whether the attempts to impose these shackles again are carried on by prerogative, or by the more formidable enemy of liberty, corruption.

It hath been observed already, that although the crown hath the sole power of creating peers, yet the independency of the peerage on the crown is secured by this; that their rights and privileges cannot be taken from them, at the will of the crown. Could the crown unmake, as well as make peers, it would be a jest to talk of three estates, since there would be virtually, and in effect, but two; and therefore our constitution hath provided against it. But the commons of Great Britain can make, and at proper seasons, and in a proper manner, unmake their representatives; by which means, many inconveniences and mischiefs are avoided, and many wise and just ends obtained. The peers of the realm can, the commons cannot, assemble in their collective body, without exceeding those numbers, amongst whom the quiet, order, decency, and solemnity of a senate may be preserved. The peers therefore sit in parliament in their collective, the commons in their representative body. The peers have an inherent, the commons a delegated right. The peers are therefore accountable for their conduct, as all other men are, to God, to their own consciences, to the tribunal of public fame, and to no other. But the commons are accountable to another tribunal, as well as to these, to that of their constituents; before which they must frequently appear, according to the true intent of our constitution, to have a censure, or approbation, passed on their conduct, by the refusal, or grant of new powers to the particular members. Thus the collective body of the people of Great Britain delegate, but do not give up; trust, but do not alienate their right and their power, and cannot be undone by having beggary or slavery brought upon them, unless they co-operate to their own undoing, and in one word betray themselves.

We cannot therefore subscribe to those two sayings of my Lord Bacon, which are quoted to this effect; " That England can never be undone, unless by parliaments; and that there is nothing, which a parliament cannot do." Great Britain, according to our present constitution, cannot be undone by parliaments; for there is something which a parliament cannot do. A parliament cannot annul the constitution; and whilst that is preserved, though our condition may be bad, it cannot be irretrievably so. The legislative is a supreme, and may be called, in one sense, an absolute, but in none an arbitrary power. " It is limited to the public good of the society. It is a power, that hath no other end but preservation, and therefore can never have a right to destroy, enslave, or designedly to impoverish the subjects; for the obligations of the law of nature cease not in society,"* &c. If you therefore put so extravagant a case as to suppose the two houses of parliament concurring to make at once a formal cession of their own rights and privileges, and of those of the whole nation to the crown, and ask who hath the right, and the means, to resist the supreme legislative power? I answer, the whole nation hath the right; and a people who deserve to enjoy liberty, will find the means. An attempt of this kind would break the bargain between the king and the nation, between the representative and collective body of the people, and would dissolve the constitution. From hence it follows, that the nation which hath a

---

* Locke's Essay on Civil Government; c. ii, Of the Extent of the Legislative Power.

right to preserve this constitution, hath a right to resist an attempt, that leaves no other means of preserving it but those of resistance. From hence it follows, that if the constitution was actually dissolved, as it would be by such an attempt of the three estates, the people would return to their original, their natural right, the right of restoring the same constitution, or of making a new one.

No power on earth could claim any right of imposing a constitution upon them; and less than any that king, those lords, and those commons, who, having been intrusted to preserve, had destroyed the former. But to suppose a case more within the bounds of possibility, though one would be tempted to think it as little within those of probability, let us suppose our parliaments, in some future generation, to grow so corrupt, and the crown so rich, that a pecuniary influence constantly prevailing over the majority, they should assemble for little else than to establish grievances, instead of redressing them; to approve the measures of the court, without information; to engage their country in alliances, in treaties, in wars, without examination; and to give money without account, and almost without stint. The case would be deplorable. Our constitution itself would become our grievance, whilst this corruption prevailed; and if it prevailed long, our constitution could not last long; because this slow progress would lead to the destruction of it as surely as the more concise method of giving it up at once. But, in this case, the constitution would help itself, and effectually too, unless the whole mass of the people was tainted, and the electors were become no honester than the elected. Much time would be required to beggar and enslave the nation, in this manner. It could scarce be the work of one parliament, though parliaments should continue to be septennial. It could not be the work of a triennial parliament most certainly: and the people of Great Britain would have none to blame but themselves; because, as the constitution is a sure rule of action to those, whom they choose to act for them, so it is likewise a sure rule of judgment to them, in the choice of their trustees, and particularly of such as have represented them already. In short, nothing can destroy the constitution of Britain, but the people of Britain; and whenever the people of Britain become so degenerate and base, as to be induced by corruption, for they are no longer in danger of being awed by prerogative, to choose persons to represent them in parliament, whom they have found by experience to be under an influence, arising from private interest, dependents on a court, and the creatures of a minister; or others, who are unknown to the people, that elect them, and bring no recommendation but that which they carry in their purses; then may the enemies of our constitution boast that they have got the better of it, and that it is no

longer able to preserve itself, nor to defend liberty. Then will
that trite, proverbial speech be verified in our case, "that the
corruptions of the best things are the worst;" for then will that
very change in the state of property and power, which improved
our constitution so much, contribute to the destruction of it; and
we may even wish for those little tyrants, the great lords and the
great prelates again, to oppose the encroachments of the crown.
How preferable will subjection to those powerful landlords,
(whom the commonalty were accustomed to serve, and by
whom, if they suffered on one hand, they had considerable advantages on the other,) how preferable, indeed, will this subjection appear to them, when they shall see the whole nation oppressed by a few upstarts in power; often by the meanest, always
by the worst of their fellow-subjects; by men, who owe their
elevation and riches neither to merit nor birth, but to the favor
of weak princes, and to the spoils of their country, beggared by
their rapine.   Then will the fate of Rome be renewed, in some
sort, in Britain.   The grandeur of Rome was the work of many
centuries, the effect of much wisdom, and the price of much blood.
She maintained her grandeur, whilst she preserved her virtue;
but when luxury grew up to favor corruption, and corruption to
nourish luxury, then Rome grew venal; the election of her magistrates, the sentences of her judges, the decrees of her senate, all
was sold: for her liberty was sold when these were sold; and her
riches, her power, her glory could not long survive her liberty.
She, who had been the envy, as well as the mistress of nations,
fell to be an object of their scorn, or their pity.   They had seen
and felt that she governed other people by will, and her own by
law.   They beheld her governed herself by will; by the arbitrary
will of the worst of her own citizens, of the worst of both sexes,
of the worst of human kind; by Caligula, by Claudius, by Nero,
by Messalina, by Agrippina, by Poppæa, by Narcissus, by Ca-
listus, by Pallas; by princes that were stupid or mad; by women
that were abandoned to ambition and to lust; by ministers that
were emancipated slaves, parasites and panders, insolent and
rapacious.   In this miserable state, the few that retained some
sparks of the old Roman spirit, had double cause to mourn in
private; for it was not safe even to mourn in public.   They
mourned the loss of the liberty and grandeur of Rome; and they
mourned that both should be sacrificed to wretches whose crimes
would have been punished, and whose talents would scarce have
recommended them to the meanest offices, in the virtuous and
prosperous ages of the commonwealth.   Into such a state, the
difference of times and of other circumstances considered, at least,
into a state as miserable as this, will the people of Britain both
fall, and deserve to fall, if they suffer, under any pretence, or by

any hands, that constitution to be destroyed, which cannot be destroyed, unless they suffer it; unless they co-operate with the enemies of it, by renewing an exploded distinction of parties; by electing those to represent them, who are hired to betray them; or by submitting tamely, when the mask is taken off, or falls off, and the attempt to bring beggary and slavery is avowed, or can be no longer concealed. If ever this happens, the friends of liberty, should any such remain, will have one option still left; and they will rather choose, no doubt, to die the last of British freemen, than bear to live the first of British slaves.

I am, sir, &c.

LETTER XVIII.

SIR:—If we had proposed nothing more to ourselves, in writing this dissertation on parties, than the entertainment, such as it is, of your readers; and our own amusement, we should not have dwelt, perhaps, so much on the nature of the British constitution, nor have recurred so often to assert the necessary independency of parliaments on the crown. But we had another motive, which we are neither afraid nor ashamed to avow. This necessary independency of parliaments, in which the essence of our constitution, and by consequence of our liberty consists, seems to be in great, not to say in imminent danger of being lost. They who are alarmed at every thing that is said in favor of our constitution, and of British liberty, and who are prejudiced against every man who writes or speaks in defence of them, may take, or affect to take, and try to give offence at this expression. But we desire to be understood, as we have explained our meaning upon some former occasion. We understand our constitution to be in danger, not only when it is attacked, but as soon as a breach is made, by which it may be attacked; and we understand this danger to be greater, or less, in proportion to the breach that is made, and without any regard to the probability or improbability of an attack. This explanation of our meaning is the better founded, because the nation hath an undoubted right to preserve the constitution not only inviolate, but secure from violations. Should corruption prevail among the members, which we trust will never happen, as notoriously as it does in the elections of parliament, we all know how much the magnanimity of our present king would scorn to take so mean an advantage over the nation; how much, on the contrary, his heroical spirit would prompt him to maintain the liberty even of a degenerate people, who might deserve no longer the enjoyment of so invaluable a blessing, but who could never deserve to have it taken from them by a prince of that family, which was raised by them to the throne, for no other reason but to preserve it. All this we know; and the nation may have, no doubt, the same confidence in every future king of the same illustrious and royal house. But this will not alter the case; nor make that, which I call danger, cease to be such. Should angels and archangels come down from heaven to govern us, the same danger would exist until the springs, from whence it arises, were cut off; not because some angels and archangels have fallen, and from being the guardians, have become the tempters and tormentors of mankind, and others therefore may fall; but because, as private liberty cannot be deemed secure under a government wherein law, the proper and sole security of it, is dependent on will; so public liberty must be in danger whenever a free constitution, the proper and sole security of it, is dependent on will; and a free constitution, like ours, is dependent on will, whenever the will of one estate can direct the conduct of all three.

Having thus explained what I mean by danger, and taken away all color for cavil, it remains that I prove this danger to be real, and not the phantom of a crazy imagination, or a prejudiced mind. This shall be done, therefore, as shortly as I am able, and by an undeniable deduction of facts.

He who undertakes to govern a free people by corruption, and to lead them by a false interest, against their true interest, cannot boast the honor of the invention. The expedient is as old as the world, and he can pretend to no other honor than that of being a humble imitator of the devil. To corrupt our parliaments hath been often attempted, as well as to divide our people, in favor of prerogative, and in order to let the arbitrary will of our princes loose from the restraints of law. We observed this in speaking of the reign of Charles the Second: but the efforts then made were ineffectual. The frugal habits of the former age were not entirely lost in that; which, I presume, may be reckoned as one cause of the noble stands that were then made by our parliaments in opposition to the court. But not to ascribe more honor than is due perhaps to our fathers, the revenue of the crown was, at that time, so small (I speak comparatively, for in every other respect it was very ample) and the profusion of that prince on his pleasures was so great, that no minister of king Charles the Second could find sums sufficient to buy a parliament. He stood, therefore, on his prerogative, strained it as far as he durst, and made all the use of it he could. The revenue of the crown was greatly increased in the reign of

king James the Second, and was given most unwisely for life.
I say most unwisely; for as a prince who hath a heart and head
to govern well, cannot stand in need of such a grant; so a prince
who hath neither, does not deserve it; and therefore, whatever
the generosity of our countrymen to their princes may carry
them to do at any time, they might leave this undone at all
times, without any reflection on their prudence, or even their
generosity. The reign of king James was short; and during
this short reign he rested on that prerogative, which he knew
was a cheaper expedient than corruption, and which he vainly
flattered himself was enough confirmed to support the measures
he took, for subverting the religion, the laws, and the liberty of
Britain. Thus were men brought, by the conduct of these two
princes, to fix their eyes on prerogative, as the sole instrument
of tyranny, and to forget that corruption had been employed,
though unsuccessfully, by king Charles, and might have been
employed with greater force, and perhaps more success, by king
James. The cry of the nation was for a free parliament, and
no man seemed to doubt, in that ferment, but that a parliament
must be free, when the influence which the crown had usurped
in the precedent reigns over the elections, was removed, as it
was by the revolution. But this general inadvertency, as well
as the particular neglect of those who took the lead in national
affairs at that time, is the more surprising, because corruption
having been so lately employed, among other means, to render
parliaments dependent on the crown, the danger of corruption
was, by consequence, one of those dangers against which the
nation had a right to be secured, as well as a promise of being
so, according to the terms of the Prince of Orange's declaration.
Those persons especially, who had exclaimed so loudly against
placemen and pensioners, in the reign of king Charles, and who
complained, at this instant, so bitterly of the undue influence
that had been employed in small boroughs chiefly, to promote
the elections of the parliamnnt which sat in the reign of king
James, ought to have been attentive, one would think, to take
the glorious opportunity that was furnished them by a new settlement of the crown, and of the constitution, to secure the independency of parliaments effectually for the future. Machiavel
observes, and makes it the title of one of his discourses, that "a
free government, in order to maintain itself free, hath need,
every day, of some new provisions in favor of liberty." The
tru h of this observation, and the reasons that support it, are
obvious. But as every day may not furnish opportunities of
making some of those new and necessary provisions, no day that
does furnish the opportunity ought to be neglected. The Romans had been so liberal in bestowing the right of citizens on

strangers, that the power of their elections began to fall into such hands as the constitution had not intended to trust with them. Quintus Fabius saw the growing evil; and being censor, he took the opportunity; confined all these new electors into four tribes; put it out of their power to turn the elections, as they had done, whilst their numbers were divided among all the tribes; freed his country from this danger; restored the constitution, according to the true intent and meaning of it, and obtained, by universal suffrage, the title of Maximus. If a spirit like this had prevailed among us, at the time we speak of, something like this would have been done: and surely something like it ought to have been done: for the revolution was, in many instances, and it ought to have been so in all, one of those renewals of our constitution that we have often mentioned. If it had been such, with respect to the elections of members to serve in parliament, these elections might have been drawn back to the ancient principle on which they had been established; and the rule of property, which was followed anciently, and was perverted by innumerable changes that length of time produced, might have been restored; by which the communities to whom the right of electing was trusted, as well as the qualifications of the electors and the elected, might have been settled in proportion to the present state of things. Such a remedy might have wrought a radical cure of the evil that threatens our constitution; whereas, it is much to be apprehended, even from experience, that all others are merely palliative; and yet the palliative must be employed, no doubt, till the specific can be procured.

But nothing of this kind was done at the revolution. Pleased that the open attacks on our constitution were defeated and prevented, men entertained no thought of the secret attacks that might be carried on against the independency of parliaments; as if our dangers could be but of one kind, and could arise but from one family. Soon after the revolution, indeed, men of all sides, and of all denominations, (for it was not a party-cause, though it was endeavored to be made such,) began to perceive not only that nothing effectual had been done to hinder the undue influence of the crown in elections, and an over-balance of the creatures of the court in parliament, but that the means of exercising such an influence, at the will of the crown, were unawares and insensibly increased, and every day increasing. In a word, they began to see that the foundations were laid of giving as great power to the crown indirectly, as the prerogative, which they had formerly dreaded so much, could give directly, and of establishing universal corruption. The first hath happened, and we pray that the last never may.

The net revenue of the crown, at the abdication of king James, amounted to somewhat more than two millions, without any tax on land or malt, and without a multitude of grievous impositions and excises, that have been since heaped on the nation. It is plain, and it was so then, that this revenue might have been so increased, as to answer annually the great annual expenses, in which we engaged soon afterwards. In this case, the people would not have had a greater, nay nor so great a burden to bear, as they had in the course of the two wars that followed; and, at the end of these wars, they would have found themselves with little or no load upon them, instead of crouching under a debt of fifty millions. That this method was not taken, furnishes matter of very melancholy reflection to the present, and will do so to future generations. But these reflections are no part of my subject. How it came to pass that a method so practicable, and so eligible, was not taken, (whether this was owing to private interest, to party-cunning of different and opposite kinds, or to an unhappy refinement in politics, that contracting national debts, under a new establishment, was an effectual expedient to attach men to this establishment,) I shall not presume to say. All three might have their share, perhaps, in determining for another measure. At least it is a point, on which the men of that time have spoken with much prejudice, and little candor. But however that might be, certain it is that we began to borrow at high interest, to anticipate and mortgage, immediately after the revolution: and having once begun, there was no remedy; we were forced to proceed in the same manner, through the course of two mighty wars. Formerly, the whole expense of the state was borne by the crown; and when this expense grew, upon extraordinary occasions, too great for the revenue of the crown to bear, the people aided the crown, if they approved the occasions of the expense. These grants were properly aids, no more: for the revenue of the crown was engaged in the first place, and therefore it might seem reasonable that the crown should have the levying and management of the whole; of these aids, as well as of the standing revenue. But it happened in this case, as it does in many; the reason of the thing ceased, and the thing continued. A separate, private revenue, or a civil list, as we commonly call it, was assigned to the crown. From that time, the former order hath been reversed. Our kings, instead of contributing most, have contributed nothing to the public charge; and the people of Britain, instead of giving occasionally aids to the crown, have taken upon themselves the whole load of ordinary and extraordinary expenses, for which they annually provide. Notwithstanding this vast alteration in the state of the revenue, and the interest of the king and the people in the management of it, the same forms of granting aids to the crown, and of levying taxes, and

of managing the public treasure, have been continued: so that
the people stand obliged (for the crown, that is trusted with the
whole, is bound for nothing) to make good all deficiencies, though
they have no share in the management of the revenue.   Our
kings, since the establishment of the civil list, have not only a
private and separate estate, but receive a kind of rent-charge out
of the public estate, to maintain their honor and dignity, nothing
else: and whether the public estate thrive, or not, this rent-charge
must be made good to them; at least, as it hath been settled on
our present most gracious monarch, if the funds appropriated
produce the double of that immense revenue of eight hundred
thousand pounds a year, which hath been so liberally given him
for life, the whole is his, without account; but if they fail in any
degree to produce it, the entire national fund is engaged to make
up the difference.   But although our kings have thus no longer
any immediate interest in the public estate, they are trusted with
the entire management of it.   They are not only stewards for
the public, but they condescend to be such for all those private
persons, who are the creditors of the public, and have the additional trouble of managing about three millions a year, on this
head.

Now this new settlement, which appears absurd in speculation, how wise soever it may have been thought contrived for
practice, hath had this evident and inevitable consequence.   As
we have annually increased our funds, and our taxes, we have
annually increased the power of the crown, and these funds and
taxes being established and laid for perpetuity, or for terms
equivalent to perpetuity, in the sense here intended, this increase
of power must not only continue, but still increase, as long as
the system of economy subsists.   How this increase of power
arises from the increase of funds and taxes, and the influence of
the crown grows, in proportion to the burthen on the people,
heavier, hath been explained so much in the debates on a late
detestable occasion, that much less needs to be said on the subject here.   If we consider in the increase of taxes, nothing more
than the increase of officers first, by which a vast number of
new dependents on the crown are created in every part of the
kingdom; (dependents as numerous, and certainly more prevalent than all the tenants and wards of the crown were anciently;)
and secondly, the powers given to the treasury, and other inferior officers, on account of these taxes, which are at least as
great and as grievous, in this free government of ours, as any
that are exercised in the most arbitrary government, on the
same occasions; if we consider this alone, we shall find reason
sufficient to conclude, that although the power of prerogative
was more open, and more noisy in its operations, yet the power

thus acquired is more real, and may prove more dangerous for this very reason, because it is more covered, and more silent. That men began to see, very soon after the revolution, the danger arising from hence to our constitution, as I said above, is most certain. No less than seven acts were made, in king William's reign, to prevent undue influences on elections; and one of the acts, as I remember, for I have it not before me, is grounded on this fact, "that the officers of the excise had frequently, by threats and promises, prevailed on electors, and absolutely debarred them of the freedom of voting."* What hath been done, or attempted to be done, since that time, in the same view, and what hath been done, or attempted to be done, both in the reign of king William and since, to prevent an undue influence on the elected, as well as on the electors, I need not recapitulate. They are matters of fresh date, and enough known. Upon the whole, this change in the state and property of the public revenue hath made a change in our constitution, not yet, perhaps, attended to sufficiently, but such a one, however, as deserves our utmost attention, since it gives a power, unknown in former times, to one of the three estates; and since public liberty is not guarded against the dangers that may arise from this power, as it was, and as it is now more than ever, against the dangers that used to arise from the powers formerly possessed or claimed by the crown. Formerly, prerogative was kept in sight, and provisions were made against the effects and encroachments of it, as often as occasion required, and opportunity offered. They who called themselves friends to the government, in those days, opposed these provisions. They who were friends to the constitution, promoted them. That the same thing should happen again, in a similar case, we must expect. But as the friends of the constitution, in times past, were not deterred, tempted, nor wearied, whilst they defended it against dangers of one kind, and by their honest perseverance delivered it down, not only safe, but more improved, to posterity; let us flatter ourselves with this agreeable hope, that the friends of the constitution, at this time, and in all times to come, will be neither deterred, tempted, nor wearied in the same generous cause, in watching and guarding it against dangers of another kind; and that they will deliver it down, in like manner, to future generations. Sure I am there are reasons, and those of no small moment, why they should be more watchful, more upon their guard, more bold, and more incessant in their endeavors, if possible, even than the ancestors of British liberty were

* Tertio Gul. et Mar.

formerly; and the enumeration of some of these reasons is an article not to be omitted on this occasion.

I am, sir, &c.

LETTER XIX.

SIR:—As the means then of influencing by prerogative, and of governing by force, were considered to be increased formerly, upon every increase of power to the crown, so are the means of influencing by money, and of governing by corruption, to be considered as increased now, upon that increase of power which hath accrued to the crown by the new constitution of the revenue since the revolution.   Nay farther.   Not only the means of corrupting are increased, on the part of the crown, but the facility of employing these means with success is increased, on the part of the people, on the part of the electors, and of the elected. Nay, farther still.   These means and this facility are not only increased, but the power of the crown to corrupt, as I have hinted already, and the proneness of the people to be corrupted, must continue to increase on the same principles, unless a stop be put to the growing wealth and power of one, and the growing depravity of the other.   We are, to be sure, in no danger from any advantage his majesty will take of this situation; but if advantage be not taken in favor of our constitution, of the present most happy reign, of the mild and beneficent temper of our heroical monarch, of the generous principle, instilled by nature, and improved by philosophy, of his royal consort, it may be supposed, for we speak hypothetically all along, as the reader will please to remember, even where the precaution is not used; it may be supposed, I say, that pretended friends to the government, and real enemies to this constitution, no matter whether they are such by principle, or become such by their crimes, will get into superior power, in some future time, and under some weak or wicked prince: and whenever this happens, the subversion of our constitution, and of our liberty by consequence, will be the most easy enterprise imaginable; because nothing can be more easy than the creation of an anti-constitutional dependency of the two houses of parliament on the crown will be in that case; and because such a dependency of the two houses is as real a subversion of our constitution as an absolute abolishment of parliaments would be.

The first of those means of corruption, that have grown up, or been increased, since the revolution, which I shall mention, is the establishment of the civil list; not so much on account of the manner in which it was originally given, as on account of that in which it hath been since given, and of the vast augmentations that have been made to it; augmentations, that may be doubled or trebled, in times to come, upon the same motives, under the same and other pretences; in short, just as speciously as they have been made. The revenue of king James the Second, as it stood at his abdication, hath been mentioned; and it would not be hard to show, by indisputable computations, that they who apprehended he might be able to govern without parliaments, or to buy parliaments, if he wanted their assistance, had good reason for such apprehensions, notwithstanding the expense he was at, over and above all the ordinary charges of the government, in maintaining against law a great standing army of sixteen or eighteen thousand men. But to go back to the reign of king Charles the Second, whose revenue was much less. The patriots of that age, even when this revenue was computed at no more than one million two hundred thousand pounds a year, took great alarm at the pecuniary influence it might create, and looked upon it, and spoke of it, as a fund for corruption. Now, if this revenue could afford a fund for corruption, when, besides maintaining the honor and dignity of the crown, it was to defray all the other expenses of the state, and among the rest, those of a small army, and a great fleet; what would the same patriots think of a revenue of eight hundred thousand pounds, or a million a year, applicable to the particular expenses of the crown alone, and not one farthing of which sacred treasure was ever diverted to any national use? They would have the same just confidence, no doubt, as we have in his present majesty; but they would say as we do, that so immense a private, or separate revenue, may become hereafter an inexhaustible fund of corruption: and therefore that the independency of parliaments is, and must be in real danger, till some remedies, as effectual against the pecuniary influence, as have been found against the prerogative of the crown, are provided. They would show that a small sum, in aid of places and pensions, of fears and expectations, might serve for the ordinary charge of annual corruption; and that a small saving reserved every year might produce, at the end of seven, a fund sufficient for the extraordinary charge of septennial and national corruption.

But again. If we suppose the civil list to become an insufficient fund for these purposes, by the profusion of some future king, (and nothing less than the most extravagant profusion can make it so,) or if we suppose that some future king may join to so many ill qualities, as leave him no means of governing but by corruption, a sordid avarice, that renders him unable to open his coffers, even for this use; yet will a very little iniquitous cunning suffice to create funds for corruption, that may come in aid of the civil list.   It is natural for men to be less frugal, when others are to pay for their want of frugality.   Our kings, therefore, may become more apt to take, and our ministers to advise such engagements, as plunge the nation, at every turn, into vast expense, since the load which fell, in part at least, on the crown formerly, falls entire on the people now.   But besides this general reason to promote a want of frugality, there may arise particular reasons, of more positive and more pernicious effect.   A weak admintstration, for instance, may pretend public necessity, when private inability alone hath formed the conjuncture; and frequent and extravagant supplies may be asked and obtained, to do, or to undo, by the weight of money, what might have been attained, or prevented, by a little foresight, and by a prudent conduct.   A wicked administration may propose to impoverish the people, to render them as submissive and as abject as the subjects, the boors, or the slaves, in some foreign countries, and to beggar them out of their sturdiness.   But there is another view, that may be common to a weak and a wicked administration both.   In such an age as we suppose, public money will be easily granted, and public accounts rarely or incuriously inspected.   The ministers, therefore, though never so weak, may be impudent enough to ask, and able enough to get frequent supplies, on national pretences, for private purposes. The consequences of this are manifold; for, in general, the more money passes through their hands, the more opportunities they have of gain; and, in particular, they may share, if they please, in every bad bargain they make for the public; and the worse their bargain, the better their share will be.   Thus an immense subsidy given to some little prince, who deals in soldiers, or an immense arrear stated in favor of these little merchants of human flesh, may be so ordered as to steal enough from the public to replenish the royal coffers, to glut the ministers, to feed some of their hungry creatures, and to bribe a parliament besides. Several of these occasional jobs may be, and, no doubt, will be contrived, in such an age, and by such means as we here suppose, and may be justly reckoned as so many auxiliary funds, belonging to the great aggregate fund of corruption.   Let us, however, break off from discoursing of these, which may be more easily and more frequently contrived under the present, but might have been contrived under the former constitution of the revenue; and let us turn our discourse, to speak of that great source of corruption, which was opened soon after the revolution, which was unknown before it, and which hath spread, since it was opened, like the box of Pandora, innumerable evils over this unhappy country.

The increase and continuance of taxes acquire to the crown, by multiplying officers of the revenue, and by arming them with formidable powers against the rest of their fellow-subjects, a degree of power, the weight of which the inferior ranks of our people have long felt, and they most, who are most useful to the commonwealth, and which even the superior ranks may feel one time or other; for I presume it would not be difficult to show how a full exercise of the powers that are in being, with, or even without some little additions to them, for the improvement of the revenue, that stale pretence for oppression, might oblige the greatest lord of the land to bow as low to a commissioner of customs, or excise, or to some subaltern harpy, as any nobleman or gentleman in France can be obliged to bow to the intendant of his province. But the establishment of public funds, on the credit of these taxes, hath been productive of more and greater mischiefs than the taxes themselves, not only by increasing the means of corruption, and the power of the crown, but by the effect it hath had on the spirit of the nation, on our manners, and our morals. It is impossible to look back, without grief, on the necessary and unavoidable consequences of this establishment; or without indignation on that mystery of iniquity, to which this establishment gave occasion, which hath been raised upon it, and carried on, for almost half a century, by means of it. It is impossible to look forward, without horror, on the consequences that may still follow. The ordinary expenses of our government are defrayed, in great measure, by anticipations and mortgages. In times of peace, in days of prosperity, as we boast them to be, we contract new debts, and we create new funds.— What must we do in war, and in national distress? What will happen, when we have mortgaged and funded all we have to mortgage and to fund; when we have mortgaged to new creditors that sinking fund which was mortgaged to other creditors not yet paid off; when we have mortgaged all the product of our land, and even our land itself? Who can answer, that when we come to such extremities, or have them more nearly in prospect, ten millions of people will bear any longer to be hewers of wood, and drawers of water, to maintain the two hundredth part of that number at ease, and in plenty? Who can answer, that the whole body of the people will suffer themselves to be treated, in favor of a handful of men, (for they who monopolise the whole power, and may in time monopolise the whole property of the funds, are indeed but a handful,) who can answer, that the whole body of the people will suffer themselves to be

treated, in favor of such a handful, as the poor Indians are, in
favor of the Spaniards; to be parcelled out in lots, as it were;
and to be assigned, like these Indians to the Spanish planters, to
toil and starve for the proprietors of the several funds?   Who
can answer, that a scheme, which oppresses the farmer, ruins
the manufacturer, breaks the merchant, discourages industry, and
reduces fraud into system; which beggars so often the fair adventurer and innocent proprietor; which drains continually a
portion of our national wealth away to foreigners, and draws
most perniciously the rest of that immense property that was
diffused among thousands, into the pockets of a few; who can
answer, that such a scheme will be always endured?   But I have
run, before I was aware, from my subject, which requires no
more than that I should take notice of the establishment of the
public funds, as it furnishes new means of corruption on the part
of the crown, and new facilities to these means, on the part of
the people.

Now this, I suppose, hath need of no proof, and of little explanation; for, first, the whole art of stockjobbing, the whole
mystery of iniquity mentioned above, arises from this establishment, and is employed about the funds; and, secondly, the main
springs that turn, or may turn, the artificial wheel of credit, and
make the paper estates that are fastened to it, rise or fall, lurk
behind the veil of the treasury.   From hence it follows, that if
this office should be ever unrighteously administered, if there
should ever be at the head of it one of those veteran sharpers, who
hath learned by experience how to improve the folly, and aggravate the misfortunes of his fellow subjects, of the innocent, of
the poor, of the widow, and of the orphan, to his own, or any
other private advantage, it follows, I say, that he must have it
in his power, and there can be no doubt of his will, to employ
two methods of corruption, without any incumbrance to the
civil list.   Such a ministerial jobber may employ the opportunities of gaining on the funds, that he can frequently create, by a
thousand various artifices, (notwithstanding the excellent provisions that have been lately made against the infamous practice
of stockjobbing, by the wisdom of the legislature, and which we
promise ourselves will be still improved,) and he may apply the
gains that are thus made, to corruption, in aid of the civil list.
He may corrupt men with their own spoils, and bribe even
those whom he reduced by his clandestine practices to that
penury which could alone make them capable of being bribed;
or, when he hath to do with men of another character, (for no
rank alone will be sufficient to raise them, in such an age, above
the most direct and prostitute corruption,) he may bribe them by
a whisper, initiate them into his mystery to gain them, and then

secure them by a participation of the same fraud and the same profit.

Though this reasoning be hypothetical, yet the suppositions are not strained, nor unnatural; for as the meanest grubs on earth have raised themselves by stockjobbing to the rank and port of noblemen and gentlemen; so many noblemen and gentlemen debase themselves to their meanness, and acquire the same spirit, by following the same trade. That luxury which began to spread after the restoration of king Charles the Second, hath increased ever since; hath descended from the highest to the lowest ranks of our people, and hath become national. Now nothing can be more certain than this, that national luxury and national poverty may, in time, establish national prostitution. Besides this, it is to be considered, that the immense wealth of particular men is a circumstance which always attends national poverty, and is, in a great measure, the cause of it. We may apply already to our country thus much at least of that which Sallust makes Cato say of the state of Rome; and I wish we could apply no more.—"Habemus luxuriam, atque avaritiam; publicè egestatem, privatim opulentiam; luxury and avarice, public want and private wealth abound." Now, as public want, or general poverty, for in that sense I take it here, will lay numbers of men open to the attacks of corruption; so private wealth will have the same effect, especially where luxury prevails, on some of those who do not feel the public want; for there is imaginary as well as real poverty. He who thought himself rich before, may begin to think himself poor, when he compares his wealth, and the expense he is able to make, with those men whom he hath been used to esteem, and perhaps justly, far inferior to himself in all respects. He who would have been ashamed to participate in fraud, or to yield to corruption, may begin to think the fault venial, when he sees men who were far below him, rise above him by fraud and by corruption; when he sees them maintain themselves by these means in an elevation which they could not have acquired by the contrary virtues if they had had them. Thus may contraries unite in their effect, and poverty and wealth combine to facilitate the means and the progress of corruption. Thus may the great thieves of the nation do more, and less reparable, mischief, by the practices they introduce and the examples they set, than by the actual robberies they commit. "Plusque exemplo quàm peccato nocent," to use an expression of Tully, in one of his books of laws.

Much more might be said concerning the increase of power which the crown hath acquired, and must continue to acquire, according to the present constitution and management of the revenue. Much more might be said to show that the power of money, as the world is now constituted, is real power, and that all power without this is imaginary; that the prince who gets prerogative alone, gets a phantom; but that he who gets money, even without prerogative, gets something real, and will be as much stronger than his neighbors, and his people too, as he hath a greater command of money. In fine, a great deal more might be said to show how much corruption is a more deadly weapon than the highest prerogative, in the hands of men who are enemies to such a constitution of government as ours is. But I hasten to a conclusion.

If then a spirit of rapine and venality, of fraud and corruption, continue to diffuse themselves, not only luxury and avarice, but every kind of immorality will follow; and the whole may be improved by such ways as have been sketched out, and by others, whenever the nation falls under a bad government, till the prince on the throne shall not be able to say, speaking of his whole people, even that which Philip the Second said, speaking of the corruption of his own court: " They all take money, except myself and Sapena." Britain will then be in that very condition in which, and in which alone, her constitution, and her liberty by consequence, may be destroyed; because the people may, in a state of universal corruption, and will in no other, either suffer others to betray them, or betray themselves. How near a progress we have made towards this state, I determine not. This I say; it is time for every man, who is desirous to preserve the British constitution, and to preserve it secure, to contribute all he can to prevent the ill effects of that new influence and power which have gained strength in every reign since the revolution; of those means of corruption that may be employed, one time or other, on the part of the crown, and of that proneness to corruption on the part of the people, that hath been long growing, and still grows. It may otherwise happen, that these causes remaining in force, their effects will become too strong to be checked, and will insure the ruin of the best constitution upon earth, whenever the men in power shall think their grandeur or their safety concerned in the ruin of it. We are not exposed at present, most certainly, to any such contingency; but the bare possibility of being so is a reason sufficient to awake and alarm every honest man. Hath not every such man, indeed, reason to be alarmed, when he hears the cause of corruption publicly pleaded, and when men are suffered, nay, paid by somebody or other, to plead this unrighteous cause, as if it was that of our most righteous government? Had we lived when the star-chamber tyrannised, and many other extravagant powers were exercised, under the authority of the crown, we should have found fault as much as we dared, no doubt, and yet have waited patiently, perhaps, for some favorable opportunity of redressing the grievances. But when we heard these acts of power justified as legal and constitutional, and the prerogative, by virtue of which they were done, claimed as a right in the crown, we should have taken the alarm, I presume, as hot as our predecessors did. Thus, in the case now before us, corruption may have been practised in some degree, perhaps, at all times. But then it hath been always kept under by the shame and danger that attended both the corrupter and the corrupted. It hath been always complained of, never defended, and endeavors have been used, from time to time, with general applause, to prevent it. But according to the principles now avowed, these endeavors were unjust; they ought to be repented of; and the acts made in consequence of them ought to be repealed: for the constitutional independency of the crown cannot be supported, unless the crown have the right and the means of taking their independency from the other parts of the legislature, by keeping the members of those assemblies under a pecuniary influence. Let no man think that the absurdity and profligacy of these doctrines secure us against the effect of them. They may soon grow into vogue, and be reputed as sacred truths as any of those falsehoods that are established by the systems of policy and religion in many other countries. What can be too absurd, or too profligate, for an absurd and profligate, or for a superstitious people?

But if we should apprehend the effects of these doctrines as little as we esteem the doctors who preach them, yet still the alarm is given by them, and it would be stupidity, or somewhat much worse than stupidity, not to take it. We despise the drummers and trumpeters of an enemy's army; (for I resume the allusion that I applied in the first of these discourses;) but when we hear the noise of their drums and trumpets, we take the alarm, and conclude the enemy is near. The friends of our constitution, therefore, are in the right to join issue upon this point with the enemies of it, and to fix upon this principal and real distinction and difference, the present division of parties; since parties we must have; and since those which subsisted formerly are quite extinguished, notwithstanding all the wicked endeavors of some men, who can have no merit but party-merit, nor safety but in faction, to revive them. If there was merit, and surely there was great merit, in opposing the asserters of prerogative formerly, when it rose so high as to endanger our liberty, there is great merit in opposing the asserters of corruption now, and in exposing the means by which this expedient may be improved to the ruin of our constitution, and therefore of our liberty. Nay, the merit is greater in some respects, if corruption be in itself, in its own nature, and in the present circumstances of the nation, and dispositions of the people, more dangerous than prerogative ever was; and if the means of establishing a government of arbitrary will, by corruption, be more likely to prove effectual than those of doing it by prerogative ever were. That it should ever become harder to save our country from the effects of corruption, than it was to defeat the efforts of prerogative, God forbid. On the whole matter, a dissertation upon parties could not wind itself up more properly, we think, than by showing that the British constitution of government deserves, above all others, the constant attention, and care to maintain it, of the people who are so happy as to live under it; that it may be weakened for want of attention, which is a degree of danger; but that it cannot be destroyed, unless the peers and the commons, that is, the whole body of the people, unite to destroy it, which is a degree of madness, and such a monstrous iniquity, as nothing but confirmed and universal corruption can produce; that since the time, when all our dangers from prerogative ceased, new dangers to this constitution, more silent and less observed, are arisen; and, finally, that as nothing can be more ridiculous than to preserve the nominal division of whig and tory parties, which subsisted before the revolution, when the difference of principles, that could alone make the distinction real, exists no longer; so nothing can be more reasonable than to admit the nominal division of constitutionists and anti-constitutionists, or of a court and a country-party, at this time, when an avowed difference of principles makes this distinction real. That this distinction is real cannot be denied, as long as there are men amongst us, who argue for, and who promote even a corrupt dependency of the members of the two houses of parliament on the crown; and others who maintain that such a dependency of the members takes away the constitutional independency of the two houses, and that this independency lost, our constitution is a dead letter, and we shall be only in a worse condition by preserving the forms of it.

To reduce therefore our present parties to this single division, our present disputes to this single contest, and to fix our principal attention on this object of danger, too long and too much neglected, hath been and is the sole design of these discourses. The design may have been insufficiently executed, but it is honest; but it is of the last importance; and whatever the enemies of our constitution, who call themselves the friends of the government, may say, to amuse and impose on the weak, ignorant, and trifling part of mankind, the importance of it will be felt every day, and every hour, more and more, till it be felt by every man in Britain. Let us hope, and endeavor by all possible means, that it may not be felt too late; and to encourage the constitutionists, or country party, in this attempt, let us consider from whom an opposition to it is to be expected.—Shall it be expected then from those, who have passed under the denomination of tories? Certainly not. They feel as much as any men in Britain, the preference that ought to be given to that system of government which was established by the revolution, and in which they took so great a share, and show themselves as ready to render that great work, which was left and still continues imperfect, complete.—Shall this opposition be expected from the dissenters? It cannot be. Shall they, who pretend to greater purity than others, become the advocates of corruption? Shall they contribute their endeavors to undermine the best constitution of government they can hope to enjoy, unless they hope to rise on the ruins of it, and to form another on their own model? As religious sects, they deserve indulgence, and they have it; but they are too wise not to see that, as a faction in the state, they would deserve none.—In fine, shall this opposition be expected from those who have been called whigs? That too is impossible. Their predecessors asserted the independency of parliaments, and struggled hard against corruption, in former reigns. When the rest of mankind embrace the same principles, and pursue the same ends, shall they renounce one, and run counter to the other? Shall they own themselves against one method of destroying our constitution, but for another? Against making kings independent on parliaments by prerogative, but for making parliaments dependent on kings by corruption? Shall they give the enemies of the revolution a plausible pretence to say that nothing more was meant by them at least, than a change of government, in which they hoped to find their particular and party account? This would be to cast black and odious colors on the revolution, indeed; more black, and more odious than any that it was in the power of a vain, forward, turbulent preacher to cast, by his frothy declamations.* But the whigs are so far from opposing the endeavors to preserve our constitution, that they co-operate to promote the success of them; and that, however personal prejudices, personal partialities, and old habits, that are daily wearing off, may be still entertained by some amongst them, all the independent men, who pass under that name, unite in the common cause of liberty and their country.—It remains, therefore, that no national party can be formed in opposition to those, who endeavor to secure the independency of parliaments against the new influence of the crown, and against corruption; nor any strength be exerted, except that of a faction, composed of the refuse of all parties, gleaned up by one who hath none for him.—I would willingly carry this

---

* Doctor Sacheverel.

farther; and, in doing so, I shall not advance a paradox, unless it be supposed, which I think would be a greater paradox, that a man may have abilities to destroy the constitution, and yet not sense enough to see his remote, as well as immediate, his family, as well as personal interest. I say, then, that if a design of raising the power of the crown above any pitch of prerogative, and of reducing parliaments to an absolute dependency, as well as a faction to support this design, be formed; the very man who forms such a design, and such a faction, must be infatuated, if he can wish very sincerely his own success. His first design, we are sure, will be that of raising a great family, and heaping upon it riches and honors. Shall his second design be that of rendering these riches and honors precarious and insecure, and of entailing servitude on his own race; for it will be impossible to exempt them from the common calamity? Nothing but despair, that is fear void of hope, arising from a consciousness of guilt, can drive any man into such a design. But, in this case, there will be fear opposed to fear, and one of these fears may be allayed by hope. The fear of being called to a severe account may be mitigated by the hope of escaping. Where is the insolent, rapacious, odious minister, that may not entertain some hope, as well as fear, when he sets before his eyes the examples of those who have gone before him? Pallas was the favorite of Agrippina. He governed like the master of the empire, and supported her pride and ambition by his counsels and services, as he had been raised to power and was maintained in it by her credit, whilst her credit lasted. Nero dismissed him; and seeing him go from court with a crowd at his heels, said pleasantly enough, as if it had been spoken of a dictator, that he went to abdicate.* But Pallas carried off the spoils of the empire with him; all scores were quitted between him and the public; and, according to the bargain he had made, he was called to no account. Many such examples might be cited to comfort with hope the most guilty minister, who is wise, if not honest enough, to stop in the career of iniquity, before the measure of it be entirely filled, pressed down, and running over. But if one of those bubbles of fortune, who thinks he always shall escape, because he always hath escaped, not content to wound a free constitution of government, should resolve to make it expire under his administration; the condition of such an one, however

---

* Nero infensius iis, quibus superbia muliebris innitebatur, demovet Pallantem curà rerum, quis à Claudio impositus, velut arbitrum regni agebat; ferebaturque, digrediente eo, magnâ prosequentium multitudine, non absurdè dixisse, ire Pallantem ut ejuraret. Sane pepigerat Pallas, ne cujus facti in præteritum interrogaretur, paresque rationes cum republicâ haberet. Tacit. An. L. 13.

he may flatter himself, or be flattered by others, must be ten
times more wretched and forlorn than the worst of those to
which his cruelty hath reduced multitudes—For what?—If he
succeeds in his sacrilegious designs, (they are of as deep a dye,
at least.)   He may hope for impunity, perhaps, to his gray hairs,
and be suffered to languish through the infirmities of old age,
with an inward remorse more pungent than any of them; but
he is sure to entail servitude on his whole race, and indelible
infamy on his memory.   If he fails, he misses of that impunity,
to which he sacrificed his country; he draws triple vengeance on
his own head; and exposes his innocent family to a thousand
misfortunes, of which it will not be the least, whether he succeeds or fails, that they descended from him.—But whatever
ministers may govern, whatever factions may arise, let the
friends of liberty lay aside the groundless distinctions, which
are employed to amuse and betray them; let them continue to
coalite; let them hold fast their integrity, and support with spirit
and perseverance the cause of their country, and they will confirm the good, reclaim the bad, vanquish the incorrigible, and
make the British constitution triumph, even over corruption.

I have now gone through the task I imposed on myself, and
shall only add these few words.   There was an engagement taken,
in the beginning of these discourses not to flatter.   I have kept
this engagement, and have spoken with great freedom; but I
hope with the justice and moderation, and decency that I intended, of persons and of things.   This freedom entitles me to
expect that no parallels, no innuendos should be supposed to
carry my sense farther than I have expressed it.   The reasonable part of mankind will not disappoint so reasonable an expectation.   But there are a set of creatures, who have no mercy on
paper, to use an expression of Juvenal,* and who are ready to
answer, even when they are absolute strangers to the subject.
Unable to follow a thread of fact and argument, they play with
words, and turn and wrest particular passages.   They have
done mine that honor, as I am told, and have once or twice
seen.   They may do the same again, whenever they please,
secure from any reply, unless they have sense enough, or their
patron for them, to take for a reply the story I am going to tell
you, and which you may find related a little differently in one
of the Spectators.   The story is this.

A certain pragmatical fellow, in a certain village, took it into
his head to write the names of the 'squire, of all his family, of
the principal parish officers, and of some of the notable members

* ——stulta est clementia——
——perituræ parcere chartæ.

of the vestry, in the margin of the whole duty of man, over against every sin, which he found mentioned in that most excellent treatise. The clamor was great, and all the neighborhood was in an uproar. At last, the minister was called in, upon this great emergency; a pious and prudent divine, and the same, for ought I know, who was a member of the Spectator's club. He heard them with patience; with so much, that he brought them to talk one after the other. When he had heard them, he pronounced that they were all in the wrong; that the book was written against sins of all kinds, whoever should be guilty of them; but that the innocent would give occasion to unjust suspicions by all this clamor, and that the guilty would convict themselves. They took his advice. The whole duty of man hath been read ever since, with much edification, by all the parishioners. The innocent have been most certainly confirmed in virtue, and we hope the guilty have been reformed from vice.

I am, sir, &c.

LETTERS

ON THE

STUDY AND USE OF HISTORY.

LETTER I.

Chantelou in Touraine, Nov. 6, 1735.

MY LORD:—I have considered formerly, with a good deal of attention, the subject on which you command me to communicate my thoughts to you: and I practised in those days, as much as business and pleasure allowed me time to do, the rules that seemed to me necessary to be observed in the study of history. They were very different from those which writers on the same subject have recommended, and which are commonly practised. But I confess to your lordship, that this neither gave me then, nor has given me since, any distrust of them. I do not affect singularity. On the contrary, I think that a due deference is to be paid to received opinions, and that a due compliance with received customs is to be held; though both the one and the other should be, what they often are, absurd or ridiculous. But this servitude is outward only, and abridges in no sort the liberty of private judgment. The obligations of submitting to it likewise, even outwardly, extend no further than to those opinions and customs which cannot be opposed, or from which we cannot deviate without doing hurt, or giving offence to society. In all these cases our speculations ought to be free: in all other cases, our practice may be so. Without any regard, therefore, to the opinion and practice even of the learned world, I am very willing to tell you mine. But, as it is hard to recover a thread of thought long ago laid aside, and impossible to prove some things, and explain others, without the assistance of many books which I have not here, your lordship must be content with such an imperfect sketch, as I am able to send you at present in this letter. The motives that carry men to the study of history are different. Some intend, if such as they may be said to study, nothing more than amusement, and read the life of Aristides or Phocion, of Epaminondas or Scipio, Alexander or Cæsar, just as they play a game at cards, or as they would read the story of the seven champions.

Others there are, whose motive to this study is nothing better, and who have the further disadvantage of becoming a nuisance very often to society, in proportion to the progress they make. The former do not improve their reading to any good purpose; the latter pervert it to a very bad one, and grow in impertinence as they increase in learning. I think I have known most of the first kind in England, and most of the last in France. The persons I mean are those who read to talk, to shine in conversation, and to impose in company; who having few ideas to vend of their own growth, store their minds with crude unruminated facts and sentences; and hope to supply, by bare memory, the want of imagination and judgment.

But these are in the two lowest forms. The next I shall mention are in one a little higher; in the form of those who grow neither wiser nor better by study themselves, but who enable others to study with greater ease, and to purposes more useful; who make fair copies of foul manuscripts, give the signification of hard words, and take a great deal of other grammatical pains. The obligation to these men would be great indeed, if they were in general able to do any thing better, and submitted to this drudgery for the sake of the public: as some of them, it must be owned with gratitude, have done, but not later, I think, than about the time of the resurrection of letters. When works of importance are pressing, generals themselves may take up the pick-axe and the spade; but in the ordinary course of things, when that pressing necessity is over, such tools are left in the hands destined to use them—the hands of common soldiers and peasants. I approve, therefore, very much the devotion of a studious man at Christ-church, who was overheard in his oratory entering into a detail with God, as devout persons are apt to do, and, amongst other particular thanksgivings, acknowledging the divine goodness in furnishing the world with makers of dictionaries! These men court fame, as well as their betters, by such means as God has given them to acquire it: and Littleton exerted all the genius he had, when he made a dictionary, though Stephens did not. They deserve encouragement, however, while they continue to compile, and neither affect wit, nor presume to reason.

There is a fourth class, of much less use than these, but of much greater name. Men of the first rank in learning, and to whom the whole tribe of scholars bow with reverence.   A man must be as indifferent as I am to common censure or approbation, to avow a thorough contempt for the whole business of these learned lives; for all the researches into antiquity, for all the systems of chronology and history, that we owe to the immense labors of a Scaliger, a Bochart, a Petavius, an Usher, and even a Marsham.   The same materials are common to them all; but these materials are few, and there is a moral impossibility that they should ever have more.   They have combined these into every form that can be given to them: they have supposed, they have guessed, they have joined disjointed passages of different authors, and broken traditions of uncertain originals, of various people, and of centuries remote from one another as well as from ours.   In short, that they might leave no liberty untaken, even a wild fantastical similitude of sounds has served to prop up a system.   As the materials they have are few, so are the very best, and such as pass for authentic, extremely precarious; as some of these learned persons themselves confess.

Julius Africanus, Eusebius, and George the monk, opened the principal sources of all this science; but they corrupted the waters.   Their point of view was to make profane history and chronology agree with sacred; though the latter chronology is very far from being established with the clearness and certainty necessary to make it a rule.   For this purpose, the ancient monuments, that these writers conveyed to posterity, were digested by them according to the system they were to maintain: and none of these monuments were delivered down in their original form, and genuine purity.   The Dynasties of Manetho, for instance, are broken to pieces by Eusebius, and such fragments of them as suited his design, are stuck into his work.   We have, we know, no more of them.   The Codex Alexandrinus we owe to George the monk.   We have no other authority for it; and one cannot see without amazement such a man as Sir John Marsham undervaluing this authority in one page, and building his system upon it in the next.   He seems even by the lightness of his expressions, if I remember well, for it is long since I looked into his canon, not to be much concerned what foundation his system had, so he showed his skill in forming one, and in reducing the immense antiquity of the Egyptians within the limits of the Hebraic calculation.   In short, my lord, all these systems are so many enchanted castles; they appear to be something, they are nothing but appearances: like them too, dissolve the charm, and they vanish from the sight.   To dissolve the charm, we must begin at the beginning of them: the expression may be odd, but it is significant.   We must examine scrupulously and indifferently the foundations on which they lean: and when we find these either faintly probable, or grossly improbable, it would be foolish to expect any thing better in the superstructure. This science is one of those that are "a limine salutandæ." To do thus much may be necessary, that grave authority may not impose on our ignorance: to do more, would be to assist this very authority in imposing false science upon us. I had rather take the Darius whom Alexander conquered, for the son of Hystaspes, and make as many anachronisms as a Jewish chronologer, than sacrifice half my life to collect all the learned lumber that fills the head of an antiquary.

LETTER II.

CONCERNING THE TRUE USE AND ADVANTAGES OF THE STUDY OF HISTORY.

LET me say something of history, in general, before I descend into the consideration of particular parts of it, or of the various methods of study, or of the different views of those that apply themselves to it, as I had begun to do in my former letter.

The love of history seems inseparable from human nature, because it seems inseparable from self-love. The same principle in this instance carries us forward and backward, to future and to past ages. We imagine that the things, which affect us, must affect posterity: this sentiment runs through mankind, from Cæsar down to the parish-clerk in Pope's Miscellany. We are fond of preserving, as far as it is in our frail power, the memory of our own adventures, of those of our own time, and of those that preceded it. Rude heaps of stones have been raised, and ruder hymns have been composed, for this purpose, by nations who had not yet the use of arts and letters. To go no farther back, the triumphs of Odin were celebrated in runic songs, and the feats of our British ancestors were recorded in those of their bards. The savages of America have the same custom at this day: and long historical ballads of their huntings and their wars are sung at all their festivals. There is no need of saying how this passion grows, among civilised nations, in proportion to the means of gratifying it: but let us observe that the same principle of nature directs us as strongly, and more generally as well as more early, to indulge our own curiosity, instead of preparing to gratify that of others. The child hearkens with delight to the tales of his nurse: he learns to read, and he devours with eager-

ness fabulous legends and novels: in riper years he applies himself to history, or to that which he takes for history, to authorised
romance: and, even in age, the desire of knowing what has
happened to other men, yields to the desire alone of relating
what has happened to ourselves. Thus history, true or false,
speaks to our passions always. What pity is it, my lord, that
even the best should speak to our understandings so seldom?
That it does so, we have none to blame but ourselves. Nature
has done her part. She has opened this study to every man
who can read and think: and what she has made the most
agreeable, reason can make the most useful, application of our
minds. But if we consult our reason, we shall be far from following the examples of our fellow-creatures, in this as in most
other cases, who are so proud of being rational. We shall
neither read to soothe our indolence, nor to gratify our vanity:
as little shall we content ourselves to drudge like grammarians
and critics, that others may be able to study with greater ease
and profit, like philosophers and statesmen; as little shall we
affect the slender merit of becoming great scholars at the expense
of groping all our lives in the dark mazes of antiquity. All
these mistake the true drift of study, and the true use of history.
Nature gave us curiosity to excite the industry of our minds;
but she never intended it should be made the principal, much
less the sole object of their application. The true and proper
object of this application is a constant improvement in private
and in public virtue. An application to any study that tends
neither directly nor indirectly to make us better men and better
citizens, is at best but a specious and ingenious sort of idleness,
to use an expression of Tillotson: and the knowledge we acquire
by it is a creditable kind of ignorance, nothing more. This
creditable kind of ignorance is, in my opinion, the whole benefit
which the generality of men, even of the most learned, reap
from the study of history: and yet the study of history seems to
me, of all other, the most proper to train us up to private and
public virtue.

Your lordship may very well be ready by this time, and after
so much bold censure on my part, to ask me, what then is the
true use of history? in what respects it may serve to make us
better and wiser? and what method is to be pursued in the study
of it, for attaining these great ends? I will answer you by quoting
what I have read some where or other, in Dionysius Halicarn.
I think, that history is philosophy teaching by examples. We
need but to cast ours eyes on the world, and we shall see the
daily force of example: we need but to turn them inward, and
we shall soon discover why example has this force. " Pauci
prudentia," says Tacitus, "honesta ab deterioribus, utilia ab noxiis

discernunt: plures aliorum eventis docentur." Such is the imperfection of human understanding, such is the frail temper of
our minds, that abstract or general propositions, though ever so
true, appear obscure or doubtful to us very often, till they are
explained by examples; and that the wisest lessons in favor of
virtue go but a little way to convince the judgment, and determine the will, unless they are enforced by the same means; and
and we are obliged to apply to ourselves what we see happen to
other men. Instructions by precept have the further disadvantage of coming on the authority of others, and frequently require
a long deduction of reasoning. "Homines amplius oculis, quam
auribus, credunt: longum iter est per præcepta, breve et efficax
per exempla." The reason of this judgment, which I quote
from one of Seneca's epistles in confirmation of my own opinion,
rests, I think, on this; that when examples are pointed out to us,
there is a kind of appeal, with which we are flattered, made to
our senses, as well as our understandings. The instruction
comes then upon our own authority: we frame the precept after
our own experience, and yield to fact when we resist speculation.
But this is not the only advantage of instruction by example; for
example appeals not to our understanding alone, but to our passions likewise. Example assuages these, or animates them; sets
passion on the side of judgment, and makes the whole man of a
piece; which is more than the strongest reasoning and the clearest
demonstration can do: and thus forming habits by repetition,
example secures the observance of those precepts which example
insinuated. Is it not Pliny, my lord, who says, that the gentlest,
he should have added the most effectual, way of commanding, is
by example? "Mitius jubetur exemplo." The harshest orders are
softened by example, and tyranny itself becomes persuasive. What
pity it is that so few princes have learned this way of commanding? But again: the force of examples is not confined to those
alone, that pass immediately under our sight: the examples, that
memory suggests, have the same effect in their degree, and a
habit of recalling them will soon produce the habit of imitating
them. In the same epistle, from whence I cited a passage just
now, Seneca says that Cleanthes had never become so perfect a
copy of Zeno, if he had not passed his life with him; that Plato,
Aristotle, and the other philosophers of that school, profited more
by the example, than by the discourse of Socrates. [But here,
by the way, Seneca mistook; for Socrates died two years according to some, and four years according to others, before the birth
of Aristotle: and his mistake might come from the inaccuracy of
those who collected for him; as Erasmus observes, after Quin-
tilian, in his judgment on Seneca.] But be this, which was
scarce worth a parenthesis, as it will; he adds that Metrodorus,

Hermachus, and Polyænus, men of great note, were formed by living under the same roof with Epicurus, not by frequenting his school. These are instances of the force of immediate example. But your lordship knows that the citizens of Rome placed the images of their ancestors in the vestibules of their houses; so that, whenever they went in or out, these venerable bustoes met their eyes, and recalled the glorious actions of the dead, to fire the living, to excite them to imitate and even to emulate their great forefathers. The success answered the design. The virtue of one generation was transfused, by the magic of example, into several: and a spirit of heroism was maintained through many ages of that commonwealth. Now these are so many instances of the force of remote example; and from all these instances we may conclude, that examples of both kinds are necessary.

The school of example, my lord, is the world: and the masters of this school are history and experience. I am far from contending that the former is preferable to the latter. I think upon the whole otherwise: but this I say, that the former is absolutely necessary to prepare us for the latter, and to accompany us whilst we are under the discipline of the latter, that is, through the whole course of our lives. No doubt some few men may be quoted, to whom nature gave what art and industry can give to no man. But such examples will prove nothing against me, because I admit that the study of history, without experience, is insufficient, but assert, that experience itself is so without genius. Genius is preferable to the other two; but I would wish to find the three together: for how great soever a genius may be, and how much soever he may acquire new light and heat, as he proceeds in his rapid course, certain it is that he will never shine with the full lustre, nor shed the full influence he is capable of, unless to his own experience he adds the experience of other men and other ages. Genius, without the improvement, at least of experience, is what comets once were thought to be, a blazing meteor, irregular in his course, and dangerous in his approach; of no use to any system, and able to destroy any. Mere sons of earth, if they have experience without any knowledge of the history of the world, are but half scholars in the science of mankind. And if they are conversant in history without experience, they are worse than ignorant; they are pedants, always, incapable, sometimes meddling and presuming. The man, who has all three, is an honor to his country, and a public blessing: and such, I trust, your lordship will be in this century, as your great-grandfather* was in the last.

I have insisted a little the longer on this head, and have made

* Earl of Clarendon.

these distinctions the rather, because though I attribute a great
deal more than many will be ready to allow, to the study of
history, yet I would not willingly even seem to fall into the ridicule of ascribing it to such extravagant effects, as several have
done from Tully down to Casaubon, La Mothe le Vayer, and
other modern pedants. When Tully informs us, in the second
book of his Tusculan disputations, that the first Scipio Africanus
had always in his hands the works of Xenophon, he advances
nothing but what is probable and reasonable. To say nothing
of the retreat of the ten thousand, nor of other parts of Xenophon's writings; the images of virtue, represented in that admirable picture the Cyropædia, were proper to entertain a soul
that was fraught with virtue, and Cyrus was worthy to be imi-
tated by Scipio. So Selim emulated Cæsar, whose commentaries were translated for his use against the customs of the
Turks; so Cæsar emulated Alexander; and Alexander, Achilles.
There is nothing ridiculous here, except the use that is made of
this passage by those who quote it. But what the same Tully
says, in the fourth book of his academical disputations, concerning Lucullus, seems to me very extraordinary. "In Asiam
factus imperator venit; cum esset Roma profectus rei militaris
rudis;" [one would be ready to ascribe so sudden a change, and
so vast an improvement, to nothing less than knowledge infused
by inspiration, if we were not assured in the same place that
they were effected by very natural means, by such as it is in
every man's power to employ] "partim percontando a peritis,
partim in rebus gestis legendis." Lucullus, according to this
account, verified the reproach on the Roman nobility, which
Sallust puts into the mouth of Marius. But as I discover the
passion of Marius, and his prejudices to the patricians, in one
case; so I discover, methinks, the cunning of Tully, and his partiality to himself, in the other. Lucullus, after he had been
chosen consul, obtained by intrigue the government of Cilicia,
and so put himself into a situation of commanding the Roman
army against Mithridates: Tully had the same government afterwards, and though he had no Mithridates, nor any other enemy
of consequence, opposed to him; though all his military feats
consisted in surprising and pillaging a parcel of highlanders and
wild Cilicians; yet he assumed the airs of a conqueror, and described his actions in so pompous a style, that the account becomes burlesque. He laughs, indeed, in one of his letters to
Atticus, at his generalship; but if we turn to those he wrote to
Cœlius Rufus, and to Cato, upon this occasion, or to those
wherein he expresses to Atticus his resentment against Cato for
not proposing in his favor the honors usually decreed to conquerors, we may see how vanity turned his head, and how im-

pudently he insisted on obtaining a triumph. Is it any strain now to suppose, that he meant to insinuate, in the passage I have quoted about Lucullus, that the difference between him and the former governor of Cilicia, even in military merit, arose from the different conjuncture alone; and that Lucullus could not have done in Cilicia, at that time, more than he himself did? Cicero had read and questioned at least as much Lucullus, and would therefore have appeared as great a captain if he had had as great a prince as Mithridates to encounter. But the truth is that Lucullus was made a great captain by theory, or the study of history, alone, no more than Ferdinand of Spain and Alphonsus of Naples were cured of desperate distempers by reading Livy and Quintus Curtius: a silly tale, which Bodin, Amyot, and others have picked up and propagated. Lucullus had served in his youth against the Marsi, probably in other wars, and Sylla took early notice of him: he went into the east with this general and had a great share in his confidence. He commanded in several expeditions. It was he who restored the Colophonians to their liberty, and who punished the revolt of the people of Mytelene. Thus we see that Lucullus was formed by experience, as well as study, and by an experience gained in those very countries, where he gathered so many laurels afterwards in fighting against the same enemy. The late Duke of Marlborough never read Xenophon, most certainly, nor the relation perhaps of any modern wars; but he served in his youth under Monsieur de Turenne, and I have heard that he was taken notice of, in those early days, by that great man. He afterwards commanded in an expedition to Ireland, served a campaign or two, if I mistake not, under king William in Flanders: and, besides these occasions, had none of gaining experience in war, till he came to the head of our armies in one thousand seven hundred and two, and triumphed not over Asiatic troops, but over the veteran armies of France. The Roman had on his side genius and experience cultivated by study: the Briton had genius improved by experience, and no more. The first therefore is not an example of what study can do alone; but the latter is an example of what genius and experience can do without study. They can do so much, to be sure, when the first is given in a superior degree. But such examples are very rare; and when they happen it will be still true, that they would have had fewer blemishes, and would have come nearer to the perfection of private and public virtue, in all the arts of peace and achievments of war, if the views of such men had been enlarged, and their sentiments ennobled, by acquiring that cast of thought, and that temper of mind, which will grow up and become habitual in every man who applies himself early to the study of history, as

to the study of philosophy, with the intention of being wiser
and better, without the affectation of being more learned.

The temper of the mind is formed, and a certain turn given to
our ways of thinking; in a word, the seeds of that moral character which cannot wholly alter the natural character, but may
correct the evil and improve the good that is in it, or do the very
contrary, are sown betimes, and much sooner than is commonly
supposed. It is equally certain, that we shall gather or not
gather experience, be the better or the worse for this experience,
when we come into the world and mingle amongst mankind,
according to the temper of mind, and the turn of thought, that
we have acquired beforehand, and bring along with us. They
will tincture all our future acquisitions; so that the very same
experience which secures the judgment of one man, or excites
him to virtue, shall lead another into error, or plunge him into
vice. From hence it follows, that the study of history has in
this respect a double advantage. If experience alone can make
us perfect in our parts, experience cannot begin to teach them
till we are actually on the stage: whereas, by a previous application to this study, we con them over at least before we appear there: we are not quite unprepared; we learn our parts
sooner, and we learn them better.

Let me explain what I mean by an example. There is scarce
any folly or vice more epidemical among the sons of men, than
that ridiculous and hurtful vanity by which the people of each
country are apt to prefer themselves to those of every other; and
to make their own customs, and manners, and opinions, the
standards of right and wrong, of true and false. The Chinese
mandarins were strangely surprised, and almost incredulous,
when the Jesuits showed them how small a figure their empire
made in the general map of the world. The Samojedes wondered much at the Czar of Muscovy for not living among them:
and the Hottentot, who returned from Europe, stripped himself
naked as soon as he came home, put on his bracelets of guts and
garbage, and grew stinking and lousy as fast as he could. Now
nothing can contribute more to prevent us from being tainted
with this vanity, than to accustom ourselves early to contemplate the different nations of the earth, in that vast map which
history spreads before us, in their rise and their fall, in their barbarous and civilised states, in the likeness and unlikeness of them
all to one another, and of each to itself. By frequently renewing
this prospect to the mind, the Mexican with his cap and coat of
feathers, sacrificing a human victim to his god, will not appear
more savage to our eyes than the Spaniard with a hat on his
head, and a gonilla round his neck, sacrificing whole nations to
his ambition, his avarice, and even the wantonness of his cru-

elty. I might show, by a multitude of other examples, how history prepares us for experience, and guides us in it: and many of these would be both curious and important. I might likewise bring several other instances, wherein history serves to purge the mind of those national partialities and prejudices that we are apt to contract in our education, and that experience for the most part rather confirms than removes: because it is for the most part confined, like our education. But I apprehend growing too prolix, and shall therefore conclude this head by observing, that though an early and proper application to the study of history will contribute extremely to keep our minds free from a ridiculous partiality in favor of our own country, and a vicious prejudice against others; yet the same study will create in us a preference of affection to our own country. There is a story told of Abgarus. He brought several beasts taken in different places to Rome, they say, and let them loose before Augustus: every beast ran immediately to that part of the circus where a parcel of earth taken from his native soil had been laid. " Credat Judæus Apella." This tale might pass on Josephus; for in him, I believe, I read it: but surely the love of our country is a lesson of reason, not an institution of nature. Education and habit, obligation and interest, attach us to it, not instinct. It is however so necessary to be cultivated, and the prosperity of all societies, as well as the grandeur of some, depends upon it so much, that orators by their eloquence, and poets by their enthusiasm, have endeavored to work up this precept of morality into a principle of passion. But the examples which we find in history, improved by the lively descriptions, and the just applauses or censures of historians, will have a much better and more permanent effect than declamation or song, or the dry ethics of mere philosophy. In fine, to converse with historians is to keep good company: many of them were excellent men, and those who were not such, have taken care, however, to appear such in their writings. It must be, therefore, of great use to prepare ourselves by this conversation for that of the world; and to receive our first impressions, and to acquire our first habits, in a scene where images of virtue and vice are continually represented to us in the colors that belong properly to them, before we enter on another scene, where virtue and vice are too often confounded, and what belongs to one is ascribed to the other.

Besides the advantage of beginning our acquaintance with mankind sooner, and of bringing with us into the world, and the business of it, such a cast of thought and such a temper of mind, as will enable us to make a better use of our experience; there is this further advantage in the study of history, that the improvement we make by it extends to more objects, and is made at the expense of other men: whereas that improvement, which is the effect of our own experience, is confined to fewer objects, and is made at our own expense. To state the account feirly, therefore, between these two improvements, though the latter be the more valuable, yet allowance being made on one side for the much greater number of examples that history presents to us, and deduction being made on the other of the price we often pay for our experience, the value of the former will rise in proportion. " I have recorded these things," says Polybius, after giving an account of the defeat of Regulus, " that they who read these commentaries may be rendered better by them; for all men have two ways of improvement, one arising from their own experience, and one from the experience of others. Evidentior quidem illa est, quæ per propria ducit infortunia; at tutior illa, quæ per aliena." I use Casaubon's translation. Polybius goes on, and concludes, " that since the first of these ways exposes us to great labor and peril, whilst the second works the same good effect, and is attended by no evil circumstance, every one ought to take for granted that the study of history is the best school where he can learn how to conduct himself in all the situations of life." Regulus had seen at Rome many examples of magnanimity, of frugality, of the contempt of riches, and of other virtues; and these virtues he practised. But he had not learned, nor had opportunity of learning another lesson, which the examples recorded in history inculcate frequently, the lesson of moderation. An insatiable thirst of military fame, an unconfined ambition of extending their empire, an extravagant confidence in their own courage and force, an insolent contempt of their enemies, and an impetuous overbearing spirit with which they pursued all their enterprises, composed in his days the distinguishing character of a Roman. Whatever the senate and people resolved, to the members of that commonwealth appeared both practicable and just. Neither difficulties nor dangers could check them; and their sages had not yet discovered, that virtues in excess degenerate into vices. Notwithstanding the beautiful rant which Horace puts into his mouth, I make no doubt that Regulus learned at Carthage those lessons of moderation which he had not learned at Rome: but he learned them by experience, and the fruits of this experience came too late, and cost too dear; for they cost the total defeat of the Roman army, the prolongation of a calamitous war which might have been finished by a glorious peace, the loss of liberty to thousands of Roman citizens, and to Regulus himself the loss of life in the midst of torments, if we are entirely to credit what is perhaps exaggeration in the Roman authors.

There is another advantage, worthy our observation, that be-

longs to the study of history; and that I shall mention here, not
only because of the importance of it, but because it leads me
immediately to speak of the nature of the improvement we
ought to have in our view, and of the method in which it seems
to me that this improvement ought to be pursued: two particulars from which your lordship may think perhaps that I digress
too long.   The advantage I mean consists in this, that the examples which history presents to us, both of men and of events,
are generally complete: the whole example is before us, and
consequently the whole lesson, or sometimes the various lessons,
which philosophy proposes to teach us by this example.   For
first, as to men; we see them at their whole length in history,
and we see them generally there through a medium less partial
at least than that of experience: for I imagine that a whig or a
tory, whilst those parties subsisted, would have condemned in
Saturninus the spirit of faction which he applauded in his own
tribunes, and would have applauded in Drusus the spirit of
moderation which he despised in those of the contrary party, and
which he suspected and hated in those of his own party.   The
villain who has imposed on mankind by his power or cunning,
and whom experience could not unmask for a time, is unmasked
at length: and the honest man, who has been misunderstood or
defamed, is justified before his story ends.   Or if this does not
happen, if the villain dies with his mask on, in the midst of
applause, and honor, and wealth, and power, and if the honest
man dies under the same load of calumny and disgrace under
which he lived, driven perhaps into exile, and exposed to want;
yet we see historical justice executed, the name of one branded
with infamy, and that of the other celebrated with panegyric to
succeeding ages.   " Præcipuum munus annalium reor, ne virtu-
tes sileantur; utque pravis dictis factisque ex posteritate et infamia metus sit."   Thus, according to Tacitus, and according to
truth, from which his judgments seldom deviate, the principal
duty of history is to erect a tribunal, like that among the Egyptians, mentioned by Diodorus Siculus, where men and princes
themselves were tried, and condemned or acquitted, after their
deaths; where those who had not been punished for their crimes,
and those who had not been honored for their virtues, received
a just retribution.   The sentence is pronounced in one case, as it
was in the other, too late to correct or recompense; but it is pronounced in time to render these examples of general instruction
to mankind.   Thus Cicero, that I may quote one instance out of
thousands, and that I may do justice to the general character of
that great man, whose particular failing I have censured so
freely; Cicero, I say, was abandoned by Octavius, and massa-
cred by Antony.   But let any man read this fragment of Aure-

lius Fuscus, and choose which he would wish to have been, the orator, or the triumvir? "Quoad humanum genus incolume manserit, quamdiu usus literis, honor summæ eloquentiæ pretium erit, quamdiu rerum natura aut fortuna steterit, aut memoria duraverit, admirabile posteris vigebis ingenium, et uno proscriptus seculo, proscribes Antonium omnibus."

Thus again, as to events that stand recorded in history; we see them all, we see them as they followed one another, or as they produced one another, causes or effects, immediate or remote. We are cast back, as it were, into former ages: we live with the men who lived before us, and we inhabit countries that we never saw.. Place is enlarged, and time prolonged, in this manner; so that the man who applies himself early to the study of history, may acquire in a few years, and before he sets his foot abroad in the world, not only a more extended knowledge of mankind, but the experience of more centuries than any of the patriarchs saw. The events we are witnesses of, in the course of the longest life, appear to us very often original, unprepared, single, and unrelative, if I may use such an expression for want of a better in English; in French I would say isolés: they appear such very often, are called accidents, and looked on as the effects of chance; a word, by the way, which is in constant use, and has frequently no determinate meaning. We get over the present difficulty, we improve the momentary advantage, as well as we can, and we look no farther. Experience can carry us no farther; for experience can go a very little way back in discovering causes: and effects are not the objects of experience till they happen. From hence many errors in judgment, and by consequence in conduct, necessarily arise. And here too lies the difference we are speaking of between history and experience. The advantage on the side of the former is double. In ancient history, as we have said already, the examples are complete, which are incomplete in the course of experience. The beginning, the progression, and the end appear, not of particular reigns, much less of particular enterprises, or systems of policy alone, but of governments, of nations, of empires, and of all the various systems that have succeeded one another in the course of their duration. In modern history, the examples may be, and sometimes are, incomplete; but they have this advantage when they are so, that they serve to render complete the examples of our own time. Experience is doubly defective; we are born too late to see the beginning, and we die too soon to see the end of many things. History supplies both these defects. Modern history shows the causes, when experience presents the effects alone: and ancient history enables us to guess at the effects, when experience presents the causes alone. Let me explain my meaning by two examples of these kinds; one past, the other actually present.

When the revolution of one thousand six hundred and eighty-eight happened, few men then alive, I suppose, went farther in their search after the causes of it, than the extravagant attempt of king James against the religion and liberty of his people. His former conduct, and the passages of king Charles the Second's reign might rankle still at the hearts of some men, but could not be set to account among the causes of his deposition; since he had succeeded, notwithstanding them, peaceably to the throne: and the nation in general, even many of those who would have excluded him from it, were desirous, or at least willing, that he should continue in it.   Now this example, thus stated, affords, no doubt, much good instruction to the kings, and people of Britain.   But this instruction is not entire, because the example thus stated, and confined to the experience of that age, is imperfect.   King James's mal-administration rendered a revolution necessary and practicable; but his mal-administration, as well as all his preceding conduct, was caused by his bigot attachment to popery, and to the principles of arbitrary government, from which no warning could divert him.   His bigot attachment to these was caused by the exile of the royal family; this exile was caused by the usurpation of Cromwell: and Cromwell's usurpation was the effect of a former rebellion, begun not without reason on account of liberty, but without any valid pretence on account of religion.   During this exile, our princes caught the taint of popery and foreign politics.   We made them unfit to govern us, and after that were forced to recall them that they might rescue us out of anarchy.   It was necessary therefore, your lordship sees, at the revolution, and it is more so now, to go back in history, at least as far as I have mentioned, and perhaps farther, even to the beginning of king James the First's reign, to render this event a complete example, and to develope all the wise, honest, and salutary precepts, with which it is pregnant, both to king and subject.

The other example shall be taken from what has succeeded the revolution.   Few men at that time looked forward enough to foresee the necessary consequences of the new constitution of the revenue, that was soon afterwards formed; nor of the method of funding that immediately took place; which, absurd as they are, have continued ever since, till it is become scarce possible to alter them.   Few people, I say, foresaw how the creation of funds, and the multiplication of taxes, would increase yearly the power of the crown, and bring our liberties, by a natural and necessary progression, into more real, though less apparent danger, than they were in before the revolution. The excessive ill husbandry practised from the very beginning of king William's reign, and which laid the foundations of all we feel and all we fear, was not the effect of ignorance, mistake, or what we call chance, but of design and scheme in those who had the sway at that time. I am not so uncharitable, however, as to believe that they intended to bring upon their country all the mischiefs that we, who came after them, experience and apprehend. No, they saw the measures, they took singly, and unrelatively, or relatively alone to some immediate object. The notion of attaching men to the new government, by tempting them to embark their fortunes on the same bottom, was a reason of state to some: the notion of creating a new, that is, a moneyed interest, in opposition to the landed interest or as a balance to it, and of acquiring a superior influence in the city of London at least by the establishment of great corporations, was a reason of party to others: and I make no doubt that the opportunity of amassing immense estates by the management of funds, by trafficking in paper, and by all the arts of jobbing, was a reason of private interest to those who supported and improved this scheme of iniquity, if not to those who devised it. They looked no farther. Nay, we who came after them, and have long tasted the bitter fruits of the corruption they planted, were far from taking such an alarm at our distress and our danger, as they deserved; till the most remote and fatal effects of causes, laid by the last generation, was very near becoming an object of experience in this. Your lordship, I am sure, sees at once how much a due reflection on the passages of former times, as they stand recorded in the history of our own, and of other countries, would have deterred a free people from trusting the sole management of so great a revenue, and the sole nomination of those legions of officers employed in it, to their chief magistrate. There remained indeed no pretence for doing so, when once a salary was settled on the prince, and the public revenue was no longer in any sense his revenue, nor the public expense his expense. Give me leave to add, that it would have been, and would be still, more decent with regard to the prince, and less repugnant if not more conformable to the principles and practice too of our government, to take this power and influence from the prince, or to share it with him; than to exclude men from the privilege of representing their fellow-subjects who would choose them in parliament, purely because they are employed and trusted by the prince.

Your lordship sees, not only how much a due reflection upon the experience of other ages and countries would have pointed out national corruption, as the natural and necessary consequence of investing the crown with the management of so great a revenue; but also the loss of liberty, as the natural and necessary consequence of national corruption.

These two examples explain sufficiently what they are intended to explain.   It only remains therefore upon this head, to observe the difference between the two manners in which history supplies the defects of our own experience.   It shows us causes as in fact they were laid, with their immediate effects: and it enables us to guess at future events.   It can do no more, in the nature of things. My lord Bacon, in his second book of the Advancement of Learning, having in his mind, I suppose, what Philo and Josephus asserted of Moses, affirms divine history to have this prerogative, that the narration may be before the fact as well as after.   But since the ages of prophecy, as well as miracles, are past, we must content ourselves to guess at what will be, by what has been: we have no other means in our power, and history furnishes us with these.   How we are to improve, and apply these means, as well as how we are to acquire them, shall be deduced more particularly in another letter.

LETTER III.

I. AN OBJECTION AGAINST THE UTILITY OF HISTORY REMOVED. II. THE FALSE AND TRUE AIMS OF THOSE WHO STUDY IT.   III. OF THE HISTORY OF THE FIRST AGES, WITH REFLECTIONS ON THE STATE OF ANCIENT HISTORY PROFANE AND SACRED.

WERE these letters to fall into the hands of some ingenious persons who adorn the age we live in, your lordship's correspondent would be joked upon for his project of improving men in virtue and wisdom by the study of history.   The general characters of men, it would be said, are determined by their natural constitutions, as their particular actions are by immediate objects. Many very conversant in history would be cited, who have proved ill men, or bad politicians; and a long roll would be produced of others, who have arrived at a great pitch of private, and public virtue, without any assistance of this kind.   Something has been said already to anticipate this objection; but, since I have heard several persons affirm such propositions with great confidence, a loud laugh, or a silent sneer at the pedants who presumed to think otherwise; I will spend a few paragraphs, with your lordship's leave, to show that such affirmations, for to affirm amongst these fine men is to reason, either prove too much, or prove nothing.

If our general characters were determined absolutely, as they are certainly influenced, by our constitutions, and if our particular actions were so by immediate objects; all instruction by precept, as well as example, and all endeavors to form the moral character by education, would be unnecessary. Even the little care that is taken, and surely it is impossible to take less, in the training up our youth, would be too much. But the truth is widely different from this representation of it; for, what is vice, and what is virtue? I speak of them in a large and philosophical sense. The former is, I think, no more than the excess, abuse, and misapplication of appetites, desires, and passions, natural and innocent, nay useful and necessary. The latter consists in the moderation and government, in the use and application of these appetites, desires, and passions, according to the rules of reason, and therefore often in opposition to their own blind impulse.

What now is education? that part, that principal and most neglected part of it, I mean, which tends to form the moral character? It is, I think, an institution designed to lead men from their tender years, by precept and example, by argument and authority, to the practice, and to the habit of practising these rules.— The stronger our appetites, desires, and passions are, the harder indeed is the task of education: but when the efforts of education are proportioned to this strength, although our keenest appetites and desires, and our ruling passions cannot be reduced to a quiet and uniform submission, yet, are not their excesses assuaged? are not their abuses and misapplications, in some degree, diverted or checked? Though the pilot cannot lay the storm, cannot he carry the ship, by his art, better through it, and often prevent the wreck that would always happen, without him? If Alexander who loved wine, and was naturally choleric, had been bred under the severity of Roman discipline, it is probable he would neither have made a bonfire of Persepolis for his whore, nor have killed his friend. If Scipio, who was naturally given to women, for which anecdote we have, if I mistake not, the authority of Polybius, as well as some verses of Nævius preserved by A. Gellius, had been educated by Olympius at the court of Philip, it is improbable that he would have restored the beautiful Spaniard.— In short, if the renowned Socrates had not corrected nature by art, this first apostle of the Gentiles had been a very profligate fellow, by his own confession; for he was inclined to all the vices Zopyrus imputed to him, as they say, on the observation of his physiognomy.

With him, therefore, who denies the effects of education, it would be in vain to dispute; and with him who admits them, there can be dispute, concerning that share which I ascribe to the study of history, in forming our moral characters, and making us better men.   The very persons who pretend that inclinations cannot be restrained, nor habits corrected, against our natural bent, would be the first perhaps to prove, in certain cases, the contrary.   A fortune at court, or the favors of a lady, have prevailed on many to conceal, and they could not conceal without restraining, which is one step towards correcting, the vices they were by nature addicted to the most.   Shall we imagine now, that the beauty of virtue and the deformity of vice, the charms of a bright and lasting reputation, the terror of being delivered over as criminals to all posterity, the real benefit arising from a conscientious discharge of the duty we owe to others, which benefit fortune can neither hinder nor take away, and the reasonableness of conforming ourselves to the designs of God manifested in the constitution of the human nature; shall we imagine, I say, that all these are not able to acquire the same power over those who are continually called upon to a contemplation of them, and they who apply themselves to the study of history are so called upon, as other motives, mean and sordid in comparison of these, can usurp on other men?

2. That the study of history, far from making us wiser, and more useful citizens, as well as better men, may be of no advantage whatsoever; that it may serve to render us mere antiquaries and scholars; or that it may help to make us forward coxcombs, and prating pedants, I have already allowed.   But this is not the fault of history: and to convince us that it is not, we need only contrast the true use of history with the use that is made of it by such men as these.   We ought always to keep in mind, that history is philosophy teaching by examples how to conduct ourselves in all the situations of private and public life; that therefore we must apply ourselves to it in a philosophical spirit and manner; that we must rise from particular to general knowledge, and that we must fit ourselves for the society and business of mankind by accustoming our minds to reflect and meditate on the characters we find described, and the course of events we find related there.   Particular examples may be of use sometimes in particular cases; but the application of them is dangerous. It must be done with the utmost circumspection, or it will be seldom done with success.   And yet one would think that this was the principal use of the study of history, by what has been written on the subject.   I know not whether Machiavel himself is quite free from defect on this account: he seems to carry the use and application of particular examples sometimes too far. Marius and Catulus passed the Alps, met, and defeated the Cimbri beyond the frontiers of Italy.   Is it safe to conclude from

hence, that whenever one people is invaded by another, the invaded ought to meet and fight the invaders at a distance from their frontiers? Machiavel's countryman, Guicciardin, was aware of the danger that might arise from such an application of examples. Peter of Medicis had involved himself in great difficulties, when those wars and calamities began which Lewis Sforza first drew and entailed on Italy, by flattering the ambition of Charles the Eighth in order to gratify his own, and calling the French into that country. Peter owed his distress to his folly in departing from the general tenor of conduct his father Laurence had held, and hoped to relieve himself by imitating his fathers's example in one particular instance. At a time when the wars with the pope and king of Naples had reduced Laurence to circumstances of great danger, he took the resolution of going to Ferdinand, and of treating in person with that prince. The resolution appears in history imprudent and almost desperate: were we informed of the secret reasons on which this great man acted, it would appear very possibly a wise and safe measure. It succeeded, and Laurence brought back with him public peace, and private security. As soon as the French troops entered the dominions of Florence, Peter was struck with a panic terror, went to Charles the Eighth, put the port of Leghorn, the fortresses of Pisa, and all the keys of the country, into this prince's hands; whereby he disarmed the Florentine commonwealth, and ruined himself. He was deprived of his authority, and driven out of the city, by the just indignation of the magistrates, and people: and in the treaty which they made afterwards with the king of France, it was stipulated, that Peter should not remain within an hundred miles of the state, nor his brothers within the same distance of the city of Florence. On this occasion Guicciardin observes, how dangerous it is to govern ourselves by particular examples; since to have the same success, we must have the same prudence, and the same fortune; and since the example must not only answer the case before us in general, but in every minute circumstance. This is the sense of that admirable historian, and these are his words——"è senza dubio molto pericoloso il governarsi con gl' esempi, se non concorrono, non solo in generale, ma in tutti i particulari, le medesime ragioni; se le cose non sono regolate con la medesima prudenza, et se oltre a tutti li altri fondamenti, non, v'ha la parte sua la medesima fortuna." An observation that Boileau makes, and a rule he lays down in speaking of translations, will properly find their place here, and serve to explain still better what I would establish. "To translate servilely into modern language an ancient author phrase by phrase, and word by word, is preposterous: nothing can be more unlike the original than such a

copy. It is not to show, it is to disguise the author: and he who
has known him only in this dress, would not know him in his
own. A good writer, instead of taking this inglorious and unprofitable task upon him, will *jouster contre l' original,* rather
imitate than translate, and rather emulate than imitate; he will
transfuse the sense and spirit of the original into his own work,
and will endeavor to write as the ancient author would have written, had he written in the same language." Now, to improve
by examples is to improve by imitation. We must catch the
spirit, if we can, and conform ourselves to the reason of them;
but we must not affect to translate servilely into our conduct, if
your lordship will allow me the expression, the particular conduct of those good and great men, whose images history sets before us. Codrus and the Decii devoted themselves to death: one,
because an oracle had foretold that the army whose general was
killed would be victorious; the others in compliance with a
superstition that bore great analogy to a ceremony practised in
the old Egyptian church, and added afterwards, as many others
of the same origin were, to the ritual of the Israelites. These
are examples of great magnanimity, to be sure, and of magnanimity employed in the most worthy cause. In the early days
of the Athenian and Roman government, when the credit of
oracles and all kinds of superstition prevailed, when heaven was
piously thought to delight in blood, and even human blood was
shed under wild notions of atonement, propitiation, purgation,
expiation, and satisfaction; they who set such examples as these,
acted an heroical and a rational part too. But if a general
should act the same part now, and, in order to secure his victory,
get killed as fast as he could, he might pass for a hero, but, I
am sure, he would pass for a madman. Even these examples,
however, are of use: they excite us at least to venture our lives
freely in the service of our country, by proposing to our imitation men who devoted themselves to certain death in the service
of theirs. They show us what a turn of imagination can operate, and how the greatest trifle, nay the greatest absurdity,
dressed up in the solemn airs of religion, can carry ardor and
confidence, or the contrary sentiments, into the breasts of
thousands.

  These are certain general principles, and rules of life and
conduct, which always must be true, because they are conformable to the invariable nature of things. He who studies history
as he would study philosophy, will soon distinguish and collect
them, and by doing so will soon form to himself a general system of ethics and politics on the surest foundations, on the trial
of these principles and rules in all ages, and on the confirmation
of them by universal experience. I said he will distinguish

them; for once more I must say, that as to particular modes of actions, and measures of conduct, which the customs of different countries, the manners of different ages, and the circumstances of different conjunctures, have appropriated, as it were; it is always ridiculous, or imprudent and dangerous to employ them. But this is not all. By contemplating the vast variety of particular characters and events; by examining the strange combination of causes, different, remote, and seemingly opposite, that often concur in producing one effect; and the surprising fertility of one single and uniform cause in the producing of a multitude of effects, as different, as remote, and seemingly as opposite; by tracing carefully, as carefully as if the subject he considers were of personal and immediate concern to him, all the minute and sometimes scarce perceivable circumstances, either in the characters of actors, or in the course of actions, that history enables him to trace, and according to which the success of affairs, even the greatest, is mostly determined; by these, and such methods as these, for I might descend into a much greater detail, a man of parts may improve the study of history to its proper and principal use; he may sharpen the penetration, fix the attention of his mind, and strengthen his judgment; he may acquire the faculty and the habit of discerning quicker, and looking farther; and of exerting that flexibility, and steadiness, which are necessary to be joined in the conduct of all affairs that depend on the concurrence or opposition of other men.

Mr. Locke, I think, recommends the study of geometry even to those who have no design of being geometricians: and he gives a reason for it, that may be applied to the present case. Such persons may forget every problem that has been proposed, and every solution that they or others have given; but the habit of pursuing long trains of ideas will remain with them, and they will pierce through the mazes of sophism, and discover a latent truth, where persons who have not this habit will never find it.

In this manner the study of history will prepare us for action and observation. History is the ancient author: experience is the modern language. We form our taste on the first, we translate the sense and reason, we transfuse the spirit and force; but we imitate only the particular graces of the original; we imitate them according to the idiom of our own tongue, that is, we substitute often equivalents in the lieu of them, and are far from affecting to copy them servilely. To conclude, as experience is conversant about the present, and the present enables us to guess at the future; so history is conversant about the past, and by knowing the things that have been, we become better able to judge of the things that are.

This use, my lord, which I make the proper and principal use of the study of history, is not insisted on by those who have written concerning the method to be followed in this study: and since we propose different ends, we must of course take different ways. Few of their treatises have fallen into my hands: one, the method of Bodin, a man famous in his time, I remember to have read. I took it up with much expectation many years ago; I went through it, and remained extremely disappointed. He might have given almost any other title to his book as properly as that which stands before it. There are not many pages in it that relate any more to his subject than a tedious fifth chapter, wherein he accounts for the characters of nations according to their positions on the globe, and according to the influence of the stars; and assures his reader that nothing can be more necessary than such a disquisition; " ad universam historiarum cognitionem, et incorruptum earum judicium." In his method, we are to take first a general view of universal history, and chronology, in short abstracts, and then to study all particular histories and systems. Seneca speaks of men who spend their whole lives in learning how to act in life, " dum vitæ instrumenta conquirunt." I doubt that this method of Bodin would conduct us in the same, or as bad a way; would leave us no time for action, or would make us unfit for it. A huge common-place book, wherein all the remarkable sayings and facts that we find in history are to be registered, may enable a man to talk or write like Bodin, but will never make him a better man, nor enable him to promote, like an useful citizen, the security, the peace, the welfare, or the grandeur of the community to which he belongs. I shall proceed therefore to speak of a method that leads to such purposes as these directly and certainly, without any regard to the methods that have been prescribed by others.

I think then we must be on our guard against this very affectation of learning, and this very wantonness of curiosity, which the examples and precepts we commonly meet with are calculated to flatter and indulge. We must neither dwell too long in the dark, nor wander about till we lose our way in the light. We are too apt to carry systems of philosophy beyond all our ideas, and systems of history beyond all our memorials. The philosopher begins with reason, and ends with imagination. The historian inverts this order: he begins without memorials, and he sometimes ends with them. This silly custom is so prevalent among men of letters who apply themselves to the study of history, and has so much prejudice and so much authority on the side of it, that your lordship must give me leave to speak a little more particularly and plainly than I have done, in favor of common sense against an absurdity which is almost sanctified.

REFLECTIONS ON THE STATE OF ANCIENT HISTORY.

The nature of man, and the constant course of human affairs, render it impossible that the first ages of any new nation which forms itself, should afford authentic materials for history. We have none such concerning the originals of any of those nations that actually subsist. Shall we expect to find them concerning the originals of nations dispersed, or extinguished, two or three thousand years ago? If a thread of dark and uncertain traditions, therefore, is made, as it commonly is, the introduction to history, we should touch it lightly, and run swiftly over it, far from insisting on it, either as authors or readers. Such introductions are at best no more than fanciful preludes, that try the instruments, and precede the concert. He must be void of judgment, and taste, one would think, who can take the first for true history, or the last for true harmony. And yet so it has been, and so it is, not in Germany and Holland alone; but in Italy, in France, and in England, where genius has abounded, and taste has been long refined. Our great scholars have dealt and deal in fables at least as much as our poets, with this difference to the disadvantage of the former, to whom I may apply the remark as justly as Seneca applied it to the dialecticians—" tristius inepti sunt. Illi ex professio lasciviunt; hi agere seipsos aliquid existimant." Learned men, in learned and inquisitive ages, who possessed many advantages that we have not, and among others that of being placed so many centuries nearer the original truths that are the objects of so much laborious search, despaired of finding them, and gave fair warning to posterity, if posterity would have taken it. The ancient geographers, as Plutarch says in the life of Theseus, when they laid down in their maps the little extent of sea and land that was known to them, left great spaces void. In some of these spaces they wrote, Here are sandy deserts, in others, Here are impassable marshes, Here is a chain of inhospitable mountains, or Here is a frozen ocean. Just so both he and other historians, when they related fabulous originals, were not wanting to set out the bounds beyond which there was neither history nor chronology. Censorinus has preserved the distinction of three eras established by Varro. This learned Roman antiquary did not determine whether the first period had any beginning, but fixed the end of it at the first, that is, according to him, the Ogygian, deluge; which he placed, I think, some centuries more backward than Julius Africanus thought fit to place it afterwards. To this era of absolute darkness he supposed that a kind of twilight succeeded, from the Ogygian deluge to the Olympic era, and this he called the fabulous age. From this vulgar era when Coræbus was crowned victor, and long after the true era when these games were instituted by Iphitus, the Greeks pretend to be able to digest their history with some order, clearness, and certainty.   Varro therefore looked on it as the break of day, or the beginning of the historical age.   He might do so the rather, perhaps, because he included by it the date he likewise fixed, or, upon recollection, that the elder Cato had fixed, of the foundation of Rome within the period from which he supposed that historical truth was to be found.   But yet most certain it is, that the history and chronology of the ages that follow are as confused and uncertain, as the history and chronology of those which immediately precede this era.

I. THE STATE OF ANCIENT PROFANE HISTORY.

The Greeks did not begin to write in prose till Pherecides of Syros introduced the custom: and Cadmus Milesius was their first historian.   Now these men flourished long after the true, or even the vulgar Olympic era; for Josephus affirms, and in this he has great probability on his side, that Cadmus Milesius, and Acusilaus Argivus, in a word, the oldest historians in Greece, were very little more ancient than the expedition of the Persians against the Greeks.   As several centuries passed between the Olympic era and these first historians, there passed likewise several more between these and the first Greek chronologers. Timæus about the time of Ptolemy Philadelphus, and Eratosthenes about that of Ptolemy Evergetes, seem first to have digested the events recorded by them, according to the Olympiads. Precedent writers mentioned sometimes the Olympiads; but this rule of reckoning was not brought into established use sooner. The rule could not serve to render history more clear and certain till it was followed: it was not followed till about five hundred years after the Olympic era.   There remains therefore no pretence to place the beginning of the historical age so high as Varro placed it, by five hundred years.

Hellanicus indeed and others pretended to give the originals of cities and governments, and to deduce their narrations from great antiquity.   Their works are lost, but we can judge how inconsiderable the loss is, by the writings of that age which remain, and by the report of those who had seen the others. For instance, Herodotus was cotemporary with Hellanicus. Herodotus was inquisitive enough in all conscience, and proposed to publish all he could learn of the antiquities of the Ionians, Lydians, Phrygians, Egyptians, Babylonians, Medes, and Persians; that is, of almost all the nations who were known in his time to exist. If he wrote Assyriacs, we have them not; but we are sure that this word was used proverbially to signify fabulous legends, soon after his time, and when the mode of publishing such relations and histories prevailed among the Greeks.

In the nine books we have, he goes back indeed almost to the Olympic era, without taking notice of it however; but he goes back only to tell an old woman's tale, of a king who lost his crown for showing his wife naked to his favorite; and from Candaules and Gyges he hastens, or rather he takes a great leap, down to Cyrus.

Something like a thread of history of the Medes and then of the Persians, to the flight of Xerxes, which happened in his own time, is carried on. The events of his own time are related with an air of history. But all accounts of the Greeks as well as the Persians, which precede these, and all the accounts which he gives occasionally of other nations, were drawn up most manifestly on broken, perplexed, and doubtful scraps of tradition. He had neither original records, nor any authentic memorials to guide him, and yet these are the sole foundations of true history. Herodotus flourished, I think, little more than half a century, and Xenophon little more than a whole century, after the death of Cyrus: and yet how various and repugnant are the relations made by these two historians, of the birth, life, and death of this prince? If more histories had come down from these ages to ours, the uncertainty and inutility of them all would be but the more manifest. We should find that Acusilaus rejected the traditions of Hesiod, that Hellanicus contradicted Acusilaus, that Ephorus accused Hellanicus, that Timæus accused Ephorus, and all posterior writers Timæus. This is the report of Josephus. But, in order to show the ignorance and falsehood of all those writers through whom the traditions of profane antiquity came to the Greeks, I will quote to your lordship a much better authority than that of Josephus; the authority of one who had no prejudice to bias him, no particular cause to defend, nor system of ancient history to establish, and all the helps, as well as talents, necessary to make him a competent judge. The man I mean is Strabo.

Speaking of the Massagetæ in his eleventh book, he writes to this effect: that no author had given a true account of them, though several had written of the war that Cyrus waged against them; and that historians had found as little credit in what they had related concerning the affairs of the Persians, Medes, and Syrians: that this was due to their folly; for observing that those who wrote fables professedly were held in esteem, these men imagined they should render their writings more agreeable, if, under the appearance and pretence of true history, they related what they had neither seen nor heard from persons able to give them true information; and that accordingly their only aim had been to dress up pleasing and marvellous relations: that one may better give credit to Hesiod and Homer, when they talk of their heroes, nay, even to dramatic poets, than to Ctesias, Herodotus, Hellanicus, and their followers: that it is not safe to give credit even to the greatest part of the historians who wrote concerning Alexander; since they too, encouraged by the greater reputation of this conqueror, by the distance to which he carried his arms, and by the difficulty of disproving what they said of actions performed in regions so remote, were apt to deceive: that indeed when the Roman empire on one side, and the Parthian on the other, came to extend themselves, the truth of things grew to be better known.

You see, my lord, not only how late profane history began to be written by the Greeks, but how much later it began to be written with any regard to truth; and consequently what wretched materials the learned men, who arose after the age of Alexander, had to employ, when they attempted to form systems of ancient history and chronology. We have some remains of that laborious compiler Diodorus Siculus, but do we find in him any thread of ancient history, I mean, that which passed for ancient in his time? What complaints, on the contrary, does he not make of former historians? how frankly does he confess the little and uncertain light he had to follow in his researches? Yet Diodorus, as well as Plutarch, and others, had not only the older Greek historians, but the more modern antiquaries, who pretended to have searched into the records and registers of nations, even at that time renowned for their antiquity. Berosus, for instance, and Manetho, one a Babylonian and the other an Egyptian priest, had published the antiquities of their countries in the time of the Ptolemys. Berosus pretended to give the history of four hundred and eighty years. Pliny, if I remember right, for I say this on memory, speaks to this effect in the sixth book of his Natural History: and if it was so, these years were probably years of Nabonassar. Manetho began his history, God knows when, from the progress of Isis, or some other as well ascertained period. He followed the Egyptian tradition of dynasties of gods and demi-gods; and derived his anecdotes from the first Mercury, who had inscribed them in sacred characters, on antediluvian pillars, antediluvian at least according to our received chronology, from which the second Mercury had transcribed them, and inserted them into his works. We have not these antiquities; for the monk of Viterbo was soon detected: and if we had them, they would either add to our uncertainty, and increase the chaos of learning, or tell us nothing worth our knowledge. For thus I reason. Had they given particular and historical accounts conformable to the scriptures of the Jews, Josephus, Julius Africanus, and Eusebius would have made quite other extracts from their writings, and would have altered and contradicted them less. The accounts they gave, therefore, were repugnant to sacred writ, or they were defective: they would have established Pyrrhonism, or have balked our curiosity.

II. OF SACRED HISTORY.

What memorials therefore remain to give us light into the originals of ancient nations, and the history of those ages, we commonly call the first ages?   The Bible, it will be said; that is, the historical part of it in the Old Testament.   But, my lord, even these divine books must be reputed insufficient to the purpose, by every candid and impartial man who considers either their authority as histories, or the matter they contain.   For what are they? and how came they to us?   At the time when Alexander carried his arms into Asia, a people of Syria, till then unknown, became known to the Greeks: this people had been slaves to the Egyptians, Assyrians, Medes, and Persians, as the several empires prevailed: ten parts in twelve of them had been transplanted by ancient conquerors, and melted down and lost in the east, several ages before the establishment of the empire that Alexander destroyed: the other two parts had been carried captive to Babylon a little before the same era. This captivity was not indeed perpetual, like the other; but it lasted so long, and such circumstances, whatever they were, accompanied it, that the captives forgot their country, and even their language, the Hebrew dialect at least and character: and a few of them only could be wrought upon, by the zeal of some particular men, to return home, when the indulgence of the Persian monarchs gave them leave to rebuild their city and to repeople their ancient patrimony. Even this remnant of the nation did not continue long entire. Another great transmigration followed; and the Jews, that settled under the protection of the Ptolemys, forgot their language in Egypt, as the forefathers of these Jews had forgot theirs in Chaldea.   More attached however to their religion in Egypt, for reasons easy to be deduced from the new institutions that prevailed after the captivity among them, than their ancestors had been in Chaldea, a version of their sacred writings was made into Greek at Alexandria, not long after the canon of these scriptures had been finished at Jerusalem; for many years could not intervene between the death of Simon the Just, by whom this canon was finished, if he died during the reign of Ptolemy Soter, and the beginning of this famous translation under Ptolemy Philadelphus. The Hellenist Jews reported as many marvellous things to authorise, and even to sanctify this translation, as the other Jews had reported about Esdras who began, and Simon the Just who finished, the canon of their scriptures. These holy romances slid into tradition, and tradition became history: the fathers of our Christian church did not disdain to employ them. St. Jerome, for instance, laughed at the story of the seventy-two elders, whose translations were found to be, upon comparison, word for word the same, though made separately, and by men who had no communication with one another. But the same St. Jerome, in the same place, quotes Aristeas, one of the guard of Ptolemy Philadelphus, as a real personage.

The account pretended to be written by this Aristeas, of all that passed relating to the translation, was enough for his purpose. This he retained, and he rejected only the more improbable circumstances, which had been added to the tale, and which laid it open to most suspicion. In this he showed great prudence; and better judgment, than that zealous, but weak apologist Justin, who believed the whole story himself, and endeavored to impose it on mankind.

Thus you see, my lord, that when we consider these books barely as histories, delivered to us on the faith of a superstitious people, among whom the custom and art of pious lying prevailed remarkably, we may be allowed to doubt whether greater credit is to be given to what they tell us concerning the original, compiled in their own country and as it were out of the sight of the rest of the world; than we know, with such a certainty as no scholar presumes to deny, that we ought to give to what they tell us concerning the copy?

The Hellenist Jews were extremely pleased, no doubt, to have their scriptures in a language they understood, and that might spread the fame of their antiquity, and do honor to their nation, among their masters the Greeks. But yet we do not find that the authority of these books prevailed, or that even they were much known among the pagan world. The reason of this cannot be, that the Greeks admired nothing that was not of their own growth, "sua tantum mirantur:" for, on the contrary, they were inquisitive and credulous in the highest degree, and they collected and published at least as many idle traditions of other nations, as they propagated of their own. Josephus pretended that Theopompus, a disciple of Isocrates being about to insert in his history some things he had taken out of holy writ, the poor man became troubled in mind for several days; and that having prayed to God, during an intermission of his illness, to reveal to him the cause of it, he learned in his sleep that this attempt was the cause; upon which he quitted the design and was cured. If Josephus had been a little more consistent than he is very often, such a story as this would not have been told by one, who was fond, as Jews and Christians in general have been, to create an opinion that the Gentiles took not their history alone, but their philosophy and all their valuable knowledge, from the Jews. Notwithstanding this story, therefore, which is told in the fifteenth book of the Jewish antiquities, and means nothing, or means to show that the divine providence would not suffer anecdotes of sacred to be mingled with profane history; the practice of Josephus himself, and of all those who have had the same design in view, has been to confirm the former by the latter, and at any rate to suppose an appearance at least of conformity between them. We are told Hecateus Abderita, for there were two of that name, wrote a history favorable to the Jews: and, not to multiply instances, though I might easily do it, even Alexander Polyhistor is called in. He is quoted by Josephus, and praised by Eusebius as a man of parts and great variety of learning. His testimony, about the deluge and tower of Babel, is produced by St. Cyril in his first book against Julian: and Justin the apologist and martyr, in his exhortation to the Greeks, makes use of the same authority, among those that mention Moses as a leader and prince of the Jews. Though this Polyhistor, if I remember right what I think I have met with in Suidas, spoke only of a woman he called Moso, " cujus scriptum est lex Hebræorum."* Had the Greek historians been conformable to the sacred, I cannot see that their authority, which was not cotemporary, would have been of any weight. They might have copied Moses, and so they did Ctesias. But even this was not the case: whatever use a particular writer here and there might make occasionally of the scriptures, certain it is that the Jews continued to be as much despised, and their history to be as generally neglected, nay almost as generally unknown, for a long time at least after the version was made at Alexandria, as they had been before. Apion, an Egyptian, a man of much erudition, appeared in the world some centuries afterwards. He wrote, among other antiquities, those of his own country: and as he was obliged to speak very often of the Jews, he spoke of them in a manner neither much to their honor, nor to that of their histories. He wrote purposely against them: and Josephus attempted afterwards, but Apion was then dead, to refute him.

---

* Μωσὼ, γυνὴ Ἑβραία· ἧς ἐςι σύγγραμμα ὁ ϖαϱ Ἑβραίοις νομος· ὡς φησιν Ἀλέξανδρος ὁ Μιλήσιος ὁ Πολυΐςωρ. Sui Lex. tom. ii. p. 583.

Ἀλέξανδρος . . . ὃς Πολυΐςωϱ . . συνέγραψε βιϐλία ἀρίϑμῦ κρείτlω. ὴ περὶ Ῥώμης βιϐλία ϖέντε. ἐν τούτοις λέγει, ὡς γυνὴ γέγονεν Ἑβραία Μωσὼ, ἧς ἐςι σύγραμμα ὁ ϖαϱ Ἑβραίοις νομος. Id. tom. i p. 105. Edit. Cantab. 1725.

Apion passed, I know, for a vain and noisy pedant; but he passed likewise for a curious, a laborious, and a learned antiquary.   If he was cabalistical, or superstitious, Josephus was at least as much so as he: and if he flattered Caligula, Josephus introduced himself to the court of Nero and the favor of Poppæa, by no very honorable means, under the protection of Aliturus a player, and a Jew; to say nothing of his applying to Vespasian the prophecies concerning the Messiah, nor of his accompanying Titus to the siege of Jerusalem.

In short, my lord, the Jewish history never obtained any credit in the world, till Christianity was established.   The foundations of this system being laid partly in these histories, and in the prophecies joined to them or inserted in them, Christianity has reflected back upon them an authority which they had not before, and this authority has prevailed wherever Christianity has spread.   Both Jews and Christians hold the same books in great veneration, whilst each condemns the other for not understanding, or for abusing them.   But I apprehend that the zeal of both has done much hurt, by endeavoring to extend their authority much farther than is necessary for the support perhaps of Judaism, but to be sure of Christianity.   I explain myself, that I may offend no pious ear.

Simon, in the preface of his critical history of the Old Testament, cites a divine of the faculty of Paris, who held that the inspirations of the authors of those books, which the church receives as the word of God, should be extended no farther than to matters purely of doctrine, or to such as have a near and necessary relation to these; and that whenever these authors wrote on other subjects, such as Egyptian, Assyrian, or other history, they had no more of the divine assistance than any other persons of piety.   This notion of inspirations that came occasionally, that illuminated the minds and guided the hands of the sacred penmen while they were writing one page, and restrained their influence while the same authors were writing another, may be cavilled against: and what is there that may not?   But surely it deserves to be treated with respect, since it tends to establish a distinction between the legal, doctrinal, or prophetical parts of the Bible, and the historical: without which distinction it is impossible to establish the first, as evidently and as solidly as the interests of religion require: at least it appears impossible to me, after having examined and considered, as well as I am able, all the trials of this kind that have been made by subtile as well as learned men.   The Old is said to be the foundation of the New, and so it is in one sense: the system of religion contained in the latter, refers to the system of religion contained in the former, and supposes the truth of it.   But the authority on which

we receive the books of the New Testament, is so far from being
founded on the authority of the Old Testament, that it is quite
independent on it; the New being proved, gives authority to
the Old, but borrows none from it; and gives this authority to
the particular parts only. Christ came to fulfil the prophecies;
but not to consecrate all the written, any more than the oral,
traditions of the Jews. We must believe these traditions as far
as they relate to Christianity, as far as Christianity refers to them,
or supposes them necessary; but we can be under no obligation
to believe them any farther, since without Christianity we should
be under no obligation to believe them at all.

It hath been said by Abbadie, and others, " That the accidents
which have happened to alter the texts of the Bible, and to dis-
figure, if I may say so, the Scriptures in many respects, could
not have been prevented without a perpetual standing miracle,
and that a perpetual standing miracle is not in the order of Providence." Now I can by no means subscribe to this opinion.—
It seems evident to my reason that the very contrary must be
true; if we suppose that God acts towards men according to the
moral fitness of things: and if we suppose that he acts arbitrarily,
we can form no opinion at all. I think that these accidents would
not have happened, or that the Scriptures would have been preserved entirely in their genuine purity notwithstanding these
accidents, if they had been entirely dictated by the Holy Ghost:
and the proof of this probable proposition, according to our
clearest and most distinct ideas of wisdom and moral fitness, is
obvious and easy. But these Scriptures are not so come down
to us: they are come down broken and confused, full of additions,
interpolations, and transpositions, made we neither know when,
nor by whom; and such, in short, as never appeared on the face
of any other book, on whose authority men have agreed to rely.

This being so, my lord, what hypothesis shall we follow?
Shall we adhere to some such distinction as I have mentioned?
Shall we say, for instance, that the Scriptures were written originally by the authors to whom they are vulgarly ascribed, but
that these authors wrote nothing by inspiration, except the legal,
the doctrinal, and the prophetical parts, and that in every other
respect their authority is purely human, and therefore fallible?
Or shall we say that these histories are nothing more than com-
pilations of old traditions, and abridgments of old records, made
in later times, as they appear to every one who reads them without prepossession, and with attention? Shall we add, that which
ever of these probabilities be true, we may believe, consistently
with either, notwithstanding the decision of any divines, who
know no more than you or I, or any other man, of the order of
Providence, that all those parts and passages of the Old Testa-

ment, which contain prophecies, or matters of law or doctrine, and which were from the first of such importance in the designs of Providence to all future generations, and even to the whole race of mankind, have been from the first the peculiar care of Providence?   Shall we insist that such particular parts and passages, which are plainly marked out and sufficiently confirmed by the system of the Christian revelation, and by the completion of the prophecies, have been preserved from corruption by ways impenetrable to us, amidst all the changes and chances to which the books wherein they are recorded have been exposed; and that neither original writers, nor later compilers, have been suffered to make any essential alterations, such as would have falsified the law of God and the principles of the Jewish and Christian religions, in any of these divine fundamental truths? Upon such hypotheses, we may assert without scruple, that the genealogies and histories of the Old Testament are in no respect sufficient foundations for a chronology from the beginning of time, nor for universal history.   But then the same hypotheses will secure the infallibility of scripture authority as far as religion is concerned.   Faith and reason may be reconciled a little better than they commonly are.   I may deny that the Old Testament is transmitted to us under all the conditions of an authentic history, and yet be at liberty to maintain that the passages in it which establish original sin, which seem favorable to the doctrine of the Trinity, which foretell the coming of the Messiah, and all others of similar kind, are come down to us as they were originally dictated by the Holy Ghost.

In attributing the whole credibility of the Old Testament to the authority of the New, and in limiting the authenticity of the Jewish Scriptures to those parts alone that concern law, doctrine, and prophecy, by which their chronology and the far greatest part of their history are excluded, I will venture to assure your lordship that I do not assume so much, as is assumed in every hypothesis that affixes the divine seal of inspiration to the whole canon; that rests the whole proof on Jewish veracity; and that pretends to account particularly and positively for the descent of these ancient writings in their present state.

. Another reason, for which I have insisted the rather on the distinction so often mentioned, is this.   I think we may find very good foundation for it even in the Bible: and though this be a point very little attended to, and much disguised, it would not be hard to show, upon great inducements of probability, that the law and the history were far from being blended together as they now stand in the Pentateuch, even from the time of Moses down to that of Esdras.   But the principal and decisive reason for separating in such manner the legal, doctrinal, and prophetical parts, from the historical, is the necessity of having some rule to go by: and, I protest, I know of none that is yet agreed upon. I content myself, therefore, to fix my opinion concerning the authority of the Old Testament in this manner, and carry it thus far only. We must do so, or we must enter into that labyrinth of dispute and contradiction, wherein even the most orthodox Jews and Christians have wandered so many ages, and still wander. It is strange, but it is true; not only the Jews differ from the Christians, but Jews and Christians both differ among themselves, concerning almost every point that is necessary to be certainly known and agreed upon, in order to establish the authority of books which both have received already as authentic and sacred. So that whoever takes the pains to read what learned men have written on this subject, will find that they leave the matter as doubtful as they took it up. Who were the authors of these Scriptures, when they were published, how they were composed and preserved, or renewed, to use a remarkable expression of the famous Huet in his Demonstration; in fine, how they were lost during the captivity, and how they were retrieved after it, are all matters of controversy to this day.

It would be easy for me to descend into a greater detail, and to convince your lordship of what I have been saying in general by an induction of particulars, even without any other help than that of a few notes which I took when I applied myself to this examination, and which now lie before me. But such a digression would carry me too far: and I fear that you will think I have said already more than enough upon this part of my subject. I go on, therefore, to observe to your lordship, that if the history of the Old Testament was as exact and authentic, as the ignorance and impudence of some rabbies have made them assert that it is; if we could believe with them that Moses wrote every syllable in the Pentateuch as it now stands, or that all the Psalms were written by David: nay, if we could believe, with Philo and Josephus, that Moses wrote the account of his own death and sepulchre, and made a sort of funeral panegyric on himself, as we find them in the last chapter of Deuteronomy; yet still would I venture to assert, that he who expects to find a system of chronology, or a thread of history, or sufficient materials for either, in the books of the Old Testament, expects to find what the authors of these books, whoever they were, never intended. They are extracts of genealogies, not genealogies: extracts of histories, not histories. The Jews themselves allow their genealogies to be very imperfect, and produce examples of omissions and errors in them, which denote sufficiently that these genealogies are extracts, wherein every generation in the course of descent is not mentioned. I have read somewhere, perhaps in the works of

St. Jerome, that this father justifies the opinion of those who think it impossible to fix any certain chronology on that of the Bible: and this opinion will be justified still better, to the understanding of every man who considers how grossly the Jews blunder whenever they meddle with chronology; for this plain reason, because their Scriptures are imperfect in this respect, and because they rely on their oral, to rectify and supply their written, traditions: that is, they rely on traditions compiled long after the canon of their Scriptures, but deemed by them of equal antiquity and authority. Thus, for instance, Daniel and Simon the Just, according to them, were members at the same time of the great synagogue which began and finished the canon of the Old Testament, under the presidency of Esdras. This Esdras was the prophet Malachi. Darius the son of Hystaspes was Artaxerxes Longimanus; he was Ahasuerus, and he was the same Darius whom Alexander conquered. This may serve as a sample of Jewish chronology, formed on their Scriptures which afford insufficient lights, and on their traditions which afford false lights. We are indeed more correct, and come nearer to the truth in these instances, perhaps in some others, because we make use of profane chronology to help us. But profane chronology is itself so modern, so precarious, that this help does not reach to the greatest part of that time to which sacred chronology extends; that when it begins to help, it begins to perplex us too; and finally, that even with this help we should not have had so much as the appearance of a complete chronological system, and the same may be said of universal history, if learned men had not proceeded very wisely, on one uniform maxim, from the first ages of Christianity, when a custom of sanctifying profane learning, as well as profane rites, which the Jews had imprudently laid aside, was taken up by the Christians. The maxim I mean is this, that profane authority be admitted without scruple or doubt, whenever it says, or whenever it can be made to say, if not "totidem verbis," yet "totidem syllabis," or "totidem literis," at least, or whenever it can be made by any interpretation to mean, what confirms, or supplies in a consistent manner, the holy writ; and that the same authority be rejected, when nothing of this kind can be done, but the contradiction or inconsistency remains irreconcilable. Such a liberty as this would not be allowed in any other case; because it supposes the very thing that is to be proved. But we see it taken, very properly to be sure, in favor of sacred and infallible writing, when they are compared with others.

In order to perceive with the utmost evidence, that the scope and design of the author or authors of the Pentateuch, and of the other books of the Old Testament, answer as little the pur-

pose of antiquaries, in history, as in chronology, it will be sufficient briefly to call to mind the sum of what they relate, from
the creation of the world to the establishment of the Persian
empire. If the antediluvian world continued one thousand six
hundred and fifty-six years, and if the vocation of Abraham is to
be placed four hundred and twenty-six years below the deluge,
these twenty centuries make almost two-thirds of the period
mentioned: and the whole history of them is comprised in
eleven short chapters of Genesis; which is certainly the most
compendious extract that ever was made. If we examine the
contents of these chapters, do we find anything like an universal history, or so much as an abridgment of it? Adam and
Eve were created, they broke the commandment of God, they
were driven out of the garden of Eden, one of their sons
killed his brother, but their race soon multiplied and peopled
the earth. What geography now have we, what history of this
antediluvian world? Why, none. The sons of God, it is said,
lay with the daughters of men, and begot giants, and God
drowned all the inhabitants of the earth, except one family.
After this we read that the earth was repeopled; but these children of one family were divided into several languages, even
whilst they lived together, spoke the same language, and were
employed in the same work. Out of one of the countries into
which they dispersed themselves, Chaldea, God called Abraham
sometime afterwards, with magnificent promises, and conducted
him to a country called Canaan. Did this author, my lord, intend an universal history? Certainly not. The tenth chapter
of Genesis names indeed some of the generations descending
from the sons of Noah, some of the cities founded, and some of
the countries planted by them. But what are bare names, naked
of circumstances, without descriptions of countries, or relations
of events? They furnish matter only for guess and dispute; and
even the similitude of them, which is often used as a clue to lead
us to the discovery of historical truth, has notoriously contributed
to propagate error, and to increase the perplexity of ancient tradition. These imperfect and dark accounts have not furnished
matter for guess and dispute alone; but a much worse use has
been made of them by Jewish rabbies, Christian fathers, and
Mahometan doctors, in their profane extensions of this part of
the Mosaic history. The creation of the first man is described
by some, as if, Preadamites, they had assisted at it. They talk
of his beauty as if they had seen him, of his gigantic size as if
they had measured him, and of his prodigious knowledge as if
they had conversed with him. They point out the very spot
where Eve laid her head the first time he enjoyed her. They
have minutes of the whole conversation between this mother of

mankind, who damned her children before she bore them, and
the serpent. Some are positive that Cain quarrelled with Abel
about a point of doctrine, and others affirm that the dispute rose
about a girl. A great deal of such stuff may be easily collected
about Enoch, about Noah, and about the sons of Noah; but I
waive any farther mention of such impertinences as Bonzes or
Talapoins would almost blush to relate. Upon the whole matter, if we may guess at the design of an author by the contents
of his book, the design of Moses, or of the author of the history
ascribed to him, in this part of it, was to inform the people of
Israel of their descent from Noah by Sem, and of Noah's from
Adam by Seth; to illustrate their original; to establish their
claim to the land of Canaan, and to justify all the cruelties committed by Joshua in the conquest of the Canaanites, in whom,
says Bochart, "the prophecy of Noah was completed, when
they were subdued by the Israelites, who had been so long
slaves to the Egyptians."

Allow me to make, as I go along, a short reflection or two on
this prophecy, and the completion of it, as they stand recorded
in the Pentateuch, out of many that might be made. The terms
of the prophecy then are not very clear: and the curse pronounced
in it contradicts all our notions of order and of justice. One is
tempted to think, that the patriarch was still drunk; and that no
man in his senses could hold such language, or pass such a sentence. Certain it is, that no writer but a Jew could impute to
the economy of Divine Providence the accomplishment of such
a prediction, nor make the Supreme Being the executor of such
a curse.

Ham alone offended; Canaan was innocent; for the Hebrew
and other doctors who would make the son an accomplice with
his father, affirm not only without, but against the express authority of the text. Canaan was however alone cursed: and he
became, according to his grandfather's prophecy, "a servant of
servants;" that is, the vilest and worst of slaves (for I take these
words in a sense, if not the most natural, the most favorable to
the prophecy, and the least absurd) to Sem, though not to Japhet,
when the Israelites conquered Palestine; to one of his uncles,
not to his brethren. Will it be said—it has been said—that
where we read Canaan we are to understand Ham, whose brethren Sem and Japhet were? At this rate, we shall never know
what we read: as these critics never care what they say. Will
it be said—this has been said too—that Ham was punished in
his posterity, when Canaan was cursed, and his descendants were
exterminated? But who does not see that the curse, and the
punishment, in this case, fell on Canaan and his posterity, exclusively of the rest of the posterity of Ham; and were therefore

the curse and punishment of the son, not of the father, properly?
The descendants of Mesraim, another of his sons, were the
Egyptians: and they were so far from being servants of servants
to their cousins the Semites, that these were servants of servants
to them, during more than fourscore years.   Why the posterity
of Canaan was to be deemed an accursed race, it is easy to account; and I have mentioned it just now.   But it is not so easy
to account, why the posterity of the righteous Sem, that great
example of filial reverence, became slaves to another branch of
the family of Ham.

It would not be worth while to lengthen this tedious letter,
by setting down any more of the contents of the history of the
Bible.   Your lordship may please to call the substance of it to
your mind, and your native candor and love of truth will oblige
you then to confess, that these sacred books do not aim, in any
part of them, at any thing like universal chronology and history.
They contain a very imperfect account of the Israelities themselves; of their settlement in the land of promise, of which, by the
way, they never had entire, and scarce ever peaceable possession;
of their divisions, apostasies, repentances, relapses, triumphs, and
defeats, under the occasional government of their judges, and
under that of their kings; of the Galilean and Samaritan captivities, into which they were carried by the kings of Assyria, and
of that which was brought on the remnant of this people when
the kingdom of Judah was destroyed by those princes who governed the empire founded on the union of Nineveh and Babylon.

These things are all related, your lordship knows, in a very
summary and confused manner: and we learn so little of other
nations by these accounts, that if we did not borrow some light
from the traditions of other nations, we should scarce understand
them.   One particular observation, and but one, I will make, to
show what knowledge in the history of mankind, and in the com-
putation of time, may be expected from these books.   The Assyrians were their neighbors, powerful neighbors, with whom they
had much and long to do.   Of this empire, therefore, if of any
thing, we might hope to find some satisfactory accounts.   What
do we find?   The Scripture takes no notice of any Assyrian kingdom, till just before the time when profane history makes that
empire to end.   Then we hear of Phul, of Teglath-Phalasser,
who was perhaps the same person, and of Salmanaser, who took
Samaria in the twelfth of the era of Nabonasser, that is, twelve
years after the Assyrian empire was no more.   Senacherib succeeds to him, and Asserhaddon to Senacherib.   What shall we
say to this apparent contrariety?   If the silence of the Bible creates
a strong presumption against the first, may not the silence of profane authority create some against the second Assyrian monarchs?

The pains that are taken to persuade, that there is room enough between Sardanapalus and Cyurs for the second, will not resolve the difficulty. Something much more plausible may be said, but even this will be hypothetical, and liable to great contradiction. So that, upon the whole matter, the Scriptures are so far from giving us light into general history, that they increase the obscurity even of those parts to which they have the nearest relation. We have therefore neither in profane nor in sacred authors such authentic, clear, distinct, and full accounts of the originals of ancient nations, and of the great events of those ages that are commonly called the first ages, as deserve to go by the name of history, or as afford sufficient materials for chronology and history.

I might now proceed to observe to your lordship how this has happened, not only by the necessary consequences of human nature, and the ordinary course of human affairs, but by the policy, artifice, corruption, and folly of mankind. But this would be to heap digression upon digression, and to presume too much on your patience. I shall therefore content myself to apply these reflections on the state of ancient history to the study of history, and to the method to be observed in it; as soon as your lordship has rested yourself a little after reading, and I after writing so long a letter.

LETTER IV.

I. THAT THERE IS IN HISTORY SUFFICIENT AUTHENTICITY TO RENDER IT USEFUL, NOTWITHSTANDING ALL OBJECTIONS TO THE CONTRARY.   II. OF THE METHOD AND DUE RESTRICTIONS TO BE OBSERVED IN THE STUDY OF IT.

WHETHER the letter I now begin to write will be long or short, I know not: but I find my memory is refreshed, my imagination warmed, and matter flows in so fast upon me, that I have not time to press it close. Since therefore you have provoked me to write, you must be content to take what follows.

I have observed already that we are apt naturally to apply to ourselves what has happened to other men, and that examples take their force from hence; as well those which history, as those which experience, offers to our reflection. What we do not believe to have happened, therefore, we shall not thus apply: and for want of the same application, such examples will not have the same effect. Ancient history, such ancient history as I have described, is quite unfit therefore in this respect to answer the

ends that every reasonable man should propose to himself in this
study; because such ancient history will never gain sufficient credit with any reasonable man. A tale well told, or a comedy or
a tragedy well wrought up, may have a momentary effect upon
the mind, by heating the imagination, surprising the judgment,
and affecting strongly the passions. The Athenians are said to
have been transported into a kind of martial phrenzy by the representation of a tragedy of Æschylus, and to have marched
under this influence from the theatre to the plains of Marathon.
These momentary impressions might be managed, for aught I
know, in such manner as to contribute a little, by frequent repetitions of them, towards maintaining a kind of habitual contempt
of folly, detestation of vice, and admiration of virtue in well-
policed commonwealths. But then these impressions cannot be
made, nor this little effect be wrought, unless the fables bear an
appearance of truth. When they bear this appearance, reason
connives at the innocent fraud of imagination; reason dis-
penses, in favor of probability, with those strict rules of criticism that she has established to try the truth of fact: but, after
all, she receives these fables as fables; and as such only she permits imagination to make the most of them. If they pretended
to be history, they would be soon subjected to another and more
severe examination. What may have happened, is the matter
of an ingenious fable: what has happened, is that of an authentic
history: the impressions which one or the other makes are in
proportion. When imagination grows lawless and wild, rambles
out of the precincts of nature, and tells of heroes and giants,
fairies and enchanters, of events and of phenomena repugnant
to universal experience, to our clearest and most distinct ideas,
and to all the known laws of nature, reason does not connive a
moment; but, far from receiving such narrations as historical, she
rejects them as unworthy to be placed even among the fabulous.
Such narrations therefore cannot make the slightest momentary
impressions on a mind fraught with knowledge, and void of
superstition. Imposed by authority, and assisted by artifice, the
delusion hardly prevails over common sense; blind ignorance
almost sees, and rash superstition hesitates: nothing less than
enthusiasm and phrensy can give credit to such histories, or
apply such examples. Don Quixote believed; but even Sancho
doubted.

What I have said will not be much controverted by any man
who has read Amadis of Gaul, or has examined our ancient traditions without prepossession. The truth is, the principal difference between them seems to be this. In Amadis of Gaul, we
have a thread of absurdities that are invented without any regard
to probability, and that lay no claim to belief: ancient traditions

are a heap of fables, under which some particular truths, inscrutable, and therefore useless to mankind, may lie concealed; which have a just pretence to nothing more, and yet impose themselves upon us, and become, under the venerable name of ancient history, the foundations of modern fables, the materials with which so many systems of fancy have been erected.

But now, as men are apt to carry their judgments into extremes, there are some that will be ready to insist that all history is fabulous, and that the very best is nothing better than a probable tale, artfully contrived, and plausibly told, wherein truth and falsehood are indistinguishably blended together. All the instances, and all the common-place arguments, that Bayle and others have employed to establish this sort of Pyrrhonism, will be quoted: and from thence it will be concluded, that if the pretended histories of the first ages, and of the originals of nations, be too improbable and too ill vouched to procure any degree of belief, those histories that have been written later, that carry a greater air of probability, and that boast even cotemporary authority, are at least insufficient to gain that degree of firm belief, which is necessary to render the study of them useful to mankind. But here that happens which often happens: the premises are true, and the conclusion is false; because a general axiom is established precariously on a certain number of partial observations. This matter is of consequence; for it tends to ascertain the degrees of assent that we may give to history.

I agree, then, that history has been purposely and systematically falsified in all ages, and that partiality and prejudice have occasioned both voluntary and involuntary errors, even in the best. Let me say without offence, my lord, since I may say it with truth and am able to prove it, that ecclesiastical authority has led the way to this corruption in all ages, and all religions. How monstrous were the absurdities that the priesthood imposed on the ignorance and superstition of mankind in the Pagan world, concerning the originals of religions and governments, their institutions and rites, their laws and customs? What opportunities had they for such impositions, whilst the keeping the records and collecting the traditions was in so many nations the peculiar office of this order of men? A custom highly extolled by Josephus, but plainly liable to the grossest frauds, and even a temptation to them. If the foundations of Judaism and Christianity have been laid in truth, yet what numberless fables have been invented to raise, to embellish, and to support these structures, according to the interest and taste of the several architects? That the Jews have been guilty of this will be allowed: and, to the shame of Christians, if not of Christianity, the fathers of one church have no right to throw the first stone at the fathers of the

other.   Deliberate, systematical lying has been practised and encouraged from age to age; and among all the pious frauds that
have been employed to maintain a reverence and zeal for their
religion in the minds of men, this abuse of history has been one
of the principal and most successful: an evident, an experimental
proof, by the way, of what I have insisted upon so much, the
aptitude and natural tendency of history to form our opinions,
and to settle our habits.   This righteous expedient was in so
much use and repute in the Greek church, that one Metaphrastus
wrote a treatise on the art of composing holy romances: the fact,
if I remember right, is cited by Baillet, in his book of the lives
of the saints.   He and other learned men of the Roman church
have thought it of service to their cause, since the resurrection
of letters, to detect some impostures, and to depose, or to unniche,
according to the French expression, now and then a reputed
saint; but they seem in doing this to mean no more than a sort of
composition: they give up some fables that they may defend
others with greater advantage, and they make truth serve as a
stalking-horse to error.   The same spirit that prevailed in the
eastern church, prevailed in the western, and prevails still.   A
strong proof of it appeared lately in the country where I am.
A sudden fury of devotion seized the people of Paris for a little
priest,* undistinguished during his life, and dubbed a saint by
the Jansenists after his death.   Had the first minister been a Jan-
senist, the saint had been a saint still.   All France had kept his
festival: and since there are thousands of eye-witnesses ready to
attest the truth of all the miracles supposed to have been wrought
at his tomb, notwithstanding the discouragement which these
zealots have met with from the government; we may assure ourselves, that these silly impostures would have been transmitted,
in all the solemn pomp of history, from the knaves of this age to
the fools of the next.

This lying spirit has gone forth from ecclesiastical to other historians: and I might fill many pages with instances of extravagant fables that have been invented in several nations, to cele-
brate their antiquity, to ennoble their originals, and to make
them appear illustrious in the arts of peace and the triumphs of
war.   When the brain is well heated, and devotion or vanity,
the semblance of virtue or real vice, and, above all, disputes and
contests, have inspired that complication of passions we term
zeal, the effects are much the same, and history becomes very
often a lying panegyric or a lying satire; for different nations
or different parties in the same nation, belie one another without
any respect for truth, as they murder one another without any

* The Abbé Paris.

regard to right or sense of humanity. Religious zeal may boast this horrid advantage over civil zeal, that the effects of it have been more sanguinary, and the malice more unrelenting. In another respect they are more alike, and keep a nearer proportion: different religions have not been quite so barbarous to one another as sects of the same religion; and, in like manner, nation has had better quarter from nation, than party from party. But in all these controversies, men have pushed their rage beyond their own and their adversaries lives: they have endeavored to interest posterity in their quarrels, and by rendering history subservient to this wicked purpose, they have done their utmost to perpetuate scandal, and to immortalise their animosity. The heathen taxed the Jews even with idolatry; the Jews joined with the heathen to render Christianity odious: but the church, who beat them at their own weapons during these contests, has had this further triumph over them, as well as over the several sects that have arisen within her own pale; the works of those who have written against her have been destroyed, and whatever she advanced, to justify herself and to defame her adversaries, is preserved in her annals, and the writings of her doctors.

The charge of corrupting history, in the cause of religion, has been always committed to the most famous champions, and greatest saints of each church; and, if I was not more afraid of tiring, than of scandalising your lordship, I could quote to you examples of modern churchmen who have endeavored to justify foul language by the New Testament, and cruelty by the Old; nay, what is execrable beyond imagination, and what strikes horror into every mind that entertains due sentiments of the Supreme Being, God himself has been cited for rallying and insulting Adam after his fall. In other cases this charge belongs to the pedants of every nation, and the tools of every party. What accusations of idolatry and superstition have not been brought, and aggravated against the Mahometans? Those wretched Christians who returned from those wars, so improperly called the holy wars, rumored these stories about the West; and you may find, in some of the old chroniclers and romance writers, as well as poets, the Saracens called Paynims; though surely they were much further off from any suspicion of polytheism, than those who called them by that name. When Mahomet the Second took Constantinople in the fifteenth century, the Mahometans began to be a little better, and but a little better known, than they had been before, to these parts of the world. But their religion, as well as their customs and manners, was strangely misrepresented by the Greek refugees that fled from the Turks: and the terror and hatred which this people had inspired

by the rapidity of their conquests, and by their ferocity, made
all these misrepresentations universally pass for truths. Many
such instances may be collected from Maraccio's refutation of
the Koran, and Relandus has published a very valuable treatise
on purpose to refute these calumnies, and to justify the Mahometans. Does not this example incline your lordship to think, that
the heathens and the Arians, and other heretics, would not appear quite so absurd in their opinions, nor so abominable in
their practice, as the orthodox Christians have represented them;
if some Relandus could arise, with the materials necessary to
their justification in his hands? He who reflects on the circumstances that attended letters, from the time when Constantine
instead of uniting the characters of emperor and sovereign pontiff in himself when he became Christian, as they were united in
him and all the other emperors in the Pagan system of government, gave so much independent wealth and power to the clergy,
and the means of acquiring so much more: he who carries these
reflections on through all the latter empire, and through those
ages of ignorance and superstition, wherein it was hard to say
which was greatest, the tyranny of the clergy or the servility of
the laity: he who considers the extreme severity, for instance of
the laws made by Theodosius in order to stifle every writing.
that the orthodox clergy, that is, the clergy then in fashion disliked; or the character and influence of such a priest as Gregory
called the great, who proclaimed war to all heathen learning in
order to promote Christian verity; and flattered Brunehault, and
abetted Phocas: he who considers all these things, I say, will
not be at a loss to find the reasons why history, both that which
was written before, and a great part of that which has been
written since the Christian era, is come to us so imperfect and
so corrupt.

When the imperfection is due to a total want of memorials,
either because none were originally written, or because they
have been lost by devastations of countries, extirpations of people, and other accidents in a long course of time; or because
zeal, malice, and policy have joined their endeavors to destroy
them purposely; we must be content to remain in our ignorance,
and there is no great harm in that. Secure from being deceived,
I can submit to be uninformed. But when there is not a total
want of memorials, when some have been lost or destroyed, and
others have been preserved and propagated, then we are in danger of being deceived: and therefore he must be very implicit
indeed who receives for true the history of any religion or nation, and much more that of any sect or party, without having the means of confronting it with some other history. A
reasonable man will not be thus implicit. He will not establish

the truth of history on single, but on concurrent testimony. If there be none such, he will doubt absolutely: if there be a little such, he will proportion his assent or dissent accordingly. A small gleam of light, borrowed from foreign anecdotes, serves often to discover a whole system of falsehood: and even they who corrupt history frequently betray themselves by their ignorance or inadvertency. Examples whereof I could easily produce. Upon the whole matter, in all these cases we cannot be deceived essentially, unless we please; and therefore there is no reason to establish Pyrrhonism, that we may avoid the ridicule of credulity.

In all other cases, there is less reason still to do so; for when histories and historical memorials abound, even those that are false serve to the discovery of the truth. Inspired by different passions, and contrived for opposite purposes, they contradict; and contradicting, they convict one another. Criticism separates the ore from the dross, and extracts from various authors a series of true history, which could not have been found entire in any one of them, and will command our assent, when it is formed with judgment, and represented with candor. If this may be done, as it has been done sometimes, with the help of authors who wrote on purpose to deceive; how much more easily, and more effectually may it be done, with the help of those who paid a greater regard to truth? In a multitude of writers there will be always some, either incapable of gross prevarication from the fear of being discovered, and of acquiring infamy whilst they seek for fame; or else attached to truth upon a nobler and surer principle. It is certain that these, even the last of them, are fallible. Bribed by some passion or other, the former may venture now and then to propagate a falsehood, or to disguise a truth; like the painter that drew in profile, as Lucian says, the picture of a prince that had but one eye. Montagne objects to the memorials of Du Bellay, that though the gross of the facts be truly related, yet these authors turned every thing they mentioned to the advantage of their master, and mentioned nothing which could not be so turned. The old fellow's words are worth quoting. " De contourner le jugement des evenemens souvent contre raison à notre avantage, et d'obmettre tout ce qu'il y a de chatouilleux en la vie de leur maistre, ils en font mestier." These, and such as these, deviate occasionally and voluntarily from truth; but even they who are attached to it the most religiously may slide sometimes into involuntary error. In matters of history we prefer very justly cotemporary authority; and yet cotemporary authors are the most liable to be warped from the straight rule of truth, in writing on subjects which have affected them strongly, " et quorum pars magna fuerunt." I am so persuaded of this from what I have felt in myself, and observed in others, that if life and health enough fall to my share, and I am able to finish what I meditate, a kind of history, from the late queen's accession to the throne, to the peace of Utrecht, there will be no materials that I shall examine more scrupulously and severely, than those of the time when the events to be spoken of were in transaction.   But though the writers of these two sorts, both of whom pay as much regard to truth as the various infirmities of our nature admit, are fallible; yet this fallibility will not be sufficient to give color to Pyrrhonism.   Where their sincerity as to fact is doubtful, we strike out truth by the confrontation of different accounts: as we strike out sparks of fire by the collision of flints and steel.   Where their judgments are suspicious of partiality, we may judge for ourselves; or adopt their judgments, after weighing them with certain grains of allowance. A little natural sagacity will proportion these grains according to the particular circumstances of the authors, or their general characters; for even these influence.   Thus Montagne pretends, but he exaggerates a little, that Guicciardin no where ascribes any one action to a virtuous, but every one to a vicious principle.   Something like this has been reproached to Tacitus: and, notwithstanding all the sprightly loose observations of Montagne in one of his essays, where he labors to prove the contrary, read Plutarch's comparisons in what language you please, I am of Bodin's mind, you will perceive they were made by a Greek. In short, my lord, the favorable opportunities of corrupting history have been often interrupted, and are now over in so many countries, that truth penetrates even into those where lying continues still to be part of the policy ecclesiastical and civil; or where, to say the best we can say, truth is never suffered to appear, till she has passed through hands, out of which she seldom returns entire and undefiled.

But it is time I should conclude this head, under which I have touched some of those reasons that show the folly of endeavoring to establish universal Pyrrhonism in matters of history, because there are few histories without some lies, and none without some mistakes; and that prove the body of history which we possess, since ancient memorials have been so critically examined, and modern memorials have been so multiplied, to contain in it such a probable series of events, easily distinguishable from the improbable, as force the assent of every man who is in his senses, and are, therefore, sufficient to answer all the purposes of the study of history.   I might have appealed, perhaps, without entering into the argument at all, to any man of candor, whether his doubts concerning the truth of history have hindered him from applying the examples he has met with in it, and from judging of the present, and sometimes of the future, by the past? Whether he has not been touched with reverence and admiration, at the virtue and wisdom of some men, and of some ages; and whether he has not felt indignation and contempt for others? Whether Epaminondas or Phocion, for instance, the Decii, or the Scipios, have not raised in his mind a flame of public spirit, and private virtue? and whether he has not shuddered with horror at the proscriptions of Marius and Sylla, at the treachery of Theodotus and Achillas, and at the consummate cruelty of an infant king? " Quis non contra Marii arma, et contra Syllæ proscriptionem concitatur? Quis non Theodoto, et Achillæ, et ipsi puero, non puerile auso facinus, infestus est?" If all this be a digression, therefore, your lordship will be so good as to excuse it.

II. What has been said concerning the multiplicity of histories, and of historical memorials, wherewith our libraries abound since the resurrection of letters happened, and the art of printing began, puts me in mind of another general rule, that ought to be observed by every man who intends to make a real improvement, and to become wiser as well as better, by the study of history. I hinted at this rule in a former letter, where I said that we should neither grope in the dark, nor wander in the light. History must have a certain degree of probability and authenticity, or the examples we find in it would not carry a force sufficient to make due impressions on our minds, nor to illustrate nor to strengthen the precepts of philosophy and the rules of good policy. But besides, when histories have this necessary authenticity and probability, there is much discernment to be employed in the choice and the use we make of them. Some are to be read, some are to be studied; and some may be neglected entirely, not only without detriment, but with advantage. Some are the proper objects of one man's curiosity, some of another's, and some of all men's; but all history is not an object of curiosity for any man. He who improperly, wantonly, and absurdly makes it so, indulges a sort of canine appetite: the curiosity of one, like the hunger of the other, devours ravenously and without distinction whatever falls in its way; but neither of them digests. They heap crudity upon crudity, and nourish and improve nothing but their distemper. Some such characters I have known, though it is not the most common extreme into which men are apt to fall. One of them I knew in this country. He joined, to a more than athletic strength of body, a prodigious memory; and to both a prodigious industry. He had read almost constantly twelve or fourteen hours a day, for five-and-twenty or thirty years; and had heaped together as much learning as could be crowded into a head. In the course of my acquaintance with him, I consulted

with him once or twice, not oftener; for I found this mass of
learning of as little use to me as to the owner. The man was
communicative enough; but nothing was distinct in his mind.
How could it be otherwise? he had never spared time to think,
all was employed in reading. His reason had not the merit of
common mechanism. When you press a watch or pull a clock,
they answer your question with precision; for they repeat exactly
the hour of the day, and tell you neither more nor less than you
desire to know. But when you asked this man a question, he
overwhelmed you with pouring forth all that the several terms
or words of your question recalled to his memory: and if he
omitted any thing, it was that very thing to which the sense of
the whole question should have led him and confined him. To
ask him a question, was to wind up a spring in his memory, that
rattled on with vast rapidity, and confused noise, till the force of
it was spent: and you went away with all the noise in your ears,
stunned and uninformed. I never left him that I was not ready
to say to him, "Dieu vous fasse la graçe de devenir moins sa-
vant!" a wish that La Mothe le Vayer mentions upon some
occasion or other, and that he would have done well to have
applied himself upon many.

He who reads with discernment and choice, will acquire less
learning, but more knowledge: and as this knowledge is collected
with design, and cultivated with art and method, it will be at all
times of immediate and ready use to himself and others.

> Thus useful arms in magazines we place,
> All rang'd in order; and disposed with grace:
> Nor thus alone the curious eye to please;
> But to be found, when need requires, with ease.

You remember the verses, my lord, in our friend's Essay on
Criticism, which was the work of his childhood almost; but is
such a monument of good sense and poetry as no other, that I
know, has raised in his riper years.

He who reads without this discernment and choice, and, like
Bodin's pupil, resolves to read all, will not have time, no, nor
capacity neither, to do any thing else. He will not be able to
think, without which it is impertinent to read; nor to act, without which it is impertinent to think. He will assemble materials
with much pains, and purchase them at much expense, and have
neither leisure nor skill to frame them into proper scantlings, or
to prepare them for use. To what purpose should he husband
his time, or learn architecture? he has no design to build. But
then to what purpose all these quarries of stone, all these mountains of sand and lime, all these forests of oak and deal?
"Magno impendio temporum, magna alienarum aurium molestia,

laudatio hæc constat, O hominem literatum! Simus hoc titulo rusticiore contenti, O virum bonum!" We may add, and Seneca might have added in his own style, and according to the manners and characters of his own age, another title as rustic, and as little in fashion, " O virum sapientia sua simplicem, et simplicitate sua sapientem? O virum utilem sibi, suis, reipublicæ, et humano generi!" I have said perhaps already, but no matter, it cannot be repeated too often, that the drift of all philosophy, and of all political speculations, ought to be the making us better men, and better citizens. Those studies, which have no intention towards improving our moral characters, have no pretence to be styled philosophical. " Quis est enim," says Tully in his Offices, " qui nullis officii præceptis, tradendis, philosophum se audeat dicere?" Whatever political speculations, instead of preparing us to be useful to society, and to promote the happiness of mankind, are only systems for gratifying private ambition, and promoting private interests at the public expense; all such, I say, deserve to be burnt, and the authors of them to starve, like Machiavel, in a jail.

LETTER V.

I. THE GREAT USE OF HISTORY, PROPERLY SO CALLED, AS DISTIN-
GUISHED FROM THE WRITINGS OF MERE ANNALISTS AND ANTI-
QUARIES. II. GREEK AND ROMAN HISTORIANS. III. SOME IDEA
OF A COMPLETE HISTORY. IV. FURTHER CAUTIONS TO BE OB-
SERVED IN THIS STUDY, AND THE REGULATION OF IT ACCORDING
TO THE DIFFERENT POSSESSIONS, AND SITUATIONS OF MEN: ABOVE
ALL, THE USE TO BE MADE OF IT (1) BY DIVINES, AND (2) BY
THOSE WHO ARE CALLED TO THE SERVICE OF THEIR COUNTRY.

I REMEMBER my last letter ended abruptly, and a long interval has since passed: so that the thread I had then spun has slipt from me. I will try to recover it, and to pursue the task your lordship has obliged me to continue. Besides the pleasure of obeying your orders, it is likewise of some advantage to myself, to recollect my thoughts, and resume a study in which I was conversant formerly. For nothing can be more true than that saying of Solon reported by Plato, though censured by him, impertinently enough in one of his wild books of laws;—" Assidue addiscens, ad senium venio." The truth is, the most knowing man, in the course of the longest life, will have always much to learn, and the wisest and best much to improve. This rule will hold in the knowledge and improvement to be acquired by the study of history; and therefore even he who has gone to this school in his youth, should not neglect it in his age. " I read in " Livy," says Montagne, what another man does not: " and Plutarch read there what I do not." Just so the same man may read at fifty what he did not read in the same book at five and twenty: at least I have found it so, by my own experience, on many occasions.

By comparing, in this study, the experience of other men and other ages with our own, we improve both: we analyse, as it were, philosophy. We reduce all the abstract speculations of ethics, and all the general rules of human policy, to their first principles. With these advantages every man may, though few men do, advance daily towards those ideas, those increated essences a Platonist would say, which no human creature can reach in practice, but in the nearest approaches to which the perfection of our nature consists; because every approach of this kind renders a man better, and wiser, for himself, for his family, for the little community of his own country, and for the great community of the world. Be not surprised, my lord, at the order in which I place these objects. Whatever order divines and moralists, who contemplate the duties belonging to these objects, may place them in, this is the order they hold in nature: and I have always thought that we might lead ourselves and others to private virtue, more effectually by a due observation of this order, than by any of those sublime refinements that pervert it.

> Self-love but serves the virtuous mind to wake;
> As the small pebble stirs the peaceful lake.
> The centre mov'd, a circle straight succeeds;
> Another still, and still another spreads:
> Friend, parent, neighbor, first it will embrace,
> His country next, and next all human race.

So sings our friend Pope, my lord, and so I believe. So I shall prove too, if I mistake not, in an epistle I am about to write to him, in order to complete a set that were written some years ago.

A man of my age, who returns to the study of history, has no time to lose, because he has little to live: a man of your lordship's age has no time to lose, because he has much to do. For different reasons therefore the same rules will suit us. Neither of us must grope in the dark, neither of us must wander in the light. I have done the first formerly a good deal; "ne verba mihi darentur; ne aliquid esse, in hac recondita antiquitatis scientia, magni ac secreti boni judicaremus." If you take my word, you will throw none of your time away in the same manner: and I shall have the less regret for that which I have misspent, if I persuade you to hasten down from the broken traditions of antiquity, to the more entire as well as more authentic histories of ages more modern. In the study of these we shall find many a complete series of events, preceded by a deduction of their immediate and remote causes, related in their full extent, and accompanied with such a detail of circumstances, and characters, as may transport the attentive reader back to the very time, make him a party to the councils, and an actor in the whole scene of affairs. Such draughts as these, either found in history or extracted by our own application from it, and such alone, are truly useful. Thus history becomes what she ought to be, and what she has been sometimes called, "magistra vitæ," the mistress, like philosophy, of human life. If she is not this, she is at best "nuntia vetustatis," the gazette of antiquity, or a dry register of useless anecdotes. Suetonius says that Tiberius used to inquire of the grammarians, "quæ mater Hecubæ? quod Achilles nomen inter virgines fuisset? quid Syrenes cantare sint solitæ?" Seneca mentions certain Greek authors, who examined very accurately whether Anacreon loved wine or women best, whether Sappho was a common whore, with other points of equal importance: and I make no doubt but that a man, better acquainted than I have the honor to be with the learned persons of our own country, might find some who have discovered several anecdotes, concerning the giant Albion, concerning Samothes the son, or Brito the grandson of Japhet, and concerning Brutus who led a colony into our island after the siege of Troy, as the others repeopled it after the deluge. But ten millions of such anecdotes as these, though they were true; and complete authentic volumes of Egyptian or Chaldean, of Greek or Latin, of Gallic or British, of French or Saxon records, would be of no value in my sense, because of no use towards our improvement in wisdom and virtue; if they contained nothing more than dynasties and genealogies, and a bare mention of remarkable events in the order of time, like journals, chronological tables, or dry and meagre annals.

I say the same of all those modern compositions in which we find rather the heads of history, than any thing that deserves to be called history. Their authors are either abridgers or compilers. The first do neither honor to themselves, nor good to mankind; for surely the abridger is in a form below the translator; and the book, at least the history, that wants to be abridged, does not deserve to be read. They have done anciently a great deal of hurt by substituting many a bad book in the place of a good one; and by giving occasion to men, who contented themselves with extracts and abridgments, to neglect, and through their neglect, to lose the invaluable originals: for which reason I

curse Constantine Porphyrogenetes as heartily as I do Gregory.
The second are of some use, as far as they contribute to preserve
public acts, and dates, and the memory of great events.   But
they who are thus employed have seldom the means of knowing
those private passages on which all public transactions depend,
and as seldom the skill and the talents necessary to put what
they do know well together: they cannot see the working of the
mine, but their industry collects the matter that is thrown out.
It is the business, or it should be so, of others to separate the
pure ore from the dross, to stamp it into coin, and to enrich, not
encumber mankind.   When there are none sufficient to this task,
there may be antiquaries, and there may be journalists or annalists, but there are no historians.

It is worth while to observe the progress that the Romans and
the Greeks made towards history.   The Romans had journalists
or annalists from the very beginning of their state.   In the sixth
century, or very near it at soonest, they began to have antiquaries, and some attempts were made towards writing of history.
I call these first historical productions attempts only or essays:
and they were no more, neither among the Romans, nor among
the Greeks.   "Græci ipsi sic initio scriptitarunt ut noster Cato,
ut Pictor, ut Piso."   It is Antony, not the triumvir, my lord, but
his grandfather the famous orator, who says this in the second
book of Tully *De Oratore:* he adds afterwards, "Itaque qualis
apud Græcos Pherecydes, Hellanicus, Acusilaus, aliique per-
multi, talis noster Cato, et Pictor, et Piso."   I know that Antony
speaks here strictly of defect of style and want of oratory.   They
were, "tantummodo narratores, non exornatores," as he expresses himself: but as they wanted style and skill to write in
such a manner as might answer all the ends of history, so they
wanted materials.   Pherecydes wrote something about Iphigenia,
and the festivals of Bacchus.   Hellanicus was a poetical historian,
and Acusilaus graved genealogies on plates of brass.   Pictor,
who is called by Livy "scriptorum antiquissimus," published, I
think, some short annals of his own time.   Neither he nor Piso
could have sufficient materials for the history of Rome; nor Cato,
I presume, even for the antiquities of Italy.   The Romans, with
the other people of that country, were then just rising out of
barbarity, and growing acquainted with letters; for those that the
Grecian colonies might bring into Sicily, and the southern parts
of Italy, spread little, or lasted little, and made in the whole no
figure.   And whatever learning might have flourished among
the ancient Etrurians, which was perhaps at most nothing better
than augury, and divination, and superstitious rites, which were
admired and cultivated in ignorant ages, even that was almost
entirely worn out of memory.   Pedants, who would impose all

the traditions of the four first ages of Rome, for authentic history, have insisted much on certain annals, of which mention is made in the very place I have just now quoted. "Ab initio rerum Romanarum," says the same interlocutor, "usque ad P. Mucium pontificem maximum, res omnes singulorum annorum mandabat literis pontifex maximus, efferebatque in album, et proponebat tabulam domi, potestas ut esset populo cognoscendi; iidemque etiam nunc annales maximi nominantur." But, my lord, be pleased to take notice, that the very distinction I make is made here between a bare annalist and a historian: "erat historia nihil aliud," in these early days, "nisi annalium confectio." Take notice likewise, by the way, that Livy, whose particular application it had been to search into this matter, affirms positively that the greatest part of all public and private monuments, among which he specifies these very annals, had been destroyed in the sack of Rome by the Gauls: and Plutarch cites Clodius for the same assertion, in the life of Numa Pompilius. Take notice, in the last place, of that which is more immediately to our present purpose. These annals could contain nothing more than short minutes or memorandums hung up in a table at the pontiff's house, like the rules of the game in the billiard-room, and much such history as we have in the epitomes prefixed to the books of Livy or of any other historian, in lapidary inscriptions, or in some modern almanacs. Materials for history they were no doubt, but scanty and insufficient; such as those ages could produce when writing and reading were accomplishments so uncommon, that the prætor was directed by law, "clavum pangere," to drive a nail into the door of a temple, that the number of years might be reckoned by the number of nails. Such in short as we have in monkish annalists, and other ancient chroniclers of nations now in being: but not such as can entitle the authors of them to be called historians, nor can enable others to write history in that fulness in which it must be written to become a lesson of ethics and politics. The truth is, nations, like men, have their infancy: and the few passages of that time, which they retain, are not such as deserved most to be remembered; but such as, being most proportioned to that age, made the strongest impressions on their minds. In those nations that preserve their dominion long, and grow up to manhood, the elegant as well as the necessary arts and sciences are improved to some degree of perfection; and history, that was at first intended only to record the names, or perhaps the general characters of some famous men, and to transmit in gross the the remarkable events of every age to posterity, is raised to answer another, and a nobler end.

II. Thus it happened among the Greeks, but much more among

the Romans, notwithstanding the prejudices in favor of the former, even among the latter. I have sometimes thought that Virgil might have justly ascribed to his countrymen the praise of writing history better, as well as that of affording the noblest subjects for it, in those famous verses,* where the different excellences of the two nations are so finely touched: but he would have weakened perhaps by lengthening, and have flattened the climax. Open Herodotus, you are entertained by an agreeable story-teller, who meant to entertain, and nothing more. Read Thucydides or Xenophon, you are taught indeed as well as entertained: and the statesman or the general, the philosopher or the orator, speaks to you in every page. They wrote on subjects on which they were well informed, and they treated them fully: they maintained the dignity of history, and thought it beneath them to vamp up old traditions, like the writers of their age and country, and to be the trumpeters of a lying antiquity. The Cyropædia of Xenophon may be objected perhaps; but if he gave it for a romance, not a history, as he might for aught we can tell, it is out of the case: and if he gave it for a history, not a romance, I should prefer his authority to that of Herodotus, or any other of his countrymen. But however this might be, and whatever merit we may justly ascribe to these two writers, who were almost single in their kind, and who treated but small portions of history; certain it is in general, that the levity as well as loquacity of the Greeks made them incapable of keeping up to the true standard of history: and even Polybius and Dionysius of Halicarnassus must bow to the great Roman authors. Many principal men of that commonwealth wrote memorials of their own actions and their own times: Sylla, Cæsar, Labienus, Pollio, Augustus, and others. What writers of memorials, what compilers of the *materia historica* were these? What genius was necessary to finish up the pictures that such masters had sketched? Rome afforded men that were equal to the task. Let the remains, the precious remains, of Sallust, of Livy, and of Tacitus, witness this truth. When Tacitus wrote, even the appearances of virtue had been long proscribed, and taste was grown corrupt as well as manners. Yet history preserved her integrity and her lustre. She preserved them in the writings of some whom Tacitus mentions, in none perhaps more than his own; every line of

* Excudent alii spirantia mollius æra,
  Credo equidem: vivos ducent de marmore vultus;
  Orabunt causas melius: cœlique meatus
  Describent radio, et surgentia sidera dicent:
  Tu regere imperio populos, Romane, memento:
  Hæ tibi erunt artes; pacisque imponere morem,
  Parcere subjectis, et debellare superbos.

which outweighs whole pages of such a rhetor as Famianus Strada. I single him out among the moderns, because he had the foolish presumption to censure Tacitus, and to write history himself: and your lordship will forgive this short excursion in honor of a favorite author.

What a school of private and public virtue had been opened to us at the resurrection of learning, if the latter historians of the Roman commonwealth, and the first of the succeeding monarchy, had come down to us entire? The few that are come down, though broken and imperfect, compose the best body of history that we have, nay the only body of ancient history that deserves to be an object of study. It fails us indeed most at that remarkable and fatal period, where our reasonable curiosity is raised the highest. Livy employed five and forty books to bring his history down to the end of the sixth century, and the breaking out of the third Punic war: but he employed ninety-five to bring it down from thence to the death of Drusus; that is, through the course of one hundred and twenty or thirty years. Apian, Dion Cassius, and others, nay even Plutarch included, make us but poor amends for what is lost of Livy. Among all the adventitious helps by which we endeavor to supply this loss in some degree, the best are those which we find scattered up and down in the works of Tully. His orations, particularly, and his letters, contain many curious anecdotes and instructive reflections, concerning the intrigues and machinations that were carried on against liberty, from Catiline's conspiracy to Cæsar's. The state of the government, the constitution and temper of the several parties, and the characters of the principal persons who figured at that time on the public stage, are to be seen there in a stronger and truer light than they would have appeared perhaps if he had written purposely on this subject, and even in those memorials which he somewhere promises Atticus to write. "Excudam aliquod Heraclidium opus, quod lateat in thesauris tuis." He would hardly have unmasked in such a work, as freely as in familiar occasional letters, Pompey, Cato, Brutus, nay himself; the four men of Rome, on whose praises he dwelt with the greatest complacency. The age in which Livy flourished abounded with such materials as these: they were fresh, they were authentic; it was easy to procure them, it was safe to employ them. How he did employ them in executing the second part of his design, we may judge by his execution of the first: and, I own to your lordship, I should be glad to exchange, if it were possible, what we have of this history for what we have not. Would you not be glad, my lord, to see, in one stupendous draught, the whole progress of that government from liberty to servitude? the whole series of causes and effects, apparent and real, public and private? those which all men saw, and all good men lamented and opposed at the time; and those which were so disguised to the prejudices, to the partialities of a divided people, and even to the corruption of mankind, that many did not, and that many could pretend they did not, discern them, till it was too late to resist them? I am sorry to say it, this part of the Roman story would be not only more curious and more authentic than the former, but of more immediate and more important application to the present state of Britain. But it is lost: the loss is irreparable, and your lordship will not blame me for deploring it.

III. They who set up for scepticism may not regret the loss of such a history: but this I will be bold to assert to them, that a history must be written on this plan, and must aim at least at these perfections, or it will answer sufficiently none of the intentions of history. That it will not answer sufficiently the intention I have insisted upon in these letters, that of instructing posterity by the example of former ages, is manifest: and I think it is as manifest, that a history cannot be said even to relate faithfully, and inform us truly, that does not relate fully, and inform us of all that is necessary to make a true judgment concerning the matters contained in it. Naked facts, without the causes that produced them, and the circumstances that accompanied them, are not sufficient to characterise actions or counsels. The nice degrees of wisdom and of folly, of virtue and of vice, will not only be undiscoverable in them; but we must be very often unable to determine under which of these characters they fall in general. The sceptics I am speaking of are therefore guilty of this absurdity: the nearer a history comes to the true idea of history, the better it informs and the more it instructs us, the more worthy to be rejected it appears to them. I have said and allowed enough to content any reasonable man about the uncertainty of history. I have owned that the best are defective, and I will add in this place an observation which did not, I think, occur to me before. Conjecture is not always distinguished perhaps as it ought to be; so that an ingenious writer may sometimes do very innocently, what a malicious writer does very criminally as often as he dares, and as his malice requires it: he may account for events, after they have happened, by a system of causes and conduct that did not really produce them, though it might possibly or even probably have produced them. But this observation, like several others, becomes a reason for examining and comparing authorities, and for preferring some, not for rejecting all. Davila, a noble historian surely, and one whom I should not scruple to confess equal in many respects to Livy, as I should not scruple to prefer his countryman Guicciardin to Thucydides in every respect; Davila, my lord, was accused, from the first publication of his history, or at least was suspected, of too much refinement and subtlety, in developing the secret motives of actions, in laying the causes of events too deep, and deducing them often through a series of progression too complicated, and too artistly wrought. But yet the suspicious person who should reject this historian upon such general inducements as these, would have no grace to oppose his suspicions to the authority of the first duke of Epernon, who had been an actor, and a principal actor too, in many of the scenes that Davila recites. Girard, secretary to this duke, and no contemptible biographer, relates, that this history came down to the place where the old man resided in Gascony, a little before his death; that he read it to him, that the duke confirmed the truth of the narrations in it, and seemed only surprised by what means the author could be so well informed of the most secret councils and measures of those times.

IV. I have said enough on this head, and your lordship may be induced, perhaps, by what I have said, to think with me, that such histories as these, whether ancient or modern, deserve alone to be studied. Let us leave the credulous learned to write history without materials, or to study those who do so; to wrangle about ancient traditions, and to ring different changes on the same set of bells. Let us leave the sceptics, in modern as well as ancient history, to triumph in the notable discovery of the ides of one month mistaken for the calends of another, or in the various dates and contradictory circumstances which they find in weekly gazettes and monthly mercuries. Whilst they are thus employed, your lordship and I will proceed, if you please, to consider more closely, than we have yet done, the rule mentioned above; that, I mean, of using discernment and choice in the study of the most authentic history, that of not wandering in the light, which is as necessary as that of not groping in the dark.

Man is the subject of every history; and to know him well, we must see him and consider him, as history alone can present him to us, in every age, in every country, in every state, in life and in death. History, therefore, of all kinds, of civilised and uncivilised, of ancient and modern nations, in short, all history that descends to a sufficient detail of human actions and characters, is useful to bring us acquainted with our species, nay, with ourselves. To teach and to inculcate the general principles of virtue, and the general rules of wisdom and good policy, which result from such details of actions and characters, comes for the the most part, and always should come, expressly and directly into the design of those who are capable of giving such details: and, therefore, whilst they narrate as historians, they hint often as philosophers; they put into our hands, as it were, on every proper occasion, the end of a clue, that serves to remind us of searching, and to guide us in the search of that truth which the example before us either establishes or illustrates.   If a writer neglects this part, we are able, however, to supply his neglect by our own attention and industry: and when he gives us a good history of Peruvians or Mexicans, of Chinese or Tartars, of Muscovites or Negroes, we may blame him, but we must blame ourselves much more, if we do not make it a good lesson of philosophy.   This being the general use of history, it is not to be neglected.   Every one may make it, who is able to read and reflect on what he reads, and every one who makes it will find in his degree, the benefit that arises from an early acquaintance contracted in this manner with mankind.   We are not only passengers or sojourners in this world, but we are absolute strangers at the first step we make in it.   Our guides are often ignorant, often unfaithful.   By this map of the country, which history spreads before us, we may learn, if we please, to guide ourselves. In our journey through it, we are beset on every side.   We are besieged, sometimes even in our strongest holds.   Terrors and temptations, conducted by the passions of other men, assault us: and our own passions, that correspond with these, betray us. History is a collection of the journals of those who have travelled through the same country, and been exposed to the same accidents: and their good and their ill success are equally instructive. In this pursuit of knowledge an immense field is opened to us: general histories, sacred and profane; the histories of particular countries, particular events, particular orders, particular men; memorials, anecdotes, travels.   But we must not ramble in this field without discernment or choice, nor even with these must we ramble too long.

As to the choice of authors, who have written on all these various subjects, so much has been said by learned men concerning all those that deserve attention, and their several characters are so well established, that it would be a sort of pedantic affectation to lead your lordship through so voluminous, and at the same time so easy, a detail.   I pass it over therefore in order to observe, that as soon as we have taken this general view of mankind, and of the course of human affairs in different ages and different parts of the world, we ought to apply, and, the shortness of human life considered, to confine ourselves almost entirely in our study of history, to such histories as have an immediate relation to our professions, or to our rank and situation in the society to which we belong.   Let me instance in the profession of divinity, as the noblest and the most important.

(1.) I have said so much concerning the share which divines of all religions have taken in the corruption of history, that I should have anathemas pronounced against me, no doubt, in the east and the west, by the dairo, the mufti, and the pope, if these letters were submitted to ecclesiastical censure; for surely, my lord, the clergy have a better title, than the sons of Apollo, to be called "genus irritabile vatum." What would it be, if I went about to show, how many of the Christian clergy abuse, by misrepresentation and false quotation, the history they can no longer corrupt? And yet this task would not be, even to me, an hard one. But as I mean to speak in this place of Christian divines alone, so I mean to speak of such of them particularly as may be called divines without any sneer; of such of them, for some such I think there are, as believe themselves, and would have mankind believe; not for temporal but spiritual interest, not for the sake of the clergy, but for the sake of mankind. Now it has been long matter of astonishment to me, how such persons as these could take so much silly pains to establish mystery on metaphysics, revelation on philosophy, and matters of fact on abstract reasoning? A religion founded on the authority of a divine mission, confirmed by prophecies and miracles, appeals to facts: and the facts must be proved as all other facts that pass for authentic are proved; for faith so reasonable after this proof, is absurd before it. If they are thus proved, the religion will prevail without the assistance of so much profound reasoning: if they are not thus proved, the authority of it will sink in the world even with this assistance. The divines object in their disputes with atheists, and they object very justly, that these men require improper proofs; proofs that are not suited to the nature of the subject, and then cavil that such proofs are not furnished. But what then do they mean, to fall into the same absurdity themselves in their disputes with theists, and to din improper proofs in ears that are open to proper proofs? The matter is of great moment, my lord, and I make no excuse for the zeal which obliges me to dwell a little on it. A serious and honest application to the study of ecclesiastical history, and every part of profane history and chronology relative to it, is incumbent on such reverend persons as are here spoken of, on a double account: because history alone can furnish the proper proofs, that the religion they teach is of God; and because the unfair manner, in which these proofs have been and are daily furnished, creates prejudices, and gives advantages against Christianity that require to be removed. No scholar will dare to deny, that false history, as well as sham miracles, has been employed to propagate Christianity formerly: and whoever examines the writers of our own age, will find the same abuse of history continued. Many and many instances of this abuse might be produced. It is grown into custom, writers copy one another, and the mistake that was committed, or the falsehood that was invented by one, is adopted by hundreds.

Abbadie says in his famous book, that the Gospel of St. Matthew is cited by Clemens, bishop of Rome, a disciple of the apostles; that Barnabas cites it in his epistle; that Ignatius and Polycarp receive it; and that the same fathers, that give testimony for Matthew, give it likewise for Mark. Nay your lordship will find, I believe, that the present bishop of London, in his third pastoral letter, speaks to the same effect. I will not trouble you nor myself with any more instances of the same kind. Let this, which occurred to me as I was writing, suffice. It may well suffice; for I presume the fact advanced by the minister and the bishop is a mistake. If the fathers of the first century do mention some passages that are agreeable to what we read in our evangelists, will it follow that these fathers had the same gospels before them? To say so is a manifest abuse of history, and quite inexcusable in writers that knew, or should have known, that these fathers made use of other gospels, wherein such passages might be contained, or they might be preserved in unwritten tradition. Besides which, I could almost venture to affirm that these fathers of the first century do not expressly name the gospels we have of Matthew, Mark, Luke, and John. To the two reasons that have been given why those who make divinity their profession, should study history, particularly ecclesiastical history, with an honest and serious application; in order to support Christianity against the attacks of unbelievers, and to remove the doubts and prejudices that the unfair proceedings of men of their own order have raised in minds candid but not implicit, willing to be informed but curious to examine; to these, I say, we may add another consideration that seems to me of no small importance. Writers of the Roman religion have attempted to show, that the text of the holy writ is on many accounts insufficient to be the sole criterion of orthodoxy: I apprehend too that they have shown it. Sure I am that experience, from the first promulgation of Christianity to this hour, shows abundantly with how much ease and success the most opposite, the most extravagant, nay, the most impious opinions, and the most contradictory faiths, may be founded on the same text; and plausibly defended by the same authority. Writers of the reformed religion have erected their batteries against tradition; and the only difficulty they had to encounter in this enterprise lay in levelling and pointing their cannon so as to avoid demolishing, in one common ruin, the traditions they retain, and those they reject. Each side has been employed to weaken the cause and explode the system of his adversary: and, whilst they have been so employed, they have jointly laid their axes to the root of Christianity: for thus men will be apt to reason upon what they have advanced. " If the text has not that authenticity, clearness, and precision which are necessary to establish it as a divine and a certain rule of faith and practice; and if the tradition of the church, from the first ages of it till the days of Luther and Calvin, has been corrupted itself, and has served to corrupt the faith and practice of Christians; there remains at this time no standard at all of Christianity. By consequence, either this religion was not originally of divine institution, or else God has not provided effectually for preserving the genuine purity of it, and the gates of hell have actually prevailed, in contradiction to his promise, against the church." The best effect of this reasoning that can be hoped for, is, that men should fall into theism, and subscribe to the first proposition; he must be worse than an atheist who can affirm the last. The dilemna is terrible, my lord. Party zeal and private interest have formed it: the common interest of Christianity is deeply concerned to solve it. Now, I presume, it can never be solved without a more accurate examination, not only of the Christian but of the Jewish system, than learned men have been hitherto impartial enough and sagacious enough to take, or honest enough to communicate. Whilst the authenticity and sense of the text of the bible remain as disputable, and whilst the tradition of the church remains as problematical, to say no worse, as the immense labors of the Christian divines in several communions have made them appear to be; Christianity may lean on the civil and ecclesiastical power, and be supported by the forcible influence of education: but the proper force of religion, that force which subdues the mind, and awes the conscience by conviction, will be wanting.

I had reason, therefore, to produce divinity, as one instance of those professions that require a particular application to the study of some particular parts of history; and since I have said so much on the subject in my zeal for Christianity, I will add this further. The resurrection of letters was a fatal period: the Christian system has been attacked, and wounded too, very severely since that time. The defence has been better made indeed by modern divines, than it had been by ancient fathers and apologists. The moderns have invented new methods of defence, and have abandoned some posts that were not tenable: but still there are others, in defending which they lie under great disadvantages. Such are various facts, piously believed in former times, but on which the truth of Christianity has been rested very imprudently in more enlightened ages; because the falsity of some, and the gross improbability of others are so evident, that, instead of answering the purpose for which they were invented, they have rendered the whole tenor of ecclesiastical history and tradition precarious, ever since a strict but just application of the rules of criticism has been made to them. I touch these things lightly; but if your lordship reflects upon them, you will find reason perhaps to think as I do, that it is high time the clergy in all Christian communions should join their forces, and establish those historical facts, which are the foundations of the whole system, on clear and unquestionable historical authority, such as they require in all cases of moment from others; reject candidly what cannot be thus established; and pursue their inquiries in the same spirit of truth through all the ages of the church; without any regard to historians, fathers, or councils, more than they are strictly entitled to on the face of what they have transmitted to us, on their own consistency, and on the concurrence of other authority. Our pastors would be thus, I presume, much better employed than they generally are. Those of the clergy who make religion merely a trade, who regard nothing more than the subsistence it affords them, or in higher life the wealth and power they enjoy by the means of it, may say to themselves, that it will last their time, or that policy and reason of state will preserve the form of a church when the spirit of religion is extinct. But those whom I mentioned above, those who act for spiritual not temporal ends, and are desirous that men should believe and practise the doctrines of Christianity, as well as go to church and pay tithes, will feel and own the weight of such considerations as these; and agree, that however the people have been, and may be still amused, yet Christianity has been in decay ever since the resurrection of letters; and that it cannot be supported as it was supported before that era, nor by any other way than that which I propose, and which a due application to the study of history, chronology, and criticism, would enable our divines to pursue, no doubt, with success.

I might instance, in other professions, the obligations men lie under of applying themselves to certain parts of history, and I can hardly forbear doing it in that of the law; in its nature the noblest and most beneficial to mankind, in its abuse and debasement the most sordid and the most pernicious. A lawyer now is nothing more, I speak of ninety-nine in a hundred at least, to use some of Tully's words, "nisi leguleius quidam cautus, et acutus præco actionum, cantor formularum, auceps syllabarum." But there have been lawyers that were orators, philosophers, historians: there have been Bacons and Clarendons, my lord. There will be none such any more, till, in some better age, true ambition or the love of fame prevails over avarice; and till men find leisure and encouragement to prepare themselves for the exercise of this profession, by climbing up to the "vantage

ground," so my Lord Bacon calls it, of science; instead of gro-
velling all their lives below, in a mean but gainful application to
all the little arts of chicane. Till this happen, the profession of
the law will scarce deserve to be ranked among the learned professions: and whenever it happens, one of the vantage grounds,
to which men must climb, is metaphysical, and the other historical knowledge. They must pry into the secret recesses of the
human heart, and become well acquainted with the whole moral
world, that they may discover the abstract reason of all laws:
and they must trace the laws of particular states, especially of
their own, from the first rough sketches to the more perfect
draughts; from the first causes or occasions that produced them,
through all the effects, good and bad, that they produced. But
I am running insensibly into a subject, which would detain me
too long from one that relates more immediately to your lordship, and with which I intend to conclude this long letter.

2. I pass from the consideration of those professions to which
particular parts or kinds of history seem to belong: and I come
to speak of the study of history, as a necessary means to prepare men for the discharge of that duty which they owe to their
country, and which is common to all the members of every society that is constituted according to the rules of right reason,
and with a due regard to the common good. I have met, in St.
Real's works, or some other French book, with a ridicule cast on
private men who make history a political study, or who apply
themselves in any manner to affairs of state. But the reflection
is too general. In governments so arbitrary by their constitution, that the will of the prince is not only the supreme, but the
sole law, it is so far from being a duty, that it may be dangerous,
and must be impertinent in men, who are not called by the
prince to the administration of public affairs, to concern themselves about it, or to fit themselves for it. The sole vocation
there is the favor of the court; and whatever designation God
makes by the talents he bestows, though it may serve, which it
seldom ever does, to direct the choice of the prince, yet I presume that it cannot become a reason to particular men, or create
a duty on them, to devote themselves to the public service.
Look on the Turkish government. See a fellow taken, from
rowing in a common passage-boat, by the caprice of the prince:
see him invested next day with all the power the soldans took
under the caliphs, or the mayors of the palace under the successors of Clovis: see a whole empire governed by the ignorance,
inexperience, and arbitrary will of this tyrant, and a few other
subordinate tyrants, as ignorant and unexperienced as himself.
In France indeed, though an absolute government, things go a
little better. Arts and sciences are encouraged, and here and

there an example may be found of a man who has risen by
some extraordinary talents, amidst innumerable examples of men
who have arrived at the greatest honors and highest posts by no
other merit than that of assiduous fawning, attendance, or of
skill in some despicable puerile amusement; in training wasps,
for instance, to take regular flights like hawks, and stoop at flies.
The nobility of France, like the children of tribute among the
ancient Saracens and modern Turks, are set apart for wars.
They are bred to make love, to hunt, and to fight: and, if any
of them should acquire knowledge superior to this, they would
acquire that which might be prejudicial to themselves, but could
not become beneficial to their country.   The affairs of state are
trusted to other hands.   Some have risen to them by drudging
long in business: some have been made ministers almost in the
cradle: and the whole power of the government has been abandoned to others in the dotage of life.   There is a monarchy, an
absolute monarchy too, I mean that of China, wherein the administration of the government is carried on, under the direction
of the prince, ever since the dominion of the Tartars has been
established, by several classes of Mandarins, and according to
the deliberation and advice of several orders of councils: the
admission to which classes and orders depends on the abilities of
the candidates, as their rise on them depends on the behavior
they hold, and the improvements they make afterwards.   Under
such a government, it is neither impertinent nor ridiculous, in
any of the subjects who are invited by their circumstances, or
pushed to it by their talents, to make the history of their own
and of other countries a political study, and to fit themselves by
this and all other ways for the service of the public.   It is not
dangerous neither; or an honor, that outweighs the danger, attends it; since private men have a right by the ancient constitution of this government, as well as councils of state, to represent to the prince the abuses of his administration.   But still
men have not there the same occasion to concern themselves in
the affairs of the state, as the nature of a free government gives
to the members of it.   In our own country, for in our own the
forms of a free government at least are hitherto preserved, men
are not only designed for the public service by the circumstances
of their situation, and their talents, all which may happen in
others: but they are designed to it by their birth in many cases,
and in all cases they may dedicate themselves to this service, and
take, in different degrees some share in it; whether they are called to it by the prince or no.   In absolute governments, all public service is to the prince, and he nominates all those that serve
the public.   In free governments, there is a distinct and a principal service due to the state.   Even the king, of such a limited

monarchy as ours, is but the first servant of the people. Among his subjects, some aré appointed by the constitution, and others are elected by the people, to carry on the exercise of the legislative power jointly with him, and to control the executive power independently on him. Thus your lordship is born a member of that order of men, in whom a third part of the supreme power of the government resides: and your right to the exercise of the power belonging to this order not being yet opened, you are chosen into another body of men, who have different power and a different constitution, but who possess another third part of the supreme legislative anthority, for as long a time as the commission or trust delegated to them by the people lasts. Freemen, who are neither born to the first, nor elected to the last, have a right however to complain, to represent, to petition, and, I add, even to do more in cases of the utmost extremity. For sure there cannot be a greater absurdity, than to affirm, that the people have a remedy in resistance, when their prince attempts to enslave them; but that they have none, when their representatives sell themselves and them.

The sum of what I have been saying is, that, in free governments, the public service is not confined to those whom the prince appoints to different posts in the administration under him; that there the care of the state is the care of multitudes; that many are called to it in a particular manner by their rank, and by other circumstances of their situation; and that even those whom the prince appoints are not only answerable to him, but, like him, and before him, to the nation, for their behavior in their several posts. It can never be impertinent nor ridiculous therefore in such a country, whatever it might be in the abbot of St. Real's, which was Savoy I think; or in Peru, under the Incas, where, Garcilasso de la Vega says, it was lawful for none but the nobility to study—for men of all degrees to instruct themselves in those affairs wherein they may be actors, or judges of those that act, or controllers of those that judge. On the contrary, it is incumbent on every man to instruct himself, as well as the means and opportunities he has permit, concerning the nature and interests of the government, and those rights and duties that belong to him, or to his superiors, or to his inferiors. This in general; but in particular it is certain that the obligations under which we lie to serve our country increase, in proportion to the ranks we hold, and the other circumstances of birth, fortune, and situation that call us to this service; and, above all, to the talents which God has given us to perform it.

It is in this view, that I shall address to your lordship whatever I have further to say on the study of history.

LETTER VI.

SINCE then you are, my lord, by your birth, by the nature of
our government, and by the talents God has given you, attached
for life to the service of your country; since genius alone cannot
enable you to go through this service with honor to yourself and
advantage to your country, whether you support or whether you
oppose the administrations that arise; since a great stock of
knowledge, acquired betimes and continually improved, is necessary to this end; and since one part of this stock must be collected from the study of history, as the other part is to be gained
by observation and experience; I come now to speak to your
lordship of such history as has an immediate relation to the great
duty and business of your life, and of the method to be observed
in this study.   The notes I have by me, which were of some
little use thus far, serve me no farther, and I have no books to
consult.   No matter; I shall be able to explain my thoughts
without their assistance, and less liable to be tedious.   I hope to
be as full and as exact on memory alone, as the manner in which
I shall treat the subject requires me to be.

I say, then, that however closely affairs are linked together in
the progression of governments, and how much soever events
that follow are dependent on those that precede, the whole connection diminishes to sight as the chain lengthens; till at last it
seems to be broken, and the links that are continued from that
point bear no proportion nor any similitude to the former.   I
would not be understood to speak only of those great changes
that are wrought by a concurrence of extraordinary events: for
instance, the expulsion of one nation, the destruction of one government, and the establishment of another: but even of those
that are wrought in the same governments and among the same
people, slowly and almost imperceptibly, by the necessary effects
of time, and flux condition of human affairs.   When such changes
as these happen in several states about the same time, and consequently affect other states by their vicinity, and by many different relations which they frequently bear to one another; then
is one of those periods formed, at which the chain spoken of is
so broken as to have little or no real or visible connection

with that which we see continue. A new situation, different
from the former, begets new interests in the same proportion of
difference; not in this or that particular state alone, but in all
those that are concerned by vicinity or other relations, as I said
just now, in one general system of policy.   New interests beget
new maxims ·of government, and new methods of conduct.
These, in their turns, beget new manners, new habits, new customs.   The longer this new constitution of affairs continues, the
more will this difference increase: and although some analogy
may remain long between what preceded and what succeeds
such a period, yet will this analogy soon become an object of
mere curiosity, not of profitable inquiry.   Such a period therefore
is, in the true sense of the words, an epocha or an era, a point
of time at which you stop, or from which you reckon forward.
I say forward; because we are not to study in the present case,
as chronologers compute, backward.   Should we persist to carry
our researches much higher, and to push them even to some
other period of the same kind, we should misemploy our time;
the causes then laid having spent themselves, the series of effects
derived from them being over, and our concern in both consequently at an end.   But a new system of causes and effects, that
subsists in our time, and whereof our conduct is to be a part,
arising at the last period, and all that passes in our time being
dependent on what has passed since that period, or being immediately relative to it, we are extremely concerned to be well
informed about all these passages.   To be entirely ignorant
about the ages that precede this era would be shameful.   Nay,
some indulgence may be had to a temperate curiosity in the
review of them.   But to be learned about them is a ridiculous
affectation in any man who means to be useful to the present
age.   Down to this era let us read history: from this era, and
down to our time, let us study it.
   The end of the fifteenth century seems to be just such a period
as I have been describing, for those who live in the eighteenth,
and who inhabit the western parts of Europe.   A little before,
or a little after this point of time, all those events happened, and
all those revolutions began, that have produced so vast a change
in the manners, customs, and interests of particular nations, and
in the whole policy, ecclesiastical and civil, of these parts of the
world.   I must descend here into some detail, not of histories,
collections, or memorials; for all these are well enough known:
and though the contents are in the heads of few, the books are
in the hands of many.   But instead of showing your lordship
where to look, I shall contribute more to your entertainment and
instruction, by marking out, as well as my memory will serve
me to do it, what you are to look for, and by furnishing a kind

of clue to your studies. I shall give, according to custom, the the first place to religion.

A VIEW OF THE ECCLESIASTICAL GOVERNMENT OF EUROPE FROM THE BEGINNING OF THE SIXTEENTH CENTURY.

Observe then, my lord, that the demolition of the papal throne was not attempted with success till the beginning of the sixteenth century. If you are curious to cast your eyes back, you will find Berenger in the eleventh, who was soon silenced; Arnoldus in the same, who was soon hanged; Valdo in the twelfth, and our Wickliff in the fourteenth, as well as others perhaps whom I do not recollect. Sometimes the doctrines of the church were alone attacked; and sometimes the doctrine, the discipline, and the usurpations of the pope. But little fires, kindled in corners of a dark world, were soon stifled by that great abettor of Christian unity, the hangman. When they spread and blazed out, as in the case of the Albigeois and of the Hussites, armies were raised to extinguish them by torrents of blood; and such saints as Dominic, with the crucifix in their hands, instigated the troops to the utmost barbarity. Your lordship will find that the church of Rome was maintained by such charitable and salutary means, among others, till the period spoken of; and you will be curious, I am sure, to inquire how this period came to be more fatal to her than any former conjuncture. A multitude of circumstances, which you will easily trace in the histories of the fifteenth and sixteenth centuries, to go no further back, concurred to bring about this great event: and a multitude of others, as easy to be traced, concurred to hinder the demolition from becoming total, and to prop the tottering fabric. Among these circumstances, there is one less complicated and more obvious than others, which was of principal and universal influence. The art of printing had been invented about forty or fifty years before the period we fix: from that time, the resurrection of letters hastened on apace; and at this period they had made great progress, and were cultivated with great application. Mahomet the Second drove them out of the east into the west; and the popes proved worse politicians than the mufties in this respect. Nicholas the Fifth encouraged learning and learned men. Sixtus the Fourth was, if I mistake not, a great collector of books at least: and Leo the Tenth was the patron of every art and science. The magicians themselves broke the charm by which they had bound mankind for so many ages: and the adventure of that knight-errant, who, thinking himself happy in the arms of a celestial nymph, found that he was the miserable slave of an infernal

hag, was in some sort renewed. As soon as the means of acquiring and spreading information grew common, it is no wonder
that a system was unravelled, which could not have been woven
with success in any ages, but those of gross ignorance, and credulous superstition. I might point out to your lordship many
other immediate causes, some general like this that I have mentioned, and some particular. The great schism, for instance, that
ended in the beginning of the fifteenth century, and in the council of Constance, had occasioned prodigious scandal. Two or
three vicars of Christ, two or three infallible heads of the church
roaming about the world at a time, furnished matter of ridicule
as well as scandal: and whilst they appealed, for so they did in
effect, to the laity, and reproached and excommunicated one another, they taught the world what to think of the institution, as
well as exercise of the papal authority. The same lesson was
taught by the council of Pisa, that preceded, and by that of
Basle, that followed the council of Constance. The horrid crimes
of Alexander the Sixth, the saucy ambition of Julius the Second,
the immense profusion and scandalous exactions of Leo the
Tenth; all these events and characters, following in a continued
series from the beginning of one century, prepared the way for
the revolution that happened in the beginning of the next. The
state of Germany, the state of England, and that of the North,
were particular causes, in these several countries, of this revolution. Such were many remarkable events that happened about
the same time, and a little before it, in these and in other nations;
and such were likewise the characters of many of the princes of
that age, some of whom favored the reformation, like the elector
of Saxony, on a principle of conscience; and most of whom
favored it, just as others opposed it, on a principle of interest.
This your lordship will discover manifestly to have been the
case; and the sole difference you will find between Henry the
Eighth and Francis the First, one of whom separated from the
pope, as the other adhered to him, is this: Henry the Eighth
divided, with the secular clergy and his people, the spoil of the
pope, and his satellites, the monks; Francis the First divided,
with the pope, the spoil of his clergy, secular and regular, and
of his people. With the same impartial eye that your lordship
surveys the abuses of religion, and the corruptions of the church
as well as court of Rome, which brought on the reformation at
this period; you will observe the characters and conduct of those
who began, who propagated, and who favored the reformation:
and from your observation of these, as well as of the unsyste-
matical manner in which it was carried on at the same time in
various places, and of the want of concert, nay even of charity,
among the reformers, you will learn what to think of the several

religions that unite in their opposition to the Roman, and yet hate one another most heartily; what to think of the several sects that have sprouted, like suckers, from the same great roots; and what the true principles are of protestant ecclesiastical policy. This policy had no being till Luther made his establishment in Germany; till Zwinglius began another in Switzerland, which Calvin carried on, and, like Americus Vesputius who followed Christopher Columbus, robbed the first adventurer of his honor; and till the reformation in our country was perfected under Edward the Sixth and Elizabeth. Even popish ecclesiastical policy is no longer the same since that era. His holiness is no longer at the head of the whole western church: and to keep the part that adheres to him, he is obliged to loosen their chains, and to lighten his yoke. The spirit and pretensions of his court are the same, but not the power. He governs by expedient and management more, and by authority less. His decrees and his briefs are in danger of being refused, explained away, or evaded, unless he negotiates their acceptance before he gives them, governs in concert with his flock, and feeds his sheep according to their humor and interest. In short, his excommunications, that made the greatest emperors tremble, are despised by the lowest members of his own communion; and the remaining attachment to him has been, from this era, rather a political expedient to preserve an appearance of unity, than a principle of conscience; whatever some bigotted princes may have thought, whatever ambitious prelates and hireling scribblers may have taught, and whatever a people, worked up to enthusiasm by fanatical preachers, may have acted. Proofs of this would be easy to draw, not only from the conduct of such princes as Ferdinand the First and Maximilian the Second, who could scarce be esteemed papists though they continued in the pope's communion; but even from that of princes who persecuted their protestant subjects with great violence. Enough has been said, I think, to show your lordship how little need there is of going up higher than the beginning of the sixteenth century in the study of history, to acquire all the knowledge necessary at this time in ecclesiastical policy, or in civil policy as far as it is relative to this. Historical monuments of this sort are in every man's hand, the facts are sufficiently verified, and the entire scenes lie open to our observation: even that scene of solemn refined banter exhibited in the council of Trent, imposes on no man who reads Paolo, as well as Pallavicini, and the letters of Vargas.

A VIEW OF THE CIVIL GOVERNMENT OF EUROPE IN THE BEGINNING OF THE SIXTEENTH CENTURY.

I. IN FRANCE.

A very little higher need we go, to observe those great changes in the civil constitutions of the principal nations of Europe, in the partition of power among them, and by consequence in the whole system of European policy, which have operated so strongly for more than two centuries, and which operate still. I will not affront the memory of our Henry the Seventh so much as to compare him to Louis the Eleventh: and yet I perceive some resemblance between them; which would perhaps appear greater, if Philip of Commines had written the history of Henry as well as that of Louis; or if my Lord Bacon had written that of Louis as well as that of Henry. This prince came to the crown of England a little before the close of the fifteenth century: and Louis began his reign in France about twenty years sooner. These reigns make remarkable periods in the histories of both nations. To reduce the power, privileges, and possessions of the nobility, and to increase the wealth and authority of the crown, was the principal object of both. In this their success was so great, that the constitutions of the two governments have had, since that time, more resemblance, in name and in form than in reality, to the constitutions that prevailed before. Louis the Eleventh was the first, say the French, " qui mit les rois hors de page." The independency of the nobility had rendered the state of his predecessors very dependent, and their power precarious. They were the sovereigns of great vassals; but these vassals were so powerful, that one of them was sometimes able, and two or three of them always, to give law to the sovereign. Before Louis came to the crown, the English had been driven out of their possessions in France, by the poor character of Henry the Sixth, the domestic troubles of his reign, and the defection of the house of Burgundy from his alliance, much more than by the ability of Charles the Seventh, who seems to have been neither a greater hero nor a greater politician than Henry the Sixth; and even than by the vigor and union of the French nobility in his service. After Louis came to the crown, Edward the Fourth made a show of carrying the war again into France; but he soon returned home and your lordship will not be at a loss to find much better reasons for his doing so, in the situation of his affairs and the characters of his allies, than those which Philip of Commines draws from the artifice of Louis, from his good cheer, and his pensions. Now from this time our pretensions on France were in effect

given up: and Charles the Bold, the last prince of the house of
Burgundy, being killed, Louis had no vassal able to molest him.
He re-united the Dutchy of Burgundy and Artois to his crown,
he acquired Provence by gift, and his son Britany by marriage:
and thus France grew, in the course of a few years, into that
great and compact body which we behold at this time. The
history of France before this period is, like that of Germany, a
complicated history of several states and several interests; sometimes concurring like members of the same monarchy, and sometimes warring on one another. Since this period, the history of
France is the history of one state under a more uniform and orderly government; the history of a monarchy wherein the prince
is possessor of some, as well as lord of all the great fieffes: and,
the authority of many tyrants centering in one, though the people are not become more free, yet the whole system of domestic
policy is entirely changed. Peace at home is better secured, and
the nation grown fitter to carry war abroad. The governors of
great provinces and of strong fortresses have opposed their king,
and taken arms against his authority and commission since that
time: but yet there is no more resemblance between the authority
and pretensions of these governors, or the nature and occasions
of these disputes, and the authority and pretensions of the vassals of the crown in former days, or the nature and occasions of
their disputes with the prince and with one another, than there
is between the ancient and the present peers of France. In a
word, the constitution is so altered, that any knowledge we can
acquire about it in the history that precedes this period, will
serve to little purpose in our study of the history that follows it,
and to less purpose still in assisting us to judge of what passes in
the present age. The kings of France since that time, more masters at home, have been able to exert themselves more abroad:
and they began to do so immediately; for Charles the Eighth,
son and successor of Louis the Eleventh, formed great designs
of foreign conquests, though they were disappointed by his inability, by the levity of the nation, and by other causes. Louis
the Twelfth and Francis the First, but especially Francis, meddled deep in the affairs of Europe: and though the superior genius
of Ferdinand called the Catholic, and the star of Charles the Fifth
prevailed against them, yet the efforts they made show sufficiently how the strength and importance of this monarchy were
increased in their time. From whence we may date likewise
the rivalship of the house of France, for we may reckon that of
Valois and that of Bourbon as one upon this occasion, and the
house of Austria; that continues at this day, and that has cost so
much blood and so much treasure in the course of it.

II. IN ENGLAND.

Though the power and influence of the nobility sunk in the great change that began under Henry the Seventh in England, as they did in that which began under Louis the Eleventh in France; yet the new constitutions that these changes produced were very different. In France the lords alone lost, the king alone gained; the clergy held their possessions and their immunities, and the people remained in a state of mitigated slavery. But in England the people gained as well as the crown. The commons had already a share in the legislature; so that the power and influence of the lords being broke by Henry the Seventh, and the property of the commons increasing by the sale that his son made of church-lands, the power of the latter increased of course by this change in a constitution, the forms whereof were favorable to them. The union of the roses put an end to the civil wars of York and Lancaster, that had succeeded those we commonly call the barons wars, and the humor of warring in France, that had lasted near four hundred years under the Normans and Plantagenets, for plunder as well as conquest, was spent. Our temple of Janus was shut by Henry the Seventh. We neither laid waste our own nor other countries any longer: and wise laws and a wise government changed insensibly the manners, and gave a new turn to the spirit of our people. We were no longer the freebooters we had been. Our nation maintained her reputation in arms whenever the public interest or the public authority required it; but war ceased to be, what it had been, our principal and almost our sole profession. The arts of peace prevailed among us. We became husbandmen, manufacturers, and merchants, and we emulated neighboring nations in literature. It is from this time that we ought to study the history of our country, my lord, with the utmost application. We are not much concerned to know with critical accuracy what were the ancient forms of our parliaments, concerning which, however, there is little room for dispute from the reign of Henry the Third at least; nor in short the whole system of our civil constitution before Henry the Seventh, and of our ecclesiastical constitution before Henry the Eighth. But he who has not studied and acquired a thorough knowledge of them both, from these periods down to the present time, in all the variety of events by which they have been affected, will be very unfit to judge or take care of either. Just as little are we concerned to know, in any nice detail, what the conduct of our princes, relatively to our neighbors on the continent, was before this period, and at a time when the partition of power and a multitude of other circumstances rendered the whole political system of Europe so vastly different from that which has existed since. But he who has not traced this conduct from the period we fix, down to the present age, wants a principal part of the knowledge that every English minister of state should have. Ignorance in the respects here spoken of is the less pardonable, because we have more, and more authentic, means of information concerning this, than concerning any other period. Anecdotes enow to glut the curiosity of some persons, and to silence all the captious cavils of others, will never be furnished by any portion of history; nor indeed can they according to the nature and course of human affairs: but he who is content to read and observe, like a senator and a statesman, will find in our own and in foreign historians as much information as he wants, concerning the affairs of our island, her fortune at home and her conduct abroad, from the fifteenth century to the eighteenth. I refer to foreign historians as well as to our own, for this series of our own history; not only because it is reasonable to see in what manner the historians of other countries have related the transactions wherein we have been concerned, and what judgment they have made of our conduct, domestic and foreign, but for another reason likewise. Our nation has furnished as ample and as important matter, good and bad, for history, as any nation under the sun: and yet we must yield the palm in writing history most certainly to the Italians and to the French, and, I fear, even to the Germans. The only two pieces of history we have, in any respect to be compared with the ancient, are, the reign of Henry the Seventh by my lord Bacon, and the history of our civil wars in the last century by your noble ancestor my lord chancellor Clarendon. But we have no general history to be compared with some of other countries: neither have we, which I lament much more, particular histories, except the two I have mentioned, nor writers of memorials, nor collectors of monuments and anecdotes, to vie in number or in merit with those that foreign nations can boast; from Commines, Guicciardin, Du Bellay, Paolo, Davila, Thuanus, and a multitude of others, down through the whole period that I propose to your lordship. But although this be true, to our shame; yet it is true likewise that we want no necessary means of information. They lie open to our industry and our discernment. Foreign writers are for the most part scarce worth reading when they speak of our domestic affairs; nor are our English writers for the most part of greater value when they speak of foreign affairs. In this mutual defect, the writers of other countries are, I think, more excusable than ours: for the nature of our government, the political principles in which we are bred, our distinct interests as islanders, and the compli-

cated various interests and humors of our parties, all these are
so peculiar to ourselves, and so different from the notions, manners, and habits of other nations, that it is not wonderful they
should be puzzled, or should fall into error, when they undertake
to give relations of events that result from all these, or to pass
any judgment upon them. But as these historians are mutually
defective, so they mutually supply each other's defects. We
must compare them therefore, make use of our discernment,
and draw our conclusions from both. If we proceed in this
manner, we have an ample fund of history in our power, from
whence to collect sufficient authentic information; and we must
proceed in this manner, even with our own historians of different
religions, sects, and parties, or run the risk of being misled by
domestic ignorance and prejudice in this case, as well as by
foreign ignorance and prejudice in the other.

III. IN SPAIN AND THE EMPIRE.

Spain figured little in Europe till the latter part of the fifteenth
century; till Castile and Arragon were united by the marriage
of Ferdinand and Isabella; till the total expulsion of the Moors,
and till the discovery of the West Indies. After this, not only
Spain took a new form, and grew into immense power; but, the
heir of Ferdinand and Isabella being heir likewise of the houses
of Burgundy and Austria, such an extent of dominion accrued
to him by all these successions, and such an addition of rank and
authority by his election to the empire, as no prince had been
master of in Europe from the days of Charles the Great. It is
proper to observe here how the policy of the Germans altered in
the choice of an emperor; because the effects of this alteration
have been great. When Rodolphus of Hapsburg was chose in
the year one thousand two hundred and seventy, or about that
time, the poverty and the low estate of this prince, who had been
marshal of the court to a king of Bohemia, was an inducement
to elect him. The disorderly and lawless state of the empire
made the princes of it in those days unwilling to have a more
powerful head. But a contrary maxim took place at this era.
Charles the Fifth and Francis the First, the two most powerful
princes of Europe, were the sole candidates; for the elector of
Saxony, who is said to have declined, was rather unable to stand
in competition with them: and Charles was chosen by the unanimous suffrages of the electoral college, if I mistake not. Another
Charles, Charles the Fourth, who was made emperor illegally
enough on the deposition of Louis of Bavaria, and about one
hundred and fifty years before, seems to me to have contributed

doubly to establish this maxim; by the wise constitutions that he
procured to pass, that united the empire in a more orderly form
and better system of government; and by alienating the imperial
revenues to such a degree, that they were no longer sufficient to
support an emperor who had not great revenues of his own.
The same maxim and other circumstances have concurred to
keep the empire in this family ever since, as it had been often
before; and this family having large dominions in the empire,
and larger pretensions, as well as dominions, out of it, the other
states of Europe, France, Spain and England particularly, have
been more concerned since this period in the affairs of Germany,
than they were before it: and by consequence the history of
Germany, from the beginning of the sixteenth century, is of importance, and a necessary part of that knowledge which your
lordship desires to acquire.

The Dutch commonwealth was not formed till near a century
later. But as soon as it was formed, nay even whilst it was
forming, these provinces, that were lost to observation among
the many that composed the dominions of Burgundy and Austria, became so considerable a part of the political system of
Europe, that their history must be studied by every man who
would inform himself of this system.

Soon after this state had taken being, others of a more ancient
original began to mingle in those disputes and wars, those councils, negotiations, and treaties, that are to be the principal objects
of your lordship's application in the study of history. That of
the northern crowns deserves your attention little, before the last
century. Till the election of Frederic the First to the crown of
Denmark, and till that wonderful revolution which the first Gustavus brought about in Sweden, it is nothing more than a confused rhapsody of events, in which the great kingdoms and
states of Europe neither had any concern, nor took any part.—
From the time I have mentioned, the northern crowns have turned their counsels and their arms often southwards, and Sweden
particularly, with prodigious effect.

To what purpose should I trouble your lordship with the mention of histories of other nations? They are either such as have
no relation to the knowledge you would acquire, like that of the
Poles, the Muscovites, or the Turks; or they are such as, having
an occasional or a secondary relation to it, fall of course into
your scheme; like the history of Italy for instance, which is sometimes a part of that of France, sometimes of that of Spain, and
sometimes of that of Germany. The thread of history that you
are to keep, is that of the nations who are and must always be
concerned in the same scenes of action with your own. These
are the principal nations of the west. Things that have no im-

mediate relation to your own country, or to them, are either too remote, or too minute, to employ much of your time: and their history and your own is, for all your purposes, the whole history of Europe.

The two great powers, that of France and that of Austria, being formed, and a rivalship established by consequence between them; it began to be the interest of their neighbors to oppose the strongest and most enterprising of the two, and to be the ally and friend of the weakest. From hence arose the notion of a balance of power in Europe, on the equal poise of which the safety and tranquillity of all must depend. To destroy the equality of this balance has been the aim of each of these rivals in his turn: and to hinder it from being destroyed, by preventing too much power from falling into one scale, has been the principle of all the wise councils of Europe, relatively to France and to the house of Austria, through the whole period that began at the era we have fixed, and subsists at this hour. To make a careful and just observation, therefore, of the rise and decline of these powers, in the two last centuries, and in the present; of the projects which their ambition formed; of the means they employed to carry these projects on with success; of the means employed by others to defeat them; of the issue of all these endeavors in war and in negotiation; and particularly, to bring your observations home to your own country and your own use, of the conduct that England held, to her honor or dishonor, to her advantage or disadvantage, in every one of the numerous and important conjunctures that happened—ought to be the principal subject of your lordship's attention in reading and reflecting on this part of modern history.

Now to this purpose you will find it of great use, my lord, when you have a general plan of the history in your mind, to go over the whole again in another method; which I propose to be this. Divide the entire period into such particular periods as the general course of affairs will mark out to you sufficiently, by the rise of new conjunctures, of different schemes of conduct, and of different theatres of action. Examine this period of history as you would examine a tragedy or a comedy; that is, take first the idea or a general notion of the whole, and after that examine every act and every scene apart. Consider them in themselves, and consider them relatively to one another. Read this history as you would that of any ancient period; but study it afterwards, as it would not be worth your while to study the other; nay as you could not have in your power the means of studying the other, if the study was really worth your while. The former part of this period abounds in great historians: and the latter part is so modern, that even tradition is authentic enough to supply the want of good history, if we are curious to inquire, and if we hearken to the living with the same impartiality and freedom of judgment as we read the dead; and he that does one, will do the other. The whole period abounds in memorials, in collections of public acts and monuments, of private letters, and of treaties. All these must come into your plan of study, my lord: many may not be read through, but all to be consulted and compared. They must not lead you, I think, to your inquiries, but your inquiries must lead you to them. By joining history and that which we call the *materia historica* together in this manner, and by drawing your information from both, your lordship will acquire not only that knowledge, which many have in some degree, of the great transactions that have passed, and the great events that have happened in Europe during this period, and of their immediate and obvious causes and consequences; but your lordship will acquire a much superior knowledge, and such a one as very few men possess almost in any degree, a knowledge of the true political system of Europe during this time. You will see it in its primitive principles, in the constitutions of governments, the situations of countries, their national and true interests, the characters and the religion of people, and other permanent circumstances. You will trace it through all its fluctuations, and observe how the objects vary seldom, but the means perpetually, according to the different characters of princes and of those who govern; the different abilities of those who serve; the course of accidents, and a multitude of other irregular and contingent circumstances.

The particular periods into which the whole period should be divided, in my opinion, are these. 1. From the fifteenth to the end of the sixteenth century. 2. From thence to the Pyrenean treaty. 3. From thence down to the present time.

Your lordship will find this division as apt and as proper, relatively to the particular histories of England, France, Spain, and Germany, the principal nations concerned, as it is relatively to the general history of Europe.

The death of queen Elizabeth, and the accession of king James the First, made a vast alteration in the government of our nation at home, and in her conduct abroad, about the end of the first of these periods. The wars that religion occasioned, and ambition fomented in France, through the reigns of Francis the Second, Charles the Ninth, Henry the Third, and a part of Henry the Fourth, ended: and the furies of the league were crushed by this great prince, about the same time. Philip the Second of Spain marks this period likewise by his death, and by the exhausted condition in which he left the monarchy he governed: which took the lead no longer in disturbing the peace of man-

kind, but acted a second part in abetting the bigotry and ambition of Ferdinand the Second and the Third.   The thirty years
war that devastated Germany did not begin till the eighteenth
year of the seventeenth century, but the seeds of it were sowing
some time before, and even at the end of the sixteenth.   Ferdinand the First and Maximilian had shown much lenity and
moderation in the disputes and troubles that arose on account of
religion.   Under Rodolphus and Matthias, as the succession of
their cousin Ferdinand approached, the fires that were covered
began to smoke and to sparkle: and if the war did not begin
with this century, the preparation for it, and the expectation of
it did.

The second period ends in one thousand six hundred and
sixty, the year of the restoration of Charles the Second to the
throne of England; when our civil wars, and all the disorders
which Cromwell's usurpation had produced, were over; and
therefore a remarkable point of time, with respect to our country.
It is no less remarkable with respect to Germany, Spain, and
France.

As to Germany; the ambitious projects of the German branch
of Austria had been entirely defeated, the peace of the empire
had been restored, and almost a new constitution formed, or an
old one revived, by the treaties of Westphalia; nay the imperial
eagle was not only fallen, but her wings were clipped.

As to Spain; the Spanish branch was fallen as low twelve
years afterwards, that is, in the year one thousand six hundred
and sixty.   Philip the Second left his successors a ruined monarchy.   He left them something worse; he left them his example and his principles of government, founded in ambition, in
pride, in ignorance, in bigotry, and all the pedantry of state.   I
have read somewhere or other, that the war of the Low Countries alone cost him, by his own confession, five hundred and
sixty-four millions, a prodigious sum in what species soever he
reckoned.   Philip the Third and Philip the Fourth followed his
example and his principles of government, at home and abroad.
At home, there was much form, but no good order, no economy,
nor wisdom of policy in the state.   The church continued to devour the state, and that monster the inquisition to dispeople the
country, even more than perpetual war, and all the numerous
colonies that Spain had sent to the West Indies: for your lordship will find that Philip the Third drove more than nine hundred
thousand Moriscoes out of his dominions by one edict, with such
circumstances of inhumanity in the execution of it, as Spaniards
alone could exercise, and that tribunal, who had provoked this
unhappy race to revolt, could alone approve.   Abroad, the conduct of these princes was directed by the same wild spirit of

ambition: rash in undertaking though slow to execute, and obstinate in pursuing though unable to succeed, they opened a new sluice to let out the little life and vigor that remained in their monarchy. Philip the Second is said to have been piqued against his uncle Ferdinand, for refusing to yield the empire to him on the abdication of Charles the Fifth. Certain it is, that as much as he loved to disturb the peace of mankind, and to meddle in every quarrel that had the appearance of supporting the Roman and oppressing every other church, he meddled little in the affairs of Germany. But, Ferdinand and Maximilian dead, and the offspring of Maximilian extinct, the kings of Spain espoused the interests of the other branch of their family, entertained remote views of ambition in favor of their own branch, even on that side, and made all the enterprises of Ferdinand of Gratz, both before and after his elevation to the empire, the common cause of the house of Austria. What completed their ruin was this: they knew not how to lose, nor when to yield. They acknowledged the independence of the Dutch commonwealth, and became the allies of their ancient subjects at the treaty of Munster: but they would not forego their usurped claim on Portugal, and they persisted to carry on singly the war against France. Thus they were reduced to such a lowness of power as can hardly be parallelled in any other case: and Philip the Fourth was obliged at last to conclude a peace, on terms repugnant to his inclination, to that of his people, to the interest of Spain, and to that of all Europe, in the Pyrenean treaty.

As to France, this era of the entire fall of the Spanish power is likewise that from which we may reckon that France grew as formidable, as we have seen her, to her neighbors, in power and pretensions. Henry the Fourth meditated great designs, and prepared to act a great part in Europe in the very beginning of this period, when Ravaillac stabbed him. His designs died with him, and are rather guessed at than known; for surely those which his historian Perefixe and the compilers of Sully's memorials ascribe to him, of a Christian commonwealth divided into fifteen states, and of a senate to decide all differences, and to maintain this new constitution of Europe, are too chimerical to have been really his: but his general design of abasng the house of Austria, and establishing the superior power in that of Bourbon, was taken up, about twenty years after his death, by Richelieu, and was pursued by him and by Mazarin with so much ability and success, that it was effected entirely by the treaties of Westphalia and by the Pyrenean treaty; that is, at the end of the second of those periods I have presumed to propose to your lordship.

When the third, in which we now are, will end, and what

circumstances will mark the end of it, I know not; but this I know, that the great events and revolutions, which have happened in the course of it, interest us still more nearly than those of the two precedent periods.   I intended to have drawn up an elenchus or summary of the three, but I doubted, on further reflection, whether my memory would enable me to do it with exactness enough: and I saw that, if I was able to do it, the deduction would be immeasurably long.   Something of this kind, however, it may be reasonable to attempt, in speaking of the last period: which may hereafter occasion a further trouble to your lordship.

But to give some breathing time, I will postpone it at present, and am in the meanwhile,

My Lord, yours, &c.

LETTER VII.

A SKETCH OF THE STATE OF HISTORY OF EUROPE, FROM THE PY-
RENEAN TREATY IN ONE THOUSAND SIX HUNDRED AND FIFTY-
NINE, TO THE YEAR ONE THOUSAND SIX HUNDRED AND EIGHTY-
EIGHT.

THE first observation I shall make on this third period of modern history is, that as the ambition of Charles the Fifth, who united the whole formidable power of Austria in himself, and the restless temper, the cruelty and bigotry of Philip the Second, were principally objects of the attention and solicitude of the councils of Europe, in the first of these periods; and as the ambition of Ferdinand the Second, and the Third, who aimed at nothing less than extirpating the protestant interest, and under that pretence subduing the liberties of Germany, were objects of the same kind in the second: so an opposition to the growing power of France, or to speak more properly, to the exorbitant ambition of the house of Bourbon, has been the principal affair of Europe, during the greatest part of the present period.   The design of aspiring to universal monarchy was imputed to Charles the Fifth, as soon as he began to give proofs of his ambition and capacity.   The same design was imputed to Louis the Fourteenth, as soon as he began to feel his own strength, and the weakness of his neighbors.   Neither of these princes was induced, I be-lieve, by the flattery of his courtiers; or the apprehension of his adversaries, to entertain so chimerical a design as this would have been, even in that false sense wherein the word universal is so often understood: and I mistake very much if either of them was of a character, or in circumstances, to undertake it. Both of them had strong desires to raise their families higher, and to extend their dominions farther; but neither of them had that bold and adventurous ambition which makes a conqueror and a hero. These apprehensions, however, were given wisely, and taken usefully. They cannot be given nor taken too soon when such powers as these arise; because when such powers as these are besieged as it were early, by the common policy and watchfulness of their neighbors, each of them may in his turn of strength sally forth, and gain a little ground; but none of them will be able to push their conquest far, and much less to consummate the entire projects of their ambition. Besides the occasional opposition that was given to Charles the Fifth by our Henry the Eighth, according to the different moods of humor he was in; by the popes, according to the several turns of their private interest; and by the princes of Germany, according to the occasions or pretences that religion or civil liberty furnished; he had from his first setting out a rival and an enemy in Francis the First, who did not maintain his cause " in forma pauperis," if I may use such an expression: as we have seen the house of Austria sue, in our days, for dominion at the gate of every palace in Europe. Francis the First was the principal in his own quarrels, paid his own armies, fought his own battles; and though his valor alone did not hinder Charles the Fifth from subduing all Europe, as Bayle, a better philologer than politician, somewhere asserts, but a multitude of other circumstances easily to be traced in history; yet he contributed by his victories, and even by his defeats, to waste the strength and check the course of that growing power. Louis the Fourteenth had no rival of this kind in the house of Austria, nor indeed any enemy of this importance to combat, till the prince of Orange became king of Great Britain: and he had great advantages in many other respects, which it is necessary to consider in order to make a true judgment on the affairs of Europe from the year one thousand six hundred and sixty. You will discover the first of these advantages, and such as were productive of all the rest, in the conduct of Richelieu and of Mazarin. Richelieu formed the great design, and laid the foundations: Mazarin pursued the design, and raised the superstructure. If I do not deceive myself extremely, there are few passages in history that deserve your lordship's attention more than the conduct that the first and greatest of these ministers held, in laying the foundations I speak of. You will observe how he helped to embroil affairs on every side, and to keep the house of Austria at bay as it were; how he entered into the quarrels of Italy against Spain, into that concerning the Valte-

line, and that concerning the succession of Mantua; without engaging so deep as to divert him from another great object of his
policy, subduing Rochelle and disarming the Huguenots.   You
will observe how he turned himself after this was done, to stop
the progress of Ferdinand in Germany.   While Spain fomented
discontents at the court and disorders in the kingdom of France,
by all possible means, even by taking engagements with the
Duke of Rohan; and for supporting the protestants; Richelieu
abetted the same interest in Germany against Ferdinand; and in
the Low Countries against Spain.   The emperor was become
almost the master in Germany.   Christian the Fourth, king
of Denmark, had been at the head of a league, wherein the
United Provinces, Sweden, and Lower Saxony entered, to oppose his progress: but Christian had been defeated by Tilly
and Valstein, and obliged to conclude a treaty at Lubec, where
Ferdinand gave him the law.   It was then that Gustavus
Adolphus, with whom Richelieu made an alliance, entered
into this war, and soon turned the fortune of it.   The French
minister had not yet engaged his master openly in the war; but
when the Dutch grew impatient, and threatened to renew their
truce with Spain, unless France declared; when the king of Sweden was killed, and the battle of Nordlingen lost; when Saxony
had turned again to the side of the emperor, and Brandenburg
and so many others had followed this example, that Hesse almost
alone persisted in the Swedish alliance: then Richelieu engaged
his master, and profited of every circumstance which the conjuncture afforded, to engage him with advantage.   For, first, he
had a double advantage by engaging so late: that of coming fresh
into the quarrel against a wearied and almost exhausted enemy;
and that of yielding to the impatience of his friends, who, pressed
by their necessities and by the want they had of France, gave
this minister an opportunity of laying those claims and establishing those pretensions, in all his treaties with Holland, Sweden
and the princes and states of the empire, on which he had projected the future aggrandisement of France.   The manner in
which he engaged, and the air that he gave to his engagement,
were advantages of the second sort, advantages of reputation
and credit; yet were these of no small moment in the course of
the war, and operated strongly in favor of France as he designed
they should, even after his death, and at and after the treaties of
Westphalia.   He varnished ambition with the most plausible
and popular pretences.   The elector of Treves had put himself
under the protection of France: and, if I remember right, he made
this step when the emperor could not protect him against the
Swedes, whom he had reason to apprehend.   No matter, the
governor of Luxemburg was ordered to surprise Treves and to

seize the elector.   He executed his orders with success, and carried this prince prisoner into Brabant. Richelieu seized the lucky
circumstance; he reclaimed the elector: and, on the refusal of the
cardinal infant, the war was declared.   France, you see, appeared the common friend of liberty, the defender of it in the
Low Countries against the king of Spain, and in Germany against
the emperor, as well as the protector of the princes of the empire,
many of whose states had been illegally invaded, and whose
persons were no longer safe from violence even in their own
palaces.   All these appearances were kept up in the negotiations
at Munster, where Mazarin reaped what Richelieu had sowed.
The demands that France made for herself were very great; but
the conjuncture was favorable, and she improved it to the utmost.
No figure could be more flattering than hers at the head of these
negotiations; nor more mortifying than the emperor's through
the whole course of the treaty.   The princes and states of the
empire had been treated as vassals by the emperor: France determined them to treat with him on this occasion as sovereigns,
and supported them in this determination.   Whilst Sweden
seemed concerned for the protestant interest alone, and showed
no other regard, as she had no other alliance; France affected to
be impartial alike to the protestant and to the papist and to have
no interest at heart but the common interest of the Germanic
body.   Her demands were excessive, but they were to be satisfied principally out of the emperor's patrimonial dominions.   It
had been the art of her ministers to establish this general maxim
on many particular experiences, that the grandeur of France was
a real, and would be a constant security to the rights and liberties of the empire against the emperor: and it is no wonder therefore, this maxim prevailing, injuries, resentments, and jealousies
being fresh on one side, and services, obligations, and confidence
on the other, that the Germans were not unwilling France should
extend her empire on this side of the Rhine whilst Sweden did
the same on this side of the Baltic.   These treaties, and the immense credit and influence that France had acquired by them in
the empire, put it out of the power of one branch of the house of
Austria to return the obligations of assistance to the other, in the
war that continued between France and Spain, till the Pyrenean
treaty.   By this treaty the superiority of the house of Bourbon
over the house of Austria was not only completed and confirmed
but the great design of uniting the Spanish and the French monarchies under the former was laid.
   The third period therefore begins by a great change of the
balance of power in Europe, and by the prospect of one much
greater and more fatal.   Before I descend into the particulars I
intend to mention, of the course of affairs, and of the political

conduct of the great powers of Europe in this third period; give me leave to cast my eyes once more back on the second. The reflection I am going to make seems to me important, and leads to all that is to follow.

The Dutch made their peace separately at Munster with Spain, who acknowledged then the sovereignty and independency of their commonwealth. The French, who had been, after our Elizabeth, their principal support, reproached them severely for this breach of faith. They excused themselves in the best manner, and by the best reasons, they could. All this your lordship will find in the monuments of that time. But I think it not improbable that they had a motive you will not find there, and which it was not proper to give as a reason or excuse to the French. Might not the wise men amongst them consider even then, besides the immediate advantages that accrued by this treaty to their commonwealth, that the imperial power was fallen; that the power of Spain was vastly reduced; that the house of Austria was nothing more than the shadow of a great name, and that the house of Bourbon was advancing, by large strides, to a degree of power as exorbitant, and as formidable as that of the other family had been in the hands of Charles the Fifth, of Philip the Second, and lately of the two Ferdinands? Might they not foresee, even then, what happened in the course of very few years, when they were obliged, for their own security, to assist their old enemies the Spaniards against their old friends the French? I think they might. Our Charles the First was no great politician, and yet he seemed to discern that the balance of power was turning in favor of France, some years before the treaties of Westphalia. He refused to be neuter, and threatened to take part with Spain, if the French pursued the design of besieging Dunkirk and Graveline, according to a concert taken between them and the Dutch, and in pursuance of a treaty for dividing the Spanish Low Countries, which Richelieu had negotiated. Cromwell either did not discern this turn of the balance of power, long afterwards when it was much more visible; or, discerning it, he was induced by reasons of private interest to act against the general interest of Europe. Cromwell joined with France against Spain, and though he got Jamaica and Dunkirk, he drove the Spaniards into a necessity of making a peace with France, that has disturbed the peace of the world almost fourscore years, and the consequences of which have well nigh beggared in our times the nation he enslaved in his. There is a tradition, I have heard it from persons who lived in those days, and I believe it came from Thurloe, that Cromwell was in treaty with Spain, and ready to turn his arms against France when he died. If this fact was certain, as little as I honor his memory, I should have some regret that he died so soon. But whatever his intentions were, we must charge the Pyrenean treaty, and the fatal consequences of it, in great measure to his account. The Spaniards abhorred the thought of marrying their Infanta to Louis the Fourteenth. It was on this point that they broke the negotiation Lionne had begun: and your lordship will perceive, that if they resumed it afterwards, and offered the marriage they had before rejected, Cromwell's league with France was a principal inducement to this alteration of their resolutions.

The precise point at which the scales of power turn, like that of the solstice in either tropic, is imperceptible to common observation: and, in one case as in the other, some progress must be made in the new direction, before the change is perceived. They who are in the sinking scale, for in the political balance of power, unlike to all others, the scale that is empty sinks, and that which is full rises; they who are in the sinking scale do not easily come off from the habitual prejudices of superior wealth, or power, or skill, or courage, nor from the confidence that these prejudices inspire. They who are in the rising scale do not immediately feel their strength, nor assume that confidence in it which successful experience gives them afterwards. They who are the most concerned to watch the variations of this balance, misjudge often in the same manner, and from the same prejudices. They continue to dread a power no longer able to hurt them, or they continue to have no apprehensions of a power that grows daily more formidable. Spain verified the first observation at the end of the second period, when, proud and poor, and enterprising and feeble, she still thought herself a match for France. France verified the second observation at the beginning of the third period, when the triple alliance stopped the progress of her arms, which alliances much more considerable were not able to effect afterwards. The other principal powers of Europe, in their turns, have verified the third observation in both its parts, through the whole course of this period.

When Louis the Fourteenth took the administration of affairs into his own hands, about the year one thousand six hundred and sixty, he was in the prime of his age, and had, what princes seldom have, the advantages of youth and those of experience together. Their education is generally bad; for which reason royal birth, that gives a right to the throne among other people, gave an absolute exclusion from it among the Mamalukes. His was, in all respects, except one, as bad as that of other princes. He jested sometimes on his own ignorance; and there were other defects in his character, owing to his education, which he did not see. But Mazarin had initiated him betimes in the mysteries of his policy. He had seen a great part of those foundations laid, on which he was to raise the fabric of his future grandeur: and as Mazarin finished the work that Richelieu began, he had the lessons of one, and the examples of both, to instruct him. He had acquired habits of secrecy and method, in business; of reserve, discretion, decency, and dignity, in behaviour. If he was not the greatest king, he was the best actor of majesty at least, that ever filled a throne. He by no means wanted that courage which is commonly called bravery, though the want of it was imputed to him in the midst of his greatest triumphs: nor that other courage, less ostentatious and more rarely found, calm, steady, persevering resolution; which seems to arise less from the temper of the body, and is therefore called courage of the mind. He had them both most certainly, and I could produce unquestionable anecdotes in proof. He was, in one word, much superior to any prince with whom he had to do, when he began to govern. He was surrounded with great captains bred in former wars, and with great ministers bred in the same school as himself. They who had worked under Mazarin worked on the same plan under him; and as they had the advantages of genius and experience over most of the ministers of other countries, so they had another advantage over those who were equal or superior to them: the advantage of serving a master whose absolute power was established; and the advantage of a situation wherein they might exert their whole capacity without contradiction; over that, for instance, wherein your lordship's great grandfather was placed, at the same time, in England, and John de Wit in Holland. Among these ministers, Colbert must be mentioned particularly upon this occasion; because it was he who improved the wealth and consequently the power of France extremely, by the order he put into the finances, and by the encouragement he gave to trade and manufactures. The soil, the climate, the situation of France, the ingenuity, the industry, the vivacity of her inhabitants are such; she has so little want of the product of other countries, and other countries have so many real or imaginary wants to be supplied by her; that when she is not at war with all her neighbors, when her domestic quiet is preserved and any tolerable administration of government prevails, she must grow rich at the expense of those who trade, and even of those who do not open a trade, with her. Her baubles, her modes, the follies and extravagances of her luxury, cost England, about the time we are speaking of, little less than eight hundred thousand pounds sterling a year, and other nations in their proportions. Colbert made the most of all these advantageous circumstances, and whilst he filled the national spunge, he taught his successors how to squeeze it; a secret that he repented having discovered, they say, when he saw the immense sums that were necessary to supply the growing magnificence of his master.

This was the character of Louis the Fourteenth, and this was the state of his kingdom at the beginning of the present period. If his power was great his pretensions were still greater. He had renounced, and the Infanta with his consent had renounced, all right to the succession of Spain, in the strongest terms that the precautions of the councils of Madrid could contrive. No matter; he consented to these renunciations, but your lordship will find by the letters of Mazarin, and by other memorials, that he acted on the contrary principle, from the first, which he avowed soon afterwards. Such a power, and such pretensions, should have given, one would think, an immediate alarm to the rest of Europe. Philip the Fourth was broken and decayed, like the monarchy he governed. One of his sons died, as I remember, during the negotiations that preceded the year one thousand six hundred and sixty: and the survivor, who was Charles the Second, rather languished, than lived, from the cradle to the grave. So dangerous a contingency, therefore, as the union of the two monarchies of France and Spain, being in view forty years together; one would imagine, that the principal powers of Europe had the means of preventing it constantly in view during the same time. But it was otherwise. France acted very systematically from the year one thousand six hnndred and sixty, to the death of king Charles the Second of Spain. She never lost sight of her great object, the succession to the whole Spanish monarchy; and she accepted the will of the king of Spain in favor of the Duke of Anjou. As she never lost sight of her great object during this time, so she lost no opportunity of increasing her power, while she waited for that of succeeding in her pretensions. The two branches of Austria were in no condition of making a considerable opposition to her designs and attempts. Holland, who of all other powers was the most concerned to oppose them, was at that time under two influences that hindered her from pursuing her true interest. Her true interest was to have used her utmost endeavors to unite closely and intimately with England on the restoration of king Charles. She did the very contrary. John de Wit, at the head of the Louvestein faction, governed. The interest of his party was to keep the house of Orange down: he courted therefore the friendship of France, and neglected that of England. The alliance between our nation and the Dutch was renewed, I think, in one thousand six hundred and sixty-two; but the latter had made a defensive league with France a little before, on the supposition principally of a war with England. The war became inevitable very soon.

Cromwell had chastised them for their usurpations in trade, and the outrages and cruelties they had committed; but he had not cured them. The same spirit continued in the Dutch, the same resentments in the English: and the pique of merchants became the pique of nations. France entered into the war on the side of Holland; but the little assistance she gave the Dutch showed plainly enough that her intention was to make these two powers waste their strength against one another; whilst she extended her conquests in the Spanish Low Countries. Her invasion in these provinces obliged De Wit to change his conduct. Hitherto he had been attached to France in the closest manner, had led his republic to serve all the purposes of France, and had renewed with the marshal d'Estrades a project of dividing the Spanish Netherlands between France and Holland, that had been taken up formerly, when Richelieu made use of it to flatter their ambition, and to engage them to prolong the war against Spain. A project not unlike to that which was held out to them by the famous preliminaries, and the extravagant barrier-treaty, in one thousand seven hundred and nine; and which engaged them to continue a war on the principle of ambition, into which they had entered with more reasonable and more moderate views.

As the private interests of the two De Wits hindered that commonwealth from being on her guard, as early as she ought to have been, against France, so the mistaken policy of the court of England, and the short views, and the profuse temper of the prince who governed, gave great advantages to Louis the Fourteenth in the pursuit of his designs. He bought Dunkirk: and your lordship knows how great a clamor was raised on that occasion against your noble ancestor; as if he alone had been answerable for the measure, and his interest had been concerned in it. I have heard our late friend Mr. George Clarke quote a witness, who was quite unexceptionable, but I cannot recall his name at present, who, many years after all these transactions, and the death of my lord Clarendon, affirmed, that the earl of Sandwich had owned to him, that he himself gave his opinion, among many others, officers, and ministers, for selling Dunkirk. Their reasons could not be good, I presume to say; but several, that might be plausible at that time, are easily guessed. A prince like king Charles, who would have made as many bad bargains as any young spendthrift, for money, finding himself thus backed, we may assure ourselves, was peremptorily determined to sell: and whatever your great grandfather's opinion was, this I am able to pronounce upon my own experience, that his treaty for the sale is no proof he was of opinion to sell. When the resolution of selling was once taken, to whom could the sale be made? To the Dutch? No. This measure would have

been at least as impolitic, and, in that moment, perhaps more
odious than the other. To the Spaniards? They were unable
to buy: and, as low as their power was sunk, the principle of
opposing it still prevailed. I have sometimes thought that the
Spaniards, who were forced to make peace with Portugal, and
to renounce all claim to that crown, four or five years afterwards,
might have been induced to take this resolution then; if the
regaining Dunkirk without any expense had been a condition
proposed to them; and that the Portuguese, who, notwithstanding their alliance with England and the indirect succors that
France afforded them, were little able, after the treaty especially,
to support a war against Spain, might have been induced to pay
the price of Dunkirk, for so great an advantage as immediate
peace with Spain, and the extinction of all foreign pretences on
their crown.   But this speculation concerning events so long ago
passed is not much to the purpose here.   I proceed therefore to
observe, that notwithstanding the sale of Dunkirk, and the secret
leanings of our court to that of France, yet England was first to
take the alarm, when Louis the Fourteenth invaded the Spanish
Netherlands in one thousand six hundred and sixty-seven: and
the triple alliance was the work of an English minister.   It was
time to take this alarm; for from the moment that the king of
France claimed a right to the county of Burgundy, the duchy
of Brabant, and other portions of the Low Countries that devolved on his queen by the death of her father Philip the Fourth,
he pulled off the mask entirely. Volumes were written to
establish, and to refute this supposed right. Your lordship no
doubt will look into a controversy that has employed so many
pens and so many swords; and I believe you will think it was
sufficiently bold in the French, to argue from customs, that regulated the course of private successions in certain provinces, to a
right of succeeding to the sovereignty of those provinces: and to
assert the divisibility of the Spanish monarchy, with the same
breath with which they asserted the indivisibility of their own;
although the proofs in one case were just as good as the proofs
in the other, and the fundamental law of indivisibility was at
least as good a law in Spain, as either this or the Salique law
was in France.   But however proper it might be for the French
and Austrian pens to enter into long discussions, and to appeal,
on this great occasion, to the rest of Europe; the rest of Europe
had a short objection to make to the plea of France, which no
sophisms, no quirks of law could evade. Spain accepted the
renunciations as a real security: France gave them as such to
Spain, and in effect to the rest of Europe. If they had not been
thus given, and thus taken, the Spaniards would not have married their Infanta to the king of France, whatever distress they

might have endured by the prolongation of the war.   These renunciations were renunciations of all rights whatsoever to the whole Spanish monarchy, and to every part of it.   The provinces claimed by France at this time were parts of it.   To claim them, was therefore to claim the whole; for if the renunciations were no bar to the rights accruing to Mary Theresa on the death of her father Philip the Fourth, neither could they be any to the rights that would accrue to her and her children, on the death of her brother Charles the Second: an unhealthful youth, and who at this instant was in immediate danger of dying; for to all the complicated distempers he brought into the world with him, the small-pox was added.   Your lordship sees how the fatal contingency of uniting the two monarchies of France and Spain stared mankind in the face; and yet nothing, that I can remember, was done to prevent it: not so much as a guaranty given, or a declaration made to assert the validity of these renunciations, and for securing the effect of them.   The triple alliance indeed stopped the progress of the French arms, and produced the treaty of Aix la Chapelle.   But England, Sweden, and Holland, the contracting powers in this alliance, seemed to look, and probably did look, no farther.   France kept a great and important part of what she had surprised or ravished, or purchased; for we cannot say with any propriety that she conquered: and the Spaniards were obliged to set all they saved to the account of gain.   The German branch of Austria had been reduced very low in power and in credit under Ferdinand the Third, by the treaties of Westphalia, as I have said already. Louis the Fourteenth maintained, during many years, the influence these treaties had given him among the princes and states of the empire.   The famous capitulation made at Frankfort on the election of Leopold, who succeeded Ferdinand about the year one thousand six hundred and fifty-seven, was encouraged by the intrigues of France: and the power of France was looked upon as the sole power that could ratify and secure effectually the observation of the conditions then made.   The league of the Rhine was not renewed, I believe, after the year one thousand six hundred and sixty-six; but though this league was not renewed, yet some of these princes and states continued in their old engagements with France: whilst others took new engagements on particular occasions, according as private and sometimes very paltry interests, and the emissaries of France in all their little courts, disposed them.   In short, the princes of Germany showed no alarm at the growing ambition and power of Louis the Fourteenth, but contributed to encourage one, and to confirm the other.   In such a state of things the German branch was little able to assist the Spanish branch against France, either in the war that ended by the Pyrenean treaty, or in that we are speaking of here, the short war that began in one thousand six hundred and sixty-seven, and was ended by the treaty of Aix la Chapelle in one thousand six hundred and sixty-eight. But it was not this alone that disabled the emperor from acting with vigor in the cause of his family then, nor that has rendered the house of Austria a dead weight upon all her allies ever since. Bigotry, and its inseparable companion, cruelty, as well as the tyranny and avarice of the court of Vienna, created in those days, and has maintained in ours, almost a perpetual diversion of the imperial arms from all effectual oppsition to France. I mean to speak of the troubles in Hungary. Whatever they became in their progress, they were caused originally by the usurpations and persecutions of the emperor: and when the Hungarians were called rebels first, they were called so for no other reason than this, that they would not be slaves. The dominion of the emperor being less supportable than that of the Turks, this unhappy people opened a door to the latter to infest the empire, instead of making their country what it had been before, a barrier against the Ottoman power. France became a sure, though secret ally of the Turks, as well as the Hungarians, and has found her account in it, by keeping the emperor in perpetual alarms on that side, while she has ravaged the empire and the Low Countries on the other. Thus we saw, thirty-two years ago, the arms of France and Bavaria in possession of Passau, and the malcontents of Hungary in the suburbs of Vienna. In a word, when Louis the Fourteenth made the first essay of his power, by the war of one thousand six hundred and sixty-seven, and sounded, as it were, the councils of Europe concerning his pretensions on the Spanish succession, he found his power to be great beyond what his neighbors, or even he perhaps thought it: great by the wealth, and greater by the united spirit of his people; greater still by the ill policy and divided interests that governed those who had a superior common interest to oppose him. He found that the members of the triple alliance did not see, or seeing did not think proper to own that they saw, the injustice, and the consequence of his pretensions. They contented themselves to give to Spain an act of guaranty for securing the execution of the treaty of Aix la Chapelle. He knew even then how ill the guaranty would be observed by two of them at least, by England and by Sweden. The treaty itself was nothing more than a composition between the bully and the bullied. Tournay, and Lisle, and Doway, and other places that I have forgot, were yielded to him: and he restored the county of Burgundy, according to the option that Spain made against the interest and the expectation too of the Dutch, when an option was forced upon her. The king of Spain compounded for his possession: but the emperor compounded at the same time for his succession, by a private eventual treaty of partition, which the Commander of Gremonville and the Count of Avers-berg signed at Vienna. The same Leopold, who exclaimed so loudly, in one thousand six hundred and ninety-eight, against any partition of the Spanish monarchy, and refused to submit to that which England and Holland had then made, made one him-self in one thousand six hundred and sixty-eight, with so little regard to these two powers, that the whole ten provinces were thrown into the lot of France.

There is no room to wonder if such experience as Louis the Fourteenth had upon this occasion, and such a face of affairs in Europe, raising his hopes, raised his ambition: and if, in making peace at Aix la Chapelle, he meditated a new war, the war of one thousand six hundred and seventy-two; the preparations he made for it, by negotiations in all parts, by alliances wherever he found ingression, and by the increase of his forces, were equally proofs of ability, industry, and power. I shall not descend into these particulars: your lordship will find them pretty well detailed in the memorials of that time. But one of the alliances he made I must mention, though I mention it with the utmost regret and indignation. England was fatally engaged to act a part in this conspiracy against the peace and the liberty of Europe, nay, against her own peace and her own liberty; for a bubble's part it was, equally wicked and impolitic. Forgive the terms I use, my lord: none can be too strong. The principles of the triple alliance, just and wise, and worthy of a king of England, were laid aside. Then, the progress of the French arms was to be checked, the ten provinces were to be saved, and by saving them the barrier of Holland was to be preserved. Now, we joined our counsels and our arms to those of France, in a project that could not be carried on at all, as it was easy to foresee, and as the event showed, unless it was carried on against Spain, the emperor, and most of the princes of Germany, as well as the Dutch; and which could not be carried on successfully, without leaving the ten provinces entirely at the mercy of France, and giving her pretence and opportunity of ravaging the empire, and extending her conquests on the Rhine. The medal of Van Beuninghen, and other pretences that France took for attack-ing the states of the Low Countries, were ridiculous. They imposed on no one: and the true object of Louis the Four-teenth was manifest to all. But what could a king of England mean? Charles the Second had reasons of resentment against the Dutch, and just ones too no doubt. Among the rest, it was not easy for him to forget the affront he had suffered, and the loss he had sustained, when, depending on the peace that was ready to be signed, and that was signed in Breda in July, he neglected to fit out his fleet; and when that of Holland, commanded by Ruyter, with Cornelius de Wit on board as deputy or commissioner of the states, burnt his ships at Chatham in June. The famous perpetual edict, as it was called, but did not prove in the event, against the election of a stadt-holder, which John de Wit promoted, carried, and obliged the Prince of Orange to swear to maintain a very few days after the conclusion of the peace at Breda, might be another motive in the breast of king Charles the Second: as it was certainly a pretence of revenge on the Dutch, or at least on the De Wits and the Louvestein faction, that ruled almost despotically in that commonwealth. But it is plain that neither these reasons, nor others of a more ancient date, determined him to this alliance with France; since he contracted the triple alliance within four or five months after the two events, I have mentioned, happened. What then did he mean? Did he mean to acquire one of the seven provinces, and divide them, as the Dutch had twice treated for the division of the ten, with France? I believe not; but this I believe, that his inclinations were favorable to the popish interest in general, and that he meant to make himself more absolute at home; that he thought it necessary to this end to humble the Dutch, to reduce their power, and, perhaps, to change the form of their government; to deprive his subjects of the correspondence with a neighboring protestant and free state, and of all hope of succor and support from thence in their opposition to him; in a word to abet the designs of France on the continent, that France might abet his designs on his own kingdom. This, I say, I believe; and this I should venture to affirm, if I had in my hands to produce, and was at liberty to quote, the private relations I have read formerly, drawn up by those who were no enemies to such designs, and on the authority of those who were parties to them. But whatever king Charles the Second meant, certain it is, that his conduct established the superiority of France in Europe.

But this charge, however, must not be confined to him alone. Those who were nearer the danger, those who were exposed to the immediate attacks of France, and even those who were her rivals for the same succession, having either assisted her, or engaged to remain neuters, a strange fatality prevailed, and produced such a conjuncture as can hardly be parallelled in history. Your lordship will observe with astonishment, even in the beginning of the year one thousand six hundred and seventy-two, all the neighbors of France, acting as if they had nothing to fear from her, and some as if they had much to hope, by helping her

to oppress the Dutch and sharing with her the spoils of that commonwealth. "Delenda est Carthago" was the cry in England,
and seemed too a maxim on the continent.

In the course of the same year, you will observe that all these
powers took the alarm, and began to unite in opposition to France.
Even England thought it time to interpose in favor of the Dutch.
The consequences of this alarm, of this sudden turn in the policy
of Europe, and of that which happened, by the massacre of the
De Wits, and the elevation of the prince of Orange, in the government of the seven provinces, saved these provinces, and stopped
the rapid progress of the arms of France. Louis the Fourteenth
indeed surprised the seven provinces in this war, as he had surprised the ten in that of one thousand six hundred and sixty-
seven, and ravaged defenceless countries with armies sufficient
to conquer them, if they had been prepared to resist. In the
war of one thousand six hundred and seventy-two, he had little
less than one hundred and fifty thousand men on foot, besides
the bodies of English, Swiss, Italians, and Swedes, that amounted
to thirty or forty thousand more. With this mighty force he took
forty places in forty days, imposed extravagant conditions of
peace, played the monarch a little while at Utrecht; and as soon
as the Dutch recovered from their consternation, and, animated
by the example of the Prince of Orange and the hopes of succor,
refused these conditions, he went back to Versailles, and left his
generals to carry on his enterprise: which they did with so little
success, that Grave and Maestricht alone remained to him of all
the boasted conquests he had made; and even these he offered
two years afterwards to restore, if by that concession he could
have prevailed on the Dutch at that time to make peace with him.
But they were not yet disposed to abandon their allies; for allies
now they had. The emperor and the king of Spain had engaged in the quarrel against France, and many of the princes of
the empire had done the same. Not all. The Bavarian continued obstinate in his neutrality, and, to mention no more, the
Swedes made a great diversion in favor of France in the empire; where the Duke of Hanover abetted their designs as much
as he could, for he was a zealous partisan of France, though the
other princes of his house acted for the common cause. I descend into no more particulars. The war that Louis the Fourteenth kindled by attacking in so violent a manner the Dutch
commonwealth, and by making so arbitrary an use of his first
success, became general, in the Low Countries, in Spain, in
Sicily, on the upper and lower Rhine, in Denmark, in Sweden,
and in the provinces of Germany belonging to these two crowns;
on the Mediterranean, the Ocean, and the Baltic. France supported this war with advantage on every side: and when your

lordship considers in what manner it was carried on against her, you will not be surprised that she did so. Spain had spirit, but too little strength to maintain her power in Sicily, where Messina had revolted; to defend her frontier on that side of the Pyrenées; and to resist the great efforts of the French in the Low Countries. The empire was divided; and, even among the.princes who acted against France, there was neither union in their councils, nor concert in their projects, nor order in preparations, nor vigor in execution: and, to say the truth, there was not, in the whole confedracy, a man whose abilities could make him a match for the Prince of Condé or the Marshal of Turenne; nor many who were in any degree equal to Luxemburg, Crequi, Schomberg, and other generals of inferior note, who commanded the armies of France. The emperor took this very time to make new invasions on the liberties of Hungary, and to oppress his protestant subjects. The Prince of Orange alone acted with invincible firmness, like a patriot, and a hero. Neither the seductions of France nor those of England, neither the temptations of ambition nor those of private interest, could make him swerve from the true interest of his country, nor from the common interest of Europe. He had raised more sieges, and lost more battles, it was said, than any general of his age had done. Be it so. But his defeats were manifestly due in a great measure to circumstances independent on him: and that spirit, which even these defeats could not depress, was all his own. He had difficulties in his own commonwealth; the governors of the Spanish Low Countries crossed his measure sometimes; the German allies disappointed and broke them often: and it is not improbable that he was frequently betrayed. He was so perhaps even by Souches, the imperial general; a Frenchman according to Bayle, and a pensioner of Louvois according to common report, and very strong appearances, He had not yet credit and authority sufficient to make him a centre of union to a whole confederacy, the soul that animated and directed so great a body. He came to be such afterwards; but at the time spoken of, he could not take so great a part upon him. No other prince or general was equal to it: and the consequences of this defect appeared almost in every operation. France was surrounded by a multitude of enemies, all intent to demolish her power. But, like the builders of Babel, they spoke different languages: and as those could not build, these could not demolish, for want of understanding one another. France improved this advantage by her arms, and more by her negotiations. Nimeguen was, after Cologne, the scene of these. England was the mediating power, and I know not whether our Charles the Second did not serve her purposes more usefully in the latter, and under the character of mediator, than he did or could have done by joining his arms to hers, and acting as her ally. The Dutch were induced to sign a treaty with him, that broke the confederacy, and gave great advantage to France: for the purport of it was to oblige France and Spain to make peace on a plan to be proposed to them, and no mention was made in it of the other allies that I remember. The Dutch were glad to get out of an expensive war. France promised to restore Maestricht to them, and Maestricht was the only place that remained unrecovered of all they had lost. They dropped Spain at Nimeguen, as they had dropped France at Munster; but many circumstances concurred to give a much worse grace to their abandoning of Spain, than to their abandoning of France. I need not specify them. This only I would observe: when they made a separate peace at Munster, they left an ally who was in condition to carry on the war alone with advantage, and they presumed to impose no terms upon him: when they made a separate peace at Nimeguen, they abandoned an ally who was in no condition to carry on the war alone, and who was reduced to accept whatever terms the common enemy prescribed. In their great distress in one thousand six hundred and seventy-three, they engaged to restore Maestricht to the Spaniards as soon as it should be retaken: it was not retaken, and they accepted it for themselves as the price of the separate peace they made with France. The Dutch had engaged farther, to make neither peace nor truce with the king of France, till that prince consented to restore to Spain all he had conquered since the Pyrenean treaty. But far from keeping this promise in any tolerable degree, Louis the Fourteenth acquired, by the plan imposed on Spain at Nimeguen, besides the county of Burgundy, so many other countries and towns on the side of the ten Spanish provinces, that these, added to the places he kept of those which had been yielded to him by the treaty of Aix la Chapelle (for some of little consequence he restored) put into his hands the principal strength of that barrier, against which we goaded ourselves almost to death in the last great war; and made good the saying of the Marshal of Schomberg, that to attack this barrier was to take the beast by his horns. I know very well what may be said to excuse the Dutch. The emperor was more intent to tyrannise his subjects on one side, than to defend them on the other. He attempted little against France, and the little he did attempt was ill-ordered, and worse executed. The assistance of the princes of Germany was often uncertain, and always expensive. Spain was already indebted to Holland for great sums; greater still must be advanced to her if the war continued: and experience showed that France was able, and would continue, to prevail against her present enemies. The triple league had stopped her progress, and obliged her to abandon the county of Burgundy; but Sweden was now engaged in the war on the side of France, as England had been in the beginning of it: and England was now privately favorable to her interests, as Sweden had been in the beginning of it. The whole ten provinces would have been subdued in the course of a few campaigns more: and it was better for Spain and the Dutch too, that part should be saved by accepting a sort of composition, than the whole be risked by refusing it. This might be alleged to excuse the conduct of the States General, in imposing hard terms on Spain; in making none for their other allies; and in signing alone: by which steps they gave France an opportunity that she improved with great dexterity of management, the opportunity of treating with the confederates one by one, and of beating them by detail in the cabinet, if I may so say, as she had often done in the field. I shall not compare these reasons, which were but too well founded in fact, and must appear plausible at least, with other considerations that might be, and were at the time, insisted upon. I confine myself to a few observations, which every knowing and impartial man must admit. Your lordship will observe, first, that the fatal principle of compounding with Louis the Fourteenth, from the time that his pretensions, his power, and the use he made of it, began to threaten Europe, prevailed still more at Nimeguen than it had prevailed at Aix: so that although he did not obtain to the full all he attempted, yet the dominions of France were by common consent, on every treaty, more and more extended; her barriers on all sides were more and more strengthened; those of her neighbors were more and more weakened; and that power, which was to assert one day, against the rest of Europe, the pretended rights of the house of Bourbon to the Spanish monarchy, was more and more established, and rendered truly formidable in such hands at least, during the course of the first eighteen years of the period. Your lordship will please to observe, in the second place, that the extreme weakness of one branch of Austria, and the miserable conduct of both; the poverty of some of the princes of the empire, and the disunion, and to speak plainly, the mercenary policy of all of them; in short, the confined views, the false notions, and, to speak as plainly of my own as of other nations, the iniquity of the councils of England, not only hindered the growth of this power from being stopped in time, but nursed it up into strength almost insuperable by any future confederacy. A third observation is this: If the excuses made for the conduct of the Dutch at Nimeguen are not sufficient, they too must come in for their share in this condemnation, even after the death of the De Wits; as they were to be condemned most justly, during the administration, for abetting and favoring France. If these excuses, grounded on their inability to pursue any longer a war, the principal profit of which was to accrue to their confederates, for that was the case after the year one thousand six hundred and seventy-three, or one thousand six hundred and seventy-four, and the principal burden of which was thrown on them by their confederates; if these are sufficient, they should not have acted, for decency's sake as well as out of good policy, the part they did act in one thousand seven hundred and eleven, and one thousand seven hundred and twelve, towards the late queen, who had complaints of the same kind, in a much higher degree and with circumstances much more aggravating, to make of them, of the emperor, and of all the princes of Germany; and who was far from treating them and their other allies, at that time, as they treated Spain and their other allies in one thousand six hundred and seventy-eight. Immediately after the Dutch had made their peace, that of Spain was signed with France. The emperor's treaty with this crown and that of Sweden was concluded in the following year: and Louis the Fourteenth being now at liberty to assist his ally, whilst he had tied up the powers with whom he had treated from assisting theirs, he soon forced the king of Denmark and the elector of Brandenburg to restore all they had taken from the Swedes, and to conclude the peace of the north. In all these treaties he gave the law, and he was now at the highest point of his grandeur. He continued at this point for several years, and in this height of his power he prepared those alliances against it, under the weight of which he was at last well nigh oppressed; and might have been reduced as low as the general interest of Europe required, if some of the causes, which worked now, had not continued to work in his favor, and if his enemies had not proved, in their turn of fortune, as insatiable as prosperity had rendered him.

After he had made peace with all the powers with whom he had been in war, he continued to vex both Spain and the empire, and to extend his conquests in the Low Countries, and on the Rhine, both by the pen and the sword. He erected the chambers of Metz and of Brisach, where his own subjects were prosecutors, witnesses, and judges all at once. Upon the decisions of these tribunals, he seized into his own hands, under the notion of dependencies and the pretence of reunions, whatever towns or districts of country tempted his ambition, or suited his conveniency: and added, by these and by other means, in the midst of peace, more territories to those the late treaties had yielded to him, than he could have got by continuing the war. He acted afterwards, in the support of all this, without any bounds or limits. His glory was a reason for attacking Holland in one thousand six hundred and seventy-two, and his conveniency a reason for many of the attacks he made on others afterwards. He took Luxemburg by force; he stole Strasburg; he bought Casal: and, whilst he waited the opportunity of acquiring to his family the crown of Spain, he was not without thoughts, nor hopes perhaps, of bringing into it the imperial crown likewise. Some of the cruelties he exercised in the empire may be ascribed to his disappointment in this view: I say some of them, because in the war that ended by the treaty of Nimeguen, he had already exercised many. Though the French writers endeavor to slide over them, to palliate them, and to impute them particularly to the English that were in their service; for even this one of their writers has the front to advance: yet these cruelties, unheard of among civilised nations, must be granted to have been ordered by the counsels, and executed by the arms of France, in the Palatinate, and in other parts.

If Louis the Fourteenth could have contented himself with the acquisitions that were confirmed to him by the treaties of one thousand six hundred and seventy-eight, and one thousand six hundred and seventy-nine, and with the authority and reputation which he then gained; it is plain that he would have prevented the alliances that were afterwards formed against him, and that he might have regained his credit amongst the princes of the empire, where he had one family alliance by the marriage of his brother to the daughter of the elector Palatine, and another by that of his son to the sister of the elector of Bavaria; where Sweden was closely attached to him, and where the same principles of private interest would have soon attached others as closely. He might have remained not only the principal, but the directing power of Europe, and have held this rank with all the glory imaginable, till the death of the king of Spain, or some other object of great ambition, had determined him to act another part. But instead of this, he continued to vex and provoke all those who were, unhappily for them, his neighbors, and, that in many instances, for trifles. An example of this kind occurs to me. On the death of the Duke of Deux Ponts, he seized that little inconsiderable duchy, without any regard to the indisputable right of the king of Sweden, to the services that crown had rendered him, or to the want he might have of that alliance hereafter. The consequence was, that Sweden entered with the emperor, the king of Spain, the elector of Bavaria, and the States General, into the alliance of guaranty, as it was called, about the year one thousand six hundred and eighty-three, and into the famous league of Augsburg, in one thousand six hundred and eighty-six.

Since I have mentioned this league, and since we may date from it a more general, and more concerted opposition to France, than there had been before; give me leave to recall some of the reflections that have presented themselves to my mind, in considering what I have read, and what I have heard related, concerning the passages of that time. They will be of use to form our judgment concerning later passages. If the king of France became an object of aversion on account of any invasions he made, any deviations from public faith, any barbarities exercised where his arms prevailed, or the persecution of his protestant subjects; the emperor deserved to be such an object, at least as much as he, on the same accounts. The emperor was so too, but with this difference relatively to the political system of the west: the Austrian ambition and bigotry exerted themselves in distant countries, whose interests were not considered as a part of this system; for otherwise there would have been as much reason for assisting the people of Hungary and of Transylvania against the emperor, as there had been formerly for assisting the people of the seven united provinces against Spain, or as there had been lately for assisting them against France; but the ambition and bigotry of Louis the Fourteenth were exerted in the Low Countries, on the Rhine, in Italy, and in Spain, in the very midst of this system, if I may say so, and with success that could not fail to subvert it in time. The power of the house of Austria, that had been feared too long, was feared no longer: and that of the house of Bourbon, by having been feared too late, was now grown terrible. The emperor was so intent on the establishment of his absolute power in Hungary, that he exposed the empire doubly to desolation and ruin for the sake of it. He left the frontier almost quite defenceless on the side of the Rhine, against the inroads and ravages of France: and by showing no mercy to the Hungarians, nor keeping any faith with them, he forced that miserable people into alliances with the Turks, who invaded the empire, and besieged Vienna. Even this event had no effect upon him. Your lordship will find, that Sobieski, king of Poland, who had forced the Turks to raise the siege, and had fixed the imperial crown that tottered on his head, could not prevail on him to take those measures by which alone it was possible to cover the empire, to secure the king of Spain, and to reduce that power who was probably one day to dispute with him this prince's succession. Tekeli and the malcontents made such demands as none but a tyrant could refuse, the preservation of their ancient privileges, liberty of conscience, the convocation of a free diet or parliament, and others of less importance. All was in vain. The war continued with them, and with the Turks, and France was left at liberty to push her enterprises,

almost without opposition, against Germany and the Low Countries. The distress in both was so great, that the States General
saw no other expedient for stopping the progress of the French
arms, than a cessation of hostilities, or a truce of twenty years;
which they negotiated, and which was accepted by the emperor
and the king of Spain, on the terms that Louis the Fourteenth
thought fit to offer. By these terms he was to remain in full
and quiet possession of all he had acquired since the years one
thousand six hundred and seventy-eight, and one thousand six
hundred and seventy-nine; among which acquisitions that of
Luxemburg and that of Strasburg were comprehended. The
conditions of this truce were so advantageous to France, that all
her intrigues were employed to obtain a definitive treaty of peace
upon the same conditions. But this was neither the interest nor
the intention of the other contracting powers. The imperial
arms had been very successful against the Turks. This success,
as well as the troubles that followed upon it in the Ottoman
armies, and at the Porte, gave reasonable expectation of concluding a peace on that side: and, this peace concluded, the emperor, and the empire, and the king of Spain would have been
in a much better posture to treat with France. With these
views, that were wise and just, the league of Augsburg was
made between the emperor, the kings of Spain and Sweden as
princes of the empire, and the other circles and princes. This
league was purely defensive. An express article declared it to
be so: and as it had no other regard, it was not only conformable to the laws and constitutions of the empire, and to the practice of all nations, but even to the terms of the act of truce so
lately concluded. This pretence, therefore, for breaking the
truce, seizing the electorate of Cologne, invading the Palatinate,
besieging Philipsburg, and carrying unexpected and undeclared
war into the empire could not be supported: nor is it possible to
read the reasons published by France at this time, and drawn
from her fears of the imperial power, without laughter. As
little pretence was there to complain, that the emperor refused
to convert at once the truce into a definitive treaty; since if he
had done so, he would have confirmed in a lump, and without
any discussion, all the arbitrary decrees of those chambers, or
courts, that France had erected to cover her usurpation; and
would have given up almost a sixth part of the provinces of the
empire, that France one way or other had possessed herself of.
The pretensions of the Duchess of Orleans on the succession of
her father, and her brother, which were disputed by the then
elector Palatine, and were to be determined by the laws and
customs of the empire, afforded as little pretence for beginning
this war, as any of the former allegations. The exclusion of the

Cardinal of Furstenburg, who had been elected to the archbishop-ric of Cologne, was capable of being aggravated: but even in this case his most Christian majesty opposed his judgment and his authority against the judgment and authority of that holy father, whose eldest son he was proud to be called.　In short, the true reason why Louis the Fourteenth began that cruel war with the empire two years after he had concluded a cessation of hostilities for twenty, was this: he resolved to keep what he had got; and, therefore, he resolved to encourage the Turks to continue the war.　He did this effectually, by invading Germany at the very instant when the Sultan was suing for peace.　Notwithstanding this, the Turks were in treaty again the following year: and good policy should have obliged the emperor, since he could not hope to carry on this war and that against France, at the same time, with vigor and effect, to conclude a peace with the least danger-ous enemy of the two.　The decision of his disputes with France could not be deferred, his designs against the Hungarians were in part accomplished, for his son was declared king, and the set-tlement of that crown in his family was made; and the rest of these, as well as those that he formed against the Turks, might be deferred.　But the councils of Vienna judged differently, and insisted even at this critical moment on the most exorbitant terms; on some of such a nature, that the Turks showed more humanity and a better sense of religion in refusing, than they in asking them.　Thus the war went on in Hungary, and proved a constant diversion in favor of France, during the whole course of that which Louis the Fourteenth began at this time; for the treaty of Carlowitz was posterior to that of Ryswic.　The em-pire, Spain, England, and Holland engaged in the war with France: and on them the emperor left the burden of it.　In the short war of one thousand six hundred and sixty-seven, he was not so much as a party, and instead of assisting the king of Spain, which it must be owned, he was in no good condition of doing, he bargained for dividing that prince's succession, as I have observed above.　In the war of one thousand six hundred and seventy-two he made some feeble efforts.　In this of one thousand six hundred and eighty-eight he did still less: and in the war which broke out at the beginning of the present century he did nothing, at least after the first campaign in Italy, and after the engage-ments that England and Holland took by the grand alliance.　In a word, from the time that an opposition to France became a common cause in Europe, the house of Austria has been a clog upon it in many instances, and of considerable assistance to it in none.　The accession of England to this cause, which was brought about by the revolution of one thousand six hundred and eighty-eight, might have made amends, and more than amends, one would think, for this defect, and have thrown superiority of power and of success on the side of the confederates, with whom she took part against France. This, I say, might be imagined, without over-rating the power of England, or undervaluing that of France; and it was imagined at that time. How it proved otherwise in the event; how France came triumphant out of the war that ended by the treaty of Ryswic, and though she gave up a great deal, yet preserved the greatest and the best part of her conquests and acquisitions made since the treaties of Westphalia, and the Pyrenees; how she acquired, by the gift of Spain, that whole monarchy for one of her princes, though she had no reason to expect the least part of it without a war at one time, nor the great lot of it even by a war at any time; in short, how she wound up advantageously the ambitious system she had been fifty years in weaving; how she concluded a war, in which she was defeated on every side, and wholly exhausted, with little diminution of the provinces and barriers acquired to France, and with the quiet possession of Spain and the Indies to a prince of the house of Bourbon: all this, my lord, will be the subject of your researches, when you come down to the latter part of the last period of modern history.

LETTER VIII.

THE SAME SUBJECT CONTINUED FROM THE YEAR ONE THOUSAND SIX HUNDRED AND EIGHTY-EIGHT.

Your lordship will find, that the objects proposed by the alliance of one thousand six hundred and eighty-nine, between the emperor and the States, to which England acceded, and which was the foundation of the whole confederacy then formed, were no less than to restore all things to the terms of the Westphalian and Pyrenean treaties, by the war; and to preserve them in that state, after the war, by a defensive alliance and guaranty of the same confederate powers against France. The particular as well as general meaning of this engagement was plain enough: and if it had not been so, the sense of it would have been sufficiently determined, by that separate article, in which England and Holland obliged themselves to assist the "house of Austria, in taking and keeping possession of the Spanish monarchy, whenever the case should happen of the death of Charles the Second, without lawful heirs." This engagement was double, and thereby relative to the whole political system of Europe, alike affected by the power and pretensions of France. Hitherto the power of France had been alone regarded, and her pretensions seemed to have been forgot; or to what purpose should they have been remembered, whilst Europe was so unhappily constituted, that the states at whose expense she increased her power, and their friends and allies, thought that they did enough upon every occasion if they made some tolerable composition with her? They who were not in circumstances to refuse confirming present, were little likely to take effectual measures against future usurpations. But now, as the alarm was greater than ever, by the outrages that France had committed, and the intrigues she had carried on; by the little regard she had shown to public faith, and by the airs of authority she had assumed twenty years together: so was the spirit against her raised to an higher pitch, and the means of reducing her power, or at least of checking it, were increased. The princes and states who had neglected or favored the growth of this power, which all of them had done in their turns, saw their error; saw the necessity of repairing it, and saw that unless they could check the power of France, by uniting a power superior to hers, it would be impossible to hinder her from succeeding in her great designs on the Spanish succession. The court of England had submitted, not many years before, to abet her usurpations, and the king of England had stooped to be her pensioner. But the crime was not national. On the contrary, the nation had cried out loudly against it, even whilst it was committing: and as soon as ever the abdication of king James, and the elevation of the prince of Orange to the throne of England happened, the nation engaged with all imaginable zeal in the common cause of Europe, to reduce the exorbitant power of France, to prevent her future and to revenge her past attempts; for even a spirit of revenge prevailed, and the war was a war of anger as well as of interest.

Unhappily this zeal was neither well conducted, nor well seconded. It was zeal without success in the first of the two wars that followed the year one thousand six hundred and eighty-eight; and zeal without knowledge, in both of them. I enter into no detail concerning the events of these two wars. This only I observe on the first of them, that the treaties of Ryswic were far from answering the ends proposed and the engagements taken by the first grand alliance. The power of France, with respect to extent of dominions and strength of barrier, was not reduced to the terms of the Pyrenean treaty, no not to those of the treaty of Nimeguen. Lorrain was restored indeed with very considerable reserves, and the places taken or usurped on the other side of the Rhine: but then Strasburg was yielded up absolutely to France by the emperor, and by the empire. The concessions to Spain were great, but so were the conquests and the encroachments made upon her by France, since the treaty of Nimeguen: and she got little at Ryswic, I believe nothing more than she had saved at Nimeguen before. All these concessions, however, as well as the acknowledgment of king William, and others made by Louis the Fourteenth after he had taken Ath and Barcelona, even during the course of the negotiations, compared with the losses and repeated defeats of the allies and the ill state of the confederacy, surprised the generality of mankind, who had not been accustomed to so much moderation and generosity on the part of this prince. But the pretensions of the house of Bourbon on the Spanish succession remained the same. Nothing had been done to weaken them; nothing was prepared to oppose them: and the opening of this succession was visibly at hand; for Charles the Second had been in immediate danger of dying about this time. His death could not be a remote event: and all the good queen's endeavors to be got with child had proved ineffectual. The league dissolved, all the forces of the confederates dispersed, and many disbanded; France continuing armed, her forces by sea and land increased and held in readiness to act on all sides, it was plain that the confederates had failed in the first object of the grand alliance, that of reducing the power of France; by succeeding in which alone they could have been able to keep the second engagement, that of securing the succession of Spain to the house of Austria.

After this peace, what remained to be done? In the whole nature of things there remained but three. To abandon all care of the Spanish succession was one; to compound with France upon this succession was another; and to prepare, like her, during the interval of peace, to make an advantageous war whenever Charles the Second should die, was a third. Now the first of these was to leave Spain, and, in leaving Spain, to leave all Europe in some sort at the mercy of France; since whatever disposition the Spaniards should make of their crown, they were quite unable to support it against France; since the emperor could do little without his allies; and since Bavaria, the third pretender, could do still less, and might find, in such a case, his account perhaps better in treating with the house of Bourbon than with that of Austria. More needs not be said on this head; but on the other two, which I shall consider together, several facts are proper to be mentioned, and several reflections necessary to be made.

We might have counter-worked, no doubt, in their own methods of policy, the councils of France, who made peace to dissolve the confederacy, and great concessions, with very suspicious generosity, to gain the Spaniards: we might have waited, like them, that is in arms, the death of Charles the Second, and have fortified in the mean time the dispositions of the king, the court and people of Spain, against the pretensions of France: we might have made the peace, which was made some time after that, between the emperor and the Turks, and have obliged the former at any rate to have secured the peace of Hungary, and to have prepared, by these and other expedients, for the war that would inevitably break out on the death of the king of Spain.

But all such measures were rendered impracticable, by the emperor chiefly. Experience had shown, that the powers who engaged in alliance with him must expect to take the whole burden of his cause upon themselves; and that Hungary would maintain a perpetual diversion in favor of France, since he could not resolve to lighten the tyrannical yoke he had established in that country and in Transylvania, nor his ministers to part with the immense confiscations they had appropriated to themselves. Past experience showed this: and the experience that followed confirmed it very fatally. But further; there was not only little assistance to be expected from him by those who should engage in his quarrel: he did them hurt of another kind, and deprived them of many advantages by false measures of policy and unskilful negotiations. Whilst the death of Charles the Second was expected almost daily, the court of Vienna seemed to have forgot the court of Madrid, and all the pretensions on that crown. When the Count d'Harrach was sent thither, the imperial councils did something worse. The king of Spain was ready to declare the archduke Charles his successor; he was desirous to have this young prince sent into Spain: the bent of the people was in favor of Austria, or it had been so, and might have been easily turned the same way again: at court no cabal was yet formed in favor of Bourbon, and a very weak intrigue was on foot in favor of the electoral prince of Bavaria. Not only Charles might have been on the spot ready to reap the succession, but a German army might have been there to defend it; for the court of Madrid insisted on having twelve thousand of these troops, and, rather than not have them, offered to contribute to the payment of them privately: because it would have been too unpopular among the Spaniards, and too prejudicial to the Austrian interest, to have had it known that the emperor declined the payment of a body of his own troops that were demanded to secure the monarchy to his son. These proposals were half refused, and half evaded: and in return to the offer of the crown of Spain to the archduke, the imperial councils asked the government of

Milan for him.   They thought it a point of deep policy to secure
the Italian provinces, and to leave to England and Holland the
care of the Low Countries, of Spain, and the Indies.   By declining these proposals the house of Austria renounced in some sort
the whole succession: at least she gave England and Holland
reasons, whatever engagements these powers had taken, to refuse
the harder task of putting her into possession by force; when
she might, and would not, procure to the English and Dutch,
and her other allies, the easier task of defending her in this possession.

I said that the measures mentioned above were rendered impracticable, by the emperor chiefly, because they were rendered
so likewise by other circumstances at the same conjuncture.   A
principal one I shall mention, and it shall be drawn from the
state of our own country, and the disposition of our people.—
Let us take this up from king William's accession to our crown.
During the whole progress that Louis the Fourteenth made
towards such exorbitant power, as gave him well-grounded
hopes of acquiring at last to his family the Spanish monarchy,
England had been either an idle spectator of all that passed
on the Continent, or a faint and uncertain ally against France,
or a warm and sure ally on her side, or a partial mediator between her and the powers confederated in their common defence.
The revolution produced as great a change in our foreign conduct, as in our domestic establishment: and our nation engaged
with great spirit in the war of one thousand six hundred
and eighty-eight.   But then this spirit was rash, presumptuous, and ignorant, ill conducted at home, and ill seconded
abroad: all which has been touched already.   We had waged
no long wars on the Continent, nor been very deeply concerned
in foreign confederacies, since the fourteenth and fifteenth centuries.   The history of Edward the Third, however, and of the
first twelve or fifteen years of Henry the Sixth might have taught
us some general but useful lessons, drawn from remote times, but
applicable to the present.   So might the example of Henry the
Eighth, who squandered away great sums for the profit of taking
a town, or the honor of having an emperor in his pay; and who
divided afterwards by treaty the kingdom of France between
himself and Charles the Fifth, with success so little answerable
to such an undertaking, that it is hard to believe his Imperial
and English majesty were both in earnest.   If they were so, they
were both the bubbles of their presumption.   But it seems more
likely that Henry the Eighth was bubbled on this occasion by
the great hopes that Charles held out to flatter his vanity: as he
had been bubbled by his father-in-law Ferdinand, at the beginning of his reign, in the war of Navarre.   But these reflections

were not made, nor had we enough considered the example of Elizabeth, the last of our princes who had made any considerable figure abroad, and from whom we might have learned to act with vigor, but to engage with caution, and always to proportion our assistance according to our abilities, and the real necessities of our allies. The frontiers of France were now so fortified, her commerce and her naval force were so increased, her armies were grown so numerous, her troops were so disciplined, so inured to war, and so animated by a long course of successful campaigns, that they who looked on the situation of Europe could not fail to see how difficult the enterprise of reducing her power was become. Difficult as it was, we were obliged, on every account and by reasons of all kinds, to engage in it: but then we should have engaged with more forecast, and have conducted ourselves in the management of it, not with less alacrity and spirit, but with more order, more economy, and a better application of our efforts. But they who governed were glad to engage us at any rate; and we entered on this great scheme of action, as our nation is too apt to do, hurried on by the ruling passion of the day. I have been told by several, who were on the stage of the world at this time, that the generality of our people believed, and were encouraged to believe, the war could not be long, if the king was vigorously supported: and there is a humdrum speech of a speaker of the house of commons, I think, who humbly desired his majesty to take this opportunity of reconquering his ancient duchy of Aquitain. We were soon awakened from these gaudy dreams. In seven or eight years no impression had been made on France, that was besieged as it were on every side: and after repeated defeats in the Low Countries, where king William laid the principal stress of the war, his sole triumph was the retaking Namur, that had been taken by the French a few years before. Unsustained by success abroad, we are not to wonder that the spirit flagged at home; nor that the discontents of those who were averse to the established government, uniting with the far greater number of those who disliked the administration, inflamed the general discontents of the nation, oppressed with taxes, pillaged by usurers, plundered at sea, and disappointed at land. As we run into extremes always, some would have continued this war at any rate, even at the same rate, but it was not possible they should prevail in such a situation of affairs, and such a disposition of minds.— They who got by the war, and made immense fortunes by the necessities of the public, were not so numerous nor so powerful, as they have been since. The moneyed interest was not yet a rival able to cope with the landed interest, either in the nation or in parliament. The great corporations that had been erected more to serve the turn of party, than for any real national use, aimed indeed even then at the strength and influence which they have since acquired in the legislature; but they had not made the same progress by promoting national corruption, as they and the court have made since. In short, the other extreme prevailed. The generality of people grew as fond of getting out of the war, as they had been of entering into it: and thus far perhaps, considering how it had been conducted, they were not much to be blamed. But this was not all; for when king William had made the peace, our martial spirit became at once so pacific, that we seemed resolved to meddle no more in the affairs of the continent, at least to employ our arms no more in the quarrels that might arise there: and accordingly we reduced our troops in England to seven thousand men.

I have sometimes considered, in reflecting on these passages, what I should have done, if I had sat in parliament at that time; and have been forced to my own self, that I should have voted for disbanding the army then, as I voted in the following parliament for censuring the partition treaties. I am forced to own this, because I remember how imperfect my notions were of the situation of Europe in that extraordinary crisis, and how much I saw the true interest of my own country in a half-light. But, my lord, I own it with some shame; because in truth nothing could be more absurd than the conduct we held. What! because we had not reduced the power of France by the war, nor excluded the house of Bourbon from the Spanish succession, nor compounded with her upon it by the peace; and because the house of Austria had not helped herself, nor put it into our power to help her with more advantage and better prospect of success—were we to leave that whole succession open to the invasions of France, and to suffer even the contingency to subsist, of seeing those monarchies united? What! because it was become extravagant, after the trials so lately made, to think ourselves any longer engaged by treaty, or obliged by good policy, to put the house of Austria in possession of the whole Spanish monarchy, and to defend her in this possession by force of arms, were we to leave the whole at the mercy of France? If we were not to do so, if we were not to do one of the three things that I said above remained to be done, and if the emperor put it out of our power to do another of them with advantage; were we to put it still more out of our power, and to wait unarmed for the death of the king of Spain? In fine, if we had not the prospect of disputing with France, so successfully as we might have had it, the Spanish succession, whenever it should be open; were we not only to show by disarming, that we would not dispute it at all, but to censure likewise the second of the three things mentioned above, and which king William put in practice, the compounding with France, to prevent if possible a war, in which we were averse to engage?

Allow me to push these reflections a little further, and to observe to your lordship, that if the proposal of sending the archduke into Spain had been accepted in time by the imperial court, and taken effect and become a measure of the confederacy, that war indeed would have been protracted; but France could not have hindered the passage of this prince and his German forces: and our fleet would have been better employed in escorting them, and in covering the coasts of Spain and of the dominions of that crown both in Europe and in America, than it was in so many unmeaning expeditions from the battle of La Hogue to the end of the war. France indeed would have made her utmost efforts to have had satisfaction on her pretensions, as ill founded as they were. She would have ended that war, as we began the next, when we demanded a reasonable satisfaction for the emperor: and though I think that the allies would have had in very many respects, more advantage in defending Spain, than in attacking France; yet, upon a supposition that the defence would have been as ill conducted as the attack was, and that by consequence, whether Charles the Second had lived to the conclusion of this war, or had died before it, the war must have ended in some partition or other; this partition would have been made by the Spaniards themselves. They had been forced to compound with France on her former pretensions, and they must and they would have compounded on these, with an Austrian prince on the throne, just as they compounded, and probably much better than they compounded, on the pretensions we supported against them, when they had a prince of Bourbon on their throne. France could not have distressed the Spaniards, nor have overrun their monarchy, if they had been united; and they would have been united in this case, and supported by the whole confederacy: as we distressed both France and them, over run their monarchy in one hemisphere, and might have done so in both, when they were disunited, and supported by France alone. France would not have acted, in such negotiations, the ridiculous part which the emperor acted in those that led to the peace of Utrecht, nor have made her bargain worse by neglecting to make it in time. But the war ending as it did, though I cannot see how king William could avoid leaving the crown of Spain and that entire monarchy at the discretion of Louis the Fourteenth, otherwise than by compounding to prevent a new war he was in no sort prepared to make; yet it is undeniable, that by consenting to a partition of their monarchy, he threw the Spaniards into the arms of France. The first partition might have taken place, perhaps,

if the electoral prince of Bavaria had lived, whom the French
and Spaniards too would have seen much more willingly than
the archduke on the throne of Spain. For among all the parties
into which that court was divided in one thousand six hundred
and ninety-eight, when this treaty was made, that of Austria
was grown the weakest, by the disgust taken at a German queen,
and at the rapacity and insolence of her favorites. The French
were looked upon with esteem and kindness at Madrid; but the
Germans were become, or growing to be, objects of contempt to
the ministers, and of aversion to the people. The electoral prince
died in one thousand six hundred and ninety-nine. The star of
Austria, so fatal to all those who were obstacles to the ambition
of that house, prevailed; as the elector expressed himself in the
first pangs of his grief. The state of things changed very much
by this death. The archduke was to have Spain and the Indies,
according to a second partition: and the Spaniards, who had expressed great resentment at the first, were pushed beyond their
bearing by this. They soon appeared to be so; for the second
treaty of partition was signed in March one thousand seven
hundred; and the will was made, to the best of my remembrance,
in the October following. I shall not enter here into many particulars concerning these great events. They will be related faithfully, and I hope fully explained, in a work which your lordship
may take the trouble very probably of perusing some time or
other, and which I shall rather leave, than give to the public.—
Something however must be said more, to continue and wind up
this summary of the latter period of modern history.

France then saw her advantage, and improved it no doubt,
though not in the manner, nor with the circumstances, that some
lying scribblers of memorials and anecdotes have advanced.
She had sent one of the ablest men of her court to that of
Madrid, the marshal of Harcourt, and she had stipulated in the
second treaty of partition, that the archduke should go neither
into Spain nor the duchy of Milan, during the life of Charles the
Second. She was willing to have her option between a treaty
and a will. By the acceptation of the will, all king William's
measures were broke. He was unprepared for war as much as
when he made these treaties to prevent one; and if he meant in
making them, what some wise, but refining men have suspected,
and what I confess I see no reason to believe, only to gain time
by the difficulty of executing them, and to prepare for making
war, whenever the death of the king of Spain should alarm mankind, and rouse his own subjects out of their inactivity and
neglect of foreign interests: if so, he was disappointed in that
too; for France took possession of the whole monarchy at once,
and with universal concurrence, at least without opposition or

difficulty, in favor of the duke of Anjou. By what has been observed, or hinted rather very shortly, and I fear a little confusedly, it is plain that reducing the power of France, and securing the whole Spanish succession to the house of Austria, were two points that king William, at the head of the British and Dutch commonwealths and of the greatest confederacy Europe had seen, was obliged to give up. All the acquisitions that France cared to keep for the maintenance of her power were confirmed to her by the treaty of Ryswic: and king William allowed, indirectly at least, the pretensions of the house of Bourbon to the Spanish succession, as Louis the Fourteenth allowed, in the same manner, those of the house of Austria, by the treaties of partition. Strange situation! in which no expedient remained to prepare for an event, visibly so near, and of such vast importance as the death of the king of Spain, but a partition of his monarchy, without his consent, or his knowledge! If king William had not made this partition, the emperor would have made one, and with as little regard to trade, to the barrier of the seven provinces, or to the general system of Europe, as had been showed by him when he made the private treaty with France already mentioned, in one thousand six hundred and sixty-eight. The ministers of Vienna were not wanting to insinuate to those of France overtures of a separate treaty, as more conducive to their common interests than the accession of his imperial majesty to that of partition. But the councils of Versailles judged very reasonably, that a partition made with England and Holland would be more effectual than any other, if a partition was to take place: and that such a partition would be just as effectual as one made with the emperor, to furnish arguments to the emissaries of France, and motives to the Spanish councils, if a will in favor of France could be obtained. I repeat it again; I cannot see what king William could do in such circumstances as he found himself in after thirty years struggle, except what he did: neither can I see how he could do what he did, especially after the resentment expressed by the Spaniards, and the furious memorial presented by Canales on the conclusion of the first treaty of partition, without apprehending that the consequence would be a will in favor of France. He was in the worst of all political circumstances, in that wherein no one good measure remains to be taken; and out of which he left the two nations, at the head of whom he had been so long, to fight and negotiate themselves and their confederates, as well as they could.

When this will was made and accepted, Louis the Fourteenth had succeeded, and the powers in opposition to him had failed, in all the great objects of interest and ambition, which they had kept in sight for more than forty years; that is from the begin-

ning of the present period. The actors changed their parts in
the tragedy that followed. The power, that had so long and so
cruelly attacked, was now to defend, the Spanish monarchy: and
the powers that had so long defended, were now to attack it.—
Let us see how this was brought about: and that we may see it
the better, and make a better judgment of all that passed from
the death of Charles the Second to the peace of Utrecht, let us
go back to the time of his death, and consider the circumstances
that formed this complicated state of affairs, in three views; a
view of right, a view of policy, and a view of power.

The right of succeeding to the crown of Spain would have
been undoubtedly in the children of Maria Theresa, that is, in
the house of Bourbon; if this right had not been barred by the
solemn renunciations so often mentioned. The pretensions of
the house of Austria were founded on these renunciations, on
the ratification of them by the Pyrenean treaty, and the confirmation of them by the will of Philip the Fourth. The pretensions of the house of Bourbon were founded on a supposition,
it was indeed no more, and a vain one too, that these renunciations were in their nature null. On this foot the dispute of right
stood during the life of Charles the Second, and on the same it
would have continued to stand even after his death, if the renunciations had remained unshaken; if his will, like that of his
father, had confirmed them, and had left the crown, in pursuance
of them to the house of Austria. But the will of Charles the
Second, annulling these renunciations, took away the sole foundation of the Austrian pretensions; for, however this act might
be obtained, it was just as valid as his father's, and was confirmed by the universal concurrence of the Spanish nation to the new
settlement he made of that crown. Let it be, as I think it ought
to be, granted, that the true heirs could not claim against renunciations that were, if I may so say, conditions of their birth: but
Charles the Second had certainly as good a right to change the
course of succession agreeably to the order of nature and the
constitution of that monarchy, after his true heirs were born, as
Philip the Fourth had to change it, contrary to this order and
this constitution, before they were born, or at any other time.—
He had as good a right, in short, to dispense with the Pyrenean
treaty, and to set it aside in this respect, as his father had to
make it: so that the renunciations being annulled by that party
to the Pyrenean treaty who had exacted them, they could be
deemed no longer binding, by virtue of this treaty, on the party
who had made them. The sole question that remained therefore
between these rival houses, as to right, was this, whether the
engagements taken by Louis the Fourteenth in the partition
treaties obliged him to adhere to the terms of the last of them

in all events, and to deprive his family of the succession which the king of Spain opened, and the Spanish nation offered to them; rather than to depart from a composition he had made, on pretensions that were disputable then, but were now out of dispute? It may be said, and it was said, that the treaties of partition being absolute, without any condition or exception relative to any disposition the king of Spain had made or might make of his succession, in favor of Bourbon or Austria; the disposition made by his will, in favor of the Duke of Anjou, could not affect the engagements so lately taken by Louis the Fourteenth in these treaties, nor dispense with a literal observation of them. This might be true, on strict principles of justice; but I apprehend that none of these powers, who exclaimed so loudly against the perfidy of France in this case, would have been more scrupulous in a parallel case. The maxim, "summum jus est summa injuria," would have been quoted, and the rigid letter of treaties would have been softened by an equitable interpretation of their spirit and intention. His imperial majesty, above all, had not the least color of right to exclaim against France on this occasion; for in general if his family was to be stripped of all the dominions they have acquired by breach of faith, and means much worse than the acceptation of the will, even allowing all the invidious circumstances imputed to the conduct of France to be true, the Austrian family would sink from their present grandeur to that low state they were in two or three centuries ago. In particular, the emperor, who had constantly refused to accede to the treaties of partition, or to submit to the dispositions made by them, had not the least plausible pretence to object to Louis the Fourteenth, that he departed from them. Thus, I think, the right of the two houses stood on the death of Charles the Second. The right of the Spaniards, an independent nation, to regulate their own succession, or to receive the prince whom their dying monarch had called to it; and the right of England and Holland to regulate this succession, to divide and parcel out this monarchy in different lots, it would be equally foolish to go about to establish. One is too evident, the other too absurd, to admit of any proof. But enough has been said concerning right, which was in truth little regarded by any of the parties concerned immediately or remotely in the whole course of these proceedings. Particular interests were alone regarded, and these were pursued as ambition, fear, resentment, and vanity directed: I mean the ambition of the two houses contending for superiority of power: the fear of England and Holland lest this superiority should become too great in either; the resentment of Spain at the dismemberment of that monarchy projected by the partition treaties; and the vanity of that nation, as well as of the princes of the house of Bourbon: for as vanity mingled with resentment to make the will, vanity had a great share in determining the acceptation of it.

Let us now consider the same conjuncture in a view of policy. The policy of the Spanish councils was this. They could not brook that their monarchy should be divided: and this principle is expressed strongly in the will of Charles the Second, where he exhorts his subjects not to suffer any dismemberment or diminution of a monarchy founded by his predecessors with so much glory. Too weak to hinder this dismemberment by their own strength, too well apprised of the little force and little views of the court of Vienna, and their old allies having engaged to procure this dismemberment even by force of arms: nothing remained for them to do upon this principle, but to detach France from the engagements of the partition treaties, by giving their whole monarchy to a prince of the house of Bourbon. As much as may have been said concerning the negotiations of France to obtain a will in her favor, and yet to keep in reserve the advantages stipulated for her by the partition treaties if such a will could not be obtained, and though I am persuaded that the marshal of Harcourt, who helped to procure this will, made his court to Louis the Fourteenth as much as the marshal of Tallard, who negotiated the partitions; yet it is certain that the acceptation of the will was not a measure definitively taken at Versailles when the king of Spain died. The alternative divided those councils, and, without entering at this time into the arguments urged on each side, adhering to the partitions seemed the cause of France, accepting the will that of the house of Bourbon.

It has been said by men of great weight in the councils of Spain, and was said at that time by men as little fond of the house of Bourbon, or of the French nation, as their fathers had been, that if England and Holland had not formed a confederacy and begun a war, they would have made Philip the Fifth as good a Spaniard as any of the preceding Philips, and not have endured the influence of French councils in the administration of their government: but that we threw them entirely into the hands of France when we began the war, because the fleets and armies of this crown being necessary to their defence, they could not avoid submitting to this influence as long as the same necessity continued; and, in fact, we have seen that the influence lasted no longer. But notwithstanding this, it must be confessed, that a war was unavoidable. The immediate securing of commerce and of barriers, the preventing an union of the two monarchies in some future time, and the preservation of a certain degree at least of equality in the scales of power, were points too important to England, Holland, and the rest of Europe, to be rested on the moderation of French, and the vigor of Spanish councils, under a prince of the house of France. If satisfaction to the house of Austria, to whose rights England and Holland showed no great regard whilst they were better founded than they were since the will, had been alone concerned; a drop of blood spilt, or five shillings spent in the quarrel, would have been too much profusion. But this was properly the scale into which it became the common interest to throw all the weight that could be taken out of that of Bourbon. And therefore your lordship will find, that when negotiations with d'Avaux were set on foot in Holland to prevent a war, or rather on our part to gain time to prepare for it, in which view the Dutch and we had both acknowledged Philip king of Spain; the great article we insisted on was, that reasonable satisfaction should be given the emperor, upon his pretensions founded on the treaty of partition. We could do no otherwise; and France who offered to make the treaty of Ryswic the foundation of that treaty, could do no otherwise than refuse to consent that the treaty of partition should be so, after accepting the will, and thereby engaging to oppose all partition or dismemberment of the Spanish monarchy. I should mention none of the other demands of England and Holland, if I could neglect to point out to your lordship's observation, that the same artifice was employed at this time, to perplex the more a negotiation that could not succeed on other accounts, as we saw employed in the course of the war, by the English and Dutch ministers, to prevent the success of negotiations that might, and ought to have succeeded. The demand I mean is that of " a liberty not only to explain the terms proposed, but to increase or amplify them, in the course of the negotiation." I do not remember the words, but this is the sense, and this was the meaning of the confederates in both cases.

In the former, king William was determined to begin the war by all the rules of good policy; since he could not obtain, nay since France could not grant in that conjuncture, nor without being forced to it by a war, what he was obliged by these very rules to demand. He intended therefore nothing by this negotiation, if it may be called such, but to preserve forms and appearances, and perhaps, which many have suspected, to have time to prepare, as I hinted just now, both abroad and at home. Many things concurred to favor his preparations abroad. The alarm, that had been given by the acceptation of the will, was increased by every step that France made to secure the effect of it. Thus, for instance, the surprising and seizing the Dutch troops, in the same night, and at the same hour, that were dispersed in the garrisons of the Spanish Netherlands, was not excused by the necessity of securing those places to the obedience

of Philip, nor softened by the immediate dismission of those
troops. The impression it made was much the same as those of
the surprises and seizures of France in former usurpations. No
one knew then, that the sovereignty of the ten provinces was to
be yielded up to the elector of Bavaria; and every one saw that
there remained no longer any barrier between France and the
seven provinces. At home, the disposition of the nation was
absolutely turned to a war with France, on the death of king
James the Second, by the acknowledgment Louis the Fourteenth
made of his son as king of England. I know what has been
said in excuse of this measure, taken, as I believe, on female
importunity; but certainly without any regard to public faith, to
the true interest of France in those circumstances, or to the true
interest of the prince thus acknowledged, in any. It was said,
that the treaty of Ryswic obliged his most Christian majesty only
not to disturb king William in his possession, he might, without
any violation of it, have acknowledged this prince as king of
England; according to the political casuistry of the French, and
the example of France, who finds no fault with the powers that
treat with the kings of England, although the kings of England
retain the title of kings of France; as well as the example of
Spain, who makes no complaints that other states treat with the
kings of France, although the kings of France retain the title of
Navarre. But besides that the examples are not apposite, because no other powers acknowledge in form the king of England
to be king of France, nor the king of France to be king of
Navarre; with what face could the French excuse this measure?
Could they excuse it by urging that they adhered to the strict
letter of one article of the treaty of Ryswic, against the plain
meaning of that very article, and against the whole tenor of that
treaty; in the same breath with which they justified the acceptation of the will, by pretending they adhered to the supposed
spirit and general intention of the treaties of partition, in contradiction to the letter, to the specific engagements, and to the whole
purport of those treaties? This part of the conduct of Louis the
Fourteenth may appear justly the more surprising, because in
most other parts of his conduct at the same time, and in some to
his disadvantage, he acted cautiously, endeavored to calm the
minds of his neighbors, to reconcile Europe to his grandson's
elevation, and to avoid all show of beginning hostilities.

Though king William was determined to engage in a war with
France and Spain, yet the same good policy, that determined
him to engage, determined him not to engage too deeply. The
engagement taken in the grand alliance of one thousand seven
hundred and one is, "To procure an equitable and reasonble
satisfaction to his imperial majesty for his pretension to the

Spanish succession; and sufficient security to the king of England, and the States General, for their dominions, and for the navigation and commerce of their subjects, and to prevent the union of the two monarchies of France and Spain." As king of England, as stadtholder of Holland, he neither could, nor did engage any further. It may be disputed perhaps among speculative politicians, whether the balance of power in Europe would have been better preserved by that scheme of partition, which the treaties, and particularly the last of them, proposed, or by that which the grand alliance proposed to be the object of the war? I think there is little room for such a dispute, as I shall have occasion to say hereafter more expressly. In this place I shall only say, that the object of this war, which king William meditated, and queen Anne waged, was a partition, by which a prince of the house of Bourbon, already acknowledged by us and the Dutch as king of Spain, was to be left on the throne of that dismembered monarchy. The wisdom of those councils saw that the peace of Europe might be restored and secured on this foot, and that the liberties of Europe would be in no danger.

The scales of the balance of power will never be exactly poised, nor in the precise point of equality either discernible or necessary to be discerned. It is sufficient in this, as in other human affairs, that the deviation be not too great. Some there will always be. A constant attention to these deviations is therefore necessary. When they are little, their increase may be easily prevented by early care and the precautions that good policy suggests. But when they become great for want of this care and these precautions, or by the force of unforeseen events, more vigor is to be exerted, and greater efforts to be made. But even in such cases, much reflection is necessary on all the circumstances that form the conjuncture; lest, by attacking with ill success, the deviation be confirmed, and the power that is deemed already exorbitant become more so; and lest, by attacking with good success, whilst one scale is pillaged, too much weight of power be thrown into the other. In such cases, he who has considered, in the histories of former ages, the strange revolutions that time produces, and the perpetual flux and reflux of public as well as private fortunes, of kingdoms and states as well as of those who govern or are governed in them, will incline to think, that if the scales can be brought back by a war, nearly, though not exactly, to the point they were at before this great deviation from it, the rest may be left to accidents, and to the use that good policy is able to make of them.

When Charles the Fifth was at the height of his power, and in the zenith of his glory, when a king of France and a pope were at once his prisoners; it must be allowed, that, his situation and that of his neighbors compared, they had as much at least to fear from him and from the house of Austria, as the neighbors of Louis the Fourteenth had to fear from him and from the house of Bourbon, when, after all his other success, one of his grandchildren was placed on the Spanish throne. And yet among all the conditions of the several leagues against Charles the Fifth, I do not remember that it was ever stipulated, that "no peace should be made with him as long as he continued to be emperor and king of Spain; nor as long as any Austrian prince continued capable of uniting on his head the imperial and Spanish crowns."

If your lordship makes the application, you will find that the difference of some circumstances docs not hinder this example from being very apposite and strong to the present purpose. Charles the Fifth was emperor and king of Spain; but neither was Louis the Fourteenth king of Spain, nor Philip the Fifth king of France. That had happened in one instance, which it was apprehended might happen in the other. It had happened, and it was reasonably to be apprehended that it might happen again, and that the Imperial and Spanish crowns might continue, not only in the same family, but on the same heads; for measures were taken to secure the succession of both to Philip the son of Charles. We do not find however that any confederacy was formed, any engagement taken, nor any war made, to remove or prevent this great evil. The princes and states of Europe contented themselves to oppose the designs of Charles the Fifth, and to check the growth of his power occasionally, and as interest invited, or necessity forced them to do; not constantly. They did perhaps too little against him, and sometimes too much for him; but if they did too little of one kind, time and accident did the rest. Distinct dominions, and different pretensions, created contrary interests in the house of Austria: and on the abdication of Charles the Fifth, his brother succeeded, not his son, to the empire. The house of Austria divided into a German and a Spanish branch: and if the two branches came to have a mutual influence on one another, and frequently a common interest, it was not till one of them had fallen from grandeur, and till the other was rather aiming at it, than in possession of it. In short, Philip was excluded from the imperial throne by so natural a progression of causes and effects, arising not only in Germany but in his own family, that if a treaty had been made to exclude him from it in favor of Ferdinand, such a treaty might have been said very probably to have executed itself.

The precaution I have mentioned, and that was neglected in this case without any detriment to the common cause of Europe, was not neglected in the grand alliance of one thousand seven hundred and one. For in that, one of the ends proposed by the war is, to obtain an effectual security against the contingent union of the crowns of France and Spain. The will of Charles the Second provides against the same contingency: and this great principle, of preventing too much dominion and power from falling to the lot of either of the families of Bourbon or Austria, seemed to be agreed on all sides; since in the partition-treaty the same precaution was taken against a union of the Imperial and Spanish crowns. King William was enough piqued against France. His ancient prejudices were strong and well founded. He had been worsted in war, overreached in negotiation, and personally affronted by her. England and Holland were sufficiently alarmed and animated, and a party was not wanting even in our island, ready to approve any engagements he would have taken against France and Spain, and in favor of the house of Austria; though we were less concerned, by any national interest, than any other power that took part in the war, either then, or afterwards. But this prince was far from taking a part beyond that which the particular interest of England and Holland, and the general interest of Europe, necessarily required. Pique must have no more a place than affection, in deliberations of this kind. To have engaged to dethrone Philip, out of resentment to Louis the Fourteenth, would have been a resolution worthy of Charles the Twelfth, king of Sweden, who sacrificed his country, his people, and himself at last, to his revenge. To have engaged to conquer the Spanish monarchy for the house of Austria, or to go, in favor of that family, one step beyond those that were necessary to keep this house on a foot of rivalry with the other, would have been, as I have hinted, to act the part of a vassal, not of an ally. The former pawns his state, and ruins his subjects, for the interest of his superior lord, perhaps for his lord's humor, or his passion: the latter goes no further than his own interests carry him; nor makes war for those of another, nor even for his own, if they are remote and contingent, as if he fought *pro aris et focis*, for his religion, his liberty, and his property. Agreeably to these principles of good policy, we entered into the war that began on the death of Charles the Second: but we soon departed from them, as I shall have occasion to observe in considering the state of things, at this remarkable conjuncture, in a view of strength.

Let me recall here what I have said somewhere else. They who are in the sinking scale of the balance of power do not easily, nor soon, come off from the habitual prejudices of superiority over their neighbors, nor from the confidence that such prejudices inspire. From the year one thousand six hundred and sixty-seven, to the end of that century, France had been constantly in arms, and her arms had been successful. She had sustained a war, without any confederates, against the principal powers of Europe confederated against her, and had finished it with advantage on every side, just before the death of the king of Spain. She continued armed after the peace, by sea and land. She increased her forces, whilst other nations reduced theirs; and was ready to defend, or to invade her neighbors whilst, their confederacy being dissolved, they were in no condition to invade her, and in a bad one to defend themselves. Spain and France had now one common cause. The electors of Bavaria and Cologne supported it in Germany: the Duke of Savoy was an ally, the Duke of Mantua a vassal of the two crowns in Italy. In a word, appearances were formidable on that side: and if a distrust of strength, on the side of the confederacy, had induced England and Holland to compound with France for a partition of the Spanish succession, there seemed to be still greater reason for this distrust after the acceptation of the will, the peaceable and ready submission of the entire monarchy of Spain to Philip, and all the measures taken to secure him in this possession. Such appearances might well impose. They did so on many, and on none more than on the French themselves, who engaged with great confidence and spirit in the war; when they found it, as they might well expect it would be, unavoidable. The strength of France however, though great, was not so great as the French thought it, nor equal to the efforts they undertook to make. Their engagement, to maintain the Spanish monarchy entire under the dominion of Philip, exceeded their strength. Our engagement, to procure some outskirts of it for the house of Austria, was not in the same disproportion to our strength. If I speak positively on this occasion, yet I cannot be accused of presumption; because, how disputable soever these points might be when they were points of political speculation, they are such no longer, and the judgment I make is dictated to me by experience. France threw herself into the sinking scale, when she accepted the will. Her scale continued to sink during the whole course of the war, and might have been kept by the peace as low as the true interest of Europe required. What I remember to have heard the Duke of Marlborough say, before he went to take on him the command of the army in the Low Countries in one thousand seven hundred and two, proved true. The French misreckoned very much, if they made the same comparison between their troops and those of their enemies, as they had made in precedent wars. Those that had been opposed to them, in the last, were raw for the most part when it began, the British particularly: but they had been disciplined, if I may say so, by their defeats. They were grown to be veteran at the peace of Ryswic, and though many had been disbanded, yet they had been disbanded lately: so that even these were easily formed anew, and the spirit that had been raised continued in all. Supplies of men to recruit the armies were more abundant on the side of the confederacy, than on that of the two crowns: a necessary consequence of which it seemed to be, that those of the former would grow better, and those of the latter worse, in a long extensive, and bloody war. I believe it proved so; and if my memory does not deceive me, the French were forced very early to send recruits to their armies, as they send slaves to their galleys. A comparison between those who were to direct the councils, and to conduct the armies on both sides, is a task it would become me little to undertake. The event showed, that if France had had her Condé, her Turenne, or her Luxemburg, to oppose to the confederates; the confederates might have opposed to her, with equal confidence, their Eugene of Savoy, their Marlborough, or their Starenberg. But there is one observation I cannot forbear to make. The alliances were concluded, the quotas were settled, and the season for taking the field approached, when king William died. The event could not fail to occasion some consternation on one side, and to give some hopes on the other; for, notwithstanding the ill success with which he made war generally, he was looked upon as the sole centre of union that could keep together the great confederacy then forming: and how much the French feared, from his life, had appeared a few years before, in the extravagant and indecent joy they expressed on a false report of his death. A short time showed how vain the fears of some, and the hopes of others were. By his death, the Duke of Marlborough was raised to the head of the army, and indeed of the confederacy: where he, a new, a private man, a subject, acquired by merit and by management a more deciding influence, than high birth, confirmed authority, and even the crown of Great Britain, had given to king William. Not only all the parts of that vast machine, the grand alliance, were kept more compact and entire; but a more rapid and vigorous motion was given to the whole: and, instead of languishing or disastrous campaigns, we saw every scene of the war full of action. All those wherein he appeared, and many of those wherein he was not then an actor, but abettor however of their action, were crowned with the most triumphant success. I take with pleasure this opportunity of doing justice to that great man, whose faults I knew, whose virtues I admired; and whose memory, as the greatest general and as the greatest minister that our country or perhaps any other has produced, I honor. But besides this, the observation I have made comes into my subject, since it serves to point out to your lordship the proof of what I said above, that France undertook too much, when she undertook to maintain the Spanish monarchy entire in the possession of Philip: and that we undertook no more than what was proportionable to our strength, when we undertook to weaken that monarchy by dismembering it, in the hands of a prince of the house of Bourbon, which we had been disabled by ill fortune and worse conduct to keep out of them. It may be said that the great success of the confederates against France proves that their generals were superior to hers, but not that their forces and their national strength were so; that with the same force with which she was beaten, she might have been victorious; that if she had been so, or if the success of the war had varied, or been less decisive against her in Germany, in the Low Countries, and in Italy, as it was in Spain, her strength would have appeared sufficient, and that of the confederacy insufficient. Many things may be urged to destroy this reasoning: I content myself with one. France could not long have made even the unsuccessful efforts she did make, if England and Holland had done what it is undeniable they had strength to do; if besides pillaging, I do not say conquering, the Spanish West Indies, they had hindered the French from going to the South Sea; as they did annually during the whole course of the war without the least molestation, and from whence they imported into France in that time as much silver and gold as the whole species of that kingdom amounted to. With this immense and constant supply of wealth France was reduced in effect to bankruptcy before the end of the war. How much sooner must she have been so, if this supply had been kept from her? The confession of France herself is on my side. She confessed her inability to support what she had undertaken, when she sued for peace as early as the year one thousand seven hundred and six. She made her utmost efforts to answer the expectation of the Spaniards, and to keep their monarchy entire. When experience had made it evident that this was beyond her power, she thought herself justified to the Spanish nation, in consenting to a partition, and was ready to conclude a peace with the allies on the principles of their grand alliance. But as France seemed to flatter herself, till experience made her desirous to abandon an enterprise that exceeded her strength; you will find, my lord, that her enemies began to flatter themselves in their turn, and to form designs and take engagemeuts that exceeded theirs. Great Britain was drawn into these engagements little by little; for I do not remember any parliamentary declaration for continuing the war till Philip should be dethroned, before the year one thousand seven hundred and six: and then such a declaration was judged necessary to second the resolution of our ministers and our allies, in departing from the principle of the grand alliance, and in proposing not only the reduction of the French, but the conquest of the Spanish monarchy, as the objects of the war. This new plan had taken place, and we had begun to act upon it, two years before, when the treaty with Portugal was concluded, and the archduke Charles, now emperor, was sent into Portugal first, and into Catalonia afterwards, and was acknowledged and supported as king of Spain.

When your lordship peruses the anecdotes of the times here spoken of, and considers the course and event of the great war which broke out on the death of the king of Spain, Charles the Second, and was ended by the treaties of Utrecht and Radstat; you will find, that in order to form a true judgment on the whole, you must consider very attentively the great change made by the new plan that I have mentioned; and compare it with the plan of the grand alliance, relatively to the general interest of Europe, and the particular interest of your own country. It will not, because it cannot, be denied, that all the ends of the grand alliance might have been obtained by a peace in one thousand seven hundred and six. I need not recall the events of that, and of the precedent years of the war. Not only the arms of France had been defeated on every side, but the inward state of that kingdom was already more exhausted than it had ever been. She went on indeed, but she staggered and reeled under the burden of the war. Our condition, I speak of Great Britain, was not quite so bad: but the charge of the war increased annually upon us. It was evident that this charge must continue to increase, and it was no less evident that our nation was unable to bear it without falling soon into such distress, and contracting such debts, as we have seen and felt, and still feel. The Dutch neither restrained their trade, nor overloaded it with taxes.— They soon altered the proportion of their quotas, and were deficient even after this alteration in them. But, however, it must be allowed, that they exerted their whole strength; and they and we paid the whole charge of the war. Since therefore by such efforts as could not be continued any longer, without oppressing and impoverishing these nations to a degree that no interest except that of their very being, nor any engagement of assisting an alliance *totis viribus* can require, France was reduced, and all the ends of the war were become attainable; it will be worth your lordship's while to consider, why the true use was not made of the success of the confederates against France and Spain, and why a peace was not concluded in the fifth year of the war. When your lordship considers this, you will compare in your thoughts what the state of Europe would have been, and that of

your own country might have beeu, if the plan of the grand
alliance had been pursued; with the possible as well as certain,
the contingent as well as necessary, consequences of changing
this plan in the manner it was chenged. You will be of opinion,
I think, and it seems to me, after more than twenty years of recollection, re-examination, and reflection, that impartial posterity
must be of the same opinion; you will be of opinion, I think,
that the war was wise and just before the change, because
necessary to maintain that equality among the powers of Europe
on which the public peace and common prosperity depends: and
that it was unwise and unjust after this change, because unnecessary to this end, and directed to other and to contrary ends.
You will be guided by undeniable facts to discover, through all
the false colors which have been laid, and which deceived many
at the time, that the war, after this change, became a war of
passion, of ambition, of avarice, and of private interest; the private interest of particular persons and particular states; to which
the general interest of Europe was sacrificed so entirely, that if
the terms insisted on by the confederates had been granted, nay
if even those which France was reduced to grant, in one thousand seven hundred and ten, had been accepted, such a new
system of power would have been created as might have exposed
the balance of this power to deviations, and the peace of Europe
to troubles, not inferior to those that the war was designed, when
it began, to prevent. Whilst you observe this in general, you
will find particular occasion to lament the fate of Great Britain,
in the midst of triumphs that have been sounded so high. She
had triumphed indeed to the year one thousand seven hundred
and six inclusively: but what were her triumphs afterwards?
What was her success after she proceeded on the new plan? I
shall say something on that head immediately. Here let me
only say, that the glory of taking towns, and winning battles, is
to be measured by the utility that results from those victories.
Victories, that bring honor to the arms, may bring shame to the
councils, of a nation. To win a battle, to take a town, is the
glory of a general, and of an army. Of this glory we had a very
large share in the course of the war. But the glory of a nation
is to proportion the end she proposes, to her interest and her
strength; the means she employs, to the ends she proposes, and
the vigor she exerts, to both. Of this glory, I apprehend, we
have had very little to boast at any time, and particularly in the
great conjuncture of which I am speaking. The reasons of ambition, avarice, and private interest, which engaged the princes
and states of the confedaracy to depart from the principles of the
grand alliance, were no reasons for Great Britain. She neither
expected nor desired any thing more than what she might have

obtained by adhering to those principles. What hurried our nation, then, with so much spirit and ardor, into those of the new plan? Your lordship will answer this question to yourself, I believe, by the prejudices and rashness of party; by the influence that the first successes of the confederate arms gave to our ministers; and the popularity that they gave, if I may say so, to the war; by ancient and fresh resentments, which the unjust and violent usurpations, in short the whole conduct of Louis the Fourteenth for forty years together, his haughty treatment of other princes and states, and even the style of his court, had created; and, to mention no more, by a notion, groundless but prevalent, that he was and would be master as long as his grandson was king of Spain, and that there could be no effectual measure taken, though the grand alliance supposed that there might, to prevent a future union of the two monarchies, as long as a prince of the house of Bourbon sat on the Spanish throne. That such a notion should have prevailed, in the first confusion of thoughts which the death and will of Charles the Second produced, among the generality of men, who saw the fleets and armies of France take possession of all the parts of the Spanish monarchy, is not to be wondered at by those that consider how ill the generality of mankind are informed, how incapable they are of judging, and yet how ready to pronounce judgment; in fine, how inconsiderately they follow one another in any popular opinion which the heads of party broach, or to which the first appearances of things have given occasion. But, even at this time, the councils of England and Holland did not entertain this notion. They acted on quite another, as might be shown in many instances, if any other besides that of the grand alliance was necessary. When these councils therefore seemed to entertain this notion afterwards, and acted and took engagements to act upon it, we must conclude that they had other motives. They could not have these; for they knew, that as the Spaniards had been driven by the two treaties of partition to give their monarchy to a prince of the house of Bourbon, so they were driven into the arms of France by the war that we made to force a third upon them. If we acted rightly on the principles of the grand alliance, they acted rightly on those of the will: and if we could not avoid making an offensive war, at the expense of forming and maintaining a vast confederacy, they could not avoid purchasing the protection and assistance of France in a defensive war, and especially in the beginning of it, according to what I have somewhere observed already, by yielding to the authority and admitting the influence of that court in all the affairs of their government. Our ministers knew therefore, that if any inference was to be drawn from the first part of this notion, it was for shortening, not prolonging, the war; for delivering the Spaniards as soon as possible from habits of union and intimacy with France; not for continuing them under the same necessity, till by length of time these habits should be confirmed. As to the latter part of this notion, they knew that it was false, and silly. Garth, the best natured ingenious wild man I ever knew, might be in the right, when he said, in some of his poems at that time,

> "——— An Austrian prince alone
> Is fit to nod upon a Spanish throne."

The setting an Austrian prince upon it was, no doubt, the surest expedient to prevent a union of the two monarchies of France and Spain; just as setting a prince of the house of Bourbon on that throne was the surest expedient to prevent a union of the Imperial and Spanish crowns. But it was equally false to say, in either case, that this was the sole expedient. It would be no paradox, but a proposition easily proved, to advance, that if these unions had been effectually provided against, the general interest of Europe would have been little concerned whether Philip or Charles had nodded at Madrid. It would be likewise no paradox to say, that the contingency of uniting France and Spain under the same prince appeared more remote, about the middle of the last great war, when the dethronement of Philip in favor of Charles was made a condition of peace *sine qua non* than the contingency of a union of the Imperial and Spanish crowns. Nay, I know not whether it would be a paradox to affirm, that the expedient that was taken, and that was always obvious to be taken, of excluding Philip and his race from the succession of France, by creating an interest in all the other princes of the blood, and by consequence a party in France itself, for their exclusion, whenever the case should happen, was not in its nature more effectual than any that could have been taken: and some must have been taken, not only to exclude Charles from the empire whenever the case should happen that happened soon, the death of his brother Joseph without issue male, but his posterity likewise in all future vacancies of the imperial throne. The expedient that was taken against Philip at the treaty of Utrecht, they who opposed the peace attempted to ridicule; but some of them have had occasion since that time to see, though the case has not happened, how effectual it would have been if it had: and he, who should go about to ridicule it after our experience, would only make himself ridiculous. Notwithstanding all this, he who transports himself back to that time, must acknowledge, that the confederated powers in general could not but be of Garth's mind, and think it more agreeable to the common interest of Europe, that a branch of Austria, than a branch of Bourbon, should gather the Spanish succession, and that the maritime powers, as they are called impertinently enough with respect to the superiority of Great Britain, might think it was for their particular interest to have a prince, dependent for some time at least on them, king of Spain, rather than a prince whose dependence, as long as he stood in any, must be naturally on France. I do not say, as some have done, a prince whose family was an old ally, rather than a prince whose family was an old enemy; because I lay no weight on the gratitude of princes, and am as much persuaded that an Austrian king of Spain would have made us returns of that sort in no other proportion than of his want of us, as I am that Philip and his race will make no other returns of the same sort to France. If this affair had been entire, therefore, on the death of the king of Spain; if we had made no partition, nor he any will, the whole monarchy of Spain would have been the prize to be fought for: and our wishes, and such efforts as we were able to make, in the most unprovided condition imaginable, must have been on the side of Austria. But it was far from being entire. A prince of the house of Austria might have been on the spot, before the king of Spain died, to gather his succession; but instead of this, a prince of the house of Bourbon was there soon afterwards, and took possession of the whole monarchy, to which he had been called by the late king's will, and by the voice of the Spanish nation. The councils of England and Holland therefore preferred very wisely, by their engagements in the grand alliance, what was more practicable though less eligible, to what they deemed more eligible, but saw become by the course of events, if not absolutely impracticable, yet an enterprise of more length, more difficulty, and greater expense of blood and treasure, than these nations were able to bear; or than they ought to bear, when their security and that of the rest of Europe might be sufficiently provided for at a cheaper rate. If the confederates could not obtain, by the force of their arms, the ends of the war, laid down in the grand alliance, to what purpose would it be to stipulate for more? And if they were able to obtain these, it was evident that, whilst they dismembered the Spanish monarchy, they must reduce the power of France. This happened; the Low Countries were conquered; the French were driven out of Germany and Italy: and Louis the Fourteenth, who had so long and so lately set mankind at defiance, was reduced to sue for peace.

If it had been granted him in one thousand seven hundred and six, on what foot must it have been granted? The allies had already in their power all the states that were to compose the reasonable satisfaction for the emperor. I say, in their

power; because though Naples and Sicily were not actually reduced at that time, yet the expulsion of the French out of Italy,
and the disposition of the people of these kingdoms, considered,
it was plain the allies might reduce them when they pleased.
The confederate arms were superior till then in Spain, and several provinces acknowledged Charles the Third. If the rest had
been yielded to him by treaty, all that the new plan required had
been obtained. If the French would not yet have abandoned
Philip, as we had found that the Castilians would not even
when our army was at Madrid, all that the old plan, the plan of
the grand alliance required, had been obtained; but still France
and Spain had given nothing to purchase a peace, and they
were in circumstances not to expect it without purchasing it.
They would have purchased it, my lord: and France, as well as
Spain, would have contributed a larger share of the price, rather
than continue the war, in her exhausted state. Such a treaty of
peace would have been a third treaty of partition indeed, but
vastly preferable to the two former. The great objection to the
former was drawn from that considerable increase of dominion,
which the crown of France, and not a branch of the house of
Bourbon, acquired by them. I know what may be said speciously enough to persuade, that such an increase of dominion
would not have augmented, but would rather have weakened
the power of France, and what examples may be drawn from
history to countenance such an opinion. I know likewise, that
the compact figure of France, and the contiguity of all her provinces, make a very essential part of the force of her monarchy.
Had the designs of Charles the Eighth, Louis the Twelfth,
Francis the First, and Henry the Second, succeeded, the dominions of France, would have been more extensive, and I believe
the strength of her monarchy would have been less. I have
sometimes thought that even the loss of the battle of St. Quentin,
which obliged Henry the Second to recall the Duke of Guise
with his army out of Italy, was in this respect no unhappy event.
But the reasoning which is good, I think, when applied to those
times, will not hold when applied to ours, and to the case I consider here; the state of France, the state of her neighbors, and
the whole constitution of Europe being so extremely different.
The objection therefore to the two treaties of partition had a real
weight. The power of France, deemed already exorbitant,
would have been increased by this accession of dominion in the
hands of Louis the Fourteenth: and the use he intended to make
of it, by keeping Italy and Spain in awe, appears in the article
that gave him the ports on the Tuscan coast, and the province of
Guipuscoa. This king William might, and, I question not, did
see; but that prince might think too, that for this very reason

Louis the Fourteenth would adhere, in all events, to the treaty of partition: and that these consequences were more remote, and would be less dangerous, than those of making no partition at all. The partition, even the worst that might have been made, by a treaty of peace in one thousand seven hundred and six, would have been the very reverse of this. France would have been weakened, and her enemies strengthened, by her concessions on the side of the Low Countries, of Germany and Savoy. If a prince of her royal family had remained in possession of Spain and the West Indies, no advantage would have accrued to her by it, and effectual bars would have been opposed to an union of the two monarchies. The house of Austria would have had a reasonable satisfaction for that shadow of right, which a former partition gave her. She had no other after the will of Charles the Second: and this may be justly termed a shadow, since England, Holland, and France could confer no real right to the Spanish succession, nor to any part of it. She had declined acceding to that partition, before France departed from it, and would have preferred the Italian provinces, without Spain and the West Indies, to Spain and the West Indies without the Italian provinces. The Italian provinces would have fallen to her share by this partition. The particular demands of England and Holland would have suffered no difficulty, and those that we were obliged by treaty to make for others would have been easy to adjust. Would not this have been enough, my lord, for the public security, for the common interest, and for the glory of our arms? To have humbled and reduced, in five campaigns, a power that had disturbed and insulted Europe almost forty years; to have restored, in so short a time, the balance of power in Europe to a sufficient point of equality, after it had been more than fifty years, that is from the treaty of Westphalia, in a gradual deviation from this point; in short to have retrieved, in one thousand seven hundred and six, a game that was become desperate at the beginning of the century. To have done all this, before the war had exhausted our strength, was the utmost sure that any man could desire who intended the public good alone: and no honest reason ever was, nor ever will be given, why the war was protracted any longer; why we neither made peace after a short, vigorous, and successful war, nor put it entirely out of the power of France to continue at any rate a long one. I have said, and it is true, that this had been entirely out of her power, if we had given greater interruption to the commerce of Old and New Spain, and if we had hindered France from importing annually, from the year one thousand seven hundred and two, such immense treasures as she did import by the ships she sent, with the permission of Spain, to the South Sea. It has

been advanced, and it is a common opinion, that we were restrained by the jealousy of the Dutch from making use of the
liberty given by treaty to them and us, and which, without his
imperial majesty's leave, since we entered into the war, we might
have taken, of making conquests in the Spanish West Indies.—
Be it so. But to go to the South Seas, to trade there if we could,
to pillage the West Indies without making conquests if we could
not, and, whether we traded or whether we pillaged, to hinder
the French from trading there; was a measure that would have
given, one ought to think, no jealousy to the Dutch, who might,
and it is to be supposed would, have taken their part in these
expeditions; or if it had given them jealousy, what could they
have replied when a British minister had told them, " That it
little became them to find fault that we traded with or pillaged
the Spaniards in the West Indies to the detriment of our common enemy, whilst we connived at them who traded with this
enemy to his and their great advantage, against our remonstrances, and in violation of the condition upon which we had
given the first augmentation of our forces in the Low Countries?"
We might have pursued this measure notwithstanding any engagement that we took by the treaty with Portugal, if I remember that treaty right: but instead of this, we wasted our forces,
and squandered millions after millions in supporting our alliance
with this crown, and in pursuing the chimerical project which
was made the object of this alliance. I call it chimerical, because it was equally so, to expect a revolution in favor of Charles
the Third on the slender authority of such a trifler as the admi-
ral of Castile; and, when this failed us, to hope to conquer Spain
by the assistance of the Portuguese, and the revolt of the Ca-
talans. Yet this was the foundation upon which the new plan
of the war was built, and so many ruinous engagements were
taken.

The particular motives of private men, as well as of princes
and states, to protract the war, are partly known, and partly
guessed, at this time. But whenever that time comes, and I am
persuaded it will come, when their secret motives, their secret
designs, and intrigues, can be laid open, I presume to say to your
lordship that the most confused scene of iniquity, and folly, that
it is possible to imagine, will appear. In the mean while, if your
lordship considers only the treaty of barrier, as my lord Townshend signed it, without, nay in truth, against orders; for the Duke
of Marlborough, though joint plenipotentiary, did not: if you
consider the famous preliminaries of one thousand seven hundred and nine, which we made a mock-show of ratifying, though
we knew that they would not be accepted; for so the Marquis
of Torcy had told the pensionary before he left the Hague, as

the said Marquis has assured me very often since that time: if you inquire into the anecdotes of Gertruydenberg, and if you consult other authentic papers that are extant, your lordship will see the policy of the new plan, I think, in this light. Though we had refused, before the war began, to enter into engagements for the conquest of Spain, yet as soon as it began, when the reason of things was still the same, for the success of our first campaign cannot be said to have altered it, we entered into these very engagements. By the treaty wherein we took these engagements first, Portugal was brought into the grand alliance; that is, she consented to employ her formidable forces against Philip, at the expense of England and Holland, provided we would debar ourselves from making any acquisitions, and the house of Austria promised, that she should acquire many important places in Spain, and an immense extent of country in America. By such bargains as this, the whole confederacy was formed, and held together. Such means were indeed effectual to multiply enemies to France and Spain; but a project so extensive and so difficult as to make many bargains of this kind necessary, and necessary for a great number of years, and for a very uncertain event, was a project into which, for this very reason, England and Holland should not have entered. It is worthy your observation, my lord, that these bad bargains would not have been continued, as they were almost to our immediate ruin, if the war had not been protracted under the pretended necessity of reducing the whole Spanish monarchy to the obedience of the house of Austria. Now, as no other confederate except Portugal was to receive his recompense by any dismemberment of dominions in Old or New Spain, the engagements we took to conquer this whole monarchy had no visible necessary cause, but the procuring the accession of this power, that was already neuter, to the grand alliance. This accession, as I have said before, served only to make us neglect immediate and certain advantages, for remote and uncertain hopes; and choose to attempt the conquest of the Spanish nation at our own vast expense, whom we might have starved, and by starving reduced both the French and them, at their expense.

I called the necessity of reducing the whole Spanish monarchy to the obedience of the house of Austria, a pretended necessity: and pretended it was, not real, without doubt. But I am apt to think your lordship may go further, and find some reasons to suspect, that the opinion itself of this necessity was not very real, in the minds of those who urged it: in the minds I would say of the able men among them; for that it was real in some of our zealous British politicians, I do them the justice to believe.— Your lordship may find reasons to suspect perhaps, that this opinion was set up rather to occasion a diversion of the forces of France, and to furnish pretences for prolonging the war for other ends.

Before the year one thousand seven hundred and ten, the war was kept alive with alternate success in Spain; and it may be said, therefore, that the design of conquering this kingdom continued, as well as the hopes of succeeding. But why then did the States General refuse, in one thousand seven hundred and nine, to admit an article in the barrier treaty, by which they would have obliged themselves to procure the whole Spanish monarchy to the house of Austria, when that zealous politician my Lord Townshend pressed them to it? If their opinion of the necessity of carrying on the war, till this point could be obtained, was real; why did they risk the immense advantages given them with so much profuse generosity by this treaty, rather than consent to an engagement that was so conformable to their opinion?

After the year one thousand seven hundred and ten, it will not be said, I presume, that the war could be supported in Spain with any prospect of advantage on our side. We had sufficiently experienced how little dependence could be had on the vigor of the Portuguese; and how firmly the Spanish nation in general, the Castilians in particular, were attached to Philip. Our armies had been twice at Madrid, this prince had been twice driven from his capital, his rival had been there, none stirred in favor of the victorious, all wished and acted for the vanquished. In short, the falsehood of all those lures, by which we had been enticed to make war in Spain, had appeared sufficiently in one thousand seven hundred and six; but was so grossly evident in one thousand seven hundred and ten, that Mr. Craggs, who was sent towards the end of that year by Mr. Stanhope into England, on commissions which he executed with much good sense and much address, owned to me, that in Mr. Stanhope's opinion, and he was not apt to despond of success, especially in the execution of his own projects, nothing could be done more in Spain, the general attachmeut of the people to Philip, and their aversion to Charles considered: that armies of twenty or thirty thousand men might walk about that country till dooms day, so he expressed himself, without effect: that wherever they came, the people would submit to Charles the Third out of terror, and as soon as they were gone, proclaim Philip the Fifth again out of affection: that to conquer Spain required a great army; and to keep it, a greater.

Was it possible, after this, to think in good earnest of conquering Spain, and could they be in good earnest who continued to hold the same language, and to insist on the same measures?

Could they be so in the following year, when the emperor Joseph died? Charles was become then the sole surviving male of the house of Austria, and succeeded to the empire as well as to all the hereditary dominions of that family. Could they be in earnest who maintained, even in this conjuncture, that "no peace could be safe, honorable, or lasting, so long as the kingdom of Spain and the West Indies remained in the possession of any branch of the house of Bourbon?" Did they mean that Charles should be emperor and king of Spain? In this project they would have had the allies against them. Did they mean to call the Duke of Savoy to the crown of Spain, or to bestow it on some other prince? In this project they would have had his imperial majesty against them. In either case the confederacy would have been broken: and how then would they have continued the war? Did they mean nothing, or did they mean something more than they owned, something more than to reduce the exorbitant power of France, and to force the whole Spanish monarchy out of the house of Bourbon?

Both these ends might have been obtained at Gertruydenberg. Why were they not obtained? Read the preliminaries of one thousand seven hundred and nine, which were made the foundation of this treaty. Inform yourself of what passed there, and observe what followed. Your lordship will remain astonished. I remain so every time I reflect upon them, though I saw these things at no very great distance, even whilst they were in transaction; and though I know most certainly that France lost, two years before, by the little skill and address of her principal minister,* in answering overtures made during the siege of Lisle by a principal person among the allies, such an opportunity, and such a correspondence, as would have removed some of the obstacles that lay now in her way, have prevented others, and have procured her peace. An equivalent for the thirty-seventh article of the preliminaries, that is, for the cession of Spain and the West Indies, was the point to be discussed at Gertruydenberg. Naples and Sicily, or even Naples and Sardinia would have contented the French, at least they would have accepted them as the equivalent. Buys and Vanderdussen, who treated with them, reported this to the ministers of the allies: and it was upon this occasion that the Duke of Marlborough, as Buys himself told me, took immediately the lead, and congratulated the assembly on the near approach of a peace; said, that since the French were in this disposition, it was time to consider what further demands should be made upon them, according to the liberty reserved in the preliminaries; and exhorted all the ministers of the allies to

* Chamillard.

adjust their several ulterior pretensions, and to prepare their demands.

This proceeding, and what followed, put me in mind of that of the Romans with the Carthaginians. The former were resolved to consent to no peace till Carthage was laid in ruins. They set a treaty however on foot, at the request of their old enemy, imposed some terms, and referred them to their generals for the rest. Their generals pursued the same method, and, by reserving still a right of making ulterior demands, they reduced the Carthaginians at last to the necessity of abandoning their city, or of continuing the war after they had given up their arms, their machines, and their fleet, in hopes of peace.

France saw the snare, and resolved to run any risk rather than to be caught in it. We continued to demand, under pretence of securing the cession of Spain and the West Indies, that Louis the Fourteenth should take on him to dethrone his grandson in the space of two months; and if he did not effect it in that time, that we should be at liberty to renew the war without restoring the places that were to be put into our hands according to the preliminaries; which were the most important places France possessed on the side of the Low Countries. Louis offered to abandon his grandson; and, if he could not prevail on him to resign, to furnish money to the allies, who might at the expense of France force him to evacuate Spain. The proposition made by the allies had an air of inhumanity: and the rest of mankind might be shocked to see the grandfather obliged to make war on his grandson. But Louis the Fourteenth had treated mankind with too much inhumanity in his prosperous days, to have any reason to complain even of this proposition. His people, indeed, who are apt to have great partiality for their kings, might pity his distress. This happened, and he found his account in it. Philip must have evacuated Spain, I think, notwithstanding his own obstinacy, the spirit of his queen, and the resolute attachment of the Spaniards, if his grandfather had insisted, and been in earnest to force him. But if this expedient was, as it was, odious, why did we prefer to continue the war against France and Spain, rather than accept the other? why did we neglect the opportunity of reducing, effectually and immediately, the exorbitant power of France, and of rendering the conquest of Spain practicable? both which might have been brought about, and consequently the avowed ends of the war might have been answered, by accepting the expedient that France offered. "France," it was said, "was not sincere: she meant nothing more than to amuse, and divide." This reason was given at the time; but some of those who gave it then, I have seen ashamed to insist on it since. France was not in a condition to act the part she had acted in former treaties: and her distress was no bad pledge of her sincerity on this occasion. But there was a better still. The strong places that she must have put into the hands of the allies, would have exposed her, on the least breach of faith, to see, not her frontier alone, but even the provinces that lie behind it, desolated: and prince Eugene might have had the satisfaction, it is said, I know not how truly, he desired, of marching with the torch in his hand to Versailles.

Your lordship will observe, that the conferences at Gertruy-denberg ending in the manner they did, the inflexibility of the allies gave new life and spirit to the French and Spanish nations, distressed and exhausted as they were. The troops of the former withdrawn out of Spain, and the Spaniards left to defend themselves as they could, the Spaniards alone obliged us to retreat from Madrid, and defeated us in our retreat. But your lordship may think perhaps, as I do, that if Louis the Fourteenth had bound himself by a solemn treaty to abandon his grandson, had paid a subsidy to dethrone him, and had consented to acknowledge another king of Spain, the Spaniards would not have exerted the same zeal for Philip; the actions of Almenara and Saragossa might have been decisive, and those of Brihuega and Villa Viciosa would not have happened. After all these events, how could any reasonable man expect that a war should be supported with advantage in Spain, to which the court of Vienna had contributed nothing from the first, scarce bread to their archduke; which Portugal waged faintly and with deficient quotas; and which the Dutch had in a manner renounced, by neglecting to recruit their forces? How was Charles to be placed on the Spanish throne, or Philip at least to be driven out of it? By the success of the confederate arms in other parts. But what success, sufficient to this purpose, could we expect? This question may be answered best, by showing what success we had.

Portugal and Savoy did nothing before the death of the emperor Joseph; and declared in form, as soon as he was dead, that they would carry on the war no longer to set the crown of Spain on the head of Charles, since this would be to fight against the very principle they had fought for. The Rhine was a scene of inaction. The sole efforts, that were to bring about the great event of dethroning Philip, were those which the Duke of Marlborough was able to make. He took three towns in one thousand seven hundred and ten, Aire, Bethune, and St. Venant: and one, Bouchain, in one thousand seven hundred and eleven. Now this conquest being in fact the only one the confederates made that year, Bouchain may be said properly and truly to have cost our nation very near seven millions sterling: for your lordship will find, I believe, that the charge of the war for that year

amounted to no less. It is true that the Duke of Marlborough
had proposed a very great project, by which incursions would
have been made during the winter into France; the next campaign might have been opened early on our side; and several
other great and obvious advantages might have been obtained:
but the Dutch refused to contribute, even less than their proportion, for the queen had offered to take the deficiency on herself,
to the expense of barracks and forage; and disappointed by their
obstinacy the whole design.

We were then amused with visionary schemes of marching
our whole army, in a year or two more, and after a town or two
more were taken, directly to Paris, or at least in the heart of
France. But was this so easy or so sure a game? The French
expected we would play it. Their generals had visited the
several posts they might take, when our army should enter
France, to retard, to incommode, to distress us in our march, and
even to make a decisive stand and to give us battle. I take what
I say here from indisputable authority, that of the persons consulted and employed in preparing for this great distress. Had
we been beaten, or had we been forced to retire towards our
own frontier in the Low Countries, after penetrating into France,
the hopes on which we protracted the war would have been
disappointed, and, I think, the most sanguine would have then
repented refusing the offers made at Gertruydenberg. But if
we had beaten the French, for it was scarcely lawful in those
days of our presumption to suppose the contrary; would the
whole monarchy of Spain have been our immediate and certain
prize? Suppose, and I suppose it on good grounds, my lord,
that the French had resolved to defend their country inch by
inch, and that Louis the Fourteenth had determined to retire
with his court to Lyons or elsewhere, and to defend the passage
of the Loire, when he could no longer defend that of the Seine,
rather than submit to the terms imposed on him: what should
we have done in this case? Must we not have accepted such a
peace as we had refused; or have protracted the war till we had
conquered France first, in order to conquer Spain afterwards?
Did we hope for revolutions in France? We had hoped for
them in Spain: and we should have been bubbles of our hopes
in both. That there was a spirit raised against the government
of Louis the Fourteenth, in his court, nay, in his family, and that
strange schemes of private ambition were formed and forming
there, I cannot doubt: and some effects of this spirit produced
perhaps the greatest mortifications that he suffered in the latter
part of his reign.

A light instance of this spirit is all I will quote at this time. I
supped, in the year one thousand seven hundred and fifteen, at

a house in France, where two persons,* of no small figure, who had been in great company that night, arrived very late. The conversation turned on the events of the precedent war, and the negotiations of the late peace. In the process of the conversation one of them† broke loose, and said, directing his discourse to me, " Vous auriez pu nous écraser dans ce tems-là: pourquoi ne l' avez-vous pas fait?" I answered him coolly, " Par ce que dans ce tems-là nous n'avons plus craint vôtre puissance." This anecdote, too trivial for history, may find its place in a letter, and may serve to confirm what I have admitted, that there were persons even in France, who expected to find their private account in the distress of their country. But these persons were a few men of wild imaginations and strong passions, more enterprising than capable, and of more name than credit. In general the endeavors of Louis the Fourteenth, and the sacrifices he offered to make in order to obtain a peace, had attached his people more than ever to him: and if Louis had determined not to go any farther than he had offered at Gertruydenberg, in abandoning his grandson, the French nation would not have abandoned him.

But to resume what I have said or hinted already; the necessary consequences of protracting the war in order to dethrone Philip, from the year one thousand seven hundred and eleven inclusively, could be no other than these: our design of penetrating into France might have been defeated, and have become fatal to us by a reverse of fortune: our first success might not have obliged the French to submit; and we might have had France to conquer, after we had failed in our first attempt to conquer Spain, and even in order to proceed to a second: the French might have submitted, and the Spaniards not: and whilst the former had been employed to force the latter, according to the scheme of the allies; or whilst, the latter submitting likewise, Philip had evacuated Spain, the high allies might have gone together by the ears about dividing the spoil, and disposing of the crown of Spain. To these issues were things brought by protracting the war; by refusing to make peace, on the principles of the grand alliance at worst, in one thousand seven hundred and six; and by refusing to grant it, even on those of the new plan, in one thousand seven hundred and ten. Such contingent events as I have mentioned stood in prospect before us. The end of the war was removed out of sight; and they, who clamored rather than argued for the continuation of it, contented themselves to affirm, that France was not enough reduced, and that

* The Dukes de La Feuillade and Mortemar.
† La Feuillade.

no peace ought to be made as long as a prince of the house of
Bourbon remained on a Spanish throne. When they would
think France enough reduced, it was impossible to guess.—
Whether they intended to join the Imperial and Spanish crowns
on the head of Charles, who had declared his irrevocable resolution to continue the war till the conditions insisted upon at Gertruydenberg were obtained: whether they intended to bestow
Spain and the Indies on some other prince; and how this great
alteration in their own plan should be effected by common consent: how possession should be given to Charles, or any other
prince, not only of Spain but of all the Spanish dominions out of
Europe, where the attachment to Philip was at least as strong
as in Castile, and where it would not be so easy, the distance
and extent of these dominions considered, to oblige the Spaniards
to submit to another government: These points, and many more
equally necessary to be determined, and equally difficult to prepare, were neither determined nor prepared; so that we were
reduced to carry on the war, after the death of the emperor
Joseph, without any positive scheme agreed to, as the scheme
of the future peace, by the allies. That of the grand alliance we
had long before renounced. That of the new plan was become
ineligible; and, if it had been eligible, it would have been impracticable, because of the division it would have created among
the allies themselves: several of whom would not have consented,
notwithstanding his irrevocable resolution, that the emperor
should be king of Spain. I know not what part the protracters
of the war, in the depth of their policy, intended to take. Our
nation had contributed, and acted so long under the direction of
their councils, for the grandeur of the house of Austria, like one
of the hereditary kingdoms usurped by that family, that it is
lawful to think their intention might be to unite the Imperial
and Spanish crowns. But I rather think they had no very determinate view, beyond that of continuing the war as long as
they could. The late Lord Oxford told me, that my Lord Somers
being pressed, I know not on what occasion nor by whom, on
the unnecessary and ruinous continuation of the war; instead of
giving reasons to show the necessity of it, contented himself to
reply, that he had been bred up in a hatred of France. This
was a strange reply for a wise man: and yet I know not whether
he could have given a better then, or whether any of his pupils
could give a better now.

The whig party in general acquired great and just popularity,
in the reign of our Charles the Second, by the clamor they raised
against the conduct of that prince in foreign affairs. They who
succeeded to the name rather than the principles of this party,
after the revolution, and who have had the administration of the

government in their hands with very little interruption ever since, pretending to act on the same principle, have run into an extreme as vicious and as contrary to all the rules of good policy, as that which their predecessors exclaimed against. The old whigs complained of the inglorious figure we made, whilst our court was the bubble, and our king the pensioner of France; and insisted that the growing ambition and power of Louis the Fourteenth should be opposed in time. The modern whigs boasted, and still boast, of the glorious figure we made, whilst we reduced ourselves, by their councils, and under their administrations, to be the bubbles of our pensioners, that is, of our allies: and whilst we measured our efforts in war, and the continuation of them, without any regard to the interests and abilities of our own country, without a just and sober regard, such an one as contemplates objects in their true light and sees them in their true magnitude, to the general system of power in Europe; and, in short, with a principal regard merely to particular interests at home and abroad. I say at home and abroad: because it is not less true, that they have sacrificed the wealth of their country to the forming and maintaining a party at home, than that they have done so to the forming and maintaining, beyond all pretences of necessity, alliances abroad. These general assertions may be easily justified without having recourse to private anecdotes, as your lordship will find when you consider the whole series of our conduct in the two wars; in that which preceded, and that which succeeded immediately the beginning of the present century, but above all in the last of them. In the administrations that preceded the revolution, trade had flourished, and our nation had grown opulent: but the general interest of Europe had been too much neglected by us; and slavery, under the umbrage of prerogative, had been well-nigh established among us. In those that have followed, taxes upon taxes, and debts upon debts, have been perpetually accumulated, till a small number of families have grown into immense wealth, and national beggary has been brought upon us; under the specious pretence of supporting a common cause against France, reducing her exorbitant power, and poising that of Europe more equally in the public balance: laudable designs no doubt, as far as they were real, but such as, being converted into mere pretences, have been productive of much evil; some of which we feel and have long felt, and some will extend its consequences to our latest posterity. The reign of prerogative was short: and the evils and the dangers, to which we were exposed by it, ended with it. But the reign of false and squandering policy has lasted long, it lasts still, and will finally complete our ruin. Beggary has been the consequence of slavery in some countries: slavery will be probably the consequence of beggary in ours; and if it is so, we know at whose door to lay it. If we had finished the war in one thousand seven hundred and six, we should have reconciled, like a wise people, our foreign and our domestic interests as nearly as possible: we should have secured the former sufficiently, and not have sacrificed the latter as entirely as we did by the prosecution of the war afterwards. You will not be able to see without astonishment, how the charge of the war increased yearly upon us from the beginning of it; nor how immense a sum we paid in the course of it to supply the deficiencies of our confederates. Your astonishment, and indignation too, will increase when you come to compare the progress that was made from the year one thousand seven hundred and six exclusively, with the expense of more than thirty millions, I do not exaggerate though I write upon memory, that this progress cost us to the year one thousand seven hundred and eleven inclusively. Upon this view your lordship will be persuaded that it was high time to take the resolution of making peace, when the queen thought fit to change her ministry towards the end of the year one thousand seven hundred and ten. It was high time indeed to save our country from absolute insolvency and bankruptcy, by putting an end to a scheme of conduct, which the prejudices of a party, the whimsy of some particular men, the private interest of more, and the ambition and avarice of our allies, who had been invited as it were to a scramble by the preliminaries of one thousand seven hundred and nine, alone maintained. The persons, therefore, who came into power at this time, hearkened, and they did well to hearken, to the first overtures that were made them. The disposition of their enemies invited them to do so, but that of their friends, and that of a party at home who had nursed, and been nursed by the war, might have deterred them from it; for the difficulties and dangers to which they must be exposed in carrying forward this great work, could escape none of them. In a letter to a friend it may be allowed me to say, that they did not escape me: and that I foresaw, as contingent but not improbable events, a good part of what has happened to me since. Though it was a duty, therefore, that we owed to our country, to deliver her from the necessity of bearing any longer so unequal a part in so unnecessary a war, yet was there some degree of merit in performing it. I think so strongly in this manner, I am so incorrigible, my lord, that if I could be placed in the same circumstances again, I would take the same resolution, and act the same part. Age and experience might enable me to act with more ability, and greater skill; but all I have suffered since the death of the queen should not hinder me from acting. Notwithstanding this, I shall not be surprised if you think that the peace of Utrecht was not answerable to the success of the war, nor to the efforts made in it. I think so myself, and have always owned, even when it was making and made, that I thought so. Since we had committed a successful folly, we ought to have reaped more advantage from it than we did: and, whether we had left Philip, or placed another prince on the throne of Spain, we ought to have reduced the power of France, and to have strenghened her neighbors much more than we did. We ought to have reduced her power for generations to come, and not to have contented ourselves with a momentary reduction of it. France was exhausted to a great degree of men and money, and her government had no credit: but they, who took this for a sufficient reduction of her power, looked but a little way before them, and reasoned too superficially. Several such there were however; for as it has been said, that there is no extravagancy which some philosopher or other has not maintained, so your experience, young as you are, must have shown you, that there is no absurd extreme, into which our party politicians of Great Britain are not prone to fall, concerning the state and conduct of public affairs. But if France was exhausted, so were we, and so were the Dutch. Famine rendered her condition much more miserable than ours, at one time, in appearance and in reality too. But as soon as this accident, that had distressed the French and frightened Louis the Fourteenth to the utmost degree, and the immediate consequences of it were over; it was obvious to observe, though few made the observation, that whilst we were unable to raise in a year, by some millions at least, the expenses of the year, the French were willing and able to bear the imposition of the tenth, over and above all the other taxes that had been laid upon them. This observation had the weight it deserved; and surely it deserved to have some among those who made it, at the time spoken of, and who did not think that the war was to be continued as long as a parliament could be prevailed on to vote money. But supposing it to have deserved none, supposing the power of France to have been reduced as low as you please, with respect to her inward state, yet still I affirm, that such a reduction could not be permanent, and was not therefore sufficient. Whoever knows the nature of her government, the temper of her people, and the natural advantages she has in commerce over all the nations that surround her, knows that an arbitrary government, and the temper of her people enable her on particular occasions to throw off a load of debt much more easily, and with consequences much less to be feared, than any of her neighbors can: that although in the general course of things, trade be cramped and industry vexed by this arbitrary government, yet neither one nor the other is oppressed; and the temper of the people, and the natural advantages of the country, are such, that how great soever her distress be at any point of time, twenty years of tranquillity suffice to re-establish her affairs, and to enrich her again at the expense of all the nations of Europe. If any one doubts of this, let him consider the condition in which this kingdom was left by Louis the Fourteenth; the strange pranks the late Duke of Orleans played, during his regency and administration, with the system of public revenue, and private property: and then let him tell himself that the revenues of France, the tenth taken off, exceed all the expenses of her government by many millions of livres already, and will exceed them by many more in another year.

Upon the whole matter, my lord, the low and exhausted state to which France was reduced, by the last great war, was but a momentary reduction of her power; and whatever real and more lasting reduction the treaty of Utrecht brought about in some instances, it was not sufficient. The power of France would not have appeared as great as it did, when England and Holland armed themselves and armed all Germany against her, if she had lain as open to the invasions of her enemies, as her enemies lay to hers. Her inward strength was great; but the strength of those frontiers which Louis the Fourteenth was almost forty years in forming, and which the folly of all his neighbors in their turns suffered him to form, made this strength as formidable as it became. The true reduction of the exorbitant power of France, I take no notice of chimerical projects about changing her government, consisted therefore in disarming her frontiers, and fortifying the barriers against her, by the cession and demolition of many more places than she yielded up at Utrecht; but not of more than she might have been obliged to sacrifice to her own immediate relief, and to the future security of her neighbors.— That she was not obliged to make these sacrifices, I affirm, was owing solely to those who opposed the peace: and I am willing to put my whole credit with your lordship, and the whole merits of a cause that has been so much contested, on this issue. I say a cause that has been so much contested; for in truth, I think, it is no longer a doubt any where, except in British pamphlets, whether the conduct of those who neither declined treating, as was done in one thousand seven hunded and six; nor pretended to treat without a design of concluding, as was done in one thousand seven hundred and nine and ten, but carried the great work of the peace forward to its consummation; or the conduct of those who opposed this work in every step of its progress, saved the power of France from a greater and a sufficient reduction at the treaty of Utrecht. The very ministers who were em-

ployed in this fatal opposition, are obliged to confess this truth.
How should they deny it?   Those of Vienna may complain that
the emperor had not the entire Spanish monarchy, or those of
Holland that the States were not made masters directly and indirectly of the whole Low Countries.   But neither they, nor any
one else that has any sense of shame about him, can deny that
the late queen, though she was resolved to treat because she was
resolved to finish the war, yet was to the utmost degree desirous
to treat in a perfect union with her allies, and to procure them
all the reasonable terms they could expect; and much better than
those they reduced themselves to the necessity of accepting, by
endeavoring to wrest the negotiation out of her hands.   The
disunion of the allies gave France the advantages she improved.
The sole question is, Who caused this disunion? and that will
be easily decided by every impartial man, who informs himself carefully of the public anecdotes of that time.   If the private anecdotes were to be laid open as well as those, and I
think it almost time they should, the whole monstrous scene
would appear, and shock the eye of every honest man.   I do
not intend to descend into many particulars at this time: but
whenever I, or any other person as well informed as I, shall
descend into a full deduction of such particulars, it will become
undeniably evident, that the most violent opposition imaginable,
carried on by the Germans and the Dutch in league with a
party in Britain, began as soon as the first overtures were made
to the queen; before she had so much as begun to treat: and
was therefore an opposition not to this or that plan of treaty,
but in truth to all treaty; and especially to one wherein Great
Britain took the lead, or was to have any particular advantage.
That the Imperialists meant no treaty, unless a preliminary and
impracticable condition of it was to set the crown of Spain on
the emperor's head, will appear from this; that prince Eugene,
when he came into England, long after the death of Joseph and
elevation of Charles, upon an errand most unworthy of so great
a man, treated always on this supposition: and I remember with
how much inward impatience I assisted at conferences held with
him concerning quotas for renewing the war in Spain, in the
very same room, at the Cockpit, where the queen's ministers had
been told in plain terms, a little before, by those of other allies,
" that their masters would not consent that the Imperial and
Spanish crowns should unite on the same head."   That the
Dutch were not averse to all treaty, but meant none wherein
Great Britain was to have any particular advantage, will appear
from this; that their minister declared himself ready and authorised to stop the opposition made to the queen's measures, by
presenting a memorial, wherein he would declare, " that his

masters entered into them, and were resolved not to continue the
war for the recovery of Spain, provided the queen would consent that they should garrison Gibraltar and Port Mahon jointly
with us, and share equally the Assiento, the South Sea ship, and
whatever should be granted by the Spaniards to the queen and
her subjects." That the whigs engaged in this league with
foreign powers against their country, as well as their queen, and
with a phrensy more unaccountable than that which made and
maintained the solemn league and covenant formerly, will appear
from this; that their attempts were directed not only to wrest the
negotiations out of the queen's hands, but to oblige their country
to carry on the war, on the same unequal foot that had cost her
already about twenty millions more than she ought to have contributed to it.   For they not only continued to abet the emperor,
whose inability to supply his quota was confessed; but the Dutch
likewise, after the States had refused to ratify the treaty their
minister signed at London towards the end of the year one
thousand seven hundred and eleven, and by which the queen
united herself more closely than ever to them; engaging to pursue the war, to conclude the peace, and to guaranty it, when
concluded, jointly with them; "provided they would keep the
engagements they had taken with her, and the conditions of pro-
portionate expense under which our nation had entered into the
war." Upon such schemes as these was the opposition to the
treaty of Utrecht carried on: and the means employed, and the
means projected to be employed, were worthy of such schemes;
open, direct, and indecent defiance of legal authority, secret
conspiracies against the state, and base machinations against
particular men, who had no other crime than that of endeavoring to conclude a war, under the authority of the queen, which
a party in the nation endeavored to prolong against her authority.   Had the good policy of concluding the war been doubtful,
it was certainly as lawful for those, who thought it good, to advise it, as it had been for those who thought it bad, to advise the
contrary: and the decision of the sovereign on the throne ought
to have terminated the contest.   But he who had judged by the
appearances of things on one side, at that time, would have been
apt to think, that putting an end to the war, or to Magna Charta,
was the same thing; that the queen on the throne had no right to
govern independently of her successor; nor any of her subjects a
right to administer the government under her, though called to it
by her, except those whom she had thought fit to lay aside.—
Extravagant as these principles are, no other could justify the
conduct held at that time by those who opposed the peace: and
as I said just now, that the phrensy of this league was more unaccountable than that of the solemn league and covenant, I might

have added, that it was not very many degrees less criminal. Some of those, who charged the queen's ministers, after her death, with imaginary treasons, had been guilty during her life of real treasons: and I can compare the folly and violence of the spirit that prevailed at that time, both before the conclusion of the peace, and, under pretence of danger to the succession, after it, to nothing more nearly than to the folly and violence of the spirit that seized the tories soon after the accession of George the First. The latter indeed, which was provoked by unjust and impolitic persecution, broke out in open rebellion. The former might have done so, if the queen had lived a little longer. But to return.

The obstinate adherence of the Dutch to this league, in opposition to the queen, rendered the conferences of Utrecht, when they were opened, no better than mock conferences. Had the men who governed that commonwealth been wise and honest enough to unite, at least then, cordially with the queen, and, since they could not hinder a congress, to act in concert with her in it; we should have been still in time to maintain a sufficient union among the allies, and a sufficient superiority over the French. All the specific demands that the former made, as well as the Dutch themselves, either to incumber the negotiation, or to have in reserve, according to the artifice usually employed on such occasions, certain points from which to depart in the course of it with advantage, would not have been obtained: but all the essential demands, all in particular that were really necessary to secure the barriers in the Low Countries and of the four circles against France, would have been so. For France must have continued, in this case, rather to sue for peace, than to treat on an equal foot. The first dauphin, son of Louis the Fourteenth, died several months before this congress began: the second dauphin, his grandson, and the wife and the eldest son of this prince, died, soon after it began, of the same unknown distemper, and were buried together in the same grave. Such family misfortunes, following a long series of national misfortunes, made the old king, though he bore them with much seeming magnanimity, desirous to get out of the war at any tolerable rate, that he might not run the risk of leaving a child of five years old, the present king, engaged in it. The queen did all that was morally possible, except giving up her honor in the negotiation, and the interests of her subjects in the conditions of peace, to procure this union with the States General. But all she could do was vain; and the same phrenzy that had hindered the Dutch from improving to their and to the common advantage the public misfortunes of France, hindered them from improving to the same purposes the private misfortunes of the house of Bourbon. They

continued to flatter themselves that they should force the queen
out of her measures, by their intrigues with the party in Britain
who opposed these measures, and even raise an insurrection
against her. But these intrigues, and those of prince Eugene,
were known and disappointed; and Monsieur Buys had the mortification to be reproached with them publicly, when he came to
take leave of the lords of the council, by the Earl of Oxford; who
entered into many particulars that could not be denied, of the
private transactions of this sort, to which Buys had been a party,
in compliance with his instructions, and, as I believe, much
against his own sense and inclinations. As the season for taking
the field advanced, the league proposed to defeat the success of
the congress by the events of the campaign. But instead of defeating the success of the congress, the events of the campaign
served only to turn this success in favor of France. At the beginning of the year, the queen, and the States, in concert, might
have given the law to friend and foe, with great advantage to
the former; and with such a detriment to the latter, as the causes
of the war rendered just, the events of it reasonable, and the
objects of it necessary. At the end of the year, the allies were
no longer in a state of giving, nor the French of receiving the
law; and the Dutch had recourse to the queen's good offices,
when they could oppose and durst insult her no longer. Even
then, these offices were employed with zeal, and with some effect,
for them.

Thus the war ended, much more favorably to France than
she expected, or they who put an end to it designed. The queen
would have humbled and weakened this power. The allies
who opposed her would have crushed it, and have raised another
as exorbitant on the ruins of it. Neither one nor the other succeeded, and they who meant to ruin the French power, preserved
it, by opposing those who meant to reduce it.

Since I have mentioned the events of the year one thousand
seven hundred and twelve, and the decisive turn they gave to
the negotiations in favor of France, give me leave to say something more on this subject. You will find that I shall do so with
much impartiality. The disastrous events of this campaign in
the Low Countries, and the consequences of them have been
imputed to the separation of the British troops from the army of
the allies. The clamor against this measure was great at that
time, and the prejudices which this clamor raised are great still
among some men. But as clamor raised these prejudices, other
prejudices gave birth to this clamor: and it is no wonder they
should do so among persons bent on continuing the war; since I
own very freely, that when the first step that led to this separation came to my knowledge, which was not an hour, by the way,

before I wrote by the queen's order to the Duke of Ormond, in the very words in which the order was advised and given, " that he should not engage in any siege, nor hazard a battle, till further order," I was surprised and hurt. So much, that if I had had an opportunity of speaking in private to the queen, after I had received Monsieur De Torcy's letter to me on the subject, and before she went into the council, I should have spoken to her, I think, in the first heat, against it. The truth is, however, that the step was justifiable at that point of time in every respect, and therefore that the consequences are to be charged to the account of those who drew them on themselves, not to the account of the queen, nor of the minister who advised her. The step was justifiable to the allies surely, since the queen took no more upon her, no not so much, by far, in making it, as many of them had done by suspending, or endangering, or defeating operations in the heat of the war, when they declined to send their troops, or delayed the march of them, or neglected the preparations they were obliged to make, on the most frivolous pretences. Your lordship will find in the course of your inquiries many particular instances of what is here pointed out in general. But I cannot help descending into some few of those that regard the emperor and the States General, who cried the loudest and with the most effect, though they had the least reason, on account of their own conduct, to complain of the queen's. With what face could the emperor, for instance, presume to complain of the orders sent to the Duke of Ormond? I say nothing of his deficiencies, which were so great, that he had at this very time little more than one regiment that could be said properly to act against France and Spain at his sole charge; as I affirmed to prince Eugene before the lords of the council, and demonstrated upon paper the next day. I say nothing of all that preceded the year one thousand seven hundred and seven, on which I should have much to say. But I desire your lordship only to consider, what you will find to have passed after the famous year one thousand seven hundred and six. Was it with the queen's approbation, or against her will, that the emperor made the treaty for the evacuation of Lombardy, and let out so great a number of French regiments time enough to recruit themselves at home, to march into Spain, and to destroy the British forces at Almanza? Was it with her approbation, or against her will, that, instead of employing all his forces and all his endeavors, to make the greatest design of the whole war, the enterprise on Toulon, succeed, he detached twelve thousand men to reduce the kingdom of Naples, that must have fallen of course? and that an opportunity of ruining the whole maritime force of France, and of ruining or subduing her provinces on that side, was lost, merely by this unnecessary

diversion, and by the conduct of prince Eugene, which left no
room to doubt that he gave occasion to this fatal disappointment
on purpose, and in concert with the court of Vienna?

Turn your eyes, my lord, on the conduct of the States, and you
will find reason to be astonished at the arrogance of the men
who governed in them at this time, and who presumed to exclaim against a queen of Great Britain, for doing what their deputies had done more than once in that very country, and in the
course of that very war.   In the year one thousand seven hundred and twelve, at the latter end of a war, when conferences for
treating a peace were opened, when the least sinister event in
the field would take off from that superiority which the allies
had in the congress, and when the past success of the war had
already given them as much of this superiority as they wanted,
to obtain a safe, advantageous, honorable, and lasting peace, the
queen directed her general to suspend till further order the operations of her troops.   In one thousand seven hundred and three,
in the beginning of a war, when something was to be risked or
no success to be expected, and when the bad situation of affairs
in Germany and Italy required, in a particular manner, that
efforts should be made in the Low Countries, and that the war
should not languish there whilst it was unsuccessful everywhere
else; the Duke of Marlborough determined to attack the French,
but the Dutch deputies would not suffer their troops to go on;
defeated his design in the very moment of its execution, if I remember well, and gave no other reason for their proceeding than
that which is a reason against every battle, the possibility of
being beaten.   The circumstance of proximity to their frontier
was urged, I know, and it was said, that their provinces would
be exposed to the incursions of the French if they lost the battle.
But besides other answers to this vain pretence, it was obvious
that they had ventured battles as near home as this would have
been fought, and that the way to remove the enemy farther off
was by action, not inaction.   Upon the whole matter; the Dutch
deputies stopped the progress of the confederate army at this
time, by exercising an arbitrary and independent authority over
the troops of the States.   In one thousand seven hundred and
five, when the success of the preceding campaign should have
given them an entire confidence in the Duke of Marlborough's
conduct, when returning from the Moselle to the Low Countries,
he began to make himself and the common cause amends, for
the disappointment which pique and jealousy in the Prince of
Baden, or usual sloth and negligence in the Germans, had occasioned just before, by forcing the French lines; when he was in
the full pursuit of this advantage, and when he was marching to
attack an enemy half defeated, and more than half dispirited;

nay when he had made his dispositions for attacking, and part
of his troops had passed the Dyle—the deputies of the States
once more tied up his hands, took from him an opportunity too
fair to be lost; for these, I think, were some of the terms of his
complaint: and in short the confederacy received an affront at
least; where we might have obtained a victory. Let this that
has been said serve as a specimen of the independency on the
queen, her councils, and her generals, with which these powers
acted in the course of the war; who were not ashamed to find
fault that the queen, once, and at the latter end of it, presumed
to suspend the operations of her troops till farther order. But
be it that they foresaw what this farther order would be. They
foresaw then, that as soon as Dunkirk should be put into the
queen's hands, she would consent to a suspension of arms for
two months, and invite them to do the same. Neither this foresight, nor the strong declaration which the Bishop of Bristol made
by the queen's order at Utrecht, and which showed them that
her resolution was taken not to submit to the league into which
they had entered against her, could prevail on them to make a
right use of these two months, by endeavoring to renew their
union and good understanding with the queen; though I can say
with the greatest truth, and they could not doubt of it at the
time, that she would have gone more than half-way to meet
them, and that her ministers would have done their utmost to
bring it about. Even then we might have resumed the superiority we began to lose in the congress; for, the queen and the
States uniting, the principal allies would have united with them:
and, in this case, it would have been so much the interest of
France to avoid any chance of seeing the war renewed, that she
must, and she would, have made sure of peace, during the suspension, on much worse terms for herself and for Spain, than
she made it afterwards. But the prudent and sober states continued to act like froward children, or like men drunk with resentment and passion; and such will the conduct be of the wisest
governments in every circumstance, where a spirit of faction and
of private interest prevails, among those who are at the head,
over reason of state. After laying aside all decency in their behavior towards the queen, they laid aside all caution for themselves. They declared " they would carry on the war without
her." Landrecy seemed, in their esteem, of more importance
than Dunkirk; and the opportunity of wasting some French provinces, or of putting the whole event of the war on the decision
of another battle, preferable to the other measure that lay open
to them; that, I mean, of trying, in good earnest, and in an honest
concert with the queen, during the suspension of arms, whether

such terms of peace, as ought to satisfy them and the other allies, might not be imposed on France.

If the confederate army had broke into France, the campaign before this, or in any former campaign; and if the Germans and the Dutch had exercised then the same inhumanity, as the French had exercised in their provinces in former wars; if they had burnt Versailles, and even Paris, and if they had disturbed the ashes of the dead princes that repose at St. Denis, every good man would have felt the horror, that such cruelties inspire: no man could have said that the retaliation was unjust. But in one thousand seven hundred and twelve, it was too late, in every respect, to meditate such projects. If the French had been unprepared to defend their frontier, either for want of means, or in a vain confidence that the peace would be made, as our king Charles the Second was unprepared to defend his coast at the latter end of his first war with Holland, the allies might have played a sure game in satisfying their vengeance on the French, as the Dutch did on us in one thousand six hundred and sixty-seven; and imposing harder terms on them, than those they offered, or would have accepted. But this was not the case. The French army was, I believe, more numerous than the army of the allies, even before separation, and certainly in a much better condition than two or three years before, when a deluge of blood was spilt to dislodge them, for we did no more, at Malplaquet. Would the Germans and the Dutch have found it more easy to force them at this time, than it was at that? Would not the French have fought with as much obstinacy to save Paris, as they did to save Mons? and, with all the regard due to the Duke of Ormond, and to prince Eugene, was the absence of the Duke of Marlborough of no consequence? Turn this affair every way in your thoughts, my lord, and you will find that the Germans and the Dutch had nothing in theirs, but to break, at any rate, and at any risk, the negotiations that were begun, and to reduce Great Britain to the necessity of continuing, what she had been too long, a province of the confederacy. A province, indeed, and not one of the best treated; since the confederates assumed a right of obliging her to keep her pacts with them, and of dispensing with their obligations to her; of exhausting her, without rule, or proportion, or measure, in the support of a war, to which she alone contributed more than all of them, and in which she had no longer an immediate interest, nor even any remote interest that was not common, or with respect to her, very dubious; and, after all this, of complaining that the queen presumed to hearken to overtures of peace, and to set a negotiation on foot, whilst their humor and ambition required that the war should be prolonged for an indefinite time, and for a purpose that was either bad or indeterminate.

The suspension of arms, that began in the Low Countries, was continued, and extended afterwards by the act I signed at Fontainebleau. The fortune of the war turned at the same time; and all those disgraces followed, which obliged the Dutch to treat, and to desire the assistance of the queen, whom they had set at defiance so lately. The assistance they had, as effectually as it could be given in the circumstances to which they had reduced themselves, and the whole alliance: and the peace of Great Britain, Portugal, Savoy, Prussia, and the States General, was made, without his Imperial majesty's concurrence, in the spring of one thousand seven hundred and thirteen; as it might have been made, much more advantageously for them all, in that of one thousand seven hundred and twelve. Less obstinacy on the part of the states, and perhaps more decisive resolutions on the part of the queen, would have wound up all these divided threads in one, and have finished this great work much sooner and better. I say, perhaps more decisive resolutions on the part of the queen, because although I think that I should have conveyed her orders for signing a treaty of peace with France, before the armies took the field, much more willingly, than I executed them afterwards in signing that of the cessation of arms; yet I no not presume to decide, but shall desire your lordship to do so, on a review of all circumstances, some of which I shall just mention.

The league made for protracting the war having opposed the queen to the utmost of their power, and by means of every sort, from the first appearance of a negotiation; the general effect of this violent opposition, on her and her ministers, was, to make them proceed by slower and more cautious steps; the particular effect of it was, to oblige them to open the eyes of the nation, and to inflame the people with a desire of peace, by showing, in the most public and solemn manner, how unequally we were burdened, and how unfairly we were treated by our allies. The first gave an air of diffidence and timidity to their conduct, which encouraged the league, and gave vigor to the opposition. The second irritated the Dutch particularly; for the emperor and the other allies had the modesty at least not to pretend to bear any proportion in the expense of the war: and thus the two powers, whose union was the most essential, were the most at variance, and the queen was obliged to act in a closer concert with her enemy who desired peace, than she would have done if her allies had been less obstinately bent to protract the war. During these transactions, my Lord Oxford, who had his correspondences apart, and a private thread of negotiation always in his hands, entertained hopes that Philip would be brought to abandon Spain in favor of his father-in-law, and to content himself with the states of that prince, the kingdom of Sicily, and the preservation of his right of succession to the crown of France. Whether my lord had any particular reasons for entertaining these hopes, beside the general reasons founded on the condition of France, on that of the Bourbon family, and on the disposition of Louis the Fourteenth, I doubt very much. That Louis, who sought, and had need of seeking peace, almost at any rate, and who saw that he could not obtain it, even of the queen, unless Philip abandoned immediately the crown of Spain, or abandoned immediately, by renunciation and a solemn act of exclusion, all pretension to that of France; that Louis was desirous of the former, I cannot doubt. That Philip would have abandoned Spain, with the equivalents that have been mentioned, or either of them, I believe likewise, if the present king of France had died, when his father, mother, and eldest brother did; for they all had the same distemper. But Louis would use no violent means to force his grandson; the queen would not continue the war to force him; Philip was too obstinate, and his wife too ambitious, to quit the crown of Spain, when they had discovered our weakness, and felt their own strength in that country, by their success in the campaign of one thousand seven hundred and ten: after which my Lord Stanhope himself was convinced that Spain could not be conquered, nor kept, if it was conquered, without a much greater army than it was possible for us to send thither. In that situation it was wild to imagine, as the Earl of Oxford imagined, or pretended to imagine, that they would quit the crown of Spain, for a remote and uncertain prospect of succeeding to that of France, and content themselves to be, in the mean time, princes of very small dominions. Philip, therefore, after struggling long that he might not be obliged to make his option till the succession of France lay open to him, was obliged to make it, and made it for Spain. Now this, my lord, was the very crisis of the negotiation; and to this point I apply what I said above of the effect of more decisive resolutions on the part of the queen. It was plain, that, if she made the campaign in concert with her allies, she could be no longer mistress of the negotiations, nor have almost a chance for conducting them to the issue she proposed. Our ill success in the field would have rendered the French less tractable in the congress: our good success there would have rendered the allies so. On this principle the queen suspended the operations of her troops, and then concluded the cessation.

Compare now the appearances and effect of this measure, with the appearances and effect that another measure would have had. In order to arrive at any peace, it was necessary to do

what the queen did, or to do more: and, in order to arrive at
a good one, it was necessary to be prepared to carry on the war,
as well as to make a show of it: for she had the hard task upon
her, of guarding against her allies, and her enemies both. But
in that ferment, when few men considered any thing coolly, the
conduct of her general, after he took the field, though he covered
the allies in the siege of Quesnoy, corresponded ill, in appearance, with the declarations of carrying on the war vigorously,
that had been made, on several occasions, before the campaign
opened. It had an air of double dealing; and as such it passed
among those, who did not combine in their thoughts all the circumstances of the conjuncture, or who were infatuated with the
notional necessity of continuing the war. The clamor could not
have been greater, if the queen had signed her peace separately:
and, I think, the appearances might have been explained as
favorably in one case, as in the other. From the death of the
emperor Joseph, it was neither our interest, nor the common interest, well understood, to set the crown of Spain on the present
emperor's head. As soon therefore as Philip had made his
option, and if she had taken this resolution early, his option
would have been sooner made, I presume that the queen might
have declared, that she would not continue the war an hour
longer to procure Spain for his Imperial majesty; that the engagements, she had taken whilst he was archduke, bound her no
more; that, by his accession to the empire, the very nature of
them was altered; that she took effectual measures to prevent,
in any future time, an union of the crowns of France and Spain,
and, upon the same principle, would not consent, much less fight,
to bring about an immediate union of the Imperial and Spanish
crowns; that they, who insisted to protract the war, intended
this union; that they could intend nothing else, since they ventured to break with her, rather than to treat, and were so eager
to put the reasonable satisfaction, that they might have in every
other case without hazard, on the uncertain events of war; that
she would not be imposed on any longer in this manner, and
that she had ordered her ministers to sign her treaty with France,
on the surrender of Dunkirk into her hands; that she pretended
not to prescribe to her allies; but that she had insisted, in their
behalf, on certain conditions, that France was obliged to grant to
those of them, who should sign their treaties at the same time as
she did, or who should consent to an immediate cessation of
arms, and during the cessation treat under her mediation.—
There had been more frankness, and more dignity in this proceeding, and the effect must have been more advantageous.
France would have granted more for a separate peace, than for
a cessation: and the Dutch would have been more influenced by

the prospect of one, than of the other; especially since this proceeding would have been very different from theirs at Munster,
and at Nimeguen, where they abandoned their allies, without
any other pretence than the particular advantage they found in
doing so. A suspension of the operations of the queen's troops,
nay a cessation of arms between her and France, was not definitive; and they might, and they did, hope to drag her back under
their, and the German yoke. This therefore was not sufficient
to check their obstinacy, nor to hinder them from making all the
unfortunate haste they did make to get themselves beaten at
Denain. But they would possibly have laid aside their vain
hopes, if they had seen the queen's ministers ready to sign her
treaty of peace, and those of some principal allies ready to sign
at the same time; in which case the mischief that followed, had
been prevented, and better terms of peace had been obtained for
the confederacy: a prince of the house of Bourbon, who could
never be king of France, would have sat on the Spanish throne
instead of an emperor: the Spanish sceptre would have been
weakened in the hands of one, and the Imperial sceptre would
have been strengthened in those of the other: France would have
had no opportunity of recovering from former blows, nor of
finishing a long unsuccessful war by two successful campaigns:
her ambition, and her power, would have declined with her old
king, and under the minority that followed: one of them at least
might have been so reduced by the terms of peace, if the defeat
of the allies in one thousand seven hundred and twelve, and the
loss of so many towns as the French took in that and the following year, had been prevented, that the other would have been no
longer formidable, even supposing it to have continued; whereas
I suppose that the tranquillity of Europe is more due, at this
time, to want of ambition, than to want of power, on the part of
France. But, to carry the comparison of these two measures to
the end, it may be supposed that the Dutch would have taken
the same part, on the queen's declaring a separate peace, as they
took on her declaring a cessation. The preparations for the
campaign in the Low countries were made; the Dutch, like the
other confederates, had a just confidence in their own troops, and
an unjust contempt for those of the enemy; they were transported
from their usual sobriety and caution by the ambitious prospect
of large acquisitions, which had been opened artfully to them;
the rest of the confederate army was composed of Imperial and
German troops: so that the Dutch, the Imperialists, and the other
Germans, having an interest to decide which was no longer the
interest of the whole confederacy, they might have united against
the queen in one case, as they did in the other; and the mischief
that followed to them and the common cause, might not have

been prevented. This might have been the case, no doubt. They might have flattered themselves that they should be able to break into France, and to force Philip, by the distress brought on his grandfather, to resign the crown of Spain to the emperor, even after Great Britain, and Portugal, and Savoy too, perhaps, were drawn out of the war; for these princes desired as little, as the queen, to see the Spanish crown on the emperor's head. But, even in this case, though the madness would have been greater, the effect would not have been worse.   The queen would have been able to serve these confederates as well by being mediator in the negotiations, as they left it in her power to do, by being a party in them: and Great Britain would have had the advantage of being delivered so much sooner from a burden, which whimsical and wicked politics had imposed, and continued upon her till it was become intolerable.   Of these two measures, at the time when we might have taken either, there were persons who thought the last preferable to the former.   But it never came into public debate.   Indeed it never could; too much time having been lost in waiting for the option of Philip, and the suspension and cessation having been brought before the council rather as a measure taken, than a matter to be debated.   If your lordship, or any one else should judge, that, in such circumstances as those of the confederaey in the beginning of one thousand seven hundred and twelve, the latter measure ought to have been taken, and the Gordian knot to have been cut rather than to suffer a mock treaty to languish on, with so much advantage to the French as the disunion of the allies gave them; in short, if slowness, perplexity, inconsistency, and indecision should be objected, in some instances, to the queen's councils at that time; if it should be said particularly, that she did not observe the precise moment when the conduct of the league formed against her, being exposed to mankind, would have justified any part she should have taken (though she declared, soon after the moment was passed, that this conduct had set her free from all engagements) and when she ought to have taken that of drawing, by one bold measure, her allies out of the war, or herself out of the confederacy, before she lost her influence on France: if all this should be objected, yet would the proofs brought to support these objections show, that we were better allies than politicians; that the desire the queen had to treat in concert with her confederates, and the resolution she took not to sign without them, made her bear what no crowned head had ever borne before; and that where she erred, she erred principally by the patience, the compliance, and the condescension she exercised towards them, and towards her own subjects in league with them.   Such objections as these may lie to the queen's conduct, in the course of this great affair; as well as objections of human infirmity to that of the persons employed by her in the transactions of it; from which neither those who preceded, nor those who succeeded, have, I presume, been free. But the principles on which they proceeded were honest, the means they used were lawful, and the event they proposed to bring about was just. Whereas the very foundation of all the opposition to the peace was laid in injustice and folly: for what could be more unjust, than the attempt of the Dutch and the Germans, to force the queen to continue a war for their private interest and ambition, the disproportionate expense of which oppressed the commerce of her subjects, and loaded them with debts for ages yet to come? a war, the object of which was so changed, that from the year one thousand seven hundred and eleven she made it not only without any engagement, but against her own, and the common interest? What could be more foolish; you will think that I soften the term too much, and you will be in the right to think so: what could be more foolish, than the attempt of a party in Britain, to protract a war so ruinous to their country, without any reason that they durst avow, except that of wreaking the resentments of Europe on France, and that of uniting the Imperial and Spanish crowns on an Austrian head? one of which was to purchase revenge at a price too dear; and the other was to expose the liberties of Europe to new dangers, by the conclusion of a war which had been made to assert and secure them.

I have dwelt the longer on the conduct of those who promoted, and of those who opposed, the negotiations of the peace made at Utrecht, and on the comparison of the measure pursued by the queen with that which she might have pursued, because the great benefit we ought to reap from the study of history, cannot be reaped unless we accustom ourselves to compare the conduct of different governments, and different parties, in the same conjunctures, and to observe the measures they did pursue, and the measures they might have pursued, with the actual consequences that followed one, and the possible, or probable consequences, that might have followed the other. By this exercise of the mind, the study of history anticipates, as it were, experience, as I have observed in one of the first of these letters, and prepares us for action. If this consideration should not plead a sufficient excuse for my prolixity on this head, I have one more to add that may. A rage of warring possessed a party in our nation till the death of the late queen: a rage of negotiating has possessed the same party of men, ever since. You have seen the consequences of one: you see actually those of the other. The rage of warring confirmed the beggary of our nation, which began as early as the revolution; but then it gave, in the last war,

reputation to our arms, and our councils too. For though I
think, and must always think, that the principle, on which we
acted after departing from that laid down in the grand alliance
of one thousand seven hundred and one, was wrong; yet must
we confess that it was pursued wisely, as well as boldly. The
rage of negotiating has been a chargeable rage likewise, at least
as chargeable in its proportion. Far from paying our debts,
contracted in war, they continue much the same, after three and
twenty years of peace. The taxes that oppress our mercantile
interest the most are still in mortgage; and those that oppress the
landed interest the most, instead of being laid on extraordinary
occasions, are become the ordinary funds for the current service
of every year. This is grievous, and the more so to any man,
who has the honor of his country, as well as her prosperity at
heart, because we have not, in this case, the airy consolation we
had in the other. The rage of negotiating began twenty years
ago, under pretence of consummating the treaty of Utrecht: and,
from that time to this, our ministers have been in one perpetual
maze. They have made themselves and us, often, objects of
aversion to the powers on the continent: and we are become at
last objects of contempt, even to the Spaniards. What other
effect could our absurd conduct have? What other return has
it deserved? We came exhausted out of long wars? and, instead
of pursuing the measures necessary to give us means and opportunity to repair our strength and to diminish our burdens, our
ministers have acted, from that time to this, like men who sought
pretences to keep the nation in the same exhausted condition,
and under the same load of debt. This may have been their
view perhaps; and we could not be surprised if we heard the
same men declare national poverty necessary to support the
present government, who have so frequently declared corruption
and a standing army to be so. Your good sense, my lord, your
virtue, and your love of your country, will always determine you
to oppose such vile schemes, and to contribute your utmost towards the cure of both these kinds of rage; the rage of warring,
without any proportionable interest of our own, for the ambition
of others; and the rage of negotiating, on every occasion, at any
rate, without a sufficient call to it, and without any part of that
deciding influence which we ought to have. Our nation inhabits
an island, and is one of the principal nations of Europe; but to
maintain this rank, we must take the advantages of this situation,
which have been neglected by us for almost half a century: we
must always remember, that we are not part of the continent,
but we must never forget that we are neighbors to it. I will
conclude, by applying a rule, that Horace gives for the conduct
of an epic or dramatic poem, to the part Great Britain ought to

take in the affairs of the continent, if you allow me to transform
Britannia into a male divinity, as the verse requires.

> Nec Deus intersit nisi dignus vindice nodus
> Inciderit.

If these reflections are just, and I should not have offered them
to your lordship had they not appeared both just and important
to my best understanding, you will think that I have not spent
your time unprofitably in making them, and exciting you by
them to examine the true interest of your country relatively to
foreign affairs; and to compare it with those principles of conduct, that, I am persuaded, have no other foundation than party
designs, prejudices, and habits; the private interest of some men,
and the ignorance and rashness of others.

My letter is grown so long that I shall say nothing to your
lordship at this time concerning the study of modern history,
relatively to the interests of your country in domestic affairs;
and I think there will be no need to do so at any other. The
History of the rebellion by your great grandfather, and his private memorials, which your lordship has in manuscript, will
guide you surely as far as they go: where they leave you, your
lordship must not expect any history; for we have more reason
to make this complaint, "abest enim historia literis nostris,"
than Tully had to put it into the mouth of Atticus, his first book
of laws. But where history leaves you, it is wanted least: the
traditions of this century, and of the latter end of the last, are
fresh. Many, who were actors in some of these events, are
alive; and many who have conversed with those that were
actors in others. The public is in possession of several collections and memorials, and several there are in private hands.
You will want no materials to form true notions of transactions
so recent. Even pamphlets, written on different sides and on different occasions in our party disputes, and histories of no more
authority than pamphlets, will help you to come at truth. Read
them with suspicion, my lord, for they deserve to be suspected;
pay no regard to the epithets given, nor to the judgments passed;
neglect all declamation, weigh the reasoning, and advert to fact.
With such precautions, even Burnet's history may be of some
use. In a word, your lordship will want no help of mine to
discover, by what progression the whole constitution of our
country, and even the character of our nation, has been altered:
nor how much a worse use, in a national sense, though a better
in the sense of party politics, the men called Whigs have made
of long wars and new systems of revenue, since the revolution;
than the men called tories made, before it, of long peace, and
stale prerogative. When you look back three or four genera-

tions ago, you will see that the English were a plain, perhaps a rough, but a good-natured hospitable people, jealous of their liberties, and able as well as ready to defend them, with their tongues, their pens, and their swords. The restoration began to turn hospitality into luxury, pleasure into debauch, and country peers and country commoners into courtiers and men of mode. But whilst our luxury was young, it was little more than elegance: the debauch of that age was enlivened with wit, and varnished over with gallantry. The courtiers and the men of mode knew what the constitution was, respected it, and often asserted it. Arts and sciences flourished, and, if we grew more trivial, we were not become either grossly ignorant, or openly profligate. Since the revolution, our kings have been reduced indeed to a seeming annual dependence on parliament; but the business of parliament, which was esteemed in general a duty before, has been exercised in general as a trade since. The trade of parliament, and the trade of funds, have grown universal. Men, who stood forward in the world, have attended to little else. The frequency of parliaments, that increased their importance, and should have increased the respect for them, has taken off from their dignity: and the spirit that prevailed, whilst the service in them was duty, has been debased since it became a trade. Few know, and scarce any respect, the British constitution: that of the Church has been long since derided; that of the State as long neglected; and both have been left at the mercy of the men in power, whoever those men were. Thus the Church, at least the hierarchy, however sacred in its origin or wise in its institution, is become a useless burden on the state: and the state is become, under ancient and known forms, a new and undefinable monster; composed of a king without monarchical splendor, a senate of nobles without aristocratical independency, and a senate of commons without democratical freedom. In the mean time, my lord, the very idea of wit, and all that can be called taste, has been lost among the great; arts and sciences are scarce alive; luxury has been increased but not refined; corruption has been established, and is avowed. When governments are worn out, thus it is: the decay appears in every instance. Public and private virtue, public and private spirit, science and wit, decline all together.

That you, my lord, may have a long and glorious share in restoring all these, and in drawing our government back to the true principles of it, I wish most heartily. Whatever errors I may have committed in public life, I have always loved my country: whatever faults may be objected to me in private life, I have always loved my friend; whatever usage I have received from my country, it shall never make me break with her: whatever usage I have received from my friends, I shall never break with one of them, while I think him a friend to my country. These are the sentiments of my heart. I know they are those of your lordship's: and a communion of such sentiments is a tie that will engage me to be, as long as I live,

My lord,

Your most faithful servant.

A PLAN

FOR A

GENERAL HISTORY OF EUROPE.

LETTER I.

I SHALL take the liberty of writing to you a little oftener than the three or four times a year, which you tell me, are all you can allow yourself to write to those you like best: and yet I declare to you with great truth, that you never knew me to busy in your life, as I am at present. You must not imagine from hence, that I am writing memoirs of myself. The subject is too slight to descend to posterity, in any other manner, than by that occasional mention which may be made of any little actor in the history of our age. Sylla, Cæsar, and others of that rank, were, whilst they lived, at the head of mankind: their story was in some sort the story of the world, and such as might very properly be transmitted under their names to future generations. But for those who have acted much inferior parts, if they publish the piece, and call it after their own names, they are impertinent; if they publish only their own share in it, they inform mankind by halves and neither give much instruction, nor create much attention. France abounds with writers of this sort, and, I think, we fall into the other extreme. Let me tell you, on this occasion, what has sometimes come into my thoughts.

There is hardly any century in history which began by opening so great a scene, as the century wherein we live, and shall, I suppose, die. Compare it with others, even the most famous, and you will think so. I will sketch the two last, to help your memory.

The loss of that balance which Lawrence of Medicis had preserved, during his time, in Italy; the expedition of Charles the

Eighth to Naples; the intrigues of the Duke of Milan, who spun, with all the refinements of art, that net wherein he was taken at last himself; the successful dexterity of Ferdinand the Catholic, who built one pillar of the Austrian greatness in Spain, in Italy, and in the Indies; as the succession of the house of Burgundy, joined to the imperial dignity and the hereditary countries, established another in the upper and lower Germany: these causes, and many others, combined to form a very extraordinary conjuncture; and by their consequences, to render the sixteenth century fruitful of great events, and of astonishing revolutions.

The beginning of the seventeenth opened still a greater and more important scene. The Spanish yoke was well-nigh imposed on Italy by the famous triumvirate, Toledo at Milan, Ossuna at Naples, and La Cueva at Venice. The distractions of France, as well as the state-policy of the queen mother, seduced by Rome, and amused by Spain; the despicable character of our James the First, the rashness of the elector Palatine, the bad intelligence of the princes and states of the league in Germany, the mercenary temper of John George of Saxony, and the great qualities of Maximilian of Bavaria, raised Ferdinand the Second to the imperial throne; when the males of the elder branch of the Austrian family in Germany being extinguished at the death of Matthias, nothing was more desirable, nor perhaps more practicable, than to throw the empire into another house. Germany ran the same risque as Italy had done: Ferdinand seemed more likely, even than Charles the Fifth had been, to become absolute master; and, if France had not furnished the greatest minister, and the North the greatest captain, of that age, in the same point of time, Vienna and Madrid would have given the law to the western world.

As the Austrian scale sunk, that of Bourbon rose. The true date of the rise of that power, which has made the kings of France so considerable in Europe, goes up as high as Charles the Seventh, and Louis the Eleventh. The weakness of our Henry the Sixth, the loose conduct of Edward the Fourth, and perhaps the oversights of Henry the Seventh, helped very much to knit that monarchy together, as well as to enlarge it. Advantage might have been taken of the divisions which religion occasioned; and supporting the protestant party in France would have kept that crown under restraints, and under inabilities, in some measure equal to those which were occasioned anciently by the vast alienations of its demesnes, and by the exorbitant power of its vassals. But James the First was incapable of thinking with sense, or acting with spirit. Charles the First had an imperfect glimpse of his true interest, but his uxorious temper, and the extravagancy of that madman Buckingham, gave Richelieu time to finish a great part of his project; and the miseries that followed in England, gave Mazarin time and opportunity to complete the system. The last great act of this cardinal's administration was the Pyrenean treaty.

Here I would begin, by representing the face of Europe such as it was at that epocha, the interests and the conduct of England, France, Spain, Holland, and the empire. A summary recapitulation should follow of all the steps taken by France, during more than twenty years, to arrive at the great object she had proposed to herself in making this treaty: the most solemn article of which the minister, who negotiated it, designed should be violated; as appears by his letters, written from the island of Pheasants, if I mistake not. After this, another draught of Europe should have its place, according to the relations, which the several powers stood in, one towards another, in one thousand six hundred and eighty-eight: and the alterations which the revolution in England made in the politics of Europe. A summary account should follow of the events of the war that ended in one thousand six hunded and ninety-seven, with the different views of king William the Third, and Louis the Fourteenth, in making the peace of Ryswic; which matter has been much canvassed, and is little understood. Then the dispositions made by the partition treaties, and the influences and consequences of these treaties; and a third draught of the state of Europe at the death of Charles the Second of Spain. All this would make the subject of one or two books, and would be the most proper introduction imaginable to a history of that war with which our century began, and of the peace which followed.

This war, foreseen for above half a century, had been, during all that time, the great and constant object of the councils of Europe. The prize to be contended for was the richest that ever had been staked, since those of the Persian and Roman empires. The union of two powers, which separately, and in opposition, had aimed at universal monarchy, was apprehended. The confederates therefore engaged in it, to maintain a balance between the two houses of Austria and Bourbon, in order to preserve their security, and to assert their independence. But with the success of the war they changed their views: and, if ambition began it on the side of France, ambition continued it on the other. The battles, the sieges, the surprising revolutions, which happened in the course of this war, are not to be parallelled in any period of the same compass. The motives, and the measures, by which it was protracted, the true reasons why it ended in a manner, which appeared not proportionable to its success; and the new political state, into which Europe was thrown by the treaties of Utrecht and Baden, are subjects on which few persons have the necessary informations, and yet every one speaks with assurance, and even with passion. I think I could speak on them with some knowledge, and with as much indifference as Polybius does of the negotiations of his father Lycortas, even in those points where I was myself an actor.

I will even confess to you, that I should not despair of performing this part better than the former. There is nothing in my opinion so hard to execute, as those political maps, if you will allow me such an expression, and those systems of hints, rather than relations of events, which are necessary to connect and explain them; and which must be so concise, and yet so full; so complicate, and yet so clear. I know nothing of this sort well done by the ancients. Sallust's introduction, as well as that of Thucydides, might serve almost for any other piece of the Roman or Greek story, as well as for those which these two great authors chose. Polybius does not come up, in his introduction, to this idea neither. Among the moderns, the first book of Machiavel's history of Florence is a noble original of this kind: and perhaps father Paul's history of benefices is, in the same kind of composition, inimitable.

These are a few of those thoughts, which come into my mind when I consider how incumbent it is on every man, that he should be able to give an account even of his leisure; and, in the midst of solitude, be of some use to society.

I know not whether I shall have courage enough to undertake the task I have chalked out: I distrust my abilities with reason, and I shall want several informations, not easy, I doubt, for me to obtain. But, in all events, it will not be possible for me to go about it this year; the reasons of which would be long enough to fill another letter, and I doubt that you will think this grown too bulky already.

Adieu.

OF THE

T R U E   U S E

OF

RETIREMENT AND STUDY.

TO THE

RT. HON. LORD BATHURST.

LETTER II.

SINCE my last to your lordship, this is the first favorable opportunity I have had of keeping the promise I made you. I will avoid prolixity, as much as I can, in a first draught of my thoughts; but I must give you them as they rise in my mind, without staying to marshal them in close order.

As proud as we are of human reason, nothing can be more absurd than the general system of human life, and human knowledge. This faculty of distinguishing true from false, right from wrong, and what is agreeable from what is repugnant to nature, either by one act, or by a longer process of intuition, has not been given with so sparing a hand as many appearances would make us apt to believe. If it was cultivated, therefore, as early and as carefully as it might be, and if the exercise of it was left generally as free as it ought to be, our common notions and opinions would be more consonant to truth than they are: and, truth being but one, they would be more uniform likewise.

But this rightful mistress of human life and knowledge, whose proper office it is to preside over both, and to direct us in the conduct of one and the pursuit of the other, becomes degraded in the intellectual economy. She is reduced to a mean and servile state, to the vile drudgery of conniving at principles, defending opinions, and confirming habits, that are none of hers. They, who do her most honor, who consult her oftenest, and obey her too very often, are still guilty of limiting her authority according to maxims, and rules, and schemes, that chance, or ignorance, or interest, first devised, and that custom sanctifies: custom, that result of the passions and prejudices of many, and of the designs of a few; that ape of reason, who usurps her seat, exercises her power, and is obeyed by mankind in her stead. Men find it easy, and government makes it profitable, to concur in established systems of speculation and practice; and the whole turn of education prepares them to live upon credit all their lives. Much pains are taken, and time bestowed, to teach us what to think; but little or none of either, to instruct us how to think. The magazine of the memory is stored and stuffed betimes; but the conduct of the understanding is all along neglected, and the free exercise of it is, in effect, forbidden in all places, and in terms in some.

There is a strange distrust of human reason in every human institution: this distrust is so apparent, that an habitual submission to some authority, or other, is forming in us from our cradles; that principles of reasoning, and matters of fact, are inculcated in our tender minds, before we are able to exercise that reason; and that, when we are able to exercise it, we are either forbid, or frightened from doing so, even on things that are themselves the proper objects of reason, or that are delivered to us upon an authority whose sufficiency or insufficiency is so most evidently.

On many subjects, such as the general laws of natural religion, and the general rules of society and good policy, men of all countries and languages, who cultivate their reason, judge alike. The same premises have led them to the same conclusions, and so, following the same guide, they have trod in the same path: at least, the differences are small, easily reconciled, and such as could not, of themselves, contradistinguish nation from nation, religion from religion, and sect from sect. How comes it, then, that there are other points, on which the most opposite opinions are entertained, and some of these with so much heat, and fury, that the men on one side of the hedge will die for the affirmative, and the men on the other for the negative? "Toute opinion est assez forte pour se faire épouser au prix de la vie," says Montagne, whom I often quote, as I do Seneca, rather for the smartness of expression, than the weight or newness of matter. Look narrowly into it, and you will find that the points agreed on, and the points disputed, are not proportionable to the common sense and general reason of mankind. Nature and truth are the same every where, and reason shows them every where alike. But the accidental and other causes, which give rise and growth to opinions, both in speculation and practice, are of infinite variety; and wherever these opinions are once confirmed by custom and propagated by education, various, inconsistent, contradictory as they are, they all pretend (and all their pretences are backed by pride, by passion, and by interest) to have reason, or revelation, or both on their side; though neither reason nor revelation can be possibly on the side of more than one, and may be possibly on the side of none.

Thus it happens that the people of Tibet are Tartars and idolaters, that they are Turks and Mahometans at Constantinople, Italians and Papists at Rome; and how much soever education may be less confined, and the means of knowledge more attainable, in France and our own country, yet thus it happens in great measure that Frenchmen and Roman Catholics are bred at Paris, and Englishmen and protestants at London. For men, indeed, properly speaking, are bred nowhere: every one thinks the system, as he speaks the language, of his country; at least there are few that think, and none that act, in any country, according to the dictates of pure unbiassed reason; unless they may be said tò do so when reason directs them to speak and act according to the system of their country, or sect, at the same time as she leads them to think according to that of nature and truth.

Thus the far greatest part of mankind appears reduced to a lower state than other animals, in that very respect, on account of which we claim so great superiority over them; because instinct, that has its due effect, is preferable to reason that has not. I suppose in this place, with philosophers, and the vulgar, that which I am in nowise ready to affirm, that other animals have no share of human reason: for, let me say by the way, it is much more likely other animals should share the human, which is denied, than that man should share the divine reason, which is affirmed. But, supposing our monopoly of reason, would not your lordship choose to walk upon four legs, to wear a long tail, and to be called a beast, with the advantage of being determined by irresistible and unerring instinct to those truths that are necessary to your well-being; rather than to walk on two legs, to wear no tail, and to be honored with the title of man, at the expense of deviating from them perpetually? Instinct acts spontaneously whenever its action is necessary, and directs the animal according to the purpose for which it was implanted in him. Reason is a nobler and more extensive faculty; for it extends to the unnecessary as well as necessary, and to satisfy our curiosity as well as our wants: but reason must be excited, or she will remain inactive; she must be left free, or she will conduct us wrong, and carry us farther astray from her own precincts than we should go without her help: in the first case, we have no sufficient guide; and in the second, the more we employ our reason, the more unreasonable we are.

Now if all this be so, if reason has so little, and ignorance, passion, interest, and custom so much to do, in forming our opinions and our habits, and in directing the whole conduct of human life; is it not a thing desirable by every thinking man, to have the opportunity, indulged to so few by the course of accidents, the opportunity "secum esse, et secum vivere," of living some years at least to ourselves, and for ourselves, in a state of freedom, under the laws of reason, instead of passing our whole time in a state of vassalage under those of authority and custom? Is it not worth our while to contemplate ourselves, and others, and all the things of this world, once before we leave them, through the medium of pure, and, if I may say so, of undefiled reason? It is not worth our while to approve or condemn, on our own authority, what we receive in the beginning of life, on the authority of other men, who were not then better able to judge for us, than we are now to judge for ourselves?

That this may be done, and has been done to some degree, by men who remained much more mingled than I design to be for the future, in the company and business of the world, I shall not deny: but still it is better done in retreat, and with greater ease and pleasure. Whilst we remain in the world, we are all fettered down more or less to one common level, and have neither all the leisure, nor all the means and advantages, to soar above it, which we may procure to ourselves, by breaking these fetters, in retreat. To talk of abstracting ourselves from matter, laying aside body, and being resolved, as it were, into pure intellect, is proud, metaphysical, unmeaning jargon: but to abstract ourselves from the prejudices, and habits, and pleasures, and business of the world, is no more than many are, though all are not, capable of doing. They who can do this may elevate their souls in retreat to a higher station, and may take from thence such a view of the world, as the second Scipio took in his dream, from the seats of the blessed, when the whole earth appeared so little to him, that he could scarcely discern that speck of dirt, the Roman empire. Such a view as this will increase our knowledge, by showing us our ignorance; will distinguish every degree of probability from the lowest to the highest, and mark the distance between that and certainty; will dispel the intoxicating fumes of phisosophical presumption, and teach us to establish our peace of mind, where alone it can rest securely, in resignation: in short, such a view will render life more agreeable, and death less terrible. Is not this business, my lord? Is not this pleasure too, the highest pleasure? The world can afford us none such; we must retire from the world to taste it with a full gust; but we shall taste it the better for having been in the world. The share of sensual pleasures, that a man of my age can promise himself, is hardly worth attention: he should be sated, he will be soon disabled; and very little reflection surely will suffice, to make his habits of this kind lose their power over him, in proportion at least as his power of indulging them diminishes. Besides, your lordship knows that my scheme of retirement excludes none of these pleasures that can be taken with decency and conveniency; and to say the truth, I believe that I allow myself more in speculation than I shall find I want in practice. As to the habits of business, they can have no hold on one who has been so long tired with it. You may object, that though a man has discarded these habits, and has not even the embers of ambition about him to revive them, yet he cannot renounce all public business as absolutely as I seem to do; because a better principle, a principle of duty, may summon him to the service of his country. I will answer you with great sincerity. No man has higher notions of this duty than I have. I think that scarce any age or circumstances, can discharge us entirely from it; no, not my own. But as we are apt to take the impulse of our own passions, for a call to the performance of this duty; so when these passions impel us no longer, the call that puts us upon action must be real, and loud too. Add to this, that there are different methods, proportioned to different circumstances and situations, of performing the same duty. In the midst of retreat, wherever it may be fixed, I may contribute to defend and preserve the British constitution of government, and you, my lord, may depend upon me, that whenever I can, I will. Should any one ask you, in this case, from whom I expect my reward? answer him by declaring to whom I pay this service; " Deo immortali, qui me non accipere modo hæc a majoribus voluit, sed etiam posteris prodere."

But, to lead the life I propose with satisfaction and profit, renouncing the pleasures and business of the world, and breaking the habits of both, is not sufficient: the supine creature, whose understanding is superficially employed, through life, about a few general notions, and is never bent to a close and steady pursuit of truth, may renounce the pleasures and business of the world, for even in the business of the world we see such creatures often employed, and may break the habits; nay he may retire and drone away life in solitude, like a monk, or like him over the door of whose house, as if his house had been his tomb, somebody wrote, " Here lies such an one." But no such man will be able to make the true use of retirement. The employment of his mind, that would have been agreeable and easy if he had accustomed himself to it early, will be unpleasant and impracticable late: such men lose their intellectual powers for want of exerting them, and, having trifled away youth, are reduced to the necessity of trifling away age. It fares with the mind just as it does with the body. He who was born with a texture of brain as strong as that of Newton, may become unable to perform the common rules of arithmetic: just as he who has the same elasticity in his muscles, the same suppleness in his joints, and all his nerves and sinews as well braced as Jacob Hall, may become a fat unwieldy sluggard. Yet farther, the implicit creature, who has thought it all his life needless, or unlawful, to examine the principles or facts that he took originally on trust, will be as little able as the other, to improve his solitude to any good purpose: unless we call it a good purpose, for that sometimes happens, to confirm and exalt his prejudices, so that he may live and die in one continued delirium. The confirmed prejudices of a thoughtful life are as hard to change as the confirmed habits of an indolent life: and as some must trifle away age because they have trifled away youth, others must labor on in a maze of error, because they have wandered there too long to find their way out.

There is a prejudice in China in favor of little feet, and therefore the feet of girls are swathed and bound up from the cradle, so that the women of that country are unable to walk without tottering and stumbling all their lives. Among the savages of America, there are some who hold flat heads and long ears in great esteem, and therefore press the one, and draw down the others so hard from their infancy, that they destroy irrecoverably the true proportions of nature, and continue all their lives ridiculous to every sight but their own. Just so, the first of these characters cannot make any progress, and the second will not attempt to make any, in an impartial search after real knowledge.

To set about acquiring the habits of meditation and study late in life, is like getting into a go-cart with a gray beard, and learning to walk when we have lost the use of our legs. In general, the foundations of a happy old age must be laid in youth: and in particular, he who has not cultivated his reason young, will be utterly unable to improve it old. "Manent ingenia senibus, modo permaneant studium et industria."

Not only a love of study, and a desire of knowledge, must have grown up with us, but such an industrious application likewise, as requires the whole vigor of the mind to be exerted in the pursuit of truth, through long trains of ideas, and all those dark recesses wherein man, not God, has hid it.

This love and this desire I have felt all my life, and I am not quite a stranger to this industry and application. There has been something always ready to whisper in my ear, whilst I ran the course of pleasure and of business,

" Solve senescentum mature sanus equum."

But my genius, unlike the demon of Socrates, whispered so softly, that very often I heard him not, in the hurry of those passions by which I was transported. Some calmer hours there were: in them I hearkened to him. Reflection had often its turn, and the love of study and the desire of knowledge have never quite abandoned me. I am not therefore entirely unprepared for the life I will lead, and it is not without reason that I promise myself more satisfaction in the latter part of it, than I ever knew in the former.

Your lordship may think this perhaps a little too sanguine, for one who has lost so much time already: you may put me in mind, that human life has no second spring, no second summer: you may ask me, what I mean by sowing in autumn, and whether I hope to reap in winter? My answer will be, that I think very differently from most men, of the time we have to pass, and the business we have to do in this world. I think we have more of one, and less of the other, than is commonly supposed. Our want of time, and the shortness of human life, are some of the principal common-place complaints, which we prefer against the established order of things: they are the grumblings of the vulgar, and the pathetic lamentations of the philosopher; but they are impertinent and impious in both. The man of business despises the man of pleasure, for squandering his time away; the man of pleasure pities or laughs at the man of business, for the same thing: and yet both concur superciliously and absurdly to find fault with the Supreme Being, for having given them so little time. The philosopher, who misspends it very often as much as the others, joins in the same cry, and authorises this impiety. Theophrastus thought it extremely hard to die at ninety, and to go out of the world when he had just learned how to live in it. His master Aristotle found fault with nature, for treating man in this respect worse than several other animals: both very unphilosophically! and I love Seneca the better for his quarrels with the Stagirite on this head. We see, in so many instances, a just proportion of things, according to their several relations to one another, that philosophy should lead us to conclude this proportion preserved, even where we cannot discern it; instead of leading us to conclude that it is not preserved where we do not discern it, or where we think that we see the contrary. To conclude otherwise, is shocking presumption. It is to presume that the system of the universe would have been more wisely contrived, if creatures of our low rank among intellectual natures had been called to the councils of the Most High; or that the Creator ought to mend his work by the advice of the creature. That life which seems to our self-love so short, when we compare it with the ideas we frame of eternity, or even with the duration of some other beings, will appear sufficient, upon a less partial view, to all the ends of our creation, and of a just proportion in the successive course of generations. The term itself is long: we render it short; and the want we complain of flows from our profusion, not from our poverty. We are all arrant spendthrifts; some of us dissipate our estates on the trifles, some on the superfluities, and then we all complain that we want the necessaries, of life. The much greatest part never reclaim, but die bankrupts to God and man. Others reclaim late, and they are apt to imagine, when they make up their accounts, and see how their fund is diminished, that they have not enough remaining to live upon, because they have not the whole. But they deceive themselves: they were richer than they thought, and they are not yet poor. If they husband well the remainder, it will be found sufficient for all the necessaries, and for some of the superfluities, and trifles too perhaps, of life: but then the former order of expense must be inverted; and the necessaries of life must be provided, before they put themseves to any cost for the trifles of surperfluities.

Let us leave the men of pleasure and of business, who are often candid enough to own that they throw away their time, and thereby to confess that they complain of the Supreme Being for no other reason than this, that he has not proportioned his bounty to their extravagance: let us consider the scholar and the philosopher: who, far from owning that he throws any time away, reproves others for doing it: that solemn mortal, who abstains from the pleasures, and declines the business of the world, that he may dedicate his whole time to the search of truth, and the improvement of knowledge. When such a one complains of the shortness of human life in general, or of his remaining share in particular; might not a man, more reasonable though less solemn, expostulate thus with him?

" Your complaint is indeed consistent with your practice; but you would not, possibly, renew your complaint if you reviewed your practice. Though reading makes a scholar; yet every scholar is not a philosopher, nor every philosopher a wise man. It cost you twenty years to devour all the volumes on one side of your library: you came out a great critic in Latin and Greek, in the oriental tongues, in history and chronology; but you was not satisfied: you confessed that these were the "literæ nihil sanantes;" and you wanted more time to acquire other knowledge. You have had this time: you have passed twenty years more on the other side of your library, among philosophers, rabbies, commentators, schoolmen, and whole legions of modern doctors. You are extremely well versed in all that has been written concerning the nature of God, and of the soul of man; about matter and form, body and spirit; and space, and eternal essences, and incorporeal substances; and the rest of those profound speculations. You are a master of the controversies that have arisen about nature and grace, about predestination and free will, and all the other abstruse questions that have made so much noise in the schools, and done so much hurt in the world. You are going on, as fast as the infirmities you have contracted will permit, in the same course of study; but you begin to foresee that you shall want time, and you make grievous complaints of the shortness of human life. Give me leave now to ask you, how many thousand years God must prolong your life, in order to reconcile you to his wisdom and goodness? It is plain, at least highly probable, that a life as long as that of the most aged of the patriarchs, would be too short to answer your purposes; since the researches and disputes in which you are engaged, have been already for a much longer time the objects of learned inquiries, and remain still as imperfect and undetermined as they were at first. But let me ask you again, and deceive neither yourself nor me; Have you in the course of these forty years, once examined the first principles, and the fundamental facts, on which all those questions depend, with an absolute indifference of judgment, and with a scrupulous exactness? with the same that you have employed in examining the various consequences drawn from them, and the heterodox opinions about them? Have you not taken them for granted, in the whole course of your studies? Or, if you have looked now and then on the state of the proofs brought to maintain them, have you not done it as a mathematician looks over a demonstration formerly made, to refresh his memory, not to satisfy any doubt? If you have thus examined, it may appear marvellous to some, that you have spent so much time in many parts of those studies, which have reduced you to this hectic condition, of so much heat and weakness. But if you have not thus examined, it must be evident to all, nay to yourself on the least cool reflection, that you are still, notwithstanding all your learning, in a state of ignorance. For knowledge can alone produce knowledge: and without such an examination of axioms and facts, you can have none about inferences."

In this manner one might expostulate very reasonably with many a great scholar, many a profound philosopher, many a dogmatical casuist. And it serves to set the complaints about want of time, and the shortness of human life, in a very ridiculous but a true light. All men are taught their opinions, at least on the most important subjects, by rote; and are bred to defend them with obstinacy. They may be taught true opinions; but whether true or false, the same zeal for them, and the same attachment to them, is every where inspired alike. The Tartar believes as heartily that the soul of Foe inhabits in his Dairo, as the Christian believes the hypostatic union, or any article in the Athanasian creed. Now this may answer the ends of society in some respects, and do well enough for the vulgar of all ranks: but it is not enough for the man who cultivates his reason, who is able to think, and who ought to think, for himself. To such a man, every opinion that he has not himself either framed, or examined strictly, and then adopted, will pass for nothing more than what it really is, the opinion of other men; which may be true or false for aught he knows. And this is a state of uncertainty, in which no such man can remain, with any peace of mind, concerning those things that are of greatest importance to us here, and may be so hereafter. He will make them therefore the objects of his first and greatest attention. If he has lost time, he will lose no more; and when he has acquired all the knowledge he is capable of acquiring on these subjects, he will be the less concerned whether he has time to acquire any farther. Should he have passed his life in the pleasures or business of the world; whenever he sets about this work, he will soon have the advantage over the learned philosopher. For he will soon have secured what is necessary to his happiness, and may sit down in the peaceful enjoyment of that knowledge: or proceed with greater advantage and satisfaction to the acquisition of new knowledge; whilst the other continues his search after things that are in their nature, to say the best of them, hypothetical, precarious and superfluous.

But this is not the only rule, by observing of which we may redeem our time, and have the advantage over those who imagine they have so much in point of knowledge over your lordship or me, for instance, and who despise our ignorance. The rule I mean is this; to be on our guard against the common arts of delusion, spoken of already; which, every one is ready to confess, have been employed to mislead those who differ from him. Let us be diffident of ourselves, but let us be diffident of others too: our own passions may lead us to reason wrong; but the passions and interest of others may have the same effect. It is in every man's power, who sets about it in good earnest, to prevent the first: and when he has done so, he will have a conscious certainty of it. To prevent the last, there is one, and but one sure method; and that is, to remount, in the survey of our opinions, to the first and even remotest principles on which they are founded. No respect, no habit, no seeming certainty whatever, must divert us from this; any affectation of diverting us from it ought to increase our suspicion: and the more important our examination is, the more important this method of conducting it becomes. Let us not be frighted from it, either by the supposed difficulty or length of such an inquiry; for, on the contrary, this is the easiest and the shortest, as well as the only sure way of arriving at real knowledge; and of being able to place the opinions we examine in the different classes of true, probable, or false, according to the truth, probability, or falsehood of the principles from whence they are deduced. If we find these principles false, and that will be the case in many instances, we stop our inquiries on these heads at once; and save an immense deal of time that we should otherwise misspend. The Mussulman who enters on the examination of all the disputes that have arisen between the followers of Omar and Ali and other doctors of his law, must acquire a thorough knowledge of the whole Mahometan system; and will have as good a right to complain of want of time, and the shortness of human life, as any Pagan or Christian divine or philosopher: but without all this time and learning, he might have discovered that Mahomet was an impostor, and that the Koran is a heap of absurdities.

In short, my lord, he who retires from the world, with a resolution of employing his leisure, in the first place to re-examine and settle his opinions, is inexcusable if he does not begin with those that are most important to him, and if he does not deal honestly by himself. To deal honestly by himself, he must observe the rule I have insisted upon, and not suffer the delusions of the world to follow him into his retreat. Every man's reason is every man's oracle: this oracle is best consulted in the silence of retirement; and when we have so consulted, whatever the decision be, whether in favor of our prejudices or against them, we must rest satisfied: since nothing can be more certain than this, that he who follows that guide in the search of truth, as that was given him to lead him to it, will have a much better plea to make, whenever or wherever he may be called to account, than he, who has resigned himself, either deliberately or inadvertently, to any authority upon earth.

When we have done this, concerning God, ourselves, and other men; concerning the relations in which we stand to him and to them; the duties that result from these relations; and the positive will of the Supreme Being, whether revealed to us in a supernatural, or discovered by the right use of our reason in a natural way—we have done the great business of our lives. Our lives are so sufficient for this, that they afford us time for more, even when we begin late: especially if we proceed in every other in-

quiry by the same rule. To discover error in axioms, or in first
principles grounded on facts, is like the breaking of a charm.
The enchanted castle, the steepy rock, the burning lake disappear: and the paths that lead to truth, which we imagined to be
so long, so embarrassed, and so difficult, show as they are, short,
open, and easy.   When we have secured the necessaries, there
may be time to amuse ourselves with the superfluities, and even
with the trifles of life.   "Dulce est desipere;" said Horace:
"Vive la bagatelle!" says Swift.   I oppose neither; not the
Epicurean, much less the Christian philosopher, but I insist that
a principal part of these amusements be the amusements of study
and reflection, of reading and conversation. You know what
conversation I mean; for we lose the true advantage of our nature and constitution, if we suffer the mind to come, as it were,
to a stand.   When the body, instead of acquiring new vigor, and
tasting new pleasures, begins to decline, and is sated with pleasures, or grown incapable of taking them, the mind may continue
still to improve and indulge itself in new enjoyments.   Every
advance in knowledge opens a new scene of delight; and the joy
that we feel in the actual possession of one, will be heightened
by that which we expect to find in another: so that, before we
can exhaust this fund of successive pleasures, death will come to
end our pleasures and our pains at once.   "In his studiis labori-
busque viventi, non intelligitur quando obrepit senectus: ita sen-
sim sine sensu ætas senescit, nec subito frangitur, sed diuturnitate
extinguitur."

This, my lord, is the wisest, and the most agreeable manner
in which a man of sense can wind up the thread of life. Happy
is he whose situation and circumstances give him the opportunity
and means of doing it!   Though he should not have made any
great advances in knowledge, and should set about it late, yet
the task will not be found difficult, unless he has gone too far
out of his way; and unless he continues too long to halt, between
the dissipations of the world, and the leisure of a retired life:

> ———Vivendi recte qui prorogat horam,
> Rusticus expectat dum defluat amnis,———

You know the rest. I am sensible, more sensible than any enemy
I have, of my natural infirmities, and acquired disadvantages:
but I have begun, and I will persist: for he who jogs forward on
a battered horse, in the right way, may get to the end of his
journey; which he cannot do, who gallops the fleetest courser of
New Market, out of it.

Adieu, my dear lord. Though I have much more to say on
this subject, yet I perceive, and I doubt you have long perceived,
that I have said too much, at least for a letter, already.   The

rest shall be reserved for conversation whenever we meet: and then I hope to confirm, under your lordship's eye, my speculations by my practice.   In the mean time let me refer you to our friend Pope.   He says I made a philosopher of him: I am sure he has contributed very much, and I thank him for it, to the making a hermit of me.

A LETTER

ON THE

SPIRIT OF PATRIOTISM.

1736.

My Lord:—You have engaged me on a subject which interrupts the series of those letters I was writing to you; but it is one which, I confess, I have very much at heart. I shall, therefore, explain myself fully, nor blush to reason on principles that are out of fashion among men, who intend nothing by serving the public, but to feed their avarice, their vanity, and their luxury, without the sense of any duty they owe to God or man.

It seems to me, that in order to maintain the moral system of the world at a certain point, far below that of ideal perfection, for we are made capable of conceiving what we are incapable of attaining; but, however, sufficient upon the whole to constitute a state easy and happy, or at the worst tolerable: I say, it seems to me, that the Author of nature has thought fit to mingle, from time to time, among the societies of men, a few, and but a few, of those on whom he is graciously pleased to bestow a larger proportion of the ethereal spirit, than is given in the ordinary course of his providence to the sons of men. These are they who engross almost the whole reason of the species; who are born to instruct, to guide, and to preserve; who are designed to be the tutors and the guardians of human kind. When they prove such, they exhibit to us examples of the highest virtue, and the truest piety: and they deserve to have their festivals kept, instead of that pack of anachorites and enthusiasts, with whose names the calendar is crowded and disgraced. When these men apply their talents to other purposes, when they strive to be great, and despise being good, they commit a most sacrilegious breach of trust; they pervert the means, they defeat, as far as lies in them, the designs of providence, and disturb, in some sort, the system of infinite wisdom. To misapply these talents is the most diffused, and, therefore, the greatest of crimes in its nature and consequences; but to keep them unexerted, and unemployed, is a crime too. Look about you, my lord, from the palace to the cottage; you will find that the bulk of mankind is made to breathe the air of this atmosphere; to roam about this globe, and to consume, like the courtiers of Alcinous, the fruits of the earth. " Nos numerus sumus, et fruges consumere nati." When they have trod this insipid round a certain number of years, and begot others to do the same after them, they have lived: and if they have performed, in some tolerable degree, the ordinary moral duties of life, they have done all they were born to do. Look about you again, my lord, nay, look into your own breast, and you will find that there are superior spirits, men who show even from their infancy, though it be not always perceived by others, perhaps not always felt by themselves, that they were born for something more, and better. These are the men to whom the part I mentioned is assigned. Their talents denote their general designation; and the opportunities of conforming themselves to it, that arise in the course of things, or that are presented to them by any circumstances of rank and situation in the society to which they belong, denote the particular vocation, which it is not lawful for them to resist, nor even to neglect. The duration of the lives of such men as these is to be determined, I think, by the length and importance of the parts they act, not by the number of years that pass between their coming into the world and their going out of it. Whether the piece be of three, or five acts, the part may be long; and he who sustains it through the whole may be said to die in the fulness of years; whilst he, who declines it sooner, may be said not to live out half his days.

I have sometimes represented to myself the vulgar, who are accidentally distinguished by the titles of king and subject, of lord and vassal, of nobleman and peasant; and the few, who are distinguished by nature so essentially from the herd of mankind, that, figure apart, they seem to be of another species, in this manner: the former come into the world, and continue in it, like German travellers in a foreign country. Every thing they meet has the grace of novelty; and they are fond alike of every thing that is new. They wander about from one object to another, of vain curiosity, or inelegant pleasure. If they are industrious, they show their industry in copying signs, and collecting mottos and epitaphs. They loiter, or they trifle away their whole time: and their presence or their absence would be equally unperceived, if caprice or accident did not raise them often to stations, wherein their stupidity, their vices, or their follies, make them a public misfortune. The latter come into the world, or at least continue in it after the effects of surprise and inexperience are over, like men who are sent on more important errands. They observe with distinction, they admire with knowledge. They may indulge themselves in pleasure; but as their industry is not employed about trifles, so their amusements are not made the business of their lives. Such men cannot pass unperceived through a country. If they retire from the world, their splendor accompanies them, and enlightens even the obscurity of their retreat. If they take a part in public life, the effect is never indifferent. They either appear like ministers of divine vengeance, and their course through the world is marked by desolation and oppression, by poverty and servitude: or they are the guardian angels of the country they inhabit, busy to avert even the most distant evil, and to maintain or to procure peace, plenty, and, the greatest of human blessings, liberty.

From the observation, that superiority of parts is often employed to do superior mischief, no consequence can be drawn against the truth I endeavor to establish. Reason collects the will of God from the constitution of things, in this as in other cases; but in no case does the Divine power impel us necessarily to conform ourselves to this will: and therefore, from the misapplication of superior parts to the hurt, no argument can be drawn against this position, that they were given for the good, of mankind. Reason deceives us not: we deceive ourselves, and suffer our wills to be determined by other motives. Montagne or Charron would say, *l'homme se pipe*, " man is at once his own sharper, and his own bubble." Human nature is her own bawd, says Tully, " blanda conciliatrix, et quasi lena sui." He who considers the universal wants, imperfections, and vices of his kind, must agree that men were intended not only for society, but to unite in commonwealths, and to submit to laws: " legum idcirco omnes servi sumus, ut liberi esse possimus."— And yet this very man will be seduced by his own passions, or the passions and examples of others, to think, or to act as if he thought, the very contrary. So he who is conscious of superior endowments, such as render him more capable, than the generality of men, to secure and improve the advantages of social life, by preserving the commonwealth in strength and splendor, even he may be seduced to think, or to act as if he thought, that these endowments were given him for the gratification of his ambition, and his other passions; and that there is no difference between vice and virtue, between a knave and an honest man, but one, which a prince, who died not many years ago, asserted, " that men of great sense were, therefore, knaves, and men of little sense were, therefore, honest." But in neither of these cases will the truth and reason of things be altered, by such examples of human frailty. It will be still true, and reason will still demonstrate, that all men are directed, by the general constitution of human nature, to submit to government, and that some men are in a particular manner designed to take care of that government on which the common happiness depends. The use that reason will make of such examples, will be only this, that since men are so apt, in every form of life and every degree of understanding, to act against their interest and their duty too, without benevolence to mankind, or regard to the Divine Will; it is the more incumbent on those who have this benevolence and this regard at heart, to employ all the means that the nature of the government allows, and that rank, circumstances of situation, or superiority of talents, give them, to oppose evil and promote good government; and contribute thus to preserve the moral system of the world at that point of perfection at least, which seems to have been prescribed to it by the great Creator of every system of beings.

Give me leave, now, my lord, to cast my eyes for a moment homeward, and to apply what I have been saying to the present state of Britain. That there is no profusion of the ethereal spirit to be observed among us, and that we do not abound with men of superior genius, I am ready to confess; but, I think there is no ground for the complaints I have heard made, as if nature had not done her part in our age, as well as in former ages, by producing men capable of serving the commonwealth. The manners of our forefathers were, I believe, in many respects better: they had more probity perhaps, they had certainly more show of honor, and greater industry. But still nature sows alike, though we do not reap alike. There are, and as there always have been, there always will be, such creatures in government as I have described above. Fortune maintains a kind of rivalship with wisdom, and piques herself often in favor of fools as well as knaves. Socrates used to say, that although no man undertakes a trade he has not learned, even the meanest; yet every one thinks himself sufficiently qualified for the hardest of all trades, that of government. He said this upon the experience he had in Greece. He would not change his opinion if he lived now in Britain. But, however, such characters as these would do little hurt, generally speaking, or would not do it long, if they stood alone. To do great hurt, some genius, some knowledge, some talents in short, natural or acquired, are necessary: less indeed, far less than are required to do good, but always some. Yet, I imagine, not the worst minister could do all the mischief he does, by the misapplication of his talents alone, if it were not for the misapplication of much better talents than his,

by some who join with him, and the non-application, or the faint
and unsteady exercise of their talents by some who oppose him,
as well as the general remissness of mankind in acquiring knowledge, and improving the parts which God has given them, for
the service of the public. These are the great springs of national
misfortunes. There have been monsters in other ages, and other
countries, as well as ours; but they never continued their devastations long, when there were heroes to oppose them. We will
suppose a man imprudent, rash, presumptuous, ungracious, insolent, and profligate in speculation as well as practice. He can
bribe, but he cannot seduce: he can buy, but he cannot gain: he
can lie, but he cannot deceive. From whence then has such a
man his strength? From the general corruption of the people,
nursed up to a full maturity under his administration; from the
venality of all orders and all ranks of men, some of whom are so
prostitute, that they set themselves to sale, and even prevent
application. This would be the answer, and it would be a true
one as far as it goes; but it does not account for the whole. Corruption could not spread with so much success, though reduced
into system, and though some ministers, with equal impudence
and folly, avowed it, by themselves and their advocates, to be
the principal expedient by which they governed, if a long and
almost unobserved progression of causes and effects did not prepare the conjuncture. Let me explain it, and apply it, as I conceive it. One party had given their whole attention, during
several years, to the project of enriching themselves, and impoverishing the rest of the nation, and, by these and other means,
of establishing their dominion under the government and with
the favor of a family, who were foreigners, and therefore might
believe that they were established on the throne by the goodwill and strength of this party alone. This party in general were
so intent on these views, and many of them, I fear, are so still,
that they did not advert in time to the necessary consequences
of the measures they abetted: nor did they consider, that the
power they raised, and by which they hoped to govern their
country, would govern them with the very rod of iron they
forged, and would be the power of a prince or minister, not that
of a party long. Another party continued sour, sullen, and inactive, with judgments so weak, and passions so strong, that
even experience, and a severe one surely, was lost upon them.
They waited, like the Jews, for a Messiah, that may never come;
and under whom, if he did come, they would be strangely disappointed in their expectations of glory and triumph, and universal
dominion. Whilst they waited, they were marked out like the
Jews, a distinct race, hewers of wood and drawers of water,
scarce members of the community, though born in the country.

All indifferent men stood as it were at a gaze: and the few who were jealous of the court, were still more jealous one. of another; so that a strength sufficient to oppose bad ministers was not easy to be formed. When this strength was formed, and the insufficiency or iniquity of the administration was daily exposed to public view, many adhered at first to the minister, and others were since gained to his cause because they knew nothing of the constitution of their own, nor of the history of other countries; but imagined wildly that things always went as they saw them go, and that liberty has been, and therefore may be, preserved under the influence of the same corruption. Others perhaps were weak enough to be frightened at first, as some are hypocritical enough to pretend to be still, with the appellations of tory and jacobite, which are always ridiculously given to every man who does not bow to the brazen image that the king has set up. Others again might be persuaded that no fatal use at least would be made of the power acquired by corruption: and men of superior parts might and may still flatter themselves, that if this power should be so employed, they shall have time and means to stop the effects of it. The first of these are seduced by their ignorance and futility; the second, if they are not hypocrites, by their prejudices; the third, by their partiality and blind confidence; the last by their presumption; and all of them by the mammon of unrighteousness, their private interest, which they endeavor to palliate and to reconcile as well as they can to that of the public: " et cæca cupiditate corrupti, non intelligunt se, dum vendunt, et venire."

According to this representation, which I take to be true, your lordship will agree that our unfortunate country affords an example in proof of what is asserted above. The German travellers I spoke of, men of the ordinary or below the ordinary size of understanding, though they are called by caprice, or lifted any other way into power, cannot do great and long mischief, in a country of liberty; unless men of genius, knowledge, and experience, misapply these talents, and become their leaders. A ministerial faction would have as little ability to do hurt, as they have inclination to do good, if they were not formed and conducted by one of better parts than they; nor would such a minister be able to support, at the head of this trusty phalanx, the ignominious tyranny imposed on his country, if other men, of better parts and much more consequence than himself, were not drawn in to misapply these parts to the vilest drudgery imaginable; the daily drudgery of explaining nonsense, covering ignorance, disguising folly, concealing and even justifying fraud and corruption: instead of employing their knowledge, their elocution, their skill, experience, and authority, to correct the administration and to guard the constitution. But this is not all: the example shows a great deal more. Your lordship's experience, as well as mine, will justify what I am going to say. It shows further, that such a conjuncture could not be rendered effectual to preserve power in some of the weakest and some of the worst hands in the kingdom, if there was not a non-application, or a faint and unsteady exercise of parts on one side, as well as an iniquitous misapplication of them on the other: and I cannot help saying, let it fall where it will, what I have said perhaps already, that the former is a crime but one degree inferior to the latter. The more genius, industry, and spirit are employed to destroy, the harder the task of saving our country becomes; but the duty increases with the difficulty, if the principles on which I reason are true. In such exigencies it is not enough that genius be opposed to genius; spirit must be matched by spirit. They, who go about to destroy, are animated from the first by ambition and avarice, the love of power and of money: fear makes them often desperate at last. They must be opposed, therefore, or they will be opposed in vain, by a spirit able to cope with ambition, avarice, and despair itself; by a spirit able to cope with these passions, when they are favored and fortified by the weakness of a nation, and the strength of a government. In such exigencies there is little difference, as to the merit or the effect, between opposing faintly and unsteadily, and not opposing at all: nay the former may be of worse consequence, in certain circumstances, than the latter. And this is a truth I wish with all my heart you may not see verified in our country, where many, I fear, undertake opposition not as a duty, but as an adventure: and looking on themselves like volunteers, not like men listed in the service, they deem themselves at liberty to take as much or as little of this trouble, and to continue in it as long, or end it as soon, as they please. It is but a few years ago that not the merchants alone, but the whole nation took fire at the project of new excises. The project was opposed not on mercantile considerations and interests alone, but on the true principles of liberty. In parliament, the opposition was strenuously enough supported for a time; but there was so little disposition to guide and improve the spirit, that the chief concern of those who took the lead seemed applied to keep it down: and yet your lordship remembers how high it continued against the projector, till it was calmed just before the elections of the present parliament, by the remarkable indolence and inactivity of the last session of the last. But these friends of ours, my lord, are as much mistaken in their ethics, as the event will show they have been in their politics.

The service of our country is no chimerical, but a real duty. He who admits the proofs of any other moral duty, drawn from the constitution of human nature, or from the moral fitness and unfitness of things, must admit them in favor of this duty, or be reduced to the most absurd inconsistency. When he has once admitted the duty on these proofs, it will be no difficult matter to demonstrate to him, that his obligation to the performance of it is in proportion to the means and the opportunities he has of performing it; and that nothing can discharge him from this obligation as long as he has these means and these opportunities in his power, and as long as his country continues in the same want of his services. These obligations, then, to the public service may become obligations for life on certain persons. No doubt they may: and shall this consideration become a reason for denying or evading them? On the contrary, sure it should become a reason for acknowledging and fulfilling them, with the greatest gratitude to the Supreme Being, who has made us capable of acting so excellent a part, and with the utmost benevolence to mankind. Superior talents, and superior rank amongst our fellow creatures, whether acquired by birth, or by the course of accidents, and the success of our own industry, are noble prerogatives. Shall he, who possesses them, repine at the obligation they lay him under, of passing his whole life in the noblest occupation of which human nature is capable? To what higher station, to what greater glory can any mortal aspire, than to be, during the whole course of his life, the support of good, the control of bad government, and the guardian of public liberty? To be driven from hence by successful tyranny, by loss of health or of parts, or by the force of accidents, is to be degraded in such a manner as to deserve pity, and not to incur blame; but to degrade ourselves, to descend voluntarily, and by choice, from the highest to a lower, perhaps to the lowest rank among the sons of Adam; to abandon the government of men for that of hounds and horses, the care of a kingdom for that of a parish, and a scene of great and generous efforts in public life, for one of trifling amusements and low cares, of sloth and of idleness, what is it, my lord? I had rather your lordship should name it than I. Will it be said that it is hard to exact from some men, in favor of others, that they should renounce all the pleasures of life, and drudge all their days in business, that others may indulge themselves in ease? it will be said without grounds. A life dedicated to the service of our country admits the full use, and no life should admit the abuse of pleasures: the least are consistent with a constant discharge of our public duty, the greatest arise from it. The common, the sensual pleasures to which nature prompts us, and which reason therefore does not forbid, though she should always direct, are so far from being excluded out of a life of business, that they are sometimes necessary in it, and are always heightened by it: those of the table, for instance, may be ordered so as to promote that which the elder Cato calls *vitæ conjunctionem*. In the midst of public duties, private studies, and an extreme old age, he found time to frequent the *sodalitates*, or clubs of friends, at Rome, and to sit up all night with his neighbors in the country of the Sabines. Cato's virtue often glowed with wine: and the love of women did not hinder Cæsar from forming and executing the greatest projects that ambition ever suggested. But if Cæsar, whilst he labored to destroy the liberties of his country, enjoyed these inferior pleasures of life, which a man who labors to save those liberties may enjoy as well as he; there are superior pleasures in a busy life, that Cæsar never knew; those, I mean, that arise from a faithful discharge of our duty to the commonwealth. Neither Montaigne in writing his essays, nor Des Cartes in building new worlds, nor Burnet in framing an antediluvian earth, no, nor Newton in discovering and establishing the true laws of nature on experiment and a sublimer geometry, felt more intellectual joys than he feels who is a real patriot, who bends all the force of his understanding, and directs all his thoughts and actions, to the good of his country. When such a man forms a political scheme, and adjusts various and seemingly independent parts in it to one great and good design, he is transported by imagination, or absorbed in meditation, as much and as agreeably as they; and the satisfaction that arises from the different importance of these objects, in every step of the work, is vastly in his favor. It is here that the speculative philosopher's labor and pleasure end. But he who speculates in order to act, goes on and carries his scheme into execution. His labor continues, it varies, it increases; but so does his pleasure too. The execution indeed is often traversed, by unforeseen and untoward circumstances, by the perverseness or treachery of friends, and by the power or malice of enemies: but the first and the last of these animate, and the docility and fidelity of some men make amends for the perverseness and treachery of others. Whilst a great event is in suspense, the action warms, and the very suspense, made up of hope and fear, maintain no unpleasing agitation in the mind. If the event is decided successfully, such a man enjoys pleasure proportionable to the good he has done; a pleasure like to that which is attributed to the Supreme Being, on a survey of his works. If the event is decided otherwise, and usurping courts, or overbearing parties prevail; such a man has still the testimony of his conscience, and a sense of the honor he has acquired, to soothe his mind and support his courage. For although the course of state affairs be to those who meddle in them like a lottery, yet it is a lottery wherein no good man can be a loser: he may be reviled, it is true, instead of being applauded, and may suffer violence of many kinds. I will not say, like Seneca, that the noblest spectacle, which God can behold, is a virtuous man suffering, and struggling with afflictions: but this I will say, that the second Cato, driven out of the forum, and dragged to prison, enjoyed more inward pleasure, and maintained more outward dignity, than they who insulted him, and who triumphed in the ruin of their country. But the very example of Cato may be urged, perhaps, against what I have insisted upon: it may be asked what good he did to Rome, by dedicating his whole life to her service; what honor to himself, by dying at Utica? It may be said, that governments have their periods, like all things human; that they may be brought back to their primitive principles during a certain time, but that when these principles are worn out in the minds of men, it is a vain enterprise to endeavor to renew them; that this is the case of all governments when the corruption of the people comes to a great pitch, and is grown universal; that when a house which is old and quite decayed, though often repaired, not only cracks, but totters even from the foundations, every man in his senses runs out of it, and takes shelter where he can, and that none but madmen continue obstinate to repair what is irreparable, till they are crushed in the ruin; just so, that we must content ourselves to live under the government we like the least, when that form which we like the most is destroyed or worn out; according to the counsel of Dolabella in one of his letters to Cicero. But, my lord, if Cato could not save, he prolonged the life of liberty: the liberties of Rome would have been lost when Catiline attacked them, abetted probably by Cæsar and Crassus, and the worst citizens of Rome; and when Cicero defended them, abetted by Cato and the best. That Cato erred in his conduct, by giving way too much to the natural roughness of his temper, and by allowing too little for that of the Romans, among whom luxury had long prevailed, and corruption was openly practised, is most true. He was incapable of employing those seeming compliances that are reconcilable to the greatest steadiness; and treated unskilfully a crazy constitution. The safety of the commonwealth depended, in that critical conjuncture, on a coalition of parties, the senatorian and the equestrian: Tully had formed it, Cato broke it. But if this good, for I think he was not an able, man erred in the particular respects I have ventured to mention, he deserved most certainly the glory he acquired by the general tenor of his conduct, and by dedicating the whole labor of his life to the service of his country. He would have deserved more, if he had persisted in maintaining the same cause to the end, and would have died, I think, with a better grace at Munda than at Utica. If this be so, if Cato may be censured, severely indeed, but justly, for abandoning the cause of liberty, which he would not, however, survive; what shall we say of those who embrace it faintly, pursue it irresolutely, grow tired of it when they have much to hope, and give it up when they have nothing to fear?

My lord, I have insisted the more on this duty which men owe to their country, because I came out of England, and continue still strongly affected with what I saw when I was there. Our government has approached nearer, than ever before, to the true principles of it, since the revolution of one thousand six hundred and eighty-eight: and the accession of the present family to the throne has given the fairest opportunities, as well as the justest reasons, for completing the scheme of liberty, and improving it to perfection. But it seems to me, that in our separate world, as the means of asserting and supporting liberty are increased, all concern for it is diminished. I beheld, when I was among you, more abject servility, in the manners and behavior of particular men, than I ever saw in France, or than has been seen there, I believe, since the days of that Gascon, who, being turned out of the minister's door, leaped in again at his window. As to bodies of men, I dare challenge your lordship, and I am sorry for it, to produce any instances of resistance to the unjust demands, or wanton will of a court, that British parliaments have given, comparable to such as I am able to cite to the honor of the parliament of Paris, and the whole body of the law in that country, within the same compass of time. This abject servility may appear justly the more wonderful in Britain, because the government of Britain has, in some sort, the appearance of an oligarchy: and monarchy is rather hid behind it than shown, rather weakened than strengthened, rather imposed upon than obeyed. The wonder, therefore, is to observe, how imagination and custom, a giddy fool and a formal pedant, have rendered these cabals, or oligarchies, more respected than majesty itself. That this should happen in countries where princes who have absolute power, may be tyrants themselves, or substitute subordinate tyrants, is not wonderful. It has happened often: but that it should happen in Britain, may be justly an object of wonder. In these countries, the people had lost the armor of their constitution: they were naked and defenceless. Ours is more complete than ever. But though we have preserved the armor, we have lost the spirit, of our constitution: and therefore we bear, from little engrossers of delegated power, what our fathers would not have suffered from true proprietors of the royal authority. Parliaments are not only, what they always were, essential parts of our constitution, but essential parts of our administration too. They do not claim the executive power: no; but the executive power cannot be exercised without their annual concurrence. How few months, instead of years, have princes and ministers now to pass, without inspection and control?   How easy, therefore, is it become, to check every growing evil in the bud; to change every bad administration, to keep such farmers of government in awe; to maintain, and revenge, if need be, the constitution?   It is become so easy, by the present form of our government, that corruption alone could not destroy us.   We must want spirit, as well as virtue, to perish. Even able knaves would preserve liberty in such circumstances as ours, and highwaymen would scorn to receive the wages, and do the drudgery of pick-pockets.   But all is little, and low, and mean among us!   Far from having the virtues, we have not even the vices, of great men.   He who had pride instead of vanity, and ambition but equal to his desire of wealth, could never bear, I do not say, to be the under-strapper to any farmer of royal authority, but to see patiently one of them, at best his fellow, perhaps his inferior in every respect, lord it over him, and the rest of mankind, dissipating the wealth, and trampling on the liberties of his country, with impunity.   This could not happen, if there was the least spirit among us.   But there is none.   What passes among us for ambition, is an odd mixture of avarice and vanity: the moderation we have seen practised, is pussillanimity, and the philosophy that some men affect, is sloth.   Hence it comes that corruption has spread, and prevails.

I expect little from the principal actors that tread the stage at present.   They are divided, not so much as it has seemed, and as they would have it believed, about measures: the true division is about their different ends.   Whilst the minister was not hard pushed, nor the prospect of succeeding to him near, they appeared to have but one end, the reformation of the government.   The destruction of the minister was pursued only as a preliminary, but of essential and indispensable necessity to that end.   But when his destruction seemed to approach, the object of his suc cession interposed to the sight of many, and the reformation of the government was no longer their point of view.   They divided the skin, at least in their thoughts, before they had taken the beast: and the common fear of hunting him down for others, made them all faint in the chase.   It was this, and this alone, that has saved him, or has put off his evil day.   Corruption, so much, and so justly complained of, could not have done it alone

When I say that I expect little from the principal actors that tread the stage at present, I am far from applying to all of them what I take to be true of the far greatest part.   There are men among them who certainly intend the good of their country, and whom I love and honor for that reason.   But these men have been clogged, or misled, or overborne by others; and, seduced by natural temper to inactivity, have taken any excuse, or yielded

to any pretence that favored it. That they should rouse, therefore, in themselves, or in any one else, the spirit they have suffered, nay, helped to die away, I do not expect. I turn my eyes
from the generation that is going off, to the generation that is
coming on the stage. I expect good from them, and from none
of them more than from you, my lord. Remember, that the opposition, in which you have engaged at your first entrance into
business, is not an opposition only to a bad administration of
public affairs, but to an administration that supports itself by
means, establishes principles, introduces customs, repugnant to
the constitution of our government, and destructive of all liberty;
that you do not only combat present evils, but attempts to entail
these evils upon you and your posterity; that if you cease the
combat, you give up the cause; and that he, who does not renew,
on every occasion, his claim, may forfeit his right.

Our disputes were formerly, to say the truth, much more about
persons than things; or, at most, about particular points of political conduct, in which we should have soon agreed, if persons
and personal interests had been less concerned, and the blind
prejudice of party less prevalent. Whether the Big-endians or
the Little-endians got the better, I believe no man of sense and
knowledge thought the constitution concerned; notwithstanding
all the clamor raised at one time about the danger of the
church, and at another time about the danger of the protestant
succession. But the case is, at this time, vastly altered. The
means of invading liberty more effectually by the constitution
of the revenue, than it ever had been invaded by prerogative,
were not then grown up into strength. They are so now; and a
bold and an insolent use is made of them. To reform the state,
therefore, is, and ought to be, the object of your opposition, as
well as to reform the administration. Why do I say as well? It
is so, and it ought to be so, much more. Wrest the power of the
government, if you can, out of the hands that have employed it
weakly and wickedly, ever since it was thrown into them by a
silly bargain made in one reign, and a corrupt bargain made in
another. But do not imagine this to be your sole, or your principal business. You owe to your country, to your honor, to
your security, to the present, and to future ages, that no endeavors of yours be wanting to repair the breach that is made, and
is increasing daily in the constitution; and to shut up, with all
the bars and bolts of law, the principal entries through which
these torrents of corruption have been let in upon us. I say, the
principal entries, because, however it may appear in pure speculation, I think it would not be found in practice possible, no,
nor eligible neither, to shut them up all. As entries of corruption
none of them deserve to be excepted; but there is a just distinc-

tion to be made, because there is a real difference. Some of these entries are opened by the abuse of powers necessary to maintain subordination and to carry on even good government, and, therefore, necessary to be preserved in the crown, notwithstanding the abuse that is sometimes made of them; for no human institution can arrive at perfection, and the most that human wisdom can do, is to procure the same or greater good, at the expense of less evil. There will be always some evil, either immediate or remote, either in cause or in consequence. But there are other entries of corruption, and these are by much the greatest, for suffering of which to continue open, no reason can be assigned, or has been pretended to be assigned, but that which is, to every honest and wise man, a reason for shutting them up; the increase of the means of corruption, which are oftener employed for the service of the oligarchy than for the service of the monarchy. Shut up these, and you will have nothing to fear from the others. By these, a more real and a more dangerous power has been granted to ministers, than was lost to the crown by the restraints on prerogative.

There have been periods when our government continued free, with strong appearances of becoming absolute. Let it be your glory, my lord, and that of the new generation springing up with you, that this government do not become absolute at any future period, with the appearances of being free. However you may be employed, in all your counsels, in all your actions, keep this regard to the constitution always in sight. The scene that opens before you is great, and the part that you will have to act, difficult. It is difficult, indeed, to bring men, from strong habits of corruption, to prefer honor to profit, and liberty to luxury; as it is hard to teach princes the great art of governing all by all, or to prevail on them to practise it. But if it be a difficult, it is a glorious attempt; an attempt worthy to exert the greatest talents, and to fill the most extended life. Pursue it with courage, my lord, nor despair of success.

> Deus hæc fortasse benigna
> Reducet in sedem vice.

A parliament, nay, one house of parliament, is able, at any time, and at once, to destroy any corrupt plan of power. Time produces every day new conjunctures. Be prepared to improve them. We read, in the Old Testament, of a city that might have escaped divine vengeance, if five righteous men had been found in it. Let not our city perish for want of so small a number: and if the generation that is going off could not furnish it, let the generation that is coming on furnish a greater.

We may reasonably hope that it will, from the first essays

which your lordship and some others of our young senators have
made in public life. You have raised the hopes of your country
by the proofs you have given of superior parts. Confirm these
hopes by proofs of uncommon industry, application, and perseverance. Superior parts, nay, even superior virtue, without
these qualities, will be insufficient to support your character and
your cause. How many men have appeared in my time, who
have made these essays with success, and have made no progress
afterwards? Some have dropped, from their first flights, down
into the vulgar crowd, have been distinguished, nay, heard of no
more! others, with better parts, perhaps with more presumption,
but certainly with greater ridicule, have persisted in making
these essays towards business all their lives, and have never been
able to advance farther, in their political course, than a premeditated harangue on some choice subject. I never saw one of
these important persons sit down after his oration, with repeated
hear-hims ringing in his ears, and inward rapture glowing in his
eyes, that he did not recall to my memory the story of a con-
ceited member of some parliament in France, who was overheard
after his tedious harangue, muttering most devoutly to himself,
Non nobis, Domine, non nobis, sed nomini tuo de gloriam!
Eloquence has charms to lead mankind, and gives a nobler
superiority than power, that every dunce may use, or fraud, that
every knave may employ. But eloquence must flow like a
stream that is fed by an abundant spring, and not spout forth
like a frothy water on some gaudy day, and remain dry the rest
of the year. The famous orators of Greece and Rome were the
statesmen and ministers of those commonwealths. The nature
of their governments, and the humor of those ages, made elaborate orations necessary. They harangued oftener than they debated: and the *ars dicendi* required more study and more exercise of mind, and of body too, among them, than are necessary
among us. But as much pains as they took in learning how to
conduct the stream of eloquence, they took more to enlarge the
fountain from which it flowed. Hear Demosthenes, hear Cicero,
thunder against Philip, Catiline, and Antony. I choose the
example of the first, rather than that of Pericles, whom he imi-
tated, or of Phocion, whom he opposed, or of any other considerable personage in Greece: and the example of Cicero rather
than that of Crassus, or of Hortensius, or of any other of the
great men of Rome; because the eloquence of these two has been
so celebrated, that we are accustomed to look upon them almost
as mere orators. They were orators indeed, and no man who
has a soul can read their orations, after the revolution of so
many ages, after the extinction of the governments, and of the
people for whom they were composed, without feeling, at this

hour, the passions they were designed to move, and the spirit they were designed to raise. But if we look into the history of these two men, and consider the parts they acted, we shall see them in another light, and admire them in a higher sphere of action. Demosthenes had been neglected, in his education, by the same tutors who cheated him of his inheritance. Cicero was bred with greater advantage: and Plutarch, I think, says, that when he first appeared, the people used to call him, by way of derision, the Greek, and the scholar. But whatever advantage of this kind the latter might have over the former, and to which of them soever you ascribe the superior genius, the progress which both of them made in every part of political knowledge, by their industry and application, was marvellous. Cicero might be a better philosopher, but Demosthenes was no less a states-man: and both of them performed actions, and acquired fame, above the reach of eloquence alone. Demosthenes used to compare eloquence to a weapon, aptly enough: for eloquence, like every other weapon, is of little use to the owner, unless he have the force and the skill to use it. This force and this skill Demosthenes had in an eminent degree. Observe them in one instance among many. It was of mighty importance to Philip, to prevent the accession of Thebes to the grand alliance that Demosthenes, at the head of the Athenian commonwealth, formed against the growing power of the Macedonians. Philip had emissaries and his ambassadors on the spot, to oppose to those of Athens, and we may be assured that he neglected none of those arts upon this occasion, that he employed so successfully on others. The struggle was great, but Demosthenes prevailed, and the Thebans engaged in the war against Philip. Was it by his eloquence alone that he prevailed, in a divided state, over all the subtilty of intrigue, all the dexterity of negotiation, all the seduction, all the corruption, and all the terror that the ablest and most powerful prince could employ? Was Demosthenes wholly taken up with composing orations, and haranguing the people in this remarkable crisis? He harangued them, no doubt, at Thebes, as well as at Athens, and in the rest of Greece, where all the great resolutions of making alliances, waging war, or concluding peace, were determined in democratical assemblies. But yet haranguing was, no doubt, the least part of his business, and eloquence was neither the sole, nor the principal talent, as the style of writers would induce us to believe, on which his success depended. He must have been master of other arts, subserviently to which his eloquence was employed, and must have had a thorough knowledge of his own state, and of the other states of Greece, of their dispositions, and of their interests relatively to one another, and relatively to their neighbors, to the Persians particularly, with whom he held a correspondence, not much to his honor in appearance, whatever he might intend by it: I say, he must have been master of many other arts, and have possessed an immense fund of knowledge, to make his eloquence in every case successful, and even pertinent or seasonable in some, as well as to direct it, and to furnish it with matter whenever he thought proper to employ this weapon.

Let us consider Tully on the greatest theatre of the known world, and in the most difficult circumstances. We are better acquainted with him than we are with Demosthenes; for we see him nearer, as it were, and in more different lights. How perfect a knowledge had he acquired of the Roman constitution of government, ecclesiastical and civil; of the original and progress, of the general reasons and particular occasions of the laws and customs of his country; of the great rules of equity, and the low practice of courts; of the duty of every magistracy and office in the state, from the dictator down to the lictor; and of all the steps by which Rome had risen, from her infancy, to liberty, to power, and grandeur, and dominion, as well as of all those by which she began to decline, a little before his age, to that servitude which he died for opposing, but lived to see established, and in which not her liberty alone, but her power, and grandeur, and dominion were lost? How well was he acquainted with the Roman colonies and provinces, with the allies and enemies of the empire, with the rights and privileges of the former, the dispositions and conditions of the latter, with the interests of them all relatively to Rome, and with the interests of Rome relatively to them? How present to his mind were the anecdotes of former times concerning the Roman and other states, and how curious was he to observe the minutest circumstances that passed in his own? His works will answer sufficiently the questions I ask, and establish in the mind of every man who reads them the idea I would give of his capacity and knowledge, as well as that which is so universally taken of his eloquence. To a man fraught with all this stock of knowledge, and industrious to improve it daily, nothing could happen that was entirely new, nothing for which he was quite unprepared, scarce any effect whereof he had not considered the cause, scarce any cause wherein his sagacity could not discern the latent effect. His eloquence in private causes gave him first credit at Rome: but it was this knowledge, this experience, and the continued habits of business, that supported his reputation, enabled him to do so much service to his country, and gave force and authority to his eloquence. To little purpose would he have attacked Catiline with all the vehemence that indignation, and even fear, added to eloquence, if he had trusted to this weapon alone. This weapon alone would have secured neither him nor the senate from the poniard of that assassin. He would have had no occasion to boast, that he had driven this infamous citizen out of the walls of Rome, " abiit, excessit, evasit, erupit," if he had not made it, beforehand, impossible for him to continue any longer in them. As little occasion would he have had to assume the honor of defeating, without any tumult, or any disorder, the designs of those who conspired to murder the Roman people, to destroy the Roman empire, and to extinguish the Roman name; if he had not united, by skill and management, in the common cause of their country, orders of men the most averse to each other; if he had not watched all the machinations of the conspirators in silence, and prepared a strength sufficient to resist them at Rome, and in the provinces, before he opened this scene of villany to the senate and the people: in a word, if he had not made much more use of political prudence, that is, of the knowledge of mankind, and of the arts of government, which study and experience give, than of all the powers of his eloquence.

Such was Demosthenes, such was Cicero, such were all the great men whose memories are preserved in history, and such must every man be, or endeavor to be, if he has either sense or sentiment, who presumes to meddle in affairs of government, of a free government I mean, and hopes to maintain a distinguished character in popular assemblies, whatever part he takes, whether that of supporting, or that of opposing. I put the two cases purposely, my lord, because I have observed, and your lordship will have frequent occasions of observing, many persons who seem to think that opposition to an administration requires fewer preparatives, and less constant application, than the conduct of it. Now, my lord, I take this to be a gross error, and, I am sure, it has been a fatal one. It is one of those errors, and there are many such, which men impute to judgment, and which proceed from the defect of judgment, as this does from lightness, irresolution, laziness, and a false notion of opposition; unless the persons, who seem to think, do not really think in this manner, but, serving the public purely for interest, and not for fame, nor for duty, decline taking the same pains when they oppose without personal and immediate reward, as they are willing to take when they are paid for serving. Look about you, and you will see men eager to speak, and keen to act, when particular occasions press them, or particular motives excite them, but quite unprepared for either: and hence all that superficiality in speaking, for want of information; hence all that confusion or inactivity, for want of concert; and all that disappointment, for want of preliminary measures. They who affect to head an opposition, or to make any considerable figure in it, must be equal, at least, to those whom they oppose; I do not say, in parts only, but in application and industry, and the fruits of both, information, knowledge, and a certain constant preparedness for all the events that may arise. Every administration is a system of conduct: opposition, therefore, should be a system of conduct likewise; an opposite, but not a dependent system. I shall explain myself better by an example. When two armies take the field, the generals on both sides have their different plans for the campaigns, either of defence, or of offence: and as the former does not suspend his measures till he is attacked, but takes them beforehand on every probable contingency, so the latter does not suspend his till the opportunity of attacking presents itself, but is alert, and constantly ready to seize it whenever it happens; and, in the mean time, is busy to improve all the advantages of skill, of force, or of any other kind that he has, or that he can acquire, independently of the plan, and of the motions of his enemy.

In a word, my lord, this is my notion, and I submit it to you. According to the present form of our constitution, every member of either house of parliament is a member of a national standing council, born, or appointed by the people, to promote good, and to oppose bad government; and if not vested with the power of a minister of state, yet vested with the superior power of controlling those who are appointed such by the crown. It follows from hence, that they who engage in opposition, are under as great obligations to prepare themselves to control, as they who serve the crown are under to prepare themselves to carry on, the administration: and that a party, formed for this purpose, do not act like good citizens, nor honest men, unless they propose true, as well as oppose false measures of government. Sure I am, they do not act like wise men, unless they act systematically, and unless they contrast, on every occasion, that scheme of policy which the public interest requires to be followed, with that which is suited to no interest but the private interest of the prince, or his ministers. Cunning men (several such there are among you) will dislike this consequence, and object, that such a conduct would support, under the appearance of opposing, a weak, and even a wicked administration; and that to proceed in this manner, would be to give good counsel to a bad minister, and to extricate him out of distresses that ought to be improved to his ruin. But cunning pays no regard to virtue, and is but the low mimic of wisdom: It were easy to demonstrate what I have asserted concerning the duty of an opposing party: and I presume there is no need of laboring to prove, that a party who opposed, systematically, a wise to a silly, an honest to an iniquitous, scheme of government, would acquire greater reputation and strength, and arrive more surely at their end, than a party who opposed, occasionally as it were, without any common system, without any general concert, with little uniformity, little preparation, little perseverance, and as little knowledge or political capacity. But it is time to leave this invidious subject, and to hasten to the conclusion of my letter before it grows into a book.

I am, my lord, &c.

THE IDEA

OF A

PATRIOT KING.

INTRODUCTION.

Dec. 1, 1738.

REVISING some letters I wrote to my Lord ***, I found in one of them a great deal said concerning the duties which men owe to their country, those men particularly who live under a free constitution of government; with a strong application of these general doctrines to the present state of Great Britain, and to the characters of the present actors on this stage.

I saw no reason to alter, none even to soften, any thing that is there advanced. On the contrary, it came into my mind to carry these considerations further, and to delineate, for I pretend not to make a perfect draught, the duties of a king to his country; of those kings particularly who are appointed by the people, for I know of none who are anointed by God to rule in limited monarchies. After which I proposed to apply the general doctrines in this case, as strongly and as directly as in the other, to the present state of Great Britain.

I am not one of those oriental slaves, who deem it unlawful presumption to look their kings in the face; neither am I swayed by my Lord Bacon's authority, to think this custom good and reasonable in its meaning, though it savors of barbarism in its institution: "Ritu quidem barbarus, sed significatione bonus." Much otherwise. It seems to me, that no secrets are so important to be known, no hearts deserve to be pryed into with more curiosity and attention, than those of princes. But many things have concurred, besides age and temper, to set me at a great distance from the present court. Far from prying into the hearts,

I scarce know the faces of our royal family. I shall therefore decline all application to their characters, and all mention of any influence which their characters may have on their own fortune, or on that of this nation.

The principles I have reasoned upon in my letter to my Lord ***, and those I shall reason upon here, are the same. They are laid in the same system of human nature. They are drawn from that source from whence all the duties of public and private morality must be derived, or they will be often falsely, and always precariously, established. Up to this source there are few men who take the pains to go: and, open as it lies, there are not many who can find their way to it. By such as do, I shall be understood and approved: and, far from fearing the censure, or the ridicule, I should reproach myself with the applause, of men who measure their interest by their passions, and their duty by the examples of a corrupt age; that is, by the examples they afford to one another. Such, I think, are the greatest part of the present generation; not of the vulgar alone, but of those who stand foremost, and are raised highest in our nation. Such we may justly apprehend too that the next will be; since they who are to compose it will set out into the world under a direction that must incline them strongly to the same course of self-interest, profligacy, and corruption.

The iniquity of all the principal men in any community, of kings and ministers especially, does not consist alone in the crimes they commit, and in the immediate consequences of these crimes: and, therefore, their guilt is not to be measured by these alone. Such men sin against posterity, as well as against their own age; and when the consequences of their crimes are over, the consequences of their example remain. I think, and every wise and honest man in generations yet unborn will think, if the history of this administration descends to blacken our annals, that the greatest iniquity of the minister, on whom the whole iniquity ought to charged, since he has been so long in possession of the whole power, is the constant endeavor he has employed to corrupt the morals of men. I say thus generally, the morals; because he, who abandons or betrays his country, will abandon or betray his friend; and because he, who is prevailed on to act in parliament without any regard to truth or justice, will easily prevail on himself to act in the same manner every where else. A wiser and honester administration may relieve our trade from that oppression, and the public from that load of debt, under which it must be supposed that he has industriously kept it; because we are able to prove, by fair calculations, that he might have provided effectually for the payment of it, since he came to the head of the treasury. A wiser and honester administration may draw us back to our former credit and influence abroad, from that state of contempt into which we are sunk among all our neighbors. But will the minds of men, which this minister has narrowed to personal regards alone, will their views, which he has confined to the present moment, as if nations were mortal like the men who compose them, and Britain was to perish with her degenerate children; will these, I say, be so easily or so soon enlarged? Will their sentiments, which are debased from the love of liberty, from zeal for the honor and prosperity of their country, and from a desire of honest fame, to an absolute unconcernedness for all these, to an abject submission, and a rapacious eagerness after wealth, that may sate their avarice, and exceed the profusion of their luxury; will these, I say again, be so easily or so soon elevated? In a word, will the British spirit, that spirit which has preserved liberty hitherto in one corner of the world at least, be so easily or so soon reinfused into the British nation? I think not. We have been long coming to this point of depravation: and the progress from confirmed habits of evil is much more slow than the progress to them. Virtue is not placed on a rugged mountain of difficult and dangerous access, as they who would excuse the indolence of their temper, or the perverseness of their will, desire to have it believed; but she is seated, however, on an eminence. We may go up to her with ease, but we must go up gradually, according to the natural progression of reason, who is to lead the way, and to guide our steps. On the other hand, if we fall from thence, we are sure to be hurried down the hill with a blind impetuosity, according to the natural violence of those appetites and passions that caused our fall at first, and urged it on the faster, the further they are removed from the control that before restrained them.

To perform, therefore, so great a work, as to reinfuse the spirit of liberty, to reform the morals, and to raise the sentiments of a people, much time is required; and a work which requires so much time, may, too probably, be never completed; considering how unsteadily and unsystematically even the best of men are apt often to proceed, and how this reformation is to be carried forward, in opposition to public fashion, and private inclination, to the authority of the men in power, and to the secret bent of many of those who are out of power. Let us not flatter ourselves: I did so too long. It is more to be wished than to be hoped, that the contagion should spread no further than that leprous race, who carry on their skins, exposed to public sight, the scabs and blotches of their distemper. The minister preaches corruption aloud and constantly, like an impudent missionary of vice: and some there are who not only insinuate, but teach the same occasionally. I say, some; because I am as far from thinking, that all those who join with him, as that any of those who oppose him, wait only to be more authorised, that they may propagate it with greater success, and apply it to their own use, in their turn.

It seems to me, upon the whole matter, that to save or redeem a nation, under such circumstances, from perdition, nothing less is necessary than some great, some extraordinary conjuncture of ill fortune, or of good, which may purge, yet so as by fire. Distress from abroad, bankruptcy at home, and other circumstances of like nature and tendency, may beget universal confusion. Out of confusion order may arise: but it may be the order of a wicked tyranny, instead of the order of a just monarchy. Either may happen: and such an alternative, at the disposition of fortune, is sufficient to make a Stoic tremble! We may be saved, indeed, by means of a very different kind; but these means will not offer themselves, this way of salvation will not be opened to us, without the concurrence, and the influence, of a Patriot King, the most uncommon of all phenomena in the physical or moral world.

Nothing can so surely and so effectually restore the virtue and public spirit essential to the preservation of liberty and national prosperity, as the reign of such a prince.

We are willing to indulge this pleasing expectation, and there is nothing we desire more ardently than to be able to hold of a British prince, without flattery, the same language that was held of a Roman emperor, with a great deal,

Nil oriturum alias, nil ortum tale fatentes.

But let us not neglect, on our part, such means as are in our power, to keep the cause of truth, of reason, of virtue, and of liberty, alive. If the blessing be withheld from us, let us deserve, at least, that it should be granted to us. If heaven, in mercy, bestows it on us, let us prepare to receive it, to improve it, and to co-operate with it.

I speak as if I could take my share in these glorious efforts. Neither shall I recall my words. Stripped of the rights of a British subject, of all except the meanest of them, that of inheriting, I remember that I am a Briton still. I apply to myself what I have read in Seneca; "officia, si civis amiserit, hominis exerceat." I have renounced the world, not in show, but in reality, and more by my way of thinking, than by my way of living, as retired as that may seem. But I have not renounced my country, nor my friends: and by my friends I mean all those, and those alone, who are such to their country, by whatever name they have been, or may be still distinguished; and though in that number there should be men, of whose past ingratitude, injustice, or malice, I might complain, on my own account, with the greatest reason. These I will never renounce. In their prosperity, they shall never hear of me: in their distress, always. In that retreat, wherein the remainder of my days shall be spent, I may be of some use to them; since, even from thence, I may advise, exhort, and warn them. "Nec enim is solus reipublicæ prodest, qui candidatos extrahit, et tuetur reos, et de pace, belloque censet; sed qui juventutem exhortatur, qui, in tanta bonorum præceptorum inopia, virtute instruit animos; qui ad pecuniam luxuriamque cursu ruentes, prensat ac retrahit, et, si nihil aliud, certe moratur; in privato publicum negotium agit."

THE IDEA OF A PATRIOT KING.

My intention is not to introduce what I have to say concerning the duties of kings, by any nice inquiry into the original of their institution. What is to be known of it will appear plainly enough, to such as are able and can spare time to trace it, in the broken traditions which are come down to us of a few nations. But those, who are not able to trace it there, may trace something better, and more worthy to be known, in their own thoughts: I mean what this institution ought to have been, whenever it began, according to the rule of reason, founded in the common rights, and interests, of mankind. On this head it is quite necessary to make some reflections, that will, like angular stones laid on a rock, support the little fabric, the model however of a great building, that I propose to raise.

So plain a matter could never have been rendered intricate and voluminous, had it not been for lawless ambition, extravagant vanity, and the detestable spirit of tyranny, abetted by the private interests of artful men, by adulation and superstition, two vices to which that staring timid creature man is excessively prone; if authority had not imposed on such as did not pretend to reason; and if such as did attempt to reason had not been caught in the common snares of sophism, and bewildered in the labyrinths of disputation. In this case, therefore, as in all those of great concernment, the shortest and the surest method of arriving at real knowledge is to unlearn the lessons we have been taught, to remount to first principles, and take nobody's word about them; for it is about them that almost all the juggling and legerdemain, employed by men whose trade it is to deceive, are set to work.

Now he, who does so in this case, will discover soon, that the notions concerning the divine institution and right of kings, as well as the absolute power belonging to their office, have no foundation in fact or reason, but have risen from an old alliance between ecclesiastical and civil policy. The characters of king and priest have been sometimes blended together: and when they have been divided, as kings have found the great effects wrought in government by the empire which priests obtain over the consciences of mankind, so priests have been taught by experience, that the best method to preserve their own rank, dignity, wealth, and power, all raised upon a supposed divine right, is to communicate the same pretension to kings, and, by a fallacy common to both, impose their usurpations on a silly world. This they have done: and, in the state, as in the church, these pretensions to a divine right have been generally carried highest by those, who have had the least pretension to the divine favor.

It is worth while to observe, on what principle some men were advanced to a great pre-eminence over others, in the early ages of those nations that are a little known to us: I speak not of such as raised themselves by conquest, but of such as were raised by common consent. Now you will find, in all these proceedings, an entire uniformity of principle. The authors of such inventions, as were of general use to the well being of mankind, were not only reverenced and obeyed during their lives, but worshipped after their deaths: they became principal gods, " Dii majorum gentium." The founders of commonwealths, the lawgivers, and the heroes of particular states, became gods of a second class, " Dii minorum gentium." All pre-eminence was given in heaven, as well as in earth, in proportion to the benefits that men received. Majesty was the first, and divinity the second, reward. Both were earned by services done to mankind, whom it was easy to lead, in those days of simplicity and superstition, from admiration and gratitude, to adoration and expectation.

When advantage had been taken, by some particular men, of these dispositions in the generality, and religion and government were become two trades or mysteries, new means of attaining to this pre-eminence were soon devised, and new and even contrary motives worked the same effect. Merit had given rank; but rank was soon kept, and, which is more preposterous, obtained, too, without merit. Men were then made kings for reasons as little relative to good government, as the neighing of the horse of the son of Hystaspes.

But the most prevalent, and the general motive was proximity of blood to the last, not to the best, king. Nobility in China mounts upwards: and he, who has it conferred upon him, ennobles his ancestors, not his posterity. A wise institution! and especially among a people in whose minds a great veneration for their forefathers has been always carefully maintained. But in China, as well as in most other countries, royalty has descended, and kingdoms have been reckoned the patrimonies of particular families.

I have read in one of the historians of the latter Roman empire, historians, by the way, whom I will not advise others to misspend their time in reading, that Sapores, the famous king of Persia against whom Julian made the expedition wherein he lost his life, was crowned in his mother's womb. His father left her with child: the magi declared that the child would be a male: whereupon the royal ensigns were brought forth, they were placed on her majesty's belly, and the princes and the satrapes prostrate recognised the embryo-monarch. But to take a more known example, out of multitudes that present themselves; Domitian, the worst, and Trajan, the best of princes, were promoted to the empire by the same title. Domitian was the son of Flavius, and the brother, though possibly the poisoner too, of Titus Vespasian: Trajan was the adopted son of Nerva. Hereditary right served the purpose of one, as well as of the other: and if Trajan was translated to a place among the gods, this was no greater a distinction than some of the worst of his predecessors obtained, for reasons generally as good as that which Seneca puts into the mouth of Diespiter in the Apokolokyntosis of Claudius; "cum sit e republica esse aliquem, qui cum Romulo possit serventia rapa vorare." To say the truth, it would have been a wiser measure to have made these royal persons gods at once: as gods they would have done neither good nor hurt; but as emperors, in their way to divinity, they acted like devils.

If my readers are ready by this time to think me antimonarchical, and in particular an enemy to the succession of kings by hereditary right, I hope to be soon restored to their good opinion. I esteem monarchy above any other form of government, and hereditary monarchy above elective. I reverence kings, their office, their rights, their persons: and it will never be owing to the principles I am going to establish, because the character and government of a Patriot King can be established on no other, if their office and their right are not always held divine, and their persons always sacred.

Now, we are subject, by the constitution of human nature, and therefore by the will of the Author of this and every other nature, to two laws. One given immediately to all men by God, the same to all, and obligatory alike on all. The other given to man by man; and therefore not the same to all, nor obligatory alike on all: founded indeed on the same principles, but varied by different applications of them to times, to characters, and to a number, which may be reckoned infinite, of other circumstances. By the first, I mean the universal law of reason; and by the second, the particular law, or constitution of laws, by which every distinct community has chosen to be governed.

The obligation of submission to both, is discoverable by so clear and so simple an use of our intellectual faculties, that it may be said properly enough to be revealed to us by God: and though both these laws cannot be said properly to be given by him, yet our obligation to submit to the civil law is a principal paragraph in the natural law, which he has most manifestly given us. In truth we can no more doubt of the obligations of both these laws, than of the existence of the lawgiver. As supreme Lord over all his works, his general providence regards immediately the great commonwealth of mankind; but then, as supreme Lord likewise, his authority gives a sanction to the particular bodies of law which are made under it. The law of nature is the law of all his subjects: the constitutions of particular governments are like the by-laws of cities, or the appropriated customs of provinces. It follows, therefore, that he who breaks the laws of his country resists the ordinance of God, that is, the law of his nature. God has instituted neither monarchy, nor aristocracy, nor democracy, nor mixed government: but though he has instituted no particular form of government among men, yet by the general laws of his kingdom he exacts our obedience to the laws of those communities, to which each of us is attached by birth, or to which we may be attached by a subsequent and lawful engagement.

From such plain, unrefined, and therefore, I suppose, true reasoning, the just authority of kings, and the due obedience of subjects, may be deduced with the utmost certainty. And surely it is far better for kings themselves to have their authority thus founded on principles incontestable, and on fair deductions from them, than on the chimeras of madmen, or, what has been more common, the sophisms of knaves. A human right, that cannot be controverted, is preferable, surely, to a pretended divine right, which every man must believe implicitly, as few will do, or not believe at all.

But the principles we have laid down do not stop here. A divine right in kings is to be deduced evidently from them: a divine right to govern well, and conformably to the constitution at the head of which they are placed. A divine right to govern ill, is an absurdity: to assert it, is blasphemy. A people may choose, or hereditary succession may raise, a bad prince to the throne; but a good king alone can derive his right to govern from God. The reason is plain: good government alone can be in the divine intention. God has made us to desire happiness; he has made our happiness dependent on society; and the happiness of society dependent on good or bad government. His intention, therefore, was, that government should be good.

This is essential to his wisdom; for wisdom consists, surely, in proportioning means to ends: therefore it cannot be said without absurd impiety, that he confers a right to oppose his intention.

The office of kings is, then, of right divine, and their persons are to be reputed sacred. As men, they have no such right, no such sacredness belonging to them: as kings, they have both, unless they forfeit them. Reverence for government obliges to reverence governors, who, for the sake of it, are raised above the level of other men: but reverence for governors, independently of government, any further than reverence would be due to their virtues if they were private men, is preposterous, and repugnant to common sense. The spring from which this legal reverence, for so I may call it, arises, is national, not personal. As well might we say that a ship is built, and loaded, and manned, for the sake of any particular pilot, instead of acknowledging that the pilot is made for the sake of the ship, her lading, and her crew, who are always the owners in the political vessel; as to say that kingdoms were instituted for kings, not kings for kingdoms. In short, and to carry our allusion higher, majesty is not an inherent, but a reflected light.

All this is as true of hereditary, as it is of elective monarchy; though the scribblers for tyranny, under the name of monarchy, would have us believe that there is something more august, and more sacred in one than the other. They are sacred alike, and this attribute is to be ascribed or not ascribed, to them, as they answer, or do not answer, the ends of their institution. But there is another comparison to be made, in which a great and most important dissimilitude will be found between hereditary and elective monarchy. Nothing can be more absurd, in pure speculation, than an hereditary right in any mortal to govern other men: and yet, in practice, nothing can be more absurd than to have a king to choose at every vacancy of a throne. We draw at a lottery indeed in one case, where there are many chances to lose, and few to gain. But have we much more advantage of this kind in the other? I think not. Upon these, and upon most occasions, the multitude would do at least as well to trust to chance as choice, and to their fortune as to their judgment. But in another respect, the advantage is entirely on the side of hereditary succession; for, in elective monarchies, these elections, whether well or ill made, are often attended with such national calamities, that even the best reigns cannot make amends for them: whereas, in hereditary monarchy, whether a good or a bad prince succeeds, these calamities are avoided. There is one source of evil the less open: and one source of evil the less in human affairs, where there are so many, is sufficient to decide. We may lament the imperfections of our human state, which is such, that in cases of the utmost importance to the order and good government of society, and by consequence to the happiness of our kind, we are reduced, by the very constitution of our nature, to have no part to take that our reason can approve absolutely. But though we lament it, we must submit to it. We must tell ourselves once for all, that perfect schemes are not adapted to our imperfect state; that Stoical morals and Platonic politics are nothing better than amusements for those who have had little experience in the affairs of the world, and who have much leisure, " verba otiosorum senum ad imperitos juvenes;" which was the censure, and a just one too, that Dionysius passed on some of the doctrines of the father of the academy. In truth, all that human prudence can do, is to furnish expedients, and to compound, as it were, with general vice and folly; employing reason to act even against her own principles, and teaching us, if I may say so " insanire cum ratione," which appears on many occasions not to be the paradox it has been thought.

To conclude this head therefore: as I think a limited monarchy the best of governments, so I think an hereditary monarchy the best of monarchies. I said a limited monarchy; for an unlimited monarchy, wherein arbitrary will, which is in truth no rule, is however the sole rule, or stands instead of all rule of government, must be allowed so great an absurdity, both in reason informed and uninformed by experience, that it seems a government fitter for savages than for civilised people.

But I think it proper to explain a little more what I mean, when I say a limited monarchy, that I may leave nothing untouched which ought to be taken into consideration by us, when we attempt to fix our ideas of a Patriot King.

Among many reasons which determine me to prefer monarchy to every other form of government, this is a principal one. When monarchy is the essential form, it may be more easily and more usefully tempered with aristocracy, or democracy, or both, than either of them, when they are the essential forms, can be tempered with monarchy. It seems to me, that the introduction of a real permanent monarchical power, or any thing more than the pageantry of it, into either of these, must destroy them and extinguish them, as a greater light extinguishes a less. Whereas it may easily be shown, and the true form of our government will demonstrate, without seeking any other example, that very considerable aristocratical and democratical powers may be grafted on a monarchical stock, without diminishing the lustre, or restraining the power and authority of the prince, enough to alter in any degree the essential form.

A great difference is made in nature, and therefore the distinction should be always preserved in our notions, between two things that we are apt to confound in speculation, as they have been confounded in practice, legislative and monarchical power. There must be an absolute, unlimited, and uncontrollable power lodged somewhere in every government; but to constitute monarchy, or the government of a single person, it is not necessary that this power should be lodged in the monarch alone. It is no more necessary that he should exclusively and independently establish the rule of his government, than it is that he should govern without any rule at all: and this surely will be thought reasonable by no man.

I would not say God governs by a rule that we know, or may know, as well as he, and upon our knowledge of which he appeals to men for the justice of his proceedings towards them; which a famous divine has impiously advanced, in a pretended demonstration of his being and attributes. God forbid! But this I may say, that God does always that which is fittest to be done, and that this fitness, whereof neither that presumptuous dogmatist was, nor any created being is, a competent judge, results from the various natures, and more various relations of things: so that, as creator of all systems by which these natures and relations are constituted, he prescribed to himself the rule, which he follows as governor of every system of being. In short, with reverence be it spoken, God is a monarch, yet not an arbitrary but a limited monarch, limited by the rule which infinite wisdom prescribes to infinite power. I know well enough the impropriety of these expressions; but, when our ideas are inadequate, our expressions must needs be improper. Such conceptions, however, as we are able to form of these attributes, and of the exercise of them in the government of the universe, may serve to show what I have produced them to show. If governing without any rule, and by arbitrary will, be not essential to our idea of the monarchy of the Supreme Being, it is plainly ridiculous to suppose them necessarily included in the idea of a human monarchy: and though God, in his eternal ideas, for we are able to conceive no other manner of knowing, has prescribed to himself that rule by which he governs the universe he created, it will be just as ridiculous to affirm, that the idea of human monarchy cannot be preserved, if kings are obliged to govern according to a rule established by the wisdom of a state, that was a state before they were kings, and by the consent of a people that they did not most certainly create; especially when the whole executive power is exclusively in their hands, and the legislative power cannot be exercised without their concurrence.

There are limitations indeed that would destroy the essential form of monarchy; or, in other words, a monarchical constitution may be changed, under pretence of limiting the monarch. This happened among us in the last century, when the vilest usurpation, and the most infamous tyranny, were established over our nation, by some of the worst and some of the meanest men in it. I will not say that the essential form of monarchy should be preserved though the preservation of it were to cause the loss of liberty. "Salus reipublicæ suprema lex esto" is a fundamental law; and, sure I am, the safety of a commonwealth is ill provided for, if the liberty be given up. But this I presume to say, and can demonstrate, that all the limitations necessary to preserve liberty, as long as the spirit of it subsists, and longer than that no limitations of monarchy, nor any other form of government, can preserve it, are compatible with monarchy. I think on these subjects, neither as the Tories, nor as the Whigs have thought; at least, I endeavor to avoid the excesses of both. I neither dress up kings like so many burlesque Jupiters, weighing the fortunes of mankind in the scales of fate, and darting thunderbolts at the heads of rebellious giants; nor do I strip them naked, as it were, and leave them at most a few tattered rags to clothe their majesty, but such as can serve really as little for use as for ornament. My aim is to fix this principle; that limitations on a crown ought to be carried as far as it is necessary to secure the liberties of a people; and that all such limitations may subsist, without weakening or endangering monarchy.

I shall be told, perhaps, for I have heard it said by many, that this point is imaginary; and that limitations, sufficient to procure good government and to secure liberty under a bad prince, cannot be made, unless they are such as will deprive the subjects of many benefits in the reign of a good prince, clog his administration, maintain an unjust jealousy between him and his people, and occasion a defect of power, necessary to preserve the public tranquillity, and to promote the national prosperity. If this was true, here would be a much more melancholy instance of the imperfection of our nature, and of the inefficacy of our reason to supply this imperfection, than the former. In the former, reason prompted by experience avoids a certain evil effectually, and is able to provide, in some measure, against the contingent evils that may arise from the expedient itself. But in the latter, if what is there advanced was true, these provisions against contingent evils would, in some cases, be the occasions of much certain evil, and of positive good in none; under a good prince they would render the administration defective, and under a bad one there would be no government at all. But the truth is widely different from this representation. The limitations necessary to preserve liberty under monarchy will restrain effectually a bad prince, without being ever felt as shackles by a good one. Our constitution is brought, or almost brought, to such a point, a point of perfection I think it, that no king, who is not, in the true meaning of the word, a patriot, can govern Britain with ease, security, honor, dignity, or indeed with sufficient power and strength. But yet a king, who is a patriot may govern with all the former; and, besides them, with power as extended as the most absolute monarch can boast, and a power, too, far more agreeable in the enjoyment as well as more effectual in the operation.

To attain these great and noble ends, the patriotism must be real, and not in show alone. It is something to desire to appear a patriot: and the desire of having fame is a step towards deserving it, because it is a motive the more to deserve it. If it be true, as Tacitus says, "contemptu famæ contemni virtutem," that a contempt of a good name, or an indifference about it, begets or accompanies always a contempt of virtue; the contrary will be true: and they are certainly both true. But this motive alone is not sufficient. To constitute a patriot, whether king or subject, there must be something more substantial than a desire of fame, in the composition; and if there be not, this desire of fame will never rise above that sentiment which may be compared to the coquetry of women; a fondness of transient applause, which is courted by vanity, given by flattery, and spends itself in show, like the qualities which acquire it. Patriotism must be founded in great principles, and supported by great virtues. The chief of these principles I have endeavored to trace; and I will not scruple to assert, that a man can be a good king upon no other. He may, without them and by complection, be unambitious, generous, good-natured; but, without them, the exercise even of these virtues will be often ill directed: and, with principles of another sort, he will be drawn easily, notwithstanding these virtues, from all the purposes of his institution.

I mention these opposite principles the rather, because, instead of wondering that so many kings, unfit and unworthy to be trusted with the government of mankind, appear in the world, I have been tempted to wonder that there are any tolerable; when I have considered the flattery that environs them most commonly from the cradle, and the tendency of all those false notions that are instilled into them by precept, and by example, by the habits of courts, and by the interested selfish views of courtiers. They are bred to esteem themselves of a distinct and superior species among men, as men are among animals.

Louis the Fourteenth was a strong instance of the effect of this education, which trains up kings to be tyrants, without knowing that they are so. That oppression under which he kept his people, during the whole course of a long reign, might proceed, in some degree, from the natural haughtiness of his temper; but it proceeded, in a greater degree, from the principles and habits of his education. By this he had been brought to look on his kingdom as a patrimony that descended to him from his ancestors, and that was to be considered in no other light: so that when a very considerable man had discoursed to him at large of the miserable condition, to which his people was reduced, and had frequently used this word, " l'etat;" though the king approved the substance of all he had said, yet he was shocked at the frequent repetition of this word, and complained of it as of a kind of indecency to himself. This will not appear so strange to our second as it may very justly to our first reflections; for what wonder is it, that princes are easily betrayed into an error that takes its rise in the general imperfection of our nature, in our pride, our vanity, and our presumption? The bastard children, but the children still, of self-love; a spurious brood, but often a favorite brood, that governs the whole family. As men are apt to make themselves the measure of all being, so they make themselves the final cause of all creation. Thus the reputed orthodox philosophers in all ages have taught, that the world was made for man, the earth for him to inhabit, and all the luminous bodies, in the immense expanse around us, for him to gaze at. Kings do no more, no, not so much, when they imagine themselves the final cause for which societies were formed, and governments instituted.

This capital error, in which almost every prince is confirmed by his education, has so great extent and so general influence, that a right to do every iniquitous thing in government may be derived from it. But, as if this was not enough, the characters of princes are spoiled many more ways by their education. I shall not descend into a detail of such particulars, nor presume so much as to hint what regulations might be made about the education of princes, nor what part our parliaments might take occasionally in this momentous affair, lest I should appear too refining, or too presumptuous, in my speculations. But I may assert in general, that the indifference of mankind upon this head, especially in a government constituted like ours, is monstrous.

I may also take notice of another cause of the mistakes of princes, I mean the general conduct of those who are brought near to their persons. Such men, let me say, have a particular duty arising from this very situation; a duty common to them all, because it arises not from their stations, which are different, but from their situation, which is the same. To enumerate the various applications of this duty would be too minute and tedious; but this may suffice, that all such men should bear constantly in mind, that the master they serve is, or is to be the king of their country: that their attachment to him, therefore, is not to be like that of other servants to other masters, for his sake alone, or for his sake and their own, but for the sake of their country likewise.

Craterus loves the king, but Hephestion loves Alexander, was a saying of the last that has been often quoted, but not censured as it ought to be. Alexander gave the preference to the attachment of Hephestion; but this preference was due undoubtedly to that of Craterus. Attachment to a private person must comprehend a great concern for his character and his interests: but attachment to one who is, or may be a king, much more; because the character of the latter is more important to himself and others; and because his interests are vastly more complicated with those of his country, and in some sort with those of mankind. Alexander himself seemed, upon one occasion, to make the distinction that should be always made between our attachment to a prince, and to any private person. It was when Parmenio advised him to accept the terms of peace which Darius offered: they were great, he thought them so; but he thought, no matter for my purpose whether justly or not, that it would be unbecoming him to accept them; therefore he rejected them, but acknowledged, that " he would have done as he was advised to do, if he had been Parmenio."

As to persons who are not about a prince in the situation here spoken of, they can do little more than proportion their applause, and the demonstrations of their confidence and affection, to the benefits they actually receive from the prince on the throne, or to the just expectations that a successor gives them. It is of the latter I propose to speak here particularly. If he gives them those of a good reign, we may assure ourselves that they will carry, and in this case they ought to carry that applause, and those demonstrations of their confidence and affection, as high as such a prince himself can desire. Thus the prince and the people take, in effect, a sort of engagement with one another; the prince to govern well, and the people to honor and obey him. If he gives them expectations of a bad reign, they have this obligation to him at least, that he puts them early on their guard; and an obligation, and an advantage it will be, if they prepare for his accession as for a great and inevitable evil; and if they guard on every occasion against the ill use, they foresee, that he will make of money and power. Above all, they should not suffer themselves to be caught in the common snare, which is laid under specious pretences of " gaining such a prince, and of keeping him by public compliances out of bad hands." That argument has been pressed more than once, has prevailed, and has been fruitful of most pernicious consequences. None indeed can be more absurd. It is not unlike the reasoning of those savages who worship the devil, not because they love him or honor him, or expect any good from him, but that he may do them no hurt. Nay, it is more absurd; for the savages suppose that the devil has, independently of them, the power to hurt them: whereas the others put more power into the hands of a prince, because he has already some power to hurt them; and trust to the justice and gratitude of one, who wants sense, virtue, or both, rather than increase and fortify the barriers against his folly and his vices.

But the truth is, that men, who reason and act in this manner, either mean, or else are led by such as mean, nothing more than to make a private court at the public expense; who choose to be the instruments of a bad king rather than to be out of power; and who are often so wicked, that they would prefer such a service to that of the best of kings. In fine, these reasons, and every other reason for providing against a bad reign in prospect, acquire a new force, when one weak or wicked prince is, in the order of succession, to follow another of the same character. Such provisions indeed are hardest to be obtained when they are the most necessary; that is, when the spirit of liberty begins to flag in a free people, and when they become disposed, by habits that have grown insensibly upon them, to a base submission. But they are necessary too, even when they are easiest to be obtained; that is, when the spirit of liberty is in full strength, and a disposition, to oppose all instances of mal-administration, and to resist all attempts on liberty, is universal. In both cases, the endeavors of every man who loves his country will be employed with incessant care and constancy to obtain them, that good government and liberty may be the better preserved and secured; but in the latter case for this further reason also, that the preservation and security of these may be provided for, not only better but more consistently with public tranquillity, by constitutional methods, and a legal course of opposition to the excesses of regal or ministerial power. What I touch upon here might be made extremely plain; and I think the observation would appear to be of no small importance: but I should be carried too far from my subject, and my subject will afford me matter of more agreeable speculation.

It is true that a prince, who gives just reasons to expect that his reign will be that of a Patriot King, may not always meet, and from all persons, such returns as such expectations deserve: but they must not hinder either the prince from continuing to give them, or the people from continuing to acknowledge them. United, none can hurt them: and if no artifice interrupts, no power can defeat, the effects of their perseverance. It will blast many a wicked project, keep virtue in countenance, and vice, to some degree at least, in awe. Nay, if it should fail to have these effects, if we should even suppose a good prince to suffer with the people, and in some measure for them, yet many advantages would accrue to him: for instance, the cause of the people he is to govern, and his own cause would be made the same by their common enemies. He would feel grievances himself as a subject, before he had the power of imposing them as a king. He would be formed in that school out of which the greatest and the best of monarchs have come, the school of affliction: and all the vices, which had prevailed before his reign, would serve as so many foils to the glories of it. But I hasten to speak of the greatest of all these advantages, and of that which a Patriot King will esteem to be such; whose ways of thinking and acting to so glorious a purpose as the re-establishment of a free constitution, when it has been shook by the iniquity of former administrations, I shall endeavor to explain.

What I have here said will pass among some for the reveries of a distempered brain, at best for the vain speculations of an idle man who has lost sight of the world, or who had never sagacity enough to discern in government the practicable from the impracticable. Will it not be said, that this is advising a king to rouse a spirit which may turn against himself; to reject the sole expedient of governing a limited monarchy with success; to labor to confine, instead of laboring to extend, his power: to patch up an old constitution, which his people are disposed to lay aside, instead of forming a new one more agreeable to them, and more advantageous to him; to refuse, in short, to be an absolute monarch, when every circumstance invites him to it? All these particulars, in every one of which the question is begged, will be thus represented, and will be then ridiculed as paradoxes fit to be ranked among the "mirabilia et inopinata" of the Stoics, and such as no man in his senses can maintain in earnest. These judgments and these reasonings may be expected in an age as futile and as corrupt as ours: in an age wherein so many betray the cause of liberty, and act not only without regard, but in direct opposition, to the most important interests of their country; not only occasionally, by surprise, by weakness, by strong temptation, or sly seduction, but constantly, steadily, by deliberate choice, and in pursuance of principles they avow and propagate: in an age when so many others shrink from the service of their country, or promote it coolly and uncertainly, in subordination to their own interest and humor, or to those of a party: in an age, when to assert the truth is called spreading of delusion, and to assert the cause of liberty and good government, is termed sowing of sedition. But I have declared already my unconcernedness at the censure or ridicule of such men as these; for whose supposed abilities I have much well-grounded contempt, and against whose real immorality I have as just indignation.

Let us come, therefore, to the bar of reason and experience, where we shall find these paradoxes admitted as plain and almost self-evident propositions, and these reveries and vain speculations as important truths, confirmed by experience in all ages and all countries.

Machiavel is an author who should have great authority with the persons likely to oppose me. He proposes to princes the amplification of their power, the extent of their dominion, and the subjection of their people, as the sole objects of their policy. He devises and recommends all means that tend to these purposes, without the consideration of any duty owing to God or man, or any regard to the morality or immorality of actions. Yet even he declares the affectation of virtue to be useful to princes: he is so far on my side in the present question. The only difference between us is, I would have the virtue real: he requires no more than the appearance of it.

In the tenth chapter of the first book of Discourses, he appears convinced, such is the force of truth, but how consistently with himself let others determine, that the supreme glory of a prince accrues to him who establishes good government and a free constitution; and that a prince, ambitious of fame, must wish to come into possession of a disordered and corrupted state, not to finish the wicked work that others have begun, and to complete the ruin, but to stop the progress of the first, and to prevent the last. He thinks this not only the true way to fame, but to security and quiet; as the contrary leads, for here is no third way, and a prince must make his option between these two, not only to infamy, but to danger and to perpetual disquietude. He represents those who might establish a commonwealth or a legal monarchy, and who choose to improve the opportunity of establishing tyranny, that is, monarchy without any rule of law, as men who are deceived by false notions of good, and false appearances of glory, and who are in effect blind to their true interest in every respect: " ne si auvegono per questo partito quanta fama, quanta gloria, quanto honore, sicurta, quiete, con satisfatione d'animo é fuggono, et in quanta infamia, vituperio, biasimo, pericolo et inquietudine incorrono." He touches another advantage which patriot princes reap: and in that he contradicts flatly the main point on which his half-taught scholars insist. He denies that such princes diminish their power by circumscribing it: and affirms, with truth on his side, that Timoleon, and others of the same character whom he had cited, possessed as great authority in their country, with every other advantage besides, as Dionysius or Phalaris had acquired, with the loss of all those advantages. Thus far Machiavel reasons justly; but he takes in only a part of his subject, and confines himself to those motives that should determine a wise prince to maintain liberty, because it is his interest to do so. He rises no higher than the consideration of mere interest, of fame, of security, of quiet, and of power, all personal to the prince: and by such motives alone even his favorite Borgia might have been determined to affect the virtues of a patriot prince; more than which this great doctor in political knowledge would not have required of him. But he is far from going up to that motive which should above all determine a good prince to hold this conduct, because it is his duty to do so; a duty that he owes to God by one law, and to his people by another. Now it is with this that I shall begin what I intend to offer concerning the system of principles and conduct by which a Patriot King will govern himself and his people. I shall not only begin higher, but descend into more detail, and keep still in my eye the application of the whole to the constitution of Great Britain, even to the present state of our nation, and temper of our people.

I think enough has been already said, to establish the first and true principles of monarchical and indeed of every other kind of government: and I will say with confidence, that no principles but these, and such as these, can be advanced, which deserve to be treated seriously; though Mr. Locke condescended to examine those of Filmer, more out of regard to the prejudices of the time, than to the importance of the work. Upon such foundations we must conclude, that since men were directed by nature to form societies, because they cannot by their nature subsist without them, nor in a state of individuality; and since they were directed in like manner to establish governments, because societies cannot be maintained without them, nor subsist in a state of anarchy; the ultimate end of all governments is the good of the people, for whose sake they were made, and without whose consent they could not have been made. In forming societies, and submitting to government, men gave up part of that liberty to which they are all born, and all alike. But why? Is government incompatible with a full enjoyment of liberty? By no means. But because popular liberty without government will degenerate into license, as government without sufficient liberty will degenerate into tyranny, they are mutually necessary to each other, good government to support legal liberty, and legal liberty to preserve good government.

I speak not here of people, if any such there are, who have been savage or stupid enough to submit to tyranny by original contract; nor of those nations on whom tyranny has stolen as it were imperceptibly, or been imposed by violence, and settled by prescription. I shall exercise no political casuistry about the rights of such kings, and the obligations of such people. Men are to take their lots, perhaps, in governments as in climates, to fence against the inconveniences of both, and to bear what they cannot alter. But I speak of people who have been wise and happy enough to establish, and to preserve, free constitutions of government, as the people of this island have done. To these, therefore, I say, that their kings are under the most sacred obligations that human law can create, and divine law authorise, to defend and maintain, in the first place, and preferably to every other consideration, the freedom of such constitutions.

The good of the people is the ultimate and true end of government. Governors are, therefore, appointed for this end, and the civil constitution which appoints them, and invests them with their power, is determined to do so by that law of nature and reason, which has determined the end of government, and which admits this form of government as the proper mean of arriving at it. Now, the greatest good of a people is their liberty: and, in the case here referred to, the people have judged it so, and provided for it accordingly. Liberty is to the collective body, what health is to every individual body. Without health no pleasure can be tasted by man: without liberty no happiness can be enjoyed by society. The obligation, therefore, to defend and maintain the freedom of such constitutions will appear most sacred to a Patriot King.

Kings who have weak understandings, bad hearts, and strong prejudices, and all these, as it often happens, inflamed by their passions, and rendered incurable by their self-conceit and presumption; such kings are apt to imagine, and they conduct themselves so as to make many of their subjects imagine, that the king and the people in free governments are rival powers, who stand in competition with one another, who have different interests, and must of course have different views: that the rights and privileges of the people are so many spoils taken from the right and prerogative of the crown; and that the rules and laws, made for the exercise and security of the former, are so many diminutions of their dignity, and restraints on their power.

A Patriot King will see all this in a far different and much truer light. The constitution will be considered by him as one law, consisting of two tables, containing the rule of his government, and the measure of his subjects' obedience; or as one system, composed of different parts and powers, but all duly proportioned to one another, and conspiring by their harmony to the perfection of the whole. He will make one, and but one, distinction between his rights, and those of his people: he will look on his to be a trust, and theirs a property. He will discern, that he can have a right to no more than is trusted to him by the constitution: and that his people, who had an original right to the whole by the law of nature, can have the sole indefeasible right to any part; and really have such a right to that part which they have reserved to themselves. In fine, the constitution will be reverenced by him as the law of God and of man; the force of which binds the king as much as the meanest subject, and the reason of which binds him much more.

Thus he will think, and on these principles he will act, whether he come to the throne by immediate or remote election. I say remote; for in hereditary monarchies, where men are not elected, families are: and, therefore, some authors would have it believed, that when a family has been once admitted, and an hereditary right to the crown recognised in it, that right cannot be forfeited, nor that throne become vacant, as long as any heir of the family remains. How much more agreeable to truth and to common sense would these authors have written, if they had maintained, that every prince who comes to a crown in the course of succession, were he the last of five hundred, comes to it under the same conditions under which the first took it, whether expressed or implied; as well as under those, if any such there be, which have been since made by legal authority: and that royal blood can give no right, nor length of succession any prescription, against the constitution of a government? The first and the last hold by the same tenure.

I mention this the rather, because I have an imperfect remembrance, that some scribbler was employed, or employed himself, to assert the hereditary right of the present family. A task so unnecessary to any good purpose, that, I believe, a suspicion arose of its having been designed for a bad one. A Patriot King will never countenance such impertinent fallacies, nor deign to lean on broken reeds. He knows that his right is founded on the laws of God and man, that none can shake it but himself, and that his own virtue is sufficient to maintain it against all opposition.

I have dwelt the longer on the first and general principles of monarchical government, and have recurred the oftener to them, because it seems to me that they are the seeds of patriotism, which must be sown as soon as possible in the mind of a prince, lest their growth should be checked by luxuriant weeds, which are apt to abound in such soils, and under which no crop of kingly virtues can ever flourish. A prince, who does not know the true principles, cannot propose to himself the true ends of government; and he who does not propose them will never direct his conduct steadily to them. There is not a deeper, nor a finer observation in all my Lord Bacon's works, than one which I shall apply and paraphrase on this occasion. The most compendious, the most noble, and the most effectual remedy, which can be opposed to the uncertain and irregular motions of the human mind, agitated by various passions, allured by various temptations, inclining sometimes towards a state of moral perfection, and oftener, even in the best, towards a state of moral depravation, is this. We must choose betimes such virtuous objects as are proportioned to the means we have of pursuing them, and as belong particularly to the stations we are in, and to the duties of those stations. We must determine and fix our minds in such manner upon them, that the pursuit of them may become the business, and the attainment of them the end, of our whole lives. Thus we shall imitate the great operations of nature, and not the feeble, slow, and imperfect operations of art. We must not proceed, in forming the moral character, as a statuary proceeds in forming a statue, who works sometimes on the face, sometimes on one part, and sometimes on another: but we must proceed, and it is in our power to proceed, as nature does in forming a flower, an animal, or any other of her productions; "rudimenta partium omnium simul parit et producit." "She throws out altogether, and at once, the whole system of every being, and the rudiments of all the parts." The vegetable or the animal grows in bulk and increases in strength; but is the same from the first. Just so our Patriot King must be a patriot from the first. He must be such in resolution, before he grows such in practice. He must fix at once the general principles and ends of all his actions, and determine that his whole conduct shall be regulated by them, and directed to them. When he has done this, he will have turned, by one great effort, the bent of his mind so strongly towards the perfection of a kingly character, that he will exercise with ease, and as it were by a natural determination, all the virtues of it; which will be suggested to him on every occasion by the principles wherewith his mind is imbued, and by those ends that are the constant objects of his attention.

Let us then see in what manner and with what effect he will do this, upon the greatest occasion he can have of exercising these virtues, the maintenance of liberty, and the re-establishment of a free constitution.

The freedom of a constitution rests on two points. The orders of it are one: so Machiavel calls them, and I know not how to call them more significantly. He means not only the forms and customs, but the different classes and assemblies of men, with different powers and privileges attributed to them, which are established in the state. The spirit and character of the people are the other. On the mutual conformity and harmony of these the preservation of liberty depends. To take away, or essentially to alter the former, cannot be brought to pass, whilst the latter remains in original purity and vigor: nor can liberty be destroyed by this method, unless the attempt be made with a military force sufficient to conquer the nation, which would not submit in this case till it was conquered, nor with much security to the conqueror even then. But these orders of the state may be essentially altered, and serve more effectually to the destruction of liberty, than the taking of them away would serve, if the spirit and character of the people are lost.

Now this method of destroying liberty is the most dangerous on many accounts, particularly on this; that even the reign of the weakest prince, and the policy of the weakest ministry, may effect the destruction, when circumstances are favorable to this method. If a people is growing corrupt, there is no need of capacity to contrive, nor of insinuation to gain, nor of plausibility to seduce, nor of eloquence to persuade, nor of authority to impose, nor of courage to attempt. The most incapable, awkward, ungracious, shocking, profligate, and timorous wretches, invested with power, and masters of the purse, will be sufficient for the work, when the people are accomplices in it. Luxury is rapacious; let them feed it: the more it is fed, the more profuse it will grow. Want is the consequence of profusion, venality of want, and dependence of venality. By this progression, the first men of a nation will become the pensioners of the last; and he who has talents, the most implicit tool to him who has none. The distemper will soon descend, not indeed to make a deposite below, and to remain there, but to pervade the whole body.

It may seem a singular, but it is perhaps a true proposition, that such a king and such a ministry are more likely to begin, and to pursue with success, this method of destroying a free constitution of government, than a king and a ministry that were held in great esteem would be. This very esteem might put many on their guard against the latter; but the former may draw from contempt the advantage of not being feared: and an advantage this is in the beginning of corruption. Men are willing to excuse, not only to others but to themselves, the first steps they take in vice, and especially in vice that affects the public, and whereof the public has a right to complain. Those, therefore, who might withstand corruption in one case, from a persuasion that the consequence was too certain to leave them any excuse, may yield to it when they can flatter themselves, and endeavor to flatter others, that liberty cannot be destroyed, nor the constitution be demolished, by such hands as hold the sceptre, and guide the reins of the administration. But alas! the flattery is gross, and the excuse without color. These men may ruin their country, but they cannot impose on any, unless it be on themselves. Nor will even this imposition on themselves be long necessary. Their consciences will be soon seared, by habit and by example: and they, who wanted an excuse to begin, will want none to continue and to complete, the tragedy of their country. Old men will outlive the shame of losing liberty, and young men will arise who know not that it ever existed. A spirit of slavey will oppose and oppress the spirit of liberty, and seem at least to be the genius of the nation. Such too it will become in time, when corruption has once grown to this height, unless the progress of it can be interrupted.

How inestimable a blessing therefore must the succession of a Patriot King be esteemed in such circumstances as these, which would be a blessing, and a great one too, in any other? He, and he alone, can save a country whose ruin is so far advanced. The utmost that private men can do, who remain untainted by the general contagion, is to keep the spirit of liberty alive in a few breasts; to protest against what they cannot hinder, and to claim on every occasion what they cannot by their own strength recover.

Machiavel has treated, in the discourses before cited, this question, "whether, when the people are grown corrupt, a free government can be maintained, if they enjoy it; or established, if they enjoy it not?" And upon the whole matter he concludes for the difficulty, or rather the impossibility, of succeeding in either case. It will be worth while to observe his way of reasoning. He asserts very truly, and proves by the example of the Roman commonwealth, that those orders which are proper to maintain liberty, whilst a people remain uncorrupt, become improper and hurtful to liberty, when a people is grown corrupt. To remedy this abuse, new laws alone will not be sufficient. These orders, therefore, must be changed, according to him, and the constitution must be adapted to the depraved manners of the people. He shows, that such a change in the orders, and constituent parts of the government, is impracticable, whether the attempt be made by gentle and slow, or by violent and precipitate measures: and from thence he concludes, that a free commonwealth can neither be maintained by a corrupt people, nor be established among them. But he adds, that " if this can possibly be done, it must be done by drawing the constitution to the monarchical form of government," "acciochè quelli huomini i quali dalle leggi non possono essere corretti, fussero da una podestá, in qualche modo, frenati." " That a corrupt people, whom law cannot correct, may be restrained and corrected by a kingly power." Here is the hinge on which the whole turns.

Another advantage that a free monarchy has over all other

forms of free government, besides the advantage of being more easily and more usefully tempered with aristocratical and democratical powers, which is mentioned above, is this. Those governments are made up of different parts, and are apt to be disjointed by the shocks to which they are exposed: but a free monarchical government is more compact, because there is a part the more that keeps, like the keystone of a vault, the whole building together. They cannot be mended in a state of corruption, they must be in effect constituted anew, and in that attempt they may be dissolved forever: but this is not the case of a free monarchy. To preserve liberty by new laws and new schemes of government, whilst the corruption of a people continues and grows, is absolutely impossible: but to restore and preserve it under old laws, and an old constitution, by reinfusing into the minds of men the spirit of this constitution, is not only possible, but is, in a particular manner, easy to a king. A corrupt commonwealth remains without remedy, though all the orders and forms of it subsist: a free monarchical government cannot remain absolutely so, as long as the orders and forms of the constitution subsist. These, alone, are indeed nothing more than the dead letter of freedom, or masks of liberty. In the first character they serve to no good purpose whatsoever: in the second they serve to a bad one; because tyranny, or government by will, becomes more severe, and more secure, under their disguise, than it would if it was barefaced and avowed. But a king can, easily to himself and without violence to his people, renew the spirit of liberty in their minds, quicken this dead letter, and pull off this mask.

As soon as corruption ceases to be an expedient of government, and it will cease to be such as soon as a Patriot King is raised to the throne, the panacea is applied; the spirit of the constitution revives of course: and, as fast as it revives, the orders and forms of the constitution are restored to their primitive integrity, and become what they were intended to be, real barriers against arbitrary power, not blinds nor masks under which tyranny may lie concealed. Depravation of manners exposed the constitution to ruin: reformation will secure it. Men decline easily from virtue; for there is a devil too in the political system, a constant tempter at hand: a Patriot King will want neither power nor inclination to cast out this devil, to make the temptation cease, and to deliver his subjects, if not from the guilt, yet from the consequence, of their fall. Under him they will not only cease to do evil, but learn to do well; for, by rendering public virtue and real capacity the sole means of acquiring any degree of power or profit in the state, he will set the passions of their hearts on the side of liberty and good government. A Patriot King is the most powerful of all reformers; for he is himself a sort of standing miracle, so rarely seen and so little understood, that the sure effects of his appearance will be admiration and love in every honest breast, confusion and terror to every guilty conscience, but submission and resignation in all. A new people will seem to arise with a new king. Innumerable metamorphoses, like those which poets feign, will happen in very deed: and, while men are conscious that they are the same individuals, the difference of their sentiments will almost persuade them that they are changed into different beings.

But, that we may not expect more from such a king than even he can perform, it is necessary to premise another general observation, after which I shall descend into some that will be more particular.

Absolute stability is not to be expected in any thing human; for that which exists immutably exists alone necessarily, and this attribute of the Supreme Being, can neither belong to man, nor to the works of man. The best instituted governments, like the best constituted animal bodies, carry in them the seeds of their destruction: and, though they grow and improve for a time, they will soon tend visibly to their dissolution. Every hour they live is an hour the less that they have to live. All that can be done, therefore, to prolong the duration of a good government, is to draw it back, on every favorable occasion, to the first good principles on which it was founded. When these occasions happen often, and are well improved, such governments are prosperous and durable. When they happen seldom, or are ill improved, these political bodies live in pain, or in languor, and die soon.

A Patriot King affords one of the occasions I mention in a free monarchical state, and the very best that can happen. It should be improved, like snatches of fair weather at sea, to repair the damages sustained in the last storm, and to prepare to resist the next. For such a king cannot secure to his people a succession of princes like himself. He will do all he can towards it, by his example and by his instruction. But after all, the royal mantle will not convey the spirit of patriotism into another king, as the mantle of Elijah did the gift of prophecy into another prophet. The utmost he can do, and that which deserves the utmost gratitude from his subjects, is to restore good government, to revive the spirit of it, and to maintain and confirm both, during the whole course of his reign. The rest his people must do for themselves. If they do not, they will have none but themselves to blame: if they do, they will have the principal obligation to him. In all events, they will have been free men one reign the longer by his means, and perhaps more; since he will leave them much better prepared and disposed to defend their liberties, than he found them.

This general observation being made, let us now descend, in some detail, to the particular steps and measures that such a king must pursue, to merit a much nobler than all those which many princes of the west, as well as the east, are so proud to accumulate.

First, then, he must begin to govern as soon as he begins to reign. For the very first steps he makes in government will give the first impression, and as it were the presage of his reign; and may be of great importance in many other respects besides that of opinion and reputation. His first care will be, no doubt, to purge his court, and to call into the administration such men as he can assure himself will serve on the same principles on which he intends to govern.

As to the first point; if the precedent reign has been bad, we know how he will find the court composed. The men in power will be some of those adventurers, busy and bold, who thrust and crowd themselves early into the intrigue of party and the management of affairs of state, often without true ability, always without true ambition, or even the appearances of virtue: who mean nothing more than what is called making a fortune, the acquisition of wealth to satisfy avarice, and of titles and ribands to satisfy vanity. Such as these are sure to be employed by a weak, or a wicked king: they impose on the first, and are chosen by the last. Nor is it marvellous that they are so, since every other want is supplied in them by the want of good principles and a good conscience; and since these defects become ministerial perfections, in a reign when measures are pursued and designs carried on that every honest man will disapprove. All the prostitutes who set themselves to sale, all the locusts who devour the land, with crowds of spies, parasites, and sycophants, will surround the throne under the patronage of such ministers; and whole swarms of little, noisome, nameless insects will hum and buzz in every corner of the court. Such ministers will be cast off, and such abettors of a ministry will be chased away together, and at once, by a Patriot King.

Some of them perhaps, will be abandoned by him; not to party fury, but to national justice; not to sate private resentments, and to serve particular interests, but to make satisfaction for wrongs done to their country, and to stand as examples of terror to future administrations. Clemency makes, no doubt, an amiable part of the character I attempt to draw; but clemency, to be a virtue, must have its bounds, like other virtues: and surely these bounds are extended enough by a maxim I have read somewhere, that frailties and even vices may be passed over, but not enormous crimes; "multa donanda ingeniis puto, sed donanda vitia, non portenta."

Among the bad company, with which such a court will abound, may be reckoned a sort of men too low to be much regarded, and too high to be quite neglected; the lumber of every administration, the furniture of every court. These gilt carved things are seldom answerable for more than the men on a chess-board, who are moved about at will, and on whom the conduct of the game is not to be charged. Some of these every prince must have about him. The pageantry of a court requires that he should: and this pageantry, like many other despicable things, ought not to be laid aside. But as much sameness as there may appear in the characters of this sort of men, there is one distinction that will be made, whenever a good prince succeeds to the throne after an iniquitous administration: the distinction I mean is, between those who have affected to dip themselves deeply in precedent iniquities, and those who have had the virtue to keep aloof from them, or the good luck not to be called to any share in them. And thus much for the first point, that of purging his court.

As to the second, that of calling to his administration such men as he can assure himself will serve on the same principles on which he intends to govern, there is no need to enlarge much upon it. A good prince will no more choose ill men, than a wise prince will choose fools. Deception in one case is indeed more easy than in the other; because a knave may be an artful hypocrite, whereas a silly fellow can never impose himself for a man of sense. And least of all, in a country like ours, can either of these deceptions happen, if any degree of the discernment of spirits be employed to choose. The reason is, because every man here, who stands forward enough in rank and reputation to be called to the councils of his king, must have given proofs beforehand of his patriotism, as well as of his capacity, if he has either, sufficient to determine his general character.

There is, however, one distinction to be made as to the capacity of ministers, on which I will insist a little: because I think it very important at all times, particularly so at this time; and because it escapes observation most commonly. The distinction I mean is that between a cunning man and a wise man: and this distinction is built on a manifest difference in nature, how imperceptible soever it may become to weak eyes, or to eyes that look at their object through the false medium of custom and habit. My Lord Bacon says, that cunning is left-handed or crooked wisdom. I would rather say, that it is a part, but the lowest part, of wisdom; employed alone by some, because they have not the other parts to employ; and by some, because it is as much as they want, within those bounds of action which they prescribe to themselves, and sufficient to the ends that they propose. The difference seems to consist in degree, and application, rather than in kind. Wisdom is neither left-handed, nor crooked: but the heads of some men contain little, and the hearts of others employ it wrong. To use my Lord Bacon's own comparison, the cunning man knows how to pack the cards, the wise man how to play the game better: but it would be of no use to the first to pack the cards, if his knowledge stopped here, and he had no skill in the game; nor to the second to play the game better, if he did not know how to pack the cards, that he might unpack them by new shuffling. Inferior wisdom or cunning may get the better of folly: but superior wisdom will get the better of cunning. Wisdom and cunning have often the same objects; but a wise man will have more and greater in his view. The least will not fill his soul, nor ever become the principal there; but will be pursued in subserviency, in subordination at least, to the other. Wisdom and cunning may employ sometimes the same means too: but the wise man stoops to these means, and the other cannot rise above them. Simulation and dissimulation, for instance, are the chief arts of cunning: the first will be esteemed always by a wise man unworthy of him, and will be therefore avoided by him, in every possible case; for, to resume my Lord Bacon's comparison, simulation is put on that we may look into the cards of another, whereas dissimulation intends nothing more than to hide our own. Simulation is a stiletto, not only an offensive, but an unlawful weapon: and the use of it may be rarely, very rarely, excused, but never justified. Dissimulation is a shield, as secrecy is armor: and it is no more possible to preserve secrecy in the administratian of public affairs without some degree of dissimulation, than it is to succeed in it without secrecy. Those two arts of cunning are like the alloy mingled with pure ore. A little is necessary, and will not debase the coin below its proper standard; but if more than that little be employed, the coin loses its currency, and the coiner his credit.

We may observe much the same difference between wisdom and cunning, both as to the objects they propose and to the means they employ, as we observe between the visual powers of different men. One sees distinctly the objects that are near to him, their immediate relations, and their direct tendencies: and a sight like this serves well enough the purpose of those who concern themselves no further. The cunning minister is one of those: he neither sees, nor is concerned to see, any further than his personal interests, and the support of his administration, require. If such a man overcomes any actual difficulty, avoids any immediate distress, or, without doing either of these effectually, gains a little time, by all the low artifice which cunning is ready to suggest and baseness of mind to employ, he triumphs, and is flattered by his mercenary train, on the great event; which amounts often to no more than this, that he got into distress by one series of faults, and out of it by another. The wise minister sees, and is concerned to see further, because government has a further concern: he sees the objects that are distant as well as those that are near, and all their remote relations, and even their indirect tendencies. He thinks of fame as well as of applause, and prefers that, which to be enjoyed must be given, to that which may be bought. He considers his administration as a single day in the great year of government; but as a day that is affected by those which went before, and that must affect those which are to follow. He combines, therefore, and compares all these objects, relations, and tendencies; and the judgment he makes, on an entire not a partial survey of them, is the rule of his conduct. That scheme of the reason of state, which lies open before a wise minister, contains all the great principles of government, and all the great interests of his country: so that, as he prepares some events, he prepares against others, whether they be likely to happen during his administration, or in some future time.

Many reflections might be added to these, and many examples be brought to illustrate them. Some I could draw from the men I have seen at the head of business, and make very strong contrasts of men of great wisdom with those of mere cunning.— But I conclude this head, that I may proceed to another of no less importance.

To espouse no party, but to govern like the common father of his people, is so essential to the character of a Patriot King, that he who does otherwise forfeits the title. It is the peculiar privilege and glory of this character, that princes who maintain it, and they alone, are so far from the necessity, that they are not exposed to the temptation, of governing by a party; which must always end in the government of a faction: the faction of the prince, if he has ability; the faction of his ministers, if he has not; and, either one way or other, in the oppression of the people. For faction is to party what the superlative is to the positive: party is a political evil, and faction is the worst of all parties. The true image of a free people, governed by a Patriot King, is that of a patriarchal family, where the head and all the members are united by one common interest, and animated by one common spirit: and where, if any are perverse enough to have another, they will be soon borne down by the superiority of those who have the same; and, far from making a division, they will but confirm the union of the little state. That to approach as near as possible to these ideas of perfect government, and social happiness under it, is desirable in every state, no man will be absurd enough to deny. The sole question is, therefore, how near to them it is possible to attain? For, if this attempt be not absolutely impracticable, all the views of a Patriot King will be directed to make it succeed. Instead of abetting the divisions of his people, he will endeavor to unite them, and to be himself the centre of their union: instead of putting himself at the head of one party in order to govern his people, he will put himself at the head of his people in order to govern, or more properly to subdue, all parties. Now, to arrive at this desirable union, and to maintain it, will be found more difficult in some cases than in others, but absolutely impossible in none, to a wise and good prince.

If his people are united in their submission to him, and in their attachment to the established government, he must not only espouse but create a party, in order to govern by one: and what should tempt him to pursue so wild a measure? A prince, who aims at more power than the constitution gives him, may be so tempted; because he may hope to obtain in the disorders of the state what cannot be obtained in quiet times; and because contending parties will give what a nation will not. Parties, even before they degenerate into absolute factions, are still numbers of men associated together for certain purposes, and certain interests, which are not, or which are not allowed to be, those of the community by others. A more private or personal interest comes but too soon, and too often, to be superadded, and to grow predominant in them: and when it does so, whatever occasions or principles began to form them, the same logic prevails in them that prevails in every church. The interest of the state is supposed to be that of the party, as the interest of religion is supposed to be that of the church: and, with this pretence or prepossession, the interest of the state becomes, like that of religion, a remote consideration, is never pursued for its own sake, and is often sacrificed to the other. A king, therefore, who has ill designs to carry on, must endeavor to divide an united people; and by blending or seeming to blend his interests with that of a party, he may succeed perhaps, and his party and he may share the spoils of a ruined nation: but such a party is then become a faction, such a king is a tyrant, and such a government is a conspiracy. A Patriot King must renounce his character, to have such designs; or act against his own designs, to pursue such methods. Both are too absurd to be supposed. It remains, therefore, that as all the good ends of government are most attainable in a united state, and as the divisions of a people can serve to bad' purposes alone, the king we suppose here will deem the union of his subjects his greatest advantage, and will think himself happy to find that established, which he would have employed the whole labor of his life to bring about. This seems so plain, that I am ready to make excuses for having insisted at all upon it.

Let us turn ourselves to another supposition, to that of a divided state. This will fall in oftener with the ordinary course of things in free governments, and especially after iniquitous and weak administrations. Such a state may be better or worse, and the great and good purposes of a Patriot King more or less attainable in it, according to the different nature of those divisions; and, therefore, we will consider this state in different lights.

A people may be united in submission to the prince, and to the establishment, and yet be divided about general principles, or particular measures of government. In the first case, they will do by their constitution what has frequently been done by the Scriptures, strain it to their own notions and prejudices; and, if they cannot strain it, alter it as much as is necessary to render it conformable to them. In the second, they will support or oppose particular acts of administrations, and defend or attack the persons employed in them; and both these ways a conflict of parties may arise, but no great difficulty to a prince who determines to pursue the union of his subjects, and the prosperity of his kingdoms independently of all parties.

When parties are divided by different notions and principles concerning some particular ecclesiastical, or civil institutions, the constitution, which should be their rule, must be that of the prince. He may and he ought to show his dislike or his favor, as he judges the constitution may be hurt or improved, by one side or the other. The hurt he is never to suffer, not for his own sake; and, therefore, surely not for the sake of any whimsical, factious, or ambitious set of men. The improvement he must always desire; but as every new mortification in a scheme of government and of national policy is of great importance, and requires more and deeper consideration than the warmth, and hurry, and rashness of party conduct admit, the duty of a prince seems to require that he should render by his influence the proceedings more orderly and more deliberately, even when he approves the end to which they are directed. All this may be done by him without fomenting division: and, far from forming or espousing a party, he will defeat party in defence of the constitution, on some occasions; and lead men, from acting with a party spirit, to act with a national spirit, on others.

When the division is about particular measures of government, and the conduct of the administration is alone concerned, a Patriot King will stand in want of party as little as in any other

case. Under his reign, the opportunities of forming an opposition of this sort will be rare, and the pretences generally weak.
Nay, the motives to it will lose much of their force, when a
government is strong in reputation, and men are kept in good
humor by feeling the rod of a party on no occasion, though they
feel the weight of the sceptre on some. Such opportunities,
however, may happen; and there may be reason, as well as pretences, sometimes for opposition even in such a reign: at least
we will suppose so, that we may include in this argument every
contingent case. Grievances then are complained of, mistakes
and abuses in government are pointed out, and ministers are
prosecuted by their enemies. Shall the prince on the throne
form a party by intrigue, and by secret and corrupt influence, to
oppose the prosecution? When the prince and the ministers are
participes criminis, when every thing is to be defended, lest
something should come out, that may unravel the silly wicked
scheme, and disclose to public sight the whole turpitude of the
administration; there is no help, this must be done, and such a
party must be formed, because such a party alone will submit to
a drudgery of this kind. But a prince, who is not in these circumstances, will not have recourse to these means. He has
others more open, more noble, and more effectual in his power:
he knows that the views of his government are right, and that
the tenor of his administration is good; but he knows that neither
he nor his ministers are infallible, nor impeccable. There may
be abuses in his government, mistakes in his administration, and
guilt in his ministers, which he has not observed: and he will be
far from imputing the complaints, that gave him occasion to
observe them, to a spirit of party; much less will he treat those
who carry on such prosecutions in a legal manner, as incendiaries, and as enemies to his government. On the contrary, he
will distinguish the voice of his people from the clamor of a faction, and will hearken to it. He will redress grievances, correct
errors, and reform or punish ministers. This he will do as a
good prince: and as a wise one, he will do it in such a manner
that his dignity shall be maintained, and that his authority shall
increase, with his reputation, by it.

Should the efforts of a mere faction be bent to calumniate his
government, and to distress the administration on groundless
pretences, and for insufficient reasons; he will not neglect, but
he will not apprehend neither, the short lived and contemptible
scheme. He will indeed have no reason to do so; for let the
fautors of mal-administration, whenever an opposition is made
to it, affect to insinuate as much as they please, that their masters
are in no other circumstances than those to which the very best
ministers stand exposed, objects of general envy and of particu-

lar malice, it will remain eternally true, that groundless opposition, in a well regulated monarchy, can never be strong and durable. To be convinced of the truth of this proposition, one needs only to reflect how many well grounded attacks have been defeated, and how few have succeeded, against the most wicked and the weakest administrations. Every king of Britain has means enough in his power, to defeat and to calm opposition. But a Patriot King, above all others, may safely rest his cause on the innocency of his administration, on the constitutional strength of the crown, and on the concurrence of his people, to whom he dares appeal, and by whom he will be supported.

To conclude all I will say on the divisions of this kind; let me add, that the case of a groundless opposition can hardly happen in a bad reign, because in such a reign just occasions of opposition must of course be frequently given, as we have allowed that they may be given sometimes, though very rarely, in a good reign; but that, whether it be well or ill grounded, whether it be that of the nation, or that of a faction, the conduct of the prince with respect to it will be the same; and one way or other this conduct must have a very fatal event. Such a prince will not mend the administration, as long as he can resist the justest and most popular opposition: and, therefore, this opposition will last and grow, as long as a free constitution is in force, and the spirit of liberty is preserved; for so long even a change of his ministers, without a change of his measures, will not be sufficient.— The former without the latter is a mere banter, and would be deemed and taken for such, by every man who did not oppose on a factious principle; that I mean of getting into power at any rate, and using it as ill, perhaps worse than the men he helped to turn out of it. Now if such men as these abound, and they will abound in the decline of a free government, a bad prince, whether he changes or does not change his ministers, may hope to govern by the spirit and art of a faction, against the spirit and strength of the nation. His character may be too low, and that of his minister too odious, to form originally even a faction that shall be able to defend them. But they may apply to their purposes, a party that was formed on far different occasions, and bring numbers to fight for a cause in which many of them would not have listed. The names, and with the names the animosity of parties, may be kept up, when the causes that formed them subsist no longer.

When a party is thus revived or continued in the spirit of a faction, the corrupt and infatuated members of it will act without any regard to right or wrong: and they who have asserted liberty in one reign, or opposed invasions of one kind, will give it up in another reign, and abet invasions of another kind; though they still distinguish themselves by the same appellation, still spread the same banner, and still deafen their adversaries and one another with the same cry. If the national cause prevails against all the wicked arts of corruption and division, that an obstinate prince and flagitious ministry can employ; yet will the struggle be long, and the difficulties, the distresses, and the danger great, both to the king and to the people. The best he can hope for, in such a case, will be to escape with a diminution of his reputation, authority, and power. He may be exposed to something worse; and his obstinacy may force things to such extremities, as they who oppose him will lament, and as the preservation of liberty and good government can alone justify. If the wicked arts I speak of prevail, faction will be propagated through the whole nation, an ill or well grounded opposition will be the question no longer, and the contest among parties will be, who shall govern, not, how they shall be governed. In short, universal confusion will follow, and a complete victory, on any side, will enslave all sides.

I have not overcharged the draught. Such consequences must follow such a conduct; and therefore let me ask, how much more safe, more easy, more pleasant, more honorable is it, for a prince to correct, if he has not prevented, mal-administration? That he may be able to rest his cause, as I said before, on the strength of the crown and the concurrence of his people, whenever any faction presumes to rise in opposition to him.

This a Patriot King will do. He may favor one party and discourage another, upon occasions wherein the state of his kingdom makes such a temporary measure necessary: but he will espouse none, much less will he proscribe any. He will list no party, much less will he do the meanest and most imprudent thing a king can do, list himself in any. It will be his aim to pursue true principles of government independently of all: and, by a steady adherence to this measure, his reign will become an undeniable and glorious proof, that a wise and good prince may unite his subjects, and be himself the centre of their union, notwithstanding any of these divisions that have been hitherto mentioned.

Let us now view the divided state of a nation in another light. In this, the divisions will appear more odious, more dangerous; less dependent on the influence, and less subject to the authority of the crown. Such will be the state, whenever a people is divided about submission to their prince, and a party is formed, of spirit and strength sufficient to oppose, even in arms, the established government. But in this case, desperate as it may seem, a Patriot King will not despair of reconciling, and re-uniting his subjects to himself, and to one another. He may be obliged, perhaps, as Henry the Fourth of France was, to conquer his own; but then, like that great prince, if he is the conqueror, he will be the father too, of his people. He must pursue in arms those who presume to take arms against him; but he will pursue them like rebellious children whom he seeks to reclaim, and not like irreconcilable enemies whom he endeavors to exterminate. Another prince may blow up the flame of civil war by unprovoked severity, render those zealous against him who were at worst indifferent, and determine the disaffection of others to open rebellion. When he has prevailed against the faction he helped to form, as he could not have prevailed if the bent of the nation had been against him, he may be willing to ascribe his success to a party, that he may have that pretence to govern by a party: and, far from reconciling the minds that have been alienated from him, and reuniting his subjects in a willing unforced submission to him, he may be content to maintain himself on that throne, where the laws of God and man have placed him, by the melancholy expedient that usurpers and tyrants, who have no other in their power, employ; the expedient of force. But a Patriot King will act with another spirit, and entertain nobler and wiser views, from first to last, and through the whole course of such a conjuncture. Nothing less than the hearts of his people will content such a prince; nor will he think his throne established, till it is established there. That he may have time and opportunity to gain them, therefore, he will prevent the flame from breaking out, if by art and management he can do it. If he cannot, he will endeavor to keep it from spreading: and, if the phrenzy of rebellion disappoints them in both these attempts, he will remember peace, like the heroic king I just now quoted, in the midst of war. Like him he will forego advantages of pushing the latter, rather than lose an opportunity of promoting the former: like him, in the heat of battle he will spare, and in the triumph of victory condescend: like him, he will beat down the violence of this flame, by his valor, and extinguish even the embers of it, by his lenity.

It may happen, that a prince, capable of holding such a conduct as this, may not have the opportunity. He may succeed to the throne after a contrary conduct has been held: and when, among other divisions which mal-administration and the tyranny of faction have increased and confirmed, there is one against the established government still in being, though not still in arms. The use is obvious, which a faction in power might make of such a circumstance under a weak prince, by ranking in that division all those who opposed the administration; or at least by holding out equal danger to him from two quarters, from their enemies who meant him no harm, and from his enemies who

could do him none.　But so gross an artifice will not impose on
a prince of another character: he will soon discern the distinctions it becomes him to make.　He will see, in this instance, how
faction breeds, nourishes, and perpetuates faction: he will observe how far that of the court contributed to form the other, and
contributes still to keep it in countenance and credit among those
who consider more what such men are against, than what they
are for.　He will observe, how much that of the disaffected gives
pretence to the other who keeps a monopoly of power and
wealth; one of which oppresses, and the other beggars, the rest
of the nation.　His penetration will soon discover, that these
factions break in but little on the body of his people, and that it
depends on him alone to take from them even the strength they
have; because that of the former is acquired entirely by his authority and purse, and that of the latter principally by the abuse
which the former makes of both.　Upon the whole, the measures
he has to pursue towards the great object of a Patriot King, the
union of his people, will appear to him extremely easy.　How
should they be otherwise?　One of the factions must be dissolved
the moment that the favor of the prince is withdrawn: and the
other is disarmed, as soon as it is marked out.　It will have no
shelter, and it must therefore be so marked out, under a good
and wise administration; for, whether the members of it avow
their principles by refusing those tests of fidelity which the law
requires, or perjure themselves by taking them, they will be
known alike.　One difference, and but one, will be made between them in the general sense of mankind, a difference arising
from the greater degree of infamy that will belong justly to the
latter.　The first may pass for fools; the latter must pass, without excuse, for knaves.

The terms I use sound harshly, but the censure is just: and it
will appear to be so in the highest degree, and upon the highest
reason, if we stop to make a reflection or two, that deserve very
well to be made, on the conduct of our jacobites; for I desire no
stronger instance on which to establish the censure, and to justify
the terms I have used.　Now all these, whether they swear or
whether they do not, are liable to one particular objection, that
did not lie against those who were, in former days, enemies to
the king on the throne.　In the days of York and Lancaster, for
instance, a man might be against the prince on the throne, without being against the constitution of his country.　The constitution conveyed the crown by hereditary right in the same family:
and he who was a Yorkist, and he who was a Lancastrian,
might, and I doubt not did, pretend in every contest to have this
right on his side.　The same constitution was acknowledged by
both: and, therefore, so much indulgence was shown by law to

both, at least in the time of Henry the Seventh, that submission
to a king *de facto* could not be imputed as a crime to either.
Thus again, to descend lower in history; when the exclusion of
the Duke of York was pressed in the reign of Charles the Second,
the right of that prince to the crown was not disputed. His
divine right indeed, such a divine right as his grandfather and
father had asserted before him, was not much regarded; but his
right by the constitution, his legal right, was sufficiently owned
by those who insisted on a law as necessary to bar it. But every
jacobite, at this time, goes beyond all these examples; and is a
rebel to the constitution under which he is born, as well as to the
prince on the throne. The law of his country has settled the
right of succession in a new family. He resists this law, and
asserts, on his own private authority, not only a right in contradiction to it, but a right extinguished by it. This absurdity is
so great, that it cannot be defended, except by advancing a
greater: and therefore it is urged, that no power on earth could
alter the constitution in this respect, nor extinguish a right to
the crown inherent in the Stuart family, and derived from a
superior, that is, from a divine, authority. This kind of plea for
refusing submission to the laws of the land, if it was admitted,
would serve any purpose as well as that for which it is brought.
Our fanatics urged it formerly, and I do not see why a conscientious fifth monarchy-man had not as much right to urge it formerly, as a jacobite has now. But if conscience, that is private
opinion, may excuse the fifth monarchy-man and the jacobite,
who act conformably to it, from all imputations except those of
madness and folly; how shall the latter be excused when he for-
swears the principles he retains, acknowledges the right he re-
nounces, takes oaths with an intent to violate them, and calls
God to witness to a premeditated lie? Some casuistry has been
employed to excuse these men to themselves and to others. But
such casuistry, and in truth every other, destroys, by distinctions
and exceptions, all morality, and effaces the essential difference
between right and wrong, good and evil. This the schoolmen
in general have done on many occasions; the sons of Loyola in
particular: and I wish with all my heart that nothing of the same
kind could be objected to any other divines. Some political reasoning has been employed, as well as the casuistry here spoken
of, and to the same purpose. It has been said, that the conduct
of those who are enemies to the establishment, to which they
submit and swear, is justified by the principles of the revolution.
But nothing can be more false and frivolous. By the principles
of the revolution, a subject may resist, no doubt, the prince who
endeavors to ruin and enslave his people, and may push this resistance to the dethronement and exclusion of him and his race:

but will it follow, that, because we may justly take arms against a prince whose right to govern we once acknowledged, and who by subsequent acts has forfeited that right, we may swear to a right we do not acknowledge, and resist a prince whose conduct has not forfeited the right we swore to, nor given any just dispensation from our oaths?

But I shall lengthen this digression no further: it is on a subject I have treated in public writings, the refutation of which never came to my hands, and, I think, never will. I return to the subject of my present discourse. And I say, that such factions as these can never create any obstruction to a prince who pursues the union of his subjects, nor disturb the peace of his government. The men who compose them must be desperate, and impotent; the most despicable of all characters, when they go together. Every honest and sensible man will distinguish himself out of their number: and they will remain, as they deserve to be, hewers of wood, and drawers of water, to the rest of their fellow subjects.

They will remain such, if they are abandoned to themselves, and to that habitual infatuation which they have not sense and spirit enough to break. But if a prince, out of goodness or policy, should think it worth his while to take them from under this influence, and to break these habits; even this division, the most absurd of all others, will not be found incurable. A man who has not seen the inside of parties, nor had opportunities to examine nearly their secret motives, can hardly conceive how little a share principle of any sort, though principle of some sort or other he always pretended, has in the determination of their conduct. Reason has small effect on numbers. A turn of imagination, often as violent and as sudden as a gust of wind, determines their conduct: and passion is taken, by others, and by themselves too, when it grows into habit especially, for principle. What gave strength and spirit to a Jacobite party after the late king's accession? The true answer is, a sudden turn of the imaginations of a whole party to resentment and rage, that were turned a little before to quiet submission, and patient expectation. Principle had as little share in making the turn, as reason had in conducting it. Men who had sense, and temper too, before that moment, thought of nothing, after it, but setting up a tory king against a whig king: and when some of them were asked, if they were sure a popish king would make a good tory king? or whether they were determined to sacrifice their religion and liberty to him? the answer was, No; that they would take arms against him if he made attempts on either; that this might be the case, perhaps, in six months after his restoration, but that, in the mean time, they would endeavor his restoration. This is no exaggerated fact: and I leave all men to judge, to what such sentiments and conduct must be ascribed, to principle or passion, to reason or madness?   What gives obstinacy without strength, and sullenness without spirit, to the jacobite tories at this time? Another turn of imagination, or rather the same showing itself in another form; a factious habit, and a factious notion, converted into a notion of policy and honor.   They are taught to believe, that by clinging together they are a considerable weight, which may be thrown in to turn the scale in any great event; and that in the mean time, to be a steady suffering party is an honor they may flatter themselves with very justly.   Thus, they continue steady to engagements which most of them wish in their hearts they had never taken; and suffer for principles, in support of which not one of them would venture further, than talking the treason that claret inspires.

It results, therefore, from all that has been said, and from the reflections which these hints may suggest, that in whatever light we view the divided state of a people, there is none in which these divisions will appear incurable, nor an union of the members of a great community with one another, and with their head, unattainable.   It may happen in this case as it does in many others, that things uncommon may pass for improbable or impossible: and, as nothing can be more uncommon than a Patriot King, there will be no room to wonder if the natural and certain effects of his conduct should appear improbable or impossible to many.   But there is still something more in this case.   Though the union we speak of be so much for the interest of every king and every people, that their glory and their prosperity must increase, or diminish, in proportion as they approach nearer to it, or are further removed from it; yet is there another interest, by which princes and people both are often imposed upon so far, as to mistake it for their own.   The interest I mean, is that of private ambition.   It would be easy to show in many instances, and particularly in this, of uniting instead of dividing, and of governing by a national concurrence instead of governing by the management of parties and factions in the state, how widely different, nay how repugnant, the interests of private ambition and those of real patriotism are.   Men, therefore, who are warmed by the first, and have no sense of the last, will declare for division as they do for corruption, in opposition to union and to integrity of government.   They will not indeed declare directly, that the two former are in the abstract preferable; but they will affirm, with great airs of sufficiency, that both are incurable; and conclude from hence, that in practice it is necessary to comply with both.   This subterfuge once open, there is no false and immoral measure, in political management, which may not be avowed and recommended. But the very men, who hope to escape by opening it, shut it up again, and secure their own condemnation, when they labor to confirm divisions, and to propagate corruption, and thereby to create the very necessity that they plead in their excuse. Necessity of this kind there is in reality none; for it seems full as absurd to say, that popular divisions must be cultivated, because popular union cannot be procured, as it would be to say that poison must be poured into a wound, because it cannot be healed. The practice of morality, in private life, will never arrive at ideal perfection: must we give up ourselves, therefore, to all manner of immorality? and must those who are charged with our instruction endeavor to make us the most profligate of men, because they cannot make us saints?

Experience of the depravity of human nature made men desirous to unite in society and under government, that they might defend themselves the better against injuries: but the same depravity soon inspired to some the design of employing societies to invade and spoil societies; and to disturb the peace of the great commonwealth of mankind, with more force and effect in such collective bodies, than they could do individually. Just so it happens in the domestic economy of particular states: and their peace is disturbed by the same passions. Some of their members content themselves with the common benefits of society, and employ all their industry to promote the public good: but some propose to themselves a separate interest; and, that they may pursue it the more effectually, they associate it with others. Thus factions are in them, what nations are in the world; they invade and rob one another: and, while each pursues a separate interest, the common interest is sacrificed by them all: that of mankind in one case, that of some particular community in the other. This has been, and must always be, in some measure, the course of human affairs, especially in free countries, where the passions of men are less restrained by authority: and I am not wild enough to suppose that a Patriot King can change human nature. But I am reasonable enough to suppose, that, without altering human nature, he may give a check to this course of human affairs, in his own kingdom at least; that he may defeat the designs, and break the spirit of faction, instead of partaking in one, and assuming the other; and that, if he cannot render the union of his subjects universal, he may render it so general as to answer all the ends of good government, private security, public tranquillity, wealth, power, and fame.

If these ends were ever answered, they were so, surely, in this country, in the days of our Elizabeth. She found her kingdoms full of factions, and factions of another consequence and danger than these of our days, whom she would have dispersed with a puff of her breath. She could not re-unite them, it is true: the papist continued a papist, the puritan a puritan; one furious, the other sullen. But she united the great body of the people in her and their common interest, she inflamed them with one national spirit: and, thus armed, she maintained tranquillity at home, and carried succor to her friends and terror to her enemies abroad. There were cabals at her court, and intrigues among her ministers. It is said too, that she did not dislike that there should be such. But these were kept within her court. They could not creep abroad, to sow division among her people: and her greatest favorite the Earl of Essex paid the price of attempting it with his head. Let our great doctors in politics, who preach so learnedly on the trite text "divide et impera," compare the conduct of Elizabeth in this respect with that of her successor, who endeavored to govern his kingdom by the notions of a faction that he raised, and to manage his parliament by undertakers: and they must be very obstinate indeed, if they refuse to acknowledge, that a wise and good prince can unite a divided people, though a weak and wicked prince cannot; and that the consequences of national union are glory and happiness to the prince and to the people; whilst those of disunion bring shame and misery on both, and entail them too on posterity.

I have dwelt long on the last head, not only because it is of great importance in itself, and at all times, but because it is rendered more so than ever at this time, by the unexampled avowal of contrary principles. Hitherto it has been thought the highest pitch of profligacy to own, instead of concealing, crimes; and to take pride in them, instead of being ashamed of them. But in our age men have soared to a pitch still higher. The first is common, it is the practice of numbers, and by their numbers they keep one another in countenance. But the choice spirits of these days, the men of mode in politics, are far from stopping where criminals of all kinds have stopped, when they have gone even to this point; for generally the most hardened of the inhabitants of Newgate do not go so far. The men I speak of contend, that it is not enough to be vicious by practice and habit, but that it is necessary to be so by principle. They make themselves missionaries of faction as well as of corruption: they recommend both, they deride all such as imagine it possible, or fit, to retain truth, integrity, and a disinterested regard to the public in public life, and pronounce every man a fool who is not ready to act like a knave. I hope that enough has been said, though much more might have been said, to expose the wickedness of these men, and the absurdity of their schemes; and to show that a Patriot King may walk more easily and successfully in other paths of government, "per tutum planumque iter religionis, jus-

titiæ, honestatis, virtutumque moralium." Let me proceed, therefore, to mention two other heads of the conduct that such a king
will hold, and it shall be my endeavor not to fall into the same
prolixity.

A king who esteems it his duty to support, or to restore, if that
be needful, the free constitution of a limited monarchy; who
forms and maintains a wise and good administration; who subdues faction, and promotes the union of his people: and who
makes their greatest good the constant object of his government,
may be said, no doubt, to be in the true interest of his kingdom.
All the particular cases, that can arise, are included in these
general characteristics of a wise and good reign. And yet it
seems proper to mention, under a distinct head, some particular
instances that have not been touched, wherein this wisdom and
goodness will exert themselves.

Now, though the true interest of several states may be the
same in many respects, yet is there always some difference to be
perceived, by a discerning eye, both in these interests, and in the
manner of pursuing them; a difference that arises from the situation of countries, from the character of people, from the nature
of government, and even from that of climate and soil; from circumstances that are, like these, permanent, and from others that
may be deemed more accidental. To illustrate all this by examples, would be easy, but long. I shall content myself therefore to mention, in some instances only, the difference that arises
from the causes referred to, between the true interest of our
country, and that of some or all our neighbors on the continent:
and leave others to extend and apply in their own thoughts the
comparison I shall hint at, rather than enlarge upon.

The situation of Great Britain, the character of her people, and
the nature of her government, fit her for trade and commerce.
Her climate and her soil make them necessary to her well being.
By trade and commerce we grow a rich and powerful nation,
and by their decay we are growing poor and impotent. As
trade and commerce enrich, so they fortify, our country. The
sea is our barrier, ships are our fortresses, and the mariners, that
trade and commerce alone can furnish, are the garrisons to defend them. France lies under great disadvantages in trade and
commerce, by the nature of her government. Her advantages,
in situation, are as great at least as ours. Those that arise, from
the temper and character of her people, are a little different perhaps, and yet upon the whole equivalent. Those of her climate
and her soil are superior to ours, and indeed to those of any
European nation. The United Provinces have the same advantages that we have in the nature of their government, more perhaps in the temper and character of their people, less to be sure

in their situation, climate, and soil. But, without descending
into a longer detail of the advantages and disadvantages attending
each of these nations in trade and commerce, it is sufficient for
my present purpose to observe, that Great Britain stands in a
certain middle between the other two, with regard to wealth and
power arising from these springs. A less, and a less constant,
application to the improvement of these may serve the ends of
France; a greater is necessary in this country; and a greater still
in Holland. The French may improve their natural wealth and
power by the improvement of trade and commerce. We can
have no wealth, nor power by consequence, as Europe is now
constituted, without the improvement of them, nor in any degree
but proportionably to this improvement. The Dutch cannot
subsist without them. They bring wealth to other nations, and
are necessary to the well being of them; but they supply the
Dutch with food and raiment, and are necessary even to their
being.

The result of what has been said is in general, that the wealth
and power of all nations depending so much on their trade and
commerce, and every nation being, like the three I have mentioned, in such different circumstances of advantage or disadvantage in the pursuit of this common interest; a good government,
and therefore the government of a Patriot King will be directed
constanly to make the most of every advantage that nature has
given, or art can procure, towards the improvement of trade and
commerce. And this is one of the principal criterions by which
we are to judge, whether governors are in the true interest of the
people or not.

It results, in particular, that Great Britain might improve her
wealth and power in a proportion superior to that of any nation
who can be deemed her rival, if the advantages she has were
as wisely cultivated, as they will be in the reign of a Patriot
King. To be convinced more thoroughly of this truth, a very
short process of reasoning will suffice. Let any man who has
knowledge enough for it, first compare the natural state of Great
Britain, and of the United Provinces, and then their artificial
state together; that is, let him consider minutely the advantages
we have for the situation, extent, and nature of our island, over
the inhabitants of a few salt marshes gained on the sea, and
hardly defended from it: and after that, let him consider how
nearly these provinces have raised themselves to an equality of
wealth and power with the kingdom of Great Britain. From
whence arises this difference of improvement? It arises plainly
from hence: the Dutch have been, from the foundation of their
commonwealth, a nation of patriots and merchants. The spirit
of that people has not been diverted from these two objects, the

defence of their liberty, and the improvement of their trade and
commerce: which have been carried on by them with uninterrupted and unslackened application, industry, order, and economy.   In Great Britain the case has not been the same, in either
respect; but here we confine ourselves to speak of the last alone.

Trade and commerce, such as they were in those days, had
been sometimes, and in some instances, before the reign of Queen
Elizabeth, encouraged and improved: but the great encourage-
ments were given, the great extensions and improvements were
made, by that glorious princess.   To her we owe that spirit of
domestic and foreign trade which is not quite extinguished.   It
was she who gave that rapid motion to our whole mercantile
system which is not entirely ceased.   They both flagged under
her successor; were not revived under his son; were checked, diverted, clogged, and interrupted, during our civil wars: and began
to exert new vigor after the restoration, in a long course of
peace; but met with new difficulties, too, from the confirmed rivalry of the Dutch, and the growing rivalry of the French.   To
one of these the pusillanimous character of James the first gave
many scandalous occasions: and the other was favored by the
conduct of Charles the Second, who never was in the true interest
of the people he governed.   From the revolution to the death
of Queen Anne, however trade and commerce might be aided
and encouragd in other respects, they were necessarily subjected
to depredations abroad, and overloaded by taxes at home, during
the course of two great wars.   From the accession of the late
king to this hour, in the midst of a full peace, the debts of the
nation continue much the same, the taxes have been increased,
and for eighteen years of this time we have tamely suffered continual depredations from the most contemptible maritime power
in Europe, that of Spain.

A Patriot King will neither neglect, nor sacrifice his country's
interest.   No other interest, neither a foreign nor a domestic,
neither a public nor a private, will influence his conduct in government.   He will not multiply taxes wantonly nor keep up
those unnecessarily which necessity has laid, that he may keep
up legions of tax-gatherers.   He will not continue national debts,
by all sorts of political and other profusion; nor, more wickedly
still, by a settled purpose of oppressing and impoverishing the
people; that he may with greater ease corrupt some, and govern
the whole, according to the dictates of his passions and arbitrary
will.   To give ease and encouragement to manufactory at home,
to assist and protect trade abroad, to improve and keep in heart
the national colonies, like so many farms of the mother country,
will be principal and constant parts of the attention of such a
prince.   The wealth of the nation he will most justly esteem to

be his wealth, the power his power, the security and the honor, his security and honor; and, by the very means by which he promotes the two first, he will wisely preserve the two last; for by these means, and by these alone, can the great advantage of the situation of this kingdom be taken and improved.

Great Britain is an island: and, whilst nations on the continent are at immense charge in maintaining their barriers, and perpetually on their guard, and frequently embroiled, to extend or strengthen them, Great Britain may, if her governors please, accumulate wealth in maintaining hers; make herself secure from invasions, and be ready to invade others when her own immediate interest, or the general interest of Europe requires it. Of all which Queen Elizabeth's reign is a memorable example, and undeniable proof. I said the general interest of Europe; because it seems to me that this, alone, should call our councils off from an almost entire application to their domestic and proper business. Other nations must watch over every motion of their neighbors; penetrate, if they can, every design; foresee every minute event; and take part by some engagement or other in almost every conjuncture that arises. But as we cannot be easily nor suddenly attacked, and as we ought not to aim at any acquisition of territory on the continent, it may be our interest to watch the secret workings of the several councils abroad; to advise, and warn; to abet, and oppose; but it never can be our true interest easily and officiously to enter into action, much less into engagements that imply action and expense. Other nations, like the Velites or light-armed troops, stand foremost in the field, and skirmish perpetually. When a great war begins, we ought to look on the powers of the continent, to whom we incline, like the two first lines, the Principes and Hastati of a Roman army: and on ourselves, like the Triarii, that are not to charge with these legions on every occasion, but to be ready for the conflict whenever the fortune of the day, be it sooner or later, calls us to it, and the sum of things, or the general interest, makes it necessary.

This is that post of advantage and honor, which our singular situation among the powers of Europe determines us, or should determine us, to take, in all disputes that happen on the continent. If we neglect it, and dissipate our strength on occasions that touch us remotely or indirectly, we are governed by men who do not know the true interest of this island, or who have some other interest more at heart. If we adhere to it, so at least as to deviate little and seldom from it, as we shall do whenever we are wisely and honestly governed, then will this nation make her proper figure: and a great one it will be. By a continual attention to improve her natural, that is her maritime strength, by collecting all her forces within herself, and reserving them to be laid out on great occasions, such as regard her immediate interests and her honor, or such as are truly important to the general system of power in Europe; she may be the arbitrator of differences, the guardian of liberty, and the preserver of that balance, which has been so much talked of, and is so little understood.

"Are we never to be soldiers?" it will be said. Yes, constantly, in such proportion as is necessary for the defence of good government. To establish such a military force as none but bad governors can want, is to establish tyrannical power in the king or in the ministers; and may be wanted by the latter, when the former would be secure without his army, if he broke his minister. Occasionally too we must be soldiers, and for offence as well as defence; but in proportion to the nature of the conjuncture, considered always relatively to the difference here insisted upon between our situation, our interest, and the nature of our strength, compared with those of the other powers of Europe; and not in proportion to the desires, or even to the wants, of the nations with whom we are confederated. Like other amphibious animals, we must come occasionally on shore: but the water is more properly our element, and in it, like them, as we find our greatest security, so we exert our greatest force.

What I touch upon here, very shortly, deserves to be considered, and re-considered, by every man who has, or may have, any share in the government of Great Britain. For we have not only departed too much from our true national interest in this respect; but we have done so with the general applause even of well meaning men, who did not discern that we wasted ourselves by an improper application of our strength in conjunctures when we might have served the common cause far more usefully, nay with entire effect, by a proper application of our natural strength. There was something more than this. Armies grew so much into fashion, in time of war, among men who meant well to their country, that they who mean ill to it have kept, and keep them still up in the profoundest peace: and the number of our soldiers, in this island alone, is almost double to that of our seamen.— That they are kept up against foreign enemies, cannot be said with any color. If they are kept for show, they are ridiculous; if they are kept for any other purpose whatever, they are too dangerous to be suffered. A Patriot King, seconded by ministers attached to the true interest of their country, would soon reform this abuse, and save a great part of this expense; or apply it, in a manner preferable even to the saving it, to the maintenance of a body of marine foot, and to the charge of a register of thirty or forty thousand seamen. But no thoughts like these, no great designs for the honor and interest of the kingdom, will be entertained, till men who have this honor and interest at heart arise to power.

I come now to the last head under which I shall consider the character and conduct of a Patriot King; and let it not be thought to be of the least importance, though it may seem, at the first mention, to concern appearances rather than realities, and to be nothing more than a circumstance contained in or implied by the great parts of the character and conduct of such a king. It is of his personal behavior, of his manner of living with other men, and, in a word, of his private as well as public life that I mean to speak. It is of that decency and grace, that bienseance of the French, that decorum of the Latins, that πρεπον of the Greeks, which can never be reflected on any character that is not laid in virtue: but for want of which, a character that is so laid will lose, at all times, part of the lustre belonging to it, and may be sometimes not a little misunderstood and undervalued. Beauty is not separable from health, nor this lustre, said the Stoics, from virtue; but as a man may be healthful without being handsome, so he may be virtuous without being amiable.

There are certain finishing strokes, a last hand as we commonly say, to be given to all the works of art. When that is not given, we may see the excellency of a general design, and the beauty of some particular parts. A judge of the art may see further; he may allow for what is wanting, and discern the full merit of a complete work in one that is imperfect. But vulgar eyes will not be so struck. The work will appear to them defective, because unfinished: so that without knowing precisely what they dislike, they may admire, but they will not be pleased. Thus in moral characters, though every part be virtuous and great, or though the few and small defects in it be concealed under the blaze of those shining qualities that compensate for them; yet is not this enough even in private life: it is less so in public life, and still less so in that of a prince.

There is a certain "species liberalis," more easily understood than explained, and felt than defined, that must be acquired and rendered habitual to him. A certain propriety of words and actions, that results from their conformity to nature and character, must always accompany him, and create an air and manner that run uniformly through the whole tenor of his conduct and behavior: which air and manner are so far from any kind or degree of affectation, that they cannot be attained except by him who is void of all affectation. We may illustrate this to ourselves, and make it more sensible, by reflecting on the conduct of good dramatic or epic writers. They draw the characters, which they bring on the scene, from nature, they sustain them through the

whole piece, and make their actors neither say nor do any thing
that is not exactly proper to the character each of them represents. " Oderint dum metuant," came properly out of the mouth
of a tyrant; but Euripides would never have put that execrable
sentence into the mouth of Minos or Æacus.

A man of sense and virtue both will not fall into any great
impropriety of character, or indecency of conduct: but he may
slide or be surprised into small ones, from a thousand reasons,
and in a thousand manners, which I shall not stay to enumerate.
Against these, therefore, even men, who are incapable of falling
into the others, must be still on their guard, and no men so much
as princes. When their minds are filled and their hearts warmed
with true notions of government, when they know their duty,
and love their people, they will not fail in the great parts they
are to act, in the council, in the field, and in all the arduous affairs
that belong to their kingly office: at least they will not begin to
fail, by failing in them. But as they are men susceptible of the
same impressions, liable to the same errors, and exposed to the
same passions, so they are likewise exposed to more and stronger
temptations than others. Besides, the elevation in which they
are placed, as it gives them great advantages, gives them great
disadvantages too, that often countervail the former. Thus, for
instance, a little merit in a prince is seen and felt by numbers: it
is multiplied, as it were, and in proportion to this effect his reputation is raised by it. But then, a little failing is seen and felt by
numbers too: it is multiplied in the same manner, and his reputation sinks in the same proportion.

I spoke above of defects that may be concealed under the blaze
of great and shining qualities. This may be the case: it has been
that of some princes. There goes a tradition that Henry the
Fourth of France asked a Spanish ambassador, what mistresses
the king of Spain had? The ambassador replied, like a formal
pedant, that his master was a prince who feared God, and had
no mistress but the queen. Henry the Fourth felt the reflection,
and asked him in return, with some contempt, " Whether his
master had not virtues enough to cover one vice?"

The faults or defects, that may be thus covered or 'compen-
sated, are, I think, those of the man, rather than those of the
king; such as arise from constitution, and the natural rather than
the moral character; such as may be deemed accidental starts of
passion, or accidental remissness in some unguarded hours; surprises, if I may say so, of the man on the king. When these
happen seldom, and pass soon, they may be hid like spots in the
sun: but they are spots still. He who has the means of seeing
them, will see them: and he who has not, may feel the effects of
them without knowing precisely the cause. When they continue

(for here is the danger, because, if they continue, they will increase) they are spots no longer: they spread a general shade, and obscure the light in which they were drowned before. The virtues of the king are lost in the vices of the man.

Alexander had violent passions, and those for wine and women were predominant, after his ambition. They were spots in his character before they prevailed by the force of habit: as soon as they began to do so, the king and the hero appeared less, the rake and bully more. Persepolis was burnt at the instigation of Thais, and Clytus was killed in a drunken brawl. He repented indeed of these two horrible actions, and was again the king and hero upon many occasions; but he had not been enough on his guard, when the strongest incitements to vanity and to sensual pleasures offered themselves at every moment to him: and, when he stood in all his easy hours surrounded by women and eunuchs, by the panders, parasites, and buffoons of a voluptuous court, they, who could not approach the king, approached the man, and by seducing the man, they betrayed the king. His faults became habits. The Macedonians, who did not or would not see the one, saw the other; and he fell a sacrifice to their resentments, to their fears, and to those factions that will arise under an odious government, as well as under one that grows into contempt.

Other characters might be brought to contrast with this; the first Scipio Africanus, for example, or the eldest Cato: and there will be no objection to a comparison of such citizens of Rome, as these were, with kings of the first magnitude. Now the reputation of the first Scipio was not so clear and uncontroverted in private as in public life; nor was he allowed by all, to be a man of such severe virtue, as he affected, and as that age required. Nævius was thought to mean him in some verses Gellius has preserved: and Valerius Antias made no scruple to assert, that, far from restoring the fair Spaniard to her family, he debauched and kept her. Notwithstanding this, what authority did he not maintain? In what esteem and veneration did he not live and die? With what panegyrics has not the whole torrent of writers rolled down his reputation even to these days? This could not have happened, if the vice imputed to him had shown itself in any scandalous appearances, to eclipse the lustre of the general, the consul, or the citizen. The same reflection might be extended to Cato, who loved wine as well as Scipio loved women. Men did not judge in the days of the elder Cato perhaps, as Seneca was ready to do in those of the younger, that drunkenness could be no crime if Cato drank: but Cato's passion, as well as that of Scipio, was subdued and kept under by his public character. His virtue warmed instead of cooling, by this indulgence to his genius or natural temper: and one may gather, from what Tully puts into his mouth, in the treatise concerning old age, that even his love of wine was rendered subservient, instead of doing hurt, to the measures he pursued in his public character.

Give me leave to insist a little on the two first Cæsars, and on Marc Antony. I quote none of them as good men, but I may quote them all as great men, and therefore properly in this place; since a Patriot King must avoid the defects that diminish a great character, as well as those that corrupt a good one. Old Curio called Julius Cæsar the husband of every wife, and the wife of every husband; referring to his known adulteries, and to the compliances that he was suspected of in his youth for Nicomedes. Even his own soldiers, in the license of a triumph, sung lampoons on him for his profusion as well as lewdness. The youth of Augustus was defamed as much as that of Julius Cæsar, and both as much as that of Antony. When Rome was ransacked by the panders of Augustus, and matrons and virgins were stripped and searched, like slaves in a market, to choose the fittest to satisfy his lust, did Antony do more? When Julius set no bounds to his debauches in Egypt, except those that satiety imposed, "postquam epulis bacchoque modum lassata voluptas imposuit," when he trifled away his time with Cleopatra in the very crisis of the civil war, and till his troops refused to follow him any further in his effeminate progress up the Nile—did Antony do more? No; all three had vices which would have been so little borne in any former age of Rome, that no man could have raised himself, under the weight of them, to popularity and to power. But we must not wonder that the people, who bore the tyrants, bore the libertines; nor that indulgence was shown to the vices of the great, in a city where universal corruption and profligacy of manners were established: and yet even in this city, and among these degenerate Romans, certain it is, that different appearances, with the same vices, helped to maintain the Cæsars, and ruined Antony. I might produce many anecdotes to show how the two former saved appearances whilst their vices were the most flagrant, and made so much amends for the appearances they had not saved, by those of a contrary kind, that a great part at least of all which was said to defame them might pass, and did pass, for the calumny of party.

But Antony threw off all decorum from the first, and continued to do so to the last. Not only vice, but indecency became habitual to him. He ceased to be a general, a consul, a triumvir, a citizen of Rome. He became an Egyptian king, sunk into luxurious effeminacy, and proved he was unfit to govern men, by suffering himself to be governed by a woman. His vices hurt him, but his habits ruined him. If a political modesty at least had made him disguise the first, they would have hurt him less, and he might have escaped the last: but he was so little sensible of this, that in a fragment of one of his letters to Augustus, which Suetonius has preserved, he endeavors to justify himself by pleading this very habit. "What matter is it whom we lie with?" says he: "this letter may find you perhaps with Tertulla, or Terentilia," or others that he names. "I lie with Cleopatra, and have I not done so these nine years?"

These great examples, which I have produced, not to encourage vice, but to show more strongly the advantages of decency in private behavior, may appear in some sort figures bigger than the life. Few virtues and few vices grow up, in these parts of the world and these latter ages, to the size of those I have mentioned; and none have such scenes wherein to exert themselves. But the truths I am desirous to inculcate will be as justly delivered in this manner, and perhaps more strongly felt. Failings or vices that flow from the same source of human nature, that run the same course through the conduct of princes, and have the same effects on their characters, and consequently on their government and their fortune, have all the proportion necessary to my application of them. It matters little whether a prince, who abandons that common decorum which results from nature and which reason prescribes, abandons the particular decorums of this country or that, of this age or that, which result from mode, and which custom exacts. It matters little, for instance, whether a prince gives himself up to the more gross luxury of the west, or to the more refined luxury of the east; whether he become the slave of a domestic harlot, or of a foreign queen; in short, whether he forget himself in the arms of one whore or of twenty; and whether he imitate Antony, or a king of Achin, who is reported to have passed his whole time in a seraglio, eating, drinking, chewing betel, playing with women, and talking of cock-fighting.

To sum up the whole and draw to a conclusion: this decency, this grace, this propriety of manners to character, is so essential to princes in particular, that whenever it is neglected their virtues lose a great degree of lustre, and their defects acquire much aggravation. Nay more; by neglecting this decency and this grace, and for want of a sufficient regard to appearances, even their virtues may betray them into failings, their failings into vices, and their vices into habits unworthy of princes and unworthy of men.

The constitutions of governments, and the different tempers and characters of people, may be thought justly to deserve some consideration, in determining the behavior of princes in private life as well as in public; and to put a difference, for instance, between the decorum of a king of France, and that of a king of Great Britain.

Louis the Fourteenth was king in an absolute monarchy, and reigned over a people whose genius makes it as fit perhaps to impose on them by admiration and awe, as to gain and hold them by affection. Accordingly he kept great state; was haughty, was reserved; and all he said or did appeared to be forethought and planned. His regard to appearances was such, that when his mistress was the wife of another man, and he had children by her every year, he endeavored to cover her constant residence at court by a place she filled about the queen: and he dined and supped and cohabited with the latter in every apparent respect as if he had had no mistress at all. Thus he raised a great reputation; he was revered by his subjects, and admired by his neighbors: and this was due principally to the art with which he managed appearances, so as to set off his virtues, to disguise his failings and his vices, and by his example and authority to keep a veil drawn over the futility and debauch of his court.

His successor, not to the throne, but to the sovereign power, was a mere rake, with some wit, and no morals; nay, with so little regard to them, that he made them a subject of ridicule in discourse, and appeared in his whole conduct more profligate, if that could be, than he was in principle The difference between these characters soon appeared in abominable effects; such as, cruelty apart, might recall the memory of Nero, or, in the other sex, that of Massalina, and such as I leave the chroniclers of scandal to relate.

Our Elizabeth was queen in a limited monarchy, and reigned over a people at all times more easily led than driven; and at that time capable of being attached to their prince and their country, by a more generous principle than any of those which prevail in our days, by affection. There was a strong prerogative then in being, and the crown was in possession of greater legal power. Popularity was, however, then, as it is now, and as it must be always in mixed government, the sole true foundation of that sufficient authority and influence, which other constitutions give the prince gratis, and independently of the people, but which a king of this nation must acquire. The wise queen saw it, and she saw too, how much popularity depends on those appearances, that depend on the decorum, the decency, the grace, and the propriety of behavior of which we are speaking. A warm concern for the interest and honor of the nation, a tenderness for her people, and a confidence in their affections, were appearances that ran through her whole public conduct, and gave life and color to it. She did great things, and she knew how to set them off according to their full value, by her manner of doing them. In her private behavior she showed great affability, she descended even to familiarity; but her familiarity was such as could not be imputed to her weakness, and was, therefore, most justly ascribed to her goodness. Though a woman, she hid all that was womanish about her: and if a few equivocal marks of coquetry appeared on some occasions, they passed like flashes of lightning, vanished as soon as they were discerned, and imprinted no blot on her character. She had private friendships, she had favorites: but she never suffered her friends to forget she was their queen; and when her favorites did, she made them feel that she was so.

Her successor had no virtues to set off, but he had failings and vices to conceal. He could not conceal the latter; and, void of the former, he could not compensate for them. His failings and his vices therefore standing in full view, he passed for a weak prince and an ill man; and fell into all the contempt wherein his memory remains to this day. The methods he took, to preserve himself from it, served but to confirm him in it. No man can keep the decorum of manners in life, who is not free from every kind of affectation, as it has been said already: but he who affects what he has no pretensions to, or what is improper to his character and rank in the world, is guilty of most consummate folly; he becomes doubly ungracious, doubly indecent, and quite ridiculous. James the First, not having one quality to conciliate the esteem or affection of his people to him, endeavored to impose on their understandings; and to create a respect for himself, by spreading the most extravagant notions about kings in general, as if they were middle beings between God and other men; and by comparing the extent and unsearchable mysteries of their power and prerogative to those of the Divine Providence. His language and his behavior were commonly suited to such foolish pretensions; and thus, by assuming a claim to such respect and submission as were not due to him, he lost a great part of what was due to him. In short, he begun at the wrong end; for though the shining qualities of the king may cover some failings and some vices that do not grow up to strong habits in the man, yet must the character of a great and good king be founded in that of a great and good man. A king who lives out of the sight of his subjects, or is never seen by them except on his throne, can scarce be despised as a man, though he may be hated as a king. But the king who lives more in their sight, and more under their observation, may be despised before he is hated, and even without being hated. This happened to king James: a thousand circumstances brought it to pass, and none more than the indecent weaknesses he had for his minions. He did not endeavor to cure this contempt and raise his character, only by affecting what he had no pretensions to, as in the former case; but he endeavored likewise most vainly to do it by affecting what was improper to his character and rank. He did not endeavor indeed to disguise his natural pusillanimity and timidity under the mask of a bully, whilst he was imposed upon and insulted by all his neighbors, and above all by the Spaniards; but he retailed the scraps of Buchanan, affected to talk much, figured in church controversies, and put on all the pedantic appearances of a scholar, whilst he neglected all those of a great and good man, as well as king.

Let not princes flatter themselves. They will be examined closely, in private as well as in public life: and those, who cannot pierce further, will judge of them by the appearances they give in both. To obtain true popularity, that which is founded in esteem and affection, they must, therefore, maintain their characters in both; and to that end neglect appearances in neither, but observe the decorum necessary to preserve the esteem, whilst they win the affections of mankind. Kings, they must never forget that they are men: men, they must never forget that they are kings. The sentiments, which one of these reflections of course inspires, will give a humane and affable air to their whole behavior, and make them taste in that high elevation all the joys of social life. The sentiments, that the other reflection suggests, will be found very compatible with the former: and they may never forget that they are kings, though they do not always carry the crown on their heads, nor the sceptre in their hands. Vanity and folly must entrench themselves in a constant affectation of state, to preserve regal dignity: a wise prince will know how to preserve it when he lays his majesty aside. He will dare to appear a private man, and in that character he will draw to himself a respect less ostentatious, but more real and more pleasing to him, than any which is paid to the monarch. By never saying what is unfit for him to say, he will never hear what is unfit for him to hear. By never doing what is unfit for him to do, he will never see what is unfit for him to see. Decency and propriety of manners are so far from lessening the pleasures of life, that they refine them, and give them a higher taste: they are so far from restraining the free and easy commerce of social life, that they banish the bane of it, licentiousness of behavior. Ceremony is the barrier against this abuse of liberty in public; politeness and decency are so in private: and the prince, who practises and exacts them, will amuse himself much better, and oblige those, who have the honor to be in his intimacy and to share his pleasures with him, much more, than he could possibly do by the most absolute and unguarded familiarity.

That which is here recommended to princes, that constant guard on their own behavior even in private life, and that constant decorum which their example ought to exact from others, will not be found so difficult in practice as may be imagined; if they use a proper discernment in the choice of the persons whom they admit to the nearest degrees of intimacy with them. A prince should choose his companions with as great care as his ministers. If he trusts the business of his state to these, he trusts his character to those; and his character will depend on theirs much more than is commonly thought. General experience will lead men to judge that a similitude of character determined the choice; even when chance, indulgence to assiduity, good nature, or want of reflection, had their share in the introduction of men unworthy of such favor. But, in such cases, certain it is that they, who judged wrong at first concerning him, will judge right at last. He is not a trifler, for instance. Be it so: but if he takes trifling, futile creatures, men of mean characters, or of no character, into his intimacy, he shows a disposition to become such; and will become such, unless he breaks these habits early, and before puerile amusements are grown up to be the business of his life. I mean, that the minds of princes, like the minds of other men, will be brought down insensibly to the tone of the company they keep.

A worse consequence, even than this, may follow a want of discernment in princes how to choose their companions, and how to conduct themselves in private life. Silly kings have resigned themselves to their ministers, have suffered these to stand between them and their people, and have formed no judgments, nor taken any measures on their own knowledge, but all implicitly on the representations made to them by their ministers. Kings of superior capacity have resigned themselves in the same manner to their favorites, male and female, have suffered these to stand between them and their most able and faithful counsellors: their judgments have been influenced, and their measures directed by insinuations of women, or of men as little fitted as women, by nature and education, to be hearkened to, in the great affairs of government. History is full of such examples; all melancholy, many tragical! sufficient, one would imagine, to deter princes, if attended to, from permitting the companions of their idle hours, or the instruments of their pleasures, to exceed the bounds of those provinces. Should a minister of state pretend to vie with any of these, about the forms of a drawing-room, the regulation of a ruelle, the decoration of a ball, or the dress of a fine lady, he would be thought ridiculous, and he would be truly so. But then are not any of these impertinent, when they presume to meddle in things at least as much above them, as those that have been mentioned are below the others? And are not princes, who suffer them to do so, unaccountably weak?

What shall I say further on this head? Nothing more is necessary. Let me wind it up, therefore, by asserting this great truth, that results from what has been already said: As he can never fill the character of a Patriot King, though his personal great and good qualities be in every other respect equal to it, who lies open to the flattery of courtiers, to the seduction of women, and to the partialities and affections which are easily contracted by too great indulgence in private life; so the prince, who is desirous to establish this character, must observe such a decorum, and keep such a guard on himself, as may prevent even the suspicion of being liable to such influences. For as the reality would ruin, the very suspicion will lessen him in the opinion of mankind: and the opinion of mankind, which is fame after death, is superior strength and power in life.

And now, if the principles and measures of conduct, laid down in this discourse, as necessary to constitute that greatest and most glorious of human beings, a Patriot King, be sufficient to this purpose; let us consider, too, how easy it is, or ought to be, to establish them in the minds of princes. They are founded on true propositions, all of which are obvious, nay, many of them self-evident. They are confirmed by universal experience. In a word, no understanding can resist them, and none but the weakest can fail, or be misled, in the application of them. To a prince, whose heart is corrupt, it is in vain to speak: and, for such a prince, I would not be thought to write. But if the heart of a prince be not corrupt, these truths will find an easy ingression, through the understanding, to it. Let us consider again, what the sure, the necessary effects of such principles and measures of conduct must be, to the prince, and to the people. On this subject let the imagination range through the whole glorious scene of a patriot reign: the beauty of the idea will inspire those transports, which Plato imagined the vision of virtue would inspire, if virtue could be seen. What in truth can be so lovely, what so venerable, as to contemplate a king on whom the eyes of a whole people are fixed, filled with admiration, and glowing with affection? A king, in the temper of whose government, like that of Nerva, things so seldom allied as empire and liberty are intimately mixed, co-exist together inseparably, and constitute one real essence? What spectacle can be presented to the view of the mind so rare, so nearly divine, as a king possessed of absolute power, neither usurped by fraud, nor maintained by force, but the genuine effect of esteem, of confidence, and affection; the free gift of liberty, who finds her greatest security in this power, and would desire no other if the prince on the throne could be, what his people wish him to be, immortal? Of such a prince, and of such a prince alone, it may be said with strict propriety and truth,

> " Volentes
> Per populos dat jura, viamque affectat Olympo."

Civil fury will have no place in this draught: or, if the monster is seen, he must be seen as Virgil describes him,

> " Centum vinctus ahenis
> Post tergum nodis, fremit horridus ore cruento."

He must be seen subdued, bound, chained, and deprived entirely of power to do hurt. In his place, concord will appear, brooding peace and prosperity on the happy land; joy sitting in every face, content in every heart; a people unoppressed, undisturbed, unalarmed; busy to improve their private property and the public stock; fleets covering the ocean, bringing home wealth by the returns of industry, carrying assistance or terror abroad by the direction of wisdom, and asserting triumphantly the right and the honor of Great Britain, as far as waters roll and as winds can waft them.

Those who live to see such happy days, and to act in so glorious a scene, will perhaps call to mind, with some tenderness of sentiment, when he is no more, a man, who contributed his mite to carry on so good a work, and who desired life for nothing so much, as to see a king of Great Britain the most popular man in his country, and a Patriot King at the head of an united people.

OF THE

STATE OF PARTIES

ACCESSION OF KING GEORGE THE FIRST.

I PERCEIVE by yours that my discourse of the character and conduct of a Patriot King, in that article which relates to party, has not entirely satisfied your expectations. You expected, from some things that I remember to have said to you in conversation, and others that have fallen on that occasion from my pen, a more particular application of those general reasonings to the present time, and to the state of parties, from the late king's accession to the throne. The subject is delicate enough, and yet I shall speak upon it what truth exacts from me, with the utmost frankness: for I know all our parties too well, to esteem any; and I am too old, and too resigned to my fate, to want, or to fear any.

Whatever anecdotes you have been told, for you are too young to have seen the passages of the times I am going to mention, and whatever prepossessions you have had, take these facts for undoubted truths: That there was no design on foot, during the four last years of queen Anne's reign, to set aside the succession of the house of Hanover, and to place the crown on the head of the Pretender to it; nor any party formed for this purpose at the time of the death of that princess, whose memory I honor, and therefore feel a just indignation at the irreverence with which we have seen it treated. If such a design had been on foot, during that time, there were moments when the execution of it would not have been difficult, or dangerous enough, to have stopped men of the most moderate resolution. Neither could a design of that nature have been carried on so long, though it was not carried into execution, without leaving some traces, which would have appeared when such strict inquisitions were made; when the papers of so many of the queen's servants were seized, and even her own papers, even those she had sealed up to be burnt after her death, were exposed to so much indecent inspection. But, laying aside all arguments of the probable kind, I deny the fact absolutely: and I have the better title to expect credit, because it could not be true without my knowledge, or at least suspicion of it; and because even they who believed it, for all who asserted it did not believe it, had no proof to produce, nor have to this hour, but vain surmises; nor any authority to rest upon, but the clamor of party.

That there were particular men, who corresponded indirectly, and directly too, with the Pretender, and with others for his service; that these men professed themselves to be zealous in it, and made large promises, and raised some faint hopes, I cannot doubt: though this was unknown to me at that time, or at least I knew it not with the same certainty, and in the same detail, that I have known it since. But if this was done by some who were in the queen's service, it was done too by some who were out of it, and, I think, with little sincerity by either.

It may well seem strange to one who carries in his breast a heart like yours, that men of any rank, and especially of the highest, should hold a conduct so false, so dangerous, always of uncertain event, and often, as it was in the case here mentioned, upon remote contingencies, and such as they themselves think the least probable. Even I think it strange, who have been much longer mingled in a corrupt world, and who have seen many more examples of the folly, of the cunning, and the perfidy of mankind. A great regard to wealth, and a total contempt of virtue, are sentiments very nearly allied: and they must possess the whole souls of men whom they can determine to such infamous duplicity, to such double treachery. In fact they do so. One is so afraid of losing his fortune, that he lays in claims to secure it, perhaps to augment it, on all sides, and to prevent even imaginary dangers. Another values so little the inward testimony of a good conscience, or the future reproaches of those he has deceived, that he scruples not to take engagements, for a time to come, that he has no design to keep; if they may serve as expedients to facilitate, in any small degree, the success of an immediate project. All this was done at the time, on the occasion, and by the persons I intend. But the scheme of defeating the protestant succession was so far from being laid by the queen and her ministers, and such a resolution was so far from being taken, that the very men I speak of, when they were pressed by the other side, that is from Versailles and St. Germains, to be more particular, and to come into a closer concert, declined both, and gave the most evasive answers.

A little before, or about, the time of the queen's death, some other persons who figured afterwards in the rebellion, entered in good earnest into those engagements, as I believe; for I do not know exactly the date of them. But whenever they took them, they took them as single men. They could answer for no party to back them. They might flatter themselves with hopes and dreams like Pompey, if little men and little things may be compared with great, of legions ready to rise at the stamp of their feet. But they had no assurance, no, nor grounds to expect any troops, except those of the highlands; whose disposition in general was known to every man, but whose insurrection, without the concurrence of other insurrections and other troops, was deemed, even by those that made them take arms afterwards, not a strength but a weakness; ruin to the poor people, and ruin to the cause. In a word, these men were so truly single in their engagements, and their measures were so unripe for action when the resolution of acting immediately was taken by them, that, I am persuaded, they durst not communicate their design to any one man of consequence that served at that time with them. What persuades me of it is this. One man, whom they thought likely to incline to them on several accounts, they attempted indirectly and at a great distance: they came no nearer to the point with him neither then, that is just before the queen's death, nor afterwards. They had indeed no encouragement to do it; for, upon this hint, and another circumstance which fell in, both he and others took several occasions to declare, that though they would serve the queen faithfully, and exclusively of all other regards or engagements, to her last breath, yet after her decease they would acknowledge the prince on whom the succession devolved by law, and to which they had sworn, and no other. This declaration would have been that of the far greatest number of the same party, and would have been stuck to by them, if the passions and private interests of another party had not prevailed over the true interest of a new family that was going to mount the throne. You may ask me now, and the question will not be at all improper, how it came to pass, if the queen and her ministers had no design to defeat the succession, that so much suspicion of it prevailed, that so great an alarm was taken and so great a clamor raised? I might answer you very shortly and very truly. By the strange conduct of a first minister, by the contests about the negotiations of the peace, and by the arts of a party.

The minds of some ministers are like the "sanctum sanctorum" of a temple I have read of somewhere: before it a great curtain was solemnly drawn; within it nothing was to be seen

but a confused group of mis-shapen, and imperfect forms, heads
without bodies, bodies without heads, and the like.   To develope
the most complicated cases, and to decide in the most doubtful,
has been the talent of great ministers: it is that of others to perplex the most simple, and to be puzzled by the plainest.   No
man was more desirous of power than the minister here intended,
and he had a competent share of cunning to wriggle himself into
it; but then his part was over, and no man was more at a loss
how to employ it.   The ends, he proposed to himself, he saw
for the most part darkly and indistinctly; and if he saw them a
little better, he still made use of means disproportionate to them.
That private correspondence with the queen, which produced
the change of the ministry in 1710, was begun with him whilst
he was secretary of state, and was continued, through him, during
the two years that intervened between his leaving the court, and
his return to it.   This gave him the sole confidence of the queen,
put him more absolutely at the head of the party that came into
power, and invested him with all the authority that a first minister could have in those days, and before any man could presume
to rival, in that rank, and in this kingdom, the rank of the ancient
mayors of the palace in France.   The tories, with whom and
by whom he had risen, expected much from him.   Their expectations were ill answered: and I think that such management as
he employed would not have hindered them long from breaking
from him, if new things had not fallen in, to engage their whole
attention, and to divert their passions.

The foolish prosecution of Sacheverel had carried party rage
to the height, and the late change of the ministry had confirmed
it there.   These circumstances, and many others relative to them,
which I omit, would have made it impossible, if there had been
honesty and wisdom enough to desire it, to bring about a coalition of the bulk of the tories and whigs at the latter end of this
reign: as it had been brought about a few years before under the
administration of my Lord Marlborough and my Lord Godolphin,
who broke it soon, and before it had time to cement, by making
such an use of it as I am unable to account for, even at this hour.
The two parties were in truth become factions in the strict sense
of the word.   I was of one, and I own the guilt; which no man
of the other would have a good grace to deny.   In this respect
they were alike; but here was the difference: one was well united,
well conducted, and determined to their future, as well as their
present objects.   Not one of these advantages attended the other.
The minister had evidently no bottom to rest his administration
upon, but that of the party at the head of which he came into
power: if he had rested it there, if he had gained their confidence,
instead of creating, even wantonly, if I may say so, a distrust of

himself in them, it is certain he might have determined them to every national interest during the queen's time, and after her death. But this was above his concepiion as well as his talents. He meant to keep power as long as he could, by the little arts by which he had got into it: he thought that he should be able to compound for himself in all events, and cared little what became of his party, his mistress, or the nation. That this was the whole of his scheme appeared sufficiently in the course of his administration; was then seen by some; and has been since acknowledged by all people. For this purpose he coaxed and persecuted whigs; he flattered and disappointed tories; and supported, by a thousand little tricks, his tottering administration. To the tory party he held out the peace, as an era when all they expected should be done for them, and when they should be placed in such fulness of power and such strength of party, "that it would be more the interest of the successor to be well with them, than theirs to be well with him." Such expressions were often used, and others of like import: and, I believe, these oracular speeches were interpreted as oracles used to be, according as every man's inclinations led him.

The contest that soon followed, by the violent opposition to the negotiations of peace, did the good hinted at above to the minister, and enabled him to amuse and banter his party a little longer. But they did great, and, in some respects, irreparable mischief to Great Britain, and to all Europe. One part of the mischief they did at home is proper to be mentioned here. They dipped the house of Hanover in our party quarrels, unseasonably, I presume to think, and unpopularly; for though the contest was maintained by two parties that pretended equally to have the national interest at heart, yet the national interest was so plainly on one side of the question, and the other side was so plainly partial, at the expense of this interest, to the emperor, the princes of the empire, and our other allies, that a successor to the crown, who was himself a prince of Germany, should have preserved, in good policy, for this very reason, the appearance at least of some neutrality. The means employed openly to break the queen's measures were indecent and unjustifiable; those employed secretly, and meditated to be employed, were worse. The ministers of Hanover, whose conduct I may censure the more freely because the late king did not approve it all, took so remarkable a share in the first, that they might be, and they were, suspected of having some in the others. This had a very bad effect, which was improved by men in the two extremes. The whigs desired nothing more than to have it thought that the successor was theirs, if I may repeat an insolent expression which was used at that time; the notion did them honor, and, though it could give no color, it gave some strength, to their opposition. The Jacobites insinuated industriously the same thing; and represented that the establishment of the house of Hanover would be the establishment of the whig party, and that the interests of Great Britain would be constantly sacrificed to foreign interests, and her wealth drained to support them under that family. I leave you to judge what ingression such exaggerations must find, on such occasion, and in such a ferment. I do not think they determined men to Jacobitism. I know they did not; but I know that they disinclined men from the succession, and made many, who resolved to submit to it, submit to it rather as a necessary evil, than as an eligible good.

This was, to the best of my observation and knowledge, the state of one party. An absurd one it was, and the consequences of it were foreseen, foretold, and pressed upon the minister at the time, but always without effect, and sometimes without any answers. He had some private intrigue for himself at Hanover: so he had at Bar. He was the bubble of one in the end: the Pretender was so of the other. But his whole management in the mean time was contrived to keep up a kind of general indetermination in the party about the succession; which made a man of great temper once say to him with passion, that " he believed no other minister, at the head of a powerful party, would not be better at Hanover, if he did not mean to be worse there."

The state of the other party was this. The whigs had appeared zealous for the protestant succession from the time when king William proposed it, after the death of the Duke of Gloucester. The tories voted for it then; and the acts that were judged necessary to secure it, some of them at least, were promoted by them. Yet were they not thought, nor did they affect, as the others did, to be thought, extremely fond of it. King William did not come into this measure, till he found, upon trial, that there was no other safe and practicable: and the tories had an air of coming into it for no other reason. Besides which, it is certain that there was at that time a much greater leaven of Jacobitism in the tory lump, than at the time spoken of here.

Now, thus far the whigs acted like a national party, who thought that their religion and liberty could be secured by no other expedient, and therefore adhered to this settlement of the crown with distinguished zeal. But this national party degenerated soon into faction; that is, the national interest became soon a secondary and subservient motive, and the cause of the succession was supported more for the sake of the party or faction, than for the sake of the nation; and with views that went more directly to the establishment of their own administration, than to a solid settlement of the present royal family. This appeared, evidently enough, to those whom noise and show could not impose upon, in the latter end of the queen's reign, and plain beyond dispute to all mankind, after her decease. The art of the whigs was to blend, as undistinguishably as they could, all their party interests with those of the succession: and they made just the same factious use of the supposed danger of it, as the tories had endeavored to make, some time before, of the supposed danger of the church. As no man is reputed a friend to Christianity beyond the Alps and the Pyrenees, who does not acknowledge the papal supremacy, so here no man was to be reputed a friend to the protestant succession, who was not ready to acknowledge their supremacy. The interest of the present royal family was, to succeed without opposition and risk, and to come to the throne in a calm. It was the interest of a faction that they should come to it in a storm. Accordingly the whigs were very near putting in execution some of the wildest projects of insurrections and rebellion, under pretence of securing what there was not sufficient disposition, nor any preparation at all made to obstruct. Happily for the public these designs proved abortive. They were too well known to have succeeded; but they might have had, and they would have had, most fatal consequences. The storm, that was not raised to disturb and endanger the late king's accession, was only deferred. To a party, who meant nothing less than engrossing the whole power of the government and the whole wealth of the nation under the successor, a storm, in which every other man should be driven from him, was too necessary, not to be conjured up at any rate, and it was so immediately after the late king's accession. He came to the throne easily and quietly, and took possession of the kingdom with as little trouble, as he could have expected if he had been not only the queen's successor, but her son. The whole nation submitted cheerfully to his government, and the queen's servants discharged the duty of their offices, whilst he continued them in their offices, in such a manner as to merit his approbation. This was signified to some of them, to the secretaries in particular, in the strongest terms, and according to his majesty's express order, before the whole council of state. He might I think, I thought then that he ought, and every man, except the Earl of O——d, who believed, or had a mind to make others believe, that his influence would be great in the new reign, expected, that he would have given his principal confidence and the principal power of the administration to the whigs: but it was scarce possible to expect, that he would immediately let loose the whole fury of party, suffer the queen's servants, who had surely been guilty of no crime against him, nor the state, to be so bitterly persecuted; and proscribe in effect every man in the country who did not bear the name of whig. Princes have often forgot, on their accession to a throne, even personal injuries received in party quarrels: and the saying of Louis the Twelfth of France, in answer to those who would have persuaded him to show severity to La Tremouille, is very deservedly famous. " God forbid," said he, " that Louis the Twelfth should revenge the quarrels of the Duke of Orleans." Other princes, who have fought their way to the throne, have not only exercised clemency, but shown favor to those who had stood in arms against them; and here again I might quote the example of another king of France, that of Henry the Fourth. But to take an example in our own country, look back to the restoration, consider all that passed from the year 1641 to the year 1660, and then compare the measures that king Charles the Second was advised to pursue, for the establishment of his government, in the circumstances of that time, with those which the late king was advised, and prevailed on, against his opinion, inclination, and first resolution, to pursue, in the circumstances I have just mentioned. I leave the conclusion to the candor and good sense of every impartial reader.

To these measures of unexpected violence, alone, it must be ascribed, that the Pretender had any party for him of strength sufficient to appear and act. These measures, alone, produced the troubles that followed, and dyed the royal ermines of a prince, no way sanguinary, in blood. I am far from excusing one party, for suffering another to drive them into rebellion. I wish I could forget it myself. But there are two observations on that event, which I cannot refuse myself to make. One is, that the very manner in which this rebellion was begun, shows abundantly that it was a start of passion, a sudden phrensy of men transported by their resentment, and nothing less than the execution of a design long premeditated and prepared. The other is, that few examples are to be found in history, perhaps none, of what happened on this occasion, when the same men, in the same country, and in the compass of the same year, were ready to rise in arms against one prince without any national cause; and then provoked, by the violence of their councils, the opposite faction to rise in actual rebellion against the successor.

These are some of the effects of maintaining divisions in a nation, and of governing by faction. I might descend into a detail of many fatal consequences that have followed, from the first false step which was taken, when the present settlement was so avowedly made, on the narrow bottom of party. But I consider that this discourse is growing into length; that I have had, and shall have occasion to mention some of these consequences elsewhere; and that your own reflections on what has been said will more than supply what I omit to say in this place. Let me therefore conclude by repeating, that division has caused all the mischief we lament, that union can alone retrieve it, and that a great advance towards this union was the coalition of parties, so happily begun, so successfully carried on, and of late so unaccountably neglected, to say no worse. But let me add, that this union can never be complete, till it become a union of the head with the members, as well as of the members with one another: and that such a union can never be expected till patriotism fills the throne, and faction be banished from the administration.

SOME REFLECTIONS

ON

THE PRESENT STATE OF THE NATION,

PRINCIPALLY WITH REGARD TO HER TAXES AND HER DEBTS, AND ON
THE CAUSES AND CONSEQUENCES OF THEM.

" Mihi autem non minori curæ est qualis respublica post mortem meam
futura sit, quam qualis hodie sit." CIC. in Læl.

———————

SINCE we are got out of a war the least successful, and the
most expensive, that this nation ever made; after having taken
part threescore years together, like principal actors, in all the
other wars and all the negotiations of the continent; it is time
surely, that we recall our attention homewards, and consider the
present state of our own country, particularly with respect to her
taxes and her debts, to the nature and application of the former,
to the rise and progress of the latter, to the necessity and to the
means of diminishing both.

The revolution of our government in one thousand six hundred and eighty-eight, makes a most remarkable era in the history of Britain on many accounts, and on none more than on
that which is the subject of these papers.   The public revenue,
in net money, amounted at that time to no more than two millions annually, which were sufficient to defray the ordinary expenses of the crown, as well as to maintain a fleet, and a greater
army than was necessary for the defence of the country at that
time.   This revenue was raised without any tax on land or malt,
and by a very few of those innumerable duties which have been
since laid, to the oppression of the landed and mercantile interest
of the nation.   These duties have been so mortgaged too, that

we are unable, at this time, to send a cock-boat to sea, or to keep
a single sentinel at Whitehall-gate without a land-tax.

The public debts, that of the bankers included, amounted to
little more than £300,000 at the beginning of this era. They
amount now to four score millions. To discover how this great
change in our national circumstances has been brought about
is surely an object of reasonable, and may be such of useful,
curiosity.

King William engaged in a necessary war with France as soon
as he came to the throne. It was necessary that he should maintain the revolution he had made, and assert his right to the crown
he had acquired by the best of all titles, the free gift of a people whom he had delivered from impending destruction, from
popery and slavery. This war might be thought necessary too
in another respect.

From the treaty of Westphalia, and from the Pyrenean, to the
accession of king William to our throne, the power and ambition of France had grown up together, and were become exorbitant. No efforts had been made sufficient to reduce, scarce
any sufficient to resist, the former. No measures had been concerted, no preparations had been made, to disappoint the latter
in that great object, the acquisition of the Spanish monarchy
to the house of Bourbon. From the revolution this alarm was
taken, which should have been taken sooner. The spirit of
our court was changed, the eyes of our people were opened,
and all men saw how necessary it was to preserve, in concert
with the Spaniards, the succession of their monarchy to the
house of Austria, instead of suffering it to fall into that of Bourbon, which was excluded from it by the most solemn engagements.

Queen Anne came to the throne at the eve of another great
war, of a war against France and Spain, which her predecessor
was ready to undertake, though he had not actually declared it
when he died, in order to procure some reasonable satisfaction
to the emperor, for a succession which had been then lost to his
family by his own fault.

King William, who engaged for so much more in the first
grand alliance, would engage for no more than this in the second.
But the private interest of her ministers, the intrigues of her
allies, and the rashness of a party, drew the queen much further:
and it must be confessed that a subserviency to the court of
Vienna, which has cost us so dear, began in her time, not in
king William's, though her heart was, what she declared it to
be, entirely English, and though he was censured, I think very
unjustly, for too great regard to foreign interests and too little for
those of Britain.

The war king William waged was not very successful; and yet if the emperor would have consented to send his second son into Spain during the life of Charles the Second, king William would have succeeded in both the objects of this war.   He had maintained himself on the throne, and had obliged France to promise that she would not disturb him in the possession of it. As to the other object, no treaties of partition would have been thought necessary by him in that case; neither would this nation have had any thing more to do, when the Spanish succession was open, than to support, with the concurrence of that whole nation, an Austrian prince who was actually on the spot with an Austrian army, and who had been already declared presumptive heir.   Thus we might have had a defensive war to make with great advantages on our side; and the events of the offensive war, which we were obliged to make afterwards, show sufficiently what would have been the success of the other.   The councils of Vienna laid us wantonly, if I may say so, under great disadvantages: and king William therefore resolved, like a wise prince, to expose neither this country nor his own to the hard task of recovering the whole Spanish monarchy out of the hands of Philip.   He accommodated his system to the circumstances of the time; and aimed at no more now than to fôrce the French and Spaniards to come into some composition about the Austrian pretensions, about trade, about barriers, and about effectual means to hinder a future union of France and Spain under one monarch.

This was all that he meant.   But they who delighted in war, because they hoped to get immensely by it, and they who amused themselves and others with vain speculations, about a thing very real in itself, about a balance of power, ensnared both England and Holland into engagements for dethroning Philip and setting up Charless in his room, though we had acknowledged the former, though the Castilians were strongly attached to him, and though he was in quiet possession of the Spanish dominions in both hemispheres.   Flattered by groundless hopes of a revolution in favor of his rival, and flushed by the first success of our arms, this precipitate engagement was approved and supported by us, notwithstanding the absurd conduct of the emperor and the wise reserve of king William, both of which should have put us more on our guard, and have made us less sanguine.

It is perhaps worth while to make an observation in this place, which was made at the time we speak of by Spaniards who acknowledged Philip the Fifth, in compliance with the will of Charles the Second, and yet were averse to the influence and authority which France assumed over them.   They observed that Cromwell had forced them to give their Infanta to Louis the

Fourteenth, by joining his arms with those of France against them, and that we went about to force them, half a century afterwards, by a new war, to an absolute dependence on France.

The court of Vienna, desirous to acquire the Italian dominions, and too indifferent about Spain and the West Indies, made her profit of our rashness. She left the whole weight of the war on England and Holland. She did worse. She not only neglected the war by contributing little or nothing to it, except the name of Austria and the claims of that family; she sacrificed the success of the common cause, for so it was called improperly enough by her, whenever any little inferior interest that seemed to be hers more immediately came in the way; by which she not only prolonged the war, but increased the annual expense of it to England and Holland, without taking any share in this expense on herself that deserves to be mentioned.

Experience was lost upon us. Our political delirium continued. It grew in some sort habitual by the artifice employed at home, and by the victories obtained abroad. The war languished however upon the whole, notwithstanding our utmost efforts; the weight of Austria grew every year heavier on us, whilst that of Spain grew every year lighter on France; the Spaniards were able to defend themselves against us at last, and the success of our enemies in Spain made them amends for our victories in Flanders.

The dethronement of Philip in favor of Charles, was become evidently a chimerical project in the year 1710, at the latest, and it became in the following year so ineligible by the death of the emperor Joseph, to whom his younger brother Charles succeeded, that one cannot conceive the men who clamored for it, even then to have been in earnest; since their aim, in that case, must have been to set the Imperial and Spanish crowns on the same head, against the common interest of Europe and the fundamental principle of the war.

But though we could not conquer Spain by a war, we might have reduced the exorbitant power of France by a peace. We might have stripped her of that barrier wherein this exorbitant power consisted chiefly, as every man, who knew what he meant when he talked of this exorbitant power, must have intended. We might have laid her as open to the incursions of her neighbors, as her neighbors were to hers: as open as she had been when a prince Casimir, or any other general of Reitres, could penetrate without a siege, and sometimes without a battle, into the heart of her provinces.

But we would not do the latter, because we could not do the former. We acted like men who thought that the exorbitant power of one family could not be reduced, unless a power as exorbitant was raised in another; and who never looked back to preceding centuries to consider the usurpations, the tyranny, and the bigotry that the house of Austria had exercised in the fulness of her power, and would exercise again if she was ever restored to the same.

We were disappointed in our great political views, after two wars that had lasted twenty-five years with a very short interval between them. We had done our utmost to defeat that scheme of ambition France had opened to herself, and of danger to all her neighbors, by the Pyrenean treaty: and, though this danger affected us less than any other nation engaged in the alliance, we had exhausted ourselves to maintain it.

When king William entered, immediately after the revolution, on this great scheme of action, the unincumbered condition of this nation, which has been hinted at above, was such, that he might have been supported in it by good management, as profusely as he was, and even more effectually, by the revenue then subsisting, by a land tax, by the excise on malt, and by some additional subsidies, all of which would have been raised within the year. A scheme of this kind was prepared and offered. It was allowed to be practicable; but it was rejected for a reason that appeared plausible in political refinement, and has proved most pernicious in its consequences. It was said that a new government, established against the ancient principles and actual engagements of many, could not be so effectually secured any way, as it would be if the private fortunes of great numbers were made to depend on the preservation of it, and that this could not be done unless they were induced to lend their money to the public, and to accept securities under the present establishment. Thus the method of funding and the trade of stock-jobbing began. Thus were great companies created, the pretended servants, but in many respects the real masters, of every administration.

I do not pretend to determine how far the wisdom of our legislature might have provided, at the beginning of the new war, against the growth and spreading of that cancerous humor, which had begun to gnaw our vitals in the former. All I am to observe is, that, a moneyed interest being firmly established at this time, and such numbers being accustomed to make immense profit at the public expense, there is no room to wonder if we proceeded on the same plan during the reign of queen Anne. We did so: and the debts contracted in this war, being added to those of the former, the whole of our debt amounted to little less than fifty millions.

Having accumulated so immense a debt, the queen put an end to the war. She could not attempt to alter the system of it whilst it continued, without throwing the whole alliance into confusion, after some of the principal allies had declared, on the death of Joseph, that they would not consent Charles should be king of Spain as well as emperor.

The interest of Britain required, no doubt, that we should turn our eyes from the continent to our own island, and that we should improve the opportunity and the advantages which a peace gave us. Whatever prejudices have been propagated industriously against that of Utrecht, thus much at least is certain. We were obliged no longer by treaties to assume any other part in the affairs of the continent, than that which the immediate interest of our country required. The opportunity and the means of diminishing taxes, reviving commerce, and paying debts were open to us.

This pacific scheme ought to have been pursued, no doubt, till we had retrieved our affairs, and recovered our former strength in some good degree, and till we were prepared to take any part in future events which our honor or interest might require. Nay, this scheme was the more necessary to be pursued; if France was left too powerful, no matter by whose fault, as I am ready to admit that she was; and if the two branches of Bourbon were to be looked upon in this century, like the two branches of Austria in the last, as inseparable allies, united by blood and by joint ambition. It was the more easy to be pursued too, because a long minority was beginning in France, and many other circumstances of characters and situation extremely favorable to it concurred in that court and country.

This should have been the scheme of our policy: but unhappily it was not. The late king as elector of Hanover, had reason, no doubt, to desire the acquisition of Bremen and Verden. Our nation contributed to it with her money, and forced it with her arms; though it was made in contradiction to the engagements that the crown of England had taken when king William gave his guaranty to the treaty of Travendal. This acquisition became the first link of a political chain, by which we were dragged back into new and expensive broils, the consequences whereof we feel at this hour.

When the king acquired these duchies, it became necessary to procure the investiture of them: and I will say, because I can demonstrate, that these investitures might have been procured, and the emperor flattered with the acquisition of Sicily, by measures as effectual, and much more consistent with former treaties and the public tranquillity, than those that were taken. The house of Austria sacrificed the success of the war to the immediate acquisition of Naples. We sacrificed all the advantages of the peace, to procure her that of Sicily in the manner we did

procure it. I have heard it said, whilst these affairs were in
transaction, that the treaty of quadruple alliance would complete
that of Utrecht. But the event has shown, and it was obvious
to foresee, that one of these treaties would unravel the system
of the other. If we had maintained the neutrality of Italy, as
we were obliged to do by treaty, even indulging the emperor in
the acquisition of Sicily, and yielding to the house of Savoy the
eventual successions which we stipulated should be given to
Spain, the intention of the treaty of Utrecht would have been
preserved, and France by concurring in these measures would
have shown her sincerity in maintaining the settlement of Europe. But when she became a party to the quadruple alliance,
she meant nothing more than to give the Spanish branch of
Bourbon an opportunity of reannexing to that crown the Italian
dominions: and we were grossly her bubbles when we triumphed
that she entered into the quadruple alliance, and made a sham
war to oblige Philip to accede io it.

As long, then, as there were hopes of obtaining an extraordinary investiture of Bremen and Verden, we flattered the emperor
at no small expense. As soon as it became apparent that this
investiture could be obtained in no other manner than it had
been granted formerly, we insulted him. We imputed to him
designs, he has constantly disowned, and we have never proved;
after which we complained of his ingratitude, we threatened
war, and we prepared for it by maintaining with great profusion
a standing army of Hessians in Germany. The same men, who
complained so lately that France had been left too powerful by
the treaty of Utrecht, and that great danger would arise from
her close connection with Spain, complained now of the too
great power of the house of Austria, and of the danger that
would arise from a good understanding between the emperor
and king Philip. In short, our politics were not only variable,
but incomprehensible to every man who knew the state and interest of Great Britain, but was not so well apprised of the several turns of interest which were to be served abroad.

When our ministers had once departed from the straight line
of British policy, the difficulty of returning to it became every
year greater, and the inclination every year less. We continued
busy and bustling in every court of Europe. We negotiated
against the emperor in concert with France, and gave her thereby the means of regaining more of that credit and influence in the
empire, which they formerly had, than she could have acquired
without our assistance. We contrived to make peace abroad
almost as chargeable to us as war. Abuses of every kind were
suffered at home. Trade was neither eased nor encouraged, and
the gradual payment of our debt was utterly neglected by a

minister rather desirous to keep his country under this oppression, than ignorant of the means to deliver her from it. Whilst we acted in this manner, France grew frugal, she made the debts she could not pay sit more lightly on her, she raised her credit, and she extended her commerce. In short, her strength increased, and ours diminished. We were reduced to a state of weakness we had never felt before; and this very weakness was urged as a reason for bearing tamely the losses our merchants sustained, and all the affronts our government received, lest we should be drawn into a war by using reprisals, the common right of nations.

As tame as we were, the insolence of the Spaniards, the reasonable impatience of our merchants, and this very tameness of our government, made a sea-war unavoidable, just before the death of the emperor Charles the Sixth; which event brought the principal powers of Europe into the field, set the whole continent in a flame, and formed one of those conjunctures wherein our honor and interest may oblige us to take a part, and for which therefore we should always be prepared.

We were in no degree so prepared, after six or seven and twenty years of peace; and yet when we took a part, we took the most lavish and the most impolitic that we could take. It was a miserable part by sea at first, and through the whole course of the war by land. I shall recall neither what we did, nor what we neglected to do; and I wish, for the honor of my country, that the whole may be buried in oblivion. Thus much only it is to my purpose to observe. First, That our councils seemed to be the echoes of those free-booters, Trenck and Mentzel, who talked of nothing less than conquering the two Alsatias and the three bishopricks, and of laying Champagne waste, whilst all our offensive projects on the Rhine were daily disappointed: and secondly, That we declined all overtures of peace, when the seat of the war was transferred, with great advantage to France, from Germany to the Netherlands, where we resolved to wage it whether the Dutch would or no, and where we were beat on every spot on which my lord Marlborough had conquered.

Every defeat in this war, like every triumph in the last, became a reason for continuing it: and this management, when no avowable reason could be given for it, gave suspicious and refining persons occasion to throw out a great deal of slander; for such I hope it was. In short, whatever the reasons were, we continued this inauspicious war so long, and we pushed it so far beyond our strength, that we were within a few months of bankruptcy, when the French granted us, miraculously, the same terms that they would have granted two or three years before:

and when they might have marched without much trouble or opposition, after taking Maestricht, into the heart of the Seven Provinces: for our last resource, a Muscovite army, was too far off to have enabled ours to make a stand.

By making the war in the Low Countries almost wholly at our own expense, and without any prospect of success, we meant to cause such a diversion to the forces of France as might leave Germany nothing to fear on the Rhine, and as might give time and opportunity to the empress queen to drive the French and Spaniards out of Lombardy. We sacrificed ourselves for these purposes: but in this war, as in the last, the court of Vienna sacrificed nothing. From the time the French had been obliged, more by the sickness of their troops and the ill conduct of their generals, than by the force of her arms, to abandon Germany, the empress queen seemed to make war just as it suited her conveniency, to save all the expense she could in the Netherlands, to plunder all she could in Italy, and to make us pay the whole immense subsidies which we gave her for both.

In the Netherlands we were outnumbered vastly by the deficiencies of her quotas: and in Italy, where we had thrown the Genoese into the arms of France and Spain, with great and just indignation against us for the treaty we had made at Worms, and had, however, obliged them to submit after the battle of Placentia, we lost the whole advantage of it by the insatiable avarice and extreme brutality of the Austrians. Yet we continued our efforts on that side still; and the sham siege of Genoa, for it was no more, and the harmless invasions of Provence and Dauphiny had no other meaning than to amuse and impose on us in the excess of our zeal.

Our expenses in every part of this strange war, particularly in the Netherlands, were made without measure, because without control; as they will be soon convinced who look into the artillery, forage, hospital, and other contingent accounts. The parliamentary aids from the year one thousand seven hundred and forty exclusively, to the year one thousand seven hundred and forty-eight inclusively, amount to £55,522,959 16s. 3d. and the new debt we have contracted to more than thirty millions, which are near twenty millions more of debt than France has contracted in the same time: a sum that will appear incredible to future generations, and is so almost to the present. There are three Reflections to be made on this state, which must add to our astonishment.—First, That the greatest part of this vast expense has been granted on account of the war, chiefly since there remained no reason for continuing it; that is, since the time when it was in our power to have a peace at least as good as that we have now obtained; and I place this era no higher than the year one thousand seven hundred and forty-seven inclusively, though I might place it higher, perhaps, on very good grounds.—Secondly, That the debt contracted in it exceeds by much that of king William's, or that of queen Anne's war; though both of them were much longer, and the last not only more widely spread, but carried into countries the distance of which and many other circumstances increased every article of our expense extraordinarily.—Thirdly, That we have thrown, by our negotiations and by the late war, into the hands of the house or Bourbon much more dominion in Italy, than would have induced the French at Gertruydenberg to have recalled Philip, and to have given up Spain and the Indies; which they were ready to do at those conferences, as Buys and Vanderdussen acquainted the ministers of the allies, in making one of their reports to that assembly.

Bad as our condition is, let us not despair. Not to despair of the commonwealth, whatever her condition be, is the principle of a true patriot, that is, of a faithful servant to his prince and country: and we may find an example to this purpose, which deserves to be quoted, in a book that is in the hands of most people, and that I hope is not unread at court, I mean the Duke of Sully's memoirs. In them we find that Henry the Fourth turned his whole application to every thing that might be useful or even convenient to his kingdom, without suffering things that happened out of it to pass unobserved by him, as soon as he had put an end to the civil wars of France, and had concluded a peace with Spain at Vervins. Is there a man, either prince or subject, who can read without the most elevated and the most tender sentiments the language he held to Sully at this time, when he thought himself dying of a great illness he had at Monceaux? " My friend!" said he, " I have no fear of death. You, who have seen me expose my life so often, when I might so easily have kept out of danger, know this better than any man. But I must confess that I am unwilling to die, before I have raised this kingdom to the splendor I have proposed to myself; and before I have shown my people that I love them like my children, by discharging them from a part of the taxes that have been laid on them, and by governing them with gentleness."

The state of France was then even worse than the state of Great Britain is now, the debts as heavy, many of the provinces entirely exhausted, and none of them in a condition of bearing any new imposition. The standing revenues brought into the king's coffers no more than thirty millions, though a hundred and fifty millions were raised on the people: so great were the abuses of that government in raising of money, and they were not less in the dispensation of it. The whole scheme of the administration was a scheme of fraud, and all who served, cheated the public, from the highest offices down to the lowest from the commissioners* of the treasury down to the under-farmers and the under-treasurers. Sully beheld this state of things, when he came to have the sole superintendency of affairs, with horror. He was ready to despair: but he did not despair. Zeal for his master, zeal for his country, and this very state seemingly so desperate, animated his endeavors: and the noblest thought, that ever entered into the mind of a minister, entered into his. He resolved to make, and he made the reformation of abuses, the reduction of expenses, and a frugal management, the sinking fund for the payment of national debts, and the sufficient fund for all the great things he intended to do, without overcharging the people.

He succeeded in all. The people were immediately eased, trade revived, the king's coffers were filled, a maritime power was created, and every thing necessary was prepared to put the nation in a condition of executing great designs, whenever great conjunctures should offer themselves. Such was the effect of twelve years wise and honest administration: and this effect would have showed itself in great enterprises against the house of Austria, more formidable in those days than the house of Bourbon has been in ours; if Henry the Fourth had not been stabbed by one of those assassins into whose hands the interest of this house, and the frenzy of religion, had put the dagger more than once.

When we consider, in these memorials, and in others which are come down to us, the deplorable condition to which France was reduced at the end of the sixteenth century, we feel some of that horror which Sully himself felt, and are ready to confess that the ruin of that kingdom, bankruptcy and confusion, must have followed, if the opportunity, which this peaceful conjuncture gave, had not been improved immediately, and as wisely, and as vigorously as it was. Shall we not see our own deplorable condition, and the necessary consequences of it in the same light? Shall we not be much more strongly affected by them? Are we not as near to bankruptcy as the French nation was at that time, and much more so than they are at this time? May not confusion follow it here as well as there? And finally, may not the joint ambition of two branches of Bourbon in some future conjuncture produce effects as fatal, and much more so to us, if we continue in our present state of impotence till such a conjuncture happens, as were to be feared by France at the time we speak of from the joint ambition of two branches of Austria? In short,

* Conseilliers dans le conseile des finances.

we have much to apprehend, unless we have the courage and the virtue to probe our domestic wounds to the bottom, and to apply immediately not palliative, but the most specific remedies. If we do this, instead of fearing others, we may become once more formidable ourselves. But this is certain, that they, who get first out of a distress common to us and to our neighbors, will give the law to the rest.

It may be said, that we have no Sullys among us. I shall not take on me to determine whether we have or no. But I will venture to say, after Sully himself, that although good princes may be wanting to good ministers; yet good ministers will never be wanting to a prince who has discernment enough to find them, who chooses them for their superior parts, experience, and integrity; and who resolves to support them, as Henry the Fourth supported Sully, against favorite mistresses, the cabals of the court, and the factions of the state.

It may be said again, that a king of France has power enough by the constitution of that government to support a minister who checks corruption, reforms abuses, and maintains a frugal management of the public revenue. But it may be asked, how a minister, who should undertake this, could be supported in a government like ours, where he would be sure to have for his enemies all those who have shared so long the public spoils, or who hope to share them, and where these enemies would have the means and opportunities of supplanting him, notwithstanding the protection of his master? I answer, by the parliament. How many ministers have there been, to whom much national mischief was imputed justly, and no one national good could be ascribed, and who were long supported by the favor of the crown, and by the concurrence of the two houses, which this favor and their own management procured them? Shall these supports be sufficient for a wicked or a weak minister; and shall innocence and ability, with the same favor and better management, be reckoned for nothing? I cannot think so ill, even of the present age, as degenerate as it is. It is degenerate no doubt: but I have heard men complain of this degeneracy, who promoted it first, and sought their excuse in it afterwards.

The delegated power of a minister, under the legal prerogatives of the crown, is sufficient to carry on a system of reformation and frugality in the ordinary course of things, if the minister really intends it: and whenever extraordinary powers are wanting for extraordinary operations, as they must be in such a state as ours, they will be effectual, if granted; and if refused, they who refuse them, not the minister, will suffer by the refusal, and be answerable to the nation for it. The moneyed man may continue to enjoy a little more revenue by this refusal: but his fortune will be more precarious, and more liable to some future reverse.   The merchant will continue to trade, the landed man to plough and sow, without even a prospect of being relieved from their servitude, not for the honest creditors alone, but for usurers and stock-jobbers, for those leeches who fill themselves continually with the blood of the nation, and never cease to suck it. The nation in the mean time will be reduced to the utmost poverty: and it behoves those particularly, who have brought us so near it, to show that this was not their object, by concurring zealously with those who have used and will continue to use their best endeavors to prevent it.

The diffculties we have to struggle with would not be so great as they are, notwithstanding the immense profusion to which the late war gave occasion and pretence, if we did not feel in this instance, as we feel in others, the fatal consequences of a precedent administration.   the payment of our debts might have been easily provided for in that time: nay, fourteen years, which are little more than two thirds of it, would have been sufficient to reduce them to twenty millions.   If this had been done, the memory of the person who was at the head of that administration, and had the sole power of it, might have deserved honor.

Let us nourish in ourselves, and cultivate in others, sentiments more elevated than these, and more worthy of the British genius. The greater our national distress and danger are, the greater should the efforts be of every particular man to relieve his country from one, and thereby to guard it against the other.   We are in a crisis that must turn either to life or death, and that cannot turn to the former unless remedies are applied much more effectual than those of monntebanks, who find their account in palliating evils and in prolonging diseases.   To palliate and to prolong would be, in our case, to kill, or to do something worse than kill, to break our constitution entirely, to render an accidental illness habitual and incurable.

One or two shillings in the pound, it is said, will be lessened this year upon land; and whatever is wanting for the current service, over and above the two shillings that remain, and the malt, will be borrowed on the credit of the sinking-fund at three per cent.   The bait will be tempting; for so must every diminution of taxes be to those who have crouched so long under the weight of so many.   But I may venture to say, that it will be no more than a bait; and that they who swallow it will have reason to repent of their rashness, when they find, as they will find very probably, that the natural effect of such measures must prevent the discharge of any considerable part of our debt, except in a term of years much longer than the prosperity and even the safety of our government admits.

I say the safety, as well as the prosperity; and some reflections very plain and obvious, though made by few, will justify me for saying so. As to the first, trade gave us wealth, wealth gave us power, and power raised our island to be, at one time, a match for France. If we desire to return into the same state, we must return by the same steps which raised us to it: and he, who should make a scheme for the payment of our debts, without a principal regard to the improvement of our trade, would make a very silly scheme. But it would be just as silly to make a scheme for both, in such a manner, as would render neither practicable.

The necessity of diminishing taxes, in order to improve our trade, becomes a good reason, not for the strange purpose to which it is applied by some, but for hastening all the operations necessary to sink our debts, in order to hasten that diminution of taxes which will become practicable, when a part of our debt is sunk, and which will facilitate extremely the discharge of the rest. The truth is, that if we defer these operations too long, we may be never able to perform them with equal advantage, nor, by keeping pace with our neighbors, to renew our strength, as fast as they are intent to renew theirs. Our neighbors have suffered by former wars, and have been exhausted by the last as well, though I apprehend not so much, as we. France, for instance, has contracted in the late war no more than one third of the additional debt we have contracted in it, as I believe on very good authority: and she has been able to assign funds, which pay the interest of this debt regularly, and sink yearly a part of the principal. I am not so well apprised of the actual state of Spain. But the treasures of the West Indies are poured into her daily; and as she has been long recovered, or recovering, from her ancient indolence and ignorance, she seems to apply herself to the augmentation of her maritime force, to the improvement of her trade, and even to that of domestic manufactures. In a word, what has been said before may be repeated here: they who get soonest out of the present common distress, will give the law to others, or be at least in a condition of not receiving it from any one.

As to national safety, we shall do well to observe how much the system of dominion and power in Europe is less favorable at present to our political interests and views, than it was when we undertook to mend it. Spain was falling, but not fallen into the hands of France, at the beginning of this century: and though the Spanish nation as well as court gave their monarchy afterwards to a prince of the house of Bourbon, that they might prevent the dismemberment of it; yet they were averse enough, by long habits of hostility, to a French government. Fortune and we have done so well at last, that these two nations are now closely united by interest and by habit, and that Spain is there-fore more than ever estranged from us; the proofs of which are not only recent, but, I fear, actual.

The frontier of France has been the great support of her ex-orbitant power, as wise men foresaw fourscore years ago, when Louis the Fourteenth began to raise that wall of brass which reaches from the Alps to the Ocean, that it would become. This frontier is now more compact than ever by the acquisition of Lorain. The branches of the house of Bourbon have taken root in Italy as well as in Spain. France has learned by experi-ence to raise and to maintain her credit, and to extend her com-merce, for the protection and support whereof she seems more attentive than ever to increase her strength by sea: a strength she will always exert with great advantage over us in some re-spects, I mean in those of order, frugal management, and strict discipline.

The whole empire, except Bavaria and Cologne, was attached to us by inclination as well as interest, in the war which began with this century. It is much otherwise now: and we may say, I fear, too truly, that the influence of France in Germany is little inferior to what it was whilst the league of the Rhine subsisted.

The Dutch commonwealth, our best ally, and in some sort a barrier to Great Britain, is in a state of dissolution; and has not, either without, or within herself, those means of recovery by conjuncture and by character, that she has had on several occa-sions from the time her government was first formed.

This short state may serve to show how difficult it will be, till we have paid a good part of our debt, and restored our country in some measure to her former wealth and power, to maintain the dignity of Great Britain, to make her respected abroad, and secure from injuries, or even affronts, on the part of her neigh-bors. This may appear easy, for aught I know, to some men. But sure I am, it would appear difficult to Burleigh and Walsing-ham, if they were to rise from the dead; notwithstanding the success they had in queen Elizabeth's reign by doing much at little expense, and by employing management much more than force.

These reflections, and such as they suggest naturally to the mind, make it evident, that the future prosperity and safety of this country depend on the speedy diminution of our national debts. Nothing else can secure us effectually against contingent events that may be of fatal consequence to both. Recent expe-rience has shown how unfit we are become in every respect, except the courage of our common seamen and soldiers, to en-gage in war. We shall not, therefore, I suppose, provoke it easily, or soon. But war may be brought upon us, though we should not provoke it, nor go to the continent to seek it. Nay, we may be reduced to the melancholy dilemma of increasing our annual expense to assert our rights, to protect our trade, and to maintain our dignity; or of sitting tamely down and sacrificing them all. I think, nay I hope, that we should not do the last: and yet we should have much greater difficulties to struggle with in our present situation, than we had in the former, great as they were, if we attempted to do, what was then so shamefully neglected. We cannot increase our expenses now, nor shall we be able to do so till some part of our national debt be discharged, without mortgaging on the remainder of the sinking fund, which would soon take away all hope of ever paying any part of this debt, and leave us nothing to mortgage but our land and our malt: whereas if a considerable part of this debt was discharged before any new war broke out, or we were reduced to any such dilemma as I have mentioned; we should find ourselves, whilst it lasted, in a much better condition of defence or offence, and we might be able, as soon as it was over, to resume the same operations, and to proceed in our great domestic concern.

These considerations will have great weight with men, who are able to combine all that is to be combined on such an important occasion, and, by reflecting on the past, and by observing the present, to judge of the future. The only effectual, and therefore necessary, remedies may appear violent, even to them: but they will consider, and every man ought to consider, that if we cannot bear our distemper, and will not bear our cure, the political body must perish. This miserable state will create justly the indignation of mankind. But this indignation should turn against those who have brought us into it, not against those who would deliver us from it. This is the language of reason dictated by public spirit: but private interest and narrow views will dictate another.

The moneyed men will complain loudly that they are exposed to perpetual reductions of interest, which have served to no other purpose than to nourish the profusion of successive administrations: and, if this was to continue, their complaints would be just, and the hardships imposed upon them intolerable. It is, therefore, just that neither they should consent to this new reduction of interest, which may be called a new tax upon them, nor the landed men to the continuance of that old and heavy tax on land, unless they have the utmost security that the whole shall be applied to its proper use. There will be still complaints; and we shall hear the melancholy condition to which the widow and the orphan, whose small but sole fortunes are in the funds, will be reduced, most pathetically displayed. The answer will be, however, obvious. If the widow and the orphan, who have their estates in money, suffer by the reduction of interest; the widow and the orphan, who have their estates in land, will suffer by the continuance of the tax upon it: and both one and the other must take their share in the common calamity of their country.

But the truth is, that the feeble voice of the widow and the orphan will be little heard. The great din will be raised by stock-jobbers and usurers, by the principal men in our great companies, who, born to serve and to obey, have been bred to command even government itself. These men will roar aloud, and endeavor, by silent intrigue, as well as by noise, to obstruct every measure that tends to emancipate government out of their hands, to make the exchequer, what it ought to be, the great spring of public credit, and the great scene of all transactions relative to public receipts and payments.

Let these men learn therefore to submit, and to reason, as old Bateman did, when the reduction of interest was agreed to in the year one thousand seven hundred and seventeen. He told my Lord Stanhope he was glad this resolution had been taken; because, though his interest diminished, he should think his principal more secure than ever. On the whole, complaints from this quarter will make little impression on a minister, who knows that, though such men have been employed whilst new debts were to be contracted every year, and the public, like an extravagant spendthrift, was obliged to deal with usurers on their own terms; yet they are not to be consulted when debts are to be paid, and the public to be taken out of their hands; who knows, in short, that his arms are longer than theirs, and makes them feel that he will keep, or not keep, measures with them according to their behavior; who pursues steadily the wise and honest design of rendering his own and every future administration independent of them.

Much opposition will arise from two other quarters, the country and the court; in which I should apprehend that the least plausible might be the most successful.

The landed man will think it hard, that he is not suffered to enjoy a little ease after having borne the burden and heat of the day, during a long course of expensive peace and of ruinous war. All that can be said, to persuade him that an immediate diminution of the land-tax is contrary to his interest, will pass for deception and paradox. He will be apt to reason like his country tenants, who are always frightened at an immediate expense, though remote, and yet great profit must be the certain consequence of it. Let such a man look back, then, and take his lesson from what is past. He will find that, whilst he winked at profusion because he was flattered by abatements on the land-tax debts, debts were contracted that have cost him much more than the continuance of that tax would have cost him. If we look back to the first ten years of his present majesty's reign, we shall find this very remarkably verified. Let the same man, after he has looked back, look forward again. He will see that, as any diminution of the land-tax to be supplied out of the produce of the sinking fund, or by borrowing even at three per cent. on the credit of it, must prevent, or retard, which may be equivalent to preventing, the discharge of any considerable part of our debt; so he will continue exposed to have the whole tax laid anew, on the first occasion either real or pretended. He may find himself, after a little respite, under the load of the same tax, and of an increased debt: and this may be all he will get by refusing to bear a little longer, for his own sake, and for an important object, what he has borne several years for the sake of others, and for the support of a most unsuccessful war; for such it may be reckoned, after the French were beat at Dettinghen.

On the other side, if he is wise enough to desire, that the four shillings in the pound be continued for a few years, he will have his share in the common benefits of diminishing public debts, increasing public credit, improving trade, and restoring national prosperity. He may entertain the comfortable hope of a time when he, or his posterity, will have no need of consenting to any tax at all on land in time of peace; since the annual produce of other funds will be sooner or later, in this method, sufficient to defray the annual expense of the government. He may acquire an advantage that will make him ample amends for what it cost him. Such of the taxes, whether of excise or of customs, as bear hardest on the poor laborers and on our own manufactures, may be reduced, gradually at least, without any considerable interruption of the operations necessary to discharge our national debt: and though he is little accustomed to think himself as much affected by other taxes, as he is by the land-tax, he will soon perceive, that a saving on every thing he eats, drinks, or wears, is a lasting and a large repayment of what this tax took from him whilst he consented to continue it. He will find himself a gainer, not only by what he saves in his expenses, but by the improvement of his estate; for the whole system of national wealth and prosperity are intimately connected.

The courtier will complain loudly, authoritatively, and pompously, that any retrenchments on our annual expenses may do more hurt, than the saving can do good. But I believe it not hard to show, that three shillings, or three shillings and sixpence in the pound on land, leaving the rest of the four shillings to go to the sinking fund, would be more than sufficient to answer all necessary expenses in time of peace. Wise men are able to do a great deal with a little: every knave or fool is ready to do a little with a great deal.   The former know that good policy consists in observing two sorts of economy, the greater and the less: to proportion, by the first, our expenses to our circumstances and to those of our neighbors, and to do it with the utmost frugality that these circumstances combined together will admit: to control, by the second, in the most strict and regular manner, the dispensation of the public treasure from the highest down to the lowest offices of the state.   It is of the utmost importance, at this time especially, that both these kinds of economy be practised.   Our well-being, even our security, depends upon them. If we do not pay our debts, we must sink under the load of them: and if we go about to pay them, without practising these two sorts of economy, the ridiculous figure which I have seen in a Dutch print, of a man toiling and sweating to cord a rope of hay, whilst an ass bites it off at the other end as fast as he cords it, will be our proper emblem.

Extreme frugality was one of the means employed by the great minister who has been quoted above: and the success he had, in similar circumstances, should .encourage the practice of the same frugality in ours.   But he employed another expedient likewise, which is not less necessary here than it was there, nor in our time than it was in his.   The expedient I mean, is that of reforming abuses.   Sully rendered this reformation no inconsiderable fund for the payment of public debts.   Whether we can do so, as effectually as he did, or no, I determine not.   But thus much is certain.   Such a reformation will make all future services be carried on at a cheaper rate for the public; and saving is often the surest way of gaining.   Materials might be collected, not for a pamphlet, but for a regular treatise under distinct heads, concerning the abuses and corruptions which prevail among us in every part of the public service, and concerning the consequences of them: I know not too whether some work of this kind should not be undertaken, as invidious as it may seem, if nothing is done to reform these abuses, and to extinguish this corruption.

They were creeping forward long ago; but since a certain period, they have advanced with very large strides.   Frauds were connived at, perhaps encouraged, and corruption was propagated formerly by principal men who had, for the most part, more ambition than avarice, and who raised, by these means, a formidable party that might support them in power.   But in process of time, and in favorable conjunctures, the contagion rose higher, and spread still wider; principal men became parties to the greatest frauds; and the highest of those who governed, and the lowest of those who were governed, contributed, in their degrees, to the universal rapine.   The greatest particular cheat, whereof any example can be found, was, I believe, that which arrears of subsidies to foreign princes, and arrears of pay to foreign troops, gave the opportunity and the means of executing.

I am sensible, that the representation I have made of the degeneracy of our age and people, may give occasion to say, that the very things I have been pleading for are impracticable. It will be asked what expectation can be entertained of raising a disinterested public spirit among men who have no other principle than that of private interest, who are individuals rather than fellow citizens, who prey on one another, and are, in a state of civil society, much like to Hobbes's men in his supposed state of nature? I must agree, though unwillingly, that the enterprise is difficult. But the more difficult it is, if nothing less can relieve us from the load of debt we lie under, nor prevent the consequences of lying under it much longer; every attempt to raise this spirit and to promote these measures, even the weakest, even mine, is commendable. The landed men are the true owners of our political vessel: the moneyed men, as such, are no more than passengers in it. To the first, therefore, all exhortations to assume this spirit should be addressed. It is their part to set the example: and when they do so, they have a right to expect that the passengers should contribute their proportion to save the vessel. If they should prove refractory; they must be told, that there is a law in behalf of the public, more sacred and more ancient too, for it is as ancient as political society, than all those under the terms of which they would exempt themselves from any reduction of interest, and consequently from any reimbursement of their principal; though this reduction and this reimbursement be absolutely necessary to restore the prosperity of the nation, and to provide for her security in the mean time. The law I mean, is that which nature and reason dictate, and which declares the preservation of the commonwealth to be superior to all other laws.

If such a co-operation of the landed and moneyed interests is once brought about, the way will lie smooth before us, and a prospect of national prosperity at the end of it will open before us yearly. Even the prospect will be of great advantage both at home and abroad. We shall feel it in the rise of our credit, in the confidence which our friends, and in the respect which our enemies, will have for us; a respect that will be due justly to a people who exert so much vigor in the midst of so much distress, and take effectual measures to restore their national strength, and to resume their former dignity, instead of languishing on, under impotence and contempt.

The man, who is not fired by such considerations as these, must have no elevation of mind, no love for his country, no regard for posterity, nor the least tincture of that public morality which distinguishes a good from a bad citizen. I know that futility, ignorance, and every kind of profligacy are general: but I know too that they are not universal, and therefore I do not despair. In all events, the merit of preserving our country from beggary, is little inferior to that of preserving it from slavery. They who engage therefore in so good a cause, and pursue it steadily in that public spirit, a revival of which can alone save this nation from misery, from oppression, and perhaps from confusion, the usual consequence of the other two; they will deserve better, I presume to say, the title of " ultimi Britannorum," even if they should be defeated by the worst subjects of Britain, than that usurer Brutus, and that severe exactor of contributions, Cassius, deserved the title of " ultimi Romanorum," when they were defeated in another manner by the worst citizens of Rome.

After all that has been said in these papers, and all that might be said, concerning the conduct of the house of Austria, from the reign of king William to the present time, it may be proper to add something by way of precaution, and to prevent very false conclusions, that many will be ready to draw from very true premises.

It is notoriously true, that a spirit of bigotry, of tyranny, and of avarice in the court of Vienna, maintained long the troubles in Hungary, which might have been appeased much sooner than they were. Thus a great and constant diversion was kept up in favor of France, even at the time when the two houses of Austria and Bourbon were struggling for that great prize, the Spanish succession, till the French troops took possession of Passau, and the malcontents of Hungary raised contributions in the very suburbs of Vienna.

It is notoriously true, that we might have had nothing more than a defensive war, as I have said in the foregoing papers, to make against France, with an Austrian prince on the throne of Spain, at the death of Charles the Second; if the emperor Leopold would have concurred in the wise and practicable measures which king William proposed.

It is notoriously true, that we might have avoided the defeat at Almanza, and have supported much better the war in Spain; if a predilection for acquisitions in Italy had not determined the councils of Vienna to precipitate the evacuation of Mantua, wherein an army of French was blocked up after the battle of Turin, and which was let loose in this manner, against the opinion of the queen and the States General, time enough to beat us at Almanza.

Finally, for I will descend no more to particulars, it is notoriously true, that we might have taken Toulon, and have carried the war into the best provinces of France, for which queen Anne had made, at a vast expense, all the necessary preparations; if the Austrians had not detached, in that very point of time, twelve thousand men on the expedition to Naples, and if prince Eugene had not shown too visibly, before persons still alive, that the taking of Toulon was the least of his objects.

These facts are sufficient to show, how much the mistaken policy of the court of Vienna has overloaded her allies during more than half a century, and has defeated the great design which these allies, and Britain in particular, carried on for her at the expense of infinite blood and treasure. Now there are many, in this kingdom, very ready to conclude from these facts, and from others of the same kind posterior to these, that our experience should teach us to neglect the interest of the house of Austria, and to be regardless of all that passes on the continent for the time to come. But surely such conclusions are very false. The principle of our conduct has been right, and our manner of pursuing it alone wrong. It was our neglect of the general interest of Europe, from the Pyrenean treaty to the revolution of our government in one thousand six hundred and eighty-eight, that gave to France a long opportunity, and the means of raising an exorbitant power. It has been zeal without knowledge, and a strange subserviency to private interests, which have almost exhausted this country, and defeated all our endeavors for the public good since that time. This we may alter. The principle of policy we cannot, as long as the division of power and property in Europe continues the same. We are an island indeed: but if a superior power gives the law to the continent, I apprehend that it will give it to us too in some great degree. Our forefathers apprehended, with reason, the exorbitant power of the house of Austria; and thought that the pretensions of Mary queen of Scots might give, even when she was a prisoner, opportunity and advantage, as they did no doubt, to this power to disturb our peace, and even to invade our island. The exorbitant power of the two branches of the house of Bourbon give surely in this respect, as well as in others, at least the same cause of apprehension now. It is, therefore, plainly our interest to maintain the rivalry between the families of Austria and of Bourbon; and for that purpose to assist the former on every occasion against the latter, as far as the common cause of Europe, not her private ambition, requires: and as far as our national circumstances may enable us to measure out our assistance in any conjuncture to her.

These are the measures and proportions, according to which alone political societies ought to unite in alliances, and to assist one another. There is a political, as well as a natural self-love; and the former ought to be, to every member of a commonwealth, the same determining principle of action, where public interest is concerned, that the latter will be to him most certainly wherever his private interest is concerned. I have heard it often said of one man, that he was a friend or an enemy to the house of Austria; and of another, that he was a friend or an enemy to the house of Bourbon. But these expressions proceed generally from passion and prepossession, as the sentiments they impute must proceed, whenever they are real, from these causes, or from one which is still worse, from corruption. A wise prince, and a wise people, bear no regard to other states, except that which arises from the coincidence or repugnancy of their several interests; and this regard must therefore vary, as these interests do, in the perpetual fluctuation of human affairs. Thus queen Elizabeth and her people opposed the house of Austria, and supported the house of Bourbon, in the sixteenth century. Thus queen Anne and her people opposed the house of Bourbon, and supported the house of Austria, in the eighteenth. The first, indeed, was done with wiser council; the last with greater force of arms. By the first, our country was enriched; by the last, it was impoverished.————

N. B.—These considerations were written thus far in the year seventeen hundred and forty-nine, but were never finished.

THE

SUBSTANCE OF SOME LETTERS,

WRITTEN ORIGINALLY IN FRENCH, ABOUT THE YEAR 1720.

TO

M. DE POUILLY.

SINCE you are so curious to know what passed in a conversation lately between one of your acquaintance and myself, wherein you have been told that I maintained a very singular paradox, I will give you some account of it, a general and short account at least, of the first part, and one more particular and more full of the last, which is called paradoxical. You led me first, in my retreat, to abstract philosophical reasonings: and, though it be late to begin them at forty years of age, when the mind has not been accustomed to them earlier, yet I have learned enough under so good a guide, not to be afraid of engaging in them, whenever the cause of God and of natural religion is concerned.

They were both concerned, very deeply on the occasion you refer to. There had been much discourse, in the company that was present, concerning the absurd opinions, which many theistical philosophers entertained of old about the Supreme Being. Many had been cited, and many reflections had been made on them, by several, when the dispute became particular between Damon* and me, he denying, and I affirming that there are sufficient proofs of the existence of one Supreme Being, the first intelligent cause of all things. You may be sure, I made use of those you furnished me with by a geometrical application of the doctrine of final causes, which shows, in various instances, what numberless chances there are against one, that intelligence and

---

* I chose to call him by this feigned name here.

design were employed in the production of each of these phenomena.

When I could not silence my adversary by these proofs though they carry probability up to a reasonable, if not to an absolute, certainty, I insisted on a proof which must give this certainty, I think, to every one who acknowledges that we are capable of demonstrative knowledge. I argued, *a posteriori*, from the intuitive knowledge of ourselves, and the sensitive knowledge of objects exterior to ourselves, which we have, up to that demonstrative knowledge of God's existence, which we are able to acquire by a due use of our reason. Here we stuck a little, and he was ready to deny all sensitive knowledge, on the chimerical notions of father Malebranche, and some other philosophers, without considering that he deprived himself, in denying the existence of God, of those expedients, by which the others pretended to account for the perception of the ideas of objects exterior to the mind, independently of any sensitive knowledge. I endeavored to show him, that to renounce sensitive knowledge, was to renounce, in some sort, humanity, and to place ourselves in some unknown rank, either above it, or below it. I endeavored to state the true notion, by stating the true bounds, of sensitive knowledge, which is not sufficient indeed to show us the inward constitutions of substances, and their real essences; but which is sufficient to prove to us their existence, and to distinguish them by their effects. I concluded this article by quoting to him a passage in the logic of Port-royal, wherein it is said, that no man ever doubted, in good earnest, whether there is an earth, a sun, and a moon, no more than he doubted, whether the whole is bigger than a part: that we may say, with our mouths, that we doubt of all these things, because we may lie; but that we cannot oblige our minds to do so: from whence it is concluded, more generally than I shall conclude, that Pyrrhonians are not a sect persuaded of what they say, but a sect of liars. He did not insist much longer, but left me to pursue my argument from intuitive and sensitive knowledge, to a demonstration of God's existence, which great and fundamental truth results necessarily from a concurrence of all the kinds of human knowledge employed in the proof of it.

I was not interrupted by him in the course of this argument, nor did he attempt to break any links of this chain of demonstration, but followed the example of all those who refuse to yield to it. They are so far from considering the degrees, the bounds, and within these, the sufficiency, of human knowledge, that they ask continually, and that others endeavor, very often, vainly to give them, knowledge concerning the divine nature and attributes particularly, which it is impossible and unnecessary we should have, even on the supposition that there is a God. Unable to break through this demonstration, they hope to weaken the effect of it, on themselves and others, by sounding high the difficulties that present themselves whenever we reason on the manner of God's existence, on his attributes, on his providence, and on many points relative to these. That is, they will not receive a demonstration, made according to the clearest and most distinct ideas that we have, and by the most precise connection of them, because there are other things which we cannot demonstrate, nor explain, for want of other ideas. This proceeding is so unreasonable, that the atheist himself does not hold it on any other occasion; but admits the truth of many propositions, though he be unable to resolve several difficulties that are, some way or other, relative to them. He reasons on this important article of human knowledge, as he would be ashamed to reason on any other.

I might have rested the argument here, because, though there are secrets of the divine nature and economy which human reason cannot penetrate, yet several of the objections to them, which atheists commonly make, even that of physical and moral evil, and the supposed unjust distribution of good and evil, which has been made in all ages, and which is now more prevalent than ever, by the joint endeavors of atheists and Christian divines, are easy to be refuted. These subjects have been so often treated between you and me, that I shall say nothing of them here, though I did not decline them there. On the contrary, if I do not flatter myself, I said enough to defeat the attack of the atheist, and to disappoint the treachery of the divine. After which I insisted, with great reason surely on my side, that these difficulties, and more of the same sort, were so little able to embarrass the theist, that, instead of being repugnant to his system, a necessary consequence of it is, that such difficulties should arise. He is so little surprised to find them, that he would be surprised not to find them. In demonstrating, to him, the existence of God, his reason has not demonstrated to him a being little raised above humanity, and about whom he may always assume on human ideas, such as the divinities of the heathen were. She has demonstrated to him the existence of an all-perfect self-existent being, the source of all existence, invisible and incomprehensible; the author, not only of all that is visible and comprehensible to his creatures, but of all that is, in the whole extent of nature, whether visible or comprehensible to them or not. From hence he concludes, and well he may, that there must be many phenomena physical and moral for which he can, and many for which he cannot, account. The system of God's attributes being, like the exercise of them, infinite, and our system of ideas and of mental operations being very narrow and imperfect, it follows necessarily, that some few parts of the former system are proportionable to the latter, and that a multitude of others are not so. A theist may suffer himself to be led into difficulties; but the atheist, take what system of atheism you please, must fall into absurdity, and be obliged to assert what implies contradiction.

I considered the Supreme Being, in all I said, as a first intelligent cause, and as the creator of the universe. From hence my antagonist took occasion to ridicule what theistical poets, philosophers, and legislators have advanced concerning the first principles or the beginning of things, and the operations of a divine wisdom and power, in the production of them, as if they had been cotemporary historians and spectators of what they related most affirmatively and circumstantially. I joined with him, for the most part, in giving them this ridicule, and expressed myself with a just indignation against them, for attempting to impose so many fictions on mankind, and for presuming to account for the proceedings of infinite wisdom and power, by the whimsies of their own imaginations. He did not spare Moses, nor I Plato. But when he went so far as to deny, on the strength of a very weak sophism, that we are obliged to ascribe the creation or formation of the world to intelligence and wisdom, he turned, I think, the ridicule on himself, for he reasoned thus:

When you investigate the proceedings of nature, you observe certain means, that seem, to you, proportioned to certain ends. You perceive too, that you cannot imitate nature any other way than by proportioning means to ends, and thus you frame that complex idea of wisdom, to which you ascribe the phenomena, and the imaginary final causes of them. But you are grossly mistaken when you assume, that nature acts by such means as seem to you proportioned to these ends.   Here is a clock which marks the hours and minutes, and strikes regularly, at certain periods, a certain number of times. The inward construction of this clock is unknown to you. But you see one made, which, by the means of certain weights, produces all the same effects. Will you assert now, that the motions of the first clock are regulated by weights, because those of the second are so? You will be much deceived if you do, for the motions of the first clock are produced and regulated by a spring.

This argument would have some force in opposition to such naturalists as Strato of Lampsacus, as Des Cartes, and as others who have made hypothetical worlds, and have pretended to account for all the phenomena by such laws of matter and motion as they have thought fit to establish. But in the present case it is a mere paralogism, and unworthy of the man who employed it, since it serves to explain and confirm that very reasoning which it is intended to oppose. The same motions are produced indeed by different means, but still these different means are proportioned alike to the same end, which proves, the very thing I would prove, the intelligence of a workman.

When we had done speaking of philosophers who admit the beginning of the world, we proceeded to those who deny it; and Damon seemed to think himself strongly intrenched in the system of its eternity. As we cannot conceive, said he, that matter was created and brought out of nothing, so we cannot conceive, neither, that matter could of itself produce motion, nor that matter and motion together could produce thought. But there arises from hence no necessity of assuming, that there is any Superior Being. Matter, motion, thought are eternal, and have been always what they are. The same nature, and the same course of things, that exist actually, have always existed.

To this it was easy to answer, that if I agreed with him in owning the eternity of the world, this concession would not infirm the proofs I had brought of an eternal Being, distinct from the world, as the workman is from his work. We may allow the world to be eternal, without allowing that it is the sole eternal Being. All that exists, has a cause of its existence, either out of itself, or in itself. It has no cause of its existence out of itself, if it is the sole eternal Being. It has this cause then within itself, and exists by the necessity of its own nature. The atheist affirms then, that it is impossible to conceive that this world should not exist; or should exist any otherwise than it does exist, both in matter and in form. This seems to me infinitely absurd; for the atheist either has no ideas in his mind when he pronounces these words, " exists by the necessity of its nature;" or he understands such a necessity of existence, that a supposition of the contrary would imply contradiction. If the atheist says, he has no idea of such a necessity, he has then no idea of the eternity of the world. If he says, as Damon did say, that he can no more conceive this world not to exist, or to exist differently from its present existence, than he can conceive the equality of twice two to four not to exist, he says nothing to the purpose; since the necessity of existence, according to him, cannot be admitted till he has given us another definition of what we are to understand by these words; and another definition, intelligible and reasonable, I think, he never will be able to give.

After having pushed this argument beyond reply, which I borrowed but did not weaken, I added, that Aristotle, and other ancient philosophers, who believed the world eternal, did not fall into the absurdity of believing it uncaused. They believed it eternal, in the order of time, but they believed it the effect of a superior cause, in the order of causality. The distinction is, per-haps, too metaphysical, but it serves to show, since they made it, to what shifts they were driven in maintaining the eternity of the world, and how little reason the modern atheist has to lean on their authority.

From refuting his opinions, I was led to advance one of my own, and to assert, that this fact, "The world had a beginning," is a fact, founded on such a tradition, as no reasonable man can refuse to accept. This is the paradox, in advancing of which, I had, not only Damon, but almost all those who were present, against me. It took up the rest of our conversation, and I will tell you, not only what I said, to support my opinion then, but what has come into my thoughts upon the same subject since.

Though we cannot have, strictly speaking, a certain knowledge of any fact whereof we have not been ourselves witnesses, yet are there several such facts whereof we cannot doubt. High probability must stand often in lieu of certainty, or we must be, every moment, at a loss how to form our opinions and to regu-late our conduct. Such is our condition, and we cannot think it unreasonably imposed, since we are able, by a right use of our reason, to ascend through various degrees from absolute impro-bability, which is little distant from evident falsehood, to that degree of probability which is little distant from evident truth. On this principle let us proceed to consider, how high this propo-sition, "The world had a beginning," stands in the scale of pro-bability. We shall find, perhaps, that it stands too high to have the proposition pass for a paradox, when I have told you what was said in conversation, and what has occurred to me since, on the same subject.

An historical fact, which contains nothing that contradicts general experience, and our own observation, has already the appearance of probability; and, if it be supported by the testi-mony of proper witnesses, it acquires all the appearances of truth; that is, it becomes really probable in the highest degree. A fact, on the other hand, which is repugnant to experience, shocks us from the first; and if we receive it afterwards for a true fact, we receive it on outward authority, not on inward conviction. Now to do so is extremely absurd; since the same experience that contradicts this particular fact, affirms this gene-ral fact, that men lie very often, and that their authority alone is a very frail foundation of assent.

It may seem a little extraordinary, and perhaps chimerical, to our first thoughts, to examine which is most conformable to ex-perience, the eternity of the world, or the beginning of it in time; and it would be really so, if, to constitute this conformity to expe-rience, it were strictly necessary, on every occasion, to cite a fact of similar kind.   But there is no such necessity in the nature of things, and this conformity may be sufficiently constituted otherwise.   Were it not so, our ignorance would produce very contrary effects, equally absurd; for this mother of superstitious credulity, would be the mother likewise of most unreasonable incredulity.

The probability of a fact, whereof there are frequent and notorious examples, may force our assent at once, like those which happen constantly in the ordinary course of things.   But still it is true, that a fact of which we find no precise example within our knowledge, may have a conformity, properly so called, with our experience.   The probability arising from this sort of conformity will not be perceived, indeed, so soon as the other, but when it is perceived, will determine alike.   This case may be compared to that of the mathematician, who arrives at truth by a long process of demonstration, and who can doubt of this truth afterward, no more than he doubted of those self-evident truths which carry instantaneous conviction to the mind.

A fact may be, in the respect we speak of here, indifferent. We may discover, in our experience, none of the same sort; and yet none that imply contradiction with it.   Such a fact, therefore, is merely new; and experience will be far from teaching us to reject any fact on this account alone.   When such facts, therefore, new to us, according to the extent of our knowledge, but not so to other men, are attested by credible witnesses, he must act very unreasonably, who refuses to give that degree of assent to them, which is proportionable to the credibility of the witnesses.   Again, the fact may be conformable to experience by a certain analogy physical or moral, if not by particular examples, and may be admitted, therefore, on proper testimony, more easily still, than one of those which I called indifferent.   One rests wholly on testimony, but experience gives to the other an indirect, if not a direct, confirmation.

Let me quote a story, which will serve to illustrate all I have been saying.   A certain king of Siam was firmly persuaded that Sommona-Codom had straddled over the gulf of Bengal; that the print of his right foot was seen at Pra-bat, and that of his left foot at Lanca.   This pious legend was certainly repugnant to his majesty's experience, the first foundation of probability: and he fell into the absurdity of believing it on the most precarious of human authorities, the authority of his priests, who had taught him, perhaps, that the merit of his faith in the legend of Sommona-Codom increased as the probability of what it contained diminished.   When the Dutch ambassador assured the same prince, that the surface of the water hardened so much in his country, during the winter, that men, and beasts, and heavy carriages passed over it, the prince treated him as a liar. He knew no example of this kind: and the seeming non-conformity to experience, in this case, had the effect which the real non-conformity to experience should have had in the other. I call this a seeming non-conformity; because although the good Siamese knew no example, in point, of what the ambassador told him, yet he might have reflected on several particular objects of his knowledge, that would have brought it up to a real conformity. He knew, for I think the art of casting cannon was known in his country, that extreme heat could give fluidity to the hardest metals: from whence he might have concluded, very naturally, that extreme cold was capable of producing a very contrary effect, that of condensing and hardening fluid substances. In his country there was no ice; but he knew that there fell sometimes on the neighboring mountains of Ava, of Pegu, and of Laos, a certain white cold and solid substance, which was nothing else than water, condensed and hardened in one season, and melting and flowing in another. He was a man of good sense, they say, and therefore we may believe that these considerations discovering to him a real, though not exact, conformity to his experience, he gave credit to the Dutchman afterwards.

Let us consider now, on our part, whether there are not facts that contain all that is necessary to establish the highest probability, though there are no examples of the same, and though we should allow, that a bare non-repugnancy to experience, or a strong analogy to it, does not afford sufficient grounds of probability. Suppose then a fact, preserved in history or tradition, which has the two conditions of non-repugnancy and of analogy, and the contrary to which cannot be asserted without absurdity. If the negative be absurd, is it not agreeable to right reason that we adhere to the affirmative?

It may be said, perhaps, that the supposition I make cannot have place in historical facts, that these are in some sort arbitrary, they may be affirmed or denied, according to the credibility of the testimony. That Julius Cæsar conquered the Britons, or that Genghiz-Khan conquered China, may be true; but it may be true, likewise that Cæsar was beat by the Britons, and that Genghiz-Khan did not even march into China. It may be said, that when such facts, as we meet with frequently in the romances of all kinds, are concerned, we may affirm that the contrary is true, or that no such events ever happened; but that it will not follow, that an historical or trraditional fact is true, because it appears to us, that to suppose the contrary is absurd. I enter no further into this disquisition, but I content myself to say, that there is, at least, one such fact conveyed to us by tradition, the truth of which we must admit, because it is absurd to assume the contrary, and because one or the other must be necessarily true. The fact I mean is this, that the world, we inhabit, had a beginning in time, and the same may be said of our whole solar system, and of the whole system of the universe. Now this fact being denied very dogmatically, and there neither being nor ever having been any living cotemporary human testimony for it or against it, we must, I think, be decided in this case, by considering, whether the beginning or eternity of the world implies any contradiction with what we know, or is repugnant to our clearest, most distinct, and best determined ideas. One of these facts must be true, since the world exists actually. If it can be shown, therefore, that the opinion of its eternity is an absurd opinion, I must be convinced that it had a commencement.

To prove the absurdity of the former, there seems to be a very obvious method, and an argument the more conclusive, because it is, in opposition to the atheist, an argument *ad hominem* an argument drawn from the only solution of one of the greatest difficulties which the theist proposes to him. If this solution be not good, he remains without a reply, and if it be good, as I think indeed that it is sufficient to answer this particular difficulty, there arises from it an argument against himself, much stronger than that which the theist opposed to him, and which I am ready to acknowledge, that he has fully answered. What is here said, requires to be explained by a deduction of particulars.

He who denies the commencement, and asserts the eternity of the world, must believe that this planet of ours has been, from all eternity, such as we see that it is. I say, that he must believe it to be so, since, if he admitted such changes in it as had overturned the whole order of physical nature, destroyed all the species of animals, and confounded all the elements in a new chaos, the dispute would be over, and he convicted, at once, of the grossest absurdity, because a God, a Δημιθργος, would be as necessary in this case, as in that of an original creation. In short, such a renewal of the world requiring no less wisdom and power than the formation of it, the dispute, on the atheist's part, would sink into a cavil about words. He is obliged therefore to maintain, that this planet of ours has been always, upon the whole, much what it is; that there have been, from eternity, the same general laws, and the same order of physical nature; an infinite succession of material causes and effects, blind causes of uniform effects, uniform in kind, if not in degree; causes, which have been effects; effects, which become causes in their turn, and proceed in this manner round the circle of eternity. When we quote to the atheist the universal consent of tradition, in affirming that the world had a beginning, he laughs at the proof, Whether he has any right to do so, will be seen presently. In the mean time, we cannot be surprised that he, who rejects a demonstration, should pay no regard to a tradition; but we may be well surprised, when, following the atheist on, we find him calling tradition to his aid, and leaning wholly upon it.

If the world is eternal, why does our knowledge of it go no further back, why have we not more ancient memorials, says the divine? The same reason, says the atheist, which hinders us from having records, where we have any, beyond two or three thousand years in a space of five or six thousand, to which, according to you, the antiquity of the world extends, is just as good to hinder us from seeing further backwards, in a longer, and even in an infinite space of time. Now here theology comes in to the aid of atheism, as it does upon more occasions than this. The history, which is ascribed to the legislator of the Jews, and which it is required that we should believe implicitly, assures us, that the world was once entirely drowned; and through the whole course of sacred, as well as profane, Scriptures, we hear of other inundations, of earthquakes, of plagues, of devastations of countries, and of captivities of people, by all, or some of which, not only numbers of men have been destroyed, but whole political societies have been lost. Thus the atheist has it in his power to make the same use of holy writ, which the divine makes of profane history; that is, he adopts whatever makes for his purpose, and rejects whatever does not. He finds ancient governments frequently dissolved, and new ones rising. The records of the former as well as their laws and customs, perish with them. The latter remain often very long in ignorance and barbarity, and have not the means, nor even the desire, of conveying the events of their own time, nor the traditions of former times by authentic records to posterity. He will not fail to observe, that all we know of ancient history, except those broken scraps of it which Jewish traditions mention, has come down to us from the Greeks; that many centuries passed, after the deluge, before Cadmus, or any one else, carried the use of letters to this people; and that this people, not having employed them to write history till many centuries afterwards, it is not astonishing that we know as little as we do concerning times more ancient than those. The atheist triumphs in this answer to the divine, and though no man abhors his cause more than I do, I think him thus far in the right. But the scene will soon change, if a theist interposes. His answer to the divine's question will indeed stand good, but out of this very answer there will arise a decisive argument against him.

When the atheist has sounded the deluge of Deucalion high,

and admitted, for the sake of his argument, that of Noah; when
he has added to these, all those other deluges, of which tradition
speaks, that of Xisuthrus, that of Ogyges, that which the Chinese
annals mention, that whereof the priests of Sais informed Solon,
and that, if it was not the same, whereof the memory had been
preserved among the people of America, besides a multitude of
devastations of other kinds, he will think himself very strong.
But the theist may ask him a very puzzling question, Was there
any thing supernatural in the production of these terrible catas-
trophes?   The divine might answer, that there was; but he could
not: for if he did, he would acknowledge the existence of a Supreme Being, which he denies.   It remains then, that all he has
said about the immutable order and laws of nature, which have
maintained the world in much the same state, and such as it is,
from all eternity, must pass for nothing, and the theist will insist,
that if such events as these, which tend directly to the dissolution
of our planet, and the extermination of the whole human race,
have been produced so often, in five or six thousand years, by
the action of blind causes, matter and motion alone, it is repugnant to common sense to believe, either that such events have
not happened an infinite number of times, in an infinite space of
time; or that having so happened, they should not have once
destroyed the world entirely, and made the supposition of a
God necessary to restore it to the state in which we see it.   The
theist will insist further against the atheist, that it is absurd to
confine these phenomena to such bounds, and to accompany
them with just such circumstances as suit his purpose.   The
purpose of the atheist required that these destructions of mankind
should happen often enough to defend his hypothesis against
that question, Why have we not more ancient memorials of the
world, and of the inhabitants of it?   What his purpose required,
is exactly answered, by the eternal complaisance of blind material causes.   The world was never entirely destroyed nor mankind entirely exterminated, nor any necessity created of a God
to restore them.   But there have been as many of these destructions, as may be improved to extricate the atheist out of the
difficulty which is laid in his way.

   The divine would sit down well satisfied with the state to
which, I suppose, the dispute is reduced by the theist, if he had
nothing more at heart, than to maintain the existence of God,
by maintaining the commencement of the world.   But he has
something more at heart, it must have commenced, it must have
been renewed, and it must have been repeopled, in the manner
Moses relates, and just at the time which he fixes, according to
the calculations that learned men have grounded on the genealogies contained in the book of Genesis.   For this purpose a sys-

tem has been invented by crowding profane into the extent of sacred chronology, and by making as many anecdotes of the former, as can be so made, seem to coincide with those of the latter. Divines would be thought to prove the latter by concurrent evidence, but in reality they assume it to be true, and by this assumption alone, can the violence, with which they drag profane anecdotes to their purpose, be in any sort excused. That I may not quote to you any of those numberless heavy writers, who have taken this task upon them, I will bring forward on this occasion M. de Meaux, the honor of the Gallican or rather of the Christian church, and the shame of that of Rome. This writer, who possessed in the highest degree the talent of seducing the imagination, when he could not convince the judgment, running over, in his discourse on universal history, those ages which succeeded the deluge, in a very agreeable manner, but on very precarious authority, makes no scruple of affirming, that there is no ancient history wherein the marks of a new 'world do not appear manifestly in these early times, and long after them. These endeavors to confirm the Mosaic system by a multitude of uncertain traditions, as well as the history itself, compiled, no doubt, from other traditions, might be sufficient to take all authority from tradition, if these authors did not mistake the notion of it, and if a just distinction, that ought to be made, did not escape them.

Tradition is first oral, the first authors of it unknown: and when it comes afterwards into history, the genealogical descent of it nothing more than tradition, and we must say, in general, very absurdly, that it proves itself, or, very truly, that it has no proof at all. From hence it follows, that particular circumstantial facts, conveyed to us by particular traditions, are destitute of historical proof. But still it will be agreeable to nature and reason, that the unanimous concurrence of many traditions, to which no contrary traditions can be opposed, may constitute the truth of a general fact. Public report, as Pliny the younger observes, relates facts in the gross, and naked of circumstances. So it must do, to deserve any credit; and so does this tradition, that the world had a beginning. It is rather a fact, resulting from the concurrence of traditions, than a fact founded on the authority of any. Nothing can be less credible than all that we read in ancient story, about the Assyrians for instance. It is a wild heap of inconsistent traditions which cannot be reconciled, nor verified for want of a historical criterion. Ctesias, it is said, boasted that he had extracted the materials of his history, whilst he was in the service of the king of Persia, out of the authentic records of that monarchy. But his account, those of other Greek writers, and even those of the Old Testament, are so contrary to

one another, and, on the whole, so improbable, that they may
be all comprehended under the name of Assyriacs, which Aristotle brought into proverbial use, and which was meant to signify all sorts of fabulous relations.   What are we now to believe
in this case?   Not any particular tradition, to be sure; but thus
much, in general, that there was an empire once founded in Asia,
to which the Assyrians gave their name.

These traditions, those of Egypt, and many of Greece, come
from those dark ages which may be called heroical or fabulous,
after Varro the most learned of the Romans.   More modern
Greeks, like echoes, repeated these traditions, and, in repeating,
multiplied them all, so that the sound of them rings still in our
ears, and they remain objects of learned curiosity.   Shall we
give credit now to the traditions, that came down from fabulous
ages, about the expedition of the Argonauts; about the war of
Thebes, and that of Troy; about the adventures of Hercules, of
Theseus, and a multitude of other romantic stories?   No, most
certainly.   It would be ridiculous to give credit to any of them.
But it is not ridiculous, it is reasonable, to be persuaded that they
had some foundation in the truth of things.   Every tradition, considered apart, may be safely denied; because no one of them has
a historical proof: but yet a truth, which may be called with
little impropriety historical, results from the combination of all
these fabulous traditions.   There were, no doubt, in unknown
ages, maritime expeditions, famous leagues, cruel wars, and heroes who rendered their names illustrious.

One tradition reports, that Perseus carried a colony into the
east; another, that Tithonus did the same "usque ad Æthiopas,"
as far as the Indies.   Is not the voyage of Io, daughter of Ina-
chus, into Egypt long before, and the expedition of the Cimme-
rians into Asia long after, famous in tradition?   Many others of
the same kind might be mentioned; and though they are all fabulous, they leave no reason to doubt, that arts and sciences, and
even barbarity, were carried from the west to the east, as well
as from the east to the west, in ages quite unknown to us; which
is enough to shake the authority of that particular history wherein it is reported, that the world was repeopled from one spot, and
by one family, after a universal deluge.   But I need insist on
this head no longer.   So many general truths, of which it is impossible to doubt, result from the concurrence of fabulous traditions, that there remains no reason to doubt of the truth of this
fact, "The world had a beginning."

Will it be said, that if there has been such a tradition, it has
not been so universal as to establish this truth, according to my
rule?   Lest this should be said, it is necessary that I prove the
universality of it; and that by showing, particularly, for what

reasons we admit other facts to be true, though founded only on tradition, it may appear that the beginning of the world is still better founded, and this important tradition advantageously distinguished from all others.

Whilst I am writing on this subject, to you, a dissertation, I had never seen before, is fallen into my hands. The author* of it pretends not only to prove, that the world had a beginning, but also, that this beginning was the same which Moses gives it. He is so fond of the second proposition, that he employs all his skill and all his learning to establish it. He ventures to assert, that the history of the world was very well known, when that of Moses became public by the spreading of the gospel; that profane history agreed with sacred, in this respect, and did not reach beyond the bounds Moses had set. One would think that these writers imagine, for this writer is a divine too, that none but themselves can read, and that they have still the advantage, which they had before the resurrection of letters, the advantage of imposing whatever they please on an ignorant world. The world had a beginning; tradition proves it had. But tradition is far from proving that it began, either in the manner Moses relates, or at the time which he is thought to have fixed. Profane and sacred history were as little agreed, when Christianity was published and the Jewish scriptures were better known, as they are at this time; notwithstanding all the pains taken by Josephus, Eusebius, and others, to reconcile them; and notwithstanding all the pains that have been taken, by modern scholars, to confirm sacred by profane anecdotes.

Let us neglect such writers, therefore, who make a show of learning, always futile, and often false. Let us examine and compare for ourselves; look into the authors, they cite; but trust neither their citations nor their reasonings. Diodorus the Sicilian, and Strabo, in the reign of Augustus; Pliny and Plutarch in those of Vespasian and Trajan, very respectable authors certainly, give us a different idea of their knowledge in the history of the world, from that which the author of this dissertation would give us. They knew a little better than this modern writer, what histories and what traditions they had of any authenticity. They made no great account of those canticles or hymns, of those inscriptions and other expedients, which had been employed, in more early times, to preserve the memory of past events, and concerning which the writer we refer to, enters into a chimerical and tiresome detail. These ancient writers looked on their histories to be more modern, and their traditions to be more ancient, than our tribe of scholars would make them, the last especially. That

* Jacquelot.

profound antiquity, wherein these men affect dogmatically to
make great discoveries, with very particular and critical exactness, was, for the others, a dark abyss, wherein they saw but
few objects, and those few rather general than particular, and,
on the whole, very imperfect.　They acknowledged, that the
first of the Greek historians had written no earlier than the time
about which the Persians began to make their expeditions into
Europe.　They confessed, that neighboring nations had some
historical monuments of a much greater antiquity; but they
confessed too, that these monuments were very imperfect and
very precarious, broken into discordant anecdotes, and mingled
up with romance and poetical fiction.　In a word, they owned
themselves able to pierce a very little way into antiquity; but
none of them pretended, that the bounds of their historical
knowledge were the bounds of antiquity.　Let us see now,
whether the beginning of the world may not be, even at this
time, reputed equivalent to the best established historical fact,
notwithstanding the avowed ignorance of the most learned and
curious inquirers, who wrote, two thousand years ago, about the
beginning of nations, and much more of the world.

The Egyptians seem to have been reputed the most ancient,
or one of the most ancient, nations of the world, by the Greeks,
from whom all our knowledge of profane history descends.-
They gave to their nation an immense antiquity, and in part,
perhaps, fabulous.　But I am at a loss, however, to discover
what means, and therefore what right, the scholars of these ages
have to decide, as dogmatically as they have done, about the
Egyptian dynasties.　Why, for instance, the Jesuit Petavius required that we should, upon his word, reject them all?　Or, why
the author of the dissertation, after touching the matter very
lightly and very superficially, should expect to be believed, when
he conjectures that there were no monuments of Egyptian antiquity later than Mœris, though he has in this the authority of
as great a man as Marsham on his side?　Dicearchus, the disciple of Aristotle, who had not, most certainly, inspired him with
much credulity in ancient traditions, had studied the antiquities
of Egypt.　Manetho had done the same in the time of Ptolemy
Philadelphus, and Eratosthenes in the time of Ptolemy Evergetes.　The first of the two was himself an Egyptian, and had
extracted his chronology and history from the books of Mercury,
that is, from the sacred and most authentic writings of the Egyptians.　Why has his chronology been called in question, or why
was it not received by Christian writers beyond a certain epocha?
Is there any pretence to say, that he altered what he found in
the books of Mercury; as we know that Julius Africanus, and
Eusebius, altered and transposed his dynasties, to make them, as

near as they could, conformable to the Mosaic chronology?—
With what front can we suspect the authenticity of books, compiled and preserved by Egyptian priests, when we receive the
Old Testament on the faith of Jewish scribes, a most ignorant
and lying race?   Were the sacred books of the Egyptians taken
from them by a king of Persia?   Diodorus says it.   But the
same Diodorus assures us, that the Egyptians purchased their
Scriptures again, and that they were restored to them by the
eunuch Bagoas: whereas the Scriptures of the Jews were lost,
more than once; and how they were recovered, the last time at
least, is unknown to us: nay, whether they were recovered at all,
in a strict sense, may be, and has been, questioned by some
Christians and Jews too.   Is the immense antiquity, which Manetho ascribed to his nation, or the tales of Osiris, and Isis, and
Typhon, too ridiculous to be admitted?   I shall not plead in
favor of them.   But, in truth, are the anecdotes of Jewish antiquity a whit more conformable to experience, to reason, and to
all our notions of things divine or human, whatever regard we
may pay to some passages in the Pentateuch, because of the use
to which they are put by theology.   No man, who has the least
pretence to candor, and who dares speak out, will assert so much.
But still, how little credit soever we may give to the particular
traditions of either sort, all of them together are the general voice
of antiquity, and extort our assent to this truth, " The world had
a beginning."

This truth seems to have been propagated by them in those
hieroglyphics, and that sacred language, wherein they recorded
whatever was most ancient and most respected.   Horus, or the
world, was represented like a youth whose beard was not yet
grown.   An egg was the famous symbol of the generation, as
well as figure, of the world; and the Thebans, who were the
most ancient Egyptian dynasty, had a hieroglyphical representation of the Divinity with an egg coming out of his mouth; which
symbol of an egg was adopted by the Phœnicians, and by the
Persians, and became an object of worship in the orgia, or mysteries of Bacchus.   These monuments came down from the first
Mercury, at whose antiquity we cannot so much as guess; for
the second, who followed, and probably very long after him, our
chronologers are obliged to place as high as the age of Moses or
of Joshua.

Sanchoniathon, that we may say something of Phœnician as
well as Egyptian traditions of this sort, is another author that
may vie, perhaps, with the most ancient for antiquity.   Bochart,
and all our divines, think fit to place him in the time of Gideon.
It is not convenient for them that he should stand backwarder.
They build their assertion on a passage concerning him in the

writings of Porphyry, who says, that Sanchoniathon had the
materials of his history from Jerombal, a priest of the god Jao.
Now Jerombal sounds too like to Jerubaal, the name Gideon
wears in Scripture, and Jao sounds too like Jehovah, to leave
any doubt on this subject in the minds of men who can make
systems and write volumes on the affinity of sounds. Sanchoniathon then, being cotemporary to Gideon, had a knowledge of
the book of Moses, and took from thence all he knew concerning
the beginning of the world; so that these two are but one and
the same tradition, according to this opinion. But there is great
reason to doubt of the first part, and the second is evidently false.
The anachronism of Porphyry, who supposed Semiramis cotemporary with the siege of Troy, will not make Sanchoniathon
cotemporary with Gideon: since the last was, unluckily, not a
priest, and since the Jerombal, from whose writings the Phœnician historian is said to have borrowed, was one. The answers
made to this objection are trifling. A pagan, it is said, might
take a general of an army for a priest, and Porphyry was guilty
of this blunder. The Jews called their chiefs or principal men
sometimes priests, it is said. Therefore Porphyry, who was no
more a Jew than he was a Christian, might make use of an appellation peculiar to the Jews. But, further, in what time soever
Sanchoniathon lived, he did not relate what he said concerning
the commencement of the world from the Mosaic history, or any
other Jewish traditions; since he affirmed positively that he derived the cosmogony from Taaut or Mercury. Have we not
reason to be surprised, as much as we are accustomed to it, at
the boldness of scholars who presume to oppose their frivolous
conjectures, to what a historian himself says of the materials
which he followed?—The second part of what is said concerning
this Phœnician historian being false, it follows that Sanchoniathon, one of the most ancient writers whose name is come down
to us, Sanchoniathon, a lover and follower of truth, according to
the etymology of his name, learned and curious in searching the
original of things, furnished with the most authentic materials
that Egypt and Phœnicia could afford him, and writing in an age
when the authenticity of these materials might be known,
affirmed the beginning of the world; and is, therefore, a voucher
of the same truth, distinct from Moses.

Whether the books of the Pentateuch were written by Moses
himself, or whether the traditions contained in them were compiled after his time, which is not at all improbable; certain it is,
that these traditions are of very great antiquity. Now these traditions confirm the same general fact, in a more circumstantial
account of it, than we may suppose that Sanchoniathon gave.
I have read that Simplicius laughed at the whole story, and at

Grammaticus for quoting some passages of it. This interpreter of Aristotle affirmed, that the whole was taken from Egyptian fables. But Simplicius might have considered, as we do, that how ridiculous soever the circumstances might be, the fact, affirmed by so many traditions, might be true, though he was led to deny it by arguments which Aristotle himself owned to be very problematical. Aristotle, who employed logic very absurdly in physics, might employ it, as absurdly, about history and tradition. Let it be, that the account Moses gives of the creation, and the cosmogony of Sanchoniathon, are alike fabulous; yet still the general fact, advanced by them, may be reputed true. The various fables annexed to it do, in effect, prove it; since it is not likely that they would have been invented, if the foundation of them had not been laid in tradition, if there had not been a stock of truth whereon to graft them.

I am as much persuaded, as Simplicius himself, that the Israelites might borrow some Egyptian traditions, as it is notorious that they borrowed many civil and religious institutions from the same people. I can believe, too, on the faith of learned men, that there is some analogy between the Mosaic account of the creation and the Phœnician cosmogony. There is nothing extraordinary to alter the state of the question in this. I can believe, too, that the six times, in which God made the world, according to an ancient tradition of the Persians, are relative to the six days in which he made it, according to the Jewish traditions. The Israelites had been slaves to the Egyptians, captives among the Chaldeans, and subjects to the Persians. They boasted their descent from Abraham; and the magi acknowledged this patriarch for their legislator, and for the institutor of their religion. The reformation, which Zoroaster made in this, was made after the return of some of the Jews, from Babylon, into their own country. But it was made, according to Hide and other modern critics, in the reign of Darius, son of Hystaspes, a little before Esdras and Nehemias went from the court of Persia to restore the religion, to settle the government, and to compile the traditions of the Jews at Jerusalem. Esdras set out from Persia and Babylonia when the disputes between the magians and the sabians ran the highest, and when the new doctrines of Zoroaster prevailed in the first fervor of reformation. Esdras, therefore, and the other Jews, who could not fail to be favorable to the first sect, and averse to the latter, might very well take, as it is highly probable that they did, the names of the months, the names of angels, many ridiculous anecdotes, and, among the rest, some concerning the creation, from the magians. The tradition was common to all these nations, but they invented and they borrowed, from one another various circumstances, in which they dressed it up dif-

ferently, each historian according to his fancy, and conformably
to the established system of his religion. This hypothesis is so
well founded, and so very probable, that our divines do nothing
better than weaken the credibility of the fact, when they assume,
on the similitude of some circumstances, that this tradition as
well as the belief of one God, was preserved by the Jews alone.

They were both much more ancient among the Persians than
Zoroaster or Zerdusht. We have to do here only with the first:
and as to that, Porphyry cites in his treatise, " De antro nym-
pharum," a certain Eubulus, who wrote the history of Mithras,
and assured in it, that Zoroaster consecrated a round grotto, such
as nature had formed it, adorned with flowers, and watered by
springs, to Mithras, the creator of all things, which grotto was
the symbol of the world, as the world is the work of Mithras. The
same reformer instituted festivals likewise to commemorate the
beginning of it; and not content with this, he descended into particulars; fixed the number of days contained in every one of the
six times that had been imagined; and marked the gradual progress of the creation in each of them.

The Chaldeans may be coupled, on this occasion, with the
Persians, as the Phœnicians and the Israelites were with the
Egyptians. They were all distinct nations; they had all their
distinct religions and traditions; but they all agreed in one, the
beginning of the world, how many different fictions soever they
might relate concerning the time and manner of this beginning.
I do not cite the Chaldaic oracles. They were as much forged
or corrupted, perhaps, as the Sibylline verses. But we have no
need of leaning on their authority. Eusebius has preserved a
remarkable passage that was in the history of Berosus. An ancient tradition of the Chaldeans reported that our world was
formed out of a chaos. All was night and water, till Bel
cut this night in two, separated the heavens from the earth,
and formed the world. The stars, the sun, the moon, and the
planets were the productions, according to this tradition, of the
same Bel, by which name the Chaldeans meant to signify the
Kneph of the orthodox Egyptians, their own invisible Mithras,
or, in one word, the Supreme Being.

I know very well that Diodorus says, the Chaldeans believed
the world eternal by its nature, and incapable of generation or
corruption. But, in the first place, the authority of Berosus
seems to deserve, on this occasion, much more credit than that
of Diodorus, not only because he was much nearer to the times
of which he speaks, but because he was a Babylonian and a
priest, and, therefore, better instructed, without doubt, than the
latter in the traditions of his own country. In the next place,
the difficulty of reconciling these two authors, does not seem in-

superable. The Greek, in the beginning of his first book, speaks of those who believed the world eternal, and of those who were of a contrary opinion. But this dispute seems to have risen among the naturalists or the learned, as he calls them, and not among those who contented themselves to know, about past events, what the history and tradition of their country taught them. Thus we may understand, and I should, I think, understand what he says of the Chaldeans; for after having said, that they maintained the eternity of the world, and believed it incapable of generation or corruption, he adds, that they believed the world to be governed by a divine providence, and every thing which happened, to be ordered by the gods, not to happen by chance. Now the greatest part of what he says being manifestly an account of philosophical opinions, and not of facts preserved in history or in tradition, it seems most natural to understand the whole in the same manner; besides which, it is to be considered, that there might be a tradition of the commencement, and that there could be none of the eternity of the world. From all which, it seems evident to me, that the whole of what Diodorus says is applicable to philosophical opinions alone, which are sometimes opposed to matters of fact sufficiently established; whereas every such hypothesis should have its foundation in fact, not to be chimerical. Berosus relates what he found in the Chaldaic traditions; and Diodorus tells us, what the opinions were of some philosophers at least. We shall see presently, that this opposition of a philosophical hypothesis to tradition was not confined to Egypt or Chaldea, and that it does not affect the truth of the proposition we defend.

Strabo relates, in his fifteenth book, that the Brachmans in India agreed with the Greeks in many things, and particularly in this, that " the world had a beginning;" to which he adds, and that " it will be destroyed." Advantage may be taken from hence to turn my own way of reasoning against me. It may be said, that, since the Brachmans believed the future destruction of the world, which could not be the subject of any tradition, and was not certainly revealed to them by prophecy, the assumed commencement of the world might be, and certainly was, merely founded, as well as its assumed destruction, on their philosophical speculations. It may be said, that we ought to explain this passage of Strabo, much as I have explained that of Diodorus, and to suppose the whole system of these Indian Brachmans philosophical.

I shall have occasion to consider, more at length, the true difference between a tradition of opinion, and a tradition of fact. But, in the mean time, I observe, that since the opinion of the future destruction of the world, founded manifestly in speculation, was entertained by the Greeks, at the same time as the opinion of its beginning, founded not less manifectly in tradition; and since Strabo assures us, that there was a great conformity between the opinions of the Greeks, and the opinions of the Indians, we may well believe that there was the same conformity between the principles on which their opinions were framed. Those among the Greeks, who believed the world had a beginning, believed it on the faith of tradition. They who imagined it would have an end, were led to imagine so both by physical and metaphysical speculation. Since they were sure it had a beginning, they concluded, from both, that it would have an end, and grafted opinion on fact. Thus it happened among the Greeks, and thus it might happen among the Indians.

I observe, in the next place, that if there was any author of equal authority, who asserted that the Brachmans believed the eternity of the world, to oppose to Strabo, as we have Berosus, to oppose to Diodorus, this circumstance might afford some pretence to say that the Brachmans, having framed, from observations of the present state of the material world, an opinion that it would be some time or other destroyed by age or accident, were led from thence, by carrying their speculations backwards, to the opinion that it had a beginning; but that as there is no such authority to oppose to Strabo, we ought to conclude, that the knowledge they had by tradition of the beginning of the world, led them to believe, on physical observation and metaphysical reasoning, its future destruction, rather than to conclude this philosophical conjecture led them to imagine, without any foundation in tradition, that the world had a beginning. So that I might very well quote the Indians, as an ancient nation who concurred in establishing the truth of this fact on the faith of their traditions.

I might go further on to the eastward, and bring the testimony of the Chinese, on the same side: a most ancient nation surely, and possessed of more ancient records, perhaps, than any other, though we have been little acquainted till very lately with their history, chronology, and traditions. But I choose to proceed in quoting authors better known to us, and shall therefore cite once more Strabo, whose authority, of all the ancient writers, is perhaps of the greatest weight. Strabo represents the Ethiopians rather barbarous than civilised; and yet this people believed a supreme immortal Being, the first cause of all things. This people therefore believed the beginning of the world, and this people could not fail to have most ancient traditions, since, as rude as they were, the use of letters had been known by them from a time immemorial. Enough has been said of the most ancient nations that are mentioned in history; and if we descend to the

Greeks, modern, with respect to them, though ancient, with respect to us, we shall find the same tradition established, and
further reasons to persuade that it was universal, allegorised, disguised, disputed, and even weakened by time; but still universally
received, and strongest as we remount highest in our inquiries
after it.   Such it was when the Greeks, from whom it has descended to us, adopted and transmitted it.   This tradition seems
to rise out of the abyss of time with the impetuosity of a great
source.   But then as the water, which spouted out with much
noise and force in the beginning, runs silently and gently on, the
further it runs; so this tradition grew weaker, but continued to
run, when the authors, whom we read at this time, began to
write.

The Egyptians were the first masters of the Greeks.   Before
any of these went into Egypt to acquire science, they had received much instruction from thence; principles of religion and
of civil government and anecdotes of antiquity.   Orpheus may
pass for the first of these Egyptian missionaries; since he came
from Egypt, though he was a Thracian.   I abandon the verses,
which had gone under his name, as easily as the Chaldaic oracles;
but that I should believe there was no such man, is too much to
require.   Aristotle asserted, as we learn in the first book of the
nature of the gods "Orpheum poetam nunquam fuisse."   But
we find in the same treatise, that Orpheus, Musæus, Hesiod, and
Homer, were reckoned among the most ancient poets.   It would
not be difficult, perhaps, to discover the principle of philosophical
interest which induced Aristotle to deny the existence of a man
so famous in all the traditions of his country, and who had been
the subject of so many fables.   What traditions of greater antiquity than Orpheus the Greeks might have, we know not.   But
he was, certainly, the principal channel, through which that of
the commencement of the world passed, from the Egyptians, to
Musæus, Hesiod, and Homer, who received it first, or were confirmed in the belief of it, by this authority, and who preserved
and propagated it in all their songs.   Pythagoras took it from
the Egyptians likewise, and from other eastern nations.   The
whole Italic school, and all those of the Ionic, who did not prefer their own speculations to a matter of fact, and Plato, the
famous founder of the Academy, followed them.   None of these
invented the fact; but all of them dressed it up and delivered it
down in different garbs, according to their different systems of
philosophy and religion.   Even the Christians, who came so
long afterwards, helped to corrupt this tradition, by interpolating
the famous verses, ascribed to Orpheus, which I have for this
reason, among others, consented to lay aside; though still, if we
believe these verses were composed by Onomacritus, and not by

Orpheus, they were composed at least as early as the age of Pisistratus, and contain, therefore, a very ancient tradition.

I might have named, as the preservers of this tradition, among the Greeks, Linus, Thamyras, and others. I might quote several Theogonias, that, it is said, were written, like that of Aristæus of the island of Proconnesus, or that of Epimenides of the island of Crete; all which would have been more ridiculous than they were, if the beginning of the world had not been established in general belief; but I will mention, particularly, that of Hesiod only. He invokes the muses to sing the divine race of those immortal gods born of the earth, of the heavens, and of night, and who have been nourished by the salt sea. He goes on to bid them sing, how the gods and the earth were first made, with the rivers and the immense sea, with the stars and the heavens, with the gods who proceeded from them, and who are the authors of all good things. The same extravagant ideas are to be found in Homer. The ocean was, according to him, the original of all things: and this notion coincides with that of Thales, who taught that all things proceeded from water as their material principle; by which he meant, no doubt, a certain chaos, wherein all the elements were confounded, till they were reduced into order; that is, till the world began.

The proofs of the universality of this tradition, muffled up almost always in allegories and fables, are so numerous that we run more risk of being lost in the multiplicity of them, than of wanting any. Abaris, the Scythian, had written concerning these generations of gods. The world was not eternal in the system of the Druids; and the ancient Etrurians had their fables concerning the beginning of it, as well as the Egyptians and the Persians. The magi, says Diogenes Laertius, taught the generation of the gods: and by these gods, they understood fire, earth, and water. One of the magi, says Herodotus, sung the same generation, in a hymn, at all the sacrifices of the Persians.

As poetry personified every thing, ancient philosophy, which was little less than poetry, animated all the elements; and every part of corporeal nature was filled with inferior divinities: for they acknowledged some that were superior, and even a Supreme Being, who, far from being born of the world, made it, and was the father of gods and men; which puts me in mind of a passage in Cicero, where it is said, of this Supreme Being, " deos alios in terrâ, alios in lunâ, alios in reliquas mundi partes spargens Deus quasi serebat."

It would have been very convenient for all the atheistical philosophers to have assumed the eternity of the world; but few of them durst do so, in opposition to this universality of tradition. They were obliged, therefore, either to reject this tradition, or to find some way of accounting for the existence of our planet, without supposing a self-existent Δημιȣργος, or architect, the first mind of Anaxagoras. They chose the last, as the most easy task; and Epicurus seemed to think his absurd system more likely to prevail, for this very reason, because it assumed that the world had a beginning conformably to tradition. The author of the dissertation, I have before me, asserts, that all the philosophers, except the Epicureans, under which name he comprehends all the atomic philosophers, held, that the world was eternal. A passage in the beginning of the fourth chapter of the treatise of Censorinus, " De Die Natali," led him into this error. What he advances may be proved false by a deduction of many particulars; but this may be said, with truth, that an opinion of the eternity of the world grew up or spread more after Aristotle. Even the latter Platonicians took part on this head with the Peripatetics. They treated their master, as St. Jerome accuses others, and might have been accused himself, of treating the Scriptures. Whatever new opinions philosophers framed, they dragged in the text of their masters to support them; which calls to my mind the proceedings of a Jew and of a Stoical philosopher. Philo found a trinity of divine hypostases in the writings of Plato. He adopted the opinion, would needs find it in the sacred writings of his fathers, and reconcile the legislator of the Jews with the founder of the Academy. Just so Cleanthes endeavored to make the fables of Orpheus, Musæus, Hesiod, and Homer agree with what he taught concerning the gods, "Ut veterrimi poetæ, qui hæc ne suspicati quidem sint, stoici fuisse videantur."* But after all, nothing can be more strongly asserted than the commencement of the world is by Plato; and even Aristotle himself acknowledged, that this philosopher thought it generated.

It may seem strange, but it is true, that we have a right to quote Aristotle himself against the eternity of the world. He falls severely on the philosophical systems, that prevailed in his time, about the manner in which it began: but he acknowledges the uniformity of this ancient tradition. How could he avoid to do so? Or how could it be otherwise, since the Greeks, in his time, had found it established among all the nations with whom they became acquainted either by commerce or by war? That happened to them, which has happened to us, in much later ages. We have pushed our discoveries through both hemispheres, and have found every where the same tradition established in the belief of mankind. The Chinese, whom I just mentioned above, would pass, like the Egyptians of old, for the

* Tully De Nat. Deor. l. 2.

most ancient race of mankind, and they have traditions and records of immense antiquity and very singular authenticity. Now these traditions and these records agree, in one general fact, with all those that have been mentioned, "the world and mankind had a beginning." Even the name of a first man is preserved, and Fohi, who was the Orpheus of the east, precedes a very little their historical age. If we cross the South sea, and visit the people of Peru or of Mexico, we find the same tradition established by universal consent, as they received it from their fathers. The world began, and Pacha Camac created it: the sun that enlightens the world now, is not eternal; there have been other suns before this. If we cross the continent of America and proceed to the islands, we find the inhabitants of them in the same belief; at least we might have found them so, whilst they preserved the primitive simplicity of their manners, and the traditions of their forefathers, and till Spanish avarice and Spanish bigotry had exterminated the whole species.

After saying so much concerning this tradition, it is necessary, I think, to consider, more particularly, what those principles are, on which reason determines us to receive general facts that have no foundation out of tradition, as we receive the most authentic historical truths. I have touched this subject already; but, to treat it with more order and clearness, let us descend into some detail of the essential differences between history and tradition. Let us consider what those attributes are which the latter wants, and for the want of which this testimony cannot produce historical probability: for if we find that there is not the same necessity of relation between these attributes and the general facts, spoken of here, as there is between these attributes and every historical account of past events; in short, if we find that such general facts are not in the case of those, in order to judge of which the rules of historical criticism have been established, it will follow, that these facts may be received for true, as well as any, and much better than several of those that are contained in history, and to the truth of which we assent.

A story, circumstantially related, ought not to be received, on the faith of tradition; since the least reflection on human nature is sufficient to show, how unsafely a system of facts and circumstances can be trusted, for its preservation, to memory alone, and for its conveyance, to oral report alone; how liable it must be to all those alterations, which the weakness of the human mind must cause necessarily, and which the corruption of the human heart will be sure to suggest. An event that is not circumstantially, is imperfectly related, not only with respect to the communication it should give, but with respect to the means we should have to judge of its probability. The means I speak of are those of comparing the different parts of a story together, and of examining how well they coincide and render the whole consistent. In one case, then, different circumstances are to be compared; in the other, all the traditions that can be collected on the same subject. Inconsistent circumstances destroy the credit of the story; repugnant traditions, that of a general event. But the silence of some histories or of some traditions will destroy the credit of neither, when all those who speak of the same thing agree. The Jewish history has preserved the memory of a Babylonian kingdom, which we call the second empire of the Assyrians, unknown to profane history and tradition, which make mention only of one. That ancient monument too of Rhamses, which Germanicus went to see in his voyage into Egypt, and the inscription on it, which contained the names of all the nations whom this prince had conquered in Asia, makes no mention of the Assyrians among those who became tributary to the Egyptian empire, as if their very name had not been known a century before the era of Nabonassar, though it mentions the Persians, the Bactrians, and others, who must have been such to the Assyrians, if an Assyrian empire had been established, as we assume, before the era of Nabonassar. Notwithstanding this silence, and the vain efforts of scholars to reconcile sacred and profane Assyriacs, it would be unreasonable to deny that there was an Assyrian empire in Asia. Upon the whole matter, that "the world had a beginning," is a general fact, even better founded than this, " there has been an Assyrian monarchy." Some ancient traditions, we have seen, do not concur with others about the latter. But I presume it would be hard to cite any body of ancient traditions, wherein the commencement of the world is not directly affirmed, or constantly supposed. There is not even the silence of tradition against it; and as to traditions that deny the fact, there neither have been, nor could be, any.

It may be thought, and it is true, in general, that history, has this advantage over tradition. The authors of authentic history are known, but those of tradition, whether authentic or unauthentic, are not known. The probability of facts must diminish by length of time, and can be estimated, at no time, higher than the value of that original authority, from which it is derived. This advantage, then, authentic history has, which no tradition can have. The degree of assent, which we give to history, may be settled, in proportion to the number, characters, and circumstances of the original witnesses; the degrees of assent to tradition cannot be so settled. Let us see, therefore, how far this difference may be thought to affect the tradition of the beginning of the world. We shall find, I think, that we are very liable to be deceived in all these respects which should constitute the authenticity of history, and that the difference I have observed cannot affect, in any sort, the true fact I assert.

We are deceived, grossly, very often about the number of witnesses, two ways. Sometimes by applying testimonies that have no true relation to the things testified, and sometimes by taking different repetitions of the same testimony, for different testimonies. Both these ways are employed with success, artfully by some, habitually by others; and numerous citations improperly brought, and carelessly or ignorantly set to account, to increase the confusion and to promote the deception. Nothing can be more ridiculous, perhaps, than to see a great part of what we find in profane antiquity applied to confirm what we find in sacred. Numerous and astonishing examples of this kind might be brought from all the writers who have endeavored to establish the authenticity of Jewish, by a supposed concurrence of profane traditions. But I pass these over. It is full as ridiculous to see all the ancient writers, who have spoken of the Assyrians and Persians, quoted as so many distinct witnesses, when they did, for the most part, nothing more than copy Ctesias, first, and one another, afterwards. Neither Ctesias, nor Moses himself, may deserve belief in all the particulars related by them; but Ctesias may be reckoned as a witness the more of some general facts, as Moses may be of some others.

That the world had a beginning is a naked fact, which neither contains nor implies any thing equivocal. It neither leans on the authority of one nation, nor of one system of traditions which many nations may adopt. Nations, the most distant in place, and the most opposite in opinions, customs, and manners, concur in affirming it. All these traditions, therefore, have had different originals, or they all proceed from one original tradition. If they had different originals, the truth of the fact is established by so great a number of independent testimonies. If they all proceed from one original tradition, the truth of the fact is established just as well; since such a tradition must have been that of one first family or society. As it would be absurd to assume that a tradition, which may be called that of mankind, could be founded originally in any thing else than the truth of a fact which concerned all mankind, and of which all mankind had once had a certain assurance; so it would be absurd to suppose that a tradition, arising in one family or society alone, could spread to all the corners of the earth, and be received alike by nations even unknown to one another, unless we suppose this family or society to be that from which all these nations, by whom this tradition was preserved, proceeded. It does not seem that this argument can be eluded.

As there is a great difference between circumstantial relations

and general naked facts, so there is likewise, between the tradition I contend for, and every other of the same kind.   That there
has been an universal deluge is a fact, as general and as naked
as this, " the world had a beginning;" but I apprehend, that the
tradition of it is not supported like that of the commencement of
the world.   Has the memory of this event been preserved among
all the ancient nations?   There are men bold enough to say so;
but the contrary is true.   The tradition of Noah's deluge is
vouched by no other authority than that of Moses: for those nations, which preserved the memory of so many particular deluges,
knew nothing of this universal deluge; and yet it is impossible
to conceive that the memory of such a catastrophe should have
been known only by one people, and that not the most ancient
neither; or being known to all, should have been preserved only
in one corner of the earth.   If this tradition then is liable to suspicion, for want of a sufficient number of testimonies, that of the
commencement of the world is liable to no suspicion; because it
has as many testimonies as can be expected on the supposition
of its truth.   Let us proceed now to consider the veracity and
probity of witnesses, and the difference between history and
tradition on this head.   History, to be authentic, must give us
not only the means of knowing the number, but of knowing the
characters, of the witnesses who vouch for it.   Tradition in general gives us the means of knowing neither; and the particular
tradition we speak of here, which is that of nations, not of men,
does not stand in need of the latter.

This condition of historical probability is even more important
than the number of witnesses; and it is by this that we are most
liable to be deceived.   There are certain follies which prevail
sometimes like epidemical maladies, and infect whole nations
with their delirium.   Such there were, of one sort, among the
Egyptians; such there were, of another sort, among the Jews;
and the predestination to universal empire may pass for another,
among the Romans.   But whatever various effects different de-
liriums may produce in different countries, there is one which
they produce alike in all, the spirit of inventing, believing, and
propagating lies.   These lies come soon to have education and
authority on their side.   It becomes the interest of particular
men, or of particular societies, to profit of the public credulity,
and when they have once done so, their lies produce such effects,
under the management of bold and artful men, as sober truth
never could.   Thus Mahomet, to go no higher, instituted a new
religion in the seventh century of ours, and founded a great empire.   Mahomet had intrepidity as well as address, and if a
miserable Jew of Asia Minor, seventy or eighty years ago, had
not wanted the former, we might have seen, very possibly, at

this hour, a new spiritual and temporal empire established by the adorers of a new Messiah. But the courage of Sabatai Sevi, to whom the Jews resorted from all parts, in a firm persuasion that he was their true Messiah, failed him, and he passes for an impostor, merely because he durst not stand an impalement.— Thus not only lies, but whole systems of lies, get into history; pass for religious truths; and serve to support, by appeals to them in after times, the original fraud. Mahomet was obliged to fly from Mecca to Medina by the unbelieving Arabs. But the Arabs now, and all those who have been converted to Mahometism, (for it would be false to say, though we hear it continually said, that this religion has been propagated by force alone and not by persuasion) go very devoutly in pilgrimage to the place from which he was driven, and the time of his flight is become their sacred era.

I dwell the longer on this point, because it is that which justifies historical Pyrrhonism the most. The ancient manner of recording events, made it easy to practise all these frauds. The priests in Egypt, in Judea, and elsewhere, were entrusted to make and to keep these records; and they were under a double obligation, if I may say so, for such they thought it no doubt, to keep them with greater regard to the system of religion, whose ministers they were, than to the truth of things. They were to keep up the credit of ancient lies, and to invent as many new ones, as were necessary to propagate the same fraud. By these means, and on these motives, the whole of history was corrupted in those nations, as we shall easily believe that it could not fail to be, when we consider the connexity between civil and ecclesiastical affairs, and their mutual influence on one another. Josephus, writing against Appion, praises this manner of preserving the memory of things, in order to bespeak approbation to the practice, which was that of his own country. He boasts much of the sincerity, and even of the inspiration, if I mistake not, of the Jewish scribes. But good sense, founded in experience, will answer, that they who record matters, concerning which they are strongly biassed by their affections, their passions and their prejudices, and wherein they have directly, or indirectly, an immediate and great private interest to serve by inventing falsehoods, or by disguising truth, are never to be received as good witnesses, unless their testimony be confirmed by collateral and disinterested evidence. That they are not to be received as such, on any other terms, we need go no further than the Jews themselves for examples. Some of their heroes and heroines may be thought justly, when we consider of the anachronisms and the blunders they commit, as fictitious as Amadis of Gaul, and their traditions no more authentic than those of archbishop Turpin.

The uncertainty of history arises principally from the causes here laid down. We are less liable to be deceived by the concurrence of authors, more independent and more indifferent than these, though they may not be all of equal credit: because when their motives and designs are not the same, when they had no common pripciple, and when they cannot be suspected to have had any concert together, nothing out the notoriety of facts can make their relations coincide. In such cases a nice examination of the veracity and probity of historians, when we can make it, is as little necessary as it is in matters of tradition, where we cannot make it. We may subscribe, at least as reasonably, to the united testimony of a great number of traditions, whose authors are unknown to us, as we may to facts reported by a great number of historians, though the authority of some of these would be otherwise very precarious.

Experience shows sufficiently, that there is no falsehood too gross to be imposed on any people, civilised or barbarous, learned or ignorant, but we shall never conceive that the same lie could be imposed on all people: because it is impossible that the same lie should flatter them all alike, or be equally well proportioned to the interest and designs of a prevalent society in every nation. What immediate or necessary relation has the beginning of the world to the predominant folly of the Egyptians, for instance, or the Chinese, or to the interest of the priests, among the former, and any of the several sects, among the latter? Since they believed the world to have had a beginning; it was very conformable to the folly of these two people to insist that they descended from the first men, and were the most ancient nations of the world; but what need had they to assume the commencement of it? Would they not have flattered their vanity more to say, that it was eternal, and that their race was coeternal with it? Once more:—What necessary relation had the beginning of the world to the favorite principle of the Jews, who believed themselves a people chosen by God, out of all the people of the earth? Could the eternity of the world make it less likely that they descended from Shem, or the vocation of Abraham more improbable, or destroy the credibility of any fact that flattered their vanity? I confess, I think not. If it be said, that this nation had nobler ideas of the Supreme Being than any other; and that it was more conformable to these ideas to believe that the world was made by God, than that it is eternal as well as he; I might deny the first proposition, and show that no nation had such mean ideas of the Divinity in many respects as this. But if I admitted it, for argument's sake, I might ask how this philosophical opinion could be passed for a matter of fact on the Egyptians, who boasted so much of their own antiquity, by a people, who had grown up among them, and who had been so long their slaves? If this tradition of the beginning of the world

had prevailed among the Jews first, who were known to few
people, and despised by those that knew them, how came it to
spread far and wide to the utmost extremities of the east and
west?   Since I have named the west, let me mention the Peruvians, and ask how the beginning of the world can be said to
have flattered the general folly of this people, or the particular
interest of their incas?   They thought their incas the children of
the sun.   To what purpose was it to make them believe that
Pacha Camac was a being superior to the sun, and that he created the world?   Would it not have been more agreeable to the
prejudices of the Peruvians, and to the interests of the incas, to
have supposed the world eternal, and themselves the offspring
of an eternal father?

Lies, that are produced by the predominant passions of people,
and by the policy of those who lead them, carry for the most
part on their fronts, if I may say so, the marks of their original:
and this observation will hold in a multitude of instances that
may be brought from history and tradition, both from facts circumstantially related, and from those that are naked, or almost
naked of circumstances.   But the tradition that affirms the beginning of the world is not in this case.   It is relative no more
to the particular character of one people than of another.   It favors no more one general principle of religion or policy than another.   In a word, force your imagination as much as you please,
you will find insurmountable difficulties in your way, if you suppose the fact invented: but all these difficulties vanish when you
suppose it true.   The universal consent of mankind follows naturally and necessarily the truth of the fact.   The antiquity of the
tradition is a consequence of the antiquity of the world, and the
great variety of fables, which have been invented about it, is a
circumstance that accompanies every event that has descended
long in oral tradition, and that has not been ascertained by cotemporary history, nay, even some that seem to heve been so
ascertained.

There remains to be spoken of, another condition of historical
probability, which it may be supposed that tradition cannot have,
and which we have seen, in the case of numbers, and veracity or
probity of witnesses, that history itself does not always furnish,
and for want of which we are often imposed upon by it.   This
condition is so essential, that neither the numbers nor characters
of witnesses will constitute probability without it.   The condition I mean is this; that the original authors were not only cotemporary but competent witnesses.   The examination whether
they were such or no may be reckoned for another advantage,
which history has, or must have, to be deemed authentic, over
tradition, by what passes every day, under our eyes, when we
see almost every public fact related, and even transmitted to

posterity, not according to truth, but according to the wrong judgments which are made by prejudice or by passion. What happens now, happened formerly, and no stronger proof of it can be required than that which we find in Arrian. He had before him the memorials of Aristobulus and of Ptolemy, two principal captains that accompanied Alexander in all his expeditions; and yet the historian was puzzled, sometimes, by the inconsistency of their relations.

On this head, the competency of original witnesses, it may be said, that if history wants it sometimes, tradition must want it always, and that tradition, especially, which I defend. I may be told, and I was told, that if every thing else, which I have advanced, was admitted, the objection, arising from the incompetency of witnesses, would be sufficient to refute me. It was urged, that whoever were the first to say there had been a monarchy of the Assyrians, might know the truth of what they said, but that they, who were the first to affirm the beginning of the world, could not know the truth of what they said, not even on the supposition that they were the first of men. This tradition, therefore, is that of an opinion, not of fact. The existence of God is a tradition too; and theists very often appeal to the universality of this tradition to prove the truth of an opinion, just as you appeal to the same universality to prove a fact. Had you proved the fact, you might have drawn from it all the arguments that can be drawn to establish, in belief, the existence of a Supreme Being. But you have amused yourself with nothing better than proving the truth of one opinion, by the tradition of another, which is a proceeding that cannot be justified; because we are as able, and probably more able judges of the opinion, than any of the ancient nations could be witnesses of the fact. As different nations have their different follies, there are some common to all mankind. As there are fictions which favor the interests and promote the designs of those who govern in all the countries of the world, the existence of one Supreme Being has been acknowledged in all ages, and if you please to say so, by all people. Superstition took hold, and policy profited of this opinion, under one form or other. Superstition abounds wherever there are men, and some kind of policy wherever there are societies. Metaphysical reasonings on the nature and attributes of a Supreme Being, may persuade philosophers that this Being, whom they assume to exist, by the necessity of his nature, created the world, which does not seem so to exist. Naturalists, in particular, may have adopted easily an opinion which saves them much pains and useless research. A first cause of infinite wisdom and power, cuts all the Gordian knots that embarrass them, and a single supposition furnishes the solution of a thousand difficulties.——All this was urged with much vehemence, by Damon, and he concluded, by putting this dilemma. If the opinion of the commencement of the world is conformable to the knowledge we have of things, and proportioned to the human understanding, as you assert, there results from thence no proof that the fact is true, but great reason to believe that men might assume it, without knowing any thing of the matter. On the other side, if this be not true, your universal tradition wants the first and principal foundation of probability which you have laid down.

I have put these objections, such as were made, and such as might have been made to me, in their full force. They seem plausible; let us see if they are unanswerable. They will not appear so, if I can show first, that the atheist begs the question when he assumes that, supposing the world to have had a beginning, even the first of men could not be competent witnesses, because they could not be competent judges, of the truth of the fact; secondly, if I can state so clearly, the distinction to be made between the tradition of an opinion, and the tradition of a fact, in our judgments about them, as to reduce to an absurdity the supposition, that the tradition we speak of, is of the first sort; and thirdly, if I can prove, by reasons drawn from the human nature and from general experience, that unless the world had really had a beginning, the opinion of its eternity would have been the opinion of all antiquity, and the commencement of it would not have been established in tradition.

The atheist begs the question, and by begging it he advances a foolish and arrogant proposition: since to be sure that the first men could not be witnesses of the beginning of the world, he must assume that he knows, very exactly, how the world we inhabit was framed, if it was framed at all. Such inconveniences happen frequently to those who combat truth. They call temerity to their aid; and they affirm, boldly, on precarious conjectures; and when they have heated their own imagination, they hope, and not always in vain, to seduce those of other men. In the defence of the truth, we shall never be reduced to any such extremity. Though the atheist must pretend to know how the material world was made, and in what manner the human race began, in order to deny that the first men were competent judges and witnesses of both. We pretend to no such knowledge: but nothing less than such knowledge can justify his denial; whereas the universality of the tradition justifies abundantly our affirmation. We may affirm, on the faith of all mankind, that the world began, much better than it can be affirmed, on the faith of a few precarious partial and inconsistent traditions, that there was an empire of the Assyrians.

To build a world is not so easy a thing as many a speculative architect has imagined. The author of the book of Genesis begins his history by it; and though we do not set to his account the use which has been made of passages in his narration, yet it is impossible to excuse all the puerile, romantic, and absurd circumstances, which nothing could produce but the habit of dealing in trifling traditions, and a most profound ignorance. It is impossible to read, what he wrote on this subject, without feeling contempt for him, as a philosopher, and horror as a divine; for he is to be considered under both these characters.

Natural philosophy made little progress among the Greeks and the Romans, and a system of the universe was very little known by them. The eastern nations knew it better; but among these we must not reckon that of the Jews. It has been said, that Pythagoras was a disciple of the prophet Ezekiel, or had some other Jewish masters. If this idle conjecture were true in fact, it would not be true, however, that he took from them his mundane system. Philolaus, who published his doctrines, had very different notions of it from those of the Jews, and from those of the other Greeks. One would think too, that some modern astronomer had dictated the hypothesis which Plutarch and Diogenes Laertius attribute to Cleanthes, the Samian. This true system, which accords so little with that of Moses, after having been long lost, was renewed in the sixteenth century by Copernicus, confirmed and improved by Galilei and Kepler, and since demonstrated by Newton. How magnificent a scene of the universe have these new discoveries opened! how much more worthy of the wisdom, the power, and the immensity of God, than all the paltry confined systems of ancient philosophers, and of Moses among the rest!

Though we know much more than they did of the works of God, yet we know as little as they did concerning the production of them. Antiquity had other makers of worlds besides Moses. Plato was one of those; and if his hypothesis be no more probable than that of the Jewish legislator, it is, at least a little more reverential to the supreme Being. The same presumptuous confidence has been seen in these ages, wherein philosophers, having greater knowledge, should have had more modesty, and have been more sensible how ignorant we remain, after all the improvements we are capable of making. Des Cartes, for instance, who had much of this presumption, and employed a great deal of artifice to make his hypotheses pass for real discoveries, acknowledged a little more need of a God than Strato avowed.— He wanted a God to create matter and to impress motion on it. But when he had assumed thus much, he thought himself able to proceed without this help, and to show, how the world was

formed, or how an universe might be formed, by the laws of
matter and motion.   I told Damon, that I thought this philosopher's ill success would hinder him from any enterprise of the
same kind; that I should, therefore, have still a right to conclude,
that he begged the question, when he asserted that it implied
contradiction to suppose the first men capable of knowing that
the world began; and I desired him further to consider with me,
whether, laying this presumption aside, we may not assume,
without any, that there might have been certain marks, by which
the first men must necessarily know that they were the first men,
and that the system of the world began.   If we find such marks,
and find them probable, by their analogy to what we know, it
will follow, I think, that the beginning of the world has some
proof *à posteriori;* whereas the eternity of it can have none
of this kind, any more than *à priori.*

However this planet of ours was formed, the first men could
not possibly be spectators of the formation of it.   Both men and
all other animals required an earth to walk on, food to nourish
them, and an atmosphere to breathe in, and the light of the sun
to conduct them.   The prior existence of the sun might be necessary too, on another account, antecedently to their creation.—
This great luminary might be necessary to the formation, as we
know that it is to the preservation, of our planet, whether that
of the moon were so or not, and whether the Arcadians were in
the right or not, when they said, that they were older than this
secondary planet.

But now, though there could be no human witnesses of the
world arising out of a chaos, and growing into that form and order wherein we see it, yet the first men might know, very certainly, that this system of things began to exist.   As it would be
ridiculous to assert, like the Thuscan author, whom Suidas mentions but does not name, that God employed twelve thousand
years in creating the universe; so is there no necessity of believing that the solar system, or even this one planet, was the work
of six days.   Such precipitation seems not less repugnant to that
general order of nature, which God established, and which he
observes in her productions, than the day of rest, which Moses
supposes God to have taken, or which the Jews invented to make
one of their institutions more respectable, is repugnant to all the
ideas we are able to frame of the Divinity.   Though it be conformable to our notions of wisdom, that every thing necessary to
man was created, when he began to exist; yet is there nothing
which obliges us to believe, that mankind began to exist in all
the parts of the world at once.

We need put our imagination to no great efforts, to believe that
all this might be: and if it might be, we may suppose that it was.

We do not, like reasoners *à priori*, imagine what may have been according to our abstract reasonings, and so conclude from possibility to actuality. We proceed much more reasonably from actuality to possibility, in a method so often, and so absurdly reversed by philosophers. A more able naturalist would succeed better in finding those marks by which the first men might know the commencement of this system. I will mention three or four which are obvious enough, and may serve to explain a matter that seemed paradoxical, and is not, perhaps, absolutely essential to my argument.

The general opinion of all those who have reasoned about the creation or formation of the world, and that which Moses himself follows, assumes that there was originally a chaos or confused mass of matter, wherein all the elements or first principles of things, which exist in the material system, were contained. Whether this mass was created or no, they thought it so necessary to be supposed, that they could not go on one step, in building a world, without it. As soon as it is supposed, " instant ardentes Tyrii," they all go to work. Every one separates and disposes these materials in his own way; the laws of mechanism are employed, according to the different plans of these architects, and a world is soon made. In one of these philosophical romances, published at the end of the last century, the ingenious author assumes that our planet was, till the deluge, in a direct situation to the sun; that is to say, that its axis was parallel to the axis of the ecliptic, or, in other words, that the ecliptic was confounded with the equator. Among several advantages which he pretends to draw from this hypothesis, the great facility of peopling the world with inhabitants is one. He thinks that animals could not have been brought forth, nor have grown up, if there had been any variety in the seasons by the obliquity of the ecliptic, and if these children of the earth, hatched, as we may say, by the sun, had been exposed, at first, to the injuries of the air, and to the cold of a winter. Had this author been opposed by his own tribe alone, and in a theological way, he might have escaped pretty well; but the natural philosophers and the mathematicians rose up against him, and battered down his hypothesis. I enter not into particulars. The conclusion drawn from all their arguments was this, that the present situation being more advantageous to the earth, in general, than any other, we ought to be persuaded that it is now the same wherein God placed it originally. But I doubt very much whether this conclusion be undeniable. The Supreme Being proportions always his means to his ends, and may therefore employ different means when different ends are to be attained. Let it be that the present obliquity of the ecliptic, which is of twenty-three degrees and twenty-nine minutes, may be in the present state of the world the most advantageous. Nothing hinders us from assuming, that another obliquity, or no obliquity at all, might be more advantageous when the present system of things began. If that of the Chevalier de Louville be true, this obliquity was of about forty-five degrees one hundréd and thirty thousand years ago. On the comparison of which two obliquities, I shall leave philosophers and mathematicians to dispute as long as they please.

What it is to my purpose to observe is, that no proof will arise, from all they can say, to convince us that the present was the original situation of the world to the sun. Infinite wisdom does not change the means, as divines would sometimes make us believe that he does, at least in the economy of the moral system, when the ends are the same. Nay, the same means serve often to accomplish different ends. But when the ends are so different, that the means of accomplishing one imply contradiction with the means of accomplishing another, we may say, very assuredly, that infinite wisdom changes the means; and, therefore, if the means of preserving the material and animal world are different from those which were necessary to˙the beginning of both, the present position of the earth may very well be thought not to have been the first. If alternate corruptions and generations are become necessary, and if the former produce the latter, it could not ·be so from the first. The first was certainly very different from those which we observe. Corruption could not then be necessary to generation. If a greater degree of heat was so for some productions, that greater degree is to be found in Burnet's hypothesis. If less, and very different degrees were necessary, these different degrees are to be found in the same hypothesis gradually lessening from the equator, and this gradation, by which different climates are formed, might be necessary for different productions to a certain distance from that climate where the sun was always in the zenith. As there were no variations in these different climates, but each enjoyed a particular and uniform season, the animals and plants, of each, were nourished and carried to the perfection of their growth, by the same principle by which they had been produced, and in a manner suitable to their nature, and to that of their climate.

Whilst it fared thus with one part of the world, the other parts were in a very different state according to this hypothesis. But far from finding any thing here, that may seem repugnant to the wisdom of the architect, this wisdom seems more fully displayed than in the hypothesis of Moses or of Plato, and this order to have much more analogy with the order of nature which we see established. These different climates appear like so many different matrices or wombs, impregnated with the original seeds of things, and wherein the first productions were formed by the inconceivable energy of divine power.   In other climates, more distant from the equator, where the influence of the sun, the first of second causes employed in these generations, was gradually less felt, the great work of the creation might advance more slowly.   In climates still more distant, this influence might become too weak to produce any considerable effects, and the great work might proceed still more slowly, or not at all.   Then, perhaps, the obliquity of the ecliptic might begin, by slow degrees, without causing any disorder in the climates already inhabited.   The first situation of the world to the sun having had its effect; another situation might become necessary for two purposes, to render those climates, where the sun was always in the zenith, more temperate; to carry the generations of animals and of the fruits of the earth forward on both sides to the north and to the south; to give a greater degree of heat, where a greater was still wanted, and to give some, where there was none at all.

We may believe, that this obliquity of the ecliptic arose much faster than the Chevalier De Louville assumed it to decrease. A minute in one hundred years is too little.   Let us suppose, on the prerogative of hypotheses, a degree, and even more, if you think fit.   In this manner, those parts of the world, which were excessively heated, cooled, and those which were frozen by cold, heated gradually.   Thus a system of final causes became, it may be, complete, and the earth having passed through the positions which were, of all possible positions, the most proper to create, might stop at that which is said to be, of all others, the most proper to preserve.

If the learned master of the Charter-house, and the able Scotch mathematician, who wrote against him, were still alive, I should expect that they would think themselves under some obligation to me for having endeavored to compromise matters between them, and to unite, in one scheme, their contrary opinions.   But since I cannot have this advantage, I must content myself with the inward satisfaction I feel, in contemplating this plausible notion, which I have advanced on grounds as good as many of those, that are not deemed paradoxical either by divines or philosophers, have been established.   They are possible, no doubt; and, I presume, they will never be demonstrated false, nor any other ways of accounting for the same things, true.   It is not however quite necessary to my purpose: for whatever circle our planet described, when her course round the sun began, we must be persuaded that the surface of it was warmed and cherished enough by the rays of the central sun to promote generation and vegetation, for which it was already prepared.—If the present obliquity of the ecliptic prevailed then, the torrid, the temperate, and the frozen zones, as we call them, might be capable of the various productions proper to them; or we may assume, very consistently, that countries more distant received, from those that were nearer the sun, such animals and such plants as their climates were fit to preserve, though not fit to generate.—In short, we need not apprehend the want of heat, even on the received hypothesis. The sun, much older probably than our world, and who has, certainly, grown older ever since, may have lost much of the force and efficacy which he had in those primeval days. Nay more; astronomers and natural philosophers agree, I think. about that perpetual expense, which all the suns of the universe are at, to enlighten, to warm, and nourish their several systems; of which expense, we must believe, that our sun has his share. They assume indeed, that the atmospheres of these suns compress so strongly the exhalations that rise from them, and drive them back with so much force and so much economy, not suffering any more than are absolutely necessary to pass, that these springs of light and heat cannot be exhausted, nor suffer any great diminution in thousands of years. But thousands of years, and God alone knows how many, are elapsed since our sun was first lighted up, and he may have therefore suffered some diminution.

These hypothetical reasonings, and others to the same purpose, may be, I think, maintained, whether we suppose this obliquity of the ecliptic to have been decreasing or increasing: for the decrease of some minutes in a century, during a space of time, even as long as that which the Egyptians imagined, will not be found inconsistent with our hypothesis. Our hypothesis wants to assume little more than this, that nature, who acts with much simplicity and uniformity, acted much in the same manner after her first productions, in those of animals for instance; and if this be granted, it will follow, evidently, that the first men were competent witnesses of the first propagations of the animal kind; which would be of itself a sufficient proof that they were such of the beginning of the world.

Nature has every where fixed certain seasons, at which all, or the greatest part of them, propagate their several species, whilst man enjoys the noble prerogative of doing the same all the year round, "Homini maximè coitus temporibus omnibus opportunus est." It is Aristotle who says this. But then this prerogative extends no further: and a term is fixed to man, as it is to the species of all other animals for the bearing their fruit. The philosopher, I have cited, descends into a particular account of these different terms, in the fifth book of his history of animals, and as we know that men are nine months in their mothers' bellies, he assures us that the camel is twelve. These animals, then, and all those who require a longer term than that of nine months, appeared later even than the second generation of human creatures, in the ordinary manner that it has been carried on from the first generation downwards. Men were by consequence witnesses of the first progagation of animals. The same proposition will hold, if we suppose them generated faster and sooner in the course of these generations, or even primevally; for, if man, for example, was but three days, or three hours in forming out of the earth, and in receiving the breath of life, it will follow, by a very fair analogy, that the same operations took up four days or four hours for the formation of a camel, and eight for that of an elephant.

I might expect to hear upon this occasion, many common-place notions advanced, to show more time required, in the process of nature, to form this animal after the image of God, than all the others, so vastly inferior to him in figure and composition. But these persons ought to reflect, that how distant soever animal may be from animal, relatively to our notion of perfection and imperfection, there can be no difference in the distance between any of them and God, who ordered this process of nature for reasons that we do not know, but certainly without regard to that dignity of nature which we imagine. The creation of a man or of an angel, in the works of God, is not more considerable than the creation of the meanest insect, nor requires that the divine energy should be exerted in a longer and more operose process of nature.

But if it is probable that the first men might see the commencement of those species of animals, whose formation require longer time than their own, it is not impossible, neither, that they might see the commencement of those species, whose formation required a less time. We may very easily imagine, that the creation had two sorts of progression, as the world has two sorts of motion. Nature might follow such an order, as we have mentioned, in every climate; but she might follow a certain general order likewise, in all climates alike. As more time was necessary for the production of one animal than another, in the same climate, so more time might be necessary to bring the same animal up to the perfection of his nature in one climate than in another. As the hare might begin to run and the sheep to feed before either man, or camel, or elephant was sufficiently formed to answer the ends of its creation; so the creation, in general, might be far advanced, or even completed, in some climates, before it was so in others. The seeds, or first principles of animal life, might have more or less force and vigor, according to the different influences of the sun, though they were scattered every where alike. The first men, therefore, who might see no more than the last acts, if I may say so, of this great drama in the countries where they themselves arose, might see the very first acts, wherein animals were brought on the stage, in other countries. They might be spectators at twice, and in a reversed order, of the whole piece.

Creation finished, propagation began, and the same instinct urged the two sexes to the same act. Instinct urged them to it first; a sense of pleasure recalled them to it afterwards; and the multiplication of their species was not a motive, probably, to these conjunctions. The revolution of some months showed them the consequences of it; and the revolution of some years showed them, that they and their offspring were born to die. Let us put ourselves, for a moment, in the place of the first men. Could they doubt that they were such? Could they doubt that all the other animals they saw, were the first of their kind likewise? Could they fail to transmit to their posterity this tradition, "the world had a beginning?" He who has a great mind to cavil, may say, that they did not know, by these marks, that the material world began, they only knew, that the animal inhabitants of it began then to exist. But if the first men could not be witnesses of their own creation, they might be such of the creation of other animals, as much as of the propagation of their own, and of every other species: so that, if they knew certainly, that the animal world began, I do not see what the atheist will gain by assuming that they were ignorant of the beginning of the material world. A God was necessary for one as much as for the other, and if tradition affirmed nothing more than the first, it would serve equally well to refute the atheist, who denies the existence of any such Being. Was it necessary to discover this great truth that they should reason logically, and transmit to posterity an opinion only? But in all cases they might know, by other marks sufficient to awaken the attention of a Samojede, or to inform a Hottentot, that the whole system then began. The lives of these men were, probably, much longer than ours; and if you compare what they must have seen in their youth, with what they must have observed in their old age, you will find that the experience of their whole lives, was one continued proof to them, that they lived in the first age of the material world. Observe it in one instance. The earth, out of which they had been created, furnished what was necessary for their subsistence.

> " per se dabat omnia tellus;
> Contentique cibis nullo cogente creatis,
> Arbuteos fœtus montanaque fraga, legebant," &c.

These were the spontaneous gifts of nature, and men had no share, at first, in the production or improvement of them. They learned, in time, to do both, to sow corn and to make bread. Trees grew up, and as they grew, they furnished a better retreat to birds, and a better shade to men. An old oak became at length to them a new phenomenon.

If it was not time to finish this article, I might easily show, in a multitude of other instances, that the first men must necessarily know that they were cotemporaries with the material world, and saw the beginning of a new order of things. But after wandering, in complaisance to the atheist, in the spaces of imagination, and to show him that, although neither the first nor the last of men were able to discover how the world was made, yet the first might know by sufficient experience, and the last by sufficient testimony, that it had a beginning, let us return into the closer precincts of reason and finish this article, as Mr. Huygens finishes his conjectures about the planetary world. After speaking of the absurdities contained in the physics of Des Cartes, he adds, "mihi magnum quid consecuti videbimur si, quemadmodum sese habeant res quæ in naturâ existunt, intellexerimus, à quo longissimè etiam nunc absumus. Quomodo autem quæque effectæ fuerint, quodque sint esse cœperint, id nequaquam humano ingenio excogitari, aut conjecturis attingi, posse," this philosopher asserts with great reason. Experimental philosophy has made great progress already, in discovering to us the things and the order of nature. Where it continues to be cultivated it will continue, doubtless, to discover more, and after all, human knowledge will stop far short of human curiosity; for this goes beyond our means of knowledge, nay, even beyond the boldest conjectures we can make.

But now, having shown the atheist, *ex abundantiâ,* how the first men might have certainty of knowledge concerning the beginning of the world, and were, therefore, authentic witnesses of the truth of this fact and authentic authors of the tradition, it is time to show that, without entering into such considerations, we must allow this tradition to be a tradition of fact, and not of opinion. This is the second of those articles that we proposed to examine in answer to the atheist's objections.—There must be some certain principles and some certain rule to distinguish between these two sorts of tradition, as the atheist seems to allow, when he distinguishes one from the other. Now these principles are not, I think, hard to find, and the rule that results from them, is simple and plain.

Common sense requires that every thing proposed to the understanding, should be accompanied with such proofs as the nature of it can furnish. He who requires more, is guilty of absurdity; he who requires less, of rashness. As the nature of the proposition decides, what proofs are exigible and what not, so the kind of proof determines the class into which the proposition is to be ranged. He, for instance, who affirms, that there is a God, advances a proposition which is an object of demonstrative knowledge alone, and a demonstration is required from him. If he makes the demonstration, we are obliged to own that we know there is a God, and the proposition becomes a judgment of nature, not merely an opinion, according to the

distinction made somewhere in Tully; though demonstrations are
sometimes called opinions, as opinions are often called demonstrations. If, by his fault or by ours, we have not a clear perception of the ideas or of the connection of them which form
this demonstration, or, if, without troubling ourselves to follow
it, we receive the proposition for true on the authority of others,
it is, indeed, opinion, not knowledge in us. But whether we
receive it, or whether we reject it, we can neither require nor
employ, with propriety, any other proofs than those which are
conformable to the nature of the proposition. Tradition is not
one of them. It may prove that men have generally believed a
God, but it cannot prove that such a Being exists. Nothing can
be more trifling, therefore, than to insist, as theists are apt to do,
on this proof, as if the opinion proved the fact; as if all men had
been alike capable of the demonstration; or, as if the demonstration was not necessary to establish the truth of the opinion.
Demonstration, indeed, is not necessary on the hypothesis, that
all men have an innate idea of God. But this hypothesis has
been, I think, long exploded. I do not remember, at least, to
have heard it maintained by more than one archbishop, two or
three ignorant monks, and as many devout ladies.

As much as I am convinced of the existence of a Supreme,
All-perfect Being, as seriously as I adore his majesty, bless his
goodness, and resign myself cheerfully to his providence, I should
be sorry to rest my conviction on the authority of any man, or
of all mankind; since authority cannot be, and demonstration is,
the sole proper proof in this case. Should I quote to the atheist
a Suphis, an Amenophis, an Orus, or any of those pretended
contemplators of divinity, he would laugh at me with reason;
though he might allow, at the same time, that these seers, who
acknowledged inferior beings, beings little raised above humanity,
were infinitely less absurd than those who had the front to assert
that they saw the invisible God, and conversed familiarly with
him. The demonstration of his existence arises from sensitive
knowledge; since it is *à posteriori* only that we can prove the
first cause to be an intelligent cause; but he is not for that
an object of sensitive knowledge. This proposition, therefore,
"there is a God," which becomes a judgment of nature, an object of demonstrative knowledge to every one who can make the
demonstration, or understand it when it is made, comes down as
an opinion only, in tradition, and can pass for nothing better on
that authority.

Is this now the case of that proposition which affirms the
beginning of the world? Reason alone can authorise the first,
and when I subscribe to the truth of it, I do this without any
regard to tradition. All that tradition tells me, is, that men
made the same judgment four or five thousand years ago. If it

told me that they made a contrary judgment, and believed the world eternal, I should make still the same on a subject concerning which, we of this age are as competent judges as the men who lived at any time before us.—This proposition, " the world had a beginning," affirms a fact long ago past, and which can, therefore, be received for true on no other authority than that of men who lived long ago, and at or near the time when this event happened. I consult my reason, indeed, to examine whether the fact implies contradiction, no more, and when I find that it does not, I receive it for true, on the faith of human testimony, which is the proper proof, to me, of every fact whereof I have not been myself a witness, and without any regard to the supposed conformity of it to the general ideas of mankind. This supposed conformity, if it be real, will add nothing to the probability of the fact, as a non-conformity will take none away. Nothing, therefore, can be more trifling than the cavil made by the atheist, when he objects that the more probable this tradition is, the more reason we have to take it for a universal tradition of opinion, not of fact. The cavil is not only trifling, but to the last degree absurd; for on this principle it will follow, that the more probable a fact is, the less reason we have to receive it, as a true fact, on historical or traditional authority. I consult my reason and my experience to discover whether the fact, I am told, may have happened possibly, and then I consult history and tradition to discover whether it has happened actually. But, according to Damon's logic, the more my reason and my experience show me the first, the more reason I have to believe that history and tradition record, in every such case, an ancient opinion, not an ancient fact.

But it is time that I should hasten to a conclusion, by showing, in the last place, that if the world had not really had a beginning, the opinion of its eternity would have been the general opinion of antiquity, and the commencement of it would not have been transmitted by tradition, either as a fact, or, perhaps, as an opinion. Though men might, in all ages, demonstrate the existence of God, they could not demonstrate alike, in any age, the commencement of the world: and, accordingly, we see that some philosophers, who believed there was a first principle, a first intelligent cause, a Supreme Being, held, at the same time, that the world was eternal, far from being induced by their theism, to believe it had a commencement. Others were, I doubt not, confirmed in the opinion that there was a God, or even led to believe it, and to seek the demonstration of it, by the proofs they had of this fact, the world had a beginning in time. It is much more probable, that the received fact gave occasion to or fortified the opinion, than that the opinion determined them to assume the fact.

The atheist, who looks on both to be nothing more than tradi-tional opinions, will be very indifferent which of them passes for the first. He blends them together, and attributes that of God's existence to the superstition of mankind, and to the policy of le-gislators. It might seem hard to attribute that of the beginning of the world to the same principles, since it seems to have little or no relation to them. He contents himself therefore, at least Damon did so with me, to insist that philosophers might easily fall into an opinion, which saved them much trouble in account-ing for the original of things, by the supposition of an eternal Being, infinitely wise and powerful. But the atheist would do well to consider, that this seeming solution of a difficulty implies a very real absurdity, for it implies that there were philosophers as soon as there were men. He would do well to consider, fur-ther, that when there were philosophers, those, who admitted the existence of such a Being, were not the less curious in their re-searches of the mechanical causes of all the phenomena. In short, he would do well to consider, that these philosophers would have cut the Gordian knots of all their difficulties, by as-suming the eternity of the world, much more easily than they could untie them, by assuming that a Being infinitely wise and powerful had made it. They might have said, in this case, once for all, things have been eternally as they are. To what purpose should we seek the original and essential causes of that which never began?

But further, if we pass over the absurdity of supposing that there were philosophers, as soon as there were men, or the im-probability of this supposition, that the commencement of the world was not believed till philosophers taught it; I would still ask, and the atheist would be puzzled to tell me, how the belief of the commencement of the world could be established, not only where philosophy and science flourished, but even universally, among nations who had no communication with these, and who were, themselves, the least civilised and the most ignorant? If it be said that, uncivilised and ignorant as they were, this opinion might arise and spread among them, because it was agreeable to their general notions, and analogous to what daily experience showed them, in innumerable instances, as well as to what they themselves were able to do; I must assert, on the contrary, this opinion was repugnant to the natural character of the human mind; to what we may feel in ourselves, and observe in all other men. All men are, in one respect, disciples of Protagoras. Unin-structed nature teaches them, like him, that man is the measure of all things; that our sensations communicate certain know-ledge; that every thing is what it appears to us to be; and that the things, which do not appear to us, are not. He who sees no inequality between two objects, affirms that they are equal, and we judge naturally of the reality of all objects by the perceptions we have of them. Ancient astronomers believed the stars to be immovably fixed in a solid firmament, and never suspected them to incline to the pole, or to decline from it. The sea was thought to have no bounds, because the bounds of it were unknown, and the celestial bodies to be incorruptible, because no changes were discerned in them. Philosophers reason often, and the vulgar always, like the roses in Fontenelle. A comparison taken from those insects, which live one day only, would have been more to his purpose; but roses were more worthy than insects to be offered to the marquis, and such a philosopher as Fontenelle might dispense with some want of precision in favor of his gallantry. Such as I have described it, is the natural character of the human mind. It infects all our judgments, moral as well as physical, till we learn to correct it by experience and a long course of reflection. This the uncivilised ignorant people, we speak of, could not do, and it was, therefore, agreeable to the general disposition of their minds, to believe that things had been always, such as they saw them to be.

This must have been universally the case, I think, in countries where the natural, unimproved character of the human mind prevailed alone. In those, which philosophy began to enlighten, some might doubt of this eternity; but some other philosophers, and the people in general, would continue to believe it. From whence can we imagine that they should derive a contrary opinion? Their experience showed them, indeed, generation and corruption; that particular things began, and then ceased to be; but they saw, on the whole, an uniform series of the same revolutions of things; their ideas were conformable to the experience which framed them, and the eternity of the world was conformable to these ideas. Such considerations may serve to show, what I have advanced, that the eternity of the world might have been the universal tradition, but that the commencement of it could not have been so, if it had not commenced, and men had not known that it had. On this hypothesis, all the consequences of it follow naturally. One consequence is, that, since the world and mankind began in time, the tradition of this beginning should be a little more or a little less obscurely, but universally known, and this consequence has followed. Another consequence is, that men, who believed the world to have been created, in the strict sense of the word, or that the confused matter of a chaos was reduced into a mundane system, must have believed, that this stupendous system was produced by some principle unknown to them, and superior to itself; for they could not fail to perceive, on the first notices of sense, and the first essays of reason, that the idea of an effect included necessarily, in it, the idea of a cause. This consequence followed likewise. Once more, although the first men could doubt no more that some cause of the world, than that the world itself, existed; yet another consequence of this great event, and of the surprise, inexperience, and ignorance of mankind, must have been much doubt and uncertainty concerning the first cause; and this likewise followed. Cudworth has endeavored to prove, many have thought, and I incline to think, that the unity of a first intelligent cause was the original belief of mankind. But if it was so, a belief soon succeeded, that gods, coadjutors to the first, in making and governing the world, as well as inferior gods, and men, and the whole material world, proceeded from this eternal source of all existence. I need not enumerate any of those various hypotheses, that arose from such absurd notions. Many of them have continued, to this day, and are held even by Christians, whom revelation as well as reason enlightens. The tradition of the fact, that the world began, and that of the opinion, that God is, have come down to us, though not entirely without opposition, from the most early ages. But the manner of God's being, and of his working in the creation, and government of the world, have been matters of dispute in all ages, ever since presumptuous mortals affected to descend into particulars, to know any thing at all of one, or any thing more of the other, than that he is self-existent and all-perfect, and that his will, relatively to his human creatures, is revealed to them in the constitution of their system.

To conclude. I am far from resting the proof of God's existence on the authority of this tradition, that the world began. I know that we are able to demonstrate this fundamental truth of all religion, whether it began or no. But since we cannot reject this tradition without renouncing almost all we know, and since it leads men to acknowledge a Supreme Being, by a proof levelled to the meanest understanding, I think we ought to insist upon it. I am the more confirmed in thinking so, by the effect it had in the dispute of which I have given you some account. Damon was embarrassed by it so much, that he had recourse at last to the wild hypothesis of Democritus and Epicurus, if we really know what that of the former was. This hypothesis is an abyss of absurdity. In that I left him, pitying from the bottom of my heart, for I love the man, his blindness and his obstinacy; the blindness of one who sees so clearly, and the obstinacy of one who shows so much candor, on other occasions.